Why You Need This New Edition

Six good reasons why you should buy this new edition of *Gender: Psychological Perspectives*

1. **10 new headline articles** on topics ranging from the incidence of women in science occupations to depression in men.

2. **New According to the Media and According to the Research features** focusing on images of feminists.

3. **Streamlined chapters** to eliminate duplication and refocus coverage onto the topics most relevant to the current study of gender.

4. **Updated tables and figures** throughout to present the most current data available.

5. **Expanded coverage of diversity issues** both in the United States and internationally.

6. More than **475 new references** presenting the latest research on gender.

PEARSON

Sixth Edition

GENDER
Psychological Perspectives

LINDA BRANNON
McNeese State University

Seminar	Chapters		
1	1	2	4
2	3	5	
3	6	8	
4	9	10	
5	7	11	12
6	14	14	

Allyn & Bacon

Boston Columbus Indianapolis New York San Francisco Upper Saddle River
Amsterdam Cape Town Dubai London Madrid Milan Munich Paris Montreal Toronto
Delhi Mexico City Sao Paulo Sydney Hong Kong Seoul Singapore Taipei Tokyo

Executive Editor: *Susan Hartman*
Project Editor: *Kara Kikel*
Editorial Assistant: *Laura Barry*
Marketing Manager: *Nicole Kunzmann*
Marketing Assistant: *Amanda Olweck*
Production Editor: *Claudine Bellanton*
Manufacturing Buyer: *Debbie Rossi*
Cover Designer/Administrator: *Kristina Mose-Libon*
Editorial Production and Composition Service: *PreMediaGlobal*

Photo credits appear on page 540, which constitutes an extension of the copyright page.

Library of Congress Cataloging-in-Publication Data
Brannon, Linda
    Gender : psychological perspectives / Linda Brannon.—6th ed.
        p. cm.
    Includes bibliographical references and index.
    ISBN-13: 978-0-205-00165-1
    ISBN-10: 0-205-00165-3
    1. Sex differences (Psychology)   2. Gender identity.   I. Title.
    BF692.2.B73 2011
    155.3—dc22

                                    2010031957

10 9 8 7 6 5 4 3 2 1   14 13 12 11 10

Allyn & Bacon
is an imprint of

www.pearsonhighered.com

ISBN 10:   0-205-00165-3
ISBN 13: 978-0-205-00165-1

Contents

3

Gender Stereotypes: Masculinity and Femininity   46

4

Hormones and Chromosomes   71

5   Theories of Gender Development   102

6   Developing Gender Identity   128

15 Treatment for Mental Disorders   397

16 How Different?   423

Preface

This book examines the topic of gender—the behaviors and attitudes that relate to (but are not entirely congruent with) biological sex. A large and growing body of research on sex, gender, and gender-related behaviors has come from psychology, sociology, biology, biochemistry, neurology, and anthropology. This research and scholarship form the basis for this book, providing the material for a critical review and an attempt to generate an overall picture of gender from a psychological perspective.

The Topic of Gender

A critical review of gender research is important for several reasons. First, gender is currently a "hot topic," and almost everyone has an opinion. These opinions are not usually based on research. Most people are not familiar with research findings; they simply know their own opinions. People's opinions are strongly influenced by their own experience, but the media cultivate a view of gender through stories and depictions in the movies, on television entertainment and news programs, and in other media. Based on these portrayals, people create images about how they believe women and men should be and attempt to re-create these images in their own lives. This personal reproduction of gender portrayals in the media is another example of what Candace West and Don Zimmerman (1987) described as "doing gender."

In *Gender: Psychological Perspectives,* I present what gender researchers have discovered, although the picture is neither simple nor complete. Research findings are complex and sometimes contradictory, but I believe that it is important to understand this research rather than draw conclusions based on only personal opinions and popular media portrayals.

Second, research is a valuable way to understand gender, despite the bias and controversy that have surrounded the research process. Although scientific research is supposed to be objective and free of personal bias, this idealistic notion often varies from the actual research process. Gender research in particular has been plagued with personal bias. Despite the bias that can enter into the research process, I believe that research is the most productive way to approach the evaluation of a topic. Others disagree with this view, including some who are interested in gender-related topics. A number of scholars, especially feminist scholars, have rejected scientific research as the best way to learn about gender.

Although I agree that science has not treated women equitably, either as researchers or as participants in research, I still believe that science offers the best chance for a fuller understanding of gender (as well as of many other topics). Some scholars disagree with this view, but I believe that science can further the goal of equity. I agree with Janet Shibley

Hyde and Kristen Kling (2001, p. 369), who said, "An important task of feminist psychology is to challenge stereotypic ideas about gender and test the stereotypes against data." My goals are consistent with that view—to examine what gender researchers have found and how they have interpreted their findings. By doing so, I hope to accomplish one of the goals that Meredith Cherland (2008) mentioned for those who teach about gender: "unsettling their students' collective views of the world and their sense of life's inevitability . . . " (p. 273). I believe that the research on gender has that potential.

The book's emphasis on gender is similar to another approach to studying gender—through examining the psychology of women. The psychology-of-women approach concentrates on women and issues unique to women, whereas the gender approach focuses on the issue of gender as a factor in behavior and in the social context in which behavior occurs. Gender research and theory draw heavily from research on the psychology of women, but the emphasis differs.

By emphasizing women and their experience, the psychology-of-women approach often excludes men, but gender research cannot. Studying both women and men is essential to an understanding of gender. Researchers who are interested in gender issues may concentrate on women or men, but they must consider both, or their research reveals nothing about gender. Therefore, this sixth edition of *Gender: Psychological Perspectives* examines the research and theory from psychology and related fields in order to evaluate the behavior, biology, and social context in which both women *and* men function.

The gender approach also reflects my personal preferences: I want a psychology of women and men. When I was completing the first edition of this book, I attended a conference session on creating a course on psychology of women. Several instructors who had created such courses led a discussion about obtaining institutional approval and the problems they had encountered, including resistance from administrators (who were mostly men) concerning a course in which the enrollment would be mostly women. One of the group advised trying for approval of a course on gender if obtaining approval for a psychology of women course was not successful. The implication was that the topic of gender included men and would be more acceptable but less desirable. I disagreed. I wanted men to be included—in the research, in my book, and in my classes. This preference comes from the belief that women and men are required in order to consider and discuss gender issues. I prefer the gender approach, and I wanted this book to reflect that attitude. As R. W. Connell (2005a) has discussed, women's efforts for change will not succeed completely without men's support and assistance. Men will need to participate to create gender equity for everyone.

My interest in gender comes from two sources—my research and my experience as a female psychologist. The research that prompted me to examine gender issues more carefully was work on risk perception related to health problems. I was interested in investigating people's perceptions of the health risks created by their behavior, such as the perceptions of health risks in smokers versus nonsmokers. In this research, I found that women and men saw their behaviors and risks in similar ways, even when the actual level of health risks differed quite a bit for men and women. My research showed gender similarities rather than gender differences.

In examining the volume of research on gender-related attitudes and behaviors, I discovered that many other researchers' findings were similar to mine—more similarities than differences. When differences appeared, many were small. I came to doubt the widespread belief that men and women are opposites. Rather, the evidence indicated that women and men are more similar than different. With the focus on differences, this view was not often voiced. Recently, this view has become more prominent. Concentrating on research findings rather than stereotypes or media portrayals, psychologists have come to conclusions of gender similarities rather than differences. Janet Shibley Hyde (2005a) has proposed a gender similarities hypothesis rather than one of gender differences, and Rosalind Barnett and Caryl Rivers (2004) have summarized this view in their book *Same Difference.*

As a female psychologist, I was forced to attend to gender issues from the outset of my career. Sexism and discrimination were part of the context in which I received my professional training and in which I have pursued my career as a psychologist. Women were a small minority in the field during my early years in psychology, but the numbers have since increased so that now women receive over half the doctoral degrees granted each year in psychology. This increase and several antidiscrimination laws have produced some improvements in equitable treatment for women in psychology (as well as in other professions and in society in general).

The psychology-of-women approach came from the women in psychology during the feminist movement of the 1960s. Most of the women in psychology have not been directly involved in the psychology of women and some are not feminists, but the presence of a growing proportion of women has changed psychology, making a psychology of gender not only possible but also, I think, inevitable.

Gendered Voices

Although I believe that research is a good way to understand behavior, including gender-related behavior, I accept the value of other approaches, including personal accounts. In traditional quantitative research, the data consist of numbers, and each participant's experience is lost in the transformation to numerical data and the statistical compilations of these data. Personal accounts and interviews do not lead to a comfortable blurring of the results. Rather, each person's account is sharply depicted, with no averaging to blunt the edges of the story. Louise Kidder (1994) contended that one of the drawbacks of personal accounts is the vividness of the data generated by reports of personal experience. I thought that such accounts could be an advantage.

Gender: Psychological Perspectives consists of an evaluation of research findings—exactly the sort of information that people may find difficult to relate to their lives. I decided that I also wanted to include some personal, narrative accounts of gender-relevant aspects of people's lives, and I wanted these accounts to connect to the research studies. The perils of vividness seemed small compared to the advantages. I believe that people's personal experiences are distilled in statistical research, but I also know that a lot of the interesting details are lost in the process.

These Gendered Voices narratives are my attempt to restore some of the details lost in statistical summaries, allowing men and women to tell about their personal experiences. Separating these stories from the text was an alternative to presenting information about gender and highlighting the relevance of research findings with vivid detail. Some of the stories are funny, showing a lighthearted approach to dealing with the frustrations and annoyances of discrimination and gender bias. Some of the stories are sad, revealing experiences of sexual harassment, violence, and abuse. All of the stories are real accounts, not fictional tales constructed as good examples. When the stories are based on published sources, I name the people presenting their experience. For other stories, I have chosen not to name those involved, to protect their privacy. I listened to my friends and students talk about gender issues and wrote down what they told me, trying to report what they said in their own words. I hope that these stories give a different perspective and add a sense of gendered experience to the volume of research reported here.

Headlines

Long before I thought of writing a book about gender, I noticed the popularity of the topic in the media. Not only are the sexes the topic of many private and public debates, but gender differences are also the topic of many newspaper, magazine, and television stories, ranging from sitcoms to scientific reporting. I had read warnings about the media's tendencies to oversimplify research findings and to "punch up" the findings to make the story grab people's attention. I wanted to examine the research on gender to try to understand what the research says, with all of its complexities, and to present the media version along with an analysis of the research findings.

Of particular concern to me was the tendency of the media and of people who hear reports of gender research to seek (or assume) a biological basis for the behavioral differences between the sexes, as though evidence of biologically based differences would be more "real" than any other type of evidence. The division of the biological realm from the behavioral realm is a false dichotomy; the two are intertwined and mutually influence each other. Even genes can be altered by environment, and experiences can produce changes in behavior as permanent as any produced by physiology. Many people hold the view that biological differences are real and permanent, whereas experience and culture produce only transient and changeable effects. This view is a myth.

Naomi Weisstein (1982) said, "Biology has always been used as a curse against women" (p. 41). The tendency to seek a biological explanation is strong and appealing to many. Unlike some other books about gender, this book spends several chapters examining biological evidence because I want to present and evaluate this research rather than ignore it. I want readers to question the extent to which the biological "curse" should apply.

To further highlight the popular conceptualizations of gender, I decided to use headlines from newspapers and popular magazines as a way to illustrate how the media represent gender. Some of the headline stories are examples of responsible journalism that seeks to present research in a way that is easy to understand, whereas other headline stories are more sensational or simplified.

The sensationalism occurs because such stories get attention, but the stories distort research findings and perpetuate stereotypical thinking about the sexes. I believe that Beryl Lieff Benderly (1989), a science reporter, was correct when she warned about media sensationalism of gender research by writing the headline "Don't believe everything you read . . ." (p. 67).

According to the Media and According to the Research

In addition to gender in the headlines, I have included two boxed features called According to the Media and According to the Research that concentrate on gender portrayals in the mainstream media. According to the Media boxes examine how gender is portrayed in magazines, television, movies, video games, Internet sources, cartoons, and fiction. The corresponding According to the Research boxes provide research findings as a more systematic counterpoint to the media portrayals. The contrast of these two presentations provides an opportunity to examine gender bias and stereotyping in the media. I hope these features lead students to question and think critically about the accuracy and fairness of the thousands of gendered images that they experience through the media.

Considering Diversity

The history of psychology is not filled with a concern for diversity or an emphasis on diversity issues, but these topics are of increasing interest and concern. Indeed, gender research is one of the major fields that represents the growing diversity in psychology. In addition, cross-cultural research has begun to provide a more comprehensive picture of psychological issues in the context of different ethnic groups within the United States as well as comparisons to other countries.

To highlight this developing research and tie it to gender issues, most chapters in this edition of *Gender: Psychological Perspectives* include a section called Considering Diversity, which focuses on diversity research. Although diversity issues enter the text at other points in the book, the creation of a section to highlight diversity ensures attention to these important issues. In some chapters, the research is sufficiently developed to present a cross-cultural review of the topic, but for other topics, cross-cultural research remains sparse, so those diversity sections present a specialized topic that relates to the chapter.

Supplements

Pearson Education is pleased to offer the following supplements to qualified adopters.

The **Instructor's Manual and Test Bank** (0205003761) is a wonderful tool for classroom preparation and management. Each chapter contains a lecture outline, multiple choice and essay questions, and a set of activities, as well as a list of useful websites and videos.

PowerPoint Presentation (0205003745) The PowerPoint Presentation is an exciting interactive tool for use in the classroom. Each chapter pairs key concepts with images from the textbook to reinforce student learning.

Acknowledgments

At the completion of any book, authors have many people to thank, and I am no exception. Without the assistance, support, and encouragement of many people, I never could have written this book, much less completed six editions. I thank all of them, but several people deserve special mention. My colleagues in the psychology department at McNeese State University were supportive and helpful. Dena Matzenbacher, Denise Arellano, Cameron Melville, Carl Bartling, Jan Disney, Chuck Robertson, and Patrick Moreno offered their expertise and assistance.

Husbands often deserve special thanks, and mine is no exception. My husband, Barry Humphus, did a great deal to hold my life together while I was researching and writing: He kept the computer working and offered me his praise, support, encouragement, and enthusiasm. I would not have attempted (much less completed) this book without him.

I would like to thank all the people who told me their personal stories for the Gendered Voices feature of the book. To respect their privacy I will not name them, with one exception. Melinda Schaefer deserves special thanks because her story was so good that hearing it made me realize that I wanted to include others' stories. Without her story, and Louise Kidder's (1994) presentation, I would not have realized how important these accounts are.

The people at Pearson have been helpful and supportive. My editor Susan Hartman and project editor Kara Kikel have supported my efforts and helped me complete the manuscript. My production editor, Claudine Bellanton, has been especially kind and helpful.

I would also like to thank reviewers who read parts of the manuscript and offered helpful suggestions, especially Florence Denmark, who took the time and careful attention to offer a review. I am honored. I am also grateful to Maggie Felton, University of Southern Indiana; Heather Hill, University of Texas at San Antonio; Mary Losch, University of Northern Iowa; Elizabeth Ossoff, Saint Anselm College; and Karen Prager, the University of Texas at Dallas. Thanks also for the suggestions from Luciane A. Berg, Southern Utah University; Christina Byme, Western Washington University; Linda Heath, Loyola University–Chicago; Marcela Raffaelli, University of Nebraska; and Stephanie Riger, University of Illinois–Chicago; Patrice Saab, University of Miami; Susan Burns, Morningside College; Katie Edwards, Ohio University; Susan Dutch, Westfield State College; Teri Nicoll-Johnson, Modesto Junior College; and Maria Lopez, Mt. San Jacinto College.

chapter 1

The Study of Gender

The first two of these headlines represent an exchange that can be described as a current skirmish in the "battle between the sexes." This exchange focused on who is more boring—men or women—with Sabine Durrant (2008) contending that men have become unbearably dull, and Neil Tweedie (2008) accusing women of being even more so. Their squabble centered on talking; Durrant cited the statistic that women talk more than men, and Tweedie accepted this gender difference, wishing that women did not talk more than men.

HEADLINES

Are Men Boring?
Telegraph, June 11, 2008

Are You Calling Us Boring?
Telegraph, June 12, 2008

Are Gender Stereotypes Boring?
New Statesman, June 23, 2008

Both Durrant and Tweedie drew on the opinions of friends and selected experts to argue that this situation was attributable to differences in men's and women's brains. This argument is prominent in evolutionary psychology, which contends that women's and men's brains have evolved in different ways that furnish modern humans with "hard-wired" gender differences (possibly including a tendency to talk in ways that the other sex may not find interesting). Evolutionary psychology holds the **essentialist view** that some "essence," or underlying biological component, makes men and women different. According to most people's views of the relationship between biology and behavior, biological differences determine behavior. Therefore, if the differences between women and men are biological, those differences are perceived as fixed and invariant (Keller, 2005). Recent changes in society would make little difference in women's and men's basic natures.

Kira Cochrane (2008) expressed another point of view in this controversy: The gender stereotypes expressed by Durrant and Tweedie, not men or women, are what is boring. She criticized the simplistic view inherent in these stereotypes, saying that those who take this position strive "to assert that men and women each have their own place and quite separate characteristics, and that these are defined not simply by social structures and norms, but by biology" (p. 22). Thus, the stereotypes are not only boring but also cast gender differences in essentialist terms.

This version of conflicts and questions is typical of many debates about gender: Which is more important, nature (biology) or nurture (culture and society)? What types of differences exist? What is the basis for these differences? What is the extent of these differences? Consistent with the position of evolutionary psychology, Durant, Tweedie, and many other people see the answers to these questions as simple and obvious: Women and men are born with biological differences that dictate the basis for different traits and behaviors. Indeed, they are so different that women are the "opposite sex," suggesting that whatever men are, women are at the other end of the spectrum. Those who hold this view find the differences obvious and important. Those such as Cochrane, who hold the biosocial view, see the answers as more complex. Drawing from research in psychology, sociology, biology, and anthropology, the differences between women and men seem to be a complex puzzle with many pieces.

Thus, the battle lines seem to be drawn between two camps, both of which look to volumes of research for support for their view and both of which see supporting evidence for their different views. Some people at some times have believed that differences between males and females are few, whereas others have believed that the two are virtually different species. These two positions can be described as the **minimalist view** and the **maximalist view** (Epstein, 1988). The minimalists perceive few important differences between women and men, whereas the maximalists believe that the two have large, fundamental differences. Many maximalists also hold an essentialist view, believing that the large differences between women and men are part of their essential biological natures. Although these views have varied over time, today both the maximalist and the minimalist views have vocal supporters, as the three headline stories demonstrate.

This lack of agreement coupled with commitment to a position suggests controversy, which is almost too polite a term for these disagreements. Few topics are as filled with emotion as discussions of the sexes and their capabilities. These arguments occur in places as diverse as playgrounds and scientific laboratories. The questions are similar, regardless of the setting: Who is smarter, faster, healthier, sexier, more capable, more emotional? Who makes better physicians, engineers, typists, managers, politicians, artists, teachers, parents, friends? Who is more likely to go crazy, go to jail, commit suicide, have a traffic accident, tell lies, gossip, commit murder? The full range of human possibilities seems to be grounds for discussion, but the issues are unquestionably important. No matter what the conclusions, at least half the human population (and most probably all of it) will be affected. Therefore, not only are questions about the sexes interesting but also the answers are important to individuals and to society. Later chapters explore the research concerning abilities and behaviors, and an examination of this research allows an evaluation of these questions.

Answers to these important questions about differences between women and men are not lacking. Almost everyone has answers—but not the same answers. It is easy to see how people might hold varying opinions about a controversial issue, but some consistency should exist among findings from researchers who have studied men and women. Scientists should be able to investigate the sexes and provide evidence concerning these important questions. Researchers have pursued these questions, obtained results, and published thousands of papers. There is no shortage of investigations—or publicity—about the sexes. Unfortunately, researchers are subject to the same problems as everyone else: They do not all agree on what the results mean—or even what they are.

In addition, many research findings on men and women are not consistent with popular opinion, suggesting that popular opinion may be an exaggeration or distortion, most likely based on people's personal experiences rather than on research. Both the past and the present are filled with examples that exaggerate differences between women and men.

People have a tendency to think in terms of opposites when considering only two examples, as with the sexes (Fausto-Sterling, 2000; Tavris, 1992). If three sexes existed, people might not have the tendency to draw comparisons of such extremes. They might be able to see the similarities as well as the differences in men and women; they might be able to approach the questions with more flexibility in their thinking. The sexual world may not actually be polarized into only two categories (as Chapter 4 explores in more detail), but people do tend to see it that way. This perception of only two sexes influences people to think of the two sexes as polar opposites. To maintain these oppositional categories, people must exaggerate the differences between women and men, which results in stereotypes that do not correspond to real people (Bem, 1993b). Although these stereotypes are not realistic, they are powerful because they affect how women and men think about themselves and how they think about the "opposite" sex.

History of the Study of Sex Differences in Psychology

Speculations about the differences between men and women probably predate history, but these issues were not part of the investigations of early psychology. Wilhelm Wundt is credited with founding modern psychology in 1879 (although there is some debate about the accuracy of this date) at the University of Leipzig (Schultz & Schultz, 2008). Wundt wanted to establish a natural science of the mind to investigate the nature of human thought processes through experimentation. Others joined Wundt, and using chemistry as the model, they devised a psychology based on an analytical understanding of the structure of the conscious mind. This approach to psychology became known as the **structuralist** school of psychology. Wundt and his followers believed that psychology could not be applied to children, the feebleminded, or species of nonhuman animals.

The structuralists were interested in investigating the "generalized adult mind" (Shields, 1975a), and therefore any individual differences, including differences between the minds of women and men, were of no concern to these early psychologists. This inattention to sex differences did not mean equal treatment of women and men by these early psychologists. The generalized adult mind on which psychology's early findings were based was a generalization drawn from data collected from and by men. Indeed, women were expressly prohibited from one of the early groups of experimental psychologists in the United States (Schultz & Schultz, 2008).

The focus of Wundt's psychology changed in the United States. Although virtually all U.S. psychologists received their training in Germany, many found the views of German psychology too limiting and impractical. As psychology grew in the United States, it developed a more practical nature. This change is usually described as an evolution to **functionalism**, a school of psychology that emphasized how the mind functions rather than its structure (Schultz & Schultz, 2008). As psychologists with a functionalist orientation started to research and theorize, they drew a wider variety of subjects into psychological research and theories, including children, women, and nonhuman animals.

The Study of Individual Differences

Among the areas of interest in functionalist psychology were the issues of adaptability and intelligence. These interests prompted the development of intelligence testing and the comparison of individual differences in mental abilities and personality traits, including sex differences. The functionalists, influenced by Darwin and the theory of evolution, tended to look for biologically determined differences, including a biological basis for sex differences. Although female psychologists pointed out the effects of social influence on women's and men's behaviors, functionalist psychologists were hesitant to acknowledge any possibility of social influence in the sex differences they found (Milar, 2000). Their findings usually supported the prevailing cultural roles for women and men.

The studies and writings of functionalists of this era tended to demonstrate that women were less intelligent than men, benefited less from education, had strong maternal instincts, and were unlikely to produce examples of success or eminence. Women were not the only group deemed inferior; people who were not white were also considered less intelligent and less capable.

Findings of the intellectual deficiencies of women did not go uncriticized. As early as 1910, Helen Thompson Woolley contended that the research on sex differences was full of the researchers' personal bias, prejudice, and sentiment (in Shields, 1975a), and Leta Stetter Hollingworth took a stand against the functionalist view of women (Shields, 1975b). These female psychologists argued against the prevailing view. Hollingworth contended that women's potential would never be known until women had the opportunity to choose the lives they would like—career, maternity, or both.

The functionalist view began to wane in the 1920s, and a new school of psychology, **behaviorism**, gained prominence. The behaviorists emphasized observable behavior rather than thought processes or instincts as the subject matter of psychology. The behaviorist view of psychology was consistent with the prevailing style of masculinity during the early 20th century—tough-minded and combative (Minton, 2000). With the change from a functionalist to a behaviorist paradigm in U.S. psychology, the interest in research on sex differences sharply decreased. "The functionalists, because of their emphasis on 'nature,' were predictably indifferent to the study of social sex roles and cultural concepts of masculine and feminine. The behaviorists, despite their emphasis on 'nurture,' were slow to recognize those same social forces" (Shields, 1975a, p. 751). Rather, behaviorists were interested in the areas of learning and memory, concentrating on studies with rats as subjects.

In addition, research on learning ignored social factors, including sex roles and sex differences. In ignoring gender, psychologists created "womanless" psychology (Crawford & Marecek, 1989), an approach that either failed to include women as participants or failed to examine gender-related factors when both men and women participated in psychological research. Until the 1970s, psychology was overwhelmingly male. As Rhoda Unger (1983–1984) commented about her education in psychology, "Even the rats were male" (p. 227).

When behaviorism dominated psychology, the only theorists who unquestionably had an interest in sex differences were those with a psychodynamic orientation—the Freudians.

Psychoanalysis

Both Freud's psychodynamic theory of personality development and his psychoanalytic approach to treatment appear in more detail in Chapter 5. However, the history of psychology's involvement in issues of sex and gender necessitates a brief description of Freud's personality theory and his approach to treatment.

Although Sigmund Freud's work did not originate within psychology, the two are popularly associated. And unquestionably, Freud's work and Freudian theory concerning personality differences between women and men have influenced both psychology and society in general. These influences have made the work of Freud very important for understanding how theorists within psychology conceptualized sex and gender.

In the United States, Freud's work began to gain popular attention in 1909, when Freud came to the United States to give a series of invited lectures at Clark University (Schultz & Schultz, 2008). Immediately after his visit, newspapers started carrying features about Freud and his theory. By 1920, interest in Freudian theory and analysis was evident both in books and in articles in popular magazines. Psychoanalysis gained popular interest, becoming almost a fad. Indeed, popular acceptance of Freud's work preceded its acceptance by academicians.

Freud emphasized the role of instinct and physiology in personality formation, hypothesizing that instincts provide the basic energy for personality and that the child's perception of anatomical differences between boys and girls is a pivotal event in personality formation. Rather than rely on genetic or hormonal explanations for sex differences in personality, Freud looked to early childhood experiences within the family to explain how physiology interacts with experience to influence personality development.

For Freud (1925/1989), the perception of anatomical differences between boys and girls was a critical event. According to Freud, the knowledge that boys and men have penises and girls and women do not forms the basis for personality differences between boys and girls. The results of this perception lead to conflict in the family, including sexual attraction to the other-sex parent and hostility for the same-sex parent. These incestuous desires cannot persist, and Freud hypothesized that the resolution of these conflicts comes through identification with the same-sex parent. However, Freud believed that boys experience more conflict and trauma during this early development, leading to a more complete rejection of their mother and a more complete identification with their father than girls experience. Consequently, Freud (1925/1989) hypothesized that men typically form a stronger conscience and sense of social values than women do.

Did Freud mean that girls and women were deficient in moral standards compared to men? Did he view women as incomplete (and less admirable) people? It is probably impossible to know what Freud thought and felt, and his writings are sufficiently varied to lead to contradictory interpretations. Thus the question of Freud's view of women has been hotly debated. Some authors have criticized Freud for supporting a male-oriented society and the enslavement of women, whereas others have defended Freud and his work as applied to women. In defense of Freud (Tavris & Wade, 1984), his view of women was not sufficiently negative to prevent him from accepting them as colleagues during a time when women were not welcome in many professions. In addition, he encouraged his daughter, Anna, to pursue a career in psychoanalysis. Freud's writings, however, reveal that he held many negative views about women and seemed to feel that they were inferior to men, both intellectually and morally.

Regardless of Freud's personal beliefs, the popular interpretation of his theory represented women as inferior to men—less ethical, more concerned with personal appearance, more self-contemptuous, and jealous of men's accomplishments (and also, literally, of their penises). Accepting the feminine role would always mean settling for inferior status and opportunities, and women who were not able to reconcile themselves to this status were candidates for therapy because they had not accepted their femininity.

Freud's theory also held stringent and inflexible standards for the development of masculinity. For boys to develop normally, they must experience severe anxiety during early childhood and develop hatred for their father. This trauma should lead a boy to identify with his father out of fear and to experience the advantages of the male role through becoming like him. Boys who do not make a sufficiently complete break with their mothers are not likely to become fully masculine but to remain somewhat feminine, thus experiencing the problems that society accords to nonmasculine men.

The psychoanalytic view of femininity and masculinity has been enormously influential in Western society. Although not immediately accepted in academic departments, the psychoanalytic view of personality and psychopathology was gradually integrated into the research and training of psychologists. Although the theory has prompted continuing controversy, interest continues, in the form of both attacks and defenses. This continuing stream of books and articles speaks to the power of Freud's theory to capture attention and imagination. Despite limited research support, Freudian theory has been and remains a force in conceptions of sex and gender.

In summary, psychological research that includes women dates back to the early 20th century and the functionalist school of psychology, but this approach emphasized sex differences and searched for the factors that distinguish men and women. When the behaviorist school dominated academic psychology, its lack of interest in sex differences created a virtually "womanless" psychology. During that same time, Freudian psychoanalysts held strong views on the sexes, but this theory proposed that women are physically and morally inferior to men. This belief in the innate inferiority of women influenced research on women. Table 1.1 summarizes psychological theories and their approaches to gender. In contrast to these male-dominated theories, some investigators emphasize the study of women.

TABLE 1.1   *Role of Gender in Psychological Theories throughout the History of Psychology*

Theory	Emphasis of Theory	Role of Gender
Structuralism	Understanding the structure of the human mind	Minimal—all minds are equivalent
Functionalism	Understanding the function of the mind	Sex differences are one type of individual difference
Behaviorism	Studying behavior in a scientific way	Minimal—behavior varies with individual experience
Psychoanalysis	Studying normal and abnormal personality development and functioning	Biological sex differences and their recognition are motivating forces

The Development of Women's Studies

Women's studies came about as a result of political, social, and intellectual developments that began in the 18th century and continue in the present (Sommers, 2008). Those developments have affected psychology and have changed society and people's daily lives.

The History of Feminist Movements

The feminist movement of the 1960s prompted the development of women's studies (Freedman, 2002). This version of feminism is referred to as the second wave of feminism. The first wave of feminism began with the campaign for changes in women's roles and legal status, focusing on voting rights for women, the availability of birth control, and other legal changes to improve women's social and economic status (Sommers, 2008). That movement experienced some success—for example, women gained the right to vote in many countries—but other legal changes did not occur.

The feminist movement of the 1960s grew out of the U.S. civil rights movement and brought about some of the changes that earlier feminist movements had sought (Nachescu, 2009). One of the most prominent changes was women's entry into the workforce in record numbers in many industrialized countries. Both professional and working-class women experienced situations of discrimination that led many to work toward legal and social changes for women. These goals fit the definition of *liberal (or egalitarian) feminism* and included people who wanted to end discrimination based on sex and extend equal rights to women (Freedman, 2002).

Some feminists believed that calling for an end to discrimination was not sufficient; equality for women required more drastic changes in society. These *radical feminists* believed that women have been oppressed by men and that this oppression has served as a model for racial and class oppression (Nachescu, 2009). According to radical feminists, the entire social system requires major change to end the subservient role that women occupy. Both liberal and radical feminism call for political activism designed to bring about changes in laws and in society.

Women had begun to enter colleges and universities in increasing numbers. These scholars pursued their interest in topics related to women, which resulted in the development of courses and curricula devoted to women's studies as an academic discipline. This emphasis was often compatible with another variety of feminism, *cultural feminism,* which also advocates social change. Inspired by Carol Gilligan's *In a Different Voice* (1982), cultural feminists advocate moving toward an acceptance and appreciation of traditionally feminine values. Cultural feminists believe that, were women in charge, many of the world's problems would disappear, because women's values of caring and relationships would eliminate them. Radical and cultural feminists have been publicized more than other types of feminism, creating an inaccurate image of feminists (see According to the Media and According to the Research later in the chapter).

Sex or Gender?

With the growing interest in women's issues came concerns about how to phrase the questions researchers asked. Those researchers who have concentrated on the differences between men and women historically have used the term **sex differences** to describe their

The first women's movement pushed for voting rights for women.

GENDERED VOICES

Is It Ok ... ?

"I consider myself a hard-core feminist," said a 20-year-old women's studies major at Tulane University in New Orleans. "But is it okay that I wear thong underwear?" (Baumgardner & Richards, 2003, p. 448). This question was typical of those posed to Jennifer Baumgardner and Amelia Richards, feminist scholars with a specific interest in young women and the feminist movement. This question exemplifies the struggle for young women to meld their personal interests and priorities with feminism, which they (and others) may not perceive as compatible with beauty, shopping, and boyfriends. Even young women who work as volunteers in rape crisis centers and women's shelters may feel that they do not meet the standards for being a feminist. Baumgardner and Richards try to reassure young women that feminism is about freedom, with many ways to achieve that goal—which may include thong underwear.

work. In some investigations, these differences were the main emphasis of the study, but for many more studies, such comparisons were of secondary importance (Unger, 1979). By measuring and analyzing differences between male and female participants, researchers have produced a huge body of information on these differences and similarities, but this information was not of primary importance to most of these researchers.

When differences between women and men began to be the focus of research, controversy arose over terminology. Some researchers objected to the term *sex differences,* contending that it carries implications of a biological basis for these differences (McHugh, Koeske, & Frieze, 1986). Critics also objected that the term has been used too extensively and with too many meanings, including chromosomal configuration, reproductive physiology, secondary sex characteristics, as well as behaviors or characteristics associated with women or men (Unger, 1979). Rhoda Unger proposed an alternative—the term **gender**. She explained that this term describes the traits and behaviors that are regarded by the culture as appropriate to women and men. *Gender* is thus a social label and not a description of biology. This label includes the characteristics that the culture ascribes to each sex and the sex-related characteristics that individuals assign to themselves. Carolyn Sherif (1982) proposed a similar definition of gender as "a scheme for social categorization of individuals" (p. 376). Both Unger and Sherif recognized the socially created differentiations that have arisen from the biological differences associated with sex, and both have proposed that use of the term *gender* should provide a useful distinction.

Unger suggested that use of the term *gender* might reduce the assumed parallels between biological and psychological sex, or at least make those assumptions explicit. If researchers had accepted and used the term consistently, then its use might serve the function Unger proposed. However, consistent usage has not yet appeared, and confusion remains. Some researchers use the two terms interchangeably, whereas others have substituted the term *gender* for the term *sex* but still fail to make any distinction (Pryzgoda & Chrisler, 2000). Although people experience some confusion in their usage, many do not use the terms interchangeably. Indeed, many people use *gender* to apply to social or psychological factors, which is consistent with Unger's proposal for the usage of the terms *sex* and *gender.*

Therefore, psychologists have attempted to draw distinctions between the concepts of *sex* and *gender.* Such distinctions pose problems, but those who use the term *gender* often intend to emphasize the social nature of differences between women and men, whereas those who use the term *sex* mean to imply biological differences. Indeed, the terminology that researchers use can indicate their point of view; researchers who are biological essentialists use the term *sex* to refer to *all* differences between men and women, whereas those who use the term *gender* want to emphasize the social nature of such differences.

Women in Psychology

The history of studying gender in psychology is lengthy, including the individual differences approach and psychoanalysis. However, women were rarely prominent psychologists. Women were admitted as students in doctoral programs from the early years of psychology, but they had a difficult time finding positions as psychologists, especially in academic settings. In 1941, a group of women who were psychologists formed the National Council of Women Psychologists to further the work of female psychologists in the war effort (Walsh, 1985). This group became the International Council of Women

According to the Media...

Feminists Are Bra-Burning Man-Haters

The media image of a feminist is a radical, man-hating woman who is uninterested in attracting (or unable to attract) men. This description is remarkably consistent throughout the United States, reported Courtney Martin (2007), who attributed this consistency to "media manufactured myths."

The image of feminists as "bra burners" originated with one of the prominent events in second-wave feminism: the protest at the 1968 Miss America pageant (Kreydatus, 2008). A group of feminist women organized a protest of the beauty pageant, arguing that its emphasis on a specific standard of beauty was degrading to women. These protests were accompanied by heavy media coverage, and one reporter used the term "bra burner" to describe these feminists. The description stuck.

The media have focused on radical feminists, probably because these feminists provide better stories. As feminism grew, the medial labels became even more uncomplimentary, including the term "feminazi," popularized by Rush Limbaugh (MediaMatters for America, 2005). The focus on radicalism and the uncomplimentary media terms helped to promote feminists as radical, bra-burning man-haters.

The third season of the television show *Veronica Mars* (2006–2007) featured a subplot that revolved around a series of campus rapes, which pitted the feminists in Lilith House against the fraternity men (Fudge & Tringali, 2007). These feminists were portrayed as "dour, shrill, unreasonable, judgmental, and vindictive" women who hated not only men but also "women who wear makeup" (p. 15). With such portrayals, no wonder women from around the country are able to describe feminists as bra-burning man-haters.

Psychologists in 1944, and despite attempts to become a division of the American Psychological Association (APA), they experienced repeated rejections.

The dramatic increase of women attending college affected psychology, and the new area of women's studies changed the discipline. Influenced by feminist scholars and their own research priorities, women expanded the earlier area of gender-related behaviors and individual differences to create a new psychology of women and gender (Marecek, Kimmel, Crawford, & Hare-Mustin, 2003; Walsh, 1985).

In 1968 psychologist Naomi Weisstein presented an influential paper, "'Kinde, Küche, Kirche' as Scientific Law: Psychology Constructs the Female." This paper influenced a generation of psychologists. In this paper, Weisstein (1970) argued that psychological research had revealed almost nothing about women because the research had been contaminated by the biases, wishes, and fantasies of the male psychologists who conducted the research. Although the criticism was aimed mostly at clinical psychology and the Freudian approach to therapy, Weisstein also charged research psychologists with finding only what they wanted and expected to find about women rather than researching women as they were. She wrote, "Present psychology is less than worthless in contributing to a vision which could truly liberate—men as well as women" (p. 231).

Weisstein's accusations came at a time when the feminist movement in society and a growing number of women in psychology wanted a more prominent place for women in the field and sought to create feminist-oriented research. Weisstein made the point that psychological research had neglected to take into account the context of behavior, without which psychologists could understand neither women nor people in general. This criticism seems to have contained a great deal of foresight (Bem, 1993a); psychological research on

ACCORDING TO THE RESEARCH . . .

Feminists Are Neither of the Above

According to research conducted on feminist women, they fail to match any of the stereotypes promoted in the media. An examination of the events of the protest during the 1968 Miss American pageant failed to show any burned bras (Kreydatus, 2008). A "freedom trash can" was part of the protest, and the protesters threw in objects they associated with "female garbage," such as bras, girdles, false eyelashes, and steno pads, but they did not set the objects on fire. The bra burning was symbolic, not literal, but the image persisted.

The notion that feminists hate men is also a widespread belief, but little research has investigated and none has supported this stereotype. One study assessed women's feminism and then tested their attitudes toward men (Anderson, Kanner, & Elsayegh, 2009). The results indicated the opposite of the stereotype: Feminists had *lower* levels of hostility toward men than women who did not identify themselves as feminists.

Some feminist scholars (Barakso & Schaffner, 2006) have contended that the media focus on the more extreme issues and members of feminist groups, which has created the image of Limbaugh's "feminazis" but fails to capture the women or the issues of feminism. As feminist Courtney Martin (2007) said, "Feminism in its most glorious, transformative, inclusive sense, is not about man-hating . . . " but about educated choices for men as well as for women, genuine equality, and a vision of gender roles that allow individuals to become their most authentic selves. This image lacks the controversy and varies from the media stereotype of feminists.

women began to change in that specific way. "During the 1970s psychological researchers made an important discovery: humans are gendered beings whose lives and experiences are (most likely) influenced by their gender" (Smiler, 2004, p. 15). Psychologists held no monopoly on women's studies. Sociologists, anthropologists, ethnologists, and biologists also became involved in questions about biological and behavioral differences and similarities between the sexes (Schiebinger, 1999).

The struggle for professional acceptance is clear in the history of the formation in the APA of a division devoted to women's issues, which did not occur until 1973. Division 35, Society for the Psychology of Women, can be directly traced to the Association for Women in Psychology, a group that demonstrated against sex discrimination and advocated for an increase in feminist psychological research at the 1969 and 1970 APA national conventions (Walsh, 1985). Unlike the earlier International Council, Division 35 goals included not only the promotion of women in psychology, but also the advancement of research on women and issues related to gender. The great volume of psychological research on sex and gender that has appeared in the past 35 years is consistent with the Division 35 goal of expanding the study of women and encouraging the integration of that research with current psychological thinking. Indeed, Division 35 members have conducted much of that research, but other disciplines have also contributed substantially. The current plethora of research on sex and gender comes from investigations in biology, medicine, sociology, communication, and anthropology, as well as psychology.

In summary, the feminist movement of the 1960s prompted a different type of research, producing results that questioned the stereotypes and assumptions about innate differences between the sexes. Not only did this research begin to examine sex differences and similarities, but these researchers also expanded ways to study women and men. This more recent orientation has led to voluminous research in the field of psychology, as well as in sociology, anthropology, communication studies, literary analysis, art, and biology.

The feminist movement questioned the roles and stereotypes for women, and soon the questioning spread to men, who began to examine how the inflexibility of gender stereotypes might harm them, too.

The Appearance of the Men's Movement

The men's movement mirrors the women's movement, beginning during the 19th-century women's suffrage movement. During that time, the women's suffrage movement was not the only challenge to society's roles for men and women. Men felt increasing threats to their masculinity by the change from agricultural to industrial society, by women entering the workforce, and by increasing demands for education, which seemed dominated by women (Minton, 2000).

The contemporary women's movement has also questioned and challenged men concerning the status quo of legal, social, and personal roles and relationships. Although some men have failed to see the problem, other men from around the world have begun to consider how these challenges pertain to their lives, too. R. W. Connell (2001) argued that societal roles constrain men, too, giving men a reason to seek change: "The gender positions that society constructs for men may not correspond exactly with what men actually are, or desire to be, or what they actually do. It is therefore necessary to study masculinity as well as men" (p. 44). Connell (2005a) also explained that men are necessary for the reform of gender roles. "Moving toward a gender-equal society involves profound institutional change as well as change in everyday life and personal conduct. To move far in this direction requires widespread social support, including significant support from men and boys" (p. 1801).

Feminist men formed groups equivalent to the consciousness-raising groups common in the women's movement (Baumli & Williamson, 1997). Although group members discussed their common problems and sought support from each other, their activities usually did not progress to the larger organizations that sought political power, as the women's groups had done. They tended to remain small and local, but a few grew into national organizations.

During the 1970s, men who were interested in furthering feminist goals joined the National Organization for Women and proclaimed themselves to be feminists. During the 1980s, masculinity and the problems of men became a focus, and other profeminist men's organizations arose. The National Organization for Men Against Sexism (NOMAS) is a profeminist men's organization that also works to obliterate racism and prejudice against gay men. This type of concern with masculinity and exploring positive options has spread to countries around the world, including Australia, Sweden, Japan, Latin America, and the Caribbean (Connell, 2001, 2005a).

Within psychology, the Society for the Psychological Study of Men and Masculinity succeeded in gaining divisional status in 1995, becoming Division 51 of the APA. The goals of this division include (1) promoting the study of how gender roles shape and constrict men's lives, (2) helping men to experience their full human potential, and (3) eroding the definition of masculinity that has inhibited men's development and has contributed to the oppression of others.

Another approach to men's groups appears in national groups that are not interested in feminist goals; indeed, some of these men are interested in restoring the traditional gender roles that they believe have been destroyed by the women's movement. These men argue that men—not women—are the oppressed sex. One such group is the National Coalition for Men (NCFM, formerly the National Coalition of Free Men), a group that opposes sexism but sees feminist groups as sexist. The men in NCFM (Baumli & Williamson, 1997) have argued that sexism oppresses men more than women.

Some men's rights groups are organized around specific issues, such as changing divorce laws or promoting joint child custody (Baumli & Williamson, 1997). Many of these men see women's rights groups as enemies because women's groups tend to oppose joint custody and no-fault divorce laws. Few in the men's movement actively promote a return of "the good old days" and a reversal of the changes brought about by the women's movement. Many participants in men's groups would like to see a less sharply gendered society, in which both women and men have choices not bound by their biological sex. What would count as fulfilling these goals differs among men, and both antifeminist and profeminist men consider themselves part of the men's movement.

Yet another variation of the men's movement came from men trying to find a masculine identity that differs from traditional masculinity. Early proponents of this view included authors such as Robert Bly (1990) and Sam Keen (1991), who contend that modern society has left men with no easy way to form a masculine identity. The culture provides inappropriate models, and fathers are often absent, providing no model at all. This deficit produces men who are inappropriately aggressive and poorly fitted to live in society, to form relationships with women, and to be adequate fathers. The straight edge (sXe) is a more recent movement with similar views. Most of those in this movement are young, single, White men who follow punk rock music but reject the drug use, violence, and sexual exploitation common in that (and in mainstream) culture (Haenfler, 2004). These men are committed to creating an alternative masculinity that is more compassionate and accepting, and this version of the men's movement has spread worldwide.

The Promise Keepers arose during the 1990s, with somewhat different objections to traditional masculinity and thus different suggestions for change (Messner, 1997; Silverstein, Auerbach, Grieco, & Dunk, 1999). This organization includes men with a shared vision of godly manhood (Bartkowski, 2000; Newton, 2004), which is part of neoconservative evangelical Christianity. It urged men to reclaim their position as head of the family, living up to their roles and keeping their commitments to their wives and children. The Promise Keepers doctrine rejects the racism that is often associated with the evangelical movement, but it does not accept homosexuality or equal partnerships with women. Promise Keepers was the model for the development of a Catholic men's movement (Gelfer, 2008). Studies of men who have participated in Promise Keepers (Newton, 2004; Silverstein et al., 1999) revealed that this movement supports men who attempt to become more nurturant, involved fathers.

The men's movement exists in many versions with diverse views and goals, and the men in these various groups do not necessarily know much about the others or endorse their views (Ford, 2004; Newton, 2004). Thus, the men's movement lacks cohesion. "Masculinities, it appears, are far from settled. From bodybuilders in the gym, to managers in the boardroom, to boys in the elementary school playground, a great deal of effort goes into the making of conventional masculinities" (Connell, 2001, p. 50). Although some

GENDERED VOICES

When I Look in the Mirror

"When you wake up in the morning and look in the mirror, what do you see?" a Black woman asked a White woman (Kimmel & Messner, 1992, p. 2).

"I see a woman," said the White woman.

"That's precisely the issue," the Black woman replied. "I see a Black woman. For me, race is visible every day, because it is how I am not privileged in this culture. Race is invisible to you, which is why our alliance will always seem somewhat false to me" (p. 2).

This exchange surprised Michael Kimmel, who examined his own thoughts and realized that when he looked into the mirror, he "saw a human being: universally generalizable. The generic person" (p. 2). Just as the White woman did not see her ethnicity, the White man saw neither his gender nor his ethnic background. His privileged status as White and male had made him blind

to these factors. He did not think of himself as White or male but as a generic human. The White woman saw femaleness—the characteristic that prompted discrimination against her. The Black woman saw both her skin color and her gender when she looked into the mirror—both had been salient in her life.

As Michael Kimmel and Michael Messner (1992, pp. 2–3) summarized these experiences, "The mechanisms that afford us privilege are very often invisible to us.... men often think of themselves as genderless, as if gender did not matter in the daily experiences of our lives. Certainly, we can see the biological sex of individuals, but we rarely understand the ways in which gender—that complex of social meanings that is attached to biological sex—is enacted in our daily lives."

men are actively exploring this process, none of the versions of the men's movement has yet exerted the impact of the women's movement in influencing public opinion and changing social policy. Table 1.2 lists some important events in both women's and men's movements and when each event occurred.

Considering Diversity

Lack of diversity was the problem that sparked women to protest their exclusion in psychology (and in society). That lack of diversity allowed men to be used as the standard (Bem, 1993b; Yoder & Kahn, 1993), which makes women appear deficient when they differ from that standard. Sandra Bem (1993b) referred to this as an *androcentric bias*, contending that this bias has permeated not only psychology and its research but also society in general. Whenever research finds a gender difference, that finding is interpreted as a disadvantage for women.

A similar concern applies to research focusing on women from various ethnic groups (Yoder & Kahn, 1993). White, privileged women have constituted the standard for research with women, and when women from other ethnic groups are included, they are compared to White, usually middle-class, college-educated women. In such a comparison, the dominant group tends to consider its own experience as the standard, and differences can be interpreted as deficiencies (Unger, 1995). That type of thoughtless bias occurred during the second wave of feminism in the United States during the 1960s and 70s and produced a rift that has not yet closed.

TABLE 1.2 *Important Events in the Women's and Men's Movements*

Women's Movement		Men's Movement
First women's rights convention, Seneca Falls, New York	1848	
	1870	15th Amendment to U.S. Constitution gives African American men the right to vote
19th Amendment to U.S. Constitution gives women the right to vote	1920	
National Council of Women Psychologists	1941	
Simon de Beauvoir's *The Second Sex* published	1952	
Betty Friedan's *The Feminine Mystique* published	1963	
The Civil Rights Act prohibits discrimination on the basis of sex	1964	1964 The Civil Rights Act prohibits discrimination on the basis of sex
National Organization for Women formed	1966	
Association for Women in Psychology demonstrates against sexism at APA convention	1969	
APA Division 35 formed	1973	
First World Conference on Women, Mexico City	1975	
United Nations Decade for Women	1976–85	1983 National Organization for Changing Men Founded
	1990	Robert Bly's *Iron John* published
Fourth World Conference on Women, Beijing, including Beijing Declaration and Platform for Action	1995	1995 APA Division 51 formed
	1995	Million Man March, Washington, DC
	1997	Promise Keepers rally, Washington, DC
United Nations 10-year review, Beijing Platform for Action	2005	

In the United States, women of color have a long history of oppression and discrimination, but they did not participate in the feminist movement of the 1960s and 1970s in the same ways that White women did. Instead, they focused on the ways that they experienced oppression and found routes to organize into groups and promote change.

Many African American women have focused their efforts on racial rather than sexual discrimination (Cole & Guy-Sheftall, 2003). When African American women addressed issues of sexism within their communities, these women were often considered disloyal to the struggle against racism for bringing up gender issues. These criticisms did not stop African American women from opposing sexism and founding several feminist organizations during the 1960s and 1970s, including the Black Women's Liberation Caucus, the Third World Women's Alliance, and the National Black Feminist Organization (Cole & Guy-Sheftall, 2003).

African American women were not the only ones who faced intersecting sources of discrimination. Latina, Asian, and Native American women also formed groups that opposed racism and sexism, creating what Becky Thompson (2002) called *multiracial feminism;* she described these interactions:

> As the straight Black women interacted with the Black lesbians, the first-generation Chinese women talked with the Native American activists, and the Latina women talked with the Black and white women about the walls that go up when people cannot speak Spanish, white women attempting to understand race knew they had a lot of listening to do. They also had a lot of truth telling to reckon with, and a lot of networking to do, among other white women and with women of color as well. (p. 343)

The interactions were not always as productive as Thompson described. Women of color often failed to find feminist group compatible with their priorities, which focused on racism and sexism, but in that order. Whitney Peoples (2008, p. 35) explained this point of view: "Feminists of color in the contemporary moment find mainstream social, political and economic landscape has not rid itself of racism, neither has feminism." The women who found feminism unwelcoming did not abandon the values of feminism; rather, they adapted them to meet their goals. Peoples described a version of feminism she calls *hip-hop feminism,* which draws from the energy of hip-hop culture to lead young women to a critical analysis of the sexism and racism that continues in U.S. society. Peoples argued that, through this analysis, women can be empowered.

Latina women in the United States were an important part of the civil rights movement for Hispanics, which began during the 1960s. Organized as part of that movement, the first National Chicana Conference took place in 1971, but almost half of the 600 who attended walked out because they objected to the focus of the conference, which was on gender issues rather than racism (Flores, 2008). This situation is similar to that of African American women, who also experienced conflicts over which source of discrimination was more important. This conflict kept many Latinas from allying themselves with feminist groups and labeling themselves as feminists.

The conflict that Latina women faced is rooted in their culture and religion. Motherhood, sacrifice to family, and subservience to men are idealized values in Hispanic culture; women become targets of criticism if they espouse feminist values that would allow them to establish equal power with husbands, live independent of men, and limit the number of children they bear (Rodríguez, 2008). The critics held that women who wanted such changes had abandoned their culture; they were no longer really Latinas. Thus, Latina women have faced challenges in identifying as feminist but have often redefined their roles and behavior in ways that are compatible with the definition of feminism. In the United States and throughout Latin America, women's groups are often oriented to access to family planning services, preventing domestic violence, increasing educational opportunities, and creating opportunities for women to gain economic power (Espino, 2007).

Native American women have also felt misgivings about the feminist movement for some of the same reasons as Latina women (Smith, 2005). Their objections to racism and their history of treatment by Whites were important to them, but so too were their experiences of sexism and violence from men. They faced criticism from men for speaking out about sexism. Thus, some Native American women avoided the term *feminist*, whereas others experienced no problems in accepting the term. Regardless of their terminology, many Native American women have organized into groups that have feminist goals, which often revolve around prevention of domestic violence and child welfare, making them similar to the goals of many women's groups.

Asian American women have also experienced difficulties in identifying themselves as feminists. Some of their reasons are similar to those of Latina and Native American women, such as the criticism of becoming too "American" and rejecting their heritage (Perez, 2003). Asian American women also experienced stereotyping that applies to their ethnicity as well as to their gender. The passivity and eroticism associated with this stereotype affects Asian American women's activism and leadership (Kawahara, Esnil, & Hsu, 2007), but violence against women has furnished an issue around which to organize, and Asian American women have become leaders in those organizations.

Asian American women have found it easier to identify themselves with feminists than women in Asia, where politics and religion form barriers to women's political participation, economic independence, and physical safety (Subramaniam, 2004; Xu, 2009). In modern India, women's movements range in social class and scope, including local-level organizations to fight against caste-based discrimination and sexual violence, national-level organizations striving to elect more women to parliament, and organizations with international affiliations (Subramaniam, 2004). Chinese women have difficulties in identifying themselves as feminists, even when their concerns and organizations match feminist goals (Shih, 2002; Xu, 2009). Women's organizations in China are also varied, often with local goals such as domestic violence and economic development. The growth of women's rights has experienced great difficulties in Muslin countries, and some debate has taken place concerning the possibility of Islamic feminism (Moghadam, 2002). However, Muslim women who have immigrated to Europe, Canada, and the United States have proclaimed themselves to be feminists and have the goal of integrating their heritage with equality for women.

Feminism in the United States been guilty of exclusion based on race and social class, and the reluctance of women of color to identify themselves with White feminists was a result. Feminists within psychology were also guilty of ignoring these factors, but diversity became a goal within psychology (Reid, 1993; Yoder & Kahn, 1993). Scholars used the same critical thinking that had led them to analyze the male bias in psychology to examine the biases within the psychology of women. As Nancy Felipe Russo (1998, p. ii) explained, "Feminist psychology is now beyond simply critiquing yesterday's findings. The challenge now is to build a knowledge base of theories, concepts, and methods to examine women's lives in all of their diversity." With the recognition that cross-cultural comparisons add to the study of women and gender, feminist psychologists value an inclusive psychology. Thus, diversity was not something that came quickly to the women's movement or to psychology, but it is now a major focus for both.

The history of the men's movement is shorter than that of the women's movement (see Table 1.2), and the timing of that movement influenced its composition. Early men's groups mostly tended to include privileged White men, but the Million Man March drew African American men together, and gay men continue to be active in pressing for changes in laws and social attitudes.

The men's movement is less united than the women's movement, encompassing more divergent perspectives. For example, the men's movement is composed of both men who are antifeminist and those who are profeminist. Groups that aim to redefine masculinity often seek to promote changes in society to make it more inclusive. However, among antifeminist, conservative men's groups, diversity is not a goal and racism may be a theme. Groups that promote a return to traditional masculinity do not strive to include diverse ethnicities, social classes, and sexual orientations among their members. Therefore, although the men's movement has a history that reflects more diversity than the women's movement, some factions of the men's movement reject goals of diversity.

■ Summary

Typically, the first thing that parents learn about their child is the child's sex, which highlights the importance of sex and gender. Beliefs about gender differences are common, but opinions vary, with some people believing in minimal differences and others holding that the differences are maximal and part of essential biological differences.

Within psychology, gender research can be traced to the functionalist school that was influential during the late 1800s. This school held that men and women differ in ability and personality (a view that received criticism at that time). Interest in sex differences (and other individual differences) faded when the behaviorist school dominated psychology, but that interest persisted in psychoanalysis. Psychoanalysts held that differences in anatomy produce personality differences in women and men, with women being inferior in a number of important ways. The feminist movement of the 1960s produced a resurgence of interest among psychologists concerning questions about gender, and research tended to question stereotypes about the sexes.

The traditional terminology—namely, the use of the term *sex differences*—has been criticized. By proposing use of the term *gender,* psychologists have tried to clarify the difference between socially determined and biologically determined differences. However, both terms continue in use, and the proposed distinction between sex differences, meaning biological differences, and gender differences, meaning socially determined differences, has not yet come into consistent use.

Ethnic and economic diversity was not a focus during the early years of the women's movement, which led women of color to experience difficulties in labeling themselves as feminists but not in forming groups oriented toward positive change for women. The men's movement has always been diverse, but some factions of the men's movement object to gays, profeminists, and various ethnic groups. Therefore, diversity remains an issue in both women's and men's movements.

■ Glossary

behaviorism   the school of psychology that emphasizes the importance of observable behavior as the subject matter of psychology and discounts the utility of unobservable mental events.

essentialist view   the view that gender differences are biologically determined.

functionalism   a school of psychology arising in the United States in the late 1800s that attempted to understand how the mind functions. Functionalists held a practical, applied orientation, including an interest in mental abilities and in gender differences in those abilities.

gender   the term used by some researchers to describe the traits and behaviors that are regarded by the culture as appropriate to men and women.

maximalist view   the view that many important differences exist between the sexes.

minimalist view   the view that few important differences exist between the sexes.

sex differences   the term used by some researchers (and considered to be inclusive by others) to describe the differences between male and female research participants.

structuralist   a school of psychology arising in Europe in the 1880s that attempted to understand the workings of the conscious mind by dividing the mind into component parts and analyzing the structure of the mind.

◼ Suggested Readings

Bem, Sandra Lipsitz. (1993). *The lenses of gender.* New Haven, CT: Yale University Press.

Bem contends that gender provides a lens, and people view the world through this lens, often failing to notice the distortions it produces. She discusses three such distorting lenses of gender: androcentrism, gender polarization, and biological essentialism. Bem argues that viewing the world through these lenses provides the basis (and biases) for organizing gender knowledge.

Connell, R. W. (2005). Change among the gatekeepers: Men, masculinities, and gender equality in the global arena. *Signs, 30,* 1801–1825.

Connell points out that societal changes toward equality of women and men will require men's participation, because men control the resources and institutions that must change for equality to occur.

Marecek, Jeanne; Kimmel, Ellen B.; Crawford, Mary; & Hare-Mustin, Rachel T. (2003). Psychology of women and gender. In Donald K. Freedheim (Ed.), *Handbook of psychology: History of psychology* (Vol. 1, pp. 249–268). New York: Wiley.

This article explores the history of women in psychology by tracing the impact of female psychologists, examining the contributions of feminist clinicians, and presenting the organizations through which women have influenced the profession of psychology.

Shields, Stephanie A. (1975). Functionalism, Darwinism, and the psychology of women: A study in social myth. *American Psychologist, 30,* 739–754.

This lively article details the history of early psychologists' research on gender differences, with all the biases showing.

2 Researching Sex and Gender

Ben Barres (2006) asked if gender matters as a response to provocative remarks by Lawrence Summers, who was the president of Harvard University. Summers contended that women's progress in scientific careers has been slow because women may lack the talent to succeed in science and engineering. His remarks were incendiary, causing a firestorm of protest (and voices of support). The suggestion that women's lack of intrinsic ability is to blame for their underrepresentation in science and engineering shows the tendency to resort to *biological essentialism* to explain gender differences. Indeed, Summers mentioned social factors and discrimination as less important than intrinsic ability for success in academic science careers (Remarks at NBER 2005). This tendency to focus on innate differences and to downplay social factors is one way that people maintain stereotypes and prejudice (Keller, 2005). Barres (2006) pointed out the consequences of this view, especially for someone in as prestigious a position as president of Harvard University.

HEADLINE

Does Gender Matter?

Nature, July 13, 2006

Barres (2006) contended that discrimination is widespread in science, but neither men nor women want to believe that the practice is common. People prefer to believe that evaluations are unbiased and that success is based on merit. Barres's contentions of discrimination come from his unique point of view as a scientist—he was born female, trained in neuroscience and began an academic career when he was a woman, underwent the process of changing his sex to male, and continued his career in neuroscience as a man. He reported many instances of discrimination during his years as a woman in science. His experiences included hearing one of his colleagues (who was unaware of his surgery) comment "Ben Barres gave a great seminar today, but then his work is much better than his sister's" (in Barres, 2006, p. 134).

Barres became suspicious of the claims of innate superiority from those who were advantaged by such claims. Instead, he argued that the evidence does not indicate innate superiority of any group in science. The arguments by Barres, Summers, and others represent a recent episode in the ongoing controversy of women's place in science, but the controversies in science go even deeper. For the past decade or so, there has been a "science war" that has debated the basic conceptions of science and its continued value in the modern world (S. Gould, 2000). Feminist scholars have been part of that debate, and gender has been one of its major topics. To understand this current battle and its impact on gender research, we must first understand the background of science and its methods.

How Science Developed

Modern science arose in the 16th and 17th centuries and came to prominence during the 19th century, bringing about radical changes in ways of knowing and understanding the world (Caplan & Caplan, 1994; Komath, 2008). Instead of looking to religion and the Bible for knowledge and wisdom, the new science looked to knowledge gathered through observation. This view represented a radical departure from traditional thought. This new scientific view assumed that the world works by a set of natural laws and that these laws can be discovered by careful, objective investigation (Dear, 2005).

Those methods depended on **empirical observation**, gathering information through evidence from the senses. This view rejected information based on authority or the presumption of supernatural powers. Instead, careful human observation furnished the material for the new science. Scientists can understand the laws of nature if they use correct methods of investigation. One of the cornerstones of scientific observation is **objectivity**, the notion that the observation is free of bias by the observer. Scientists must be careful to remain objective and not allow their personal feelings and biases to affect research. Critics have argued that science has fallen short of this ideal, contending that the required level of objectivity may not be possible (Cosgrove & McHugh, 2008).

Increasing girls' participation in science is a first step toward increasing the number of female scientists.

During the 18th and 19th centuries, science proliferated in Europe and spread throughout the Western world. Research in chemistry, physics, biology, and medicine created new products, medicines, and industries. This proliferation of science was related to the social and political context of Europe, but the development of technology based on science was an important factor in the adoption of the scientific method by other cultures (Komath, 2008). The social sciences of psychology, sociology, and anthropology developed as part of the growing enthusiasm for science. These social sciences used the natural sciences as models, adopting the same assumptions and methods.

What is necessary to conduct scientific research? What makes scientific investigation different from other ways of gaining knowledge? What techniques do scientists use to accomplish these goals, and what are the limitations for each? The following sections explore these questions, with an emphasis on the social sciences, and then examine the critiques of science that have led to the current "science wars."

Approaches to Research

Traditional science remains the dominant approach to research. This approach follows the empiricist tradition, which includes observation and data collection. This research usually follows the procedure of **quantification**, turning observations into numbers, so it is referred to as **quantitative research**. Numbers are the **data** for quantitative research. Data are not the same as the observed phenomenon, but rather are representations of some facet of the phenomenon the researcher considered important. For example, a researcher interested in attitudes toward gay men might ask people to rate their feelings about gay men based on a description of characteristics and behaviors furnished by the researcher. These ratings might range from *very negative* to *very positive* on a 7-point scale. Thus, the data for this study would be numbers obtained from each participant's rating, and each number would represent a participant's attitude in this research study. Quantitative researchers usually analyze their studies by performing statistical analyses of their quantitative data.

Some scholars have raised objections to quantitative research, claiming that quantification fails to capture important aspects of the situations under study; that is, something is lost in the process of turning observations into numbers. An alternative to the quantitative approach is **qualitative research**, which focuses on understanding the complexity of the situation rather than trying to reduce the situation to numbers. In addition to a different philosophy of research, qualitative studies include a different set of methods.

Both quantitative and qualitative researchers have a variety of methods available to them. Any particular research question may be approached using a number of different methods, and each has advantages and disadvantages (Hyde & Durik, 2001). Thus, researchers must examine their research question and decide which method is appropriate.

Quantitative Research Methods

The method of collecting information is critically important in science. By following specific rules, researchers collect information that meets the requirements of science. Scientific information must be observable not only to the researcher but also to others; that is, it must be observable by anyone. This requirement is intended to minimize bias and lead to some level of objectivity.

Another rule of gathering information in science requires systematic observation; scientists must follow some plan or system to gather information. Everyone makes observations, but most people in most circumstances do so in a personal, nonsystematic way, which can lead people to notice certain things while ignoring others. This selective perception may result in distortion and bias. Scientists strive to be systematic in their observations in order to gather information that more accurately reflects the situations they have observed. This procedure does not mean that scientists are free of personal biases; as humans, they are subject to the same perceptual distortions (and even biases) as other humans. Although they cannot avoid personal opinions, scientists are supposed to strive to treat information fairly (Gould, 2000; Mahoney, 2003). Working with observable information and adopting a systematic plan to gather data are strategies to help researchers minimize bias.

The use of numbers in quantitative research has led to an erroneous impression about science—namely, that science is precise. People tend to believe that numbers lend precision, when actually numbers are only one way to summarize certain characteristics of a situation. The process of quantification does not make science precise; it really does the opposite, omitting some aspects of the situation and concentrating on only one.

For example, a researcher who is interested in investigating campus attitudes toward gay, lesbian, and bisexual students might choose to study how such students rate their college campus. The researcher might ask students to rate their progress toward a degree, how their instructors interact with them, how they are treated in the dorms, whether they have ever been threatened by other students, and other such questions. The data might consist of rating each question on a scale ranging from 1 to 7; these numerical ratings would be the data. The researcher can analyze these numbers to determine the results of the study, but the process of turning people's attitudes and experiences into numbers loses many details of their feelings and experiences.

An additional narrowing of the observations in science comes from the specification of a **variable** or several variables in research studies. A variable is the factor of interest in a research study. The term comes from the notion that the factor varies or potentially has more than one value (as opposed to a constant, which has only one value). Most things vary, so finding a variable of interest is not nearly as difficult as restricting a study to only a few variables. For example, variables include family income, level of anxiety, number of hours of practice, gender of participants, and so forth. Studies typically include only a few variables, and this restriction limits what researchers know about a situation.

Quantitative research can be divided into two types: experimental and descriptive. Each approach has advantages and limitations that the other does not. Experimental research is highly prized because a carefully conducted experiment allows researchers to draw conclusions about cause-and-effect relationships. This type of information is difficult to obtain through any other method, and psychology researchers conduct experimental studies if they can do so. However, this method has requirements that make it unsuited to all research situations.

Descriptive research methods help investigators answer "what" questions. That is, descriptive research can tell what types of things exist, including great detail about those things and even the extent of relationships among various things. Descriptive research methods include surveys and correlational studies as well as methods that overlap with qualitative research.

Experimental Designs.   To obtain information about cause and effect, researchers do **experiments**. This type of design allows researchers to answer "why" questions—questions with answers that involve explanations rather than descriptions. An experiment involves the manipulation of one factor, called the **independent variable (IV)**, and the measurement of another factor, called the **dependent variable (DV)**, while attempting to hold all other factors constant. By manipulating the IV, the experimenter tries to create a change in the value of the DV. By holding all other factors constant, the experimenter restricts the change in the DV to the manipulation of the IV. Detecting change requires some basis for comparison, so the simplest version of an experiment requires two conditions, consisting of two different levels of the IV. The manipulation may be more elaborate, with three, four, or more levels of the IV; experiments may also include more than one IV.

The DV is the variable that the experimenter measures. Choosing and quantifying DVs can also be complex. In psychological research, DVs are always some type of behavior or response. By using such DVs, psychology is placed among the sciences that require empirical subject matter—behavior and responses that can be observed and measured.

The logic of experimental design holds that the manipulation of the IV should produce a change in the value of the DV if the two are causally related. When the experimenter also holds other factors constant, the only source of change in the DV should be the manipulated change in the IV. Thus, in a well-designed experiment, the changes in the value of the DV can be entirely attributed to the manipulation of the IV. That is, the changes in the IV caused the changes in the DV.

An example of an experiment on the topic of sexual orientation is difficult to devise. Sexual orientation is not available as an IV—researchers cannot change participants' sexual orientation for the purposes of an experiment. However, Laura Madson (2000) conducted an experiment about people's tendency to infer sexual orientation based on physical appearance. She reasoned that people tend to make inferences about behaviors and characteristics based on appearance. Her research included pretesting to find photographs of people whose gender was unclear (physically androgynous), and she matched these photographs to those of equally attractive people who were clearly male or female, thus manipulating physical appearance as the IV. She asked college students to rate the people pictured in the photos on a variety of measures, including traits, behaviors, and sexual orientation. In this study, perception of sexual orientation was a DV that the researcher measured. The results were consistent with Madson's predictions: Participants were more likely to rate the people in the physically androgynous photos as homosexual than the people whose physical appearance in the photos was more typically feminine or masculine.

Gender research such as Madson's defines sexual orientation as a social category. Researchers who use this approach investigate how sexual orientation is one piece of information in a complex system of beliefs and expectations about behavior. Gender is another variable that can be used this way in experimental studies. Rather than manipulate information about physical appearance, researchers may provide information about the gender of the target to determine participants' reaction to this information. This approach allows gender to become an IV because researchers can manipulate the gender of a character in a description or photo and yet hold all other factors in the description constant. According to Kay Deaux's (1984) review of this approach, the results indicated that gender is an important piece of information that people use in forming impressions and interacting with people: "The focus is not on how men and women actually differ, but how people *think* that they differ" (Deaux, 1984, p. 110). This approach is especially well suited to investigating stereotypes, attitudes, and conceptions of gender and issues related to gender, such as sexual orientation.

Although the logic of experimental design is simple, creating conditions to effectively manipulate one factor while holding all other factors constant is far from simple. Such a situation would be almost impossible in a naturalistic setting, because any one change would result in many others. Therefore, almost all experiments take place in laboratories. These settings offer the possibility of the necessary control, but they open experiments to the criticism of artificiality.

Experiments are prized because, carefully designed and conducted, this method allows conclusions to be made concerning causality. If the experiment is not done carefully, however, interpretation of causality can be in error. The participants in the Madson study saw photographs of people whom they rated based on their appearance. These participants may have behaved differently in a more naturalistic situation; evaluating photos or descriptions differs from evaluating actual people. In addition, the laboratory situation may prompt different behavior than would occur in a more realistic context. Because participants in a laboratory setting are always aware that their behavior is of interest to researchers, they may behave differently than they would in a natural setting. This possibility limits the extent to which researchers can generalize their results to other situations. The artificiality of the situation and its limitations in generalizing results to other situations are drawbacks of the experimental method. Despite some disadvantages, researchers have a prejudice in favor of experiments, prizing them above other methods (perhaps inappropriately), and leading scientists to conduct experiments whenever they can.

Ex Post Facto Studies.

Researchers cannot always perform experiments. Some variables of interest are beyond possible manipulation, for either practical or ethical reasons. For example, researchers might want to know about the effect of brain damage on memory. To do an experiment, researchers would be required to select a group of people and perform the surgery that causes brain damage in half of them while leaving the other half with undamaged brains. Obviously, this research is unethical, but the question that prompted it—Does brain damage influence memory?—is still of interest. Sexual orientation is similar; it is a variable of interest, but researchers cannot manipulate sexual orientation by assigning people to groups and changing their sexual orientation.

Researchers interested in the question about brain damage and memory have at least two choices. They might choose to do the experiment with nonhuman subjects (although some would object to the ethics of this research, too), but the problems of generalizing the findings to humans would be a severe limitation. Another choice would be the **ex post facto** (or **quasi-experimental**) **study**. In this type of study, researchers might select people who have sustained brain damage in the area of interest and enlist these individuals as research participants, contrasting them with a group of people who have not experienced brain damage of any sort, or with those who have damage in some other area of the brain. Both groups would participate in the assessment of memory. Therefore, the presence of brain damage would be the **subject variable** (or *participant variable*)—the characteristic of interest in the participants—and the scores on the memory test would be the DV.

Such an ex post facto study would not be a true experiment, because the researchers did not produce the brain damage while holding all other factors constant. Instead, the researchers entered the picture *after* the manipulation had occurred through accidents. With no opportunity for precision in creating the values of the IV or in holding other factors constant, the ex post facto study lacks the controls of an experiment that would allow researchers to draw conclusions about cause-and-effect relationships (Christensen, 2004).

Ex post facto research is one type of quasi-experimental research, meaning that it shares some characteristics with but does not meet the definition of experimental research. The missing elements are random assignment of participants to groups, manipulation of an IV, and control of other variables. The similarities include a contrast of two or more groups and measurement of a DV. These similarities can lead to misinterpretations of these studies and incorrect attributions of causality. Researchers are usually careful to use the correct language to interpret their findings from ex post facto studies, but people who read the research may not be appropriately cautious, leading to misunderstandings of research findings from ex post facto studies.

Gender and sexual orientation of participants are both subject variables, characteristics of the participants that exist prior to their taking part in a study. These characteristics can be the basis for division of participants into contrasting groups. This research design has a long history in psychology and has constituted the traditional approach to gender research. In 1974 two psychologists, Eleanor Maccoby and Carol Nagy Jacklin, published *The Psychology of Sex Differences,* a comprehensive review of research-based psychological findings about gender-related differences. These authors collected more than 2,000 studies in which gender was a subject variable, and they organized the findings around different topics, such as aggression and verbal ability. Maccoby and Jacklin then evaluated the findings for each topic, determining how many studies failed to find a difference, how many studies supported a difference, and the direction of the differences for those comparisons that showed differences. Maccoby and Jacklin's book was soon accepted as a classic in this type of research review.

Studies with gender as a subject variable remain a common choice in gender research in psychology and may be applied to the study of sexual orientation. Nathan Berg and Donald Lien (2002) conducted such a study, comparing heterosexual and nonheterosexual individuals (subject variable) in terms of income (dependent variable). These researchers wanted to know if being gay, lesbian, or bisexual was related to differences in earnings. They asked more than 4,000 participants the number and sex of their sexual partners within the past 5 years, which allowed Berg and Lien to construct categories of heterosexual and nonheterosexual. They also asked about income and performed an analysis comparing the incomes of individuals in these two categories. Their results indicated that sexual orientation is related to income, but in a complex way that interacts with participants' gender. Heterosexual men earned more than gay and bisexual men, but heterosexual women earned less than lesbian and bisexual women. These researchers were restricted from interpreting their results in terms of cause and effect because their use of the ex post facto method did not allow such conclusions, and some other uncontrolled variables (such as discrimination against gay men, marital status, or career choice) may have been important in these results. However, Berg and Lien were able to conclude that sexual orientation is a factor in income level.

The studies that approach gender as a subject variable are also ex post facto studies, with all of the limitations of this method. That is, these studies do not and cannot reveal that gender *causes* differences in any behavior. This caution is difficult for many people to keep in mind, and those who are not familiar with research methods have a tendency to believe that gender-related differences in behavior have biological sex as the underlying cause (Keller, 2005). This reasoning contains two errors: (1) incorrectly attributing causality to a research method that cannot demonstrate cause-and-effect relationships and (2) reducing the many variables that coexist with biological sex to the subject variable gender. Therefore, an erroneous interpretation of such studies can lead people to conclusions for which there is no research evidence.

Figure 2.1 illustrates some of the differences between experimental and ex post facto designs, using sexual orientation as an example. In the experimental design, researchers often randomly divide the participants into groups in order to keep individual differences equal among the groups. Random assignment would be *very* unlikely to yield groups based on sexual orientation. The ex post facto design, on the other hand, assigns participants to groups on the basis of some factor that the participants already possess, such as sexual orientation or gender. In this type of design, the researcher might have one group consisting of women and another of men. Indeed, thousands of studies use this design to study gender-related differences and similarities.

Gender can be an IV in an experiment if the researcher manipulates the gender of some target person whom the participants rate, evaluate, or react to. This approach makes

Experimental Design—Sexual Orientation as a Social Category

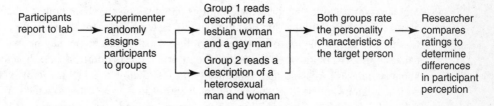

Ex Post Facto Design—Sexual Orientation as a Subject Variable

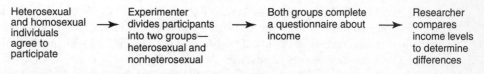

FIGURE 2.1 *Two Designs with Sexual Orientation as a Variable*

gender a social category. In addition, the subject variable of gender can be included in a study that manipulates an IV to study each variable as well as the variables in combination. Therefore, ex post facto designs can examine gender as a subject variable, experimental designs can study gender as a social category to which participants react, and studies can use gender as a subject variable combined with additional, manipulated IVs. These approaches are not equivalent, and each yields information that requires careful interpretation of findings.

Unlike experimental and ex post facto studies, other types of quantitative research do not concentrate on comparisons and differences. Instead, these methods focus on describing characteristics or attitudes of participants, determining the relationship (correlation) between variables, and other descriptions of variables. These variables may include gender, sexual orientation, or many others; these methods fit within the category of *descriptive research*. Surveys and correlational studies are examples of such descriptive methods.

Surveys.   In a **survey**, researchers construct a questionnaire, choose a group of people to respond to the questionnaire, collect the data, and analyze the data to yield results. This method sounds deceptively simple; almost anyone can think of questions to ask. However, the method is filled with choices and pitfalls. For example, researchers using this method must decide about the wording of questions (e.g., "Do you agree . . ." versus "Do you disagree . . ."), the answer format (respondents give answers in their own words versus respondents choose from a set of answers), the appearance of the questionnaire (number of pages, size of type, page layout), the choice of people responding (representative of the entire population versus a select group, such as first-time parents or gay men), the number of people needed (what number will give a good estimate for accuracy), and the method of administration (face-to-face interview, telephone interview, mailed questionnaire). Unwise choices on any of these decisions may result in a survey that does not allow the researcher to answer the question that prompted the research or, worse, may give the researcher an answer that is misleading.

The main limitation of surveys is inherent in the method: Surveys pose questions rather than make direct measurements. That is, surveys rely on self-reports rather than direct observations of behavior, which requires participants to be both honest when they are asked about their attitudes and opinions and to have a good memory when they are asked to report on past behavior. Both tasks may present problem: People may lie, withhold the truth, or simply not know or remember the information. In addition, participants' beliefs about social standards and their tendency to present themselves in a favorable way are biases that can invalidate a question or even an entire survey. Despite the wide variety of information that can be obtained through the survey method, that information is limited not only by its descriptive nature but also by its potential inaccuracy.

Despite the disadvantages, surveys offer the advantages of allowing researchers to ask people about things that the researchers could not easily (or possibly ethically) observe directly. Thus, the method is flexible and useful in a variety of situations. Surveys are very commonly used for measuring people's attitudes. Psychologists, sociologists, market researchers, and political pollsters all use this method to help decide how people feel about a wide variety of issues.

For example, Robert Brown and his colleagues (Brown, Clarke, Gortmaker, & Robinson-Keilig, 2004) surveyed gay, lesbian, and bisexual university students as well as other university students, faculty, staff, and residence hall assistants concerning the campus climate and sexual orientation. Gay, lesbian, and bisexual students are more likely to "come out"—that is, to reveal their sexual orientation—in college than in high school because college is typically a less hostile climate than high school. Nevertheless, colleges often fail to be supportive of students with nonheterosexual sexual orientations. These researchers used the survey method and were careful to choose a sample that yielded representative data from heterosexual and nonheterosexual students. They also included representatives from faculty and staff to better understand several facets of campus climate. Also, they asked questions about a variety of factors to try to examine the general campus climate, acceptance by various social groups, progress in academic programs, and acceptance by faculty.

The results from this study indicated that gay, lesbian, and bisexual students found the campus climate less accepting of their sexual orientation than heterosexual students did. In addition, heterosexual students rated the campus climate for nonheterosexuals as more accepting than gay, lesbian, and bisexual students reported. That is, students who were not heterosexual found less acceptance than heterosexual students believed they would. This difference in point of view is not surprising but does highlight how discrimination may be less visible to those who are doing the discriminating than to those who are the targets of such discrimination. This survey also found that resident assistants were more supportive of gay, lesbian, and bisexual students than others and that freshman students were less accepting than older students. Like many other surveys, this research yielded many results based on the varied responses from participants. Indeed, one conclusion of the study emphasized how valuable these different perspectives are in understanding the campus climate for nonheterosexual students.

Correlational Studies.   If researchers want to know about the relationship between two specific variables rather than information about several variables, they may conduct a **correlational study**, another type of descriptive method. Correlational studies allow researchers to determine both the strength and types of relationships between the variables under study.

To conduct a correlational study, researchers must choose two variables, create an operational definition of the variables, measure these variables, and then analyze the relationship between them. An **operational definition** is a definition of a variable in terms of the operations used to obtain data on that variable rather than in terms of the concepts underlying the variable. Operational definitions are one method that researchers use to be more specific about the variables they study. An operational definition provides instructions about how to measure the two variables in a correlational study.

To perform the analysis of the data, researchers calculate a correlation coefficient by analyzing their data using the correlation coefficient formula. The results reveal the strength or magnitude of the relationship between two variables. A number of variations on the correlation coefficient exist, but the most common is the *Pearson product–moment correlation coefficient,* symbolized by the letter r. The results of the analysis yield a number that varies between $r = +1.00$ and $r = -1.00$. Correlations that are close to $r = +1.00$ indicate a strong positive relationship, which means that as scores on one variable increase, those on the other also increase. Correlations that are close to $r = -1.00$ indicate a strong negative relationship, which means that as one measurement increases, the other decreases. Correlations that are close to $r = 0.00$ indicate little or no relationship between the two variables.

For example, Michelle Davies (2004) examined the correlation between attitudes toward gay men and other attitudes. She questioned more than 500 people, assessing not only their emotional attitudes toward gay men (such as "Gay men are disgusting") but also their attitudes about civil rights for gays (such as "Gay men should have the same civil rights as anyone else"), attitudes about women (such as "Women seek to gain power and control over men"), attitudes about masculinity (such as "Sometimes fists are the only way to get out of a bad situation"), and attitudes about male sexuality (such as "Men should always take the initiative when it comes to sex"). She performed a correlational analysis of these attitudes and found a moderately strong positive correlation ($r = 0.42$) between attitudes toward gay men and attitudes toward women; that is, people who held negative attitudes about gay men also tended to have hostile attitudes about women. She found an even stronger correlation ($r = 0.51$) between negative attitudes toward gay men and attitudes of masculine toughness; that is, people who tended to have negative attitudes toward gay men also agreed with the notion that men should be tough. The results showed no relationship ($r = 0.01$) between attitudes toward gay men and attitudes about civil rights. Thus, this correlational study demonstrated that attitudes toward gay men relate to other attitudes, including those about women and masculinity but not about civil rights.

Like other descriptive methods, correlational studies do not reveal why the relationship exists. However, making such deductions may be very tempting. Indeed, a causal relationship may exist between two variables that have a high correlation, but the method does not allow that conclusion to be made. Even a high correlation would not allow a researcher to know the source of the relationship: Did changes in one variable produce changes in the other, or vice versa? Another possibility is that both variables may be causally related to a third variable that was not part of the study. Indeed, Davies (2004) suggested that the correlations in her study all related to an underlying attitude about traditional gender roles. In any case, a conclusion of causality is not legitimate on the basis of the evidence from a correlational study. Thus, the information that researchers obtain and the conclusions that they may draw from correlational studies exclude causality but include information on the existence and strength of relationships.

In summary, different quantitative research methods yield different types of information. Experimental research allows researchers to explain *why* a relationship exists between IVs and DVs because this method yields information about cause-and-effect relationships. A quasi-experimental method, the ex post facto study, is similar to an experiment in the designation of variables (called subject or participant variables) and DVs, but these designs differ from true experiments in that they use the existing values of the subject variable rather than create the values of the IV through manipulation. Descriptive research methods include surveys and correlational studies. Such studies help to answer questions about *what* occurs; that is, they describe what exists but reveal no information about causality.

Qualitative Research Methods

Researchers who use qualitative methods often believe that the quantification process removes important information. This belief leads qualitative researchers to collect different data and to resist reducing their data to numbers. Such researchers may collect extensive reports or interviews, which they transcribe and attempt to organize and understand. This strategy makes statistical analysis difficult or impossible.

Qualitative researchers also reject the notion that they should be detached and impartial; instead, they accept the subjectivity of the research process and attempt to form cooperative relationships with those whom they study. By interacting with research participants as equals, they try to understand the meaning and context of the phenomena they study. Some researchers advocate an even more active role, striving to bring a voice to individuals and groups that have been pushed to the margins and striving to change social and political situations (Zavos & Biglia, 2009).

The methods of qualitative research are not necessarily different from those of quantitative research. That is, the methods themselves do not create qualitative or quantitative research; the key to the difference is the type of data collected. However, qualitative researchers tend to use a different selection of methods than quantitative researchers, including case studies, interviews, ethnography, and focus groups.

Case Studies.   A **case study** is an intensive study of a case—that is, a single person or a small sample of people. Several different factors determine which case might be a good candidate for study. The person may be typical and thus reflective of many other people, or the person may be unusual and thus of interest. The unusual cases are more common for case studies. Researchers conducting case studies often spend days or months interviewing or observing in order to write a case study.

Brent Bilodeau (2005) reported on two cases of transgendered individuals who discussed the development of their identities during college. Both individuals had been born female, but Jordan said that she failed to accept herself as a girl from the earliest time that she understood the concept of gender. Nick spoke of gender as a performance that she had created with interesting variations. Neither individual accepted the divisions of gender that their families and society furnished; each found multiple ways to transgress gender boundaries. During college, both individuals explored their gender identities and found support and guidance through the lesbian, bisexual, and transgendered (LGBT) campus organization. This support was critical in the process, as Jordan explained: "More dialogue happened. [It] became a place for me to have a voice and for others to ask those 'burning questions' " (Bilodeau, 2005, p. 36). These two cases present a fascinating picture of two unusual cases of the development of gender identity and how college is a critical time for that development. The cases are clearly not representative for most individuals and may not be typical of other transgendered individuals, but the in-depth exploration included details that no other method captures.

Interviews.   **Interviews** can take many forms, but qualitative interviews differ from interviews conducted as part of survey research in both format and goals. Survey interviews are quantitative, including a uniform set of questions to which all respondents reply. The uniformity of responses allows statistical analysis, but such analysis is not the goal of qualitative interviews. These interviews can take the form of oral or life histories, or the interview may be oriented around a narrower topic.

Andrea Daly and her colleagues (Daley, Solomon, Newman, & Mishna, 2007) used the interview method to study LGBT students' experience of bullying in school. After selecting nine key informants for their sexual orientation, gender, and ethnic diversity, the researchers conducted semi-structured interviews to understand these students' experiences with bullying. The interviews were coded and analyzed for themes, resulting in several commonalities. One category encompassed bullying that occurred when individuals crossed gender boundaries—when men's behavior was too "feminine" and women's was too "masculine." The types of bullying also varied according to the gender of the bully; men were more likely to perform physical attacks against gay men but to sexually harass and assault lesbians. By crossing gender boundaries, however, gay men became targets for the harassment and gossip that is more typical of women's experience. These researchers also found that sexual orientation and ethnicity intersected, creating situations in which LGBT young people were not always aware of what made them targets—their sexual orientation or their ethnicity. Both factors added to the risks. As one participant said, "The more 'isms' you have to deal with, the harder it is" (Daly et al., 2007, p. 22).

Ethnography.   **Ethnography**, one of the most common qualitative methods, has a long tradition in anthropology, in which qualitative research has been more common than in psychology. However, this method is compatible with research in psychology—observation and recording of behavior and events (Stewart, 2003). Researchers using this method spend time becoming immersed in the situation they are studying, which necessitates attention to context. For anthropologists, this situation is typically another culture; for psychologists and sociologists, the situation may be a school, company, or hospital. By becoming part of the situation, the researcher can gather and interpret information situated in the context in which it occurs.

Phyllis Dalley and Mark David Campbell (2006) conducted an ethnographic study in a Canadian high school, investigating the processes through which heterosexuality was maintained as the norm and other sexuality was pushed to the margins. They observed students at school as they interacted with peers at school events and in corridors, focusing on five marginalized female students who were friends and two gay male students over a 3-year period. They observed how the expectation for heterosexuality silenced the two gay male students. On the other hand, the five straight female students used lesbianism to challenge and question the heterosexual norm of the school. Thus, the context of this school and its expectations for heterosexuality were not played out equally for female and male students.

Focus Groups.   The focus group is another qualitative method that psychologists have borrowed; this method is more common in communications and marketing research than in psychology (Kleiber, 2004). A **focus group** is a discussion centered on a specific topic. The group can consist either of people brought together for the purpose of the discussion or of people who belong to some existing group, such as a family or sorority. Groups usually consist of 6 to 8 people but rarely more than 12. Focus groups are similar to interviews in terms of the questions and topics that can be explored. However, this method allows group members to interact with each other as well as with the researcher, making the focus group more similar to naturally occurring situations than the interview method is (Wilkinson, 1999).

Camille Lee (2002) also investigated sexual orientation issues in high school, but she used the focus group approach, studying a group of seven students who were members of the Gay/Straight Alliance at their high school. This group included gay, lesbian, bisexual (GLB), and straight students questioned over a 2-year period. Lee was interested not only in the opinions of GLB students but also in how the heterosexual students changed in reaction to their participation in the alliance. She found positive changes for all students, including an increased sense of safety for the GLB students and a diminished assumption of heterosexuality among the straight students. The analysis also indicated an improvement in school, which suggests the value of positive action by schools concerning sexual orientation issues.

Table 2.1 presents both quantitative and qualitative research methods, along with advantages and limitations of each approach.

Researchers' Choices

The use of qualitative research methods has expanded in acceptance and frequency, especially since the 1990s (Rennie, Watson, & Monteiro, 2002), but these methods still constitute a minority of the research, even in the area of gender (Marchel & Owens, 2007). Researchers steeped in the quantitative tradition may fail to accept qualitative investigations as "legitimate" research (Weil, 2008). An analysis of two leading journals, *Feminism & Psychology* and *Psychology of Women Quarterly,* revealed that the interview method was the most common qualitative approach (Wilkinson, 1999). It accounted for

TABLE 2.1   *Advantages and Limitations of Quantitative and Qualitative Research Methods*

Method	Advantage	Limitation
Quantitative Methods		
Survey	Examines a variety of topics without being intrusive	Relies on self-reports rather than direct observation of behavior
Correlational study	Allows determination of strength and direction of relationship between two variables	Cannot reveal any information about causality
Experiment	Allows determination of cause-and-effect relationships	Conducted in laboratory situations that are artificial; can investigate only a few variables at a time
Qualitative Methods		
Case study	Reveals extensive information about one case	Cannot be generalized to other cases
Interview	Allows researchers to question participants extensively about a topic	Does not yield a standard set of answers; may include only a few participants
Ethnography	Allows researchers to become immersed in a situation and to understand the contexts in which behavior occurs	Data collection is not systematic, which may lead to focusing on some and overlooking other information
Focus group	Allows extensive exploration of a topic as well as observation of the interaction among group members	Does not yield a standard set of data, making the information difficult to analyze

over 50% of the research articles in *Feminism & Psychology* but only 17% of research articles in *Psychology of Women Quarterly*. Other qualitative methods accounted for much lower percentages, and no other qualitative method represented more than 2% of the research studies in these journals. Therefore, the majority of psychology research is quantitative research—even those studies published in journals featuring feminist scholarship.

Qualitative research offers alternatives to traditional quantitative research methods in terms of philosophy and methods. A comparison of the two approaches appears in Table 2.2. Qualitative researchers emphasize context and acknowledge that subjectivity is part of the research process; they become involved in the research situation, interact with participants in order to understand the patterns of their behavior, and sometimes endeavor to bring about change in the situations they research (Zavos & Biglia, 2009). Researchers who use these methods believe that this approach offers advantages over the traditional quantitative approach, and the rise of qualitative research has polarized the teaching of research methods (Tashakkori & Teddlie, 2003). Some researchers see no room for qualitative research (Capaldi & Proctor, 2005), whereas others (Onwuegbuzie & Leech, 2005) have called for a combination of qualitative and quantitative methods as a pragmatic way to approach social science research.

Lisa Bowleg (2008) reported on research that included both quantitative and qualitative approaches, focusing on the perceptions and experiences of African American lesbians. Bowleg contended that researchers have approached the combination of gender, ethnicity, and sexual orientation by choosing each of these factors as variables and questioning participants about which of these factors presents problems for them. She reported on findings from such questions, which revealed that 49% agreed or strongly agreed that racism was a more serious issue in their lives than homophobia. However, Bowleg also argued that such a quantitative approach separates factors that intersect in complex ways; the separation loses much of the experience of African American lesbians. Bowleg's qualitative research included an analysis of narratives of the experience of Black lesbians. For

TABLE 2.2   *Comparison of Quantitative and Qualitative Research*

Quantitative Researchers	Qualitative Researchers
Often work in laboratories	Rarely work in laboratories
Strive to detach themselves from the situation to attain objectivity	Immerse themselves in the situation and accept subjectivity as part of the process
Attempt to study a representative group of individuals to be able to generalize	May seek unusual individuals because they are interesting cases
Create a distinction between researchers and participants	Treat participants as equals
Collect data in the form of numbers	Collect information that is not reduced to numbers
Attempt to control the influence of variables other than the independent variable(s)	Attempt to understand the complexity of the situation as it exists
Use statistics to analyze their data	Do not use statistics to analyze their information

example, in narratives of the influence of racism and sexism, the reports tended to focus on racism but to also include frustrations concerning the sexism and homophobia that these women had encountered. Their experiences were part of a social context in which racism, sexism, and homophobia combined in inseparable ways that qualitative research is much more likely to capture than a quantitative approach would.

Gender Bias in Research

Despite the long history and success of science, some modern scholars have questioned its assumptions and procedures, starting what has become known as the "science wars" (Gould, 2000). One criticism is that science grew not only from the activities of men but also from a gendered, masculine bias that is inherently part of science. According to this view, this masculine bias affects our modern conception of science, including the thinking of the men and women who do scientific work. Harvard President Lawrence Summers expressed this bias when he suggested that women may be inherently less capable of being scientists than men are.

Another criticism of science contends that science is incapable of revealing an objective picture of the natural world because objective reality does not exist. These critics are **constructionists**, who emphasize the subjective nature of all knowledge, including scientific knowledge. The constructionists argue that "we do not discover reality, we invent it" (Hare-Mustin & Marecek, 1988, p. 455). That is, science does not lead researchers to map a realistic picture of the world but to construct views of the world in ways that reflect social and personal perceptions and biases. Scholars who take this view have cited the study of gender as a particularly good example of the distortions and misrepresentations of science.

Sources of Bias

Bias can enter research at many levels, beginning with the very framework of science. The philosophers whose work spurred the founding of science were all men, and Evelyn Fox Keller (1985) argued that these philosophers introjected a masculine bias into the very conceptual foundation of science. She interpreted the emphasis on rationality and objectivity in science as masculine values, and she contrasted those masculine elements of science with the feminine elements of nature—feeling and subjectivity. Keller discussed what she interpreted as the gendering of science and nature: masculine for science and feminine for nature. Thus, even at its inception, science carried connotations of maleness, rationality, and dominance. According to Keller, not only have women been discouraged from the pursuit of science as a profession but also the activity of science itself suggests masculinity (see According to the Media and According to the Research). The culture of science was and remains masculine (Schiebinger, 2007), and female scientists cite this as more important than innate ability for women's exclusion from science careers (van Anders, 2004).

Theories are another potential source of bias in science. The study of gender is full of examples in which speculations and theories have attained a status in which they are mistaken for results. Freud's theory is probably the most prominent example, with its

ACCORDING TO THE MEDIA...

Scientists Are Men (or Act Like Men)

In the movies, scientists are most often male and more often mad or bad than good. If they are good, they are generally bumbling incompetents. These depictions go back to the era of silent film and continue to the present in movies and on television. "The movies have always been full of insane chemists, demonic doctors and obsessive inventors who, whether purposely or inadvertently, unleash malevolent forces that neither they nor anyone else can control" (Ribalow, 1998, p. 26). Some scientists in the movies want to do evil, but even with noble motivations, movie scientists often cause serious problems when they fail to understand the implications of their actions. Both evil and well-meaning scientists are portrayed as obsessive, self-centered, personally cold, and removed from society.

Women have been in the background more often than playing leading characters in media portrayals of science. In children's science programming, about 80% of the women were in secondary or supporting roles, and the proportion of male to female scientists was 2 to 1 (Steinke & Long, 1996). That proportion is similar in feature films that appeared between 1991 and 2001 (Steinke, 2005), making women much less frequent media scientists than men.

Female scientists are not "mad scientists" or bungling nerds as often as male scientists (Flicker, 2003). They may be evil but are more likely to be masculine women, "old maids," world experts, or lonely heroines. The masculine women and unmarried women who have given up on romance were more common in older films. During the 1990s, the female scientist was most often the "brainy babe" (Ribalow, 1998). This female version of the scientist was sometimes the extraordinarily talented expert, such as the female scientists in *Mimic, Jurassic Park,* and *Twister,* or the lonely heroine, such as Dr. Ellie Arroway (in *Contact*), Dr. Emma Russell (in *The Saint*), and Dr. Amy Barnes (in *Volcano*). A variety of female scientists who are brainy babes obsessively dedicated to their work appear in TV's several versions of *CSI: Crime Scene Investigation* and as Dr. Temperance "Bones" Brennan in *Bones*.

Although female scientists have begun to be portrayed as brainy and competent (Steinke, 2005), they are definitely babes: Female scientists in film and on television tend to be young and extraordinarily good looking (Flicker, 2003). Indeed, many are too young to be the world-class experts they portray. However, female scientists often have to withstand challenges from their male colleagues, who question their competence and make sexist remarks. Romance has been a common theme for these movie scientists, but family and children have not. Most female scientists in films have been unmarried, and the married female scientists tend to be childless.

To sum up, female scientists appear much less frequently than male scientists in the movies. When they appear, they are portrayed as driven, outspoken, obsessive, and dedicated—characteristics common to male scientists.

emphasis on the importance of biological sex differences in building personality. Research has not supported this theory (see Chapter 5 for more on Freud), and supporters of the theory speak with unearned authority.

Additional bias in research on gender (and many other topics) comes from the procedures involved in planning studies and evaluating results. Researchers' values enter the research process as early as the planning stage of studies, influencing the choice of problem to investigate and the choice of questions to ask (Harding & Norberg, 2005; Rolin, 2004). Publications place too much emphasis on results and too little emphasis on the conceptualization of the questions underlying the research process, often ignoring the social and political aspects and implications of research (Harding, 2001; Harding & Norberg, 2005). The

▚ ACCORDING TO THE RESEARCH ...

Women in Science Face Barriers

The images of female scientists in the media may furnish models for girls and thus help to orient girls to pursue careers in science and engineering, a goal that has proven difficult. However, some of the portrayals do not present enticing images of scientific careers, and thus the media image of female scientists may discourage girls from pursuing such careers (Jones, 2005).

Depictions of female scientists have increased in the movies, and that change is accurate: The number of women working in science and engineering has increased over the past 35 years. An analysis of feature films (Steinke, 2005) indicated that about one-third of films that portrayed scientists or engineers included women in those roles, which is actually *higher* than the 20% of women working in these fields (Kohlstedt, 2004). It is easier to become a female scientist in the movies than in real life.

The frequency of female scientists in the media is not the only inaccuracy of science at the movies, but male scientists receive worse treatment than their female counterparts. Male scientists appear as inept social bunglers or evil geniuses (Jackson, 2008). Female film scientists appear professional and competent (Steinke, 2005), which is correct, but this description also applies to male scientists. Unfortunately, the portrayals of challenges to that competence and harassment by male colleagues are also correct.

Surveys of female scientists (Rosser, 2004; Settles, Cortina, Malley, & Stewart, 2006) have revealed that women in science face barriers that their male colleagues do not. Two of those barriers appear in films about female scientists: challenges to competence and sexual harassment. Such negative experiences were more common among women in the natural sciences than in the social sciences, and female scientists reported such negative experiences as factors in decisions to leave their departments or even their jobs. Female scientists who perceived that their work environment included a sexist climate, gender discrimination, and sexual harassment reported lower job satisfaction and poorer productivity than female scientists who experienced more supportive work environments.

Another barrier faced by female scientists often fails to appear in films—the conflict between work and family demands. Films avoid depicting this dilemma by portraying female scientists as single or childless (Steinke, 2005). Research on the success of female scientists (Bentley & Wise, 2004) revealed that this depiction may not be accurate; female scientists often marry and have children. However, family commitments hampered scientific success for women compared to men.

Thus, research on women in science shows a growing number of women pursuing careers in science but also barriers that block their success. Those barriers are similar to the movie image of female scientists in terms of harassment and lack of acceptance by their male colleagues, but in addition, women in science face problems of balancing career and family in ways that the movies fail to show.

answers that researchers find depend on the questions they ask; the planning and questioning aspects of the process are critically important, therefore, but often neglected.

When researchers formulate their studies, they ask questions and choose methods of gathering information that will allow them to answer their questions. Most researchers know what they expect to find when they ask a question, so research is not free of the values and expectations of the scientists, even at this stage of the research (Cisneros-Puebla & Faux, 2008). In quantitative research, these expectations lead to the formulation of a **hypothesis,** a statement about the expected outcome of the study. Researchers test hypotheses by gathering data and analyzing them to obtain results. The researchers can then decide whether the results support or fail to support their hypothesis.

To evaluate the data collected from studies, quantitative researchers usually use statistical tests. Many different statistical tests exist, but all of those used to evaluate research data have a common goal—to allow the researcher to decide whether the results are statistically significant. A **statistically significant result** is one due to reasons other than chance alone. If researchers are careful in the design of their studies, they can attribute significant results to the factors they have identified in their studies. The procedure for determining the statistical significance of a result involves choosing the appropriate statistical test and analyzing the data using that statistic. If the analysis indicates significant effects, then the researchers can conclude that their results were not due to chance alone—that is, the study worked as hypothesized. If the analysis does not indicate a significant effect, then the researchers cannot claim that their results are due to anything but chance or that their study worked as hypothesized. Researcher bias may enter both at the stage of planning and at the point of data analysis. For example, an analysis of many studies on the topic of gender development (Tennenbaum & Leaper, 2002) revealed that studies with male first authors showed larger gender differences than studies with female first authors.

Researchers are constrained from making claims about factors that do not produce significant results, because these results are not considered "real," and researchers are not allowed to have confidence in the validity of nonsignificant results. When researchers obtain statistically significant results, they have confidence that their research has revealed effects that probably are not due to chance. However, the term *significant* may be misleading, because people who are not sophisticated in the logic of statistical evaluation may believe that statistically significant means *important* or *large*.

A large or important result is not only statistically significant but also significant in practical terms. The concepts of statistical significance and practical significance are not the same. A result is statistically significant when it is unlikely to have occurred solely on the basis of chance. A result has **practical significance** when it is important to everyday life. For example, a low correlation ($r = 0.20$) can indicate a statistically significant relationship if the number of people participating in the study was sufficiently large (what constitutes a large sample varies with the design and statistic), but this magnitude of correlation does not reveal a strong relationship between the two variables in the correlation. That is, this correlation would have little practical significance. Confusion between these two concepts can result: "Reasonable people who are repeatedly exposed to findings reported as significant mean differences or nonchance factors . . . sometimes begin to think and talk as if those differences were actually true in most individual cases" (Bernstein, 1999, p. x). Such misunderstandings can lead people to believe that results mean more than they actually do and apply to everyone when they actually do not.

The gender difference in mathematics performance is one such well-publicized difference (Maccoby & Jacklin, 1974). Are boys really better at math than girls? If so, how much better? Do all boys do better than all girls? One way to answer these questions is to examine the amount of overlap in the distribution of math scores for boys and girls. Figure 2.2 shows some possibilities for the distributions of math scores for boys and girls. Group A of this figure shows two distributions with no overlap. If this figure represented the mathematics performance of boys and girls, then all boys would do better than all girls. Group B shows the performance of boys and girls overlapping slightly. If this figure represented the performance of boys and girls, then most boys would do better than most girls. A few girls would do

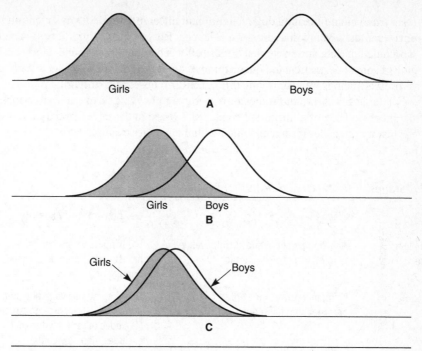

FIGURE 2.2   *Distributions with Varying Degrees of Overlap*

better than a few boys, but no girls would do better than boys with the highest performance. Group C shows a lot of overlap between the performance of the two groups. If this figure represented performance, many girls would do better at math than many boys.

Hyde (1981, 2005a) contended that the upper range of difference in mathematical performance between men and women is no more than 1%. With this level of difference, only a small percentage of the distribution of math scores for boys and girls fails to overlap, and most of the scores for the two are in the same range. Figure 2.2C comes closer to this distribution of math ability than the other parts of Figure 2.2. These gender-related differences in math performance are sufficiently large to show a statistically significant difference but not large enough to have any practical significance when applied to the performance of most boys and most girls. This magnitude of difference would not lead educators to create different math classes for boys and girls because their abilities were so dissimilar, nor would counselors advise girls to avoid math courses because of their lack of ability. With this level of overlap, Lawrence Summers should not speculate about women's lack of innate ability.

Studies that do not find hypothesized differences in outcomes are less likely to be published than studies that offer support for the hypotheses. Thus, a strong prejudice exists in favor of findings that show differences rather than findings that do not succeed in showing differences; that is, there is a prejudice against findings that suggest similarities (Greenwald, 1975; Hyde, 2005a). This tendency prompts researchers to highlight the differences they find and to dismiss other nonsignificant results. Indeed, researchers may omit any mention of failure to find a difference, such as a gender-related difference, but researchers who find statistically significant differences will always mention the differences and the level of statistical significance. Researchers cannot discuss an effect they have failed to find, and they must discuss effects that they have found. However, the omission of some information and the mention of other information can lead to a distorted view of overall findings by magnifying differences and obscuring similarities.

Table 2.3 shows the stages of research and how bias can enter at various points in the process. The possibilities for gender bias listed in the table are only a few examples; the history of gender research is filled with many other examples.

TABLE 2.3   *Stages of Research and Potential for Bias*

Stage	Ways Bias Can Enter	Gender-Related Example
Finding a problem to investigate	Allowing personal and societal values to influence choice of topic	Studying heart disease rather than breast cancer in middle-aged populations
Selecting variables	Using inaccurate, incomplete, or misleading definitions	Defining rape as vaginal penetration accompanied by force or threat of force (excludes other forced sexual acts and excludes men as victims)
Choosing a design	Choosing a design that does not allow for the evaluation of context	Testing participants in a situation that is anxiety-provoking for women but not for men
Formulating a hypothesis	Failing to consider the validity of the null hypothesis	Always hypothesizing gender differences rather than similarities
	Following a theory that is biased	Following Freudian theory to hypothesize that women have weak superegos
Collecting data	Permitting personal bias to influence measurement; using a definition of the behavior that is too narrow	Defining battering as the number of police reports of domestic violence
Analyzing results	Allowing personal values and expectation to guide the choice of which factors to evaluate	Failing to make a comparison of female and male participants
Interpreting results	Failing to report effect sizes	Interpreting a gender difference in a way that makes it seem large when it is not
	Interpreting gender differences as due to biological factors when no biological data exist	Claiming that boys' advantage in math is biological when no biological data have been collected
Publication bias	Publication of findings showing significant gender differences	Publication and media attention for findings of gender differences, but no attention for findings of similarities

Ways to Deal with Bias in Science

Those who criticize the bias in science have proposed two very different strategies for dealing with this problem. The constructionists deny the possibility of objectivity and thus reject the basic tenets of science. The extreme of this position calls for abandoning science as a way to deal with its inevitable bias. That position is unlikely to prevail: Science has been too successful and is too widely accepted. Nevertheless, some scholars advocate radical transformation in collecting and analyzing information. Other researchers argue that scientists must try harder to do good science.

Advocating Transformation.   Several scholars have argued that feminist research has the power to transform research with women and even the discipline of psychology. Historian Londa Schiebinger (1999, 2003) asked a broader question about the influence of feminism on all of science. She evaluated the possibility that feminism and its criticisms of traditional science have changed modern science. Her conclusions were both positive and negative. On the one hand, Schiebinger contended that feminism (and the presence of women) has brought about some changes in science. On the other hand, nothing has changed in science's basic assumptions or approach. The criticisms concerning masculinist bias in science may be founded, and the women who enter the profession of scientific research must play by the rules of science. In that sense, feminism has not changed science. Women have changed science in terms of what questions researchers ask and possibly how those results are interpreted. Research on issues important to women—such as incest and sexual abuse of children, rape and sexual assault, sexual harassment, spouse abuse, and achievements by women—has increased dramatically within the past 30 years, parallel to the increase in women in psychology (Worell, 1996). In addition, extending research to understudied populations has been a force in expanding psychology research beyond White, middle-class college students (Worell & Etaugh, 1994). Women in psychology have managed to change psychology research more than to transform science itself.

Scholars who claim that research should center on women advocate a more radical transformation. This view is *feminist standpoint epistemologies* (Campbell & Wasco, 2000; Harding, 2004, 2006; Harding & Norberg, 2005), and scholars who take this view claim that women have a unique point of view and different cognitive processes that have been ignored. These researchers believe that the analytical categories that are appropriate for men may not be appropriate for women and that research should remedy these shortcomings by devising methods to study the unique experience of womanhood. Rather than push women's issues to the margins, feminist standpoint scholars make those issues the center (Anderson, 2002; Harding, 2006).

As a way of gaining additional information about women and their experience, the feminist standpoint epistemologies have considerable value and appeal. Some feminist scholars have rejected traditional quantitative research as impoverished in capturing the female experience and have opted for more qualitative approaches. Such methods allow researchers to be subjective and interpretive, which qualitative researchers believe is critical in studying behavior.

The feminist standpoint epistemologies have the disadvantage of perpetuating the emphasis on gender differences that they criticize (Cosgrove, 2003) and carry the risk of emotionally harming participants (Sampson, Bloor, & Fincham, 2008). The growing interest in qualitative research and its increasing frequency in psychology journals speak to the greater support of these changes in research, but in departing radically from accepted methodology, these studies are difficult for mainstream science to accept (Riger, 1992; Whelan, 2001). Less radical changes, however, are easier to accept and enact. Thus, decreasing bias in gender research is a more feasible goal.

Decreasing Bias.   Those scholars who advocate a more objective study of gender can be termed *feminist empiricists* (Campbell & Wasco, 2000; Riger, 1992). These feminist researchers have argued that the development of a feminist methodology may not benefit research on women and gender-related behaviors. "A distinctive set of feminist methods for psychological research are not only futile but dangerous," and "any method can be misused in sexist ways" (Peplau & Conrad, 1989, p. 380). This view rejects the notion that methodology is gendered or that feminist research must be conducted by women or exclusively on women. Instead, some feminist psychologists (Hyde & Durik, 2001; McHugh & Cosgrove, 2004) argue that the use of diverse and appropriate methods is best for the study of women and gender-related behaviors.

To adequately study gender contrasts, research must include men (or boys) as well as women (or girls). Such comparisons are the subject matter of gender similarities and differences, and this research cannot include only one sex or the other. However, the necessary research must differ from much prior research, because so much of the existing research concerning gender is filled with serious bias.

Several groups of feminist empiricist researchers have alerted researchers to the potential for inadvertently introducing sexist bias into research and have presented some suggestions for conducting nonsexist psychological research. Maureen McHugh and her colleagues (McHugh, Koeske, & Frieze, 1986) acknowledged that psychology research has included biases, some of them unintentional. An unwarranted confidence in traditional research methods is one source of bias. In addition, bias can come from the theories and explanations researchers use as well as from inappropriate labeling and definitions.

Unwarranted confidence in traditional research methods occurs, for example, when psychologists accept that observations of behavior are objective (McHugh & Cosgrove, 2004). Observations are not necessarily free of sexist (or other) biases, because the observer may be biased and the *context* of the observation is rarely included in the analysis of the situation. The process of measurement itself fails to capture critical aspects of experience. For example, capturing the multitude of factors that relate to bullying for LGBT young people is a difficult research objective (Daley et al., 2007), and this situation impedes the development of programs to decrease this problem.

Gender may be part of the context of research and yet go unmentioned in a study. For example, the gender of the participants may be a subject variable in a study, but the gender of the experimenter usually is not. The gender of the experimenter may affect the behavior of participants, yet researchers rarely consider this factor.

Bias in an explanatory system occurs when researchers use broad terms (such as *hormones* or *modeling*) to explain specific behaviors. Appropriate explanations should take many factors into account, including social, cultural, biological, and situational factors. Inappropriate labeling and definitions occur in gender research when differences exist and one variation is labeled in a derogatory way. For example, the controversy over Lawrence

Summers's remarks concerning women in science provoked research asking "Why aren't more women in science?" (Ceci & Williams, 2007). Londa Schiebinger (2008) highlighted the subtle sexism in that question by asking why there aren't research initiatives to determine why so few men are involved with child care and domestic labor. The focus of the research on women's participation in science is deficit: Women must have something wrong with them, or they would be engineers and scientists in numbers similar to men. Researchers should avoid placing value-laden labels on behaviors before they have evidence of the value, consider the context of the behavior, include both women and men in research on gender-related behaviors, or give appropriate emphasis to topics of interest to both men and women (McHugh et al., 1986). It may not be possible to eliminate gender bias in research, but such bias can be decreased. Critical thinking can lead to an appropriate skepticism and a reformulation for gender research that includes a step-by-step consideration of how bias can enter the study of gender at any point (Caplan & Caplan, 1994).

Specific analysis techniques can reduce the bias in evaluating research, depending on the technique chosen. The development and use of a statistical technique called **meta-analysis** allow researchers to evaluate results from many studies and thereby determine the overall size of various effects. This information is related to the concept of practical significance because it can reveal which results are small and which are large. Janet Hyde (2007a) explained that "Meta-analysis is a statistical method that allows the researcher to synthesize the statistical findings from numerous studies of the same question" (p. 259). She contended that meta-analysis is preferred over evaluations that count the outcomes or combine probabilities from various studies because meta-analysis allows similar studies to be combined and statistically evaluated. Researchers have performed hundreds of meta-analyses related to gender (Hyde, 2005a), which have contributed to the finding that gender-related differences are nonexistent or small in most cases and large enough to be practically significant for only a few variables. That is, meta-analyses have revealed more gender similarities than gender differences.

Analysis and reporting results also require changes (Hyde, 1994). Researchers should conduct all appropriate significance tests and report all (even nonsignificant) findings and sizes of effects, exercising caution in interpreting results so as to make appropriate conclusions, and applying appropriate scientific standards to ensure that findings are not misused. All of these suggestions are intended to make the research on sex and gender more scientifically rigorous and thus eliminate the biases that have been so common in this area, creating a feminist empiricism.

■ Summary

The present and past of gender research offers examples of bias, and one such example came from Harvard President Lawrence Summers, who set women seething when he suggested that women may be inherently less suited to science than men. This episode is only one example of the controversies surrounding women in science.

Science as a method of gathering information can be traced back to the 16th century and rests on philosophical traditions that assert the advantages of an objective, observation-based understanding of the world. By using descriptive methods such as correlational studies and surveys, researchers gather and evaluate information that leads them to understand the world. By using the experimental method, researchers can develop an understanding of the cause-and-effect relationship between an independent variable and a dependent variable. Although the ex post facto method resembles experimentation, it differs in procedure and in the type of information it yields; ex post facto studies do not involve the manipulation of independent variables and do not allow the determination of causality.

All studies with gender as a subject variable are ex post facto designs, and none has the ability to reveal the cause of any differences they might show. Gender can be an independent variable in experimental studies when, for example, the researcher manipulates the description of targets, identifying some as male and some as female. This type of approach treats gender as a social category and, like all laboratory research, suffers from artificiality.

Dissatisfaction with traditional quantitative research has led to a growing interest in qualitative research methods among psychologists. These methods include case studies, interviews, ethnography, and focus groups. Researchers using these approaches acknowledge that they are part of the research process, try to treat their participants as equals, and attempt to preserve the complexity of the situations they study.

Bias can enter the research process at any point, and the history of gender studies is filled with examples of bias. Some have argued that science has a masculinist bias, and theories such as Freud's psychodynamic theory have a clear bias against women. Any of the steps in conducting research can be contaminated by personal bias. In addition, studies that reveal gender-related differences may show a difference that is statistically significant—that is, not due to chance. Yet the difference may not have any practical significance; for instance, it may not reveal large, important differences between women and men.

Solutions to the bias in science include an abandonment of science, which is unlikely, or drastic revisions to research methodology. Some feminist scholars advocate abandoning the traditional scientific method and adopting alternatives that center on women and that use different methods of gaining information, especially qualitative research methods such as ethnography and interview studies. The term *feminist standpoint epistemologies* applies to those who want to create a woman-centered approach to researching the female experience. Less drastic revisions include recommendations for making researchers more careful. Those researchers who advise taking care to avoid sexist bias in research can be described as *feminist empiricists.* In psychological research, feminist empiricists are more numerous than feminist standpoint epistemologists. Some psychologists have considered the problems and proposed solutions for carrying out nonsexist research. Some feminist scholars argue against excluding any method and propose a more varied and objective feminist empiricism.

■ Glossary

case study   a qualitative method that focuses on gathering extensive information about a single person or a small group.

constructionists   a group of critics of science who argue that reality is constructed through perception and is inevitably subject to bias. Included in this bias is all scientific observation, thus excluding science from its claim of objectivity.

correlational study   a descriptive research method that requires researchers to measure two factors known to occur within a group of people to determine the degree of relationship between the two factors.

data   representations, usually in numerical form, of some facet of the phenomenon that the researcher observes.

dependent variable (DV)   the factor in an experiment that the experimenter measures to determine whether the manipulation of the independent variable has an effect.

descriptive research methods   a group of research methods, including naturalistic observation, surveys, and correlational studies, that yield descriptions of the observed phenomena.

empirical observation   collecting information through direct observation.

ethnography   a type of qualitative research in which the researcher becomes immersed in a situation in order to make observations and interpretations of that situation.

experiment   a type of study in which a researcher manipulates an independent variable and observes the changes in a dependent variable; only through experiments can researchers learn about cause-and-effect relationships.

ex post facto (quasi-experimental) study   a type of nonexperimental research design that involves the comparison of subjects, who are placed in contrast groups, on the basis of some preexisting characteristic of the subjects.

focus group   a qualitative research method consisting of a discussion involving a group of people centered around a specific topic.

hypothesis   a statement about the expected outcome of a study.

independent variable (IV)   the factor in an experiment that the experimenter manipulates to create a difference that did not previously exist in the participants.

interview   a type of qualitative study in which respondents are interviewed in order to determine patterns or commonalities among their responses.

meta-analysis   a statistical analysis that allows the evaluation of many studies simultaneously.

objectivity   the notion that observation is free of bias by the observer.

operational definition   a definition of a variable in terms of operations used to obtain information on that variable, rather than in terms of concepts underlying that variable.

practical significance   an important result with practical implications; different from statistical significance.

qualitative research   research that focuses on understanding complexity and context rather than distilling situations to sets of numbers.

quantification   the process of turning observations into numerical data.

quantitative research   research that uses numerical data and statistical analysis.

statistically significant result   a result obtained by analysis with statistical tests and found unlikely to have been obtained on the basis of chance alone.

subject variable   a characteristic of the subjects, such as gender, that allows researchers to form contrast groups in quasi-experimental studies.

survey   a descriptive research method involving the measurement of attitudes through the administration and interpretation of questionnaires.

variable   a factor of interest to researchers; something that can have more than one value, as opposed to a constant, which has only one constant value.

■ Suggested Readings

Hyde, Janet Shibley; & Durik, Amanda M. (2001). Psychology of women and gender in the 21st century. In Jane S. Halonen & Stephen F. Davis (Eds.), *The many faces of psychological research in the 21st century.* Retrieved July 19, 2010 from http://teachpsych.org/resources/e-books/faces/script/Ch08.htm
In this online volume sponsored by the Society for the Teaching of Psychology, Hyde and Durik review the methods of psychology as they have been used to research women and gender.

Mahoney, Michael J. (2003). Minding science: Constructivism and the discourse of inquiry. *Cognitive Therapy and Research, 27,* 105–123.
Mahoney's very personal account of science includes a review of the history of science, the ideal procedures of scientific investigation, and the many ways in which that ideal is not realized in the work and politics of science.

Marecek, Jeanne. (2003). Dancing through minefields: Toward a qualitative stance in psychology. In P. M. Camic, J. E. Rhodes, & L. Yardley (Eds.), *Qualitative research in psychology: Expanding perspectives in methodology and design* (pp. 49–69). Washington, DC: American Psychological Association.
Marecek reviews the status of qualitative work in psychology, pointing out that such studies have a long history in psychology and much to offer to investigators.

Riger, Stephanie. (1992). Epistemological debates, feminist voices: Science, social values, and the study of women. *American Psychologist, 47,* 730–740.
Many subsequent articles discuss this topic, but this excellent article clearly outlines the different positions and ongoing debates about the scientific method. Although the article is not easy reading, Riger does a fine job of summarizing these complex issues.

3 Gender Stereotypes: Masculinity and Femininity

Kenyon Smith is a member of the Aquamaids, an organization for synchronized swimmers. This situation has created "great material" for comics; synchronized swimmers are funny "when the joke is on a person of the nonfemale sex" (Newman, 2008, p. A1). The image of a young man performing the "twists and splits and head down pirouettes" of synchronized swimming may be comical to some people, but Kenyon Smith's case has a "not-so-comical" part. He is extraordinarily good at synchronized swimming; he has won competitions. But he will never win an Olympic gold medal in synchronized swimming because he is not allowed to be part of the U.S. team.

HEADLINE

This Swimmer Is in Deep End of Gender Wars

Wall Street Journal,
March 17, 2008

Synchronized swimming is one of the few sports that is exclusive to women. Olympic officials barred Smith from the team, as they had Bill May in 1994. May went on to swim with Cirque du Soleil's water show, but Kenyon Smith has no place in which he can follow his talent, training, and choices. In his case, the image of this sport as female has solidified into rules that prohibit a man from pursuing the sport. Kenyon Smith is one of many cases for whom gender stereotypes have led to prejudice and discrimination.

In this chapter, we examine stereotyping, including the historical origins of today's gender stereotypes. We also look at how gender functions for today's women and men and influences how people think of and treat women and men. Indeed, the phenomenon of stereotyping is so important and pervasive that it can serve as a framework for our examination of psychological perspectives on gender in future chapters.

History of Stereotypes of Women and Men

A **gender stereotype** consists of beliefs about the psychological traits and characteristics of, as well as the activities appropriate to, men or women. These beliefs often have something to do with the behaviors typically performed by women and men in a particular culture, but gender stereotypes are more generalized beliefs and attitudes about masculinity and femininity. Such attitudes do not have a perfect relationship with observed behaviors: When people associate a pattern of behavior with either women or men, they may overlook individual variations and exceptions and come to believe that the behavior is inevitably associated with one gender but not the other. Therefore, gender stereotypes go beyond behaviors, forming categories that may not correspond to reality.

Gender stereotypes are very influential; they affect conceptualizations of women and men. They establish social categories that represent what people think. Even when beliefs vary from reality, the beliefs can be very powerful forces in judgments of self and others. Therefore, the history, development, and function of stereotypes are important topics in understanding the impact of gender on people's lives.

The current gender stereotypes, especially those about women, reflect beliefs that appeared during the 19th century, the Victorian era (Lewin, 1984c). Before the 19th century, most people lived and worked on farms, where men and women worked together. The Industrial Revolution changed the lives of a majority of people in Europe and North America by moving men outside the home to earn money and leaving women at home to manage households and children. This separation forced men and women to adapt to different environments and roles. As men coped with the harsh business and industrial world, women were left in the relatively unvarying and sheltered environments of their homes. These changes produced two beliefs: the Doctrine of Two Spheres and the Cult of True Womanhood.

The Doctrine of Two Spheres is the belief that women's and men's interests diverge—women and men have their separate areas of influence (Lewin, 1984a). For women, the areas of influence are home and children, whereas men's sphere includes work and the outside world. These two spheres have little overlap, which has allowed them to be seen as opposites. This notion of women and men as opposites has been influential in how people think about women and men and has also guided psychology's attempts to measure masculinity and femininity.

The Cult of True Womanhood

The Cult of True Womanhood arose between 1820 and 1860. "The attributes of True Womanhood, by which a woman judged herself and was judged by her husband, her neighbors, and society could be divided into four cardinal virtues—piety, purity, submissiveness, and domesticity" (Welter, 1978, p. 313). The Cult of True Womanhood held that the combination of these characteristics provided the promise of happiness and power to the Victorian woman, and without these no woman's life could have real meaning.

Piety was a virtue that society viewed as more natural to women than men. Religious studies were seen as compatible with femininity and deemed appropriate for women, whereas other types of education were thought to detract from women's femininity. These other types of education included studying through formal means and even reading romantic novels—either of which might lead women to ignore religion, become overly romantic, and lose their virtue, or purity (that is, their virginity).

Although women were seen as uninterested in sex, they were vulnerable to seduction. The loss of the second virtue, purity, was a "fate worse than death." Having lost her purity, a woman was without value or hope. Men, on the other hand, were not naturally as religious and thus not naturally as virtuous as women. According to this view of True Womanhood, men were, at best, prone to sin and seduction, and at worst, brutes. True Women would withstand the advances of men, dazzling and shaming them with their virtue.

The third virtue of the Cult of True Womanhood was submissiveness, a characteristic not true of and not desirable in men (Welter, 1978). Women were expected to be weak, dependent, and timid, whereas men were supposed to be strong, wise, and forceful. Dependent women wanted strong, not sensitive, men. These couples formed families in which the husband was unquestionably superior and the wife would not consider questioning his authority.

The last of the four virtues, domesticity, was connected to both submissiveness and to the Doctrine of the Two Spheres. True Women were wives whose concern was with domestic affairs—making a home and having children: These domestic duties included cooking and nursing the sick, especially a sick husband or child.

Table 3.1 summarizes the elements of the Cult of True Womanhood. Women who personified these virtues passed the test of True Womanhood, but the criteria were too demanding for any woman to meet. Nonetheless, these virtues were held as attainable, and women tried to meet these ideals. Remnants linger in our present-day culture and influence current views of femininity.

Masculinities

The 19th-century idealization of women also had implications for men, who were seen as the opposite of women in a number of ways. Women were passive, dependent, pure, refined, and delicate; men were active, independent, coarse, and strong. The Victorian ideal of manhood was the basis for what Joseph Pleck (1981, 1995) referred to as the Male Sex Role Identity (now called the Male Gender Role Identity). Pleck discussed the Male Gender Role Identity as the dominant conceptualization of masculinity in our society and as a source of problems, both for society and for individual men.

R. W. Connell (1995) explored the historical origins of attitudes toward masculinity, looking back into 16th-century Europe and the changing social and religious climate to trace the development of individualism. He contended that industrialization, world exploration,

TABLE 3.1 *Elements of Stereotyping of Women and Men*

The Cult of True Womanhood	Male Sex Role Identity
Piety: True Women were naturally religious.	*No Sissy Stuff:* A stigma is attached to feminine characteristics.
Purity: True Women were sexually uninterested.	*The Big Wheel:* Men need success and status.
Submissiveness: True Women were weak, dependent, and timid.	*The Sturdy Oak:* Men should have toughness, confidence, and self-reliance.
Domesticity: True Women's domain was in the home.	*Give 'Em Hell:* Men should have an aura of aggression, daring, and violence.

Sources: Based on "The Male Sex Role: Our Culture's Blueprint of Manhood and What It's Done for Us Lately" (p. 12), by Robert Brannon, in Deborah S. David and Robert Brannon (Eds.), *The Forty-Nine Percent Majority,* 1976, Reading, MA: Addison-Wesley; and "The Cult of True Womanhood: 1820–1860," by Barbara Welter, in Michael Gordon (Ed.), *The American Family in Social-Historical Perspective* (2nd ed.), New York: St. Martin's Press.

◻ GENDERED VOICES

Gendered Food

A college senior related how gender stereotypes intruded into eating at a restaurant with her boyfriend: "When my boyfriend and I go out to dinner, I usually order a steak, and he orders a big salad. More than half of the time, the food server puts the salad in front of me, and my boyfriend gets the steak. If the servers don't write down the order, the stereotypes take over."

and civil wars became activities associated with men and formed the basis for modern masculinity. Pleck (1984) also reviewed the social climate, focusing on the late 19th century, and citing examples of the increasing concern that men were not as manly as they once had been. Being a good provider became an increasingly difficult role for men to fulfill (Bernard, 1981; Faludi, 1999); failure at this role endangered their masculinity. Education became increasingly important for employment, but early-childhood education became the province of women, and Pleck discussed how these female elementary school teachers tried to make boys into well-behaved pupils—in other words, "sissies." This issue remains part of a debate over boys in the classroom (Kimmel, 2000; Sommers, 2000).

The prohibition against being a sissy and the rejection of the feminine are strong components of modern masculinity. According to Robert Brannon (1976), No Sissy Stuff is one of the four themes of the Male Sex Role. Another theme, The Big Wheel, describes men's quest for success and status as well as their need to be looked up to. The Sturdy Oak component describes men's air of toughness, confidence, and self-reliance, especially in a crisis. Finally, the Give 'Em Hell aspect of the Male Sex Role reflects the acceptability of violence, aggression, and daring in men's behavior. Table 3.1 summarizes these elements.

The more closely a man conforms to these characteristics, the closer he is to being a "real man." This idealization of masculinity is equally as unrealistic as the "true woman" of the Cult of True Womanhood. However, even men who are fairly successful in adopting the Male Gender Role Identity may be poorly adjusted, unhappy people; this role prohibits close personal relationships, even with wives or children, and requires persistent competition and striving for achievement. These difficulties lead men to make significant departures from the role's requirements.

Pleck (1981, 1995) proposed a new model, which he called Sex Role Strain (now Gender Role Strain), which departs in many ways from the Male Gender Role Identity. Pleck argued that during the 1960s and 1970s, both men and women started to make significant departures from their traditional roles. Nevertheless, the Male Gender Role Identity retained a powerful influence over what both men and women believe men should be. Many men deviate from the role, and some even believe that the role is harmful to society and to them personally, which makes adherence to the role a strain. Even men who succeed feel the strain in doing so, and the toxic components of the role present problems even for the successful. A review of research on male gender role ideology (Levant & Richmond, 2007) confirmed that strain occurs and problems are associated with strong adherence to traditional masculinity.

Connell (1987, 1995, 2005b) argued that gender has been constructed as part of each society throughout history, a view that is consistent with the belief that gender is something that people do rather than part of what people are (West & Zimmerman, 1987). This construction of masculinity includes both sanctioned and less accepted behaviors. Thus, masculinity varies with both time and place, creating a multitude of masculinities. For each society, Connell contended that one version of masculinity is sanctioned as the one to which men should adhere, which he termed *hegemonic masculinity.* This version of masculinity attempts to subordinate femininity as well as less accepted versions of masculinity, such as male homosexuality. Like Pleck, Connell recognized many disadvantages to this narrow, dominant form of masculinity and saw many problems for society and for individual men who adhere to it.

Despite the notion that masculinity has undergone drastic changes in the past two decades, evidence indicates little change in hegemonic masculinity and strong representation of the four themes of the Male Gender Role (Bereska, 2003). Boys and men are still supposed to be stoic, aggressive, dependable, and not feminine.

Conceptualizing and Measuring Masculinity and Femininity

The history of gender stereotypes suggests that differences should be easy to understand. Indeed, the concepts of *male* and *female* are relatively easy for people to understand because these words relate to biological differences. The concepts of masculine and feminine are much less closely related to biology and thus much more difficult to separate into two nonoverlapping categories: "One can be more or less feminine. One cannot be more or less female" (Maccoby, 1988, p. 762). Nonetheless, these dimensions seem important—perhaps critically important—and psychologists have attempted to conceptualize and measure masculinity and femininity along with other important personality traits. Unfortunately, psychologists' efforts to measure masculinity and femininity have a long history but not a great deal of success (Constantinople, 1973; Hoffman, 2001; Lewin, 1984a, 1984b). The problems began with the first measures developed, and no measurement technique used since has escaped serious criticism.

Lewis Terman (who adapted the Binet intelligence test into the Stanford-Binet test) and Catherine Cox Miles constructed the Attitude Interest Analysis Survey, a 456-item test that appeared in 1936 (Lewin, 1984a). This test yielded masculinity–femininity (MF) scores that lay along a continuum with strong masculinity lying at one extreme and strong femininity at the other. The test was not valid in any way other than distinguishing men from women (Lewin, 1984a). This test is no longer used, but its existence influenced others to develop measurements of masculinity and femininity.

When the MF scale of the Minnesota Multiphasic Personality Inventory (MMPI) appeared in 1940, it soon became the most common measure of masculinity and femininity, largely because of its inclusion in this personality test developed to measure psychological disorders (Lewin, 1984b). This scale was also unidimensional and bipolar, with masculinity and femininity at opposite ends of the scale. The psychologists who developed the MMPI were not really interested in measuring masculinity and femininity; they were more interested in measuring homosexual tendencies in men. As a result of this interest, their **validation** procedure included a comparison of the MF responses of 13 homosexual men to the responses of 54 heterosexual male soldiers. They used the responses of the 13 homosexual men as a standard for femininity, thus defining femininity as the responses of these men.

The test makers knew that the scale should not be used as a valid measure of femininity (after all, they had used no women in their standardization), and they were initially tentative in describing its use for a heterosexual population. But the test was soon extended to thousands of people, and the reservations disappeared. "It is rather staggering to realize that *the femininity dimension of this popular test was 'validated' on a criterion group of 13 male homosexuals!*" (Lewin, 1984b, p. 181; emphasis in original). The scale was not even very successful in diagnosing homosexuality in men, and this confusion of masculinity–femininity and sexual orientation posed a problem for understanding both concepts.

An alternative means of conceptualizing masculinity and femininity used the terms *instrumental* and *expressive,* with men's behaviors considered instrumental and women's behaviors as expressive (Lewin, 1984b). This distinction was based on an analysis of families around the world, with the conclusion that men occupy the role of autonomous- and achievement-oriented leaders, whereas women provide nurturance and support. This terminology has become important to those who have attempted to reconceptualize and measure psychological masculinity and femininity. Even more important were the realizations that femininity and masculinity may not be best conceptualized as opposite ends of one continuum.

In 1974 Sandra Bem published a different approach to the measurement of masculinity and femininity by separating the dimensions of masculinity and femininity and by adding the concept of **androgyny**. She proposed that some people have characteristics associated with both masculinity and femininity; that is, some people are androgynous. The androgyny concept requires both masculinity and femininity in combination, making it incompatible with a unidimensional view of masculinity–femininity. Instead, Bem constructed two scales to capture her concept of androgyny. Her test the Bem Sex Role Inventory (BSRI) included one scale to measure masculinity and another to assess femininity. Figure 3.1 illustrates the difference between the traditional unidimensional approach to personality measurement and Bem's two-dimensional approach.

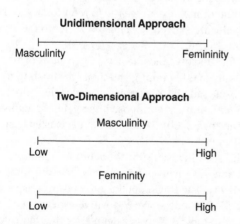

FIGURE 3.1 *Two Approaches to the Measurement of Femininity and Masculinity*

People who take the BSRI respond to 60 characteristics by rating how well each of these characteristics applies to them on a 7-point scale ranging from *Always or almost always true* to *Never or almost never true*. Of the 60 items, 20 represent cultural stereotypes of masculinity (ambitious, independent, competitive), 20 represent femininity (gentle, warm, understanding), and 20 are filler items. Scores on the masculinity and femininity scales yield four different possibilities: masculine, feminine, androgynous, and undifferentiated. People who score high on the masculinity scale and low on the femininity scale would be classified *masculine,* whereas people who score high on the femininity scale and low on the masculinity scale would be considered *feminine.* These people not only accept cultural stereotypes of masculinity or femininity, but they also reject the other role. Bem labeled those people who score high on both scales *androgynous* and those who score low on both scales *undifferentiated,* classifications that do not appear in traditional tests of masculinity–femininity. Androgynous people evaluate themselves as having many of the characteristics that our culture associates with men and women, whereas those people who are undifferentiated endorse few traits of either gender.

The concept of androgyny experienced a rapid growth in popularity, prompting the development of another test, the Personal Attributes Questionnaire (PAQ) (Spence, Helmreich, & Stapp, 1974). Designed to overcome problems with the BSRI (see Spence & Helmreich, 1978), the PAQ also identified people as masculine, feminine, androgynous, and undifferentiated. Both tests have undergone revisions and continue to be in use.

Not all researchers agree that the concept of androgyny offers improvements. Critics contend that tests that measure androgyny have provided no revolutionary reconceptualization of the measurement of masculinity and femininity and have validity problems (Choi & Fuqua, 2003; Choi, Fuqua, & Newman, 2008; Ward, Thorn, Clements, Dixon, & Stanford, 2006). Indeed, many researchers now refer to scores on these two scales in terms of instrumentality and expressiveness rather than masculinity and femininity. Janet Spence (1985; Spence & Buckner, 2000), one of the developers of the PAQ, has acknowledged the weaknesses of this conceptualization of masculinity and femininity and now uses the terms *instrumental* and *expressive* to describe the traits that such tests measure. Some researchers have adopted David Bakan's (1966) terminology of *agentic* to refer to the assertive, controlling tendencies that are associated with men and *communal* to refer to the concern with the welfare of others associated with women.

Any change in terminology fails to solve the underlying problems of first defining the underlying qualities of masculinity and femininity and then constructing instruments to assess those qualities. Spence discussed the conceptual inadequacies of psychology's measurements of masculinity and femininity and proposed that gender identity is multifactorial and complex (Spence & Buckner, 2000). Thus, none of the existent tests provides adequate assessments of these constructs.

Other research (Ricciardelli & Williams, 1995; Woodhill & Samuels, 2003) has tested an alternative conceptualization that involves positive and negative dimensions for masculinity, femininity, and androgyny. The PAQ contains only positive aspects of masculinity and femininity, and the BSRI includes mostly positive aspects of both but has some examples of negative femininity. Table 3.2 gives examples of the four categories of positive and negative masculinity and femininity. Positive and negative androgyny consist of combinations of the positive and negative traits from both.

TABLE 3.2 *Examples of Positive and Negative Femininity and Masculinity*

Femininity		Masculinity	
Positive	Negative	Positive	Negative
Patient	Timid	Strong	Aggressive
Sensitive	Weak	Confident	Bossy
Devoted	Needs approval	Firm	Sarcastic
Responsible	Dependent	Forceful	Rude
Appreciative	Nervous	Carefree	Feels superior

Source: From "Desirable and Undesirable Gender Traits in Three Behavioral Domains," by Lina A. Ricciardelli and Robert J. Williams, 1995, *Sex Roles, 33,* pp. 637–655. Adapted by permission of Springer.

Research that has shown positive effects associated with androgyny may be biased by the consideration of only those positive aspects. Research into the concept of negative and positive androgyny (Woodhill & Samuels, 2003) indicated that the separation of positive and negative aspects of masculinity, femininity, and androgyny was a useful addition. This study measured positive and negative aspects of all three orientations and found that people with positive androgyny showed better mental health and well-being than all other groups, and a later study (Levant et al., 2006) confirmed the mental health benefits of androgyny. However, people with positive masculinity and positive femininity were only slightly less mentally healthy, but the presence of negative masculinity, femininity, or androgyny—especially negative masculinity—was less conducive to health and well-being (Woodhill & Samuels, 2003).

Although the terms *masculinity* and *femininity* are meaningful to most people, psychologists have not yet managed to measure them in theoretically meaningful and valid ways. Problems exist both in the measurement of masculinity and femininity as well as in the concept of androgyny (Constantinople, 1973; Lewin, 1984b; Woodhill & Samuels, 2003). In answering the question "Are MF tests satisfactory? [The answer is] No. There is no evidence that the MF tests of the last 60 years provide a valid measure of the relative femininity of women or the relative masculinity of men" (Lewin, 1984b, p. 198). The MF tests purport to measure masculinity and femininity, but actually measure gender stereotypes rather than personality characteristics. The tests that include the concept of androgyny offer some improvement but do not solve the problem.

The Process and Implications of Stereotyping

Psychologists have struggled with conceptualizing and measuring femininity and masculinity, and they have also grappled with understanding the process and implications of stereotyping. Despite the negative connotations of the term *stereotyping,* some theorists have minimized the negative aspects of the process. The simplification that is inherent in stereotyping leads to streamlined cognitive processing, which may be an advantage (Macrae & Bodenhausen, 2000). The limits on children's cognitive abilities make gender stereotyping a normal part of children's cognitive development (Martin & Halverson, 1981). Therefore, the function of gender stereotyping can be understood as a useful way to approach the complexities of social cognition, including gender. Stereotypes do not lead inevitably to bias (Perrin, Heesacker, & Shrivastav, 2008), but a great deal of evidence indicates that stereotyping produces such a magnitude of distortions and incorrect generalizations that its disadvantages are overwhelming (Bobo, 1999; Glick & Fiske, 2001; Hegarty & Pratto, 2004).

Stereotyping, Prejudice, and Discrimination

Gender stereotypes provide not only descriptions of how people think about women and men but also prescriptions about what women and men should be, which means that gender stereotyping places limits and evaluations on what traits and behaviors are allowed (Prentice & Carranza, 2002). The process of stereotyping results in the formation of cognitive categories, and people have the tendency to use one of those categories as the norm and the others as deviant from the norm (Hegarty & Pratto, 2004). For example, in forming cognitive categories for men and women, men are cast as the norm; in categorizing sexual orientation, heterosexuality is the norm. This process leaves women and gays and lesbians as deviant from the norm categories. Thus, perceived differences will be attributed to the "deviants" rather than the norm categories, which tends to create negative evaluations for women, gays, and lesbians. Such negative evaluations should create problems, and prejudice and discrimination are among the effects that flow from stereotyping.

Prejudice is a negative evaluation of an entire group, which allows prejudiced people to react to members of the group without any personal contact or without knowing anything about people in the group as individuals. *Discrimination* is behavior that holds people or groups apart from others and results in different treatments for those people. Thus, prejudice is an attitude, but discrimination is behavior. People may be prejudiced yet not actively discriminate, but the two often go together. Perceptions of women and men are important in these processes.

Perceptions of Women and Men

Perception is the basis for the cognitive processing that can become a stereotype. The perception that men cannot (or should not) be synchronized swimmers provides a foundation for Kenyon Smith being in the "deep end of gender wars," as the headline story for this chapter suggested (Newman, 2008, p. A1). But how do these perceptions become stereotypes?

The content of gender stereotypes may be analyzed into four separate components that people use to differentiate male from female—traits, behaviors, physical characteristics, and occupations (Deaux & Lewis, 1984). All these components are relatively independent, but people associate one set of features from each of these with women and another set with men. On the basis of knowledge of one dimension, people extend judgments to the other three. Figure 3.2 shows the components of this model; the arrows indicate the associations people make among components. For example, given a gender label for a target person, people will make inferences concerning the person's appearance, traits, gender role behaviors, and occupation. Information about one component can affect inferences made about the others, and people will attempt to maintain consistency among the components.

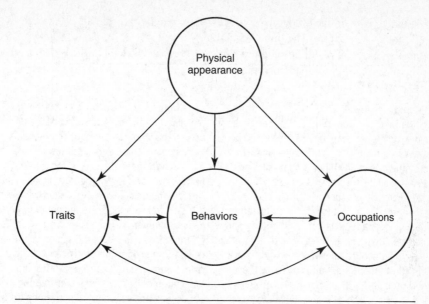

FIGURE 3.2 *Components of Deaux and Lewis's Model of Gender Stereotyping*

Physical features seem to be central: People viewed men and women as differing more in physical features than in psychological characteristics (Deaux & Lewis, 1984), but research with children (Miller, Lurye, Zosuls, & Ruble, 2009) suggests that the application of stereotype components may not be equal: Girls were described in terms of physical appearance, whereas descriptions of boys focused more on traits and activities. As Figure 3.2 shows, when people have information about behaviors, they make inferences about traits, and information about occupations can affect judgments about behaviors. However, physical appearance affected judgments about the other components more strongly than information about traits, behaviors, or occupations influenced judgments about appearance. In addition, specific personal information can outweigh gender as a factor in subsequent judgments about a person. For example, men who were described as managing the house or taking care of children were also judged as likely to be emotional and gentle. Such counterstereotypical information about men also increased the likelihood that such men would be judged as likely to be homosexual—"those who don't fit the mold in one way . . . are often confused with those who do not fit in another way" (Sell, 2004, p. 134).

Although the participants in a stereotyping study (Deaux & Lewis, 1984) saw differences in the physical characteristics, traits, behaviors, and occupations of women and men, their ratings of the two categories reflected the possibility that women may have some characteristics more typical of men, or men may have some characteristics more typical of women. That is, people do not view the stereotypes for women and men as separate, dichotomous categories but as probabilistic and overlapping. Participants judged the probability of a man and woman having certain characteristics on a scale of 0 (no chance) to 1.00 (certainty). The participants judged the probability that a man would be strong as 0.66, a high probability but not a certainty. However, they also judged the chances that a

ACCORDING TO THE MEDIA . . .

White Men Are in Charge

In both television commercials and entertainment programming, White men are more common, more prominent, and more dominant than others. According to content analyses of commercials, White male characters were more prominent than any other group (Coltrane & Messineo, 2000; Ganahl, Prinsen, & Netzley, 2003). Women tended to be cast into supporting roles, and male prominence extended even to those who appeared in voice only: Male voices narrated commercials more than 10 times more often than female voices. The patterns of men in positions of authority and men as the voice of authority exist in the United Kingdom, Europe, Australia, Asia, and the United States (Furnham & Mak, 1999) as well as in Saudi Arabia (Nassif & Gunter, 2008) and Spain (Valls-Fernández & Martínez-Vincente, 2007).

In U.S. entertainment programming, women have a history of underrepresentation. Despite increases in female characters during the 1980s and 1990s, women have failed to reach parity, even in the 21st century (Greenberg & Worrell, 2007). Women's roles also tend to be less significant and less serious (Harwood & Anderson, 2002). This pattern also emerged in an analysis of feature films (Eschholz, Bufkin, & Long, 2002). Women are more likely to be shown as dependent, and around the world, women appear more often at home than in other settings (Furnham & Mak, 1999).

Women are not the only stereotyped group on television. In the United States, African Americans appeared in the background of commercials more often than as main characters, and they were often subordinate to Whites (Coltrane & Messineo, 2000). Additional stereotyping appeared in the portrayal of African American men, who tended to be shown as aggressive but less likely to be shown in home settings or with women. African Americans were less visible, failing to get the attention that White women received. The proportion of African Americans in television commercials (Coltrane & Messineo, 2000) and entertainment programming (Harwood & Anderson, 2002) was not substantially different from their proportion in the actual population—about 11%. However, African Americans were concentrated in a small number of entertainment programs, which tended to "ghettoize" these characters.

Hispanics were drastically underrepresented in television commercials (Coltrane & Messineo, 2000) and entertainment programming (Greenberg & Worrell, 2007) as well as in feature films (Eschholz et al., 2002). In addition, entertainment television depicted Hispanics in less positive ways than any other ethnic group. Therefore, television's depiction of the world is disproportionately White and dominated by men.

woman would be strong as 0.44, a lower probability but far from unlikely. Although these judgments reflected stereotypical views of the relative strength of men and women, participants saw the possibility of each sex being strong or not.

Therefore, adults and children use several dimensions to categorize men and women, drawing inferences on one dimension based on information from another. What traits are stereotypically associated with these categories? Studies in the 1960s and 1970s often found evidence for beliefs that matched elements of the Male Gender Role Identity or the Cult of True Womanhood, and recent studies have also found remnants of these beliefs (Lueptow, Garovich-Szabo, & Lueptow, 2001). (See According to the Media and According to the Research for examples of stereotyping in the media and its potential effects.) However, some recent research has reflected changes in attitudes.

Beliefs held by college students in the 1960s showed strong acceptance of gender stereotypes by both college men and women (Rosenkrantz, Vogel, Bee, Broverman, & Broverman,

ACCORDING TO THE RESEARCH . . .

Biased Media Portrayals Perpetuate Stereotyping

When people see women and ethnic minorities portrayed in stereotypical ways, those presentations influence the way they think about and judge individuals from those groups: "Most viewers do not just consume the images and storylines in the media and just walk away untouched" (Eschholz et al., 2002, p. 301). Rather, media portrayals influence people's perceptions of women and ethnic minorities. That is, biased portrayals perpetuate stereotyping (Brescoll & LaFrance, 2004). Several studies using the "priming" technique demonstrated this effect. In one study (Murphy, 1998), participants read a fake autobiography about an African American man who was aggressive, lazy, unintelligent, and criminal—the most prominent of the negative characteristics associated with this ethnic group. This presentation primed participants to accept negative views of African American men, affecting their later judgments of Rodney King (receiving a beating from police) and Magic Johnson (being infected with HIV). Participants who read neutral or counterstereotypical stories made judgments that differed significantly. Two later studies (Dixon, 2008; Dixon & Azocar, 2007) showed similar effects. Another priming study (Brown Givens & Monahan, 2005) demonstrated that negative video portrayals of African American women affected subsequent judgments about an African American woman in a job interview.

Another view of the power of stereotyping on television (and in other media) is through its representation of various groups (Harwood & Anderson, 2002). This position holds that the way ethnic groups, women, children, and older people appear in the media reflects their power and vitality in society. Groups that are minimized, distorted, or marginalized are at risk because these portrayals make the groups seem less significant than they really are. Thus, media content is important not only for the power that it exerts on individuals' views but also for how it reflects and shapes cultural values.

Concerning gender stereotypes on television, there is bad news and good news. The bad news is that stereotypical portrayals of women and ethnic minorities abound on television, and these presentations have the power to do harm. Regardless of people's knowledge that "it's only on television," these messages are persuasive and powerful (Eschholz et al., 2002). The good news is that the media can also work to counteract stereotyping. Commercials and programming that present counterstereotypical information can counteract stereotypes. These presentations can offer models who behave in ways contrary to stereotypes and open behavioral possibilities (Browne, 1998). Therefore, the media tend to perpetuate negative stereotypes, but programming can—and sometimes does—counteract stereotyping.

1968). Table 3.3 (page 58) shows how some of the items that differentiated women and men match the components in the Cult of True Womanhood and Male Gender Role Identity. Not all of the traits these college students named match these categories; for example, one of the characteristics of women was "talkative," which does not fit into traits for the Cult of True Womanhood, and college students in the 1960s did not mention sexual purity as a defining trait of women. They did, however, mention several characteristics of men that relate to sex, including "worldly" and "talks freely with men about sex," which matches the suggestion (Good & Sherrod, 2001) for an additional component of the Male Gender Role—Be a Stud. Both the women and men in early studies (Broverman, Vogel, Broverman, Clarkson, & Rosenkrantz, 1972; Rosenkrantz et al., 1968) gave more positive ratings to the characteristics associated with men than with women, which suggests that these stereotypes include gender bias.

Have subsequent changes prompted decreased bias? Administrations of the Attitudes Toward Women Scale (AWS) to students at the same university over a 20-year period

TABLE 3.3   *Stereotypical Traits of Men and Women Matched to Descriptions from Rosenkrantz et al. (1968)*

Men		Women	
Male Gender Role Identity Component	**Stereotypic Traits in Study**	**Cult of True Womanhood Component**	**Stereotypic Traits in Study**
Give 'Em Hell	Aggressive Not uncomfortable about being aggressive Adventurous Competitive	Pious	Religious
Sturdy Oak	Unemotional Hides emotions Not excitable in a minor crisis Able to separate feelings from ideas	Submissive	Aware of feelings of others Gentle Tactful Quiet
Big Wheel	Dominant Skilled in business Knows the ways of the world Acts as a leader Self-confident Ambitious Worldly	Domestic	Neat in habits Strong need for security
No Sissy Stuff	Never cries Not dependent Direct Thinks men are superior to women Not conceited about appearance	Purity	Does not use harsh language

Source: Based on "Sex-Role Stereotypes and Self-Concepts in College Students" by P. Rosenkrantz, S. Vogel, H. Bee, I. Broverman, and D. M. Broverman, 1968, *Journal of Consulting and Clinical Psychology, 32,* p. 291. Adapted by permission of Helen Bee.

showed that college students in the United States (Spence & Hahn, 1997) and Canada (Loo & Thorpe, 1998) became more egalitarian between the 1970s and the 1990s. A meta-analysis of studies that used the AWS revealed a positive relationship between feminist attitudes and the year of administration—but a stronger relationship for women (Twenge, 1997). Two additional studies (Diekman & Eagly, 2000; Prentice & Carranza, 2002) showed larger changes in the stereotypes for women than for men. Another study (Bolzendahl & Myers, 2004) indicated a liberalization of gender roles over the past 30 years. A study that examined age and endorsement of stereotypical personality traits (Strough, Leszczynski, Neely, Flinn, & Margrett, 2007) found that women who were adolescents during or after the feminist movement of the 1960s endorsed more masculine

⬛ GENDERED VOICES

The Problem Disappeared

"Our car was having some problem, and my wife took it to be repaired," a man said. "She called me from the auto repair place, furious with the treatment she had received. The men there were stonewalling her—failing to listen to what she was telling them and treating her as though she couldn't possibly be capable of relating problems concerning an automobile. She was steamed.

"I went down there, and the problem disappeared. I was a man and apparently privy to the innermost secrets of automobiles. They treated me as though I would understand everything perfectly. Both my wife and I thought it was really absurd."

"One of my friends was upset that it cost $3.20 to get her shirt dry-cleaned," a woman told me. "She asked them why it was so much—the shirt was a tailored, plain shirt. They told her that women's blouses cost more than men's shirts, regardless of the style, because women's clothes don't fit on the standard machine for pressing and must be hand-pressed. She wondered if that was really true, and she gave the shirt to a male friend to take to the same dry cleaners. The problem apparently disappeared, because they charged him $1.25 for the very same garment. Isn't that beyond stereotyping?"

personality traits than older women did. Therefore, these studies show that attitudes toward women have become more egalitarian and less biased, which signals some changes in the traditional stereotypes of women, but attitudes toward men have not shown parallel changes.

The stereotype for men seems to be more stable, and men may be the victims of more stringent stereotyping than women. Kenyon Smith, the synchronized swimmer in the headline story for this chapter, is an example. The story mentioned how a woman pursuing a sport dominated by men would be praised for her skill and courage, but Kenyon was not (Newman, 2008). College students who described their views of women and men applied more stereotypical terms to men than to women (Hort, Fagot, & Leinbach, 1990). Masculinity is also viewed as more difficult to maintain and more easily threatened (Vandello, Bosson, Cohen, Burnaford, & Weaver, 2008) and more strongly determined by biology (Smiler & Gelman, 2008). In addition, men are the targets of some negative attitudes. Assessments of women's attitudes toward men have revealed that women hold ambivalent (Glick & Fiske, 1999; Glick et al., 2004) and negative (Stephan, Stephan, Demitrakis, Yamada, & Clason, 2000) attitudes toward men. The ambivalence includes feelings of hostility toward men and their gender role combined with admiration and attraction. The disapproving attitudes originate with women's negative contacts with men more than with the influence of negative stereotypes of men. Indeed, the results of a study (Edmonds & Cahoon, 1993) of evaluations of same- and other-gender individuals showed that women tended to believe that men held higher degrees of bias concerning women than the men expressed. That is, women showed negative stereotyping of men.

Some evidence suggests that a process moderates the application of gender stereotypes: Men and women may not apply stereotypes to themselves as strictly as they apply these stereotypes to others. U.S. college students hold stereotypical beliefs about gender, but they have also shown that they are willing to exempt themselves from these stereotypes (Williams & Best, 1990). That is, these students rated themselves as varying from the stereotype. By allowing such personal exceptions as routine, people decrease the power of stereotypes to control and restrict their lives.

Therefore, some of the positive attitudes about men and negative attitudes about women found in earlier studies seem to show some changes. More recent studies have shown a shift toward greater acceptance of gender role flexibility for women and an increase in positive attitudes toward women. But how—and when—do these stereotypes develop?

Development of Stereotypes in Children

In order to develop gender stereotypes, children must have gender knowledge, which begins to develop during the first years of their lives. By age 2 years, children apply gender labels, which predicts future behavior based on gender (Zosuls et al., 2009). Children as young as 3 years old start to show signs of gender stereotyping (Martin & Little, 1990). This development is not uniform or simple; 6-year-old children showed a pattern of selective stereotyping in which they made gender-stereotypical judgments about children whose toy interests were similar to their own but failed to make stereotypical judgments for children whose interests were different from their own. This behavior probably reflected a more complete development of knowledge about self and others like self, which extended to gender. As they get older, children's gender stereotyping becomes stronger (Martin, Wood, & Little, 1990). By age 4 some strong gender stereotyping appears, such a girls' fondness for pink, frilly dresses (Ruble, Lurye, & Zosuls, 2007). Between ages 8 and 10 years, children make stereotypical judgments for both genders (Martin et al., 1990).

This pattern of stereotype development appears in Table 3.4. Children in the first stage have learned characteristics and behaviors associated directly with each gender, such as the toy preferences of each. However, in this stage, children have not learned the many indirect associations with gender, associations that are essential for the formation of stereotypes. In the second stage, children have begun to develop the indirect associations for behaviors associated with their own gender but not yet for the other gender. In the third stage, children have learned these indirect associations for the other gender as well as their own, allowing them to make stereotypical judgments of both women and men.

A specific cognitive process called **illusory correlation** allows children (and adults) to form and maintain stereotypes (Sherman et al., 2009). This process may be described

TABLE 3.4 *Stages of Gender Stereotype Development*

Stage	Gender Knowledge	Status of Gender Stereotypes
1	Behaviors and characteristics directly associated with gender	Undeveloped
2	Beginnings of indirect associations with gender for own sex but not other sex	Self-stereotype but none for other sex
3	Complex, indirect gender-related associations for same and other sex	Stereotypes for self and other sex

Source: Based on data from "The Development of Gender Stereotype Components," by C. L. Martin, C. H. Wood, and J. K. Little, 1990, *Child Development, 61,* pp. 1891–1904.

as "the erroneous perception of covariation between two events when no correlation exists, or the perception of a correlation as stronger than it actually is" (Meehan & Janik, 1990, p. 84). The cognitive process of category accentuation also aids stereotyping, exaggerating existing differences (Sherman et al., 2009). Gender fits into this conceptualization; people perceive that relationships exist between gender and various behaviors when no relationship exists or when the relationship is not as strong as their perception indicates, and people accentuate the existing differences to sharpen the categories.

Illusory correlation operates in 2nd- and 4th-grade children in a way that is consistent with developing gender stereotypes (Meehan & Janik, 1990; Susskind, 2003). Furthermore, children's tendency to gender stereotype creates distortions in their memory for gender-related information. The perception of correlations can be an important factor in maintaining stereotypes for both children and adults; when people believe that activities are related to one or the other gender, they feel comfortable thinking in terms of these categorizations. This perceptual bias acts to maintain stereotypes. However, one study (Susskind, 2003) indicated that children do not ignore counterstereotypical information, and the presentation of such information may be a way to diminish gender stereotyping. Thus, when children see fathers cooking and mothers performing home repairs, these observations may act to decrease stereotyping by breaking down illusory correlations.

Gender stereotyping follows age-related trends similar to the development of other gender knowledge. That is, young children show less gender stereotyping than older children (Durkin & Nugent, 1998), men are subject to harsher stereotyping than women, and girls stereotype less strongly than boys. Younger children look for male–female differences and try to understand and categorize such differences (Martin & Ruble, 2004; Miller et al., 2009), whereas older children are more acceptant of deviations from gender stereotypes. Studying gender stereotyping in individuals ranging from kindergarten children to college students showed that the gender stereotyping increases to a point between ages 5 and 7 and then becomes more flexible with age (Biernat, 1991; Trautner et al., 2005). Another period of inflexibility occurs during adolescence, followed by greater flexibility during young adulthood (Lobel, Nov-Krispin, Schiller, Lobel, & Feldman, 2004). However, the tendency to rely on the stereotype is always present, and both children and adults showed a tendency to attribute gender-stereotypical traits to women, men, and children, including a reluctance to attribute feminine characteristics to males and a tendency to associate femininity with being childlike (Powlishta, 2000).

Therefore, the development of gender stereotypes begins early, with 3-year-olds knowing about gender-related differences in behavior. As children acquire information about gender, they become capable of forming and maintaining elaborate stereotypes for men and women, including a conceptualization of masculinity and femininity. Even when adults become less tied to gender stereotypes, those stereotypes may not lose their power to influence attitudes and behavior.

Explicit and Implicit Stereotyping

In evaluating stereotyping, researchers ask people to give their evaluations or opinions about individuals or groups. This procedure yields *explicit attitudes* because people are explicitly, consciously aware of the opinions they furnish. However, people also have underlying components to their attitudes that they may not know about on a conscious level, called **implicit attitudes**. These implicit attitudes may differ from or be more extreme than a person's explicit attitudes. Research indicates that gender stereotyping includes such implicit components.

Assessing implicit attitudes is more difficult than asking people what their explicit opinions are. Those who study implicit attitudes ask participants to make judgments about the similarity or compatibility of word pairs and measure how long it takes people to react to these pairs, a process called the Implicit Association Test (Greenwald & Banaji, 1995). Shorter reaction times mean closer associations. Thus stereotypical associations should be faster than counterstereotypical associations, a hypothesis confirmed by research (Greenwald & Farnham, 2000; to take the Implicit Association Test, go to https://implicit.harvard.edu/implicit/). Over the past 25 years, it has become less acceptable to express gender and ethnic bias, but people still harbor those prejudices, and the Implicit Association Test reveals these biases (Kawakami & Dovidio, 2001; Rudman, Greenwald, & McGhee, 2001).

The technique of functional magnetic resonance imaging (fMRI) has allowed researchers to observe human brains during various cognitive activities. Through use of this technique, researchers have investigated how stereotypes function at the level of the brain. One research team (Mitchell, Ames, Jenkins, & Banaji, 2009) found that a specific brain area was activated when participants thought about a man or a woman in stereotypical ways, such as a woman enjoying shopping. Another team of researchers (Knutson, Mah, Manly, & Grafman, 2007) asked participants about their explicit attitudes concerning gender and ethnicity and then scanned their brains using fMRI while they performed the Implicit Association Test. The results indicated that activation of different areas of the brain accompanied explicit gender and ethnic biases, whereas another area of the brain was more active when implicit bias took place. These studies confirm the existence of gender stereotyping on the physiological level.

Negative Effects of Stereotyping

Overt prejudice and discrimination are obvious negative effects of stereotyping, but as we have seen, those overt effects have diminished. However, implicit stereotyping continues, which opens the possibility that the negative effects of stereotyping may be taking more subtle forms. Stereotype threat and benevolent sexism are two effects of gender stereotyping that are negative but also less obvious than explicit prejudice and discrimination.

Stereotype Threat.   Stereotypes have the power to prompt prejudice and discrimination from others. In addition, members of stereotyped groups may handicap themselves by accepting the negative evaluations of others. In 1995, Claude Steele and Joshua Aronson reported on a study that showed how the existence of negative stereotypes affects those who are part of the stereotyped groups. They proposed that people feel threatened when they believe that their performance will identify them as examples of their group's negative stereotype. Steele and Aronson labeled this situation **stereotype threat** because the presence of these negative stereotypes threatens performance and self-concept. Even if the person does not believe or accept the stereotype, the threat of being identified with a negative stereotype can be an ever-present factor that puts a person in the spotlight and creates tension and anxiety about performance.

Stereotype threat can cause people to fear confirming a stereotype and thus to perform more poorly than they otherwise might.

By manipulating expectations of the implications of taking a test, Steele and Aronson showed that those expectations affected participants' performance. Steele and Aronson's early research focused on African Americans and academic achievement, but Steele (1997) drew on the stereotype of women and math to expand the scope of stereotype threat. He demonstrated a decrease in math performance in women who believed that the test they were taking was a test of mathematics ability; these women performed worse than women who thought the test was just another test. African Americans and women performed more poorly than White men, who are not threatened by negative stereotypes of their abilities in math. Women who accepted the negative stereotype about women and math ability showed greater susceptibility to stereotype threat than women who were less accepting of the stereotype, which affected math performance and career expectations for the two groups of women (Schmader, Johns, & Barquissau, 2004).

How influential is stereotype threat? A meta-analysis of experimental studies on stereotype threat (Nguyen & Ryan, 2008) indicated a small to moderate effect overall, but the influence was stronger for some groups and some situations. For example, women experienced more of a performance decrease when the cues concerning their group membership were subtle rather than blatant. Minority ethnic groups are even more influenced by stereotype threat than are women, but some people get a double dose of stereotype threat, such as Latina women, who were affected by stereotype threat on a test of mathematical and spatial ability (Gonzales, Blanton, & Williams, 2002).

Stereotype threat applies to a variety of people in many situations. The critical elements include the perception that one is a member of a stereotyped group and a situation that evokes the stereotype. For example, White men can be threatened by stereotypes of math ability when reminded that Asians are superior at math (Smith & White, 2002). Another study (Koenig & Eagly, 2005) used the stereotype that men are not socially sensitive and demonstrated poorer performance for men reminded of this stereotype. Yet another study (Kirnan, Alfieri, Bragger, & Harris, 2009) showed that women and ethnic minority members who took an employment test were affected by stereotype threat when they filled out demographic information before taking the test, but similar individuals who furnished this information after completing the test were not affected.

Children begin to be subject to stereotype threat when they become aware of the stereotyping that others do (between ages 6 and 10 years). Those from stigmatized groups (such as African American and Latino children) became aware of others' stereotyping before children from more privileged groups (McKown & Weinstein, 2003). This knowledge builds the basis for stereotype threat, and children with knowledge of the stereotyping process from stigmatized groups were more likely to exhibit the negative performance effects of stereotype threat than other children.

Although stereotype threat appears to be easily summoned, additional research suggests that nullifying stereotype threat may not be too difficult. Just the suggestion that men and women perform equally well on a test was enough to avert the effects of stereotype threat on a math test (Smith & White, 2002) and so was a request for demographic information after rather than before people complete the test (Kirnan et al., 2009). Discussing the existence of stereotype threat also diminished its effects for women's performance on a math test (Johns, Schmader, & Martens, 2005). Research on brain function (Krendl, Richeson, Kelley, & Heatherton, 2008; Wraga, Helt, Jacobs, & Sullivan, 2007) has revealed the area of the brain activated by stereotype threat and different areas that become more active when stereotype threat is nullified. Therefore, stereotypes that individuals carry around with them may threaten their performance in situations that match the stereotyped ones, but nullifying those stereotypes may avoid these negative effects.

Benevolent Sexism.   Psychology's traditional view of prejudice holds that people within a group (the in-group) form negative feelings about those in another group (the out-group) (Allport, 1954). The identification of the out-group may include stereotyping that sharpens the difference between the two groups and erases the individual differences of those people in the out-group. The results of prejudice include a combination of increased feelings of worth for people in the in-group and a devaluation of those in the out-group. For example, women and people of color are frequent targets of derogatory public remarks based on ethnicity and gender (Nielsen, 2002). Every one of the African Americans in this study reported that he or she had been the target of offensive racist remarks made by a stranger in public. Does gender fit into this model? Are men and women in-groups and out-groups to each other?

Listening to the conversations of groups of women or men saying terrible things about the other may seem to confirm this contention, but research results are not consistent with such a view. Although women are the targets of various types of discrimination in terms of economic, political, educational, and professional achievement, attitudes about women are not uniformly negative. Indeed, one line of research from Alice Eagly and her colleagues (Eagly, Mladinic, & Otto, 1991) showed that women as a category receive more *favorable* evaluations than men. Results from a meta-analysis (Feingold, 1998) indicated that women received slightly more favorable ratings than men. Thus, people in general have positive feelings about the characteristics stereotypically associated with women, which is not consistent with an overall prejudice against women.

Peter Glick, Susan Fiske, and their colleagues (Fiske, Cuddy, Glick, & Xu, 2002; Glick & Fiske, 2001; Glick et al., 2000) have researched this puzzle in gender stereotyping and formulated an answer that demonstrates another negative yet subtle effect of stereotyping. Their focus has been on separating positive from negative aspects of sexism (prejudice based on sex or gender). They call the negative aspects *hostile sexism,* which includes negative attitudes toward women. They also proposed the concept of **benevolent sexism**, which they defined as positive attitudes that nonetheless serve to belittle women and keep them subservient. Benevolent sexism is represented in the attitudes that women deserve special treatment, should be set on a pedestal, and should be revered. Despite the positive nature of these beliefs, people who hold such attitudes tend to see women as weaker, more in need of protection, and less competent than men (Fiske et al., 2002).

Ironically, it may be the favorable traits stereotypically associated with women that serve to perpetuate their lower status (Glick & Fiske, 2001). When people see women as warm and caring but less competent than men, they may give women positive evaluations but still feel that women need men to protect and take care of them. Thus, women's subservience is justified. When women accept these stereotypes, they endorse prejudice against themselves and help to perpetuate negative stereotyping (Jost & Kay, 2005; Sibley, Overall, & Duckitt, 2007). Indeed, these stereotypes are consistent with romantic chivalry and thus are attractive to women and men (Viki, Abrams, & Hutchinson, 2003). This type of benevolent prejudice may rationalize racism as well as sexism, casting the dominant group as benevolent protectors rather than oppressors.

Research on the contents of stereotypes (Eckes, 2002; Fiske et al., 2002; Wade & Brewer, 2006) has shown that combinations of two dimensions—competence and warmth—capture many beliefs about stereotyped groups. The mixed values of low competence–high warmth and high competence–low warmth have been of most interest to researchers, but the two other combinations of high warmth–high competence and low warmth–low competence also occur. Figure 3.3 (page 66) shows these combinations, the feelings associated with each, and examples. Research on this stereotype content model (Eckes, 2002; Fiske et al., 2002) confirmed that people evaluated a number of lower-status groups (women, ethnic minority groups, older people, disabled people) as less competent but warm and thus rated them positively. People from some high-status groups were not so well liked; they were respected and judged as competent but not warm. Indeed, finding examples of women who receive ratings high in both warmth and competence is difficult (Cikara & Fiske, 2009). Therefore, this view promotes a complex analysis of the components of stereotypes as well as a broad view of the effects of such stereotyping as it applies to gender and other stereotyped categories.

Men are not exempt from ambivalent sexism; the stereotypic characteristics of men can also be analyzed into hostile and benevolent components that are analogous to those that apply to women (Glick & Fiske, 1999; Glick et al., 2004). However, hostile attitudes toward men do not erase men's dominant status because men are perceived as "bad but bold," characteristics that are not necessarily consistent with men kind but signal that they should be in charge.

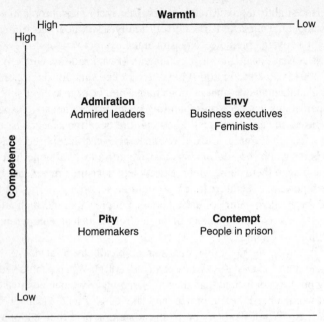

FIGURE 3.3 *Combinations of the Two Dimensions of the Stereotype Content Model and Examples of Each Combination*

Considering Diversity

Gender stereotypes affect how women and men think of themselves and how they evaluate their own behaviors as well as the behaviors of others. "Although every individual belongs to at least one sexual, racial, and social class category simultaneously, such categories do not have an equal social meaning" (Unger, 1995, p. 427). How do different societies construct masculinity and femininity? Do cultures around the world stereotype gender-related behaviors in ways that are similar to those in North America?

Stereotypes exist for ethnicity as well as for gender, and these stereotypes may interact. Evidence exists that African American and White women hold similar conceptualizations of womanhood (Settles, Pratt-Hyatt, & Buchanan, 2008). But whether ethnic or gender stereotypes are more important varies according to situation. For example, young Hispanic American women were able to use their ethnic identity as a positive factor in becoming successful students, but young Hispanic men often found that their ethnic identity was a handicap in becoming a good student (Lasley Barajas & Pierce, 2001). For African American college students, the situation of attending a predominantly White or predominantly African American campus contributed more heavily to feeling of being stereotyped than gender did (Chavous, Harris, Rivas, Helaire, & Green, 2004).

Cross-cultural investigations of gender stereotypes have often sought universals but have found both similarities and differences in the concepts of masculinity and femininity.

One investigation (Williams & Best, 1990) took place in 30 different countries in North America, South America, Europe, Asia, Africa, and Oceania. College students in these countries rated a list of 300 adjectives according to the extent to which each was more frequently (and thus stereotypically) associated with men or women. The results revealed more similarities than differences in these gender stereotypes. Six adjectives were associated with males in all of the cultures—*adventurous, dominant, forceful, independent, masculine,* and *strong*—and three adjectives were identified with females in all cultures—*sentimental, submissive,* and *superstitious*. In addition, a long list of adjectives appeared as male-associated or female-associated in a large majority of the cultures, and only a few adjectives were male-associated in one culture and female-associated in another. These findings furnish evidence for similarities in gender stereotypes across cultures, but the similarities were far short of being universal.

A reanalysis of some of these data in terms of the Five Factor Model of personality (Williams, Satterwhite, & Best, 1999) revealed even more similarities across cultures than the original analysis. Using averages for 25 countries, differences in gender stereotypes appeared in all five factors. Participants scored the male stereotype higher in Extraversion, Conscientiousness, Emotional Stability, and Openness to Experience and placed the female stereotype higher on Agreeableness. Not all countries adhered to this pattern, and individuals within the countries did not necessarily believe they fit the stereotypes. Later research (Costa, Terracciano, & McCrae, 2001) confirmed a pattern of cross-cultural gender differences but also reported that these gender differences were small.

Despite cross-cultural similarities of gender stereotypes, not all cultures hold the same views of what traits, characteristics, and patterns of behavior men and women should exhibit. One cross-cultural review (Gibbons, Hamby, & Dennis, 1997) found that no single gender distinction applied to all cultures.

Japan was one of the cultures that showed a different pattern of gender stereotypes than many others (Williams & Best, 1990; Williams et al., 1999). Research on gender roles in Japan (Sugihara & Katsurada, 2002) showed that the characteristics that differentiate women and men in the United States, such as independent, assertive, and self-reliant, do not do so in Japan. Indeed, these characteristics are not considered desirable for either Japanese women or men. As Richard Nisbett (2003) discussed, Asian culture promotes the development of strong family ties and obligations, making conformity and obedience valued traits for everyone. In the United States and Europe, these characteristics would be considered feminine, but in Japan, they are not gendered. In China, another Asian culture, the ideal man is a warrior but also a cook, a teacher, an artist, and a musician (Chia, Moore, Lam, Chuang, & Cheng, 1994). People in both Japan (Sugihara & Katsurada, 2002) and China (Hong, Veach, & Lawrenz, 2003) exhibit gender stereotyping, but these societies hold varying views of what women and men should be, and thus the contents of their gender stereotypes differ from the Western stereotypes of gender.

Other cross-cultural research on gender stereotypes has shown that some of those stereotypes are inaccurate. For example, many people in the United States believe that people in their society are less guilty of gender stereotyping than others. Research comparing Italian and American men (Tager & Good, 2005) showed that Italian male students endorsed traditional masculinity less than American male students. Another misconception about gender applies to Arab women, whom many see as veiled, passive, and secluded within the home. Research on Arab women in the United States (Read, 2003) showed that Arab women are more diverse and less traditional than the stereotype suggests, especially Arab women who are Christian rather than Muslim.

Going beyond variation in specific gender-related characteristics, some scholars have asked questions concerning how gender stereotyping creates gender-related attitudes that are common over many cultures. The prevalence of male dominance has prompted a broader question: Are men dominant and women subordinate in all cultures? Is this pattern universal and thus the basis for most gender stereotyping?

The answer from anthropology to the question of universal male dominance is "no" (Bonvillain, 2000; Marler, 2006; Salzman, 1999). Some societies have included equal access to resources and power for both women and men. But egalitarian cultures tend to be simple, pastoral societies rather than complex, industrialized cultures. Many more societies have placed men rather than women in positions of power and control; few have enacted egalitarian arrangements. A possible reason for this dominance is men's tendency to a social dominance orientation versus women's greater emphasis on forming relationships (Pratto, Sidanius, & Levin, 2006; Sidanius, Pratto, & Bobo, 1994). Research on sexist attitudes (Christopher & Mull, 2006; Sibley, Wilson, & Duckitt, 2007) confirmed the relationship between social dominance orientation and sexist attitudes among men.

Another view is based on the conflicts that come from women and men living in male-dominated societies that depend on and value women. This situation sets up attitudes that demean women yet still include positive components. Peter Glick, Susan Fiske, and their colleagues (2000) have delineated the concepts of benevolent and hostile sexism toward women, which relate to the stereotypically positive (warm, nurturing) and negative (incompetent, need to be cared for) characteristics of women. These researchers demonstrated the implications of these two components of gender stereotypes in a large (more than 15,000 people) cross-cultural study in 19 countries around the world. They found a positive relationship between hostile and benevolent sexism in every one of the 19 nations: Higher hostile sexism scores were related to higher benevolent sexism scores. They explained the connection as being a result of the relationships between men and women in male-dominated cultures, which create both women's subordination and their value as sexual and domestic companions and caregivers. For such systems to remain stable, both women and men must hold attitudes that support the system, and these ideologies form a complementary system that maintains societies in which men dominate. Thus, gender stereotypes seem to perpetuate sexist discrimination in many cultures (Désert & Leyens, 2006).

Similar research on hostile and benevolent attitudes about men (Glick et al., 2004) revealed similar patterns across 16 nations. Ratings of men were not as positive as ratings of women; participants saw men as more ruthless, unfeeling, and self-centered than women. However, both female and male participants tended to see men as more powerful and bold. Ratings of men as "bad but bold" are consistent with their dominant position in societies.

Results from these studies on benevolent and hostile attitudes toward women and men show that both men and women hold these attitudes. Although women and men were likely to have more positive opinions of their own sex, both endorsed beliefs of hostility and benevolence. Furthermore, the degree of acceptance of hostile and benevolent sexism predicted the level of gender inequality in these societies. Thus, these stereotypes are related to the continuance of gender inequality in many countries.

As the Glick and colleagues (2000) results showed, women often hold more egalitarian views of women and women's roles than men endorse, but even this difference is not universal. No differences in attitudes toward women appeared in a study (Gibbons et al., 1997) of people in Malaysia or Pakistan, and men in Brazil expressed more liberal views of women than women did. The distinction between traditional beliefs and beliefs concerning equal opportunity and equal power might apply to all cultures, but the specifics of what constitutes traditionalism vary. The division of activities and behaviors into male and female domains is universal, without worldwide agreement about what those activities and characteristics are. Such divisions of activities, however, form the basis for gender roles and furnish the potential for gender stereotyping.

■ Summary

The term *gender stereotype* refers to the beliefs associated with the characteristics and personalities appropriate to men and women. Current stereotypes of women and men have been influenced by historical views of women and men. The Cult of True Womanhood that arose during Victorian times held that women should be pious, pure, submissive, and domestic. For men, several models of masculinity show gender role stereotypes. One of these is the Male Gender Role Identity, which holds that to be successful as men, males must identify with the elements of that role, including the need to avoid all feminine activities and interests, have an achievement orientation, suppress emotions, and be aggressive and assertive.

The concepts of masculinity and femininity have a long history in the field of psychology as personality traits measured by various psychological tests. The first such test was the Attitude Interest Analysis Survey, which conceptualized masculinity and femininity as opposite poles of one continuum. The Minnesota Multiphasic Personality Inventory still uses this unidimensional approach. A more recent approach to the measurement of masculinity and femininity includes the concept of androgyny. Several tests have adopted this strategy, including the Bem Sex Role Inventory and the Personal Attributes Questionnaire. These tests include separate scales for masculinity and femininity, allowing classification of people as not only masculine or feminine but also as androgynous. However, some critics have argued that none of the personality tests that purport to measure masculinity and femininity does so. At present, the underlying concepts of masculinity and femininity remain elusive.

Gender stereotypes have four different aspects—physical characteristics, traits, behaviors, and occupations. Each aspect may vary independently, but people make judgments about one based on information about another, to form an interdependent network of associations. People use this network of information in making deductions about gender-related characteristics.

Gender stereotyping begins early in development and results in simplified cognitive processing that allows children to make easier decisions and judgments but also leads children to hold rigid rules for gender-related behavior. Stereotyping is maintained by the illusion that more activities and characteristics are associated with gender than actually are. Children become more flexible in applying gender rules after about age 7, allowing themselves more exceptions for individual variation. Adolescents go through another period of rigid stereotyping, followed by greater flexibility during adulthood. Stereotyping may not be necessary for adults, but the process continues during adulthood, along with its negative implications.

Stereotypes have explicit components that people are aware of but also implicit components that are unconscious. Assessment of implicit stereotypes reveals that even people who say that they reject gender stereotypes may accept them on an unconscious level. Thus, stereotyping may take a subtle form.

Negative aspects of stereotyping include not only prejudice and discrimination but also stereotype threat and benevolent sexism. Stereotype threat occurs when people feel that their performance in certain situations will identify them as examples of their group's negative stereotype. This perception may negatively affect their performance. Invoking stereotype threat is easy, but dispelling it may also be easy. Benevolent sexism consists of positive attitudes that nonetheless serve to belittle women and keep them subservient.

Hostile sexism and benevolent sexism are related, and both women and men hold such attitudes.

Cross-cultural research on gender roles and gender stereotyping indicates that all cultures delegate different roles to men and women, but what traits are associated with each show some cultural variation. Gender stereotypes have more similarities than differences across cultures, with the male stereotype fitting the instrumental, or agentic, model and the female stereotype fitting the expressive, or communal, model.

■ Glossary

androgyny   a blending of masculinity and femininity, in which the desirable characteristics associated with both men and women are combined within individuals.

benevolent sexism   positive attitudes that nonetheless serve to belittle women and keep them subservient.

gender stereotype   the beliefs about the characteristics associated with, and the activities appropriate to, men or women.

illusory correlation   the incorrect belief that two events vary together, or the perception that the relationship is strong when little or no actual relationship exists.

implicit attitudes   attitudes that people hold on an unconscious level, which may differ from their explicit, conscious attitudes.

stereotype threat   a phenomenon that occurs in situations in which the presence of negative stereotypes affects the performance of those to whom the stereotype applies.

validation   the process of demonstrating that a psychological test measures what it claims to measure; the procedure that demonstrates the accuracy of a test.

■ Suggested Readings

Hegarty, Peter; & Pratto, Felicia. (2004). The differences that norms make: Empiricism, social constructionism, and the interpretation of group differences. *Sex Roles, 50,* 445–453.

Hegarty and Pratto offer a social cognitive theory called norm theory, which they use to explain how group differences become stereotypes.

Hoffman, Rose Marie. (2001). The measurement of masculinity and femininity: Historical perspective and implications for counseling. *Journal of Counseling and Development, 79,* 472–485.

This review traces psychologists' attempts to measure masculinity and femininity, including a critique of criticism by others.

Kite, Mary E. (2001). Changing times, changing gender roles: Who do we want women and men to be? In

Rhoda Unger (Ed.), *Handbook of the psychology of women and gender* (pp. 215–227). New York: Wiley. Kite reviews gender belief systems, gender stereotypes and their measurement, and what men and women think of men and women. In addition, she carefully considers the cost of violating these gender stereotypes.

Levant, Ronald F.; & Richmond, Katherine. (2007). A review of research on masculinity ideologies using the male role norms inventory. *Journal of Men's Studies, 15* (2), 130–146.

This review presents the concept of gender role strain and the research on its assessment over a period of 15 years.

4 Hormones and Chromosomes

"It's easy to dis your period, especially if you get premenstrual syndrome and feel irritable and crampy the week before it starts. But did you know that your mind is most insightful during PMS?" (Ribeiro, 2006, p. 67). This statement may be a shock to both women and men, who have come to accept the several days before the beginning of menstruation as a dreaded time that includes mood swings, food cravings, irritability, and depression. The contention that the premenstrual period may include more creative problem-solving and greater intuitive ability contradicts the bad publicity given to PMS. Is it possible that PMS has positive as well as negative symptoms? Might the positive outweigh the negative?

HEADLINES

PMS Makes You Smarter!
CosmoGirl!, February 2006

Father Nature: The Making of a Modern Dad
Psychology Today,
March–April 2002

"According to popular perceptions, men are supposedly driven by their hormones (primarily testosterone) to compete for status, to seek out sex and even to be violent—conditions hardly conducive to raising kids," but Douglas Carlton Abrams (2002, p. 38)* contended that hormones also prepare men to be fathers. He argued that changes in hormone levels occur to prospective fathers as well as to prospective mothers, creating behaviors that prime men to become good fathers.

Both these popular articles considered the role of hormones in a variety of behaviors, and both make radical claims that go against popular beliefs. This chapter includes a consideration of these claims and also poses several questions concerning the role of hormones in the development of male and female bodies as well as the behavior of women and men. What role do hormones play in physical development and ongoing behavior? Are hormones the key to the differences between males and females? Or are chromosomes the key?

This chapter begins to answer these questions with an exploration of the contribution of biology—chromosomes and the effect of hormones—on human development from conception throughout prenatal development and again during puberty. Additional questions about the influence of hormones appear in an examination of individuals who fail to develop according to a clear female or male pattern of physiology. Finally, this chapter examines the role of hormones in adult behavior, including an examination of PMS and the role of testosterone in behavior.

---

*Reprinted with permission from *Psychology Today* magazine. (Copyright © 2002 Sussex Publishers, LLC)

The Endocrine System and Steroid Hormones

Hormones are substances released from **endocrine glands** to circulate throughout the body in the bloodstream. Receptors on various organs are sensitive to specific hormones, which produce many different actions at various sites. Although the body contains many endocrine glands that secrete a variety of hormones, **steroid hormones** are the ones that relate to reproduction and differences between the sexes. The reproductive organs, the ovaries and testes, are the **gonads**. These organs are obviously among the physical characteristics differentiating the sexes and are also essential to reproduction, but the ovaries and testes are not the only endocrine glands that are important for sexual development and functioning.

Two brain structures, the hypothalamus and the pituitary gland, are essential in regulating the production of sex hormones. The complex action of the hypothalamus results in the production of a class of hormones called **releasing hormones**, including gonadotropin-releasing hormone. This hormone acts on the **pituitary gland**, prompting it to release other hormones. **Tropic hormones** are among those products, including gonadotropins. These hormones circulate through the bloodstream and stimulate the ovaries and testes to release their hormones. Thus, the release of hormones by the gonads is the result of a cascade of events, beginning with the hypothalamus and then the pituitary. Figure 4.1 summarizes the action of these glands and hormones.

Gonadal hormones are called steroid hormones and consist of two main classes, **androgens** and **estrogens**. Although people tend to think of androgens as male hormones and estrogens as female hormones, that belief is inaccurate—each sex produces both types of hormones. The most common of the androgens is **testosterone**, and the most common of the estrogens is **estradiol**. Men typically produce a greater proportion of androgens than estrogens, and women typically produce a greater portion of estrogens than androgens. The gonads also secrete a third type of hormone, the **progestins**. The most common progestin is progesterone, which plays a role in preparing a woman's body for pregnancy. Men also secrete progesterone, but its function for the male body is unknown (Pinel, 2009).

The gonads are not the only glands that produce steroid hormones; the adrenal glands also produce small amounts of both hormones. These hormones are important in differentiating male and female.

Stages of Differences between the Sexes

Humans (and most other animals) are sexually dimorphic; that is, they come in two different physical versions—female and male. This **sexual dimorphism** is the result of development that begins with conception and ends at puberty, resulting in men and women who are capable of sexual reproduction. One way to conceptualize sexual dimorphism is to consider it the product of five stages of development: genetic, gonadal, hormonal, internal genitalia, and external genitalia (Kaplan, 1980). The *genetic stage* refers to the inheritance of the chromosomes related to sex. The *gonadal stage* includes the development of the gonads. The *hormonal stage* begins during prenatal development, with the secretion of androgens and estrogens but also occurs at puberty, producing mature, functional gonads. The stage at which

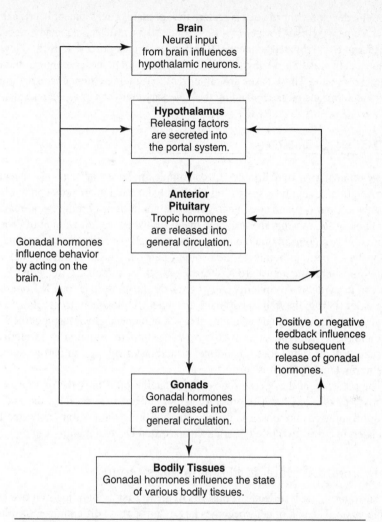

FIGURE 4.1 *A Summary Model of the Regulation of Gonadal Hormones*

Source: From *Biopsychology* (2nd ed.), by John P. J. Pinel, 1993, Boston: Allyn & Bacon. Copyright © 1993 by Allyn & Bacon. Reprinted by permission.

internal genitalia, the internal reproductive organs, develop occurs prenatally and affects not only the ovaries and testes but also other internal structures relating to reproductive functioning. The **internal genitalia** consist of the internal structures related to reproduction: ovaries, Fallopian tubes, uterus, and upper vagina in women; testes, prostate gland, seminal vesicles, and vas deferens in men. The **external genitalia** are reproductive structures that can be seen without internal examination: clitoris, labia, and vaginal opening in women; and penis and scrotum in men. These developments result in differences that are apparent at birth but occur later during prenatal development than the development of internal genitalia.

In the development of sex characteristics, prenatal development is critically important. For a clear pronouncement of "It's a boy" or "It's a girl," a great many prenatal events must occur in a coordinated sequence. When this complex process fails to follow the typical sequence, the result is a baby whose sex may be ambiguous, combining characteristics of male and female. These cases are rather rare, but their existence is revealing because they provide a means of understanding the necessary elements of typical development.

Sexual Differentiation

The development of sexual differences is a complex process that starts at conception—the fertilization of an ovum by a sperm cell. Most cells in the human body contain 23 pairs of chromosomes, but ova and sperm carry half that amount of chromosomal material. The combination of the two into the fertilized ovum furnishes the full amount of genetic material, with half coming from the mother's ovum and half from the father's sperm.

Of the 23 pairs of human chromosomes, pair number 23 is the one that is critical. Although most chromosomes are X shaped, only those in pair 23 are called **X chromosomes**. An individual who inherits two of these X chromosomes (one X from the mother and the other X from the father) will have the genetic endowment to develop according to the female pattern. Individuals who inherit one X and one **Y chromosome** (the X from the mother and the Y from the father) will have the genetic information to develop according to the male pattern. Therefore, the normal female pattern is XX in chromosome pair 23, and the normal male pattern is XY.

The presence of the XY chromosome constellation is only the first factor that produces male physiology, and its presence is not sufficient to produce the male pattern. Other configurations are possible for pair 23, but those patterns are abnormalities, discussed later, in the section titled "Variations in Sexual Development."

Development of Male and Female Physiology

After conception, the fertilized ovum starts to grow, first by dividing into two cells, then four, and so on. The ball of cells becomes larger and starts to differentiate, forming the basis for different structures and organs. Within the first 6 weeks of prenatal development, no difference exists between male and female embryos, even in their gonads. Both the embryos with the XX pattern and those with the XY pattern have the same structures, and this replication signifies that both types of embryos have the potential to develop into individuals who look like and have the internal reproductive organs of either boys or girls.

The Reproductive Organs.   Both male and female embryos have a **Wolffian system**, which has the capacity to develop into the male internal reproductive system, and a **Müllerian system**, which has the capacity to develop into the female internal reproductive system. During the third month of prenatal development, two processes typically begin occurring in fetuses with the XY chromosome pattern to further the developing male pattern.

The first involves the production of androgens. A gene on the Y chromosome prompts the development of fetal testes, which produce androgens (Hiort, Thyen, & Holterhus, 2005). The presence of androgens stimulates the development of the Wolffian system, which further increases production of testosterone and stimulates development of the male pattern. The second process that prompts male development is the production of Müllerian-inhibiting substance, which causes the Müllerian system to degenerate. Therefore, one type of secretion prompts the Wolffian system to develop into the male internal reproductive organs (masculinization), and the other causes the female Müllerian system to degenerate (defeminization). These actions result in male internal reproductive organs in the fetus. Figure 4.2 shows how the male reproductive system develops from

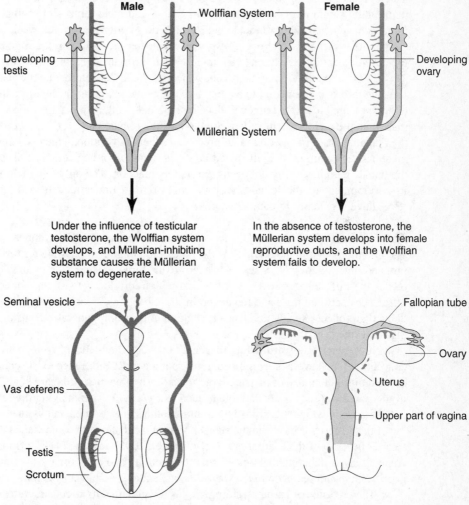

At 6 weeks, all human fetuses have the antecedents of both male (Wolffian) and female (Müllerian) reproductive ducts.

Male   Wolffian System   **Female**

Developing testis

Developing ovary

Müllerian System

Under the influence of testicular testosterone, the Wolffian system develops, and Müllerian-inhibiting substance causes the Müllerian system to degenerate.

In the absence of testosterone, the Müllerian system develops into female reproductive ducts, and the Wolffian system fails to develop.

Seminal vesicle

Fallopian tube

Ovary

Uterus

Vas deferens

Upper part of vagina

Testis

Scrotum

FIGURE 4.2   *Development of Internal Reproductive Systems*

Source: From *Biopsychology* (2nd ed.), by John P. J. Pinel, 1993, Boston: Allyn & Bacon. Copyright © 1993 by Allyn & Bacon. Reprinted by permission.

the Wolffian system, creating testes, vas deferens, and seminal vesicles. This figure also illustrates how both male and female reproductive structures originate from the same prenatal structures.

Differentiation of the ovaries also occurs through the action of genes (Hiort et al., 2005), but the fetal ovaries produce few estrogens, suggesting that the development of female reproductive system requires no surge of fetal hormones. In female embryos, the Wolffian system degenerates and the Müllerian system develops, resulting in ovaries, uterus, Fallopian tubes, and the upper part of the vagina. Figure 4.2 also shows how the female reproductive system develops from the Müllerian system.

Six weeks after conception, the external genitalia of male and female fetuses are also identical, with the potential to develop into either. The structures that will become the penis and scrotum in males and the clitoris, outer and inner labia, and vaginal opening in females have not yet differentiated but begin to do so after the seventh week of gestation. Again, the presence of androgens, especially testosterone, is important. Figure 4.3 shows the development of the external genitalia for both the male and female patterns.

Prenatal production of androgens generates the male pattern, and the absence of androgens results in an incomplete version of the female pattern. If few or no hormones of either type are present, a fetus will develop external genitals that appear more like the female than the male structures. Development of the female pattern is less well understood than the male pattern and often interpreted as a "default" option, which is a mistake. "The most basic meaning of default is 'failure to act; inaction or neglect'. The development of the female periphery is by no means typified by inaction. The only thing that is defaulted in development of the female body is our failure to understand how it is regulated" (Breedlove, Cooke, & Jordan, 1999, p. 9).

The Nervous System.   During prenatal development, the hormones that produce sexual dimorphism in the body also affect the brain, making it possible for the brain structure and function to vary by sex. However, sexual dimorphism of the brain is not as obvious as the differences between female and male reproductive systems. In addition, the differences between male and female brains have been researched much more fully for rodents than for humans, which leads to caution concerning generalizations of these findings (Breedlove et al., 1999).

Investigations of structural differences between the brains of women and men have concentrated on several specific structures, but a gender difference exists concerning the entire brain: The brains of men are larger than those of women (Leonard et al., 2008). Part of the size difference is attributable to men's larger body size, making the ratio of brain weight to body weight nearly—but not quite—the same for men and women. The meaning of this difference has been the subject of heated debate, with some claims that men are smarter because of their larger brains (McDaniel, 2005) and others (Witelson, Beresh, & Kigar, 2006) concluding that type of cognitive activity and brain organization interact with brain volume and sex in complex ways that prevent any simple conclusion.

The presence of prenatal androgens has the potential to affect structures throughout the brain, and some structures differ for women and men (Breedlove et al., 1999). However, many brain structures contain receptors that are sensitive to androgens and estrogens, creating the possibility for influence not just during prenatal development but also later in the life span and especially during puberty (Ahmed et al., 2008; Peper et al., 2009).

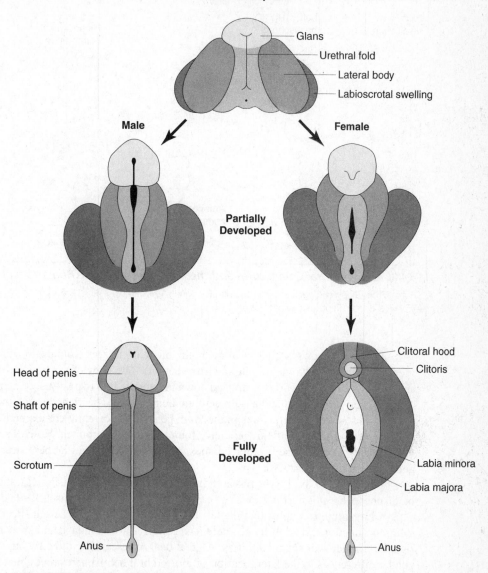

FIGURE 4.3 *Development of Male and Female External Genitalia*

Source: From *Biopsychology* (2nd ed.), by John P. J. Pinel, 1993, Boston: Allyn & Bacon. Copyright © 1993 by Allyn & Bacon. Reprinted by permission.

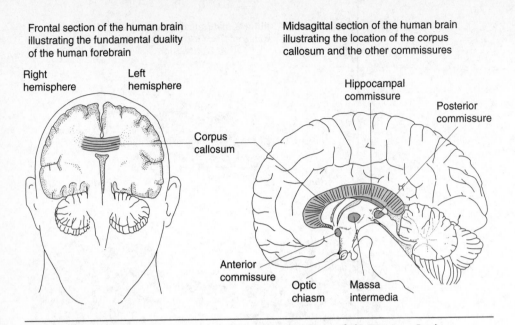

Frontal section of the human brain illustrating the fundamental duality of the human forebrain

Right hemisphere   Left hemisphere

Corpus callosum

Midsagittal section of the human brain illustrating the location of the corpus callosum and the other commissures

Hippocampal commissure

Posterior commissure

Anterior commissure

Optic chiasm   Massa intermedia

FIGURE 4.4 *Cerebral Commisures and the Hemispheres of the Human Brain*

Source: From *Biopsychology* (2nd ed.), by John P. J. Pinel, 1993, Boston: Allyn & Bacon. Copyright © 1993 by Allyn & Bacon. Reprinted by permission.

Figure 4.4 shows two views of the brain, one view as seen from the top, and another view as seen cut down the middle (a cross section). The view of the brain from the top shows that the cerebral cortex is divided down the middle into two halves, or hemispheres. This division forms a left and a right cerebral hemisphere. The view through the midsection shows some of the structures in the brain beneath the cerebral cortex, including several structures in which researchers have found sexual dimorphism. However, when the overall factor of brain size is removed, most of the sex differences in these structures disappear (Leonard et al., 2008).

Beginning in the 1800s, research indicated that, despite appearances, the cerebral hemispheres are not mirror images of each other (Springer & Deutsch, 1998). The concept of **lateralization** holds that the left and right hemispheres are each specialized for different functions; the left hemisphere is specialized for language and speech, and the right hemisphere for spatial abilities. A great deal of research and theory have explored gender differences in the lateralization of the cerebral hemispheres, but a meta-analysis (Sommer, Aleman, Bouma, & Kahn, 2004) and a critical review (Wallentin, 2009) indicated that lateralization of function does not differ significantly for women and men.

The evidence for sexual dimorphism in the brain is strongest for a small section of the hypothalamus called the **sexually dimorphic nucleus (SDN)**. This structure is larger in male rats and in men than in female rats and in women (Gorski, 1987; Swaab & Fliers, 1985). Although its function is not understood, that function may be related to sexual behavior or gender identity (Garcia-Falgueras & Swaab, 2008). This nucleus is very sensitive to testosterone and estrogen, so the presence or absence of these hormones influences

◼ GENDERED VOICES

Will I Be Smarter?

Male brains are larger than female brains, and this situation has led to much debate regarding the relative intelligence of women and men. The relationship between brain weight and intelligence is not entirely clear and has been the topic of research and debate for over a century. The initial belief that larger brains make for greater intelligence has been abandoned—under that metric, elephants would be smarter than humans. The measurement of the ratio of brain weight to body size puts humans at the top of the scale, and thus it has been accepted (by humans, at least) as the standard.

Although the ratio of brain weight to body size among species is an index of intelligence, the variations within species are difficult to interpret. The difference in brain weight between men and women falls into this debate. When considering the ratio of brain weight to body size, the interpretation of gender difference varies; some authorities argue that this gender difference is reduced, others contend that it is eliminated, and some even claim that it is reversed (see Breedlove, 1994, for a brief summary of this argument). The division of opinion may reflect a controversy regarding what measurement to use to define body size. Should the measurement be body weight, height, or skin surface? Each of these measurements has both advocates and opponents.

When I explained these arguments and problems to one of my classes, a student listening to this lecture posed a question that frames the problem: "If I lose weight, does that mean that I will be smarter?" She wasn't serious, but her question highlights the obvious absurdity of using individual body weight in the calculation of intelligence.

its development. In humans, gender differences in this structure do not exist at birth. Between birth and ages 2 to 4 years, the number of cells in this structure increases rapidly (Swaab, Gooren, & Hofman, 1995). The number of cells begins to decrease in girls but not in boys, creating a sexual dimorphism that peaks in young adulthood to middle age (Breedlove, 1994). Otherwise, the differences in structure between female and male brains are small. Table 4.1 summarizes the results of studies on structural differences between women's and men's brains.

TABLE 4.1 *Summary of Brain Differences between Men and Women*

Structure	Difference
Cerebral hemispheres	Men may be more lateralized than women for language and spatial functions
Sexually dimorphic nucleus (SDN) of hypothalamus	SDN in men is 2.5 times larger than in women
Splenium of corpus callosum	Early studies indicated larger and more bulbous splenium in women; later studies found an interaction with age and gender
Anterior commissure	Evidence for sexual dimorphism is sketchy
Massa intermedia of the thalamus	Evidence for sexual dimorphism is sketchy

In addition to brain differences, other nervous system structures show gender differences. For example, one of the nervous system sex differences is in the **spinal nucleus of the bulbocavernosus** (Watson, Freeman, & Breedlove, 2001). The spinal nucleus of the bulbocavernosus is 25% larger in men than in women. These neurons aid in the ejaculation of sperm in men and constrict the opening of the vagina in women. These spinal neurons are present in both male and female rats at birth, but the neurons die in female rats to a greater extent than in women. In male rats, the presence of androgens allows these neurons to survive, but environmental factors also affect the survival of these neurons. Therefore, there is a larger difference between the nervous systems of male and female rats than male and female humans, and a simple generalization from rats to humans would be invalid.

Another caution is related to interpretations for sex and gender differences in understanding hormonal versus social factors. The tendency exists to see a one-way chain of causality in which genetic and hormonal influences produce physiology, which in turn, produces behavior. As S. Marc Breedlove (1994) pointed out, this reasoning is false because it is impossible to separate biological from social influences and because the causality goes both ways. He contended that it is possible to concentrate on either biological or psychological measurements, but because biologists and psychologists are studying the same phenomena, any distinctions they make are illusory. In addition, social influences can affect behavior, which can alter the brain. For example, any change in the number, size, or connection of neurons in the structure of the brain constitutes a biological measurement, but such alterations will have psychological implications in terms of behavioral changes. Conversely, behavior can affect brain chemistry, which can alter brain structure, resulting in biological changes. Breedlove warned against confusing biological measures and biological influences, claiming that psychological and biological influences are impossible to separate.

Gonadal, hormonal, genital, and brain organization are not sufficient to produce sexually interested and sexually active people capable of reproduction. Such changes depend on the activating effects of hormones during puberty.

Changes during Puberty

The levels of circulating hormones are low during infancy and childhood, but these levels increase before puberty, the onset of sexual maturity. The changes that occur during this period include not only fertility but also the characteristic adolescent growth spurt and the development of secondary sex characteristics. These characteristics constitute the differences between male and female bodies other than reproductive ones (see Figure 4.5). Both sexes experience the growth of body and pubic hair and the appearance of acne. Young men experience the growth of facial hair, larynx enlargement, hairline recession, and muscle development, whereas young women experience breast development, rounding of body contours, and menarche—the beginning of menstruation. All of these changes are prompted by changes in the release of hormones.

The adolescent growth spurt is the result of muscle and bone growth in response to increased release of growth hormone by the pituitary. Increased production of tropic hormones by the pituitary act on the adrenal glands and the gonads to increase production of gonadal and adrenal hormones. As puberty begins, the pituitary starts to release two gonadotropic hormones into the bloodstream—**follicle-stimulating hormone (FSH) and luteinizing hormone (LH)**. These hormones stimulate the gonads to increase their

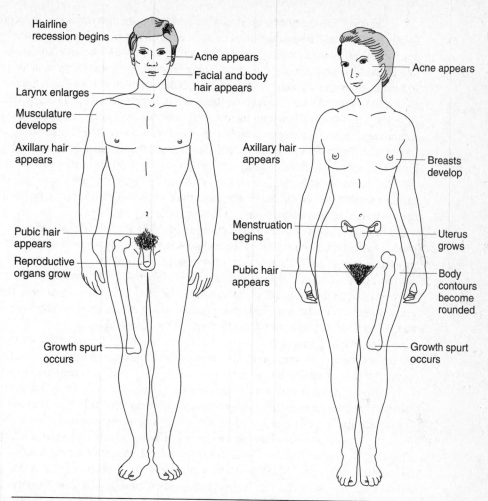

FIGURE 4.5 *Changes Occurring in Males and Females during Puberty*

Source: From *Biopsychology* (2nd ed.), by John P. J. Pinel, 1993, Boston: Allyn & Bacon. Copyright © 1993 by Allyn & Bacon. Reprinted by permission.

production of estrogens and androgens. Increased circulation of these gonadal hormones results in maturation of the genitals, that is, the development of fertility as well as the development of secondary sex characteristics.

In adolescent boys and adult men, the production of androgens is proportionately higher than their production of estrogens; in adolescent girls and in women, the production of estrogens is proportionately higher than their production of androgens. Again, it would be inaccurate to think of androgens as "male" hormones and estrogens as "female" hormones. An example of the influence of one hormone on both sexes is the growth of pubic and underarm hair; the androgen produced by both boys and girls results in the growth of pubic and underarm hair in both.

LH and FSH, the hormones that initiate puberty, are also important for reproduction. In girls and women, the production of these two hormones varies cyclically, whereas in boys and men, their production is not cyclic (but neither is it entirely steady). The cyclic variation of LH and FSH produces the menstrual cycle, beginning with an increase in the production of luteinizing hormone releasing factor and follicle-stimulating hormone releasing factor by the hypothalamus. These actons cause the pituitary to produce LH and FSH. FSH stimulates follicles, a group of cells within the ovaries, to mature an ovum. LH causes the follicle to rupture and release the ovum, which begins to travel down the Fallopian tube toward the uterus. The remainder of the follicle starts to produce the hormone progesterone, which prepares the uterus to receive and implant the ovum, if it happens to be fertilized. Then all of these hormone levels begin to decline. If the ovum is fertilized, pregnancy will produce an increase in estradiol and progesterone, but if the ovum is not fertilized, the prepared lining of the uterus is shed in menstruation, and the cycle starts again.

In boys, puberty causes the maturation of internal and external genitalia, including growth of the penis, seminal vesicles, and prostate. The maturation of seminal vesicles and prostate is necessary for ejaculation of seminal fluid, and sperm production is necessary for fertility. FSH is involved in the production of sperm. LH contributes to the maturation of sperm, but its main function is to stimulate the production of testosterone. Testosterone is controlled by feedback to the hypothalamus, which can inhibit or prompt the production of LH and FSH, which in turn can affect the production of sperm.

The role of hormones is essential in the regulation of fertility and clearly important for sexual activity in some animals. In rats, for example, the cyclic production of hormones by the females relates to sexual receptivity, and male rats respond to that receptivity. Hormone levels are also important for the development and maintenance of sexual interest. Rats that have their gonads removed before puberty fail to develop any interest in sexual activity. If their gonads are removed after puberty, their sexual interest fades.

In humans, the relationship between hormonal levels and sexual interest is less clear-cut. Hormones are also important for the development of sexual interest in humans (Bancroft, 2002), but sexual interest usually precedes puberty (Hyde & Jaffee, 2000). Around age 10, many children begin to show great curiosity (and perhaps even feelings) concerning sex. One possible mechanism for this development is the maturation of the adrenal glands, which occurs at this time and produce both androgens and estrogens. Nevertheless, people who do not undergo puberty generally fail to develop much interest in sexual activity (Meyer-Bahlburg, 1980), so hormonal events during preadolescence and puberty may form a cascade of circumstances crucial for the development of sexual interest.

The story is even more complex concerning the maintenance of sexual activity in humans who experience a decline of hormone levels. Such declines can occur for a number of reasons, including removal of the gonads or decreased hormone production associated with aging. For men, removal of the testes tends to produce a decrease in sexual activity, but the extent and rate of decrease varies enormously from person to person (Bancroft, 2002). Some men experience the significant and rapid loss of either ability to get erections or ability to ejaculate or both. Other men experience a slowly decreasing interest in sexual activity, followed by difficulty in ejaculating, and then by loss of ability to achieve erections. Few men remain unaffected by loss of androgens, though replacement testosterone can reverse the decline in sexual interest and possibly in sexual performance. Testosterone replacement therapy has increased with the creation of the testosterone patch and testosterone gel, and its short-term effects are clear (Sullivan, 2003). However, its long-term safety remains unestablished.

On the other hand, women's sexual interest seems less affected by the removal of ovaries. Indeed, some women report increased sexual motivation after such surgery. One possibility is that the hormones that are important for the maintenance of sexual interest in women are androgens, and so a decrease in estrogen is not critical. Adrenal androgens may be sufficient to maintain sexual interest. Another possibility is that humans are so little controlled by their hormones that drastic physical changes in sexually mature adults are mediated by experience and expectation.

In summary, LH and FSH produce the changes in reproductive and secondary sex characteristics associated with puberty. In girls, these changes produce cyclic variations in hormone levels that are associated with the maturation and release of an ovum approximately every month. If this ovum is fertilized by a sperm, the fertilized ovum will implant in the uterus, and pregnancy will occur. If no fertilization occurs, the lining of the uterus is shed in menstruation, and the process will reoccur. In boys, the changes during puberty produce growth of the penis and maturation of the internal reproductive system, which will allow them to produce and ejaculate sperm. In addition to the physical changes associated with boys' bodies and reproductive systems, raised levels of gonadal hormones seem to be related to the development of sexual interest. Individuals who do not undergo puberty do not develop motivation to participate in sexual activity. However, the maintenance of sexual interest in humans is not directly related to the levels of hormones but instead depends on experience and expectancy.

Variations in Sexual Development

A number of events relating to the development of the reproductive system can, but usually do not, vary from the typical patterns during prenatal development. Problems can originate at several points, beginning before conception with the formation of the mother's ovum or the father's sperm. Yet other problems can arise when the prenatal hormones are not consistent with the genetic configuration of the developing fetus. These variations provide contrasts to typical development and highlight the complexities of defining male and female.

Beginning with the single cell that is the fertilized ovum, males differ from females in their chromosomes, but the presence of the XX or XY sex chromosome pattern does not guarantee the development of a normal boy or girl. Variations sometimes occur in the assortment of chromosomes carried by the sperm and ova. Instead of the typical 23, sometimes chromosomes are missing or extra ones appear. Several types of chromosomal variations have direct effects on the development of the internal reproductive system, the external genitalia, or both, with resulting hormonal differences.

Variations in Number of Sex Chromosomes.   Variations from the typical number of sex chromosomes produce syndromes that often affect reproductive organs, genitalia, hormone production, fertility, growth, intelligence, and other aspects of development. **Turner syndrome** (or *Turner's syndrome*) occurs when the fertilized ovum has only one chromosome of pair 23—that is, one X. This syndrome is usually described as X0, where the zero stands for the missing chromosome (Ranke & Saenger, 2001). Individuals with Turner syndrome appear female at birth, because their external genitals develop according to the female pattern. Their prenatal development begins normally, but their Müllerian systems degenerate, producing individuals with no functioning ovaries, and their brains vary in small ways from those of other women (Cutter et al., 2006). At birth the appearance of the external genitalia prompts identification as female, but without ovaries, they produce no estrogens, so they do not undergo puberty or produce ova. With hormone supplements, they appear female but are not fertile.

Another mistake in chromosome number is the presence of an extra X chromosome—the XXX configuration (Harmon, Bender, Linden, & Robinson, 1998). Individuals with the XXX configuration develop prenatally as female, but women with the XXX pattern may have normal intelligence or may have developmental disabilities that affect cognitive ability. They also may have problems that affect their reproductive ability, including menstrual irregularities or amenorrhea (absence of menstrual periods) that results in sterility, but they may not. Women with this chromosomal pattern have been known to have children. Individuals with the XXXX pattern and XXXXX pattern have also been identified (Linden, Bender, & Robinson, 1995). These individuals tend to have more severe developmental problems and are very likely to be seriously developmentally disabled as well as sterile.

Klinefelter syndrome is characterized by the XXY configuration, and this variation is the most common of the sex chromosome abnormalities occurring in 1 case per 1,000 male births (Wattendorf & Muenke, 2005). Individuals with Klinefelter syndrome have male internal and external genitalia, but their testes are small and usually cannot produce sperm, resulting in sterility. They may also develop breasts and a feminized body shape during puberty. Like other people with extra chromosomal material, individuals with Klinefelter syndrome have an increased chance of developmental disabilities. Other configurations of chromosomes are similar to Klinefelter syndrome, including XXXY and XXXXY, which produce more severe problems in the skeletal and reproductive systems as well as severe developmental disabilities.

The XYY chromosome pattern was the subject of a great deal of publicity during the 1960s. Articles appeared linking the XYY gene pattern to "aggressive tendencies" and "criminality" (Hubbard & Wald, 1993). These sensational reports were largely unfounded; the early association of XYY with imprisonment was based on faulty research. The large majority of XYY men are not aggressive or criminal. They tend to be very tall and may be more likely to be in prison than men with the XY chromosome pattern (Witkin et al., 1976). However, their offenses were no more likely to be violent than other inmates. Thus, the presence of an extra Y chromosome produces an increased risk for developmental disabilities but not a tendency to higher levels of aggression.

In summary, missing or extra sex chromosomes often affect the development of the sexual organs and more often affect other areas of development, especially intelligence. Both missing chromosomes (Turner syndrome) and extra chromosomes (Klinefelter syndrome) result in sterility, but individuals with the XXX pattern and the XYY pattern may be fertile. This extra chromosomal material does not make individuals "hypermasculine" or "superfeminine." Indeed, extra chromosomes produce developmental problems rather than adding anything useful.

Problems Related to Prenatal Hormone Exposure.

The presence of the XY chromosome pattern is not necessary (or sufficient) for the development of male internal or external genitalia; the hormone testosterone is the key to these developments.

Therefore, a fetus that is genetically female (XX pattern) can be masculinized by the addition of testosterone during the period of the third and fourth months of prenatal development. Typically, female fetuses do not produce testosterone during this important period, but prenatal exposure to androgens may occur, either through the action of tumors in the adrenal gland or through the pregnant woman's inadvertent or intentional exposure to androgens.

Congenital adrenal hyperplasia (CAH, also called *adrenogenital syndrome*) occurs when the adrenal gland decreases its production of the hormone cortisol, which prompts an increase in adrenal androgens. For a male fetus, relatively few problems occur; for a boy, increased androgen production accelerates the onset of puberty. For a developing female fetus, however, the presence of excessive androgens produces masculinization of the external genitalia. The excess androgens occur too late to affect the internal genitals, which are usually normal, but these girls are born with a clitoris that may look very much like a small penis. If their genitals appear atypical at birth, physicians often recommend to parents that surgical correction should be performed so that the genitals will have a more typical female appearance. This procedure has become very controversial (Cohen-Kettenis, 2005b; Meyer-Bahlburg et al., 2004), partly because the surgery may damage nerves to the clitoris, producing permanent problems in sexual responsiveness.

These girls interest researchers because their brains were exposed to androgens during prenatal development, which may affect their behavior, gender identity, and sexual orientation. Hormone exposure is not their only difference—the early medical and parental attention focused on their genitals makes these girls different from others. Research has suggested that CAH is associated with play activities more typical of boys than girls; that is, these girls are more likely to be "tomboys" (Berenbaum, 2006; Hines, Brook, & Conway, 2004). As adults, women affected by CAH are more likely than other women to show reduced heterosexual interest, but as girls (Meyer-Bahlburg et al., 2004) and as women (Berenbaum, 2006), those affected by CAH showed neither gender confusion nor dissatisfaction. Indeed, the majority of women affected by CAH become heterosexual women satisfied with their female gender identity.

Androgen insensitivity syndrome occurs in XY male fetuses whose body cells are insensitive to androgens. The androgens produced by their fetal testes will not induce masculinization because the androgen receptors in their bodies do not function normally (Mazur, 2005; Simpson, 2001). These fetuses will develop as though no androgens were present, and at birth the XY baby will appear to be a girl. The internal genitalia are not female, however, because the production of Müllerian-inhibiting substance caused the normal degeneration of the Müllerian system and the presence of the Y chromosome prompted the development of testes (that remain within the abdominal cavity). Thus, these individuals have undescended testes, but their external genitalia appear female.

Individuals with androgen insensitivity syndrome (and their families) can be completely unaware of the disorder. Complicating the diagnosis, their testes produce sufficient estrogen to prompt breast development, increasing their feminine appearance. They have no ovaries, Fallopian tubes, or uterus, so they will not reach **menarche**, the beginning of menstruation. Nor will they grow pubic hair, a characteristic under the control of the androgens, to which they are insensitive. No amount of added androgens will reverse this condition, because their body cells are insensitive to it. Indeed, the levels of androgens circulating in their bloodstream are within the normal range for men, but their bodies are "deaf" to these hormones.

Individuals with androgen insensitivity syndrome are identified as girls at birth, raised as girls, and have no reason to doubt their gender identification for years. At puberty they grow breasts and begin to look like young women, giving them no reason to imagine they are anything but women. Typically, few suspicions arise concerning any abnormality until they fail to grow pubic hair and fail to reach menarche. Even then these symptoms may be discounted for several years due to the variability of sexual development.

When gynecological examination reveals the abnormality of their internal genitalia, these individuals and their families learn that they are, in some sense, men. This information contradicts years of gender role development; some of these individuals have difficulty adjusting to this information. No treatments exist to masculinize these individuals, so no attempt is made to change them. A longitudinal study of individuals with androgen insensitivity syndrome (Hines, Ahmed, & Hughes, 2003) indicated that they are similar to other women in gender identity, esteem, and well-being. Despite their male chromosomes, these individuals are women in terms of gender identity, physical appearance, and behavior.

All of these examples of variation in sexual development illustrate individuals born with characteristics of both sexes. The modern term for these conditions is **intersexuality** or *disorders of sexual development* (*DSD*). The traditional diagnosis for these individuals was **hermaphroditism**, which was restricted to individuals who have both ovarian and testicular tissue—either an ovary on one side of the body and a testicle on the other side, or both types of tissue combined into a structure called an ovotestis. This condition is extremely rare, with no more than 60 cases being identified in Europe and North America within the last century (Money, 1986).

Another provocative example of intersexuality comes from individuals with a genetic enzyme (5-alpha-reductase) deficiency that prevents chromosomal males from developing male external genitalia during the prenatal period (Cohen-Kettenis, 2005a; Herdt, 1994). Like individuals with androgen insensitivity syndrome, these babies may appear more female than male at birth and are often identified as girls. The appearance of their external genitals is ambiguous, not truly female but definitely not male. Unlike people with androgen insensitivity syndrome, these individuals respond to androgens during puberty and develop masculine characteristics. That is, their voice deepens, their muscles develop, their testes descend into the scrotum, and their penis enlarges. For those identified as girls, they no longer fit into that category. However, most of these individuals do not clearly fit into the category of male, either.

An early study of these intersex individuals (Imperato-McGinley, Guerrero, Gautier, & Peterson, 1974) indicated that the majority had made at least fairly successful transitions to the male role, but an analysis of studies on this topic (Berenbaum, 2006; Cohen-Kettenis, 2005a) indicated that about 40% of individuals with this syndrome retained a female gender identity. A few individuals identified themselves as men but dressed and lived the social role of women, not clearly fitting either role. Indeed, the New Guinea culture in which this form of intersexuality is relatively common acknowledges the existence of individuals who do not fit either sex by devising a third category of sex to describe them (Herdt, 1981).

A third sex or some continuum for sex seems a better choice than the two categories of male and female (Fausto-Sterling, 2000). The intersex individuals represent cases in which chromosomal, hormonal, gonadal, and genital sex are not consistent. As Sheri Berenbaum (2006) pointed out, the determination of sex does not necessarily require complete consistency. For example, individuals with androgen insensitivity syndrome have a male chromosome configuration and normal levels of androgens, but they look and feel female—they are female in their own opinion and in the opinion of society (Mazur, 2005). Although individuals with 5-alpha-reductase deficiency usually identify as either male or female, some experience difficulties. If hormones and chromosomes were the determining factors in gender identity, then these individuals should all become male, and individuals with androgen insensitivity syndrome would be male. Such is not the case. If exposure to prenatal androgens were the determining factor for gender identity, girls with CAH would experience many problems. They do experience more problems with their gender identity than other girls, but a majority of them have no gender confusion or dissatisfaction (Berenbaum, 2006). Although hormones play a very important role in determining reproductive physiology, sex and gender are more than the function of hormones.

Hormones and Behavior Instability

In addition to their role in sexual development and activity, hormones are widely considered to affect other behaviors. The concept of premenstrual syndrome (PMS) and its many negative effects have received wide publicity, making the headline "PMS Makes You Smarter!" a surprising statement. Another of the widely publicized influences of hormones is the effect of testosterone on aggression, making the headline contention that hormones prepare men to be fathers another surprising statement. Rather than positive effects, people tend to attribute unstable, problem behavior to "raging hormones." Which view is correct? What types of behavioral effects do hormones produce?

Premenstrual Syndrome

The notion that women's reproductive systems affect their mood is ancient (Chrisler & Caplan, 2002), but the concept of PMS is quite modern—it can be traced to the 1960s. During this time, Katharina Dalton published research (reviewed by Parlee, 1973) suggesting that women experience a wide variety of negative emotional, cognitive, and physical effects due to the hormonal changes that precede menstruation. These effects became known as a *syndrome,* although the list of symptoms extended to over 150, and some of the symptoms were mutually exclusive (such as *elevated mood* and *depression*).

The symptoms associated with the premenstrual phase of the cycle include headache; backache; abdominal bloating and discomfort; breast tenderness; tension or irritability; depression; increased analgesic, alcohol, or sedative use; decreased energy; and disruption in eating, sleeping, sexual behavior, work, and interpersonal relationships (Dickerson, Mazyck, & Hunter, 2003). The most common among these symptoms are tension and irritability, and the widespread belief is that hormones are the underlying cause.

Recall that the cyclic variation of LH and FSH produces the menstrual cycle by affecting the release of estrogens and progesterone. In the middle of the cycle, the follicles produce larger amounts of one of the estrogens (estradiol) than during other times of the cycle, and this increase produces a surge of LH and FSH. This surge causes the release of the matured ovum, and the remainder of the follicle then starts to produce progesterone. Therefore, during the ovulatory phase of the cycle, estrogen levels are higher than progesterone levels. During the premenstrual phase of the cycle, both estradiol and progesterone are falling, and progesterone is at a higher level than estradiol. During the menstrual phase, the levels of both hormones are relatively low. Figure 4.6 shows the levels of hormones during the different phases of the cycle.

All of the hormonal changes that occur during the menstrual cycle have been candidates for the underlying cause of PMS (Dickerson et al., 2003). The possibilities include an excess of estrogens, falling progesterone levels, and the ratio of estrogens to

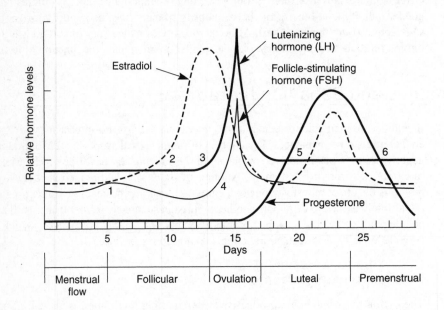

Phases of the Human Menstrual Cycle

1. In response to an increase in FSH, small spheres of cells called ovarian follicles begin to grow around individual egg cells (ova).

2. The follicles begin to release estrogens such as estradiol.

3. The estrogens stimulate the hypothalamus to increase the release of LH and FSH from the anterior pituitary.

4. In response to the LH surge, one of the follicles ruptures and releases its ovum.

5. The ruptured follicle under the influence of LH develops into a corpus luteum (yellow body) and begins to release progesterone, which prepares the lining of the uterus for the implantation of a fertilized ovum.

6. Meanwhile, the ovum is moved into the Fallopian tube by the rowing action of ciliated cells. If the ovum is not fertilized, progesterone and estradiol levels fall and the walls of the uterus are sloughed off as menstrual flow and the cycle begins once again.

FIGURE 4.6   *Hormones during the Menstrual Cycle*

Source: From *Biopsychology* (2nd ed.), by John P. J. Pinel, 1993, Boston: Allyn & Bacon. Copyright © 1993 by Allyn & Bacon. Reprinted by permission.

progesterone. However, hormonal differences show no relationship with symptoms (Hsiao, Liu, & Hsiao, 2004). This failure to tie any pattern of hormonal changes to the experience of PMS is a major problem for the concept of PMS.

But might these hormonal changes make women smarter, as one of the headline articles for this chapter contended? The article focused on the differences in cognitive ability in the two hemispheres of the cerebral cortex (see Figure 4.4), contending that different types of cognition arise from each hemisphere and that the hormonal changes that occur during the premenstrual period amplify some and suppress other types of thinking. Early research in this area (Kimura, 1989, 1992) indicated that hormonal changes in both women's and men's brains produce cognitive effects, but more recent research has revealed that these effects are more complex (Fernández et al., 2003; Hausmann, 2005) or possibly do not exist (Halari et al., 2005). Even research that has shown differences in cognition related to hormone level has demonstrated only very small effects—nothing that would produce behaviors that might make a person "smarter."

The lack of relationship between hormone levels and the experience of PMS also presents a problem for diagnosis; there is no hormone or laboratory test for PMS (Freeman, 2003), and the diagnostic criteria have presented problems for researchers (Weisz & Knaapen, 2009). About 12% of women in France reported premenstrual problems serious enough to interfere with their lives (Potter, Bouyer, Trussell, & Moreau, 2009). Almost 19% of women in the United States report menstrual-related problems (Strine, Chapman, & Ahluwalia, 2005), but these problems include menstrual symptoms—heavy flow and cramping—as well as symptoms associated with PMS—anxiety, depression, and sleep problems. Even women who experience no troublesome problems associated with menstruation still report premenstrual symptoms (Gonda et al., 2008). Confusing the diagnosis of PMS even further is the related diagnosis of premenstrual dysphoric disorder (PMDD). This disorder was added to the fourth edition of the *Diagnostic and Statistical Manual of Mental Disorders,* the official guidelines for diagnosing mental disorders published by the American Psychiatric Association. PMDD is a more severe version of PMS; its treatment includes prescription antidepressant drugs.

Distinguishing among premenstrual symptoms, PMS, and PMDD presents a challenge for researchers and clinicians (Weisz & Knaapen, 2009; Yonkers, Pearlstein, & Rosenheck, 2003). About half the women seeking treatment from a gynecology practice reported that they experienced symptoms of PMS, but about a third of that group did not meet the criteria for PMS. In other studies (McFarlane Martin, & Williams, 1988; McFarlane & Williams, 1994), about half the women who met and about half who failed to meet diagnostic criteria consistent with PMS reported that they had it. A random survey of women (Deuster, Adera, & South-Paul, 1999) indicated that only 8.3% experienced PMS. These results suggest that the *belief* in PMS is more widespread than PMS. What has contributed to the widespread belief that most women are victims of their hormones and suffer not only during their menstrual periods but also during the two or three weeks before (which totals three out of four weeks of the month)? Media publicity may be one answer (see According to the Media and According to the Research), but researchers have explored some additional possibilities.

Two longitudinal studies by Jessica McFarlane and her colleagues (McFarlane et al., 1988; McFarlane & Williams, 1994) offer some insight into beliefs about PMS. Both studies involved instructing women (and men) to keep records of their daily moods without

Although the diagnosis of PMS is controversial, many women are willing to label their symptoms as this disorder.

knowing that the menstrual cycle was the focus of the study (to avoid bias by alerting participants to the topic of the study). Both studies included women who were cycling normally, women who were taking oral contraceptives and thus not ovulating, and men. The main result of the study by McFarlane and her colleagues (1988) was that no differences in mood stability appeared when comparing the young men and the young women who participated in the study. All participants experienced similar mood changes within a day as well as from day to day. Also, the men and women reported similar variability in mood during the 70 days of the study. These results offer no support for the existence of PMS.

A second study (McFarlane & Williams, 1994) recruited participants who were older than the typical college students and lasted at least 12 weeks to cover more menstrual cycles. The analysis for this study included an evaluation of each participant's cyclic mood variation over time. This study also revealed that people experienced cyclic mood variations but not in the PMS pattern. In comparing women who were cycling normally to women taking oral contraceptives and to the men, the women who were cycling normally reported *more pleasant moods* during and immediately after their periods than in the ovulatory or premenstrual periods (McFarlane et al., 1988), and few reported emotional symptoms consistent with PMS (McFarlane & Williams, 1994). The headline story contended that women's periods present advantages, but it did not mention this one.

Why do so many women believe that they have PMS? One reason is perception of the signals that predict the onset of menstruation. Women around the world experience premenstrual symptoms, recognizing their bodies' signals that their periods are going to start (Adewuya, Loto, & Adewumi, 2009; Lee, So-Kum Tang, & Chong, 2009; Miller, 2002). Some people are more responsive than others in interpreting body signals. Comparing women who showed higher sensitivity to bodily cues to those who showed less revealed that women with high body sensitivity reported more emotional responses during the premenstrual periods than women less sensitive to their bodies' changes (Schnall, Abrahamson, & Laird, 2002). Indeed, the experience of physical symptoms is a major factor in accepting PMS (Kiesner, 2009). Consistent with the contentions from the headline article, about half of the women reported positive emotional changes, including greater energy and happiness.

Recognizing symptoms of an impending menstrual period also allows women to attribute negative moods to PMS rather than to some other source (such as stress, pressure at work or school, or relationship conflicts). This cognitive process of attribution allows for distortion of cognitive processes that maintain beliefs in PMS, even if an individual's experience does not. For example, by imagining that all women have PMS and by believing that one's own symptoms are less severe than the norm, a woman can feel superior to the average woman (Chrisler, Rose, Dutch, Sklarsky, & Grant, 2006). Women (and the men around them) may be more comfortable in attributing negative emotions to PMS rather than accepting those negative emotions as part of the self (Chrisler, 2008; Chrisler & Caplan, 2002). After all, women are supposed to be sweet, kind, and nurturant; if they behave otherwise, PMS is a good excuse.

Both women and men are willing to attribute moody behavior to PMS (Koeske & Koeske, 1975). When furnished with information about a woman's cycle, both men and women tended to use this information to partly explain the woman's emotional behavior. If people believe that these symptoms are associated with the premenstrual period as well as menstruation, they can apply this explanation at least half the time—the week (or two) before and the week during menstruation. When they experience the same situations and reactions at other phases of their cycle, they seek other explanations. In this way, PMS can become a self-perpetuating myth for the women who react to problems, stresses, and irritations in their lives as well as for the people who observe the reactions.

Does this explanation of PMS mean that the syndrome is not "real"? Are women imagining all their premenstrual symptoms? And what about those women who experience very serious symptoms that meet the diagnosis of PMDD? None of the findings on expectancy and attribution of symptoms indicates that the symptoms are not real; women are not imagining their discomfort, irritation, anxiety, bloating, sleep problems, and cramps. They may, however, be misattributing these symptoms to PMS when other explanations would be more accurate. For example, a recent study (Szollos, Thyrum, & Martin, 2006) found that anxiety varied across the menstrual cycle in some women, and those women often showed symptoms consistent with PMS. A survey of women in the United States (Strine et al., 2005) indicated that women who reported severe menstrual problems also reported problems with depression, anxiety, and stress. Perhaps the concept of PMS provides a convenient label—it is more acceptable to label women's distress as PMS rather than to consider and address more complex

▨ ACCORDING TO THE MEDIA . . .

PMS Is a Joke

For many years, television did not mention any type of menstrual process, either in its entertainment programming or in advertising. Indeed, until the 1970s, television advertising was not permitted to show women's underwear on women; ads had to use mannequins as models (Independent TeleWeb). Even before PMS could be mentioned on television, it was a topic in sitcoms (Parsons, 2004). In 1973, the character of Gloria in the sitcom *All in the Family* expressed unreasonable irritation that the show clearly indicated as being attributable to premenstrual tension, but PMS was not named.

Over the next 20 years, PMS continued to be the topic of humor on television, and it began to be named (Parsons, 2004). Menarche, the beginning of menstruation, and menopause, the ending of menstrual periods, were portrayed on dramas as well as comedies in ways that educated as well as entertained (Kissling, 2002). PMS, on the other hand, appeared only as a comedy

ploy. Women in sitcoms such as *Taxi, Married with Children,* and *Roseanne* showed symptoms of PMS, but those symptoms were always confined to the emotional rather than physical symptoms. Actress Patricia Heaton won an Emmy award for her portrayal of PMS in "Bad Moon Rising," an episode of *Everybody Loves Raymond* aired in 2000.

In these sitcoms, the male characters suffer more than the female characters from the female characters' PMS (Parsons, 2004). These puzzled men bear the brunt of angry outbursts, crying spells, mood swings, and temper tantrums, without any suggestion in the script that the men's behavior might contribute to their partners' irritation. These programs are funny, but "women's bad moods are often blamed on PMS, regardless of whether or not they are menstruating. Thus, negative expressions of anger or sadness are not validated. Troubled women get blamed for their PMS and PMS gets blamed for women's troubles" (Parsons, 2004, p. 23).

---

sources for problems, such as work and relationships that produce tension, stress, anxiety, and depression (Chrisler et al., 2006; Chrisler & Caplan, 2002).

The possibility that serious premenstrual symptoms are really other disorders is consistent with the treatment for PMDD, which consists of antidepressant drugs (Daw, 2002). Thus, women who respond favorably to these drugs may actually experience depression that is exacerbated by hormonal variations (Miller & Miller, 2001). As some researchers contend, PMDD may be a created disorder with little validity as a separate diagnosis (Flora & Sellers, 2003).

In summary, PMS has received wide publicity and wide acceptance, but research has failed to confirm a biological basis, and emotional symptoms are subject to expectation and attribution. It may be convenient to explain women's negative moods in terms of PMS or even PMDD, but it is probably not accurate to do so.

Testosterone and Aggression

Douglas Carlton Abrams's (2002) headline article "Father Nature" contained the subtitle "If testosterone is the defining hormone of masculinity, it's time to redefine manhood" (p. 38). This subtitle acknowledges the bad publicity associated with testosterone by way of its hypothesized link to aggression and violence. Abrams took another route, exploring research on men's hormonal changes during their partners' pregnancies and speculating

▓ ACCORDING TO THE RESEARCH . . .

PMS Is Not So Funny

About 19% of women in the United States between the ages of 18 and 55 report some type of distress associated with menstruation (Strine et al., 2005). Many of these unpleasant symptoms are not associated with PMS but rather with the menstrual period, such as heavy bleeding or painful cramping. However, PMS was among the problems mentioned by these women. The list of symptoms associated with PMS is extensive, numbering over 100 (Chrisler & Caplan, 2002). The most commonly mentioned symptom is fluid retention, especially in the breasts and abdomen, rather than the emotional symptoms portrayed on sitcoms (Parsons, 2004). Other symptoms include additional physical manifestations such as acne, headaches, aches or pain in the muscles or joints, fatigue, sleep problems, alterations in sex drive, cravings for sweet or salty food, and constipation or diarrhea, as well as emotional symptoms such as bursts of energy, sadness, depression, anxiety, tension, moodiness, and feeling out of control. To present such

symptoms as amusing requires substantial insensitivity to the women who experience these symptoms.

Television sitcoms portray men as the victims of women's PMS, but some research (Skatssoon, 2005) suggested that men may be more than innocent bystanders: Women who lived with men were more likely to report PMS than women who lived with other women. Consistent with portrayals on television, research indicates that women often experience problems during the premenstrual period that involve relationship issues. PMS researcher Jane Ussher (in Skatssoon, 2005) reported that, when asked to describe situations in which they had experienced PMS, women often told about relationship problems. She offered an alternative explanation: Women's anger may be justified, but they are willing to blame themselves and their PMS for their angry reactions. This interpretation is quite consistent with television sitcoms but may not be best for women's health or, in the long run, for their relationships.

that the increase in the hormone prolactin and decreases in testosterone may allow men to become more nurturant toward their newborn babies. This article explained that testosterone is the "primary" hormone for men but that other hormones are also important in their behavior. Do men's hormones prepare them to be warriors, fathers, or both? And how does testosterone affect women's behavior?

The most common assumption (and the greatest amount of research) involves the role of testosterone in aggression. This relationship has three possibilities: (1) Testosterone may cause increases in aggression, (2) aggressive behavior may cause increases in testosterone levels, or (3) levels of testosterone and aggression may be mediated through some other biological or social mechanism (Ramirez, 2003). Although many people assume the first possibility, evidence indicates that the second and third possibilities are more likely.

Research on the relationship between testosterone levels and aggression indicates complex rather than a simple, linear relationship. James Dabbs and his colleagues (Dabbs, 2000) conducted dozens of studies on hormone levels and behavior in both men and women. These studies revealed that high testosterone levels were related to impulsive and antisocial (what Dabbs called "rambunctious") behaviors, but few studies found a link to aggressive or violent behaviors.

Within the normal range of testosterone (which varies by a great deal), testosterone may not be a major factor in behavior. However, for men with the highest levels of testosterone, problems appeared in a variety of behaviors. For example, U.S. military veterans

Contrary to its popular image, testosterone may play a role in preparing men to be nurturant fathers.

showed a positive relationship between testosterone level and drug and alcohol abuse, antisocial behavior, and affective disorders (Dabbs, Hopper, & Jurkovic, 1990). Men whose testosterone fell within the upper 10% of testosterone levels had a history of trouble with parents, teachers, and classmates as well as a history of drug use and more instances of going AWOL (absent without leave) while in the military (Dabbs & Morris, 1990). Men with high levels of testosterone also tend to have lower-status occupations, which may indicate that high testosterone levels are related to behaviors that make success less likely, such as impulsiveness and antisocial behavior (Dabbs, 1992, 2000).

A comparison of college students and young men who were delinquents showed higher testosterone levels in the delinquents (Banks & Dabbs, 1996). An assessment of the testosterone levels in two college fraternities showed that men in the "rowdy" fraternity had higher testosterone levels than did the men in the fraternity with a reputation for academic success and social responsibility (Dabbs, Hargrove, & Heusel, 1996). For engineers working in the same company, those with high testosterone levels were more likely to quit or be fired than those with lower testosterone levels (Heusel & Dabbs, 1996). Although high testosterone levels seem to be related to problem behavior, those behaviors are not necessarily examples of aggression or violence.

A more specific example of the relationship between testosterone and violence appeared in a study of male prisoners (Dabbs, Carr, Frady, & Riad, 1995). Those prisoners who had committed crimes against individuals involving sex and violence had higher testosterone levels than did prisoners who had committed property crimes. The prisoners

TABLE 4.2 *Relationship of Testosterone to Various Behaviors in Men and Women*

Behaviors Associated with Higher Testosterone Levels	
In Men	**In Women**
Lower-status occupations	Unprovoked violence among prisoners
Drug and alcohol abuse among veterans	
Antisocial disorders among veterans	
Affective disorders among veterans	
Trouble getting along with parents, teachers, and classmates among veterans	
Delinquent behaviors while young	
Membership in a "rowdy" fraternity	
Job loss	
Incarceration for crimes involving sex or violence	
Rule violations and personal confrontations among prisoners	

Behaviors Not Associated with Higher Testosterone Levels	
Personality traits among students	Violent criminal acts
	Prisoner versus student status

with higher levels of testosterone also were more likely to be involved with rule violations and personal confrontations while in prison. Table 4.2 summarizes the findings from research by Dabbs and his colleagues. Confirming this body of research, meta-analyses (Archer, Graham-Kevan, & Davies, 2005; Book & Quinsey, 2005) have shown a small relationship between testosterone levels and aggression in men and in delinquent boys (van Bokhoven et al., 2006) and adolescent girls with conduct disorder (Pajer et al., 2006).

Women also produce testosterone, and Dabbs and his colleagues investigated the relationship between testosterone levels and aggression in women. One study (Dabbs, Ruback, Frady, Hopper, & Sgoutas, 1988) focused on inmates in a women's prison, contrasting their testosterone levels with those of female college students. Within the prison group, women with the highest levels of testosterone had the highest incidence of unprovoked violence. In addition, testosterone levels differed among inmates convicted of unprovoked violence, defensive violence, theft, drugs, and other crimes—inmates who had committed acts of unprovoked violence had the highest testosterone levels. Women who had committed violence in protecting themselves, such as those who had murdered an abusive spouse, had the lowest levels of testosterone in the prison group.

Interestingly, the mean levels of testosterone were similar for the inmates and the college students, and both averages fell within the normal range for women. The failure to find differences between women convicted of crimes and female students indicates that aggression and violence are influenced by factors other than testosterone level, including SES, which moderated the relationship between testosterone and problem behavior in men. For women as for men, testosterone may be more closely related to rambunctious behavior rather than violence (Dabbs, 2000). Thus, the evidence is weak that testosterone is the underlying cause of aggression.

Although the evidence is lacking that testosterone causes aggression, a causal relationship might still exist in the other direction—aggression may cause increases in testosterone. Although this relationship is not what most people imagine, both laboratory experiments and descriptive field studies have demonstrated this effect. In two laboratory studies (Carré & McCormick, 2008 Carré, Putman, & McCormick, 2009), no initial relationship appeared between testosterone level and aggressive behavior, but men who behaved aggressively showed raised testosterone levels. Another laboratory study showed that symbolic aggression produce an effect—handling a gun increased testosterone levels in men (Klinesmith, Kasser, & McAndrew, 2006).

An early field study (Booth, Shelley, Mazur, Tharp, & Kittok, 1989) examined the relationship between testosterone levels and winning versus losing in tennis competition. Players showed increases of testosterone on days when they played, and their hormone levels were highest before the game. The effects of winning and losing were complex, moderated by players' evaluations of their performance; players who felt positively about their performance tended to have higher testosterone levels after games.

Later research has produced findings consistent with this early study. Competition boosts testosterone levels, and the effects apply to both women and men. For example, athletic competition increased testosterone levels in both male and female soccer players (Edwards, Wetzel, & Wyner, 2006). For female rugby players, testosterone levels were higher on the days of matches and increased during the matches (Bateup, Booth, Shirtcliff, & Granger, 2002). An examination of hormone levels among male and female rowing competitors also showed effects of competition (Kivlighan, Granger, & Booth, 2005). Both of the studies that included male and female athletes showed different patterns of testosterone changes for women and men that related to social relationships with teammates. For male soccer players, playing on the home field increased testosterone levels significantly more than playing "away" games (Wolfson & Neave, 2004), which indicates that factors in addition to competition may be important in increasing testosterone levels. Therefore, research evidence suggests that competition raises testosterone, but the findings also hint that other factors may be important in the equation.

Another possibility for a relationship holds that violence and aggression are the product of an interaction in which testosterone is only one component (Ramirez, 2003). Other components include psychological and environmental factors such as personality factors or peer influence. Some research has shown that the personality factor of sensation seeking shows a stronger relationship with testosterone level than does aggression and testosterone (Aluja & Torrubia, 2004). Testosterone exposure and personality factors showed no relationship (Cohen-Bendahan, Buitelaar, van Goozen, Orlebeke, & Cohen-Kettenis, 2005), so the influence must come from an indirect link between testosterone and aggression mediated through some psychological or social variable. Two social variables, peer influence and parenting, have shown a link. Peer influence appeared as a factor in two studies of adolescent boys (Rowe, Maughan, Wrotman, Costello, & Angold, 2004; Vermeersch, T'Sjoen, Kaufman, & Vincke, 2008). Testosterone levels and physical aggression were unrelated, but aggression was related to associations with deviant peers. Family influence appeared as a factor in a study with boys and girls with high testosterone levels, who showed problem behaviors in bad family environments but not when their relationships with parents were positive (Booth,

Johnson, Granger, Crouter, & McHale, 2003). These results suggest that aggression may be related to testosterone indirectly, through an interaction with other factors.

Our headline story about testosterone and fathering contended that hormones push men toward nurturing as well as aggressive behaviors, and a model called the challenge hypothesis (Archer, 2006) explains how testosterone may relate to aggression and to nurturing. That is, testosterone may play a role in making men warriors and fathers. The challenge hypothesis arose to explain mating and paternal behaviors of birds, but the hypothesis is consistent with the complex actions of testosterone in humans. According to this view, testosterone levels rise at puberty to support reproduction. Competition and challenges boost testosterone levels, which may result in aggressive behaviors (which further increase testosterone levels). However, caring for offspring lowers testosterone and is compatible with nurturing. The model's application to humans is recent, but it may provide an integrated explanation for the complexities of testosterone action.

Considering Diversity

"The polarity of male-female is taken to be an absolute in modern Western cultures" (Sell, 2004, p. 133). This point of view creates limited possibilities for cultural variations in sexual development; biological sex is a matter of chromosomes and hormones. However, non-Western cultures include a variety of possibilities in how they divide those categories, including a category for a third sex.

In Western cultures, individuals born with some intersex condition are evaluated as abnormal and in need of medical attention, but in some cultures, these individuals are considered special (Sell, 2004). For example, a high frequency of 5-alpha-reductase deficiency produces individuals with normal male internal genitalia and with external genitals that more closely resemble a girl's than a boy's—a clitoris-like penis, an unfused scrotum that resembles labia, and undescended testes. At birth, these babies are sometimes identified as boys but are more often identified and reared as girls. At puberty they produce testosterone and become "masculinized": Their penis grows, their testes descend, they grow facial hair, and their musculature increases. That is, they change from individuals who look more like girls to ones who look more like boys. This rare disorder is more common in the Dominican Republic and New Guinea than in most other parts of the world (Herdt, 1981, 1994), and these two cultures have a term for a third sex, one that is neither male nor female but that starts out as female and becomes male. Even after these individuals develop masculine characteristics, the Sambia culture of New Guinea does not grant them full male status, but they may gain prestige and power in their culture as healers or shamans.

More than 130 Native American societies identified individuals whose "spirit" did not match the sex of their bodies. Modern anthropologists often classify these individuals as *berdaches*—men or women who adopted the gender-related behaviors of the other gender (Roscoe, 1993; Wieringa, 1994), but Native American societies had specific terms in their languages; contemporary Native American scholars prefer the term *two-spirit people*. These individuals were not intersex, but instead individuals who chose to blend masculine and feminine roles. The tradition of men who adopted characteristics of women was more common, but both male and female two-spirit people existed. Lakota, Navajo, Crow, and Zuni societies all included two-spirit people who were not thought of as homosexual but as a merging of feminine and masculine spirits, which they attained through a blessing from the spirits, achieving high spiritual status in their societies. Not all Native American societies were acceptant of these individuals, but most accepted these departures from ordinary gender roles rather than viewing them as deviations.

India also has a "third sex," the *hijras,* who are men who wish to become women (Reddy, 2005). These men may be intersex (individuals whose genitals are not clearly male or female), transvestites (men who dress in women's clothing), or transgendered men (who wish to or have undergone genital surgery to become female). The hijras trace their origin to Hindu mythology as men who worship the goddess Bedhraj Matá, sacrifice their genitals to her, and live without sexuality. Hijras are believed to have the power to confer fertility and thus are welcomed at weddings and births.

In several cultures, women can assume the male gender role (Sell, 2004). For example, several African societies allow "female husbands." These women assume the male role and receive recognition as men. They may have wives, but they may also be a wife, conferring a status that is neither male nor female. In northern Albania, women may also become men in the form of "sworn virgins," who dress and behave as men but who do not form any type of sexual relationships with women or men (Littlewood, 2002).

Thus, some cultures have a category for a third sex, providing for individuals whose biology has not clearly designated them male or female and for those who choose to blend roles. In addition, some cultures designate a category for third sex as anyone who fails to fit clearly within the two categories designated by their society. This classification arose after 1900 with the movement of women into the workforce in Europe and North America (Murat, 2005). These "emancipated" women performed jobs that removed them from the female gender role but did not make them into men, resulting in a failure to fit into either gender category. Many Western women are categorized as a third sex in Muslim countries, such as Afghanistan (Sweetland, 2004), when they perform jobs that these cultures consider the domain of men and fail to wear the clothing considered proper for women. Thus female journalists, attorneys, physicians, and professors fit into this category.

■ Summary

Several steroid hormones are important to sexual development and behavior, including the androgens, the estrogens, and the progestins. Men and women produce all of these hormones, but women produce proportionately more estrogens and progestins, whereas men produce more androgens. The prenatal production of these hormones prompts the bodies and brains of fetuses to organize in either the male or the female pattern. During puberty, these hormones work toward developing fertility and prompt the production of secondary sex characteristics, such as facial hair for men and breasts for women. The role of hormones in the activation and maintenance of sexual interest and activity is less clear in humans than in other species, but humans who do not experience the surge of hormones associated with puberty tend not to develop much interest in sex. Testosterone, one of the androgens, plays a role in maintaining sexual activity in men and possibly in women as well.

Sexual development may be conceptualized as consisting of five stages—genetic, gonadal, hormonal, internal genitalia, and external genitalia—all of which usually proceed according to either the male or the female pattern. The first stage in sexual development is genetic, the inheritance of either XX or XY chromosomes of pair 23. Although the inheritance of chromosomes is the beginning of the pattern, embryos are not sexually dimorphic until around 6 weeks into gestation, when those with the XY pattern develop testes. Androgens produced by the fetal testes masculinize the fetus. During the third month of gestation, androgens direct the development of external male genitalia.

The female pattern is not as dependent on the presence of estrogens as the male pattern is on androgens. After the sixth week of pregnancy, those individuals with the XX pattern of chromosomes start to develop the Müllerian structures, which become the ovaries, Fallopian tubes, uterus, and upper vagina. In addition, their Wolffian structures start to degenerate. An absence of all steroid hormones will allow the feminization of external genitalia, but the internal reproductive organs do not develop normally.

Prenatal hormones also affect brain development, producing differences in the brains of males versus females. Several brain structures are affected, but the sexually dimorphic nucleus of the hypothalamus shows the biggest difference. Its function is not known.

Variances from the typical female or male patters may occur at any stage of sexual development, beginning with the inheritance of the X and Y chromosomes. A number of disorders exist that create individuals with fewer or more sex chromosomes than typical, and some of these configurations produce problems with the development of internal or external genitalia. In addition, several of these disorders produce individuals with developmental disorders, especially lowered intelligence. Individuals with Turner syndrome (X0) appear to be female but lack ovaries; individuals with Klinefelter syndrome (XXY) appear to be male, often with feminized body contours, but have nonfunctional testes; XXX individuals are female and may vary little from XX individuals; XYY individuals are tall males who may be reproductively normal but with low intelligence.

Even having 46 chromosomes does not guarantee typical development in subsequent stages, and several types of intersexuality exist. These cases of individuals who have the physiology of both males and females highlight the complexity of sexual development and suggest that many components contribute to gender identity and functioning.

Media reports tend to indicate a role for hormones in two areas of problem behavior—premenstrual syndrome (PMS) and aggression. Careful research has indicated that the premenstrual phase of the cycle often includes some physical symptoms, but it also suggests that expectation and attribution, not hormones, are the factors that underlie widespread reports of PMS. Both women and men may attribute behavioral symptoms to PMS and the more severe PMDD, when those symptoms may actually indicate other problems.

Research on the role of testosterone in aggression has revealed that the relationship is not a simple, linear one. Men with higher-than-average testosterone levels tend to engage in a wide variety of antisocial behaviors but usually not violence. Indeed, studies of competition or aggress and testosterone show that aggression increases testosterone rather than the other way around. Another possibility is that testosterone and aggression are mediated through some other factor, such as personality or peer influence.

The role of hormones in sexual development is not subject to cultural variation, but how culture delineates the sexes varies enormously. In addition to male and female, some cultures define a third sex. In some non-Western cultures, intersex individuals may be considered to be a third sex. Another basis for a third sex was a belief common among Native American societies that allowed for a melding of the two spirits, male and female, in an individual. The hijras in India are another group designated a third sex. Women who take the roles of men may vary from the female gender role so much that they are no longer considered women but some third sex.

■ Glossary

androgen insensitivity syndrome   a disorder in which body cells are unable to respond to androgens, resulting in the feminization of chromosomal males.

androgens   a class of hormones that includes testosterone and other steroid hormones. Men typically produce a greater proportion of androgens than estrogens.

congenital adrenal hyperplasia (CAH)   a disorder that results in masculinization, producing premature puberty in boys and masculinization of the external genitalia in girls; also called *adrenogenital syndrome*.

endocrine glands   glands that secrete hormones into the circulatory system.

estradiol   the most common of the estrogen hormones.

estrogens   a class of hormones that includes estradiol and other steroid hormones. Women typically produce a greater proportion of estrogens than androgens.

external genitalia   the reproductive structures that can be seen without internal examination: clitoris, labia, and vaginal opening in women and penis and scrotum in men.

follicle-stimulating hormone (FSH)   the gonadotropic hormone that stimulates development of gonads during puberty and development of ova during the years of women's fertility.

gonads   reproductive organs.

hermaphroditism   a disorder in which individuals have characteristics of both sexes.

hormones   chemical substances released from endocrine glands that circulate throughout the body and affect target organs that have receptors sensitive to the specific hormones.

internal genitalia   the internal reproductive organs, consisting of the ovaries, Fallopian tubes, uterus, and upper vagina in women; and testes, seminal vesicles, vas deferens, and prostate gland in men.

intersexuality   a more modern term for hermaphroditism.

Klinefelter syndrome   the disorder that occurs when a chromosomal male has an extra X chromosome, resulting in the XXY pattern of chromosome pair 23. These individuals have the appearance of males, including external genitalia, but they may also develop breasts and a feminized body shape. Their testes are not capable of producing sperm, so they are sterile.

lateralization   the concept that the two cerebral hemispheres are not functionally equal but rather that each hemisphere has different purposes.

luteinizing hormone (LH)   the gonadotropic hormone that prompts sexual development during puberty and also causes a maturing ovum to be released.

menarche   the first menstruation.

Müllerian system   a system of ducts occurring in both male and female embryos that forms the basis for the development of the female internal reproductive system—ovaries, fallopian tubes, uterus, and upper vagina.

pituitary gland   an endocrine gland within the brain that produces tropic hormones that stimulate other glands to produce yet other hormones.

progestins   a group of steroid hormones that prepares the female body for pregnancy; their function for the male body is unknown.

releasing hormones   hormones produced by the hypothalamus that act on the pituitary to release tropic hormones.

sexual dimorphism   the existence of two sexes—male and female—including differences in genetics, gonads, hormones, internal genitalia, and external genitalia.

sexually dimorphic nucleus (SDN)   a brain structure in the hypothalamus, near the optic chiasm, that is larger in male rats than in female rats and larger in men than in women.

spinal nucleus of the bulbocavernosus   a collection of neurons in the lower spinal cord that control muscles at the base of the penis.

steroid hormones   hormones related to sexual dimorphism and sexual reproduction that are derived from cholesterol and consist of a structure that includes four carbon rings.

testosterone   the most common of the androgen hormones.

tropic hormones   hormones produced by the pituitary gland that influence the release of other hormones by other glands, such as the gonads.

Turner syndrome   the disorder that occurs when an individual has only one chromosome of pair 23, one X chromosome. These individuals appear to be female (have the external genitalia of females) but do not have fully developed internal genitalia. They do not produce estrogens, do not undergo puberty, and are not fertile.

Wolffian system   a system of ducts occurring in both male and female embryos that forms the basis for the development of the male internal reproductive system—testes, seminal vesicles, and vas deferens.

X chromosome   one of the possible alternatives for chromosome pair 23. Two X chromosomes make a genetic female, whereas genetic males have only one X chromosome in pair 23.

Y chromosome   one of the possible alternatives for chromosome pair 23. One X and one Y chromosome make a genetic male, whereas genetic females have two X chromosomes in pair 23.

■ Suggested Readings

Berenbaum, Sheri A. (2006). Psychological outcome in children with disorders of sex development: Implications for treatment and understanding typical development. *Annual Review of Sex Research, 17,* 1–38.

Berenbaum's thoughtful article evaluates variations of sexual development, exploring the complexity of the biology and psychology of gender development.

Breedlove, S. Marc; Cooke, Bradley M.; & Jordan, Cynthia L. (1999). The orthodox view of brain sexual differentiation. *Brain, Behavior and Evolution, 54,* 8–14.

This article is not easy reading, but it is a thorough and careful review of the research. Breedlove and his colleagues are also careful to acknowledge the interaction of biology and experience in the development of gender differences in the nervous system.

Chrisler, Joan C. (2008). PMS as a culture-bound syndrome. In J. C. Chrisler, C. Golden, & P. D. Rozee (Eds.), *Lectures on the psychology of women* (4th ed.; pp. 155–171). New York: McGraw-Hill.

Chrisler's critical summary of the concept of PMS highlights the problems with this syndrome and leads the reader to be skeptical of the widespread acceptance of PMS as a disorder.

Pinel, John P. J. (2009). *Biopsychology* (7th ed.). Boston: Allyn & Bacon.

For more details about the action of the endocrine system, the brain's involvement in endocrine function, sexual development, and some of the things that can go wrong, see Chapter 13 of this biopsychology textbook.

chapter
5 Theories of Gender Development

Journalist Kathleen Deveny (2007) expressed her concern about Paris Hilton, Britney Spears, and Lindsay Lohan, who meet the definition of girls who behave badly. And who are very visible when they do. "They seem to be everywhere and they may not be wearing underwear. Tweens adore them and teens envy them" (p. 41).[*]

HEADLINE

Girls Gone Bad?
Newsweek, February 12, 2007

Deveny disapproved of the pantyless partying but also of the adoration, including that of her 6-year-old daughter, who "loves, loves, loves" Lindsay Lohan. Deveny expressed dismay over the effect these "images of oversexed, underdressed celebrities" are having on girls and young women (p. 41).

Deveny and millions of other parents are concerned about the influence of celebrities' behavior on their daughters (and possibly on their sons as well). Many consider Paris, Britney, and Lindsay to be bad models of gender role behavior for tweens and teens. The definition of a **gender role** is the socially significant activities that men and women engage in with different frequencies. The origin of the concept of *role* was not within social science; the term can be traced to theater, where an actor's part was printed on a roll of paper. The word *role* was French for *roll,* and this usage is particularly meaningful, if we consider that the role, or the part a person plays, differs from the person. Therefore, gender roles are like a script that men and women follow to fulfill their appropriate masculine or feminine parts. Social scientists use the term *role* to mean expected, socially encouraged patterns of behavior exhibited by individuals in specific situations.

Do the media images of Lindsay Lohan, Britney Spears, and Paris Hilton influence the behavior of tweens and teens? Deveny interviewed a first-grade teacher, who reported that the 7-year-old girls in her class imitate Britney and Lindsay, singing their songs with suggestive lyrics and flirting with boys. Parents' worries may be at least partially founded—the bad girls who are "young, beautiful and rich, unencumbered by school, curfews or parents" may seem very attractive to girls (Deveny, 2007, p. 42).

These images and their power to shape attitudes and behavior are important for social learning theory, one of the theories of gender development. But imitating gendered

---

[*]From Newsweek, February 12, 2007. © 2007 Newsweek, Inc. All rights reserved. Used by permission and protected by the Copyright Laws of the United States. The printing, copying, redistribution, or retransmission of the Material without express written permission is prohibited.

behavior is not the extent of developing **gender identity**, which is how individuals come to identify themselves as male or female. How that process occurs is unquestionably important but also controversial, and several very different theories attempt to explain how individuals come to accept themselves as female or male. Social learning theory emphasizes the importance of models and experiences, but the psychodynamic approach does not look to role models to explain the development of gender identity. Gender schema theory holds that the process involves much more than modeling. Each of these theories has advocates and supporting evidence, which requires an examination of the theories and the evidence.

The Psychodynamic Approach to Personality

Sigmund Freud, a Viennese neurologist, devised a theory that emphasizes the differences between personality development and functioning of men and women. Freud's theory was controversial when he developed it, during the last part of the 19th century, and remains so, partly because his theory casts women as inferior to men. Countering the sexism in Freud's theory, Karen Horney proposed an alternative psychodynamic theory of personality and gender development. Nancy Chodorow and Ellyn Kaschak have devised contemporary versions of psychodynamic personality theory. Thus, some of Freud's basic assumptions about personality remain in these contemporary theories.

Freud's Theory of Personality

Freud's theory hypothesizes the existence of the **unconscious**, a region of the mind that functions beyond conscious personal awareness. He described the basic energy for personality development and functioning with a word that is most often translated as "instinct" but might also be translated as "drive" or "impulse" (Feist & Feist, 2009). Freud hypothesized that the life (or sexual) instinct and the death (or aggressive) instinct furnish the dynamic energy for personality development and functioning. That is, these **instincts** are the forces that underlie thought and action.

Freud's View of Gender Identity Development.   Freud's medical background led him to accept these instinctive forces as biologically determined. The role of biology was also important in Freud's theory of personality development, which he described in terms of **psychosexual stages**. Starting at birth, these stages continue through adulthood in a sequence named according to the regions of the body that were most important for sexual gratification. The early stages were the most important for personality development, emphasizing the importance of early childhood for personality formation.

By hypothesizing that the first psychosexual stage began at birth, Freud described infants as sexual beings and explained many of their actions as sexually oriented. Freud termed the first psychosexual stage the *oral stage,* during which babies receive sexual gratification from oral activities. During the *anal stage,* the child receives pleasure from excretory functions. The *phallic stage* begins in children around 3 or 4 years and is the first of Freud's psychosexual stages that describes a different course of personality development for boys and

GENDERED VOICES

Big Guns

"I just joined a gun club," a man told me, "and the men in the club do appear to have a relationship with their guns that seems symbolic to me. Of course, guys who own guns are pretty macho, but I have noticed two distinct styles, one of which seems more Freudian than the other.

"One style concentrates on shooting, and those men seem to like weapons that allow accuracy. Those types of guns tend to be rifles and are pretty lightweight. Maybe

that's symbolic, but the other style concentrates on the size of the weapon. With some of these guns, it's just not possible to shoot accurately, but they are big guns with lots of firepower. That's all that some of these guys go for, that's all they talk about—how many guns they have and how big they are. They don't really want to shoot targets, but they want to shoot, and they seem to love their big guns. It's pretty embarrassing, in a symbolic sense."

girls (Freud, 1933/1964). During this stage, sexual pleasure shifts from the anal region to the genitals; children begin to focus on their genitals, and they gain pleasure from masturbation. Parents are often disturbed by their children's masturbation and try to discourage or prevent this activity, furnishing one source of frustrated development during this stage.

Freud believed that the focus on genital activity resulted in a sexual attraction to the parent of the other sex and an increasing desire to have sex with this parent. These dynamics occur on an unconscious level, outside of children's awareness, and set the stage for the **Oedipus complex**. Freud used the Greek tragedy *Oedipus Rex* as an analogy for the interactions that occur within families during the phallic stage. According to the story, the oracle prophesied that Oedipus would kill his father and marry his mother, and this prophecy came true. Freud hypothesized that all boys feel jealousy, hatred, and aggression directed toward their fathers and sexual longing for their mothers. In boys, these family interactions result in competition with their fathers for their mothers' affections and growing hostility of the fathers toward their sons.

Boys in the phallic stage concentrate on their genitals and prize their penises. They notice the anatomical differences between girls and boys, which leads them to realize that everyone does not have a penis (Freud, 1925/1989). The realization that girls lack penises is shocking, disturbing, and threatening because, boys reason, penises must be removable. Indeed, boys come to fear that their fathers will remove their penises because of the boys' hostility toward their fathers and affection for their mothers. Thus, boys experience the **castration complex**, the belief that castration will be their punishment. Boys believe that girls have suffered this punishment and are thus mutilated, inferior creatures.

These feelings of anxiety, hostility, and sexual longing are intense and produce great turmoil for boys. All possibilities seem terrible: to lose their penises, to be the recipient of their fathers' hatred, or to be denied sex with their mothers. To resolve these feelings, boys must end the competition with their fathers and deny their sexual wishes for their mothers. Both goals can be met through identification with their fathers. This identification accomplishes several goals. First, boys no longer feel castration anxiety, because they have given up the sexual competition that originated such feelings. Second, boys no longer feel hostility toward their fathers; they now strive to be like their fathers rather than competing with them. Third, boys no longer desire their mothers sexually, but instead, they receive some vicarious sexual gratification from the identification with their fathers, who have a sexual relationship with the mothers. By identifying with their fathers and becoming masculine, boys develop a sexual identity that includes sexual attraction to women. Therefore, identification with fathers is the mechanism through which boys resolve the Oedipus complex and develop a masculine identity.

Freud hypothesized a slightly different resolution to the Oedipus complex in girls. During the phallic stage, girls also notice the anatomical differences between the sexes. Aware that they do not have penises, girls become envious of boys and experience *penis envy* (Freud, 1925/1989). Freud hypothesized that penis envy is the female version of the castration complex and that girls experience feelings of inferiority concerning their genitals. Their clitorises are so much smaller than penises, and they perceive their vaginas as wounds that result from their castration. Furthermore, girls hold their mothers responsible for their lack of penises and develop feelings of hostility toward them. Fathers become the object of their affection, and girls wish to have sex with their fathers and to have babies. Freud saw both the desire for sex and the wish for a baby as substitutes for penises and as expressions of penis envy.

The feelings that accompany the male Oedipus complex—hostility and competition— are also present in the female version. Girls, however, cannot experience the castration complex in the same way that boys do, because girls have no penises to lose. Thus, girls do not experience the trauma of the phallic stage as strongly as boys. Girls must still surrender their sexual desires for their fathers and identify with their mothers, but the process is not as quick or as complete as it is for boys (Freud, 1933/1964).

After the resolution of the Oedipus complex, children enter the *latency stage,* during which little overt sexual activity occurs. This stage lasts until puberty, when physiological changes bring about a reawakening of sexuality and entry into the *genital stage.* During the genital stage, individuals will desire a genital relationship with people of the other sex. The regions of the body that have furnished sexual pleasure during childhood are now secondary to genital pleasure obtained through intercourse.

Table 5.1 (page 106) shows Freud's psychosexual stages and the types of gender-related differences that he hypothesized for these stages. Development is similar for girls and boys in several stages but differs drastically in the phallic stage. Freud also believed that women have a more difficult time achieving a mature sexual relationship than men. He described the sexuality of the phallic stage, with its emphasis on masturbation, as immature sexuality that should be replaced in the genital stage with mature, heterosexual intercourse. For men, such activity involves their penises, but women must redirect their sexual impulses away from their clitorises and toward their vaginas.

Freud believed that girls have little awareness of their vaginas until puberty and that the redirection of their sexual energies is another difficult task for women. Freud believed that women who failed to achieve pleasure from vaginal intercourse had not achieved the mature, genital type of sexuality that signaled adequate personality development.

Freud and Women.   Freud knew that his theory was uncomplimentary to women, because his female associates, such as Karen Horney, told him so (Gay, 1988). He gave the matter a great deal of thought and heard many criticisms but never changed his mind about women being, essentially, failed men. Although Freud may have thought women were

TABLE 5.1 *Freud's Psychosexual Stages and Gender-Related Differences in Each Stage*

Stage	Gender-Related Difference
Oral	None
Anal	None
Phallic	Boys notice that they have penises and that girls do not
	Girls notice that boys have penises and that they do not
	Oedipus complex
	Boys experience extreme trauma connected with the Oedipus complex, undergo stronger identification with their fathers, and develop a stronger sense of morality
	Girls experience less Oedipal trauma, undergo weaker identification with their mothers, and develop a weaker sense of morality
Latency	None
Genital	Women must transfer their sexual pleasure from their clitorises to their vaginas, making mature sexuality more difficult for them
	Men's penises remain the center of their sexuality, making mature sexuality easier for them

inferior in some ways, intelligence was not among them. Freud considered that an intelligent, independent woman deserved credit and praise and might be "virtually as good as a man" (Gay, 1988, p. 507).

Freud seemed to have held contradictory attitudes about women (Feist & Feist, 2009). On the one hand, Freud was a proper Victorian gentleman who expected women to be sweet, pleasant, and subservient. On the other hand, he admired women who were intelligent and "masculine" in their pursuit of intellectual achievement and careers. Freud acted on both beliefs. His wife, Martha, held the role of wife and mother and shared none of his professional life. Feminists were prominent among the intellectual circles of Vienna and Germany where psychoanalysis gained prominence, and many women participated in these discussions (Kurzweil, 1995).

Although Freud contended that the sexes could never be equal and disparaged the efforts of feminists, who argued for the equality of men and women, he also admitted women into the ranks of psychoanalytic training at a time when women were admitted to few professions (Tavris & Wade, 1984). The person who carried on his work was his daughter, Anna, whom he encouraged to become an analyst. However, his most intimate personal friends were all men.

Therefore, Freud's attitudes about women and their personalities showed some inconsistency. Freud undoubtedly held negative attitudes about women, and he expressed his lack of understanding and his uncertainty about women in several of his papers. One of Freud's last statements about women appeared in his 1933 paper "Femininity." He concluded with a tentative statement about women, acknowledging his awareness of the criticisms and also his own far-from-complete understanding:

> That is all I had to say to you about femininity. It is certainly incomplete and fragmentary and does not always sound friendly. But do not forget that I have only been describing women in so far as their nature is determined by their sexual function. It is true that that influence extends very far; but we do not overlook the fact that an individual woman may be a human being in other respects as well. If you want to know more about femininity, inquire from your own experiences of life, or turn to the poets, or wait until science can give you deeper and more coherent information. (Freud, 1933/1964, p. 135)

Other researchers and theorists have attempted the last alternative rather than the first two. In general, they have sought other information about personality and gender. One of those theorists was Karen Horney, a colleague of Freud.

Horney's Theory of Personality

Horney was one of the first German women to enter medical school, in which she specialized in psychiatry. After completing a training analysis with one of Freud's close associates, she began to attend seminars and to write papers on psychoanalysis (Feist & Feist, 2009). Soon, however, Horney became a vocal critic of Freud's theory of personality, especially concerning gender differences in personality development. Horney reexamined Freud's concepts of penis envy, inferiority feelings in women, and the masculinity complex (the expression of masculine behavior and attitudes in women). In addition, Horney's interpretation of feminine **masochism** (deriving pleasure from pain) differed from the Freudian version.

Her re-examination included pointing out the masculine bias in psychoanalytic theory (Miletic, 2002; Quinn, 1987). Although she argued for a course of personality development that differed from Freud's view, Horney stayed within the framework of psychodynamic theory, as shown by her acceptance of the unconscious as a motivating force in personality, her emphasis on sexual feelings and events in personality development, and her belief in the importance of early childhood experiences for personality formation. She differed from Freud in her interpretation of the significance of the events of early childhood and her growing belief in the importance of social rather than instinctual forces in personality development.

Part of Horney's reinterpretation of psychoanalysis was an alternative view of the notion of penis envy, the feelings of envy that girls have when they discover that boys' penises are larger than their own clitorises. Horney argued that penis envy was a symbolic longing for the social prestige and position that men experience, rather than a literal physical desire for penises. Indeed, she hypothesized that men envy women's capability to reproduce and proposed the concept of *womb envy*. She interpreted the male strivings for achievement as overcompensation for their lack of ability to create by giving birth.

Horney believed that men fear and attribute evil to women because men feel inadequate when comparing themselves to women. To feel more adequate, men must see women as inferior, which keeps men from contending with their own feelings of inferiority. She explained that men still retain the feelings of inferiority that originated with the perception of the small size of their penises during childhood, when they initially noticed them. Therefore, men go through life needing to prove their masculinity, and failures make men constantly vulnerable to feelings of inferiority. This resentment can lead men to attempt to diminish

TABLE 5.2   *Points of Agreement and Disagreement in Horney's and Freud's Psychoanalytic Theories*

Concept	Horney's Theory	Freud's Theory
Existence of unconscious	Yes	Yes
Importance of early childhood experiences	Yes	Yes
Gender differences in personality	Yes	Yes
Source of differences	Social	Biological
Feelings of envy for other gender	Men envy women's ability to give birth	Women envy men's penises
Feelings of inferiority	Constant need to perform sexually leads men to feel inferior	Lack of penises leads women to feel inferior
Masculinity complex	Driven by girls' lack of acceptance of femininity and identification with their fathers	Driven by girls' feeling of inferiority
Masochism	Socially determined part of development that is abnormal for women as well as men	Biologically determined, inevitable part of feminine development; abnormal in men

women, and these attempts may succeed, leaving women with feelings of inferiority. Therefore, female inferiority originates with male insecurities rather than, as Freud hypothesized, with the female perception of inferior genitals. These female feelings of inferiority are perpetuated by men's behavior toward women and by the masculine bias in society.

Table 5.2 shows the points of agreement and disagreement between Horney's and Freud's psychodynamic theories. As this table shows, both theories accept the importance of unconscious forces and early childhood experiences. However, the difference in their interpretations of the importance and causes of other events makes the two theories substantially different.

Contemporary Psychodynamic Theories of Personality Development

Freud's theory of personality appeared during the late 19th and early 20th centuries in a Victorian culture that viewed women as passive, dependent, and intellectually inferior to men. This view of women was easy for Freud to accept, not only because it was the view of his culture but also because his female patients reflected these characteristics. Freud built his theory on the basis of observing his patients, many of whom were upper-class, bored, unhappy women who lived in a repressive society that assumed women's inferiority. The extent to which their experiences reflect that of contemporary women is questionable, but Freud's female patients and the culture in which they lived influenced his view of women.

During the time that Freud formulated his theory, a feminist movement was active in Europe and the United States (Kurzweil, 1995), and Freud's theory was never popular among those women and men who believed in and worked for fair treatment for women, both by society and in personal relationships. That discontent also emerged during the 1970s, when feminist scholars turned their attention to gender development (Bell, 2004). Some created psychodynamic theories of personality development that not only removed the objectionable elements of Freud's theory but also created revisions of his theory that are compatible with a positive view of women. Sociologist Nancy Chodorow (1978, 1979, 1994, 2005) and psychologist Ellyn Kaschak (1992) have formulated psychodynamic theories that are significant departures from Freud's view. Chodorow's theory proposes a progression of development that gives women advantages, and Kaschak's theory replaces the emphasis on male psychological development with a woman-centered view of personality. Both theories are examples of feminist psychoanalytic theory.

Chodorow's Emphasis on Mothering.

Like Freud, Chodorow (1979) expressed pessimism about any potential equality between men and women. Unlike Freud (who concentrated on the perception of anatomical differences), Chodorow's reasons for believing in the continuation of inequality focused on the early experiences of children in relation to their mother. Chodorow's theory concentrates on the **pre-Oedipal period** during early childhood, before the Oedipus complex, and centers on the process of being mothered by a woman.

Although Chodorow (1978) acknowledged that women are not unique in their capacity to care for infants, she also granted that mothers (or other women) provide most nurturing, and fathers (or other men) do little caregiving. Thus, Chodorow explained how this early relationship between mother and infant makes a permanent imprint on personality development—an imprint that differs for boys and girls. Chodorow described babies as having no sense of self versus other people or the world; infants are one with the world, and most of their world is their mother. The early mother–daughter relationship is closer than the mother–son relationship, because mothers and daughters are of the same sex. Infants have no initial perception of their sex or gender, but mothers always know about the sex of their infants and treat girls and boys differently.

Chodorow (1978) hypothesized that when children start to develop a sense of self and separate from their mothers, events differ for girls and boys. Girls have an easier task in developing a sense of self because they have already identified with their mothers. This identification gives them an advantage in developing a separate identity, because this identity will likely be feminine and much like their mothers. Boys, on the other hand, have a more difficult time in developing separate identities because they too have already identified with their mothers. To become masculine, boys must reject the femininity of their mothers and develop an identity that is not only separate but also different. Thus, boys have a more difficult task than girls in accomplishing these developmental goals of separation and identity.

But according to Chodorow, girls never separate from their mothers as completely as boys do. The gender similarity is something that both mothers and daughters know, and this similarity influences each one. One study (Benenson, Morash, & Petrakos, 1998) confirmed the difference in emotional closeness between daughters and sons, as Chodorow's theory hypothesizes. Boys must work to accomplish their separation, even with the aid of their mothers. This effort extracts a price. Chodorow (1978) described the aftermath of boys' separation in terms of their rejection of all femininity and the development of fear and mistrust of the feminine. Chodorow thus explained the almost worldwide denigration of women by men as a by-product of boys' efforts to distinguish and separate themselves from their mothers. On the other hand, girls have no such need,

According to Chodorow's theory, girls are similar to their mothers, which eases the course of their gender development.

and they accept their mothers and the feminine role without the turbulence that boys experience. Girls grow into women and reproduce their early relationships with their mothers in their own mothering.

Table 5.3 shows the differences between Chodorow's feminist psychoanalytic theory and traditional psychoanalytic theory. Notice that the differences lie not only in the

TABLE 5.3   *Differences between Chodorow's Feminist Psychodynamic Theory and Traditional Freudian Theory*

	Stages	Gender-Related Outcome
Chodorow's Theory	Pre-Oedipal stages	Boys work toward separation from mother, rejecting femininity. Girls retain connectedness with mother, becoming feminine
	Oedipus conflict	Gender differences have already emerged
Freud's Theory	Pre-Oedipal stages	No gender-related differences emerge
	Oedipus conflict	Family dynamics and perception of differences in genitals prompt personality differences

outcomes but also in the stage of development that each theory hypothesizes to be important in personality development and in gender-related differences.

Thus, Chodorow's psychodynamic theory represents an alternative to Freud's theory. Although she retained the emphasis on early childhood, Chodorow concentrated on the pre-Oedipal period and on the early infant–mother relationship. She also hypothesized a different course of personality development for boys than for girls, but in Chodorow's theory girls have an easier time in developing gender. Their similarity to their mothers makes femininity an easier identity to develop than boys, who must find ways to separate themselves from their mothers and find masculine gender identity.

Kaschak's Antigone Phase.   Like Freud, Ellyn Kaschak's (1992) psychodynamic theory drew from the Oedipus legend in the Greek plays by Sophocles. Kaschak argued that the minor changes Freud made to accommodate women in his female Oedipus complex were inadequate. Instead, Kaschak casts female personality development in terms of Antigone, Oedipus's daughter (and half-sister). In Sophocles's plays, Antigone was the daughter of Oedipus and Jocasta (who was Oedipus's mother). After Oedipus learned of his incest with Jocasta, he destroyed his eyes, and Antigone then became her father's guide and caretaker. Antigone sacrificed an independent life to care for her blind father, and he considered it his right to have this level of devotion. Kaschak (1992) interpreted personality development of men and women in similar terms: "As Oedipus' dilemma became a symbol for the dilemma of the son, so might that of Antigone be considered representative of the inevitable fate of the good daughter in the patriarchal family" (p. 60).

Men grow and develop in societies that allow them power, both in those societies and in their families. In taking this power, men come to consider women their possessions. Women grow and develop in situations of subservience in which they are men's possessions, and women's lives and personalities reflect this status. Kaschak hypothesized that many men and women never resolve these complexes because the social structure perpetuates differential power for women and men, encouraging both to adhere to these different roles.

For men, an unresolved Oedipus complex results in treating women as extensions of themselves rather than as independent people. With this sense of entitlement, men tend to seek power and sex in self-centered ways that may be destructive to others, such as family violence, incest, and rape. Consistent with Kaschak's formulation, Michael Johnson (1995; Johnson & Leone, 2005) researched family violence and proposed that some men engage in systematic violence within their families because they feel that they have the right to do so. He called this form of family violence *patriarchal terrorism.*

When women fail to resolve the Antigone phase, they allow themselves to be extensions of others rather than striving for independence. Girls learn that men are important and their own wishes are less so, thus limiting their lives with this knowledge. Among those limits are restrictions on what women may do in the world and conforming to a limited sexuality, all defined and controlled by men. In addition, women learn to deny their physicality and try to make their bodies invisible, and this denial can be expressed in terms of eating disorders. These limits can lead to feelings of self-hatred and shame and the need to form relationships with others to feel self-worth.

Women who successfully resolve the Antigone phase achieve separation from their fathers and other men to become independent people. This independence allows them to form relationships with women, which Kaschak believes to be a problem for women who have not

TABLE 5.4   *Possible Outcomes of Personality Development According to Kaschak*

	Not Resolved	Resolved
Men (Oedipal phase)	Patriarchical	Nonpatriarchical
	Gaining power a major goal	Gaining power not a major issue
	See women as extensions of self—they have the right to have women serve them	See women as independent
	Sexually self-centered	Sexually unselfish
Women (Antigone phase)	Accept subservience	Reject subservient role
	Passive and dependent	Assertive and independent
	Accept male-defined sexuality	Define their own sexuality
	Deny their own needs, including physical needs	Accept and express their own needs
	Cannot form friendships with other women	Form friendships with other women

resolved the Antigone phase. In their relationships with men, women who have resolved these issues are able to stop making men central to their lives and can form interdependent, flexible relationships. Men who resolve their Oedipus complex relinquish their grandiosity and drive for power, see women as whole persons rather than possessions, and come to see themselves as individuals who act within boundaries and limits, rather than as kings. Table 5.4 shows the four possibilities in Kaschak's view of personality development—men and women who have and have not resolved major developmental issues.

Is feminist psychodynamic theory an improvement over traditional psychoanalytic theory? All versions of psychoanalytic theory have the shortcoming of relying heavily on unconscious mental processes to explain important events in personality development, which poses problems for scientific testability. Therefore, any psychoanalytic theory shares the problem of providing adequately observable research evidence.

Both traditional and modern psychoanalytic theories emphasize the importance and inevitability of gender differences, but other theories of gender development do not share this view. Several theories concentrate on the social factors in children's lives to explain how gender develops. The influence of social factors forms the foundation for social learning theory, cognitive developmental theory, and gender schema theory.

Social Learning Theory

Social learning theory explains gender development in the same way that it explains other types of learned behaviors, by classifying gender development as learned behaviors. This possibility was what distressed Kathleen Deveny (2007); if gender development proceeds through learning gende related behaviors, then behaviors of Lindsay Lohan and Paris

Hilton would offer girls the opportunity to learn "bad" behaviors from media coverage of these celebrities' misbehavior.

Social learning theory emphasizes the influence of the social environment, including the media. Biological sex differences furnish the basis for gender identity, but social learning theorists contend that a great many other characteristics and behaviors that have no relation to sex have been tied to gender. In this view, gender identity development is determined by social factors (Bandura, 1986; Bandura & Bussey, 2004; Bussey & Bandura, 1999).

The social learning approach is a variation of traditional learning theory, which includes the principles of operant conditioning developed by B. F. Skinner. **Operant conditioning** is a form of learning based on applying **reinforcement** and **punishment**. A reinforcer is any stimulus that increases the probability that a behavior will recur. A behavior is more likely to be repeated in the future if that person (or animal) has received a reinforcer after performing the behavior in the past. On the other hand, a person is less likely to repeat a behavior in the future if that person has been punished after performing the behavior. Punishment is any stimulus that decreases the probability that a behavior will recur. The reinforcements and punishments in each individual's history contribute to present and future behavior. Thus, future behavior can be predicted from past experience. Table 5.5 gives an example of how reinforcements and punishments can work to mold gender-related behaviors.

Traditional learning theorists reject all concepts of internal mental processes and terminology in their explanations of behavior, relying on objectively observable behaviors, but social learning theory extends learning theory to include cognitive processes. This addition changes the focus of learning by emphasizing the importance of observation. Social learning theorists consider observation more important than reinforcement in the process of learning. To these theorists, learning is cognitive, whereas performance is behavioral. The social learning approach thus separates learning from performing learned behaviors, and it investigates factors that affect both (Mischel, 1966, 1993).

Observation provides many opportunities for learning, including the learning of gender-related behaviors among children (Bandura & Bussey, 2004; Bussey & Bandura, 1999). The social environment provides children with examples of male and female models who perform different behaviors, including behaviors that vary by gender. The models who influence children include mothers, fathers, and siblings, but also many others, both real people and media images of boys, girls, men, women, and cartoon characters. In observing these many male

TABLE 5.5 *Results of Reinforcement and Punishment for Gender-Related Behaviors*

Behavior	Consequences	Result
Little girl plays with doll	*Reinforcement:* Her mother praises her toy choice	Girl plays with doll again
Little girl plays with truck	*Punishment:* Her mother scolds her for choosing a truck	Girl does not play with truck again
Little boy plays with doll	*Punishment:* His mother scolds him for choosing a doll	Boy does not play with doll again
Little boy plays with truck	*Reinforcement:* His mother praises his toy choice	Boy plays with truck again

According to the Media . . .

Girls Are in the Background in Children's Television

Children's television programming has always been oriented toward boys. Programming executives believe that boys will not watch cartoons with female lead characters (Thompson & Zerbinos, 1995), and early analyses of cartoon programming indicated that male characters outnumbered female characters by more than 3 to 1. A later analysis (Leaper, Breed, Hoffman, & Perlman, 2002) found that boys were more numerous in traditional action cartoons (such as *Spiderman*) but not in nontraditional adventure (such as *Reboot*) or in comedy cartoons. In both analyses, female characters were less visible, important, and active, but more polite, romantic, and supportive. These characteristics are stereotypically feminine and cast girls and women in traditional roles.

Cartoon programming changed from the 1970s to the 1990s, going from an emphasis on cartoons featuring pratfalls to those with continuing adventures (Thompson & Zerbinos, 1995). Female characters became more independent, assertive, intelligent, competent, and responsible and less emotional and tentative. The male characters continued to behave in stereotypical ways for men, giving orders and being brave and aggressive. Female superhero characters are also brave and aggressive, but they are less common than male superheroes and show some

stereotypically feminine behavior, such as emotionality (Baker & Raney, 2007).

Pokémon cartoons contain characters that are consistent with stereotypical gender depictions but also those that vary (Ogletree, Martinez, Turner, & Mason, 2004). Unfortunately, the "good" Pokémon trainers tend to be consistent with gender stereotypes, whereas the "bad" trainers behave in nonstereotypical ways. Thus, these cartoons still contain a high degree of gender-stereotypical portrayals, presented as desirable behavior.

Television advertising oriented toward children also has a history of biased gender portrayals, but changes have also occurred (Larson, 2001). The number of girls in commercials now equals the number of boys, but girls are still in the background in terms of activities. The advertisements oriented toward boys contain more action, competition, control, and destruction, whereas those oriented toward girls contain more limited activity and more nurturing (Johnson & Young, 2002). Commercials convey clear messages about which toys are for girls and which are for boys; few advertisements offer attractive portrayals of children deviating from gender stereotypes (Pike & Jennings, 2005). All of these presentations tend to leave girls in the background.

and female models, children have abundant opportunities to learn. However, not all models have the same influence for all children, and not all behaviors are equally likely to be imitated.

The differential influence of models relates to their power or prestige as well as to the observer's attention and perception of the similarity between model and observer. Children tend to be more influenced by powerful models than by models with less power (Bussey & Bandura, 1984), but children are also more influenced by models who are similar to them. This similarity extends to gender, with children more likely to imitate same-sex models than other-sex models and models of similar age (Grace, David, & Ryan, 2008).

Observing the consequences of a behavior is another important factor in performing a learned behavior. If people observe a behavior being rewarded, then they are more likely to perform that behavior than if they see the same behavior punished or unrewarded. Social learning theorists believe that reinforcement and punishment are not essential for learning, which occurs through observation. Instead, reinforcement and punishment are more important to performance, affecting the likelihood that a learned behavior will be performed in circumstances similar to those observed.

Children develop in an atmosphere in which they are exposed to models of gender-stereotypic behaviors "in the home, in schools, on playgrounds, in readers and storybooks,

ACCORDING TO THE RESEARCH...

Gender Depictions on Television Convey a Message

Cartoons and advertisements on children's television tend to portray gender-related behaviors in stereotypical ways, selling not only products but also gender ideology (Lewin-Jones & Mitra, 2009). Television provides many more opportunities for children to observe stereotypical gender behaviors than actual experience does (Bussey & Bandura, 1999). Research indicates that children not only notice but also are influenced by gender portrayals in cartoons and in advertisements, but some evidence hints that television can easily send more positive messages.

Interviews with children between ages 4 and 9 years (Thompson & Zerbinos, 1997) showed that 78% noticed that cartoons contained more male than female characters, and 68% noticed that boys talked more in cartoons. Of elementary school children who watched the Pokémon cartoons, less than 50% could name a female Pokémon character, and children were much more likely to name a male than a female character or trainer as a favorite (Ogletree et al., 2004).

Gender-related perceptions of cartoon characters influenced 4- to 9-year-old children's thoughts about their careers (Thompson & Zerbinos, 1997). Children who noticed the gender differences in the cartoon characters' behavior tended to be more likely to envision themselves in a gender-stereotypical job than did children who were less aware of the gender portrayals in cartoons. This tendency was stronger for boys than for girls. In contrast, the children who noticed characters behaving in nonstereotypical ways were the ones who were more likely to see themselves in nontraditional jobs. This tendency applied to both girls and boys.

Children exposed to gender-stereotypical television advertising for boys' toys were more likely to say that the toys were appropriate for boys rather than for either boys or girls (Pike & Jennings, 2005). However, changing the gender of the child in the advertisement to a girl was successful in prompting significantly more children to say that the advertised toy could be for either girls or boys, but boys were affected more strongly.

Therefore, the gendered presentation of characters in cartoons has the power to do harm. Children notice and are influenced by these stereotypical presentations, and young children take this information into account when they imagine themselves in an occupation. But counterstereotypical portrayals have the power to alter stereotypes.

and in representations of society on the television screens of every household" (Bandura, 1986, p. 93). These presentations do two things. First, all children are exposed to both female and male models, so all children learn the gender-related behaviors associated with *both* genders. Second, children learn which behaviors are gender-appropriate for them. Children learn that certain behaviors are rewarded for girls but not for boys; for other behaviors, the rewards come to boys and not to girls.

For example, children see girls rewarded for playing with dolls, whereas they see boys discouraged and ridiculed for this same behavior. Children see boys rewarded for playing with toy trucks, but they may see girls discouraged from that behavior. Both boys and girls learn how to play with dolls and trucks, but they are not equally likely to do so due to the differential rewards they have seen others receive. Their learning is not based on observation of merely a few models; the world is filled with examples of men and women who are rewarded and punished for gender-related behaviors. The portrayals of gender-related behavior are especially stereotypical in the media (Lauzen, Dozier, & Horan, 2008; Signorielli, 2004) and offer a multitude of sexist examples for children to model (see According to the Media and According to the Research). Therefore, children may behave in ways different from their parents, including expressing sexist views that their parents do not endorse.

Not all observed consequences are consistent with each other; some people are rewarded and others punished for the same behavior. But consistency is not necessary for children to learn gender-related behaviors (Bandura, 1986). Children observe many models; they notice the consistencies among the behaviors of some models and start to overlook the exceptions. As more same-sex models exhibit a behavior, the more likely children are to connect that behavior with one or the other sex. Through this process, behaviors come to be gendered, although these behaviors may have no direct relationship to sex. Children learn to pay attention to sex and the activities associated with each, and thus they become selective in their modeling.

Children experience many sources of modeling and reinforcement, and these sources influence the development of gender-related behaviors (Bussey & Bandura, 1999). Beginning before birth, parents often have some preference for a boy or a girl—more often for a boy.

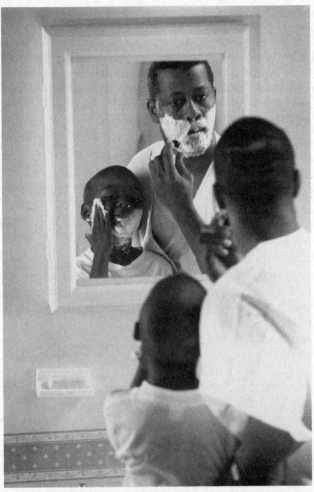

Parents are powerful models for developing gender-related behaviors.

▣ GENDERED VOICES

I Wouldn't Know How to Be a Man

"I never thought of myself as very feminine, but I wouldn't begin to know how to be a man," said a woman in her 30s. "There are thousands of things about being a man or being a woman that the other doesn't know. It takes years to learn all those things. I have been struck several times by the differences in women's and men's experience, by small things.

"During college one of my roommate's boyfriends decided to paint one of his fingernails. It was an odd thing to do, but he said that it was an experience he hadn't had, and he just wanted to try it. What was interesting was that he didn't know how to go about it—didn't know how to hold the brush, which direction to apply the polish. It was interesting to watch him. That was the first time that I really thought, 'Men and women have some unique experiences that the other does not know.' I've had that thought several times since then, usually about small experiences or skills that women have and men don't.

"I'm sure that it works the other way, too. There's a world of little experiences that are part of men's lives that women don't have a clue about. For example, I wouldn't know how to go about shaving my face. In some sense, these experiences are trivial, but they made me think about the differences between the worlds of women and men."

When their children are infants, parents interact differently with their sons and daughters. For example, young children do not show strong preferences for gender-typical toys, but when parents choose toys for play, they tend to pick masculine toys for boys and feminine or neutral toys for girls (Wood, Desmarais, & Gugula, 2002). Parents are not alone in these preferences; in one study (Campenni, 1999), adults who were not parents showed even more stereotypical toy choices than parents did.

Studies that observe parental interactions with children have confirmed gender differences in treatment. Mothers and fathers created different amounts of emotional availability during interactions with their toddlers, and the gender of the child also influenced the situation (Lovas, 2005). Sons received were involved in less positive interactions than daughters. An early study that examined toy choices (Fagot & Hagan, 1991) found larger differences than a more recent study (Wood et al., 2002) on the topic, but the tendency persisted to choose "masculine" toys when playing with boys and "feminine" or gender-neutral toys for girls. During the preschool years, boys come to believe that their fathers disapprove of cross-gender toy choices and behave accordingly, rejecting these toys (Raag & Rackliff, 1998). Thus, parents encourage some and discourage other gender-related behaviors.

Social learning theory hypothesizes that these forces affect gender-related thinking, and children come to develop gender knowledge and gender standards for their own behavior. In children age 2 to 4 years, behavior typical of the same sex was more common than behavior typical of the other sex for all ages of children (Bussey & Bandura, 1992). The younger children in the study reacted to their peers in gender-stereotypical ways but did not regulate their own behavior by these same standards, whereas the older children did both. These results indicate that these 4-year-olds had begun to develop a coherent set of standards that they applied to their gender-related behaviors.

When children start interacting with peers outside the home, these other children become a major source of both modeling and approval. Children's play groups tend to be gender segregated, especially in school settings. Children often put a great deal of effort into maintaining this segregation and even begin to use insults and severe prohibitions aimed at those who attempt to join an other-sex group (Thorne, 1993). The formation of relationships, including the gender composition of play groups, is a topic explored in Chapter 9.

The differential treatment of boys and girls is enhanced by parents' and teachers' expectations and encouragement during the school years. Both parents and teachers are more likely to urge boys to persist in solving problems than they are to urge girls. By the time children reach adolescence, their models and reinforcements tend to encourage boys toward careers and sexual expression and girls toward domesticity and physical attractiveness (Peters, 1994). Therefore, children develop in environments that contain many sources of social learning that will lead to differences in the gender-related behaviors of boys and girls, including the "girls gone bad" celebrities whom Deveny (2007) feared as models for girls such as her 6-year-old daughter.

In summary, social learning theory views the development of gender-related behaviors as part of the overall development of many behaviors that children learn through observation and modeling. This theory emphasizes the contribution of the social environment to learning and behavior. Social learning theory sees learning, which occurs through observation, as cognitive and separate from performance, which is behavioral. Whether a learned behavior is performed depends on the observed consequences of the behavior and the observers' beliefs about the appropriateness of the behavior. Thus, children have many opportunities to observe gender-related behaviors from a wide variety of models, to develop beliefs about the consequences of those behaviors, and to exhibit appropriate gender-related behaviors as a result of their observation of these models.

Cognitive Theories of Gender Development

Sandra Bem (1985) criticized social learning theory, arguing that the theory portrays children as too passive; she believed that children are more actively involved in developing gender identity than social learning theory hypothesizes. Bem argued that children do not exhibit a gradual increase in gender-related behaviors, but rather form cognitive categories for gender and then acquire gender-related knowledge around these categories. In addition, research evidence suggests that children may develop stronger gender stereotypes than their parents convey, which implies that children actively organize information about gender. Thus, another way to look at gender development places an emphasis on cognition. These theories include cognitive developmental theory and gender schema theory.

Cognitive Developmental Theory

The cognitive developmental theorist Lawrence Kohlberg (1966) described this theory by saying, "Our approach to the problems of sexual development starts directly with neither biology nor culture, but with cognition" (p. 82). Cognitive developmental theory views the acquisition of gender-related behaviors as part of children's general cognitive development. This development occurs as children mature and interact with the environment, forming an increasingly complex and accurate understanding of their bodies and the world around them.

The cognitive developmental approach follows Jean Piaget's theory of cognitive development, which places the development of gender-related concepts into the realm of increasing cognitive abilities and which emphasizes children's active role in organizing their own thoughts (see Ginsburg & Opper, 1969). Piaget described four stages of cognitive development, beginning at birth and ending during preadolescence, throughout which children achieve cognitive maturity. During childhood, limitations in cognitive abilities lead children to have problems in classifying objects according to any given physical characteristic such as size or color. During their elementary school years, children gain in cognitive abilities but may still have difficulty in dealing with abstractions, such as the ability to imagine hypothetical situations—"what if." Piaget believed that once children reach cognitive maturity, at around age 11 or 12 years, they no longer have any cognitive limitations on their understanding. (Although lack of information may be a limitation at this or any age, this problem is different from the limits on cognitive ability that appear during childhood.) Thus, Piaget explained cognitive development as a series of stages leading to an increasing ability to understand physical reality and deal with abstract, complex problems. Infants are capable of almost no abstract thought, but by preadolescence, children have fewer limitations on their cognitive abilities.

Cognitive developmental theorists see the development of gender-related behaviors as part of the larger task of cognitive development. Very young children, lacking a concept of self, can have no concept of their gender. Most 2-year-olds are unable to apply the words *boy* or *girl* consistently to self or others; thus, they fail at **gender labeling**. When children use gender labels correctly, they still lack critical gender knowledge—young children do not see gender as a permanent feature. They believe that a boy can become a girl if he wishes or that a girl might become a boy if she dressed in boys' clothing (Kohlberg, 1966). That is, young children lack **gender constancy**, the belief that gender will remain the same throughout life. This concept rarely appears before age 4. According to cognitive developmental theory, gender constancy is essential for the development of gender identity; children begin to develop a gender identity based on a classification of self and others as irreversibly belonging to one gender or the other.

This gender constancy is part of children's growing ability to classify objects based on physical criteria. These cognitive developments in conceptualizing gender parallel other cognitive changes in children. Below age 5 or 6 years, children have an incomplete understanding of the qualities of physical objects, and their misunderstanding of gender is part of this limitation. By around age 6 years, children have developed a correct, if concrete, understanding of physical reality, including gender identity. Cognitive developmental theory sees changes that occur in gender identity as part of this process, and the mistakes that children make concerning gender identity are seen as part of their general cognitive limitations during the course of development. Consistent with this contention, a study that assessed children's ability to tell the difference between appearance and reality (Trautner, Gervai, & Németh, 2003) confirmed that understanding reality develops before or concurrently with gender constancy.

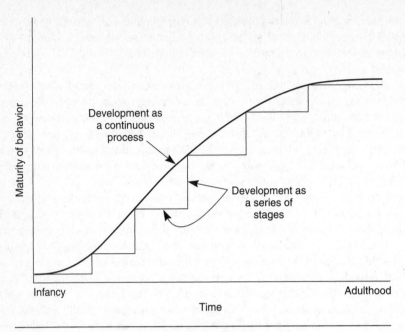

FIGURE 5.1 *Two Views of Development*

The cognitive developmental approach is similar to the social learning approach in its emphasis on the role of cognition. However, the two approaches differ in several ways. Cognitive developmental theory hypothesizes that development moves through a series of discrete stages. Each stage has internal consistency and a set of differences that delineate it from successive stages. Social learning theory sees development as more continuous and not bounded by stages. Although the environment and culture are important in cognitive developmental theory (Martin, Ruble, & Szkrybalo, 2004), those factors are even more important for social learning theory (Bandura & Bussey, 2004). Figure 5.1 illustrates the difference between development as a continuous process and as a series of stages.

Cognitive developmental theory views the acquisition of gender-related behaviors as a by-product of the cognitive development of gender identity. Children begin to adopt and exhibit gender-related behaviors because they adopt a gender identity and strive to be consistent with this identity. On the other hand, social learning theory hypothesizes that children come to have a gender identity because they model gender-related behaviors. Through the performance of these behaviors, children conform to either the masculine or the feminine social roles of their culture. Thus, social learning theory sees gender identity as coming from performance of gender-related behaviors, whereas cognitive developmental theory sees gender-related behaviors as coming from the cognitive adoption of a gender identity.

When children develop an understanding of categories, including gender categories, they tend to concentrate on the classification rules and show a great reluctance to make exceptions. Applied to gender, this strategy leads to classifying all women and all men by invariant physical or behavioral characteristics. Therefore, cognitive developmental theory predicts that children will develop gender stereotypes as part of their process of developing gender identity (Martin, Ruble, & Szkrybalo, 2002). As Chapter 3 described, a great deal of research evidence substantiates the notion that children form stereotypical gender concepts beginning early in their lives. Children as young as 2 years old exhibit stereotypical gender-related knowledge, and this level of knowledge relates to their comprehension of gender identity and gender constancy (Kuhn, Nash, & Brucken, 1978; Poulin-Dubois, Serbin, Eichstedt, Sen, & Beissel, 2002). The process of acquiring gender stereotypes has also been related to the development of gender constancy (Warin, 2000).

One problem with cognitive developmental theory comes from its emphasis on gender constancy as the primary force underlying the development of gender identity. Although Kohlberg's predictions are not completely clear on this point (Stangor & Ruble, 1987), he hypothesized that gender constancy is pivotal in developing gender identity; all other facets of gender identity stem from establishing gender constancy. Although the interpretation of what constitutes gender constancy remains a point of contention (Ruble et al., 2007), research has failed to substantiate the primacy of gender constancy (Martin & Little, 1990), leaving a major component of this theory in doubt.

Another problem with cognitive developmental theory comes from the need to treat gender the same as any other cognitive category. As Sandra Bem (1985) put it, "The theory fails to explicate why sex has primacy over other potential categories of the self such as race, religion, or even eye color" (p. 184). This theory fails to explain why children choose gender as a primary domain around which to organize information. Gender schema theory addresses this problem by extending the concepts in cognitive developmental theory.

Gender Schema Theory

Gender schema theory is an extension of the cognitive developmental theory. A **schema** is "a cognitive structure, a network of associations that organizes and guides an individual's perceptions" (Bem, 1981, p. 355). Piaget used the term *schema* (plural, *schemata* or *schemas*) to describe how cognitions are internalized around various topics; gender schema theory hypothesizes that children develop gender-related behaviors because they develop schemata that guide them to adopt such behaviors. In this view, gender-related behaviors appear not only as a result of general cognitive development but also as a specific result of developing gender schemata.

According to gender schema theory, the culture also plays a role in gender development, providing the reference for the formation of gender schemata. Not only are children ready to encode and organize information about gender but they also do so in a social environment that defines maleness and femaleness (Bem, 1985). As children develop, they acquire schemata that guide their cognitions related to gender. These schemata influence information processing and problem solving in memory and also regulate behavior (Martin & Halverson, 1981; Martin, Ruble, & Szkrybalo, 2002, 2004; Wilansky-Traynor & Lobel, 2008). Gender schema theorists believe that children use these schemata to develop a concept of self versus others, and each child's gender schema is included in that child's self-schema, or self-concept. In addition, gender schemata can provide a guide for concepts of personal masculinity and femininity, including personal judgments about how people personally fit, or fail to fit, these schemata (Janoff-Bulman & Frieze, 1987). Thus, gender schema theory provides an explanation for the concepts of masculinity and femininity and how people apply these concepts to themselves.

Bem (1985) emphasized the process rather than the content of gender schemata. The information in the schemata is not as important as the process of forming schemata and acting in ways that are consistent with them. Gender schema theory predicts that cognitive changes accompany schema formation, leading to alterations in the ways that children process gender-related information, which changes the ways in which they behave (Martin et al., 2004). Confirming these predictions, gender-schematic preschoolers behaved in more gender-typical ways than less schematic children (Levy, Barth, & Zimmerman, 1998; Wilansky-Traynor & Lobel, 2008).

Gender schema theory also predicts that developing gender schemata increases accuracy and memory for gender-consistent information compared to gender-inconsistent information. A number of studies have demonstrated such memory effects in both children and adults. Gender-typed college students tended to remember words in clusters related to gender—for example, the women's proper names in one cluster and the men's names in another (Bem, 1981). This schematicity did not affect the number of words remembered, but the organization of memory differed according to participants' gender schemata. In addition, participants with strong gender schemata were faster at making gender-related judgments that were consistent with their gender schemata than they were at making judgments inconsistent with their schemata. A study with both children and adults (Cherney, 2005) found that the effects of gender schemata appeared in incidental but not in an intentional memory task. A study with college students (Harper & Schoeman, 2003) found that gender was a strong cognitive organizing principle that affected stereotyping. A longitudinal study with children in Hong Kong (Lobel, Bar-David, Gruber, Lau, & Bar-Tal, 2000) demonstrated that the process of developing gender schemata is similar for these Asian children and results in similar changes in cognitive processing. Thus, gender schema theory has some validity across cultures.

The types of differences found among gender-schematic college students prompted further research using a similar approach, but with participants of various ages. A review of the research on gender schema and information processing (Stangor & Ruble, 1987) indicated that children with well-defined gender schemata tend to remember gender-consistent information better than gender-inconsistent information. For example, when children see drawings, photos, or videotapes in which men and women perform activities such as cooking and sewing or driving a truck and repairing appliances, gender-schematic children remember the gender-typical pairings (women cooking and sewing and men driving trucks and repairing appliances) better than the gender-atypical pairings (women driving trucks and repairing appliances and men cooking and sewing). In addition, children tend to change their memories to fit the gender-typical activities, such as remembering a man driving a truck when he was pictured as cooking. This tendency to distort memory in ways consistent with gender schemata suggests that the development of gender schemata influences the way that people interpret information (Martin & Ruble, 2004).

In developing gender schemata, children become increasingly ready to interpret information in terms of gender. A tendency to interpret information in gender-schematic terms may lead to gender stereotyping—exaggerated and narrow concepts of what is appropriate and acceptable for each gender. The formation of gender stereotypes can be understood as a natural reflection of the use of gender schemata (Martin & Halverson, 1981; Martin et al., 2002). Some of the effects of gender stereotyping are positive, such as increased ease in classifying behaviors and objects, which can give children the feeling that the environment is manageable and predictable. But stereotyping can also have negative effects, leading to inaccurate perceptions and failures to accept information that does not fit the stereotype. Thus, the existence of gender schemata prompts the formation of gender stereotypes, with both positive and negative consequences.

In summary, gender schema theory extends the cognitive developmental theory by hypothesizing the existence of gender schemata, cognitive structures that internally represent gender-related information and guide perception and behavior. Children internalize their schemata for masculinity or femininity to form a self-concept, or self-schema, for gender-related behaviors. Research has indicated that gender schemata can affect the processing of gender-related information and can lead to gender stereotyping.

Which Theory Is Best?

Each of these theories of gender development presents an orderly pattern of development, but the research shows a complex pattern with many components that do not necessarily match the theories. That is, none of the theories is able to explain all the data from research on gender identity development.

Social learning theory predicts a process of learning gender roles that results in a gradual matching of gender-related behaviors to the culturally prescribed pattern through modeling and reinforcement of gender-appropriate behaviors. Although the research shows that children begin learning information consistent with gender at an early age, gender knowledge consists of several different concepts that do not appear incrementally. The finding that children learn gender labeling before gender-typical toy and clothing preferences indicates a pattern of gender knowledge development that social learning theory does not predict.

Research has substantiated the influence of parents, siblings, and peers in directing gender-related behaviors. Social learning theory predicts that family, peers, teachers, and media images of men and women affect children in their learning and performance of gender-appropriate behaviors. Modeling can be a powerful force in prompting the performance of gender-related behaviors (Bandura & Bussey, 2004; Bussey & Bandura, 1984, 1992, 1999), and same-sex siblings, parents, peers, and teachers are all important influences in the child's development of gender flexibility (Bronstein, 2006). These findings are consistent with the predictions of social learning theory.

Social learning theory allows that girls and boys might differ not only in their gender-related behaviors but also in their cross-gender behaviors. The male gender role carries more power, and power is one of the factors that affects children's modeling. During childhood, boys are discouraged from performing feminine behaviors, whereas girls may not be discouraged from performing behaviors typical of boys (Kane, 2006). These differences lead to the prediction that boys should be more strongly gender-typed than girls, and research supports this difference. Cognitive developmental theory does not allow for a different pattern of development for boys and girls, whereas gender schema theory hypothesizes that parental attitudes and family patterns may produce variations in individual schemata. This theory does not specifically address differences in schemata between girls and boys but allows for the possibility.

Cognitive developmental theory hypothesizes that gender identity comes about through cognitive changes that occur by way of general cognitive development. Research has indicated that gender development produces cognitive changes in accuracy and memory for gender-related information, but gender schema theory also predicts that cognitive changes come with the development of gender schema, making findings that support these cognitive changes applicable to either theory.

The prediction that gender constancy is the basis for developing all other gender knowledge presents problems. Indeed, research has shown that gender constancy develops late, with many other components of gender knowledge appearing earlier. This failure is a serious problem for cognitive developmental theory. Another problem for this theory is that gender development continues during adolescence. According to cognitive developmental theory, children undergo no additional cognitive changes after early adolescence, but research has shown that late adolescence is a time during which individuals gain flexibility of gender beliefs. Understanding the development of gender flexibility is a goal for researchers in this area (Martin & Ruble, 2004).

Gender schema theory predicts that children develop a cognitive organization for gender—a schema—that forms the basis for their understanding of gender and directs their gender-related behaviors. The types of cognitive changes that this theory predicts have been found in modes of information processing, such as accuracy of judgments and memory effects. In preschool children, gender schematicity was a significant predictor of masculine and feminine gender-typed behaviors, but gender constancy was not related (Levy et al., 1998). Children also showed memory bias for characters in children's books, recalling more gender-stereotypical behaviors and emotions than the books portrayed (Frawley, 2008). In addition, women in traditional versus nontraditional jobs have different conceptualizations of gender-appropriate behavior (Lavallee & Pelletier, 1992), a finding consistent with gender schema theory.

Gender development seems to consist of several different cognitive abilities. One team of researchers (Hort, Leinbach, & Fagot, 1991) proposed that the cognitive components of gender development do not have a great deal of coherence; they postulated that such knowledge varies among individual children of the same age and stage of cognitive development. That is, gender knowledge may not fall into a pattern sufficiently coherent to be called a schema.

It is evident from this discussion that all of the social theories of gender development make predictions that research has supported, and all make predictions that research has failed to confirm. Table 5.6 (page 125) compares these theories. The picture drawn from the research shows that gender development presents a more complex process than any of the theories can fully explain. Gender development consists of separate components—gender labeling, preferences for gender-typed activities, gender stereotyping, and gender constancy. These components appear to develop in a pattern, but the pattern does not exactly conform to any of those predicted by the theories. Thus, all of the social theories of personality development have been useful and have been partially confirmed, but none is without weaknesses.

TABLE 5.6   *Comparison of Theories of Gender Development*

	Psychodynamic Theories	Social Learning Theory	Cognitive Developmental Theory	Gender Schema Theory
Gender differences develop through . . .	Early childhood interactions with parents	Reinforcement and observation of models	General cognitive development, especially gender constancy	Development of gender-specific schemata
Children's participation involves . . .	Passively moving through stages	Choosing which models to imitate	Organizing information about physical world	Developing schemata specific to gender
Gender development begins . . .	During Oedipal period (Freud); during pre-Oedipal period (Chodorow)	As soon as the culture emphasizes it, usually during infancy	During preschool years	During preschool years
Gender development proceeds . . .	Through resolution of Oedipus complex (Freud); through identification with or separation from mother (Chodorow)	Gradually becoming more like adult knowledge	Through a series of stages	Through development of schemata
Gender development finishes . . .	With identification with same-sex parent	During adulthood, if at all	During late childhood or preadolescence	During late childhood
Girls and boys . . .	Develop very different personalities; girls are inferior (Freud); boys have a more difficult time separating from mother (Chodorow)	May develop different gender knowledge as well as different gender-related behaviors	Develop similar cognitive understanding of gender	May develop different structures and schemata, depending on parents and family patterns

◼ Summary

Psychoanalytic theory, originated by Freud, is the traditional approach to psychodynamic personality theory and relies on the concepts of unconscious forces and biologically determined instincts to explain personality development and functioning.

Freud's theory hypothesized a series of psychosexual stages—oral, anal, phallic, latency, and genital—to account for the influence of childhood experiences on adult personality. Gender differences appear during the phallic stage, with its

Oedipus complex in which children are attracted to their other-sex parent and feel fear and hostility toward their same-sex parent. Boys experience a more traumatic and a more complete resolution of the Oedipus complex than girls.

Horney disputed Freud's view that women inevitably experience inferiority by arguing that social, not biological, forces form the basis for personality differences between the sexes. Her analysis of the differences in personality development between men and women showed that men have feelings of inferiority compared to women, especially regarding women's ability to give birth. Horney hypothesized that men try to feel more adequate by disparaging women.

Feminist psychoanalytic theories include those originated by Nancy Chodorow and Ellyn Kaschak. Chodorow's theory emphasizes the primacy of the early relationship with mothers and hypothesizes that boys have a more difficult time separating themselves from the feminine than do girls. Men's success in forming a masculine identity results in a denial of all that is feminine, including a rejection of female values. Kaschak's theory relies on the Oedipus legend, hypothesizing that Oedipus personifies men's drives for power and feelings of entitlement, whereas Antigone, the faithful daughter, represents women's self-sacrifice. She maintained that patriarchal culture perpetuates these roles and makes resolving these complexes difficult for men and women.

Alternatives to psychodynamic theory include social learning theory and several cognitive theories that explain how infants come to identify themselves as male or female, to understand gender, and to behave in ways that their culture deems gender-appropriate. The social learning approach relies on the concepts of observational learning and modeling to explain how children learn and perform gender-related behaviors. Initially the family, and later the broader culture, provide models and reinforcements for adopting certain gender-related behaviors while discouraging others. Research has supported the power of children's family and social surroundings to influence the development of gender-related behaviors, but the orderly pattern of gender development that occurs is not consistent with this theory.

Cognitive theories include cognitive developmental theory and gender schema theory. Cognitive developmental theory holds that gender identity is a cognitive concept that children learn as part of the process of learning about the physical world and their own bodies. Children younger than 2 years have no concept of gender and cannot consistently label themselves or others as male or female. When children have developed gender constancy, the understanding that gender is a permanent personal characteristic that will not change with any other physical transformation, their gender identity is developed. However, research has indicated that gender constancy is among the last types of gender knowledge to be acquired, which presents a problem for this theory.

Gender schema theory is an extension of cognitive developmental theory that explains gender identity in terms of schemata—cognitive structures that underlie complex concepts. When children acquire a gender schema, they change the way that they deal with information concerning gender and also change their behavior to conform to gender roles. This theory suggests that gender stereotyping is a natural extension of the process of developing gender schemata, and that children become stereotypical in their gender behavior and judgments.

Psychodynamic theories have little research support, and gathering such evidence is difficult for these theories because they draw on unconscious factors. Evaluating the social and cognitive theories of gender development leads to the conclusion that although each has supporting research, this research fails to confirm any one theory to the exclusion of the others.

◼ Glossary

castration complex   in Freudian theory, the unconscious fear that the father will castrate his son as a punishment for the son's sexual longings for his mother.

gender constancy   the knowledge that gender is a permanent characteristic and will not change with superficial alterations.

gender identity   individual identification of self as female or male.

gender labeling   the ability to label self and others as male or female.

gender role   a set of socially significant activities associated with being male or female.

instincts   in Freudian theory, the drives or impulses that underlie action, thought, and other aspects of personality functioning, which include the life, or sexual, instinct and the death, or aggressive, instinct.

masochism   feelings of pleasure as a result of painful or humiliating experiences.

Oedipus complex   in Freudian theory, the situation that exists during the phallic stage in which the child feels unconscious hostility toward the same-sex parent and unconscious sexual feelings for the opposite-sex parent. Freud used the story of Oedipus as an analogy for the family dynamics that occur during the phallic stage of personality development.

operant conditioning   a type of learning based on the administration of reinforcement or punishment. Receiving reinforcement links the reinforcement with the behavior that preceded it, making the behavior more likely to be repeated.

pre-Oedipal period   time during early childhood, before the phallic stage and the Oedipus complex. Some feminist psychoanalytic theorists, including Chodorow, have emphasized the importance of this period for personality development.

psychosexual stages   in Freudian theory, the series of stages ranging from birth to maturity through which the individual's personality develops. These stages are the oral, anal, phallic, latency, and genital stages.

punishment   any stimulus that decreases the probability that a behavior will be repeated.

reinforcement   any stimulus that increases the probability that a behavior will be repeated.

schema   (plural, *schemata* or *schemas*) an internal cognitive structure that organizes information and guides perception.

unconscious   in Freudian theory, a region of the mind functioning beyond a person's conscious awareness.

◼ Suggested Readings

Bem, Sandra Lipsitz. (1985). Androgyny and gender schema theory: A conceptual and empirical integration. In Theo B. Sonderegger (Ed.), *Nebraska Symposium on Motivation, 1984: Psychology and gender* (pp. 179–226). Lincoln: University of Nebraska Press.
Bem evaluates the other theories of gender development and presents gender schema theory, the research supporting her theory, along with advice about raising nonsexist children.

Bussey, Kay; & Bandura, Albert. (1999). Social-cognitive theory of gender development and differentiation. *Psychological Review, 106,* 676–713.
This lengthy article presents information in support of social learning theory and makes an argument that this theory is sufficient to explain gender development.

Chodorow, Nancy. (1978). *The reproduction of mothering: Psychoanalysis and the sociology of gender.* Berkeley: University of California Press.

With its psychoanalytic terminology, Chodorow's book is difficult reading, but it offers a compelling alternative to Freud's theory and has influenced many of the scholars who take the feminist standpoint on personality development.

Martin, Carol Lynn; & Ruble, Diane. (2004). Children's search for gender cues: Cognitive perspectives on gender development. *Current Directions in Psychological Science, 15,* 67–70.
Martin and Ruble briefly summarize cognitive developmental and gender schema theory and the evidence that supports the cognitive view of gender development. Their emphasis is on the active role that children take in understanding how to deal with gender.

chapter

6 Developing Gender Identity

Since he could speak, Brandon, now 8, has insisted that he was meant to be a girl . . . He spoke his first full sentence at a local Italian restaurant: "I like your high heels," he told a woman in a fancy red dress . . . At the toy store, Brandon would head straight for the aisles with the Barbies or the pink and purple dollhouses . . . One weekend, when Brandon was 2½, she [his mother Tina] took him to visit her 10-year-old cousin. When Brandon took to one of the many dolls in her huge collection—a blonde Barbie in a pink sparkly dress—Tina let him bring it home. He carried it everywhere, "even slept with it, like a teddy bear." (Rosin, 2008, p. 56)

HEADLINE

A Boy's Life

The Atlantic, November 2008

Brandon is one of a small minority of boys who behaves in ways that are typically associated with girls. Like Brandon, some of these boys wear girls' clothing and prefer playing with dolls over playing sports. These gender-atypical behaviors prompt concerns among parents, as they did with Brandon's mother. Parents of such children know that their sons' behavior is different, but feminism and the burgeoning men's movement have made parents hesitant to apply restrictions to their sons that they would not impose on their daughters. Brandon's parents decided to let him live as a girl. Other parents do not know what these atypical behaviors mean. Most fear that these behaviors signal that their sons will be gay, but the publicity about transgendered individuals has led some parents to consider that possibility.

Boys who fail to fit the narrow restrictions of the male gender role concern not only parents but peers and their parents as well. Some experts (Pollack, 1998) have called for the type of expansion of the male gender role that has occurred for girls and women. The development of gender role behaviors is more rigidly fixed for boys than for girls, yet boys are more likely to express a desire to be girls than the other way around. The children who experience *gender dysphoria,* a dissatisfaction with their biological sex, provide puzzling cases for gender development.

This chapter first traces the process of gender development, then examines several sources of influence in the process of gender development, and finally considers those individuals for whom the process diverges.

Gender Identity Development

Traditionally, a child's sex was announced at birth, but now many parents know their child's sex during prenatal development, which allows for gender differentiation even *before* a child is born. In either event, the pinks and blues appear early in children's lives. All social theories of gender development rate this type of differential treatment as important in causing children to attend to and adopt particular behaviors. But to what extent do typical gender behaviors signal the adoption of gender identity? Is it possible to behave in ways that are not typical for one gender or the other and yet have a firm notion of one's gender identity? Does Brandon's behavior in the headline story signal confusion over male gender identity or indicate only behaviors that are not typical for the male gender role?

Most people think of gender identity and gender role as the same thing, but many researchers have found it necessary to separate these concepts. The concept of **gender identity** refers to identifying and accepting the self as male or female. *Gender role* behaviors are those behaviors that are typically associated with males or females. Thus, children may behave in ways that are not typical for their gender and still have a clear gender identity, but exhibiting gender atypical behaviors may signal some problem in the development of gender identity.

For gender identity to develop, an individual must have some understanding of the categories of male and female, such as the characteristics that distinguish the two, what labels apply to each gender, what activities are associated with each category, and how she or he fits into one or the other category. Research indicates that these elements of gender identity are separable and develop at different times during childhood. This process might start early in infancy.

Development during Childhood

Some research indicates that infants possess the ability to tell the difference between male and female faces. Although infants' thoughts are difficult to study, one approach involves showing an infant objects such as photos of faces and measuring how long these objects hold the infant's attention. When infants see something new, they tend to gaze at the novel object; when they grow bored, their gaze shifts from the object. By noting when infants attend to an object and when they grow bored, researchers can deduce which stimuli infants can distinguish and which they cannot.

Results using such a procedure showed that infants had the ability to distinguish between women and men (Fagot & Leinbach, 1994). Infants 7, 9, and 12 months old could distinguish male from female faces, mainly by using hair length as the distinguishing cue. Infants may be able to make such distinctions even earlier than 6 months of age, when they show a preference for female over male faces, possibly based on the amount of experience with each type of face (Ramsey-Rennels & Langlois, 2006). This ability gives infants some basis to begin to make gender distinctions, but 9½-month-old infants showed no sign of gender differences in communication or gestures (Stennes, Burch, Sen, & Bauer, 2005). By age 24 months, however, children showed differences in gender-related vocabulary.

By age 24 months, toddlers also showed some knowledge of gender-typical activities (Serbin, Poulin-Dubois, & Eichstedt, 2002). When presented with photographs of women and men performing gender-typical or gender-atypical activities, these young children attended longer to those performing gender-atypical activities. This attention reflected their knowledge of what activities were and were not typical of men and women. Another study of children between 12 and 24 months old (Serbin, Poulin-Dubois, Colburne, Sen, & Eichstedt, 2001) showed that girls (but not boys) demonstrated some knowledge of gender-typical toys. These results suggest that gender knowledge begins to develop early, which is a first step toward possessing a gender concept or identity. Even though infants can distinguish between men and women, they use hair length to signal gender, thus missing the true basis of the distinction.

The Sequence of Childhood Gender Role Development.   Children may understand gender words before they produce them, but by age 24 months, both boys and girls use words that denote gender (Stennes et al., 2005). That is, they use gender labels to refer to women (or girls) and men (or boys). However, children sometimes misuse gender words by applying them incorrectly or inconsistently. For example, a child may label all people she likes or all members of her family as "girls" and all others as "boys." Even at this early age, children use more words to refer to their own gender than to the other.

Toddlers under age 18 months fail at gender labeling (Fagot & Leinbach, 1989), and few 20-month-olds succeed (Levy, 1999). By age 24 months, 67% of 24-month-olds were correct in their gender labeling (Campbell, Shirley, & Caygill, 2002). In a longitudinal study (Zosuls et al., 2009), the average age for the appearance of gender labeling was 19 months (17 months for girls and 21 months for boys). Therefore, children begin to use gender labels slightly before age 2, and between ages 2 and 3 years, the ability develops to use gender words accurately.

Labeling is a necessary step in the sequence of gender development, but success in this task does not assure correct performance on other types of gender knowledge (Levy, 1999). When children can consistently apply gender labels, they often do so on the basis of some external and irrelevant physical characteristic, such as clothing or hairstyle. Knowledge of gender-related behaviors and the traits and behaviors associated with each gender develop after gender labeling (Zosuls et al., 2009). Children between ages 20 and 28 months showed some indication of understanding for the categories of male and female (Levy, 1999), including objects associated with each category. Three-year-old participants were able to label the sexes, form groupings based on gender, and exhibit some knowledge of the behaviors typically associated with women and men (Martin & Little, 1990; Ruble & Martin, 1998). One longitudinal study of children between ages 2 and 3 (Campbell, Shirley, & Candy, 2004) failed to find patterns of development that would explain the relationship among these elements of gender identity, but another longitudinal study (Zosuls et al., 2009) found that gender labeling predicted gender-typed play.

At age 3, most children lack gender constancy; they do not understand that being female or male is a permanent, unchangeable feature. Young children may believe that they can change their sex if they want to or that changes in clothing or hair length will change their sex. The concept of gender constancy is very important in cognitive developmental theory. Kohlberg (1966) contended that developing gender constancy is the basis for other

Boys who have not developed gender constancy may believe that they can become women and even have babies.

gender development. Research has suggested that this concept develops later than others, casting doubt on Kohlberg's version of that theory.

Reformulations of cognitive developmental theory place less emphasis on gender constancy, acknowledging that this concept may be multifaceted, complex, and not the sole criterion for gender development (Martin et al., 2002; Ruble, Martin, & Berenbaum, 2006). **Gender constancy** may consist of two separable components: *gender stability,* the knowledge that gender is a stable personal characteristic, and *gender consistency,* the belief that people retain their gender even when they adopt behaviors or superficial physical features associated with the other gender. For example, a child who shows gender stability will say that she was a girl when she was a baby and will be a woman when she grows up. A child who shows gender consistency will say that a boy will remain a boy even if he grows long hair or puts on a dress. Children may show gender stability without gender consistency, but never the other way around (Chauhan, Shastri, & Mohite, 2005; Martin & Little, 1990; Ruble et al., 2007). Many children develop gender stability before age 6, but some children in early elementary school may not have attained gender consistency (Ruble et al., 2007; Warin, 2000); they can be confused by changed appearance or gender-atypical names.

Some research (Ruble et al., 2007) suggests that gender stability may be more important than gender consistency for the development of other, gender-related behaviors. For children who have developed both aspects of gender constancy, gender becomes a very salient aspect of their lives: They are more concerned about gender-appropriate behavior and making same-gender friends (Warin, 2000). Children who develop gender

■ GENDERED VOICES

You Could Be a Boy One Day and a Girl the Next

"When my daughter was 2 or 3 years old, she clearly had no concept of gender or the permanence of gender," a man told me. "She would say that she was a girl or a boy pretty much randomly, as far as I could tell. One day, she would say one, and maybe even later the same day, the other—for both herself and others. You could be a boy one day and a girl the next. This lack of permanence also extended to skin color. She would say that your skin was the color of your clothes, so that changed from day to day, too. One day, you were blue; the next day, your skin was red. I thought that was very odd, even more odd than being a boy one day and being a girl the next.

"She's 5 years old now, and gender is a very salient characteristic for her. She seems to realize that she is a girl, and I think that she knows that she will always be a girl, but she is very concerned with gender and gender-related things—as though she is working on sorting out all this information and making sense of it."

constancy become motivated to adopt gender-typical behaviors, causing them to avoid some activities and engage in others (Newman, Cooper, & Ruble, 1995). Children who are gender constant, therefore, have the motivation to conform to gender roles. The pattern is regular: first gender labeling, then gender stereotype knowledge and gender preferences, and then the two components of gender constancy—gender stability and gender consistency. Table 6.1 shows these four stages of development of gender knowledge.

But at what point have children developed the sense of being male or female that is defined as gender identity? That question is surprisingly difficult to answer. Some say that gender labeling signals gender identity because children are able to categorize on the basis of gender and categorize themselves. Others argue that children do not really have a gender identity until they exhibit gender consistency; before this point, they misunderstand critical elements of gender. Thus, the sequence of development is less controversial than the point at which gender identity is established.

Differences between Girls and Boys.   The course of gender development shows some differences between boys and girls. Such a difference is reasonable, given the greater

TABLE 6.1   *Stages of Developing Gender-Related Knowledge*

	Gender Labeling	Gender Preferences or Knowledge	Gender Constancy
Stage 1	No	No	No
Stage 2	Yes	No	No
Stage 3	Yes	Yes	As gender stability
Stage 4	Yes	Yes	Yes

Source: Data from "The Relation of Gender Understanding to Children's Sex-Typed Preferences and Gender Stereotypes," by C. L. Martin and J. Little, 1990, *Child Development, 61,* pp. 1434–1435.

◼ GENDERED VOICES

Raising a Sissy

"Being twins, my brother and I were closer than most brothers and sisters. We didn't look alike, but we were together a lot," a college student told me. "We had different interests. I was the one who went outside and helped my dad, while my brother stayed inside with my mother. Everybody always said I should have been the boy and he should have been the girl.

"He didn't want to play alone, so he played with me and my friends—dolls, or whatever we played. He never got to choose. And when we played dolls, he got the one that was left after me and my friend chose the ones we wanted. My mom said, 'Let him play with the Ken doll—you have two Ken dolls—don't make him play with a Barbie,' but we didn't. So he got the Barbie with one arm missing or something.

"I always liked the outdoor activities, and my brother didn't. I was so upset that I couldn't join the Cub Scouts. My dad was a troop leader, and I just couldn't understand why I couldn't join; I had always done outdoor things with my dad. Besides, the Brownies did wimpy things, and the Cub Scouts did neat stuff. I was so ticked off.

"When we were in about the 7th grade, I told my mother, 'Mom, you're raising a sissy,' and I told her that my brother should stop hanging around with her and start doing things more typical of boys. She was really angry with me for saying so.

"Did we change as we grew up? I don't consider myself very feminine—I don't take anything off anybody. My mom can't believe that her daughter acts like I do. I still like outdoor activities—camping, hiking, bicycling. I don't think I've changed as much as my brother has. I wouldn't consider him a sissy now. In high school he played football, and he started being more in line with what everyone would consider masculine. As an adult, he's not a sissy at all, but I'm still kind of an adult tomboy."

pressure placed on boys to adopt the typical and approved gender role (Sandnabba & Ahlberg, 1999). As the mother in Rosin's (2008) headline story reported, boys experience a more severe version of gender socialization. Girls are allowed greater leeway in behaving in ways typical of boys than boys are allowed in acting like girls (Kane, 2006; Martin, 1995; O'Brien et al., 2000). That is, being a "tomboy" is more acceptable than being a "sissy." Indeed, tomboys are judged to be as attractive as their nontomboy sisters (Bailey, Bechtold, & Berenbaum, 2002). Many women reported positive attitudes toward tomboys (Morgan, 1998), but many women who were tomboys also said that they recall pressures to adopt more feminine behaviors (Carr, 2004, 2007).

Feminine boys experience more serious problems. College men and women (Martin, 1995), elementary school boys (Zucker, Wilson-Smith, Kurita, & Stern, 1995), and parents of young children (Kane, 2006; Sandnabba & Ahlberg, 1999) all expressed negative opinions. Thus it is not surprising that boys begin to show greater knowledge of the male gender role than the female gender role, beginning as early as age 18 months (Stennes et al., 2005). By age 3, boys tend to show greater stability of gender-typed preferences (Powlishta, Serbin, & Moller, 1993). However, girls develop gender knowledge faster than boys (Poulin-Dubois et al., 2002; Ruble et al., 2007), and they tend to be more knowledgeable about both male and female gender roles than boys are (O'Brien et al., 2000).

Gender schema theory predicts that children attend to and master information about their own gender more rapidly than about the other gender (Levy & Fivush, 1993). Research has confirmed these predictions: Young children have better-organized knowledge of events and behaviors stereotypically associated with their own rather than the other gender (Levy, 1999; Martin, Wood, & Little, 1990). In addition, children evaluate their own gender more positively than the other gender, with girls saying that "girls are better" and boys contending that "boys are better."

Later Development

The emphasis on the sequence of gender development during early childhood has led to the widespread belief that gender development is complete by about age 6 years. This belief has resulted in less research conducted with older children, adolescents, or adults. Some researchers have explored the many dimensions of gender identity, but the majority of the research on continuing gender development has concentrated on the development of gender stereotypes and role flexibility.

Several studies have concentrated on middle childhood, examining the relationship between gender-related behavior during this time and during adolescence. One study (McHale, Kim, Whiteman, & Crouter, 2004) assessed children around age 11 to determine how and with whom they spent their free time and the relationship of these activities to behavior in early adolescence. The results indicated that boys spent more time in gender-typed activities and more time with other boys, whereas girls participated in a greater variety of activities and interacted with both boys and girls. The patterns of activities predicted gender-typed behaviors two years later, which suggests that by middle childhood, children exhibit some stability in term of gender-typed patterns of activities.

Two studies (Carver, Yunger, & Perry, 2003; Egan & Perry, 2001) explored the dimensions of gender identity in relation to adjustment and acceptance by peers for 4th- through 8th-grade children. These studies assessed the children's gender identity, how pressured they felt to conform to gender-typical behavior, and how highly they valued their own gender. The results indicated that children with stronger gender identities showed better adjustment and acceptance by peers, but pressure to conform to gendered behavior prompted negative reactions. These studies suggest that gender identity is multidimensional and that children who have less well-established gender identities may face problems in terms of self-esteem and social acceptance, which is consistent with Brandon's experience. His attraction to girls' clothing and activities led to teasing and bullying by his peers.

Early in the course of gender development, knowledge and behaviors remain closely related—with greater knowledge comes stricter application of gender stereotypes. Cognitive development allows children to expand their knowledge of gender roles to include flexibility (Ruble et al., 2007; Trautner et al., 2005). As children pass through middle childhood into adolescence, they become more capable of recognizing that the individuals in the categories of male and female vary among themselves and not just between the categories. Studies of adolescents and adults have explored this process of increasing gender flexibility.

Most studies have found a linear relationship between gender flexibility and age— that is, as age increases, so does gender flexibility (Bartini, 2006; Katz & Ksansnak, 1994; Welch-Ross & Schmidt, 1996). When children acquire gender role knowledge, they tend to apply it inflexibly, but with an increasing comfort with gender role comes an increasing willingness to make exceptions, especially when the standard is applied to self rather than others. However, one longitudinal study (Alfieri, Ruble, & Higgins, 1996) found that the transition to junior high school is an event that prompted short-lived increase of gender flexibility, followed by fairly rigid stereotyping during junior high school that persisted during high school.

Some indications of inflexible gender stereotyping may be the result of different research methods used and variations in the measurement of flexibility (Liben & Bigler, 2002; Signorella, Bigler, & Liben, 1993). For example, when forced to choose whether a behavior is performed by or an occupation is held by women or men, children are likely to show increasing evidence of gender stereotyping as they get older. If allowed the option to indicate that both may perform the behavior or either can have that occupation, even middle school children show signs of gender flexibility. This difference highlights the importance of the format and wording of questions, especially in research with children.

In addition, gender role flexibility may include attitudes and behaviors and apply to self and others, casting gender flexibility as a multidimensional concept. A longitudinal study of children in the 6th and 7th grades (Bartini, 2006) revealed that these components are separable, and their developmental trajectories differ from each other and for girls and boys. Flexibility in attitudes increased over time, whereas self-perceptions and behaviors showed little change during middle school. A study with adolescents (Leszczynski & Strough, 2008) indicated flexibility: The gender-related behaviors changed in response to situational factors such as the gender of the person with whom the adolescents interacted and the instructions for performing the task.

Children, adolescents, and even adults vary in their gender role flexibility, and several researchers have explored factors that relate to flexibility versus inflexibility. In one study (Katz & Ksansnak, 1994), a complex pattern of gender role flexibility appeared: Both family and peer social environment influenced gender-related behavior, but participants showed a general increase in tolerance for gender-atypical activities for self and others with increasing age. Another study (Welch-Ross & Schmidt, 1996) found that increases in gender role knowledge preceded increases in gender role flexibility, with flexibility developing during middle childhood. Other studies have found that gender flexibility increased with age during childhood to adolescence (Trautner et al., 2005) and from adolescence to young adulthood (Lobel et al., 2004).

Figure 6.1 (page 136) shows the course of development for gender knowledge and for application of gender-related rules over the life span. The knowledge component and application of gender-related rules increase throughout childhood, indicating decreases in flexibility. During adolescence, application of gender-related rules declines, signaling increased flexibility.

Girls are more likely than boys to endorse gender flexibility throughout adolescence (Crouter, Whiteman, McHale, & Osgood, 2007; Signorella et al., 1993). Girls show more flexibility in their own activity preferences and greater tolerance for gender-atypical behaviors in others. Research has shown that both adolescent girls (Burt & Scott, 2002) and women (Carter, Hall, Carney, & Rosip, 2006; Kulik, 2002) were more likely to endorse egalitarian gender roles than were boys and men. These attitudes apply not only to the United States but also to European countries (Frieze et al., 2003).

Some research has traced the correlates of both gender flexibility and inflexibility in men. Men who were stereotypically masculine tended to see women as stereotypically feminine; that is, men who show little gender flexibility in their own roles also show little toward women (Hudak, 1993). In adolescents, inflexibility increases as traditional young men approach high school graduation and begin to contemplate marriage and careers (Jackson & Tein, 1998). Young men who are less strongly gender-typed tend to be more flexible in their

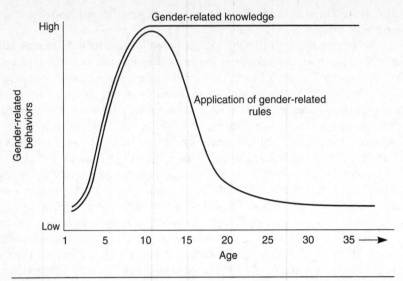

FIGURE 6.1   *Course of Knowledge and Application of Gender-Related Rules for Behavior throughout the Life Span*

application of gender rules than more strongly gender-typed men (Lobel et al., 2004). The experience of bachelorhood also seems to promote more flexible attitudes; men who lived longer on their own expressed more egalitarian attitudes concerning women's careers and sharing housework (Pitt & Borland, 2008). Also, greater flexibility appeared in men whose early life experiences included nurturing fathers and mothers in the workforce as well as an adult relationship with a feminist women (Christian, 1994). These findings suggest that both parenting and the social environment are related to gender flexibility. Table 6.2 summarizes influences on gender flexibility and inflexibility.

It is apparent that gender identity continues to develop during adolescence and even into adulthood. When children have developed the cognitive and motivational components of gender identity, they tend to be inflexible in applying their understanding of these rules; they are intolerant of gender-atypical behavior in themselves and even more so in others. Young children appear to be tolerant of gender flexibility, but this apparent tolerance is due to a lack of understanding of gender-typed behaviors. Children are "sexist piglets" who apply rigid rules of gender-related behavior to themselves and to others, but this inflexibility reaches a peak and then dissipates as individuals progress through middle childhood, adolescence, and young adulthood.

Influences on Gender Identity Development

The process of developing gender identity begins early in childhood and continues into adulthood. Although this process can be divided into stages, individuals vary in how rapidly they proceed through the stages and in the outcome of their gender identity

TABLE 6.2 *Factors in the Development of Gender-Related Attitudes in Children*

Children Who Exhibit Inflexible Attitudes about Gender	Children Who Exhibit More Flexible Attitudes about Gender
Are male	Are female
(Bryant, 2003; Burt & Scott, 2002; Crouter, Whiteman, McHale, & Osgood, 2007; Frieze et al., 2003; Kulik, 2002)	
Are between 5 and 7 years old	Are older children, adolescents, or young adults
(Bartini, 2006; Lobel et al., 2004; Trautner et al., 2005; Welch-Ross & Schmidt, 1996)	
Have parents who exhibit traditional attitudes concerning gender-related behaviors	Have parents who question traditional attitudes concerning gender-related behaviors
(Tennenbaum & Leaper, 2002)	
Are men who have lived with their families and then in college dorms or with wives	Are men who have lived on their own as bachelors
(Pitt & Borland, 2008)	
Interact more with parents	Interact less with parents
(Levy, 1989)	
Have same-gender siblings who are gender-inflexible	Have same-gender siblings who are gender-flexible
(Katz & Ksansnak, 1994)	
Have same-gender peers who are gender-inflexible	Have same-gender peers who are gender-flexible
(Katz & Ksansnak, 1994)	
Are more likely to have mothers who are homemakers	Are more likely to have mothers who work outside the home
(Levy, 1989; Riggio & Desrochers, 2005)	
Live in two-parent homes dominated by fathers	Live in single-parent families with mothers
(Friedman et al., 2007; Mandara et al., 2005; McHale et al., 2005; Sidanius & Pena, 2003; Slavkin & Stright, 2000)	
Live in families with both boys and girls	Live in families with children all the same sex
(McHale, Crouter, & Tucker, 1999)	
Are high school boys who are seniors and who are contemplating careers and marriage	Are high school girls who have mothers who work outside the home
(Jackson & Tein, 1998)	

development. The most obvious difference is whether a person develops a male or female gender identity. The factors that influence the process are another consideration. Not only biology but also family, peers, and media exert influences on gender identity development.

Biological Factors and Gender Development

The most obvious biological influence for gender identity is the configuration of the external genitalia, which lead to labeling an individual as male or female. This pronouncement prompts a host of social factors to swing into action. But what role do biological factors such as genes and prenatal exposure to hormones play a role in gender identity development?

The evolutionary view holds that adaptations during human evolutionary history have shaped gender-related behaviors, including the development of gender identity. One example is the gender difference in toy preference, which develops early in childhood (Alexander, 2003). Evolutionary psychologists argue that characteristics of typically masculine and feminine toys express evolved tendencies for girls to nurture and for boys to explore the environment. These tendencies do not determine gender identity, but evolutionary psychologists propose that they provide the basis for its development.

Researchers have also explored the genetic basis for gender-typed behaviors. Comparing twins with nontwins, one study (Iervolino, Hines, Golombok, Rust, & Plomin, 2005) concluded that gender-typed behaviors in 3- to 4-year-olds have a genetic component but are also influenced by environmental factors. The contribution of genetics and environment was not equal for boys and girls; genetics contributed more to girls' behavior than to boys'.

The presence of prenatal testosterone prompts development of reproductive organs but also has the potential to influence brain development in ways that may affect gender-typed behaviors. The evidence for hormonal influences on gender-related behaviors comes from research on girls with a disorder called congenital adrenal hyperplasia and boys who have experienced sexual reassignment during early childhood.

As discussed in Chapter 4, *congenital adrenal hyperplasia* (*CAH*) is a disorder resulting in female fetuses that are exposed to high levels of androgens. These girls usually are born with "masculinized" genitalia, identified as intersex individuals, and treated medically and surgically to make their genitalia appear more female. Studies have examined their childhood behavior, often finding that girls with CAH engage in play behavior more typical of boys than of girls (Berenbaum & Hines, 1992; Hines et al., 2004; Zucker, 2001). Nonetheless, the vast majority of girls with CAH accept themselves as women and develop female gender identity (Berenbaum, 2006). No index of hormonal exposure or masculinization of genitalia predicts which of these girls will develop a female gender identity and which will have difficulties in establishing a gender identity. Thus, prenatal exposure to testosterone seems to be more strongly related to gender-related behaviors than to gender identity.

Testosterone exposure also exerts prenatal effects when the exposure levels are within the normal range (Hines, Golombok, Rust, Johnston, & Golding, 2002). Examining gender-typical behaviors and blood samples taken from mothers during pregnancy, results revealed that girls who were high in masculine activities had mothers whose testosterone level was higher during pregnancy. A similar study (Auyeung et al., 2009) found a relationship between prenatal testosterone levels in amniotic fluid and male-typical play activities during childhood for both boys and girls.

Another line of evidence for a biological basis for gender identity comes from boys who have experienced sex reassignment during childhood. Such boys are rare, and the drama surrounding one case made headlines. The case involved a boy (known as John) who lost his penis when he was 7 months old in a mishap during circumcision (Colapinto, 2000). His parents received medical advice to have sex reassignment surgery performed to change him into a girl. When he was 2 years old, they did so (creating Joan); the case was followed by researchers to determine the difficulties of such a transition. Although reports of the reassignment indicated that Joan developed a female gender identity, those reports were untrue. Throughout childhood, Joan refused to conform to many behaviors typical of girls. When she was an adolescent, Joan found out her history and sought sex reassignment surgery to become male again. Joan became John and made a successful adjustment to a male gender identity, which suggested that gender identity is a biological phenomenon.

The John/Joan case contrasts with a similar situation but a different outcome—a boy whose penis was destroyed at age 2 months and who underwent sex reassignment at age 7 months (Bradley, Oliver, Chernick, & Zucker, 1998). This case, however, identified herself as a girl. Despite some behaviors that were more typically associated with boys and some sexual attraction to women, at age 26, this individual had no question about her female gender identity.

One type of girl is very high in masculine interests and activities—tomboys. These girls like boys' games, prefer boys as playmates, and often shun activities that girls usually prefer. A study of tomboys (Bailey et al., 2002) examined how different tomboys were from their sisters and brothers. The results indicated that tomboys were more masculine than their sisters and even more masculine than CAH girls in terms of toy and playmate preferences. Their gender identities varied, with some tomboys showing poor identification with the female gender role, but others showed the extremes of female gender identity combined with behaviors more typical of boys. Despite the belief that their atypical behavior signals a lesbian sexual orientation, such is not always the case (Showfety, 2008). No evidence exists that these girls experienced any abnormal hormone exposure during gestation, and thus there is no evidence of a biological basis for their gender atypical behavior.

What does this research convey about the biological basis of gender identity? The evidence indicates that both genetics and prenatal exposure to testosterone influence gender-related behaviors, especially during childhood. The relation to gender identity is much less clear. Babies may arrive primed to identify as male or female, but gender identity is not entirely dependent on any biological factor. Of course, the appearance of the external genitals is also the main signal for a cascade of social influences, making a distinction between the biological and other influences virtually impossible to disentangle.

Family Environment and Gender Development

Despite claims that parents have little influence in children's development (Harris, 1998; Knafo & Schwartz, 2009), the family context is critically important, including its role in gender development. Susan Witt (1997, p. 253) summarized the influences that shape gender attitudes: "These attitudes and behaviors are generally learned first in the home and are then reinforced by the child's peers, school experience, and television viewing. However, the strongest influence on gender role development seems to occur within the family setting, with parents passing on, both overtly and covertly, their own beliefs about gender." Families, however, consist of more than parents (and sometimes fewer than two parents); siblings are also part of the family environment that influences gender development.

A majority of the research investigating family influences on gender development has concentrated on parents and how their gender-related attitudes and behaviors influence their children. This influence may take place through four processes (Leaper, 2002). One process is modeling; children observe parents' behavior. A second possibility for influence is differential treatment of sons and daughters. A third avenue of influence is through the types of opportunities that parents furnish or encourage, such as toys, play activities, and household chores. A fourth possibility for parents' influence comes through the extent to which parents monitor and supervise their children's friends and activities.

Parents' gender ideologies are influential on children's gender development in both overt and subtle ways. A great deal of research indicates that fathers and mothers treat their sons and daughters differently with respect to verbal and emotional interactions, toy choices, encouragement of gender-typed play, sports participation, mathematics and science achievement, and monitoring of children's behavior (Leaper, 2002; Moon & Hoffman, 2008). The dimension that has received the most study is how traditional or nontraditional parents are in terms of their gender beliefs and attitudes and how these parental differences are imparted to children (Tennenbaum & Leaper, 2002). However, parents tend to differ from each other in terms of traditionalism, with fathers being more traditional than mothers (Kulik, 2002; Sidanius & Pena, 2003) and spending less time with children (Tennenbaum & Leaper, 2002). Despite the decreased contact, evidence suggests that fathers may exert greater influence than mothers in pushing children toward adopting traditional gender roles (Friedman, Leaper, & Bigler, 2007; Sidanius & Pena, 2003), especially their sons (Peters, 1994). This effect is not restricted to families in the United States but also occurs in Canada, Sweden, and Australia as well.

For ethnic groups within the United States, situations vary. African American fathers tend to be more egalitarian than fathers in other ethnic groups in the United States (Hill, 2002). In African American families without fathers, the gender role orientations were even less traditional; boys expressed lower and girls expressed higher evaluations of their masculinity (Mandara, Murray, & Joyner, 2005). Hispanic families differ; Hispanic women and men recalled less egalitarian families, with differences in parental attitudes and treatment for boys and girls during childhood and adolescence (McHale, Updegraff, Shanahan, Crouter, & Killoren, 2005; Raffaelli & Ontai, 2004). Boys were allowed more freedom and privileges, whereas girls were expected to perform more household chores. These differences in treatment were more pronounced for Hispanic families that were more strongly affiliated with Hispanic culture than for those more acculturated to the United States.

Evidence from families without fathers (MacCallum & Golombok, 2004) indicates that these children experience closer relationships with their mothers, and sons show more feminine (but no less masculine) behaviors than children from two-parent families. Children with lesbian mothers (Sutfin, Fulcher, Bowles, & Patterson, 2008) experienced less gender-stereotyped environments and held less traditional attitudes than children in heterosexual couples. Without fathers, children, especially girls, develop less traditional gender roles (Slavkin & Stright, 2000). Single-parent families headed by mothers produced children who were higher in traits considered masculine (more independent, assertive, and self-reliant) than two-parent families, in which girls reported more of a mixture of masculine and feminine traits. Women who work outside the home provide nontraditional models and have

When parents share household chores, children have the opportunity to observe nonstereotypical behaviors, which is related to increases in gender role flexibility.

daughters who showed more gender role flexibility (Levy, 1989) and sons and daughters who expressed more egalitarian attitudes toward family life (Riggio & Desrochers, 2005) than other children. Thus, mothers are more likely to encourage gender egalitarianism than are fathers, and the presence of a father pushes children toward traditional gender roles.

Parents may differ in their gender-related attitudes, but even parents with a commitment to gender equality often continue to create very different environments for boys and girls by continuing to model gender-stereotypical behavior in the household and through the environments they create for their children (Sabattini & Leaper, 2004). For example, most parents continue to demonstrate traditional divisions of household chores and also make different choices for clothing, room decorations, and toys for girls versus boys. Parents talk differently to daughters than to sons (Leaper, Anderson, & Sanders, 1998); the stories that they tell differ according to children's gender (Fiese & Skillman, 2000). One study (Peters, 1994) found that adolescent sons got to use the family car more than adolescent daughters, who were more restricted in their curfews than the sons. Another big difference in gender socialization within families lies in the area of household chores, which tend to be sharply gendered. This gendering applies both to parents who perform household work and to the chores assigned to daughters versus sons (Antill, Goodnow, Russell, & Cotton, 1996; Shellenbarger, 2006). This division affects skills as well as attitudes.

The presence and the gender of siblings also influence gender socialization within families: "Through their everyday interactions, siblings can influence each other by serving as models, advisors, social partners and combatants" (McHale, Crouter, & Whiteman, 2003, p. 140). The presence of siblings also alters the family context in ways that relate to gender.

For example, Israeli children with younger siblings developed gender constancy earlier than others (Karniol, 2009). Another study (Levy, 1989) showed that children who interacted more with their parents showed *less* gender role flexibility than children who spent less time with their parents, and children with fewer siblings showed *more* gender role flexibility than those with more brothers and sisters. Indeed, siblings may be more important than parents in developing gender role flexibility (Katz & Ksansnak, 1994). Same-sex siblings showed an especially important effect in the development of gender flexibility—either increasing or decreasing flexibility, depending on siblings' attitudes.

Longitudinal studies have demonstrated the influence of siblings by measuring first-born and second-born children, following them over years. Results from one study (McHale, Updegraff, Helms-Erikson, & Crouter, 2001) indicated that the qualities of first-born children during the first year assessment appeared in second-born children three years later. Another study (Crouter et al., 2007) indicated that boys with younger brothers in families with traditional gender ideology became more traditional over time, but other configurations of sibling and families did not; all other children and adolescents became more egalitarian over time. Therefore, sibling influences are not a simple matter of modeling, and birth order appears to be important in the process.

The gender composition of siblings may also interact in ways that are important for gender socialization. A study that compared families with a girl and a boy to families with siblings of only one sex found stronger gender typing in the latter (McHale, Crouter, & Tucker, 1999), and once again, fathers were influential in creating traditional gender role ideology. The mixed-gender siblings seemed to be related to traditional gender roles—one child of each gender is available to do the activities stereotypically associated with chores (Crouter, Manke, & McHale, 1995). When the children are all boys, someone still has to do the dishes—a situation that may prompt flexibility.

Therefore, families are important for gender socialization in many ways, including parents' attitudes and behavior, the gendered environment of the home, and the complex influence of siblings. Gender socialization also occurs outside the family environment, and as children get older, they encounter a wide variety of others who send messages about gender and gender-related behaviors.

Peers and Gender Development

Interaction with age-mates also influences children and adolescents to adopt gender-typical behaviors. Beginning about age 3 years, children develop a preference for same-sex playmates (Maccoby, 2002). These preferences become stronger over the next few years, making gender segregation one of the most prominent features of elementary school children's peer interactions. Indeed, elementary school children spend between 50% and 60% of their time with same-gender peers (Martin & Fabes, 2001). Adults often urge children toward same-gender peers, but even when adults try to get children to play in mixed-gender groups, the tendency toward gender segregation usually prevails. Reactions from peers concerning gender-related behaviors furnish information that contributes to self-concept (Smith & Leaper, 2006).

The types of relationships and activities that occur in groups of girls typically differ from those in groups of boys (Maccoby, 2002). Boys tend to be rougher, more competitive, more likely to form a hierarchy, and less likely to play near adults. Girls often (but not always) find boys' activities and interaction style unappealing; so many girls do not want to play with boys. Those girls who do face challenges in developing a "tomboy" gender identity (Paechter & Clark, 2007). Boys resist girls joining their play groups, even during elementary school, and both peers and parents exert increasing pressure on tomboy to relinquish their atypical activities and become more feminine.

Boys who do not maintain gender segregation face harsher sanctions, as Brandon in this chapter's headline story demonstrated. Both girls and boys devalued children who violated gender norms for appearance and, to a lesser extent, for behaviors (Blakemore, 2003; Horn, 2007). Boys, however, received harsher judgments than girls. During the school years, children and adolescents tend to have inflexible gender roles, so peer pressure acts to maintain traditional gender-related behaviors. Part of that pressure is bullying directed at children who fail to conform to gender roles, especially boys (Young & Sweeting, 2004). Therefore, peers often operate as the "gender police," acting to maintain inflexible gender roles for children and adolescents.

Peers may also act to promote gender flexibility, which often occurs during the college years. Research with college students (Bryant, 2003) demonstrated that both men and women became less traditional in their gender attitudes during four years of college. Consistent with other research, women were less traditional than men, but both changed during college. One important influence was their peers. Therefore, peers may act to promote or to curtail gender flexibility and do each at different times during development.

The Media and Gender Development

Print, broadcast, film, and electronic media are an integral part of daily life for most people in developed countries, and gender portrayals are daily events for those who are exposed to these media. Children, adolescents, and adults learn about gender from entertainment programming, advertisements, video games, and news reports. These media begin to influence children as early as parents do. Entertainment programs show men, women, boys, and girls in a wide variety of situations, and these programs transmit messages about what is desirable and attractive in each gender. Advertising sends signals about gender as well as sells products. News reports cover gender research, and examining the style of the news report as well as the content reveals the attitude behind the story (Brescoll & LaFrance, 2004).

Media portrayals can be so powerful and persuasive that these depictions become the standard on which people judge what is normal and desirable for their own lives. Indeed, the media can be more important than personal experience in shaping attitudes and behavior, and this view is compatible with the *cultivation theory* of media effects (Gerbner, Gross, Morgan, & Signorielli, 1994). This theory holds that depictions in the media cultivate beliefs and attitudes about the real world, leading people to imagine that their lives should match the media depictions.

One reason that the media have become so persuasive is the tendency toward what Gregg Easterbrook (1996) called **synthesized realism**, a mixture of actual information with phony details blended into a realistic portrayal that is really fiction. When this mixture is done with sufficient skill, people cannot tell the difference. Thus, people absorb information that is a toxic blend of reality and fiction and use this information as a basis by which to judge their own (and others') behavior. Children are especially vulnerable because their cognitive limitations make them unable to think critically about the portrayals, leaving them even more vulnerable to media misinformation.

Gender Bias in the Media.   A number of analyses have revealed how the media provide inaccurate and systematically biased information about gender. One of the prime assumptions is that women and men are different. As Janet Bing (1999, p. 5) said, "The media continue to seek new ways to ask 'How are men and women different?'" By assuming difference, drawing women and men into stereotypical categories, and then presenting these stereotypical depictions as attractive, the media perpetuate restrictive roles for both men and women. These depictions appear in television entertainment programming, television commercials, movies, magazines, music videos, and video games.

Television is almost unavoidable for people in the United States. Most homes have at least one (and many have more than one) television. Although pediatricians recommends against television viewing for children younger than 3 years old, 1-year-olds average over 2 hours of viewing per day, and 3-year-olds average over 3 hours (Christakis et al., 2004), presenting many opportunities to influence all who view them, including very young children. Adolescents watch less television than children, but those who were heavy viewers during childhood continue that habit (Marshall, Gorely, & Biddle, 2006).

Male characters on television are older and occupy more prestigious positions than female characters (Glascock, 2001; Signorielli, 2004). Men also are more often the leading characters in drama and adventure programs, activities that take them away from home and family relationships (Lauzen, Dozier, & Horan, 2008). These representations devalue women by making them less visible and credible on television and limit men by restricting them to aggressive, competitive roles. Indeed, men are disproportionately depicted as police officers and criminals in television dramas (Scharrer, 2001). In television entertainment programming, female characters are younger, less likely to be employed, and more likely to appear in secondary and comedy roles than are male characters (Signorielli, 2004). Women are also less likely to use the plot device of directly addressing the audience, which builds rapport and trust (Lauzen & Deiss, 2009). Thus, women are less visible and less significant than men on television entertainment programming. The situation is similar in television advertising (see According to the Media and According to the Research).

The underrepresentation of women also occurs in movies. In top-grossing movies from the 1940s through the 1980s, women appeared less frequently than men (Bazzini, McIntosh, Smith, Cook, & Harris, 1997). This underrepresentation was true for women in both primary and secondary roles, and it applied more strongly to older than younger women. In addition, older women were portrayed in less favorable ways than older men. The underrepresentation and age bias have continued; an analysis of the 100 top films in the United States in 2002 (Lauzen & Dozier, 2005) revealed a similar pattern. Thus, the lower visibility for women extends to movies.

Some people (including network programmers and studio executives) argue that television and movies furnish entertainment, and people know that the depictions are not accurate. Despite the knowledge that entertainment programming is fictional, the gender messages on those programs have the power to influence people when they experience similar characters in real life (Murphy, 1998). Knowing that a character is fictional does not decrease that character's appeal—they can still influence attitudes and beliefs

(Ziegler & Stoeger, 2008). Therefore, media portrayals have the power to influence, and this process occurs for people of all ages.

Children and Media.

For children, television is probably the most influential of the media because it is such a part of most children's lives (Witt, 2000). Preschool children average about 30 hours a week of TV viewing, including about 20,000 commercial advertisements a year. Television has the power to teach positive attitudes and behaviors, but researchers, critics, and parents worry about the negative messages that children receive. Many of those concerns have centered on the topics of violence and encouragement for smoking and drinking, but perpetuating gender stereotypes has also been an issue.

Gender bias in programming for adults also appears in children's television (Witt, 2000). Boys are portrayed as more powerful, smart, ambitious, competitive, and violent; girls appear as more timid, warm, sensitive, peaceful, and attractive. An analysis of children's favorite TV programs suggested that both girls and boys chose programs with more gender-neutral portrayals as their favorites (Aubrey & Harrison, 2004). Favorite programs still contained gender stereotyping, especially for the male gender role, and some children were more attracted than other to these stereotypical portrayals.

These gender biases in children's entertainment programming appear in advertisements on children's television more strongly than in adult programming (Hentges, Bartsch, & Meier, 2007). Commercials are of great interest for children's television viewing because children attend to the commercials more than to the regular programming (Larson, 2003). According to one analysis (Larson, 2001), when commercials depict girls and boys together, the gender stereotyping is minimal. However, when either gender appears alone in a commercial, gender stereotypes abound, and children see girls in kitchen settings and boys being violent. Similar stereotyping appeared in a study that examined the voice-overs for children's commercials (Johnson & Young, 2002). A longitudinal analysis of television advertising directed toward children (Maher & Childs, 2003) indicated a shift toward gender-neutral advertising since 1975. However, gender stereotyping remained prevalent in more subtle forms. For example, when an advertisement features both a girl and a boy, the main character is likely to be the boy; when an advertisement has a voice-over, the voice is likely to be male. Gender bias has decreased, but not disappeared, from advertising on children's television.

Older children and adolescents have expanded opportunities for media influence, including films and video games as well as print media such as comics, magazines, and literature. Reading has become less popular and video games more popular leisure activities for children and adolescents (Nippold, Duthie, & Larsen, 2005). Video games were sharply gendered during the early years of their development, but girls and women began to enter the world of gaming in larger numbers in the mid-1990s (Williams, 2003). Nevertheless, the video game market remains strongly oriented toward boys and men, and the portrayals of girls and women in video games tend to be very stereotypical (Dickerman, Christensen, & Kerl-McClain, 2008; Ivory, 2006).

Adolescents watch less television than children or adults, but they too receive messages from the programming they see (Signorielli, 1998). For adolescent girls as for women, television, magazines, movies, and music videos send the message that looks count, often more than anything else. The most important aspects are body image and weight. Most of the attractive girls and women on television are very thin, and this message comes across to adolescent girls (Hentges et al., 2007). Indeed, adolescent girls who

According to the Media...

Women Are Young, Attractive, and Subordinate—in Television Commercials

Looking at television commercials in countries around the world, women and men usually vary in the roles they play, the products they promote, and the settings they occupy, but they also differ in their presence. In some countries, such as the United States (Ganahl, Prinsen, & Netzley, 2003), Great Britain (Furnham, Pallangyo, & Gunter, 2001), and Spain (Valls-Fernández & Martínez-Vincente, 2007), men are more common characters in advertisements than women are; in other countries, such as Japan, Taiwan, and Malaysia (Bresnahan, Inoue, Liu, & Nishida, 2001) and in Saudi Arabia (Nassif & Gunter, 2008), representation is more equal. However, even in countries with an equal frequency of female and male characters, the portrayals are stereotypical, not equal.

One common difference around the world in television advertising is the presentation of female characters that are younger than their male counterparts. This age difference appeared in analyses of television advertising in the United States (Ganahl et al., 2003), Great Britain and Zimbabwe (Furnham et al., 2001), Korea (Kim & Lowry, 2005), Turkey (Uray & Burnaz, 2003), Hong Kong, Indonesia, and throughout Europe (Furnham & Mak, 1999). Also, women are significantly more likely to appear in advertisements for personal care products (Bresnahan et al., 2001; Ganahl et al., 2003), which emphasize the value of the product in improving beauty. The combination of age and attractiveness results in a preponderance of attractive young women in television advertising.

The young, attractive women in television commercials may also be portrayed as dependent or subordinate (Furnham & Mak, 1999; Furnham et al., 2001; Ganahl et al., 2003; Kim & Lowry, 2005), less authoritative and credible than men (Uray & Burnaz, 2003), and less intelligent than men (Furnham et al., 2001). Women are more likely than men to appear in home settings and with children (Nassif & Gunter, 2008), which emphasizes another stereotype. Thus, in television advertising around the world, women's image represents an idealized female stereotype.

watched more hours of romantic television oriented toward young women reported lower body satisfaction than girls who watched fewer hours of TV (Eggermont, Beullens, & van den Bulck, 2005). Television and movies also send messages about the importance of getting and keeping a boyfriend as well as unrealistic images of career possibilities.

Despite being more plentiful and powerful in media portrayals, adolescent boys also are subject to unflattering and unrealistic television and movie depictions (Greven, 2002). The prominence of violence is the most dramatic feature associated with boys in the media, and concern over bullying has led to various depictions of such situations successfully resolved by violence. In addition, adolescent boys often appear as inept with girls and obsessed with sex. This combination furnishes the material for many teen comedies in which boys appear as stereotypes.

The widespread gender stereotyping that appears in the media, combined with the power of the media to shape attitudes and behavior, has led several groups to formulate guidelines for helping parents to teach their children to be media literate. Children Now (2006) is an advocacy organization for children that collects information about media influence and bias and also strives to counteract some of the negative effects that media can convey, including gender stereotyping. The American Academy of Pediatrics (2003) also advocates for media education and provides materials to help parents teach their children how to analyze media messages in critical ways. Thus, the power of media portrayals is

ACCORDING TO THE RESEARCH . . .

Women's Roles Have Changed More Than Commercials Portray

Women's roles have changed a great deal over the past 30 years, but television's portrayals have not kept pace. Although the number of female characters and their roles have altered since early 1970s television (Ganahl et al., 2003; Nassif & Gunter, 2008), these alterations do not represent the actual changes in women's employment and responsibilities. Women's lives have changed more than commercials portray.

Women's roles have changed in many countries around the world. As Kwangok Kim and Dennis Lowry (2005, p. 901) described the situation, "television commercials are a lagging social indicator of role changes." Women have entered the workforce, professions, and politics not only in North America, Australia, and Europe but also in Korea (Kim & Lowry, 2005); Japan, Taiwan, and Malaysia (Bresnahan et al., 2001); and Turkey (Uray & Burnaz, 2003).

Gender stereotyping has decreased in commercials in Great Britain (Furnham & Saar, 2005) and Portugal (Neto & Silva, 2009) more than in the United States

(Ganahl et al., 2003) but remains high in Poland (Furnham & Saar, 2005), Zimbabwe (Furnham et al., 2001), and throughout Europe (Furnham & Mak, 1999). An analysis of prime time commercials in Japan, Malaysia, and Taiwan (Bresnahan et al., 2001) indicated that the majority depicted women and men in nonstereotypical situations, which would more closely match women's lives. Another analysis of commercials on Korean television (Eun & Kim, 2006) indicated that a transition occurred between 1985 and 2005; women and men started performing similar rather than gender-stereotyped activities.

These images may even be losing the power to shape women's aspirations. A study that tested the power of commercials to influence women's career aspirations (Yoder, Christopher, & Holmes, 2008) reported that an earlier study had found that exposure to sexist commercials diminished women's aspirations, but their study did not. Indeed, women's career aspirations had become similar to men's. The study hinted that sexist advertising has not lost all its power, but that influence seems diminished.

well recognized, and individuals as well as organizations are attempting to counter these powerful messages that include gender stereotyping.

Considering Diversity

Most children adopt the gender-related behaviors typical for their biological sex, but Brandon, whose story began this chapter, did not and experienced increasing pressure to do so (Rosin, 2008). For example, one study (Raag & Rackliff, 1998) showed that most 4- and 5-year-old boys believed that their fathers would think it was "good" if they played with boys' toys and "bad" if they played with girls' toys. None of the boys who imagined their fathers would disapprove actually played with girls' toys in an observed play situation. Thus, children feel pressure to adopt gender-typical behaviors, and boys experience more pressure than girls.

As William Pollack (1998) emphasized, most children show behaviors that represent a combination of the typical masculine and feminine, which does not indicate any type of gender confusion or dissatisfaction. For example, one 5-year-old boy wanted a pink bicycle because pink was his favorite color (Rosenfeld, 1998). His parents knew that the color would be a problem, but they accepted his choice; the salesman did not and tried to convince him that a "boy's" color would be much better. His choice created problems—peers, including the girls, teased him for having a pink bicycle. Boys who make many such cross-gender choices face a great deal of social censure, bullying, and even violence (Young & Sweeting, 2004).

What behaviors signal variation in gender-typical behaviors and what behaviors indicate some problem in developing gender identity? As Brandon's mother learned, this question is difficult to answer, and even experts disagree. One way to understand children with atypical gender behavior is to focus not only on the gender-atypical behavior but also on the extent to which they exhibit gender-typical behaviors (Knafo, Iervolino, & Plomin, 2005). Like Brandon, some other boys exhibit preferences and play behaviors more typical of girls, but these boys may either like or reject activities typical of boys. Likewise, tomboys may accept or reject activities typical of girls. Children, especially girls, who combine gender-typical and -atypical behaviors may be well accepted. However, the combination of persistent gender-atypical behaviors and rejection of gender-typical behaviors may be indicative of problems, such as gender identity disorder.

Gender identity disorder is among the classifications of behavior disorders in the American Psychiatric Association's *Diagnostic and Statistical Manual of Mental Disorders* (DSM) (American Psychiatric Association, 2000), making it an official psychiatric diagnosis. According to the fourth edition of the DSM (DSM-IV-TR), exhibiting interests and behaviors typical of the other gender is not sufficient to result in this diagnosis. Children must exhibit four of five of the following symptoms: (1) cross-sex behaviors, (2) cross-sex toy and activity preferences, (3) cross-sex peer affiliation, (4) cross-dressing, and, (5) a stated desire to be the other sex.

Richard Green (1987) conducted a longitudinal study of boys who showed signs of gender identity disorder to discover differences between these boys and others who had more typical gender role development. His study indicated that some of these boys had received reinforcement and others were ignored by parents for their cross-gender behaviors. This observation is consistent with later research (Knafo et al., 2005), which indicated that gender identity disorder has an environmental component, although it may also have a genetic component.

The majority of boys in Green's study did not develop a completely heterosexual sexual orientation but experienced sexual attraction to men or to both women and men (Green, 1987; Zucker & Bradley, 1995). Indeed, for both boys and girls with symptoms of gender identity disorder, nonheterosexual sexual orientation has been a more common long-term outcome than seeking sexual reassignment (Dreger, 2009; Drummond, Peterson-Badali, Bradley, & Zucker, 2008).

Determining which children will continue in their dissatisfaction with their sex is a critical issue for action (Dreger, 2009). One important criterion is the expressed lack of acceptance, even hatred, of one's own sex (Zucker, 2002). This component of gender identity disorder is called *gender dysphoria*; the persistence of gender dysphoria into adolescence is a better predictor of seeking a change to the other sex than similar feelings during childhood or attraction to cross-gender behavior (Dreger, 2009).

Studies on girls with gender dysphoria are much less common than research with boys. Green (1987) chose not to include girls in his study because too few girls showed symptoms of gender identity disorder. Boys are more than six times more likely than girls to receive a clinical referral (Zucker, Bradley, & Sanikhani, 1997), and one factor in this situation is the greater social tolerance for cross-gender behaviors of girls (Lippa, 2008). Indeed, girls tend to see advantages in being boys (Baumgartner, in Tavris & Wade, 1984). When asked what would happen if they changed sex, elementary school girls imagined advantages, whereas boys imagined disaster. Adults make similar judgments, believing that being male offers advantages and being female presents disadvantages (Cann & Vann, 1995). The widespread perception of advantages for males may be a factor in considering boys abnormal when they want to change their sex. However, a follow-up study of girls with gender identity disorder (Drummond et al., 2008) found that the percentages of nonheterosexual and gender dysphoric women were similar to Green's (1987) findings of boys.

The individuals who experience these symptoms also encounter many negative consequences of their cross-gender behaviors from parents and peers, and the lack of acceptance and failure to fit in with peers may constitute a situation that produces the most distress for children with gender identity disorder (Bartlett, Vasey, & Bukowski, 2000). As they grow into adolescents, some individuals with gender identity disorder come to identify with their biological sex, whereas others experience increasing dissatisfaction with their bodies and continue efforts to have a body of the other sex.

The adolescents and adults who continue to experience gender dysphoria may say they feel "trapped in the wrong body," a sentiment that many people find perplexing. How could a person fail to understand and accept his or her sex? Some research has hinted that the difference may originate in the brain (Molo et al., 2006). Brain scans of individuals with gender identity disorder were more similar to those of the other sex than their own biological sex, which suggests a situation very much like what individuals with gender identity disorder describe—their brains don't match their bodies. Others find these studies unpersuasive (Bailey & Triea, 2007) and contend that advocates of hormonal and surgical interventions urge unnecessary action.

A growing number of vocal individuals advocate acceptance of gender dysphoric individuals and treatment with hormones and surgical sexual reassignment (Rosin, 2008). The term **transsexual** describes these individuals, and those who are in the process of acquiring a new sex sometimes refer to themselves as *transgendered individuals*. These concepts and terminology confuse many people, who assume that biological sex, gender, and sexual orientation all go together (Carr, 2005). All are actually separable. Feeling "trapped in the wrong body" (gender dysphoria) does not mean that the person is homosexual (has feelings of sexual attraction for people of one's own sex). *Transvestism* (dressing in clothing appropriate to the other gender) is associated with gender identity disorder but may also occur as a sexual fetish (receiving sexual pleasure from the behavior) rather than an expression of gender dissatisfaction. Thus, these phenomena may overlap, but they are separable. For example, a large majority of gay men and lesbians have no gender dysphoria and no gender identity confusion. Only 17% of male transvestites reported feeling trapped in a man's body (Docter & Prince, 1997). Therefore, dissatisfaction with one's gender may be associated with gender-atypical behaviors, but most individuals who exhibit these behaviors do not do so as part of gender identity disorder.

During childhood and adolescence, these individuals typically experience problems, most often associated with depression, and individuals who seek sexual reassignment face challenges (Splete, 2005). Although transsexuals face problems in being accepted by society, sexual reassignment is often successful in resolving many of their problems (Cohen-Kettenis, Delemarre-van de Waal, & Gooren, 2008; de Cuypere et al., 2005; Rehman, Lazer,

Benet, Schaefer, & Melman, 1999; Smith, van Goozen, & Cohen-Kettenis, 2001). After surgery, their gender dysphoria disappears, their overall health is good, and their sexual functioning improves.

Gender identity disorder is a rare and controversial disorder. Indeed, controversy exists over its classification as a disorder, with authorities criticizing its inclusion in the DSM (Bartlett et al., 2000; Langer & Martin, 2004; Lev, 2005) and others defending this diagnosis (Zucker & Bradley, 1995; Zucker & Spitzer, 2005). As children, individuals who exhibit gender dysphoria and cross-gender behaviors are subject to diagnosis and treatment to make them accept their biological sex as their gender identity. If they develop sexual attraction to people of the same gender (homosexual sexual orientation), they are not subject to treatment; the American Psychiatric Association has not considered homosexuality a disorder for over 25 years. If individuals experience persistent gender dysphoria as adolescents and adults, they are free to seek sexual reassignment surgery. Some authorities (and some transsexuals) consider this situation contradictory: Why consider gender identity disorder a problem in children but not for adults? Why should it be considered a disorder rather than a difference to be accepted?

■ Summary

The process of gender development may begin during infancy, but between ages 2 and 3, most children learn to apply gender labels and to understand some behaviors and features as stereotypically associated with gender. Their understanding of gender is far from complete, however, and children may be 6 or 7 years old before they have a complete understanding of all the components of gender, including gender constancy, gender consistency, and gender stability.

When children develop an understanding of gender, they tend to be rigid and inflexible in their application of gender rules to themselves and others, but the peak period of inflexibility is relatively short and occurs between ages 5 and 7. Gender stereotyping is not as strong during adolescence and adulthood, indicating that additional gender development occurs after childhood.

Biology influences gender development, but its effects are difficult to separate from social influences because the identification of a child's genitals as male or female prompts a cascade of social events related to gender development. Prenatal hormone exposure affects gender-typed behaviors more than gender identity.

Families exert an important influence on the gender socialization of children. Parents may convey gendered messages through modeling, different treatment of boys and girls, creating opportunities for different types of behaviors, and differential monitoring of activities. Traditional families tend to have children with more traditional gender attitudes, and fathers tend to be the family member whose influence promotes traditional gender behaviors. Even parents who attempt to avoid gender stereotyping have difficulties; the tendency to assign girls and boys gender-typical chores is strong, and both parents and siblings often create a gendered environment for children. Peers also tend to push children and adolescents toward inflexible gender role behaviors.

The media influence all members of society, and that influence includes gender stereotyping in television entertainment programming and commercials, movies, video games, comics, and literature. Girls and boys are subject to similar gender stereotyping in programming oriented toward children, even educational television and children's books. Thus, media exposure is a strong force in establishing and perpetuating traditional gender roles.

The large majority of children develop gender identities that are consistent with their biological sex, but some do not. Those children who express preferences and enact behaviors typical of the other gender and reject those typical of their own prompt concern among parents, but a diagnosis of gender identity disorder requires a persistent identification with and desire to be the other gender. As they mature, many of these individuals do not continue with their gender dysphoria (but many do develop nonheterosexual sexual orientation); other do and seek sexual reassignment surgery to fulfill their wish to be the other gender. The treatment and even the diagnosis of gender identity disorder is controversial.

◼ Glossary

gender constancy   the knowledge that gender is a permanent characteristic and will not change with superficial alterations.

gender identity   individual identification of self as female or male.

gender identity disorder   a disorder that occurs when a child rejects the gender role that corresponds to biological sex and adopts cross-gender behaviors and possibly a cross-gender identity.

synthesized realism   a mixture of actual information with phony details into a realistic portrayal that is really fiction.

transsexual   an individual who receives hormonal and surgical treatment to be changed to the other sex.

◼ Suggested Readings

Dreger, Alice. (2009). Gender identity disorder in childhood: Inconclusive advice to parents. *Hastings Center Report 39* (1), 26–29.
This short article summarizes the controversy concerning gender identity disorder in the form of advice to parents of children who express atypical gender behavior.

Pollack, William. (1998). *Real boys.* New York: Holt.
The first two chapters of Pollack's book about boys explore the rigid gender role socialization that boys undergo and the damage that this socialization can do to boys.

Ruble, Diane N.; Martin, Carol Lynn; & Berenbaum, Sheri A. (2006). Gender development. In N. Eisenberg, W. Damon, & R. M. Lerner (Eds.), *Handbook of child psychology, Vol. 3* (pp. 858–932). Hoboken, NJ: Wiley.
This thorough review of gender development examines the biological, social, and cognitive approaches and attempts an integration.

chapter

7

Intelligence and Cognitive Abilities

HEADLINE

Lost in Space
Vogue, June 2001

Brain research, the hot science specialty and the bane of a feminist's existence, says that we are, on average, profoundly different from men. Researchers who look at everything from the size of the brain (theirs is bigger) to the speed at which it ages (theirs deteriorates faster) to the effect of sex hormones come to a single, unnerving conclusion: Biology is a good chunk of destiny. Recent studies suggest that while women may excel at reading a map, men may be quicker at processing that information and putting it into good use on the road. In other words, we are hot-wired to get lost more often than the guys are. (Stabiner, 2001, p. 142)*

Citing the importance of biological differences, Karen Stabiner's (2001) headline article argued that women are "Lost in Space." In her trek to explore gender differences, Stabiner and her husband participated in an orienteering course in which they had to find their way around in the woods, and she talked to several prominent cognitive researchers about gender and spatial ability. Neither of these strategies supplied a great deal of evidence to back up her claims that women do more poorly on finding their way or that the ability to get around in the world is wired into the brain.

The long-held belief that women get lost and men never ask directions is an enduring gender stereotype that relates to cognitive differences in spatial abilities. This gender contrast is one of many that this chapter will evaluate. Do women and men have different cognitive abilities, do they use distinct strategies, or both? If such contrasts exist, are they expressions of hormonal or brain differences between the sexes, or do these distinctions represent different learning and experience?

Like Janet Hyde (2005b, 2007b), one of the experts Stabiner consulted, some researchers contend that gender differences do not exist, whereas Doreen Kimura (2007), another expert, has argued that they do exist and that they have a biological basis. The research in the area of cognitive abilities is filled with complex findings and strongly held (but opposing) views; dozens of articles have appeared in the popular press and thousands in the research literature.

This level of controversy reflects the strong feelings that this topic has produced. To what extent do gender differences explain intelligence and cognitive abilities? Are such

---

*Copyright © by Karen Stabiner. Originally published in *Vogue*. Reprinted by permission of the author.

contrasts sufficiently large to explain the distribution of men and women into different areas of study and occupations, or do these findings represent insignificant distinctions in how women and men think? Do differences apply only to specific cognitive abilities or to overall intelligence?

Cognitive Abilities

Other than defining intelligence as "how smart a person is" (a trivial and circular definition), an acceptable definition of this concept has been difficult to formulate. Indeed, heated debate over the nature of intelligence has occurred throughout the history of intelligence testing, a controversy within but not confined to psychology. The prominence of this concern highlights the importance of the issue; understanding intelligence and the abilities that contribute to intelligence is a basic question for understanding humans.

Psychologists have been concerned with the concept of intelligence since the 1890s (Schultz & Schultz, 2008). However, the current view of intelligence was most influenced by the creation of the intelligence test in 1905. This test, formulated by Alfred Binet, Victor Henri, and Théodore Simon, measured a variety of mental abilities related to school performance, including memory, attention, comprehension, vocabulary, and imagination. A version of this test—the Stanford-Binet—appeared in the United States in 1916, and the intelligence testing movement became an important part of psychology, especially in the United States.

The prevailing view of intelligence during the 19th and early 20th centuries was that women's intellect was inferior to men's (Lewin, 1984a; Shields, 1975a). Lewis Terman, who adapted the Binet-Simon test into the Stanford-Binet, did not believe in the intellectual inferiority of women and had no trouble accepting the results of this test, which revealed no average differences between the intelligence of men and that of women. Indeed, the scores on the early versions of the Stanford-Binet showed that women scored slightly higher than men, but after some minor adjustment of items, the average scores for women and girls were equal to those of men and boys (Terman & Merrill, 1937).

Although IQ test scores are equal, the gender prejudice of the 19th century has lasted into the 21st century: Both women and men judge women's intelligence as lower than men's (Furnham, Callahan, & Akande, 2004). Such contrasts occur when students estimate their own intelligence, when college students estimate their parents' intelligence, and when parents judge their children's intelligence (Furnham, Reeves, & Budhani, 2002). This difference crops up around the world, including Europe, the United States, Asia, the Middle East, and in some countries in Africa (von Stumm, Chamorro-Premuzic, & Furnham, 2009). South Africa was an exception; both Whites (Furnham et al., 2004) and Blacks (Furnham, Ndlovu, & Mkhize, 2009) showed few gender differences or higher estimates of men's than women's intelligence.

With the development of the intelligence testing movement came increased attention to the various abilities included within these tests. In the Stanford-Binet, most test items could be classified as verbal; that is, most questions require the understanding and use of language. Psychologist David Wechsler created an alternative intelligence test that divided abilities into the categories of verbal and performance skills. The verbal subtests require those being tested to provide verbal answers by performing certain tasks: supplying factual knowledge (information), defining vocabulary items (vocabulary), performing basic arithmetic computation (arithmetic), repeating a series of digits (digit span), understanding similarities between objects (similarities), and properly interpreting social conventions (comprehension).

The performance subtests of Wechsler's test require no verbal responses, but instead people respond by performing some action. The performance subtests include arranging pictures into a sensible story (picture arrangement), duplicating designs with blocks (block design), completing pictures that have some missing part (picture completion), assembling cut-up figures of common objects (object assembly), and learning and rapidly applying digit symbol codes (digit symbols) (Gregory, 1987). Figure 7.1 shows samples of the types of items on the Wechsler tests.

Verbal Subtests	Sample Items
Information	How many wings does a bird have? Who wrote *Paradise Lost*?
Digit span	Repeat from memory a series of digits, such as 3 1 0 6 7 4 2 5, after hearing it once.
General comprehension	What is the advantage of keeping money in a bank? Why is copper often used in electrical wires?
Arithmetic	Three men divided 18 golf balls equally among themselves. How many golf balls did each man receive? If 2 apples cost 15¢, what will be the cost of a dozen apples?
Similarities	In what way are a lion and a tiger alike? In what way are a saw and a hammer alike?
Vocabulary	This test consists simply of asking, "What is a _____?" or "What does _____ mean?" The words cover a wide range of difficulty or familiarity.

Performance Subtests	Description of Item
Picture arrangement	Arrange a series of cartoon panels to make a meaningful story.
Picture completion	What is missing from these pictures?
Block design	Copy designs with blocks (as shown at right).
Object assembly	Put together a jigsaw puzzle.
Digit symbol	

1	2	3	4
X	III	I	O

Fill in the symbols:

3	4	1	3	4	2	1	2

FIGURE 7.1   *Sample Test Items Similar to Items on Wechsler's Tests of Intelligence*

Source: From *The World of Psychology,* by Ellen R. Green Wood and Samuel E. Wood, 1993, Boston: Allyn & Bacon. Copyright © 1993 by Allyn & Bacon. Reprinted with permission.

Unlike the Stanford-Binet, Wechsler's test showed differences between the scores of men and women; women scored higher on the verbal subtests, and men scored higher on the performance subtests. Although the combined scores on the Wechsler tests do not show gender contrasts, the subtest scores always have. These differences parallel the bias in men's estimates of their own intelligence, which stem from men's estimation of their spatial and mathematical abilities as higher than women's (Rammstedt & Rammsayer, 2002). This bias applies more strongly to men who rated themselves as more masculine; these men rated their spatial and mathematical reasoning higher than women's abilities. But the same men also rated themselves lower in musical ability than women. These results fall in line with stereotypes of abilities, as do results that indicate men judged themselves higher in intellectual ability but lower in social and emotional intelligence than women (Petrides, Furnham, & Martin, 2004; von Stumm et al., 2009). Thus, Wechsler subtests and self-estimates conform to gender stereotypes of abilities.

Similarly, Eleanor Maccoby and Carol Jacklin's (1974) review of gender differences in intellectual performance found differences on verbal, mathematical, and spatial tasks that were consistent with stereotypes. More recent research, however, has revealed that the patterns of gender differences in these cognitive abilities are smaller yet more complex than the early reviews suggested.

Part of the complexity comes from the tests used to assess these various cognitive abilities. The term *abilities* is somewhat inaccurate, because the assessments have been tests of performance or achievement, such as the Scholastic Assessment Test (SAT, which was formerly called the Scholastic Aptitude Test), a test used for college admissions. Such tests do not measure innate abilities, so findings of gender differences do not necessarily mean that women and men are inherently different in what these tests measure. Rather, variations imply only different levels of current performance; generalizations to innate ability are incorrect. Differences in performance might come from distinct biological endowment, but could also come from social roles, parental encouragement, school courses, leisure activities, or motivation to perform well on the test.

Verbal Performance

The tasks that researchers have used to study verbal ability include not only the verbal subtests of the Wechsler tests but also a great variety of tests related to language, reading, and writing (see Table 7.1 on page 156). This variation may be one reason why research on verbal performance has not yielded entirely consistent results (Sanders, Sjodin, & de Chastelaine, 2002). When taking the variety of verbal tasks into account, literature reviews (Halpern, 2000; Maccoby & Jacklin, 1974) have come to the conclusion that girls and women have some advantages in verbal performance. These advantages include the rapidity and proficiency with which girls acquire language compared to boys, an advantage that girls maintain throughout elementary school. The National Assessment of Educational Progress tests the achievement of a representative sample of students in 4th, 8th, and 12th grades and shows an advantage in reading and writing for girls at all of these grade levels (Coley, 2001). The advantage in writing ability is large and persists throughout college (Halpern et al., 2007; Willingham, Cole, Lewis, & Leung, 1997).

One gender stereotype of women's verbal behavior is not correct: Women do not talk more than men. Two studies (Leaper & Ayres, 2007; Mehl, Vazire, Ramirez-Esparza,

TABLE 7.1 *Examples of Different Measures of Verbal, Quantitative, and Spatial Abilities*

Verbal	Quantitative	Spatial
Vocalizations during infancy	Pointing to a member of a set	Reproducing geometric forms
Visual-motor association	Estimating proportion	Matching geometric shapes
Talking to mother	WISC arithmetic subtest	Reading maps
Verbalization in free play	Digit-processing task	Matching photos for orientation
Parents' reports of speech problems	Digit-symbol subtest of WAIS	Distance perception
Complete sentences	Math achievement	Assembling puzzles
Anagram task	Math reasoning	Rotating shapes
Carrying out simple and complex tasks	Problem solving	Reproducing patterns
Judgment of grammatical sentences	Addition	Disembedding figures
Verbal imitation	Subtraction	Angle matching
Verbal reproduction of story	Arithmetic computation	Maze performance
Reading speed	Number arrangement	Localization of a spatial target
Reading vocabulary	Math subtests for SAT	Discrimination of triangles and
Reading comprehension	General Aptitude Test Battery	mirror-image reversals
Errors in similes	ACT	Distinguishing right from left, east from
Spelling		west, and top from bottom
Punctuation		Rod-and-frame task
Synonyms and antonyms		Matching pictures to objects
Verbal subtests from:		Seguin Form Board
Peabody Picture Vocabulary		Spatial subtests from:
Illinois Test of Psycholinguistic		Differential Aptitude Test
Ability		General Aptitude Test Battery
Expressive Vocabulary Inventory		Piaget's water-level task
WISC		Making judgments about moving
		objects
		WISC Block Design

Source: Adapted from *The Psychology of Sex Differences* (pp. 76–97), by Eleanor Maccoby and Carol Jacklin, 1974. Stanford, CA: Stanford University Press. Adapted by permission of Stanford University Press.

Statcher, & Pennebaker, 2007) have evaluated speaking behavior in women and men and found no significant difference in the number of words uttered each day.

Meta-analysis is a statistical technique that combines the results from many studies to estimate the size of certain effects, and this technique offers advantages over the literature review approach. Janet Hyde has completed several meta-analyses, one including the studies from Maccoby and Jacklin's (1974) literature review (Hyde, 1981) and a later one examining additional studies (Hyde & Lin, 1988). The results of these meta-analyses revealed gender-related differences in verbal performance are small; about 1% of the difference in verbal ability relates to gender, leaving the other 99% related to other factors. A later analysis of many meta-analyses (Hyde, 2005a) confirmed that, despite the stereotype, verbal abilities of women and men are quite similar. The differences exist in writing—women write more quickly and fluently—and in language development—girls develop language earlier than boys, but boys catch up (Wallentin, 2009).

Mathematical and Quantitative Performance

Research on mathematical and quantitative performance presents a complex picture in which changes during adolescence, patterns of course selection, and attitudes toward math make the assessment of underlying ability impossible. Most studies with children younger than age 13 show either no gender differences or certain advantages for girls in mathematical performance, defined as proficiency in arithmetic computation (Fennema, 1980; Hyde, Fennema, & Lamon, 1990). By age 13, gender differences favoring boys begin to appear in many of the assessments of mathematical performance (Spelke, 2005). Girls who excel at arithmetic computation do not become women who are poor at such tasks; the difference in performance arises from the assessments for what constitutes mathematical and quantitative performance. Rather than consist of arithmetic computation, the tests of quantitative ability during the middle and high school years begin to include tasks that draw on a variety of cognitive abilities, as Table 7.1 shows.

Despite the stereotype that girls and women do more poorly in mathematics than boys and men, research indicates little difference in performance (Leahey & Guo, 2001; Hyde, 2005a). For example, examining scores from standardized tests administered to the population of 12th-grade high school students, no gender differences appear (Willingham et al., 1997). However, for scores on standardized tests such as the mathematics section of the SAT (SAT-M) and the quantitative test of the Graduate Record Examination (GRE), men score higher than women (Gallagher, Levin, & Cahalan, 2002). Using the technique of meta-analysis to evaluate many studies of mathematics performance, men's scores were slightly higher than women's (Hyde, 1981, 2005b). Thus, some measures of mathematics performance indicate an advantage for women, some show an advantage for men, and yet others suggest no advantage either way. These seemingly contradictory findings are the result of different measures of quantitative performance.

Analyzing quantitative abilities into different skills and ages reveals a complex pattern related to gender (Hyde, Fennema, & Lamon, 1990; Spelke, 2005). Girls and women have a small advantage in math computation, which draws on their better abilities to rapidly retrieve information from memory (Camarata & Woodcock, 2006; Halpern, 2004). By the 10th grade, boys begin to show an advantage (Leahey & Guo, 2001), possibly because some math problems draw on spatial skills, in which boys tend to excel. By 12th grade, boys' scores exceed girls' scores by about 1%, which represents a very small difference. Boys' advantage is largest for geometry, which is consistent with the view that spatial skills are important in this area. Table 7.2 (page 158) summarizes the findings on math performance.

A large gender difference in higher-level mathematics appeared in several studies, showing that, in selected groups of mathematically gifted students, males have a large advantage over females (Benbow & Stanley, 1980, 1983). In early studies, boys outnumbered girls by over 12 to 1, but those ratios have changed. Programs that recruit mathematically talented students now find about twice as many boys as girls (Spelke, 2005).

As the disproportionate number of boys gifted in mathematics suggests, the variation in mathematical performance is not uniform for women and men. Men's performance shows more variability than women's performance (Lehre, Lehre, Laake, & Denbolt, 2009; Lubinski & Benbow, 2007). That is, men are more likely to score in the upper *and* lower ends of the performance distribution than women are. More men exhibit mathematical deficits than women, but men are also more likely to be more numerous in the upper range of these abilities, as the studies of talented adolescents in the United States demonstrate. This

TABLE 7.2   *Gender-Related Differences in Mathematics Performance*

Mathematics Skill	Group	Advantage
Arithmetic computation	Elementary school students	Girls
Math concepts	Elementary school students	Girls
Problem solving	Middle school students	No difference
SAT Mathematics subtest	13-year-old gifted students	Boys
Math concepts	High school students	Boys
Problem solving	High school students	Boys
SAT Mathematics subtest	College-bound students	Boys
Advanced Placement Calculus test	College-bound students	Boys
Numerical Ability subtest of DAT	Grades 8–12	No difference
Math performance	Representative group of 12th-grade students	No difference
Mathematics subtest of GRE	College students	Men
Arithmetic computation	Adults in general population	Women
Math performance	Adults in general population	No difference

variability, however, is not universal and fails to appear in some cultures in which girls are more common in the upper end of the distribution of math performance (Penner, 2008a).

The classification of students as mathematically gifted often involves a standardized test, and this type of test has been part of the controversy related to gender differences in math performance. Some standardized tests have consistently revealed a male advantage, including the mathematics subtests from the SAT and the Preliminary Scholastic Assessment Test (PSAT), the quantitative section of the Graduate Record Examination (GRE), and the Advanced Placement Program calculus exam (Spelke & Grace, 2007; Willingham et al., 1997). The gender-related differences in performance on these tests demonstrate a variety of influences, including the possibility that the selection of test items and test format give advantages to men that are not really related to mathematics ability (Spelke, 2005). For example, men do better than women on multiple-choice format tests and on tests with time limits (Willingham & Cole, 1997). Both characteristics are common to the mathematics tests that show a male advantage but have no relationship to math ability.

For as long as the Educational Testing Service (ETS) has collected information on gender, the Mathematics section of the SAT has shown substantial differences, even

◼ GENDERED VOICES

Math Class Is Tough

"Math class is tough," according to Teen Talk Barbie, introduced by the Mattel Toy Company in 1992. Teen Talk Barbie was the company's second talking Barbie, but this particular phrase unleashed a furor. Many women and women's groups protested the perpetuation of the idea that women find math more difficult than men do; they feared that this popular toy's proclamation would reinforce and perpetuate the stereotype that math is not for girls. Mattel soon dropped that phrase from Barbie's repertoire (Smith & White, 2002).

among young women whose math grades are equal to or better than young men's grades (Gallagher et al., 2002). Indeed, the SAT "overpredicts" men's grades in college math classes; that is, men's grades are not as high as the test scores predict they will be (Spelke, 2005). Likewise, the test "underpredicts" women's college math grades; women's grades are higher than the tests predict. Indeed, women's grades are higher than men's grades in the same college math classes. Thus the SAT Mathematics section fails to achieve its stated purpose—to predict college grades accurately (Spelke & Grace, 2007).

The bias in the SAT has several implications. First, as the Educational Testing Service advises, colleges should not rely on the SAT alone for decisions about entrance and scholarships. Indeed, a growing number of colleges and universities have gone a step further, eliminating the SAT as part of their admissions criteria (FairTest *Examiner,* 2006). Second, researchers must accept that they cannot use the SAT as a standard for assessing mathematics ability (Spelke & Grace, 2007). The evidence of its bias makes it unsuitable for this purpose.

What, then, are the gender differences in quantitative ability and performance? Gender differences in attitudes toward math and motivation to pursue mathematics play a role in women's and men's quantitative experiences. Elementary school students do not perceive math as a male domain (Heyman & Legare, 2004), but mathematically gifted middle school students (especially boys) expressed beliefs that men were more naturally talented at math than women, and so did their parents and teachers (Leedy, LaLonde, & Runk, 2003). These perceptions lead to the acceptance of math as a male domain (Kimball, 1995;

Despite the stereotype of math as a male domain, high school girls now enroll in as many math courses as high school boys.

Nosek, Banaji, & Greenwald, 2002). Both children and parents share this cultural perception, resulting in differential beliefs concerning boys' and girls' math abilities. When girls
are good at math, they are more often the target of bullying than boys (although being a
math "nerd" places both at risk for bullying; Boehnke, 2008).

Individuals who hold the belief that accomplishments originate from natural talent
rather than from work tend to experience doubts in their abilities and loss of confidence and
motivation when they encounter difficulties, and this tendency applies to girls more strongly
than to boys (Dweck, 2007). This attitude may play a critical role in not only the motivation
to pursue mathematics but other academic performance as well.

Girls' perception that math is a male domain may lead them to believe that they are
unlikely to succeed in the subject and to perceive that math is not important or valuable to
them (Eccles, 1987, 2007). The combined lack of confidence and the belief that math is
not important to their future form a powerful disincentive for girls during high school,
when they have the option to choose elective math courses. Until the 1990s, girls enrolled
in fewer math courses than boys, but that situation changed, and enrollment is now similar
(Spelke, 2005).

Janis Jacobs and Jacquelynne Eccles (1992) proposed and validated a model for the
gender-related factors that influence self-perceptions about abilities, including math ability.
Figure 7.2 presents that model, and an examination of that figure reveals that several factors
are important. One is biological sex, which affects children's beliefs about their abilities.
Another component is gender stereotypes and an interaction of sex with gender stereotyping, such as the stereotype that math is a male domain. Research indicated that accepting this
stereotype predicted college women's changing career plans and leaving academic fields that
require mathematics (Schmader, Johns, & Barquissau, 2004). A longitudinal analysis of career choices in young women (Eccles, 2007) showed that, consistent with the model, expectations for success and the value of taking courses mediated enrollment.

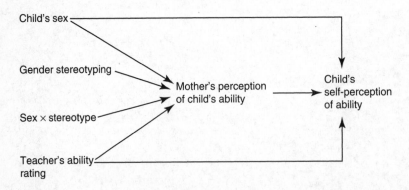

FIGURE 7.2   *Path of Influence for Perception of Abilities*

Source: Adapted from "The Impact of Mothers' Gender-Role Stereotypic Beliefs on
Mothers' and Children's Ability Perceptions," by Janis E. Jacobs and Jacquelynne S.
Eccles, 1992, *Journal of Personality and Social Psychology, 63,* p. 935. Copyright
1992 by American Psychological Association. Adapted by permission of Janis E.
Jacobs and the American Psychological Association.

GENDERED VOICES

The Problem with Being Good at Math

Cornelia Dean, science editor for *The New York Times*, recounted her experience with what it's like to be a girl in junior high school who is good at math (Dean, 2005). Dean reported that when she was in the 7th grade, she was enrolled in an experimental school for "brainiacs," in which all the students took a mathematics aptitude test. Her results and her classmates' reactions changed her life: "The results were posted and everyone found out I had scored several years ahead of the next brightest kid. A girl really good in math! What a freak! I resolved then and there on a career in journalism" (Dean, 2005, p. F3).

Beliefs about competence may not be the only problem in encouraging girls to pursue mathematics; some evidence (Jacobs, Davis-Kean, Bleeker, Eccles, & Malanchuk, 2005) indicates that girls may have the talent but not the interest in studying math. Indeed, a survey of children from around the world (Sanchez, Zimmerman, & Ye, 2004) revealed that high school students in the United States tend to think that mathematics is difficult and not all that interesting. Girls expressed these opinions more strongly than boys. In addition, girls with high proficiency in math tend to do well in verbal performance as well (Ceci, Williams, & Barnett, 2009). This combination gives these girls the ability to pursue a variety of careers, not only mathematics. Thus, motivating girls to pursue math is a challenge, and parents and teachers do not pressure girls and boys equally to pursue the study of mathematics. Without these sources of social support to study math, girls choose not to do so in larger numbers than boys.

In summary, gender-related differences in mathematics performance do not exist in the general population, and the stereotype of math as a male domain is not based on performance. Among students, girls and boys do not differ in mathematics performance until high school. At this time, boys begin to show higher average levels of math performance on standardized tests and confidence in their ability at math. These differences persist throughout adulthood. The stereotype of math as a male domain lingers, affecting girls, boys, parents, and teachers to give contrasting encouragement to girls and boys. Despite the disappearing performance differences between boys and girls in math classes and on some standardized tests, encouraging girls to pursue mathematics remains a challenge.

Spatial Performance

Variation has existed in the definitions of verbal ability and quantitative ability, but researchers have defined spatial ability in an even wider variety of ways. Table 7.1 includes some of these definitions. Any of these tasks represents a reasonable way to measure the concept of spatial abilities, but they vary sufficiently to yield results that may not be consistent from study to study. The variations in the definition of what constitutes spatial ability have not hindered many people from accepting the notion that men are better at these tasks than women.

Despite some disagreement over how to categorize spatial abilities (Voyer, Voyer, & Bryden, 1995), a four-category approach captures some of the complexity of the area. Three categories include spatial perception, mental rotation, and spatial visualization (Linn & Petersen, 1986); a fourth type of spatial task is spatiotemporal or targeting ability. **Spatial perception** includes the ability to identify and locate the horizontal or vertical planes in the presence of distracting information. Examples of measures of spatial perception are the rod-and-frame task and Piaget's water-level task, both shown in Figure 7.3. These tasks usually show gender-related differences, with boys and men outperforming girls and women. The magnitude of this variation is small during childhood and adolescence, but fairly large for adults.

Mental rotation includes the ability to visualize objects as they would appear if rotated in space. An example of a measure of this type of ability also appears in Figure 7.3. The gender-related difference for this spatial ability is fairly large, with boys and men scoring substantially higher than girls and women on speed and accuracy of mentally rotating objects (Hyde, 2005a; Voyer et al., 1995).

Spatial visualization refers to the ability to process spatial information so as to understand the relationship between objects in space, such as the ability to see a figure embedded in other figures (also shown in Figure 7.3), find hidden figures in a drawing or picture, or imagine the shape produced when a folded piece of paper is cut and then unfolded. Gender distinctions do not always appear on measures of these tasks. When such differences appear, men show a small advantage.

A fourth category of spatial ability is called **spatiotemporal ability** (Halpern, 2000). This ability involves judgments about moving objects in space, such as predicting when a moving object will arrive at a target or aiming and throwing. This spatial ability has been less researched than the others. Some research on this ability indicated that men's ability is higher than women's, but other research (Barral & Debû, 2004) found that women were more accurate (but slower) than men in aiming and throwing.

An additional complication in assessing gender differences in spatial ability comes from the possibility that some tasks labeled "spatial" may include other components. For example, men performed better than women on a paper-and-pencil version of a mental rotation task, but the differences were reduced (Monahan, Harke, & Shelley, 2008) or eliminated (Parsons et al., 2004) in a computerized, virtual reality version of the mental rotation task. Gender role and expectancy influenced women's performance on an embedded figures test; highly feminine women did better when the task was presented as an empathy test, but more masculine women did better when the same task was described as a spatial ability task (Massa, Mayer, & Bohon, 2005). Similarly, the male advantage on the rod-and-frame task disappeared when a human figure replaced the rod and the task was presented as a measure of empathy (Naditch, in Caplan, MacPherson, & Tobin, 1985). In this situation, women outperformed men. Altering the expectations for the task changed performance in these two studies, even though the tasks remained the same and required the same spatial abilities. Thus, what researchers define as measures of spatial ability may include other components.

Several research findings provide evidence against a simple conclusion for a male advantage on spatial tasks, including findings that women show an advantage on some

Mental rotation
Which figure on the right is identical to the figure in the box?

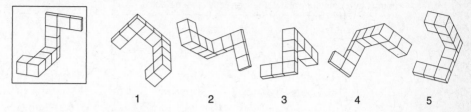

| 1 | 2 | 3 | 4 | 5 |

Piaget's water-level problem
This glass is half filled with water. Draw a line across the glass to indicate the top of the water line.

Rod-and-frame test
Ignore the orientation of the frame and adjust the position of the rod so that it is vertical.

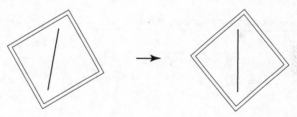

Disembedding
Find the simple figure on the left embedded in one of the four more complex figures on the right.

FIGURE 7.3 *Spatial Tasks Favoring Men*

spatial tasks (Halpern, 2000; Montello, Lovelace, Golledge, & Self, 1999). Women tend to do better on tasks of perceptual speed in which people must rapidly identify matching items. Women also outperform men on tasks in which people must remember the placement of a series of objects (Levy, Frick, & Astur, 2005), especially for recently moved objects

Study the objects in group **A** for one minute and cover it up. Then look at group **B** and put an X through the figures not in the original array. Score one point for each item correctly crossed out, and subtract one point for each item incorrectly crossed out.

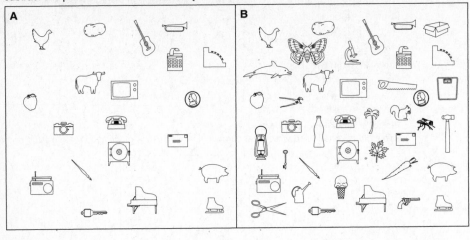

Identification of matching items

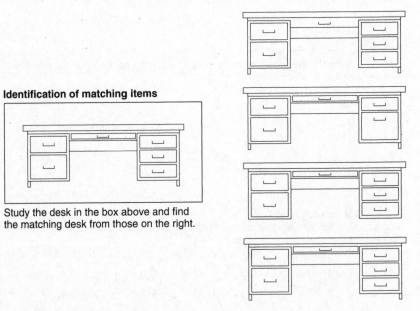

Study the desk in the box above and find the matching desk from those on the right.

FIGURE 7.4 *Spatial Tasks Favoring Women*

(Honda & Nehei, 2009). Examples of these tasks appear in Figure 7.4. An additional complication comes from the finding that gender differences appear in some age groups but not in others, that differences are subject to change with variations in testing procedure, and that gender variations in some spatial abilities seem to be decreasing (Voyer et al., 1995).

These various findings raise the question: Do men really have better spatial abilities than women? The answer is not a simple yes or no. Of the many spatial abilities, men show an advantage in some, and women show an advantage in others. Men in the United States produce reliably better scores than women in spatial perception, such as Piaget's water-level task and a large advantage in mental rotation (Hyde, 2005a). That advantage disappeared when researchers (Ortner & Sieverding, 2008) presented a male stereotype before participants performed a mental rotation task. Training can also decrease this difference (see According to the Media and According to the Research). The embedded figures task has also yielded complex results for gender and ethnic background, suggesting that men have no clear advantage for this measure of spatial ability (Kühnen et al., 2001).

Women's advantage in spatial abilities appears on measures of perceptual speed and on memory for the placement of objects. Therefore, of the gender differences in spatial abilities that exist, a number favor men, a few favor women, and some vary by gender, culture, context, expectation, or some combinations of these factors.

Other Cognitive Abilities

Verbal, mathematical, and spatial abilities are important and have been the subjects of extensive research, but these are only three of many cognitive abilities. Memory, creativity, musical ability, and nonverbal communication are all abilities that have been researched. Gender has rarely been the emphasis of these studies, and much of the research has failed to show gender-related differences. A consideration of these other cognitive abilities is important for perspective on comparisons of gender-related cognitive abilities, because the gender differences in verbal, mathematics, and spatial performance have been given so much attention.

As the headline story for this chapter suggested, one of the persistent stereotypes about men's and women's cognitive abilities is the male advantage in following directions and wayfinding. As the experience of Karen Stabiner (2001) and her husband illustrated, both men and women have developed strategies that allow them to find their way, but those strategies tend to differ by gender. Men are more likely than women to use a strategy that involves orienting to directions and forming an abstract map of the area, whereas women are more likely to use landmarks to find their way (Cherney, Brabec, & Runco, 2008; Nori & Giusberti, 2006). Which of these strategies is best? It depends on the situation. In laboratory situations, such as abstract mazes and virtual reality situations, the directional strategy leads to fewer errors and more rapid problem solution (Malinowski, 2001; Saucier et al., 2002). When allowed to use their preferred strategy in a real-world situation, the gender differences disappear. That is, women are worse at directions only when they are forced to use the strategy that men typically prefer. In terms of women's ability to find their way, they do as well as men (Bosco, Longoni, & Vecchi, 2004). A combination of the two strategies is actually the most effective (Schmitz, 1999).

Memory performance can draw from either verbal or spatial abilities, depending on the type of material. The majority of tasks that psychologists have studied fall into the category of verbal learning and memory. According to Maccoby and Jacklin's (1974) review of research in this area, few gender-related differences exist. However, some studies have found a female advantage for verbal material (Kimura & Clarke, 2002). Some studies have found an advantage for men for visual or spatial material (Herlitz & Rehnman, 2008), but other studies (Lewin, Wolgers, & Herlitz, 2001) have shown no gender differences in this ability.

ACCORDING TO THE MEDIA . . .

Video Games Are for Boys

Popular video games are oriented to boys. Both arcade games and home video games contain primarily male characters, lots of action and violence, and plots attractive to boys and men (St. John, 2002). The websites that promote these video games contain similar content of violence, sexualized depictions of women, and ethnic stereotypes (Robinson, Callister, Clark, & Phillips, 2008).

The most common portrayal of women in video games consists of nothing—literally. Less than 14% of characters in a sample of video games were female (Beasley & Collins Standley, 2002). When women appear in video games, sometimes they are helpless and in need of rescue; sometimes they are evil and need to be conquered. Female characters also appear in the background as supporters of male characters (Dickerman, Christensen, & Kerl-McClain, 2008). Occasionally female characters get to be heroes, but they are cast in the role of female warrior, such as Buffy the Vampire Slayer (Labre & Duke, 2004) and Lara Croft, Tomb Raider (Jansz & Martis,

2007). Regardless of their role, they are often large-breasted and provocatively dressed.

The amount of violence in video games is an area of concern (Dill, Gentile, Richter, & Dill, 2005; Williams, 2003). Early video games tended to depict spaceships and aliens, but human or humanlike characters are now more common. Thus, players have repeated exposure to chasing and doing violence to both male and female characters. In addition, 21% of the games include violence directed specifically toward women. These games give players the opportunity to act within a situation in which women are the designated targets of video violence.

The combination of themes for boys, few female characters, and fewer attractive, powerful female characters makes video games more appealing to boys than to girls. The portrayals of women as victims, targets, or sex objects put girls in the position of seeing unflattering depictions of female characters, choosing from the limited range of games for girls, or avoiding video games altogether.

Some of the gender-related variations in memory seem strongly related to the gender-stereotypical nature of the task and to the match between stereotyping and the gender of the learner. For example, when women and men were asked to memorize a shopping list and directions to a particular place, the differences were in a predictable direction—women better at the shopping list and men at the directions (Herrmann, Crawford, & Holdsworth, 1992). Furthermore, the labeling of the task influenced women's and men's memories. When people heard that the shopping list pertained to groceries, women showed an advantage, but when the same list was described as pertaining to hardware, men's memories were better. An extension of this study (Colley, Ball, Kirby, Harvey, & Vingelen, 2001) demonstrated again that memory performance depended on a combination of the labeling of the task and the gender of the learner rather than the skill of either women or men as learners. Consistent with gender stereotyping, women tend to be better at recalling details of personal appearance (Mast & Hall, 2006). Thus, memory may depend on factors other than ability, with men and women performing according to their attention, interests, and expectations based on stereotypes.

Creativity is a term that researchers have defined in a variety of ways, leading to a great diversity of findings. Studies of kindergarten children (Pollatou, Karadimou, & Gerodimos, 2005), children in grades 4 through 8 (Rejskind, Rapagna, & Gold, 1992), 5th- and 7th-grade students in China and Germany (Shi, Xu, Zhou, & Zha, 1999), college students

ACCORDING TO THE RESEARCH . . .

Video Games Can Improve Spatial Skills

Despite the bad news about video games—violence and sexist portrayals—playing these games may develop boys' cognitive skills, especially spatial performance. That is, boys' enthusiasm for video games may contribute to their advantage in performance on spatial tasks.

Boys play video games more than girls (Marshall, Gorley, & Biddle, 2006; Robinson et al., 2008), and their choice of games also differs. Girls were more common among those classified as "logic and skill players," whereas boys were most common in the category "action and stimulation players" (Quaiser-Pohl, Geiser, & Lehmann, 2006). Individuals in the latter category scored higher on tests of mental rotation, suggesting either that players who are good at this skill select these games or the games develop this skill. Some research suggests the latter possibility—playing video games develops spatial performance.

Several studies have trained participants using video games to determine the benefit for boosting spatial performance (Cherney, 2008; Feng, Spence, & Pratt, 2007). The results indicate that gaming increases performance for both males and females, with women's performance boosted more than men's. In addition, the spatial ability that increases most is the one on which women's scores are lowest—mental rotation. Even minimal practice can prompt significant improvement.

The design and marketing of video games for boys puts girls at a double disadvantage. Girls may find these games unattractive and avoid this type of activity. Boys have a greater incentive to participate in activities that boost skills on which they already have higher performance, whereas girls have lower motivation to play video games that could improve their spatial skills. However, there is some good news: Improvements in spatial performance are also possible through other types of computer use (Terlecki & Newcombe, 2005) and even other types of spatial activities, such as music, visual art, and athletics (Ginn & Pickens, 2005). Thus, girls have several ways that they can gain experiences that may improve their performance on spatial tasks.

(Goldsmith & Matherly, 1988), and adults in the Canary Islands (Matud, Rodríguez, & Grand, 2007) have failed to show gender-related differences in various types of creativity. In a wide-scale review of research on creativity (Baer, 2008), few gender differences appeared; measures of creativity, self-assessments of creativity, and judgments of the creative products of males and females of various ages fail to show marked gender differences.

When researchers define creativity in terms of achievement, the gender differences are large. Men's advantage, however, may not be due to greater creative ability but rather to access to training, parental and societal encouragement, and limited acceptance of women in creative fields (Baer, 2008). A study of women who have become successful musicians (Stremikis, 2002) showed that these women focused on professional success, often from young ages, and conformed less to gender stereotypes than did women who have not pursued such careers. If gifted girls were encouraged to devote themselves to their talents in the same ways that boys are encouraged, the gender differences would be smaller.

Nonverbal communication includes a variety of behaviors related to conveying and receiving information through gestures, body position, and facial expressions, and some gender differences exist in both expressing and interpreting nonverbal behaviors (Hall, Coats, & Lebeau, 2005). Women are more likely than men to make and keep eye contact and touch themselves. In addition, their facial expressions are more revealing of their emotions (Thunberg & Dimberg, 2000). One large contrast is women's tendency to

GENDERED VOICES

It's Not Something on the Y Chromosome

"I don't think that it's something on the Y chromosome," a 13-year-old girl said, referring to the ability to play percussion. "But some boys act like it is. The boys in the school band are used to me because I've played percussion all through junior high school with them, but when I go to competitions, the boys act like I shouldn't be playing percussion. Almost like it's an insult that a girl should be playing."

She explained that lots of girls play in the school band. There is generally no prejudice against girls who are musicians, but the band is gender segregated by musical instrument. The instruments toward the front of

the band are more "feminine," such as violins, clarinets, and cellos. The instruments toward the back are more "masculine," such as tubas and the percussion instruments: "There are lots more girls toward the front of the band, and the boys dominate the back.

"At the all-city band competition, it was especially bad. The boys who played percussion were especially obnoxious, acting like I shouldn't be trying. They acted like it was their right as boys to be able to play drums or other percussion—like there was something on the Y chromosome that gave them the gift. Well, I guess they were really surprised when I won."

smile; women smile more often than men do (LaFrance, Hecht, & Levy Paluck, 2003). This tendency may not reveal more pleasant moods for women. Rather, smiling may reflect their subordinate status.

Indeed, gender differences in nonverbal behavior may relate to power and status. Early research by Sara Snodgrass (1985, 1992) showed that no gender distinctions existed in the ability to read cues of people's motives, feelings, and wishes. Instead, she found that people in subordinate positions were better at reading the nonverbal behaviors of those in dominant positions. Later research (Snodgrass, Hecht, & Ploutz-Snyder, 1998) explored the possibility that those in dominant positions send better cues, which leads those in subordinate positions to interpret the situation better. These findings suggest that gender is not a direct factor in interpreting nonverbal behavior; status is more important. Other research (Hall et al., 2005) has confirmed the importance of status and power in various types of nonverbal behaviors and the relationship of gender to many measures of status and power.

Although the gender differences are small in verbal, mathematical, and spatial abilities, variations are even smaller or nonexistent in other cognitive abilities such as memory, creativity, musical ability, and nonverbal communication. The studies that have revealed gender-related differences in performance in these areas have shown that they come from stereotypes, gender roles, and expectations rather than from ability differences.

Source of the Differences

If stereotypes, roles, and expectations shape performance on aptitude and achievement tests, then are these factors the source of differences between men and women? Does biology play no role in the gender distinctions in cognitive performance? The possibility that cognitive gender differences can be traced to biology appeals to many people, possibly because it offers a simple answer to many complex questions. The tendency to resort to biological essentialism is strong in the media (Brescoll & Lafrance, 2004), which affects people's acceptance of such explanations. In the headline article for this chapter, Stabiner (2001) claimed that the gender differences in wayfinding are "hardwired." This view has prompted theories and research concerning the source of gender differences in cognitive performance.

Biological Evidence for Gender Differences in Cognitive Abilities

Several theories have proposed a biological basis for gender differences in cognitive abilities. These theories concentrate on genes, hormones, or structural variations in the brain that create functional differences in cognition. One biologically based view emphasizes the role of evolution, which has built different brains for men and women (Silverman, Choi, & Peters, 2007). Following this explanation, distinct role demands of men and women in the hunter–gatherer societies of prehistory posed different task demands and resulted in different brain organization. Thus, men should be better at spatial tasks because their evolutionary history included traveling to hunt, whereas women stayed home; women should be better at verbal tasks because they talked to their children. Although the logic of these stories may be appealing, these speculations are impossible to confirm or disconfirm; those early societies are gone and can no longer be observed.

Also, alternative stories make as much sense. For example, more remote periods in prehistory when prehumans were tree dwellers would present similar selection pressures for spatial abilities for both females and males (Benderly, 1987). For example, poor spatial abilities would result in falling out of trees, which would not be conducive to survival and reproduction. Humans are the product of evolutionary history, but the strategy of hypothesizing which evolutionary pressures resulted in what types of cognitive abilities has many possible versions and no way of confirming these hypotheses (Bleie, 2003; Newcombe, 2007). Thus, this view is not useful as a scientific explanation.

Another biologically based theory relies on the role of prenatal testosterone exposure on brain development. Recall from Chapter 4 that, beginning at about 6 weeks in prenatal development, male fetuses begin to produce androgens that exert masculinizing effects. These androgens have the potential to affect the developing nervous system, perhaps producing changes in the structure and function of the brain. Examining the function of the brains of women exposed to prenatal androgens should provide one test of this hypothesis. Studies of these girls have not always indicated enhanced spatial performance (Malouf, Migeon, Carson, Petrucci, & Wisniewski, 2006), but a meta-analysis (Puts, McDaniel, Jordan, & Breedlove, 2008) showed an advantage. Another study (Mueller et al., 2008) suggested that girls with a more severe form of the disorder (and thus greater testosterone exposure) were the ones whose spatial performance was increased. These results implicate testosterone exposure during brain development as a factor in spatial performance, but a study that measured hormone levels in men and women (Halari et al., 2005) found no relationship to spatial or verbal performance. Thus, exposure to testosterone during prenatal development may exert effects that influence adult performance, but hormonal levels during adulthood may not underlie gender differences in cognitive performance.

Another strategy for studying sex differences in cognition involves using brain imaging technology to determine whether women's and men's brains function differently while performing cognitive tasks. This strategy makes use of brain imaging technology such as positron emission tomography (PET) and functional magnetic resonance imaging (fMRI), which can detect metabolic changes in the brain that accompany heightened neural activity (Pinel, 2009). This approach allows researchers to determine the similarities and differences in the function (rather than the structure) of female and male brains during varying cognitive tasks.

Several studies using brain imaging have found the expected (and some unexpected) variations in brain processing during cognitive tasks. The expected findings include greater activity in the left hemisphere during verbal performance and greater activity in the right hemisphere during spatial tasks. In addition, these studies have shown some distinctions in the activation patterns of men's and women's brains. For example, women's brains showed a higher level of metabolic activity than men's brains during a verbal memory task (Ragland, Coleman, Gur, Glahn, & Gur, 2000), and the difference related to better performance. Unexpectedly, men's performance was equal to women's on a working memory task, but men's brains showed a higher level of activation during the task (Bell, Willson, Wilman, Dave, & Peterson, 2006). Both men's and women's left hemispheres were more active during a verbal task (Baxter et al., 2003), but women's right hemispheres were also active during this task. In a comparison of brain activation during a verbal and a spatial task (Gur et al., 2000), the expected differences appeared in both women and men, but other, unexpected areas of the brain were also active, including left hemisphere activation for women when they performed the spatial task.

Do such results suggest that men and women use their brains differently? Possibly, but the studies also tend to show that the patterns of activation are more similar than not and that some male or female brains do not react in the pattern that is typical for their sex. These results present a complex picture of brain function, which is summarized in Table 7.3. However, as brain researcher Ruben Gur and his colleagues (1995, p. 531) commented, "the brains of men and women are fundamentally more similar than different."

Researchers have concentrated on gender differences to try to understand the intricacies of how brains function. Many of these research projects have become headlines that have sensationalized small distinctions, leaving people with the impression that hormones or brain structures produce large, important gender differences in cognition. The evidence

TABLE 7.3   *Patterns of Brain Activation in Women and Men during Various Tasks*

Type of Task	Activation Pattern	Activation Occurs in	Performance Advantage
Verbal memory	Higher brain metabolic activity	Women	Yes
Verbal task	Left hemisphere more active	Both	No
	Right hemisphere active	Women	No
Spatial task	Right hemisphere more active	Both	No
	Left hemisphere active	Women	No
Verbal rhyming task	Left hemisphere active	Both	No
	Right hemisphere active	Women	No
Mental rotation	Activation in three lobes of cerebral cortex	Both	No
Working memory	Right hemisphere more active	Men	No

indicates that, under some circumstances, men's and women's brains (on the average) function differently. The variation from person to person is much larger than the contrast between women and men. However, the research indicates that hormonal and functional brain differences influence cognitive performance in men and women.

Evidence for Other Sources of Gender Differences

Although many people have a tendency to think in terms of either biological or environmental influences, almost all researchers accept that both contribute to cognitive performance. Furthermore, separating biological from environmental factors is virtually impossible. Therefore, the list is extensive for other sources of gender differences in cognitive performance.

Training and experience play an obvious role in cognitive performance. An example of this effect appeared in a study of spatial performance in secondary school students (Tlauka, Williams, & Williamson, 2008) that examined differences not only among boys and girls but among individuals in each group. The results indicated that students who participated in physical education showed better spatial performance than those who did not. A second study (Roberts & Bell, 2000) showed that men's advantage on a spatial task disappeared when the women in the study were allowed to familiarize themselves with the computer that was part of the study before they performed the mental rotation task. Another study (Scali, Brownlow, & Hicks, 2000) suggested that the gender difference in spatial task performance could be erased by the directions that researchers give to participants. When these researchers told the participants that accuracy was very important, gender differences appeared, but other instructions failed to produce the expected male advantage. All of these studies suggest that performance on spatial tasks—the type of task on which the largest gender difference appears—can change with experience and with instructions.

Another environmental factor that is capable of affecting cognitive performance is *stereotype threat,* a term originated by Claude Steele (Steele & Aronson, 1995). As discussed in Chapter 3, stereotype threat describes situations in which the presence of negative stereotypes affects the performance of those to whom the stereotype applies. Many studies have indicated that stereotype threat is a factor in women's poorer performance in mathematics, but the effect applies to a wide variety of situations. For example, the performance of college women was worse on a math test when they heard that men do better on this type of test, but men's performance declined when they heard that Asians outperform Whites (Smith & White, 2002). Stereotype threat also applies to performance on a mental rotation task (Burns, Peterson, Bass, & Pascoe, 2002), and women with a feminine gender role orientation performed more poorly on a spatial task when the task was described as a spatial task than when the same task was presented as an empathy task (Massa et al., 2005). However, women's performance on a mental rotation task increased when they were reminded of their status at the selective, private school they attended (McGlone & Aronson, 2006).

Therefore, in addition to the biological factors that affect performance on cognitive tasks, a variety of experiences, instructions, and expectations also contribute. These factors form a complex interaction with biological factors influencing behavior and behavior influencing biology (Halpern, 2004). In addition, the factors that influence academic choices are critically important. Choices are rooted in a cultural setting influenced by gender roles and stereotypes, parental pressure, and teacher perception. Refer to Figure 7.2, which illustrates a model that captures the influences on self-perception of abilities. These perceptions affect the choices that may lead to very different paths for girls and boys.

Implications of Gender-Related Differences

As reviewed in previous sections of this chapter, gender-related differences in cognitive performance are small. These small differences should mean equally small differences in scholastic and occupational achievement for which these abilities are required, as well as small differences in confidence in mental abilities. Instead, there are large contrasts in the choices that men and women make concerning careers and also in their confidence in their abilities. These choices and levels of confidence may be mediated through social beliefs about the abilities of men and women. People's behavior may be more closely related to their images of what men and women can do than to what women and men actually do.

Misunderstandings of gender research have contributed to these images. Hyde (2005b) has discussed the ways in which research on gender-related cognitive differences has led to erroneous beliefs about these abilities. Her meta-analyses have been important in demonstrating that the magnitude of these distinctions is small and appear to be decreasing. These small differences mean that a factor, such as gender, that accounts for 1% of the variance in an ability leaves 99% of the difference in that ability due to other factors. Figure 7.5 presents two distributions of scores that have a 99% overlap, leaving a 1% difference. This figure shows how similar the two distributions are. If 1% of the variance in verbal ability were due to gender, we would not know much about any specific person's verbal ability by knowing that person's gender, because too much variation in verbal ability would be due to other factors.

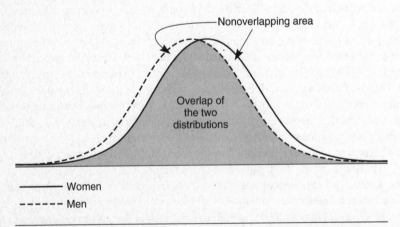

FIGURE 7.5   *An Example of Two Distributions with 99% Overlap*

Note: This distribution represents differences similar to those for verbal ability in men and women.

Stereotypes based on gender differences in these cognitive abilities will lead to incorrect conclusions about the abilities of men and women, because women and men vary more from one person to another than from one gender to another. With only a small percentage of the variance attributable to gender, individual differences overwhelm any gender difference.

Even small differences can have larger implications, as one computer simulation study (Martell, Lane, & Emrich, 1996) showed. Researchers created an organization with eight levels. A computer algorithm then simulated promotion based on ability within this hypothetical organization, with a 5% and a 1% difference in ability (with women having less ability than men, of course). With an initially equal number of women and men in the hypothetical workforce, the simulation resulted in 35% of the top-level jobs going to women (for the 1% deficit). When women were given a 5% deficit in ability, they ended up in 29% of the top-level positions.

Does this simulation mirror workplace situations? Probably not. Few cognitive abilities show as much as a 5% difference between women and men, mental rotation being an exception. Mental rotation shows about a 9% difference, which is enough to make a sizable difference for any occupation that relies entirely on mental rotation. However, no occupation relies entirely on one mental ability, and many factors contribute to workplace success (Valian, 2007). The simulation also varied from actual employment situations in another respect: An equal number of men and women were hired, which is true of almost no occupation. The selection factors begin years prior to employment and result in a much greater gender inequality in most occupations than in this simulation. For example, consider the gender gap in engineering and in fashion design—engineering is male dominated, whereas fashion design is female dominated. Both require a high degree of spatial abilities; indeed, a study of college students (Esgate & Flynn, 2005) indicated that students in fashion design showed the highest average levels of spatial abilities of any group of college majors. Thus, ability is often not the most important selection factor that operates to produce gender differences in employment or careers.

People's beliefs allow small distinctions in cognitive abilities to have a large impact. When parents, teachers, and children come to accept that boys are better at math than girls, this acceptance leads to differential expectations for math achievement. Even when achievement is similar, parents have different beliefs about the underlying reasons. Parents in the United States (Yee & Eccles, 1988) and in Finland (Räty, Vänshä, Kasanen, & Kärkkäinen, 2002) explained the mathematics success of their sons in terms of natural talent and their daughters in terms of hard work. The belief that math achievement is due to a "gift" for the topic is a dangerous one, leading teachers, parents, children, and the general public to judge who should pursue the subject and the careers that rely on math (Dweck, 2007). These beliefs affect the attitudes that individuals hold concerning their abilities and the choices that girls and boys make concerning their elective math courses, which may create lifelong consequences for attitudes toward the subject as well as career options. Although the gender-related differences in cognitive abilities are small, people throughout society largely accept these differences, which magnifies the differences.

In summary, meta-analysis has shown that the magnitude of gender differences is small for verbal, quantitative, and spatial abilities. Gender differences in these three areas account for between 1% and 5% of the variation, which is smaller than variations from person to person. However, the gender stereotyping of cognitive domains has magnified small differences, thus perpetuating the belief that gender-related differences exist and that there are large contrasts in the abilities of women and men.

Considering Diversity

Most of the studies on cognitive abilities have focused on European Americans in the United States, and many imagine that these results apply to other groups. Cross-cultural research indicates otherwise. Studies on various ethnic groups in the United States and research in other countries have indicated that cognition varies with culture. Indeed, cultural variations may be larger than those related to gender.

Some cultures show patterns of spatial performance similar to those in the United States. For example, males showed better performance than females in Japan, Ecuador, and Ireland (Flaherty, 2005), in Ghana and Norway (Amponsah, 2000), in Kuwait (Alansari, Deregowski, & McGeorge, 2008), and in a world-wide study of 40 countries (Silverman et al., 2007). However, spatial performance varied among the cultures. For example, people in Ecuador scored lower than those in Japan and Ireland (Flaherty, 2005), and students in Japan scored higher than those in Canada (Silverman, Phillips, & Silverman, 1996). Indeed, the women in some cultures scored higher than the men in other countries, indicating that variations exist across cultures even when the pattern of gender differences is similar to that found in the United States.

A program of cross-cultural research on gender differences in spatial perception has revealed large cultural distinctions. One result from the Auca Indians, a Stone Age culture living in the Amazon basin (Pontius, 1997b), revealed a very dissimilar pattern of gender differences in spatial performance from that in the United States. In this culture, the women outperformed the men in block design tasks in which U.S. men have an advantage over women. Boys and girls in northwestern Pakistan perform similarly in spatial abilities. A study of children in eastern Ecuador (Pontius, 1997a) failed to find gender differences in a mental rotation task. A study with Norwegian 6th-grade students (Manger & Eikeland, 1998) also failed to reveal gender differences in spatial visualization. Therefore, a variety of cultures fail to show the gender contrasts typical of those in the United States.

Richard Nisbett (2003) also questioned the universality of gender differences in cognitive processes, concentrating instead on the contrast between Western and Eastern cognitive styles. Nisbett argued that a long tradition of analytic, individualistic thought in Western cultures and a similarly long tradition of holistic, relational thinking in Eastern cultures has produced very distinct ways of thinking. He described studies that demonstrated a tendency among people in China, Japan, and Korea to notice and remember a wider variety of things in a picture, to be more influenced by the context of an event, and to have difficulty in separating the situation from the person. This dependence on situation led to poorer performance on the rod-and-frame test, one of the tests for spatial performance, than that by people in the United States (Ji, Peng, & Nisbett, 2000). A comparison of people from two Western countries (United States and Germany) and two non-Western countries (Russia and Malaysia) supported cross-cultural differences by revealing that the people from Russia and Malaysia had more trouble seeing figures embedded in a drawing (Kühnen et al., 2001). Nisbett (2003) contended that his research has isolated few gender differences that are as large as cultural differences in cognitive processes.

■ Summary

The assessment of intelligence and cognitive abilities has a long history in psychology, dating from the development of the intelligence test. The Stanford-Binet, an early intelligence test, showed no gender differences, but the Wechsler tests revealed advantages on verbal tasks for women and girls and advantages in performance tasks for men and boys.

Assessing gender differences in various types of cognitive performance is complicated by the definition of what the assessments measure, and verbal, mathematics, and spatial performance have all been defined in various ways. Despite the stereotypical views of women's advantage in verbal abilities and men's advantage in mathematics and spatial performance, the research shows a more complex picture. Women and men have advantages and disadvantages in each of these categories, depending on the skill. Individual differences are much more important than gender in each of these cognitive abilities.

The verbal advantage that was once associated with women is not only small but also disappearing, except for performance on writing tasks. Boys and men perform better on some types of standardized mathematics tests, but girls and women make better math grades. Men show an advantage in performing spatial visualization and mental rotation tasks and an occasional advantage on spatial perception tasks, but women show advantages on tasks of perceptual speed and memory for placement of objects. Therefore, any conclusion about a male advantage in spatial ability is overly simplistic.

Other cognitive abilities show no gender-related differences. These abilities include learning and memory, creativity, musical ability, and the ability to read nonverbal cues. Some studies have shown gender differences in these abilities, but these studies have fallen along gender-stereotypical lines. Studies on wayfinding have revealed variations in strategies, with women preferring landmarks and men preferring position orientation. These strategy differences do not give any advantage for success in finding one's way, especially in real-world situations. The differential achievement for men and women in creative arts and music reflects variance in social support and access to these careers rather than contrasts in ability.

Both biological and social theories attempt to explain gender differences in cognitive abilities. The biological theories have focused on prenatal hormone exposure and their effects on developing brain structures. The results from brain imaging studies suggest that gender variations exist in patterns of brain activity, but few differences appear in performance.

Theories that emphasize the social aspects of gender-related cognitive differences hypothesize that biological distinctions become magnified and selected through cultural and experiential processes, producing larger variations in women's and men's choices than in their abilities. Beliefs in ability differences and the choices women and men make have huge implications for their lives.

Studies of other cultures and other ethnic groups have revealed that the advantage for men in mathematics and spatial ability tests may be the result of testing a limited group. White college students in the United States show larger gender differences from other groups around the world. However, cross-cultural research on cognition indicates that cultural influences on thought may be large.

■ Glossary

mental rotation   a subtype of spatial ability that includes the ability to visualize objects as they would appear if rotated in space.

spatial perception   a subtype of spatial ability that includes the ability to identify and locate the horizontal or vertical in the presence of distracting information.

spatial visualization   a subtype of spatial ability that refers to the ability to process spatial information so as to understand the relationship between objects in space, such as the ability to see a figure embedded in other figures, find hidden figures in a drawing or picture, or imagine the shape produced when a folded piece of paper is cut and then unfolded.

spatiotemporal ability   a subtype of spatial ability that involves judgments about moving objects in space, such as making a judgment about when a moving object will arrive at a target.

■ Suggested Readings

Dweck, Carol S. (2007). Is math a gift? Beliefs that put females at risk. In S. J. Ceci & W. M. Williams (Eds.), *Why aren't more women in science: Top researchers debate the evidence* (pp. 47–55). Washington, DC: American Psychological Association.
Dweck's provocative article examines the belief that mathematics achievement is due to talent, the negative effects of this belief, its impact on women, and some possibilities for remedying this situation.

Halpern, Diane F. (2004). A cognitive-process taxonomy for sex differences in cognitive abilities. *Current Directions in Psychological Science, 13,* 135–139.
Halpern proposes an alternative way to look at gender differences in cognition, examining the processes that underlie various broad abilities rather than trying to break down the abilities into specific tasks. She also criticizes simplistic thinking about the roles of nature and nurture in explaining gender differences in cognition.

Hyde, Janet Shibley. (2005). The gender similarities hypothesis. *American Psychologist, 60,* 581–592.
Hyde presents an analysis of all the meta-analyses that have evaluated gender differences and concludes that the evidence supports a hypothesis of gender similarities, not differences. Those findings apply to almost all types of cognitive performance, with the exception of mental rotation, which shows medium to large advantages for men.

Emotion

The tear running down his father's cheek shocked Robert Westover, who had never seen his father cry (Hales, 2005). The occasion for the tear was Robert's graduation from the same Marine Corps boot camp from which his father had graduated. Growing up in a military family as one of four brothers, Robert learned that "Showing emotion is a no-can-do among men" (in Hales, 2005, p. 104). He and his brothers had learned to be loud and competitive, and like other boys, he had learned to choke back any tears and to show no fear.

HEADLINES

Big Boys Don't Cry—And Other Myths About Men and Their Emotions
Reader's Digest, October 2005

There's No Crying in Business
Fortune, October 18, 2004

Like many other men, Robert had trouble communicating his emotions to his wife. He felt that women want men to be emotionally forthcoming but also to be strong. "Women are asking us to perform these incredible emotional gymnastics, and it is messing with our heads. Men don't have a road map or a role model to show us how to be both emotional and strong" (in Hales, 2005, p. 104). Men such as Robert have learned the lessons of the male gender role, which include displaying a restricted range of emotions (Brannon, 1976), but such men have also experienced distress in needing to express emotions they have learned to suppress. They may need to cry yet feel that they should not.

For women, the problem with crying is almost the opposite; women cry in situations that men consider inappropriate. Businessman Stanley Bing (2004) recounted a situation in which a female executive had been humiliated by a male superior and started crying in a business meeting. All the men were both embarrassed and angry—at her (not at the man who bullied her). Bing (2004, p. 352) reported that crying has been "leached out" of boys; "for the most part, men have solved the problem of public crying. Now, having come so far, you women have to do the same." He noted that women have been allowed to cry as an expression of emotion but not permitted to express their anger (even justifiable anger). This gender role socialization is a disadvantage in the male-dominated business world, in which crying is a sign of weakness.

Thus, crying may present problems for both men and women: men because they aren't allowed and women because they are. As these headline articles suggest, gender is important to the experience and expression of emotion.

Gender in the Experience and Expression of Emotion

Emotion has been a subject of interest in the field of psychology since its early years as a discipline. Even before psychologists began experimental investigations of behavior, emotion was a topic of interest to philosophers. From the start, Western philosophers tended to conceptualize emotions as irrational and to place emotion opposite the rational thought processes (Averill, 1982). This attitude shaped the rational–emotive dichotomy that persists today (and conveniently corresponds to gender stereotypes). "From the 19th century onwards, rationality and emotionality have largely become associated with the supposedly different natures of men and women, the former fitted for productive labor and the latter for household and emotional labor" (Fischer, 1993, p. 303). This emotional double standard holds that women are more emotional than men, but only for a restricted range of emotions—happiness, sadness, disgust, fear, and surprise.

Anger is notably absent from the list of emotions stereotypically associated with women but is more strongly associated with men. One way to conceptualize this situation is to classify the emotions associated with women as expressions of powerlessness and those associated with men as expressions of power, which fits with the social and economic situations in many countries. This classification was confirmed in an analysis of data about emotions in 37 countries around the world (Fischer, Rodriguez Mosquera, van Vianen, & Manstead, 2004).

The stereotypes of overemotional women and restrained men are among the most prevalent in the United States. A study on stereotyping of emotion (Plant, Hyde, Keltner, & Devine, 2000) showed a bias in identifying anger with men and not women. Participants tended to interpret women's reactions as sadness rather than anger and had trouble seeing women as angry, even when women's expressions were clearly angry. Similar findings appeared in a study of preschool children who responded to stories (Parmley & Cunningham, 2008). In situations in which the responses were not clear, these children tended to interpret the women's responses as indicating sadness, but in men, the same responses were interpreted as anger. These studies demonstrate that gender stereotypes for emotionality are very strong and begin early in life.

But the gender stereotypes for emotion may not be entirely correct; women may experience and yet not express it. Indeed, the experience of emotion may differ substantially from its expression for both men and women. People can experience an emotion and yet manifest no overt behavior that signals their inner experience. Paul Ekman (1984) defined the concept of **display rules** as "overlearned habits about who can show what emotion to whom and when they can show it" (p. 320). These display rules make it possible to experience one emotion and display another or to display no emotional reaction at all despite the internal experience of strong emotion. In addition, the learning of display rules provides an explanation for the variability of emotion from person to person and from culture to culture. The difference in display rules also explains why women cry more than men, as this chapter's headline articles highlighted.

An examination of reports of emotion for a representative sample of U.S. residents showed that men and women reported experiencing emotion with similar frequencies (Simon & Nath, 2004). The emotions, however, differed. Men reported more experiences of

Display rules prohibit men from openly expressing
emotions such as sadness.

positive emotions such as excitement and calm, and women recounted more experiences of
anxiety and sadness. No difference appeared in the experience of anger. Age and educational
level were involved with reports of emotions, but the one factor that made the biggest difference between the women and men in this survey was living with young children. Women
who lived with young children experienced more negative emotions than those who did not.

The findings from this survey are inconsistent with the stereotypes for emotion in several ways. First, the negative effect of children on emotional experience is inconsistent with
one of the most cherished stereotypes: maternal instinct. Mothering and the joys of that experience are the basis for the association of women with emotionality. Second, the gender
similarity in the experience of anger flies in the face of abundant crime statistics and
barroom brawls. This chapter investigates the inconsistency between gender stereotypes and
findings about women's and men's emotional experiences by examining two varieties of
emotional experience: maternal behavior (a "feminine" expression of emotion) and aggression

(a "masculine" expression of emotion). By examining both, we can contrast research findings with the stereotypes.

The Myth of Maternal Instinct

The concept of instinct holds that an instinctive behavior is determined by biological factors and is largely insensitive to environmental or situational conditions. The concept of an instinctive basis for material behavior can be traced to Charles Darwin (1872) and the 19th century (Shields, 2002). During that time, both women's intellectual inferiority and their emotional reactions to infants and children were widely accepted. Scientific thought held that women could not be as intellectually developed as men because their energies were required to go toward reproduction and caregiving. Nature had suited them to focus on immediate situations rather than abstract ones (hence their intellectual inferiority) and to be more perceptive and emotional (hence their attraction to small and helpless beings). The notion that women are endowed with the urge to nurture continues today (Cole, Jayaratne, Cecchi, Feldbaum, & Petty, 2007), with men's beliefs in maternal instinct stronger than women's endorsement of a biologically determined trait for maternal behavior.

Maternal instinct is not so well established among scientific researchers. According to primatologist Sarah Blaffer Hrdy (1981, 1999), observations of various primate species have changed academic opinions of mothers, fathers, and infants. Evolutionary biology places primary emphasis on producing offspring and the factors related to this success, making sexual selection a prominent topic. However, success in evolutionary terms includes not only having offspring but also having offspring that live long enough to have offspring themselves, so the processes of motherhood and nurturing young are of paramount importance. The study of nonhuman primates brings a wider perspective to the topic of mothering and parental care. Rather than aggression or a lack of male involvement, these studies have shown that male primates' involvement with infants varies from being the primary caretaker to showing benign disinterest. This research (Hrdy, 1999) reveals little dangerous aggression toward infants from adult males within the social group (although males from other social groups can be very dangerous). Differences for paternal involvement vary enormously across species; some males formed numerous relationships with infants and young primates, even those they had not fathered, whereas other males of the same species were less involved with the young (Silverstein, 1993). The evidence from studies of various primate species does not offer consistent support for the concept of maternal instinct (and paternal disinterest). The behavior of primates offers no evidence for biological invariance of nurturing among females and lack of nurturing among males.

Despite the lack of support for the concept of maternal instinct, the notion has lingered longer than belief in other instincts (Cole et al., 2007). As Judith Lorber (1997, p. 13) quipped, "Believing is seeing," so researchers tended to avoid research in this area or, if they did, had trouble accepting their own observations. One of these hard-to-convince scientists was psychologist Harry Harlow, whose research ironically provided evidence *against* the validity of the concept of maternal instinct.

Maternal Deprivation and Its Consequences for Nurturing. During the
1950s, Harry Harlow and his colleagues (including his wife, Margaret) conducted a series of experiments concerning affection and attachment—of mothers for their babies, of babies for

their mothers, of fathers for their babies, of children for each other, and so forth. One of Harlow's questions concerned the effects of maternal deprivation on children, but ethics prevented him from using humans as participants. Instead, he chose to experiment on monkeys.

Harlow's (1971) research on maternal deprivation originated from his desire to raise infant monkeys in a controlled environment, but he noticed that isolation-reared infant monkeys behaved abnormally. They stared into space for hours, circled their cages or rocked repetitively for long periods of time, and repeatedly injured themselves, especially when humans approached (Harlow & Harlow, 1962). Not only did these young monkeys behave oddly when alone, they also exhibited abnormal behavior when placed in a social group of other monkeys. They failed to fit into the social group; they fought more and interacted less than monkeys raised normally. They were also sexually abnormal; they appeared interested in sex but unable to mate. Thus, Harlow noticed that the experience of maternal deprivation seemed to have permanent effects on the social and sexual behavior of these monkeys.

Isolation also affected the monkeys' maternal behavior. When the isolated female monkeys became mothers themselves, they made spectacularly poor ones. These monkey mothers were negligent and abusive, refusing to allow their infants to nurse and sometimes beating them for trying to establish physical contact. Such negligent and abusive behavior did not support the concept of maternal instinct but rather suggested that the experience of isolation from their mothers affected their nurturing behavior. This research suggests that caregiving is dependent on experience and not on instinct.

Harlow (1959) initially believed that being mothered was the critical experience that would allow a monkey to become an adequate mother, but a series of subsequent studies revealed that other social experiences could substitute. Physical contact was critically important in learning "mothering." Harlow and his colleagues constructed two types of surrogate mothers, one a wire "mother" and the other a cloth-covered wire "mother." Neither type of surrogate was very much like a real mother monkey; neither moved, held the infants, or responded to them in any way. Although the surrogate mothers were unresponsive, the infants were not. The infants strongly preferred the cloth-covered surrogates to the wire surrogates, even if the wire surrogate was the sole source of food. Infants nursed from the wire "mother" but clung to the cloth-covered surrogate for hours and ran to it when frightened. Harlow concluded that the cloth-covered surrogates provided some comfort that the wire surrogates could not, and he called this factor *contact comfort,* the security provided by physical contact with a soft, caring, or comforting object. However, even these monkeys did not become socially, sexually, or maternally normal, indicating that the cloth surrogate had failed to provide all the experiences that are necessary for normal monkey development.

Additional research showed that the experiences that promote normal nurturing and caregiving in monkeys involve contact with other monkeys. Despite the logic of modeling and imitation, such contact does not have to include the experience of being mothered. That is, being a good mother does not require being adequately mothered. Harlow and Harlow (1962) reported that age-mates can provide the social experiences necessary for normal development. The study involved separating infant monkeys from their mothers and raising them together as a group. Although these monkeys showed some abnormal behavior as infants—they clung together practically all the time they were together in their cage—these infants developed into normal adolescent monkeys. Another study in which infants were raised with their mothers but without peer contact showed that mothering alone would not be adequate for normal development; some contact with peers appeared to be essential.

TABLE 8.1 *Types of Deprivation and Effects on Nurturing in Monkeys*

Type of Deprivation	Adequacy of Nurturing
No deprivation—contact with mother and peers	Normal
Complete isolation	Inadequate and abusive
Wire or cloth "mother"	Inadequate
Contact with mother only	Inadequate
Contact with peers but not with mother	Normal

Therefore, the studies by Harlow and his colleagues demonstrated that maternal behavior is not the product of instinct in monkeys. Other research has confirmed these findings for other nonhuman primates (Smith, 2005), and additional research has demonstrated similar effects in rats (Melo et al., 2006). As Table 8.1 shows, nurturing and caregiving are not behaviors that appear in all females. Instead, specific social experiences are necessary for the development of adequate maternal (and other social) behaviors. Without these experiences, adequate maternal behaviors fail to appear.

Attachment.   Although research has demonstrated no innate, fixed pattern of caregiving, the contention that nurturing behavior has innate components has not disappeared from psychological theory. Instead, that notion has been transformed into other concepts, such as attachment and bonding. The concept of **attachment** originated with John Bowlby (1951), who studied infants raised in group homes that often deprived them of some elements of care, including the opportunity to form a relationship with an adult (usually the mother). Young humans require a great deal of care, and understanding the mutual interaction of caregiver and infant is an important factor in children's survival and well-being (Hrdy, 1999). Attachment may have components that begin during pregnancy and extend for months or years, resulting in processes of mutual attachment between caregiver and child (Hofer, 2006). Attachment is not restricted to mother–infant attachment, but can also occur between fathers and infants, or with any others who happen to be present during the critical time period, but attachment to mothers occurs more often than with others. Infants for whom this process goes wrong are at risk.

The concept of **bonding** is a variation on the idea of maternal instinct because bonding also depends on innate components that are known to occur in the early interaction between infant and caregiver. The concept was popularized with published research (Klaus & Kennell, 1976) contending that in the first few hours after children's birth, their attachment to mothers is critically important. Other researchers have failed to confirm these results, and the concept has been subject to critical review (Anderson, Moore, Hepworth, & Bergman, 2003). As Harlow's research suggests, contact is important, and skin contact shortly after birth may serve to facilitate the development of mothering behaviors (Mortimer, 2007). But the few hours after birth are not a magical period for attachment. This lack of research support has not deterred those who believe that bonding is critical. For example, recent advice from pediatricians (Kennell & McGrath, 2005) instructed hospital staff to keep "mother and infant always together in the first hours and days after delivery" to promote bonding (p. 775). The more valid concept of attachment is not so limited in time or so simple to accomplish.

Gender and Caring for Children. Recent research has explored hormonal involvement in mothers' preparation to nurture. During late pregnancy, delivery, and especially nursing, hormonal changes occur that may "prime" mothers to tend their babies (Hrdy, 1999; Mortimer, 2007). These hormonal events are not sufficient to prompt maternal behavior, even in rats, so the existence of biological circumstances related to mothering is not the same as maternal instinct. Indeed, the investigation of attachment need not be limited to mothers and infants but extends to a variety of relationships (Woollett & Marshall, 2001). However, through circumstance as well as physiology, women remain the primary caregivers for children in the great majority of cultures, whereas fathers' involvement varies (Parke, 2002). In some species and in some human cultures, fathers have virtually no contact with their children, whereas in some species and other human cultures, fathers are primary caregivers.

The circumstances of childbearing and nursing place many women in continued contact with children. Indeed, this association with caregiving is the basis for the classification of women as more nurturant than men (Doucet, 2006). Possible explanations for gender-related differences in nurturing behavior include responsiveness to children and pleasure in taking care of children. That is, perhaps girls and women respond more quickly and strongly to children or derive greater satisfaction from caring for children than men do, or both.

Gender differences in responsiveness to babies appear by age 3 years (Blakemore, 1998) and increase throughout childhood (Melson, 2001). Many of the studies that have reported gender differences in responsiveness to babies relied on self-report measures that are subject to biases from expectation (Berman, 1980), but some studies have measured behavioral reactions. One study (Melson & Fogel, 1988) found that preschoolers' interest in babies was similar before age 4, but with age, involvement with an infant in a play situation increased for girls and decreased for boys. In a naturalistic situation, girls showed more interest and nurturance toward babies than boys did, even at age 3 (Blakemore, 1998). This pattern was stronger for boys whose parents held traditional gender roles than for boys with more egalitarian parents. Therefore, parental and social encouragement are clearly factors in responsiveness to infants.

Girls' responsiveness to babies may not reflect a complete picture of nurturance. Boys tended to care for and nurture pets as they became less interested in babies (Melson, 2001). This behavior may represent the tendency for boys to become aware of the gender role they should follow, which does not include caring for babies. Boys still have the capacity to be nurturant caregivers, which they express by their feelings for and behavior toward pets. Boys may be as nurturant as girls, but in different ways.

The differences in patterns of child care—namely, that women perform the vast majority of child care—complicate comparisons of the pleasure that women and men derive from these activities. Some fathers are involved in all aspects of child care, but the accepted role for fathers is helper, whereas the role for mothers is primary caregiver. Although fathers in the United States approximately tripled the time they spend in child care between 1965 and 2000 (Wang & Bianchi, 2009), the manner in which they interact with their children have remained much the same. Mothers provide primary care and fathers are playmates (Laflamme, Pomerleau, & Malcuit, 2002). Thus, contrasts of the pleasure of nurturing experienced by mothers and fathers are not based on a direct comparison of the satisfaction each derives from specific caregiving activities, but rather on a comparison of their roles as mothers or fathers and the type of caregiving each provides. Within the context of these differences, men's experience is more positive than women's (Larson & Pleck, 1999).

◘ GENDERED VOICES

If Men Mothered

"I think that men could do as good as women at taking care of children," two college students told me. Both the young man and the young woman said that they believed that women have no instinctive advantage in nurturing children. Both of them said that the differences were due to experience rather than inherent biological factors. Indeed, both said that they believed there were few differences in ability to care for children.

"Well, men can't breast-feed," the young man said, "but I think that is about the only advantage women have except for experience. They have a lot more experience in caring for children. Girls babysit, and boys don't." He knew how difficult it was for men to get experience caring for young children because he had attempted to obtain such experience. He had volunteered to care for the young children in his church while their parents attended the service and had answered advertisements for babysitters. Neither of these efforts had met with enthusiasm from others; he had gotten the impression that wanting to care for children was considered odd for a man. He considered the possibility that people might think he was a pedophile, when all he really wanted was to learn to be more nurturant.

"I think if men were responsible for caring for children, there would be more changes in men than in children. If men had to learn to care for children, then they would. It wouldn't be automatic, because they don't have the experience, but they could learn. I don't believe in maternal instinct—that women have some innate advantage over men in caring. But women do have more experience, and men would have to learn the skills they lack.

"Men would learn to care for children if they had to, and they would become more nurturant in other aspects of their lives, maybe even in their careers. They might not care so much about competition and high-status careers."

The young woman had a slightly different view: "I think that the children would be different. This opinion is based on my own family and the differences between my mother and my father. My father was more willing to let us be on our own, but my mother was more involved. My mother took care of us, but my father let us make our own decisions. Maybe that wouldn't be good for young children, but I think I would have learned to be more self-reliant with my father's style of caretaking. But maybe if he had been the one who had to look out for us, he would have been as protective as my mother was."

However, men have few models for being involved fathers (Maurer & Pleck, 2006) and feel the strain of trying to construct a fathering role in which they become the type of father they want to be, which often is at odds with their role as breadwinner and societal expectations for masculinity (Doucet, 2006; Silverstein, Auerbach, & Levant, 2002).

The time and effort mothers spend in child care lead to feelings of both satisfaction and dissatisfaction (Renk et al., 2003). The experience of involvement in parenting, coupled with their feelings on the social value of nurturing children, produce satisfaction; the loss of freedom and the irritation of attending to the demands of small children can lead to dissatisfaction. In addition, many mothers held expectations that their partners would participate more fully in child care than they did, which led to feelings of being burdened. Indeed, the experience of greater negative emotionality among women is attributable to the presence of young children in the household (Simon & Nath, 2004).

Traditional gender roles are often enacted in the child-care situation, but gay fathers experience child care with the gender factor removed. The majority of gay fathers are men who have fathered children in heterosexual relationships. These men do not often get custody of their children, but an increasing number of gay couples are adopting or choosing surrogacy in order to become fathers (Miller & Ramirez, 2009; Silverstein et al., 2002). These men are highly motivated to become fathers, and they place a high value on relationships with their children. Without an automatic division of gender roles, gay fathers struggle with devising a "degendered" system of child care. They tend to divide child care more evenly than do heterosexual couples and to be more satisfied with this division of labor. Contrary to general beliefs, gay fathers are as able as heterosexual fathers to parent and to help their children develop (Armesto, 2002).

A study of heterosexual fathers who participated in the care of their children (Risman, 1989) revealed fathers' feelings and behavior that were similar to those of women who provided similar levels of care—satisfaction and frustration. Therefore, the greater pleasure that women derive from caring for children is likely a function of their greater involvement with their children, and men who have similar levels of involvement experience similar feelings.

If no instinctive force compels women toward and men away from nurturing, why, then, have men been involved so little in caring for children? Powerful social forces operate to prevent fathers from becoming more intimately involved with their children. In industrialized societies, fathers hold the role of breadwinner, which usually takes them outside the home and away from their children's lives (Maurer & Pleck, 2006). The traditional pattern of the male breadwinner who is a distant, uninvolved father has undergone changes over the past 40 years (Pleck & Pleck, 1997), but the well-publicized image of the "new" father who is involved with children's upbringing is an overstatement for most families, in which mothers provide substantially more care than fathers do (Finley & Schwartz, 2008; Wood & Repetti, 2004). Men and women who hold traditional gender role ideologies tend to believe that child care is "women's work," which makes the men reluctant to participate and the women reluctant for their husbands to do so (Wood & Repetti, 2004).

Fathers are now more involved with their children than in past decades, and an increasing number of fathers feel motivated to be more intimately involved in their children's lives (Cook, Jones, Dick, & Singh, 2005). For these men, few institutional supports exist to help them become more involved in child care, but many barriers prevent increased involvement (Doucet, 2006). Their childhood socialization tends to push them away from learning how to care for children, which leaves men feeling less capable of child-care tasks (Sanderson & Sanders Thompson, 2002). Being male in the world of young children makes some men feel as though they are moving through "estrogen-filled worlds," which are unfamiliar territory (Doucet, 2006, p. 696). Nevertheless, research indicates that the children, mothers, and fathers all can benefit from positive involvement by fathers in their children's lives (Maurer & Pleck, 2006; Pleck, 1997).

The Prominence of Male Aggression

Aggression has also been attributed to instinct. This conceptualization includes gender differences, with explanations of an evolutionary advantage for male aggression (Dabbs, 2000). The standard version says that during human prehistory, while the women were at home caring for the children, the men were out hunting and defending the group against various threats. In both the hunting and the defending, aggressive actions could be adaptive and even essential. Thus, women became passive homebodies and men became aggressive conquerors.

This view of human prehistory may be fictionalized, based more on the theorists' personal views than on prehistoric human behavior. There have been questions about both the idea of female passivity and the notion of the adaptive advantage of aggression (Hrdy, 1981, 1999; Weisstein, 1982). Women in the hunter–gatherer societies of prehistory probably not only gathered plants for food but also participated in small-game (and perhaps even large-game) hunting, thus making them essential contributors to their groups' food supply and far from passive. As for aggression, it can offer advantages if directed at the proper targets outside the group, but it can also be disruptive and dangerous within a group (de Waal, 2000). The men in these societies must have needed to become selectively rather than pervasively aggressive; natural selection would not favor those who were aggressive in all situations.

A definition of aggression turns out to be difficult to formulate in completely behavioral terms. The notion that human aggression is behavior directed toward another person intended to cause harm (Anderson & Bushman, 2002) relies on the intention of the aggressor and thus is not entirely behavioral. This difficulty in definition is not confined to theorists and researchers; not all people agree on which behaviors should be included and which consequences of these behaviors constitute harm, but intention is important to people's assessment of aggression (Krieglmeyer, Wittstadt, & Strack, 2009). Actions such as hitting, kicking, and biting obviously fit into the definition of aggression, but aggression can cause not only physical but also psychological harm. The terms *relational aggression* and *social aggression* have been applied to behaviors that harm others through damage to personal relationships, such as sulking, group exclusion, or the "silent treatment." *Indirect aggression* is a term applied to harm created through indirect means, such as arranging for someone to be blamed for a serious mistake at work or mocking someone's actions (Bjorkqvist, 1994). Despite the difference in terminology, these concepts are similar (Archer & Coyne, 2005).

Anger and Aggression.   Anger and aggression seem intimately related: Anger is the internal emotion, and aggression is its behavioral reaction. However, the two are not inevitably connected; a person can experience anger and take no action, aggressive or otherwise, but a person can also act aggressively without feeling anger, such as the careful planning of harm to another for personal benefit (Anderson & Bushman, 2002).

Several types of investigations have explored people's experience of anger and the connection to aggression in laboratory experiments, interviews, and surveys. Interviews and surveys have the advantage of tapping into personal experiences in ways that laboratory experiments cannot, but both have the disadvantage of relying on self-reports and lacking direct measurements of either anger or aggression. Several such studies have concentrated on children and their experience of anger. One study (Peterson & Biggs, 2001) asked 3-, 5-, and 8-year-olds about emotional situations, including anger. Five-year-old boys were most likely to label anger, and both girls and boys were more likely to label anger than any other emotion. An assessment of self-reports of anger (Hubbard et al., 2002) found no gender differences in anger for 2nd-grade girls and boys or among 4th- and 5th-grade rural, urban, and suburban students (Buntaine & Costenbader, 1997).

Studies of self-reports of anger in adults have revealed surprisingly few gender differences. Surveys of adults in eight European countries (Scherer, Wallbott, & Summerfield, 1986), in 37 nations around the world (Fischer et al., 2004), and community residents

(Averill, 1982) and college students in the United States (Taylor & Risman, 2006) found no gender differences in the reported frequency of anger. An analysis of meta-analyses (Archer, 2004) confirmed these findings. The targets of anger, however, varied by gender and by relationship with the angry person. For example, women in countries with a great deal of gender inequality were more often angry with strangers than people with whom they had close relationships, but the pattern was the opposite for women in cultures with greater gender equality (Fischer et al., 2004). In general, women experienced more anger in more egalitarian societies, which is consistent with the notion that anger is an emotion of the powerful.

The tendency for women to cry when they feel angry appeared in the cross-cultural survey of emotion (Fischer et al., 2004) and in a study in which women explored their emotions (Crawford, Kippax, Onxy, Gault, & Benton, 1992). These investigations are consistent with Bing's (2004) headline story about crying in business meetings. For women, crying is a common expression of emotion, even in response to anger. As Bing contended, girls are allowed to cry as an acceptable means of expressing anger, whereas physical aggression is less acceptable. However, crying is discouraged among boys, and men are much less likely to cry than women (Lombardo, Cretser, & Roesch, 2001). Indeed, men often misinterpret women's crying as sadness or grief, which would be inappropriate in situations that provoke anger. This tendency for women to cry in situations in which men would not may be a major reason that women receive the label of "overemotional."

Gender role rather than gender may have a stronger relationship with anger and the expression of anger. Masculinity (rather than being male) showed a relationship to the expression of anger and aggression, and femininity (rather than being female) was related to the suppression of anger (Kopper & Epperson, 1996). Masculinity was also important in men's fear of emotion, with more masculine men showing greater fear of emotion (Jakupcak, Tull, & Roemer, 2005). Masculinity also related to higher levels of anger and to expression of hostility. Emotional skillfulness mediates the expression of aggression (Mansfield, Addis, Cordova, & Dowd, 2009). These studies show the importance of the traditional male gender role in anger and how anger becomes an accepted emotion for men, whereas other emotions are not.

In summary, the relationship between anger and aggression is far from automatic, with feelings of anger occurring far more often than acts of aggression. Of the studies that have explored gender differences in the experience of anger, few have confirmed the stereotypes. Instead, these studies have shown that men and women both experience anger. Other studies have indicated that gender role—more than gender—shows a relationship to anger and emotion.

Developmental Gender Differences in Aggression. Observing gender differences in aggression during the early months and even early years of life is very difficult, because what counts as aggression in an infant is virtually impossible to define. Rather than attempting to assess aggression in young children, researchers have used other behaviors, beginning with children's activity level during infancy. Some studies have failed to find a gender difference in activity level, but Maccoby and Jacklin's (1974) review concluded that boys showed higher activity levels than girls. Maccoby and Jacklin found little evidence for gender differences in aggression in early childhood, but a review of meta-analyses on aggression came to a different conclusion: Gender differences in physical aggression appear early during childhood and persist throughout adulthood

(Archer, 2004). Studies during early childhood are most often based on observation, and some research (Ostrov, Crick, & Keating, 2005) has shown that observers tend to demonstrate gender biases in evaluating what counts as aggression in children, which may be a biasing factor in these studies of early childhood.

Another way to understand the development of aggression is through longitudinal research—in studies that test the same group of people over many years. Several longitudinal studies have focused on aggression, including early childhood in Canada (Baillargeon et al., 2007), childhood to preadolescence in Canada (Côté, Vaillancourt, LeBlanc, Nagin, & Tremblay, 2006), childhood to middle age in Finland (Kokko & Pulkkinen, 2005), and three generations of participants in the Columbia County Longitudinal Study in the United States (Dubow, Huesmann, & Boxer, 2003; Eron, 1987; Huesmann, Eron, Lefkowitz, & Walder, 1984; Lefkowitz, Eron, Walder, & Huesmann, 1977). These studies employed multiple methods of assessing aggression, including not only observation but also reports from the participants as well as from parents, teachers, and peers.

The results from all three longitudinal studies revealed several commonalities. First, aggression tends to decrease over development, with younger children showing higher levels of aggression—especially physical aggression—than older children. This finding may seem counterintuitive; people appear to become more aggressive, especially as they reach adolescence, but this conclusion is not correct. As they mature into middle childhood, children become increasingly capable of controlling their aggression, and most do so (Côté et al., 2006).

Second, some children exhibit a higher degree of aggression than other children, and these individuals exhibit a stable, high level of aggression from childhood to adulthood. This stability maintained for both boys and girls, but boys were more likely to be classified in the group with the highest levels of aggression (Côté et al., 2006; Lefkowitz et al., 1977) and with more stable aggression (Kokko & Pulkkinen, 2005). These aggressive children tended to see themselves as aggressive, rated others as such, and saw the world as a dangerous place in which aggression was an appropriate response.

Third, parenting styles relate to the development of aggression in children. Parents who were less nurturant and harsher in their discipline tended to have children who behaved more aggressively than the children brought up by more nurturant and acceptant parents (Côté et al., 2006; Lefkowitz et al., 1977). Aggressive adults tend to use parenting strategies that create aggressive children, propagating a cycle of violence. Table 8.2 shows the stability of aggression among the participants in the Columbia County Longitudinal Study, the longest of the longitudinal studies.

A component of the Columbia County Longitudinal Study (Eron, Huesmann, Brice, Fischer, & Mermelstein, 1983) investigated the influence of watching violent television programs; the researchers found that the violence on television acted as an effective model for aggressive children. Indeed, the preference for violent television programs at age 8 was a good predictor of how aggressive the male adolescents would be at age 19. An additional longitudinal study (Huesmann, Moise-Titus, Podolski, & Eron, 2003) demonstrated a relationship between watching violent television programs during childhood and aggression in young adulthood, 15 years later. Those children who were most strongly influenced saw the TV violence as more realistic and also tended to identify with the aggressive television characters. Both boys and girls were subject to this influence.

From early in the lifespan, boys and men exhibit higher levels of physical aggression than girls and women, and these differences are higher during middle childhood and

TABLE 8.2 *Aggression over the Life Span*

Children Identified at 8 Years of Age by Their Peers as Aggressive toward Other Children		
At Age 8	**At Age 18**	**At Age 30**
Had less nurturant and acceptant parents	Were still rated by peers as aggressive	Were more likely to have a criminal record
also	*also*	*also*
Preferred violent TV programs	Rated themselves as aggressive	Were more likely to abuse spouse
	also	*also*
	Rated others as aggressive	Were more likely to have DWI (DUI) conviction
	also	*also*
	Saw the world as a dangerous place	Were more likely to have traffic violations
		also
		Were more likely to use severe punishment with children

adolescence than during other ages (Archer, 2004). Girls exhibit opposition and defiance of parents as often as boys do (Lahey et al., 2000), but they are less likely to fight. Boys also use higher levels of verbal aggression than girls, but girls and women exhibit similar or higher levels of social and indirect aggression (Archer, 2004). Between ages 2 and 8, some children replace the tendency for physical aggression with indirect aggression (Côté, Vaillancourt, Barker, Nagin, & Tremblay, 2007). The tactic of hurting others by ostracizing, excluding them from the group, and gossiping is especially prevalent among adolescent girls who exhibit high levels of aggression. Books such as *Queen Bees and Wannabes* (Wiseman, 2002) and the movie *Mean Girls* portrayed this age group and these tactics, but among children from age 10 to 14, boys showed higher levels of indirect aggression than girls (Salmivalli & Kaukiainen, 2004). During adulthood, both men and women tend use indirect aggression, especially in the workplace, because physical aggression is obviously unacceptable in such situations (Archer, 2004).

Both boys and girls are discouraged from being physically aggressive, but they are not held to the same standards; boys are allowed to be more aggressive than girls—"boys will be boys." By middle childhood, both boys and girls have developed different expectations about expressing aggression (Anderson, 2005; Perry, Perry, & Weiss, 1989). Boys expected less parental disapproval for their aggression, and both expected less parental disapproval for aggression against a boy than against a girl. Even with general parental disapproval for aggression (Valles & Knutson, 2008), children learn about circumstances under which their aggression is more acceptable and more effective, and boys learn different rules for displaying aggression than girls learn—aggression is part of the male but not the female gender role. By adolescence, the gender differences in physical aggression are even larger than during childhood, and again, parental behavior is important. Parents monitored girls' behavior more strictly than boy's behavior (Carlo, Raffaelli, Laible, & Meyer, 1999), and this difference was a significant mediating factor in the higher levels of aggression exhibited by boys.

Boys tend to enact the most serious types of aggression more often than girls do (Archer, 2004). Some girls appear in the same range of violence as the most aggressive boys, but a study of girls in gangs (Campbell, 1993) showed that high levels of male and female violence tended to serve different purposes. Men used aggression to exert control over others, whereas women's aggression usually represented a loss of emotional self-control. This gender difference may apply to women and men in general and represent different meanings even for similar behaviors (Alexander, Allen, Brooks, Cole, & Campbell, 2004). The violence in male gangs is consistent with this interpretation; boys in gangs used aggression and violence to gain social recognition and to get money. Girls in gangs also used violence to create recognition, but unlike boys, they did not seek money as much as they sought to avoid becoming victims by creating a reputation for being tough. As other research has indicated (Keltikangas-Jarvinen, 2002), some groups allow and even encourage violence, and under some circumstances, aggression can have high benefits and low costs. These gang girls represent an extreme, but their use of and benefit from violence are similar to those of their male counterparts, even though their goals differ from those of boys.

Therefore, a developmental trend occurs toward a decrease in aggression from middle childhood to young adulthood, and gender-related differences appear in the use of aggression. Boys and girls tend to use different strategies and behaviors in their displays of aggression. Boys tend to use more confrontational, physical aggression as well as indirect aggression; girls tend to be less aggressive than boys, and their aggression is more likely to be indirect or relational rather than physical. Despite its lower frequency, aggression during adolescence and adulthood is more dangerous than childhood aggression. With their size, strength, and greater likelihood of owning a weapon, adolescent boys become more likely to use aggression that causes serious damage and violations of the law than are adolescent girls.

Gender Differences in Aggression during Adulthood. If gender-related differences in aggression decrease during development, then gender differences should be smaller during adulthood than earlier in development. Reviews of the experimental research on aggression have confirmed these conclusions, finding that the differences between aggression in men and women are not as large as most people imagine, but significant differences exist in styles and circumstances.

In addition to the early reviews of gender and aggression, the technique of meta-analysis has allowed a more systematic review of this massive research area. Indeed, a review of meta-analyses has appeared (Archer, 2004), providing an even more comprehensive picture of the findings on this topic.

One early review (Frodi, Macaulay, & Thome, 1977) focused on laboratory studies, and under controlled laboratory conditions, the gender differences in aggression are small. When women were provoked or felt justified, they became as aggressive as men. The factor of provocation was the topic of one meta-analysis (Bettencourt & Miller, 1996), which showed that gender differences decreased or disappeared with some types of provocation.

TABLE 8.3 *Gender Differences in Situations That Provoke Anger and Aggression*

For Children*	
Type of Provocation	**Tendency toward Anger**
Being hit accidentally	Boys report more anger
Not being invited to a party	Girls report more anger

For Adults**	
Type of Provocation	**Tendency toward Aggression**
No provocation	Men respond with much more aggression in everyday contacts
Physical attack	Men respond with slightly more aggression
	Men consider attacks more serious

Insults:
   Insensitive behavior
   Condescending behavior
   Impolite treatment
   Rude comments
	Women consider insults more serious
	Women respond with more aggression

Frustrations:
   Not able to succeed
   Not able to finish task
   Recognize own inability
   Traffic congestion
	Men respond with more aggression

Negative feedback concerning intelligence	Men respond with much more aggression Women are much less angered by this type of provaction

Sources: *From "Self-Reported Differences in the Experience and Expression of Anger between Boys and Girls," by Roberta L. Buntaine and Virginia K. Costenbader, 1997, *Sex Roles,* 36, pp. 625–637. **From "Gender Differences in Aggression as a Function of Provocation: A Meta-analysis," by Ann Bettencourt and Norman Miller, 1996, *Psychological Bulletin,* 119, pp. 422–447.

For example, women do not as readily respond aggressively to insults to their intelligence as men do, but both respond similarly to the frustration of someone blocking their path in traffic. This analysis showed that some of the gender differences found in experimental research are due to the various provocations researchers have used. Table 8.3 summarizes some gender-related differences in tendencies to respond with anger and aggression for both children and adults.

When the definition of aggression includes the infliction of psychological or social harm, women may be as aggressive or more aggressive than men (Archer, 2004; Richardson, 2005). These situations are more common among adults than those involving physical aggression (Bjorkqvist, 1994), so this type of aggression is important. Although not without the danger of retaliation, relational and indirect aggression are less risky than physical confrontation, making it a less dangerous choice, especially for women. The focus on physical aggression is the major reason that research has shown men to be more aggressive than women. With more comprehensive definitions of aggression and in more naturalistic situations, gender differences are smaller (Richardson, 2005).

Aggression can be a very effective way of exerting power and forcing others to behave according to one's wishes (Cassidy & Stevenson, 2005; Hawley & Vaughn, 2003). When considering aggression as a method of exerting power, women may be reasonably concerned about the potential for reprisal; the size and strength differential between men and women makes women more vulnerable to the effects of aggression. Women's reluctance to use physical aggression may relate to their fear of retaliation. Men's tendency to use physical aggression may relate to their training and experiences and to their belief in its effectiveness as a control strategy (Campbell & Muncer, 2008). In addition, the compatibility of aggression with the male gender role makes aggression a way to demonstrate masculinity (Anderson, 2005).

◻ GENDERED VOICES

He Said/She Said: Intimate Partner Violence

Two studies (Eisikovits et al., 2002; Winstok et al., 2002) reported on men who had beaten their partners and women who had stayed with their abusive partners. The men's stories reflected their beliefs that they were provoked into violence and reflected how they felt justified in hitting their partners.

He said:

> She starts making those faces and talking ugly, and this is expressed in a million ways. "You make yourself coffee, I won't do it for you." So after I hit her, she becomes a real disciplined child, just like I used to like her. After a month or two, slowly, slowly, she becomes self-confident again and gets out of line. (Winstok et al., 2002, p. 136)
>
> I am unable to beat her to death. I give her a slap and that's all, no more than that. Just to deter her. Stop it and that's it. She's getting just what she deserves, no more, sometimes less, but never more. (Winstok et al., 2002, p. 135)

These abusive men told stories about trying to silence their partners' voices.

The women's stories reflect a different view of these violent situations. Some abused women told stories about how uncontrollable and unpredictable their partners' violence was.

She said:

> Most of the time everything is OK. But sometimes we're sitting talking about something and the argument starts. From the argument ... he ... erupts just like a volcano, he raises his voice, and then I say something, and then he raises his voice some more and then I do too.... And we're screaming and arguing and not listening to each other. And it goes wherever it goes.... (Eisikovits et al., 2002, p. 142)

Other women told about how they recognized and managed their partners' escalation of violence.

She said:

> I prefer not to answer him at all, because I know that if I answer back it'll only get worse. Slowly I understood that if I shut up his anger would be less than if I answer him back. (Eisikovits et al., 2002, p. 142)

These abused women told stories about how their voices were silenced.

The concept of demonstrating masculinity is consistent with the reports of different experiences of aggression for women and men (Graham & Wells, 2001). A random sample of Canadian women and men reported their last experience of physical aggression, and results revealed that men were more likely than women to report involvement in some sort of violence. For men, the most common report was a fight with another man, usually in a public place such as a bar, with men as the more common perpetrators and the more common victims of violence. For women, the most common report was a conflict with a male partner or friend, many of which fit the description of intimate partner violence. Women also perpetrate physical violence, but the context is often in private settings and directed toward partners or children (Archer, 2000; Richardson, 2005).

The dynamics of partner conflicts and the escalation to violence are complex (Eisikovits, Winstok, & Gelles, 2002; Winstok, Eisikovits, & Gelles, 2002). Studies of partner violence indicate that women initiate violence as often as men, but the outcome is not equal; women are much more likely to sustain serious injuries or to be killed in such encounters (Archer, 2000; Richardson, 2005). The context of violence makes a great deal of difference to its recognition in terms of crime statistics. Domestic violence is less likely than public violence to result in arrest, so women who commit violent acts in private are not as likely as men to be involved in the criminal justice system.

Gender and Crime.   Despite fairly small gender difference in aggression, the statistics on societal aggression reveal large differences. Men commit many more criminal acts than women do, and their arrest and incarceration rates are much higher. According to the statistics for the United States (Federal Bureau of Investigation [FBI], 2008), men are about 3.5 times more likely than women to be arrested for various types of offenses, such as murder, robbery, vandalism, fraud, and drunkenness. Although not all of these violations involve violence, many do; as Table 8.4 (page 194) shows, such offenses are more likely to be committed by men than by women. However, increases in violent crimes committed by girls and women have occurred in more categories of crime over the past 15 years than for boys and men (FBI, 2008). Those increases have been slight, leaving the disproportionate levels of arrest shown in Table 8.4.

Not all crimes result in arrest, and the possibility exists that the ratio of crimes committed by men and women is closer to equal than the arrest rates suggest. Indeed, violent acts performed by women are evaluated differently than similar behavior by men (Anderson, 2005). However, surveys have indicated that although the reported rates of crime exceed the arrest rates, men still outnumber women in committing crimes (Steffensmeier & Allan, 1996). Crime was so strongly associated with men before the 1970s that most criminologists and officials in the criminal justice system assumed that crime was an almost exclusively male problem.

Prompted by the increase of criminal activity among women during the 1970s, research interests turned to female offenders. One hypothesis about this increase focused on the women's movement—equal opportunity applied to crime—but research indicated that female offenders tended to be traditional rather than feminist in their beliefs. In addition, the increase in crimes committed by women has been attributed more to nonviolent rather than violent crimes (Small, 2000). Therefore, the gender difference in violent crime persists, and the role of gender in criminal behavior and in treatment by the justice system remains unclear (Goodkind, Wallace, Shook, Bachman, & O'Malley, 2009).

TABLE 8.4 *Percentage of Male and Female Offenders Arrested for Various Offenses*

Offense	Men	Women
Murder	89.3%	10.7%
Rape	99.0%	1.0%
Robbery	88.5%	11.5%
Aggravated assault	78.7%	21.3%
Burglary	84.7%	15.3%
Larceny/theft	60.0%	40.0%
Motor vehicle theft	81.9%	18.1%
Arson	84.5%	15.5%
Forgery	61.6%	38.4%
Fraud	55.6%	44.4%
Embezzlement	48.7%	51.3%
Vandalism	82.8%	17.2%
Prostitution	29.4%	70.6%
Drug abuse violations	80.7%	19.3%
Domestic violence	75.4%	24.6%
Drunkenness	84.1%	15.9%
Disorderly conduct	73.0%	27.0%
Curfew violation/loitering	69.8%	30.2%
Runaway	43.7%	56.3%
All arrests	77.8%	24.2%

Source: Based on information from "Crime in the United States 2007," Federal Bureau of Investigation, Table 33. Retrieved August 28, 2009, from http://www.fbi.gov/ucr/cius2007/data/table_33.html.

Men are not only more likely to commit acts of violence, they are also more likely than women to be the victims of crime (see According to the Media and According to the Research). Boys are much more likely than girls to use confrontation and aggression as strategies for managing conflict, making male-against-male violence a common occurrence and physical aggression between boys and girls less common. Despite their lower rate of victimization, women are more likely than men to fear being the victims of crime. Early research indicated large differences, but later research (Schafer, Huebner, & Bynum, 2006) has revealed than men also fear crime victimization. Men, however, have a greater fear of being the victim of property crime, whereas women fear personal victimization. Indeed, the fear of sexual assault overwhelms fear of other crimes for women (Lane, Gover, & Dahod, 2009). This fear is not entirely unrealistic; sexual violence toward women is common.

Sexual Violence.   Although women's fears of sexual violence have some basis, the sexual assault they fear is not the most common that women experience—women fear stranger rape when sexual violence from acquaintances and intimates is a more common experience (U.S. Department of Justice Statistics, 2008). Based on reported cases, only about 30% of rapes and attempted rapes are by strangers. In addition, rape often goes unreported, making the official estimates lower than actual occurrences.

A classic study of U.S. college students (Koss, Gidycz, & Wisniewski, 1987) clarified the rate of sexual violence. Asking both men and women about their sexual behaviors revealed that 15.4% of the women reported being raped since the age of 14 years, and another 12.1% reported experiences that met the legal criteria for attempted rape. These rates yielded estimates for rape that were 10 to 15 times greater than the arrest rates for this crime, as well as perpetration rates that were 2 to 3 times higher than official estimates for the risk of rape, suggesting that many rapes go unreported. The findings from this study provoked controversy, but subsequent research has confirmed these figures. Sexual coercion and violence are common experiences, and most incidents go unreported.

Not only does rape go unreported to legal authorities, many women are reluctant to tell anyone about being raped. Although this reluctance is common, women from some ethnic backgrounds are more reluctant than others. Despite a similarity in the numbers of attempted and completed rapes for African American and European American women, African American women are significantly less likely to tell anyone about being raped (Donovan & Williams, 2002). Women from both ethnic groups had difficulty in identifying attacks by their acquaintances as "real" rape.

Asian Americans hold more negative attitudes toward women as rape victims than European Americans do (Lee, Pomeroy, Yoo, & Rheinboldt, 2005), especially first-generation Asian Americans (Devdas & Rubin, 2007). Both Asian American men and women were more likely than European Americans to endorse rape myths, such as the myth that rape is the woman's fault and that most rapes are stranger rape (Lee et al., 2005). Asian American men had more negative attitudes about women than any other group, so Asian American women's acceptance of blame for rape may make them particularly unlikely to report this crime.

Rape invokes a stigma for two reasons: (1) the sexual nature of the crime and (2) the tendency to blame the victim. The stigma is even more severe when men are the victims (Doherty & Anderson, 2004), resulting in men being even less likely to report the offence than women (Sable, Danis, Mauzy, & Gallagher, 2006). Male victims of rape or other types of sexual coercion have been accorded much less attention than have female victims, partly because they are not victimized as often, and partly because of the difficulty of accepting that men can be raped (Chapleau, Oswald, & Russell, 2008; Struckman-Johnson & Struckman-Johnson, 1994). This difficulty applies to victimized men because men tend to blame victims more than women do (Schneider, Mori, Lambert, & Wong, 2009) and whose masculine self-identity is threatened by their victimization (Pino & Meier, 1999).

Despite the barriers to recognizing the situation, a growing body of research indicates that men are sexually coerced and victimized by women as well as by men in ways similar to women's experience of coercion: through bribery, threats of withdrawal of affection, intoxication, physical intimidation, physical restraint, and physical harm (Krahé, Scheinberger-Olwig, & Bieneck, 2003). Both men and women are victims of sexual coercion, and both are censured for being victimized (Sable et al., 2006). The problem of female victimization is much more urgent because of its frequency and because women are more traumatized by coercive sexual experiences than men are (Rickert, Vaughan, & Wiemann, 2003). Therefore, a great deal of research has concentrated on understanding the characteristics of men who rape and coerce women into sex.

Diana Scully (1990) studied convicted rapists by conducting extensive interviews that revealed some of their motivation and attitudes. Her results revealed that the rapists

According to the *Media*...

Women Are Stalked by Crazed Killers and Queen Bees

Since the 1970s, the "slasher" film has undergone several waves of popularity and continues to capture large audiences, especially among adolescents ("Horror Show," 2006). *The Texas Chainsaw Massacre* was one of the early films of this genre and exemplified many of the common elements of slasher movies, including a maniac killer with frightening weapons stalking young women. In these movies, young women (often dressed very scantily) run screaming with fear, only to be pursued, menaced, caught, and killed. Some of the films showed the action of stalking through the eyes of the slasher, who was always a man. Thus, slasher movies portray more young female victims terrorized and then killed by men than other genres of film (Sapolsky, Molitor, & Luque, 2003).

During the 1990s, a version of slasher movie appeared that differed from those in the 1970s and 1980s. In these slasher movies, which are usually sequels to earlier movies, a lone woman survives the carnage (King, 2005; Trencansky, 2001). Although this survivor is a woman, other women and men are dead, and any remaining men are completely ineffective in stopping the killing; the woman manages to overcome the menacing murderer and seeks vengeance. These "final girls" are strong, resourceful, and capable—that is, they adopt masculine values and behavior rather than cower in terror waiting to be slaughtered (Keisner, 2008). By adopting masculine behavior, these images fail to empower the women who watch but rather send messages of female vulnerability. More common in recent slasher movies, the final girl lives long enough to be rescued by a man, another disempowering message.

Some movies portray women as menacing and even as killers—"mean girls movies," including films such as *The Craft, Foxfire,* and *Jawbreaker* (King, 2005). These movies feature competition and cattiness among girls, with one girl experiencing threats or violence from mean girls or violence and mistreatment from men. The main character finally triumphs, usually through more violence. These movies actually feature higher depictions of violence toward women than slasher movies. Thus from crazed killers and queen bees, girls and women are the targets of movie violence.

---

had not experienced an unusually high level of treatment for psychopathology or an unusually high rate of childhood physical or sexual abuse. Their family histories were filled with instability and violence, but so were the backgrounds of other felons in the study. The rapists were able to form relationships with women, but their attitudes toward women showed a combination of beliefs: women belong "on a pedestal," and men have the right to treat women with violence. Many of these rapists told Scully that they planned their actions because they were angry with their wives or girlfriends and wanted to do violence to some woman. These men reported that the common characteristic of their victims was their vulnerability; they were in the right place at the wrong time—usually alone somewhere at night. Their physical appearance made no difference—many of the rapists had trouble describing their victims. This disregard for appearance highlights the violence of the act and argues against a sexual motive for this type of rape.

Scully's sample underrepresented rapists who were acquainted with their victims; acquaintance rape is less often reported and prosecuted, and convictions are less than stranger rape. The violent attack by a stranger is the vision of rape that women fear, yet the most common experience of rape is an attack by an acquaintance, termed *date rape*, or *acquaintance rape*. One survey (Koss et al., 1987) of rape and attempted rape included questions that allowed participants to estimate their involvement in various types of sexual coercion. A total

ACCORDING TO THE RESEARCH . . .

Men Are More Often the Victims of Violent Crime, and Women Are Most Often Killed by Intimate Partners

In slasher movies, women are the ones who are stalked and killed by men, but most murderers are male (FBI, 2008). Men are also more likely than women to be the victims of such crimes. Indeed, men are more involved in all types of crimes than women are, but especially violent crime. This evidence makes the movie image of the maniac killer stalking beautiful young women inaccurate in several ways.

First, most people who commit murder kill people whom they know well, rather than people whom they do not know or know only slightly. This pattern is more applicable to female rather than male murder victims. Second, most people with psychological problems are not violent. Of those people who are violent and have psychological problems, most commit crimes that lead to their prompt arrest, giving them no opportunity to continue with a series of killings. Indeed, serial and mass murder are much more common in the media than in real life. Third, young women are not the most typical victims; young African American men are disproportionately the

victims of violence in the United States (U.S. Census Bureau [USCB], 2009a).

When women are the victims of violence, crazed killers are rarely the perpetrators. Instead, husbands and boyfriends are more likely to be the ones who harm women. Women are more likely to be assaulted or killed by men whom they love than by strangers (Heise, Ellsberg, & Gottemoeller, 1999). Therefore, the portrayal of deranged, menacing stalkers with female victims is not how most real-world violence occurs, nor is the image of the female hero who prevails over menacing criminals accurate. For most female and male victims, violence has a familiar male face.

Girls and women cause harm to others, but not as portrayed in movies with mean girls. These films present women enacting a high level of physical violence, whereas women's aggression tends to take the form of relational and indirect aggression (Archer, 2004). Thus, the movie depictions of women as victims and women as perpetrators are both inaccurate.

of 54% of the women in the survey reported some type of forced or coerced sexual activity, but only 25% of the men in the survey admitted to some level of sexual aggression. The discrepancy in the rates for men and women is not due to a few sexually predatory men, but rather to some degree of denial or failure by many men to recognize their own sexual aggression. This failure to recognize sexual aggression also occurred among the convicted rapists in Scully's study and in a study with a representative sample of U.S. residents (Laumann, Gagnon, Michael, & Michaels, 1994). All of these researchers have found that men may have trouble recognizing their own behavior as sexually coercive.

Neil Malamuth and his colleagues (in Malamuth, 1996) have worked toward developing a model to predict sexual aggression. Drawing from the fields of evolutionary psychology and feminist scholarship, Malamuth proposed that the convergence of two factors relate to rape: (1) high levels of uncommitted, impersonal sex and (2) hostile masculinity—hostility toward and desire to dominate women. When combined, these two factors relate to men's use of sexual coercion. Figure 8.1 presents this model and the paths leading toward coercive sexuality. Malamuth's research team has conducted several studies that support the model and its ability to predict coercive tactics to obtain sex, and research with Asian American and European American men (Hall, Teten, DeGarmo, Sue, & Stephens, 2005) has also confirmed this model.

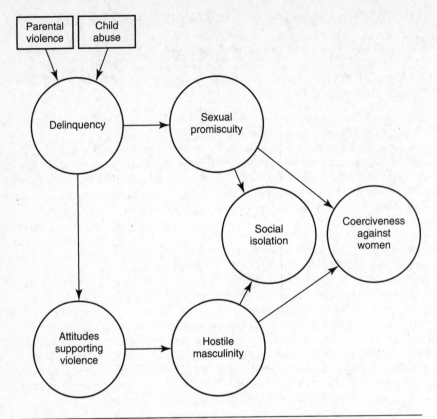

FIGURE 8.1   *Model of Characteristics of Men Who Are Coercive against Women*

Source: Adapted from "The Characteristics of Aggression against Women: Testing a Model Using a National Sample of College Students," by N. Malamuth, R. Sockloskie, M. P. Koss, and J. Tanaka, 1991, *Journal of Consulting and Clinical Psychology, 52,* p. 676. Adapted by permission of Neil Malamuth and the American Psychological Association.

A meta-analysis of studies on attitudes toward rape (Murnen, Wright, & Kaluzny, 2002) also confirmed elements of Malamuth's model. The combination of hostility toward women, male dominance, and an acceptance of violence showed a moderately strong relationship to sexual aggression. Additional research (Hill & Fischer, 2001; Ryan, 2004) has identified a sense of entitlement as an important component in sexual aggression. That is, men who feel that they are entitled to have sex, even if women refuse, are more likely to be sexually aggressive. In addition, both men and women make excuses and rationalizations for men's sexual aggression (Weiss, 2009), which allows this unacceptable behavior to continue

In summary, male aggression is not a myth, but the notion that men are aggressive and women are passive is not true. Both genders experience similar levels of anger, but men are more likely to express their anger as physical aggression. This likelihood can be traced to different social expectations and reinforcements for aggression experienced by boys and girls. As adults, men are more likely to be violent in public, to use aggression to gain power over others, and to experience legal problems associated with their aggression. Women are more likely to be violent in private, to use indirect or social aggression, and to respond violently if they feel justified in doing so and protected from retaliation. These patterns of aggression show gender-related differences, but they do not suggest that aggression is a male instinct or even a male domain.

Expressivity and Emotion

The similarities in the feelings that men and women experience and the differences in their behavior suggest that the gender differences in emotion may occur in the way emotions are expressed. Research has confirmed that men hold negative attitudes about emotional expression (Jakupcak et al., 2005; Wong, Pituch, & Rochlen, 2006), and women reported that they express their emotions more freely than men (Simon & Nath, 2004). However, the notion of large gender differences in emotional expression is possible only by using a selective definition of what counts as emotion (Shields, 2002). By concentrating on the emotions of fear and sadness in women and by overlooking aggression in men, women could be considered more expressive than men. This difference in expressivity can be explained by differences in display rules: Men and women are supposed to restrain displays of certain emotions, yet are free to show others. This selectivity reinforces gender stereotyping of emotions.

In his discussion of compliance with the Male Gender Role Identity model, Robert Brannon (1976) listed four criteria, two of which relate to these gender differences in emotionality: (1) No Sissy Stuff, meaning men must avoid anything vaguely feminine, such as crying or fear, and (2) Give 'Em Hell, meaning men are proud to display anger and aggression. (See Chapter 3 for a discussion of all four components.) The stereotype holds that men must avoid all things feminine and women are emotional; thus, the display of most emotion is prohibited. Anger is acceptable, however, because it is the essence of "giving 'em hell." These two components are essential elements of the display rules for men, which allow women to express more of what they feel, with the penalty of being stereotyped for their display (Shields, 2002).

Psychologists have used three types of measurements to assess emotion: self-reports, observed behavior, and physical arousal. The influence of gendered display rules appears in the results from studies on expressivity. When researchers have used participants' self-reports to measure emotion, they often find that women are more emotional than men. For example, one review of self-reports of emotionality (Maccoby & Jacklin, 1974) showed that girls and women were more likely than boys and men to admit to feelings of fear and anxiety. When researchers have used observations of participants' behavior in public, they have measured the enactment of display rules and the potential bias of observers, who may be influenced by the stereotypes governing emotion. Such studies tend to find gender differences (Eagly & Steffen, 1986), although the differences are not large, on the average. When researchers unobtrusively measure behavior in private, participants are more likely to display their emotions, and such studies often fail to show gender differences (Eisenberg & Lennon, 1983).

Women learn a slightly different set of display rules for emotion than men do, and the behavior of both men and women tends to conform to their display rules. Thus, women should be more nurturant than men, and in self-reports and in public behavior, they are. Boys and men should not be interested in babies or responsive to them, and under some

◼ GENDERED VOICES

They Put a Lot of Effort into Showing Nothing

I talked to a psychologist who had been employed as a therapist in a prison, and he told me that the prisoners exhibited what he considered to be an inappropriate level of emotion—none. He said, "I thought they put a lot of effort into showing no emotion. Their goal seemed to be to show no sign of any emotion. For example, even if they were hurt, their faces didn't change expression. Every once in a while, I would see a slip, and a prisoner would show some sign of pain when he got hurt. I assume that they had feelings that were similar to anyone's, but their expression of emotion was very abnormal.

"Showing no emotion didn't mean that they let things go. They would retaliate against another prisoner who had hurt them, even if it was mostly an accident and he hadn't meant to hurt anyone. But they didn't show any emotion when they were hurt or when they hurt the other guy. It was part of the prison society to keep their faces like masks, showing nothing about what they felt, closing themselves off from the others."

circumstances, they are not. However, boys tend to nurture pets, and men who care for children may be as nurturant and responsive as women who perform these tasks. According to these display rules, men should be more physically aggressive than women, and in self-reports and in public behavior (including criminal violence), they are. However, women experience anger as strongly as men do, and when they feel justified (and anonymous), women are as likely to show physical aggression similarly to men. Relational and indirect aggression involve doing harm indirectly, and women exhibit this type of aggression, sometimes more than men. Therefore, the gender differences in emotion are strongly related to circumstances and social learning of display rules and cannot be attributed to biologically determined differences due to instinct.

Considering Diversity

Research on diversity and emotion has tended to focus on the universals of emotion rather than on cross-cultural differences, but one study that examined ethnic groups within the United States (Durik et al., 2006) found both differences and similarities. African American, Hispanic Americans, and European American participants all held gendered stereotypes of emotions, but European Americans' views were more gender polarized than the other groups, and gender often interacted with ethnicity. These results present a complex picture of the influences of gender, culture, and emotion.

A major approach to understanding the basics of human emotions and the commonalities across cultures has emphasized facial expressions as a reflection of emotional experience. Paul Ekman (1984, 1992), who is the leading proponent of this position, has traced his view back to Darwin and the notion that facial expressions reflect basic emotional experiences for humans and nonhuman animals. People's conceptualizations of emotion are consistent with this view—people classify some emotions as basic and agree that both humans and nonhuman animals experience these basic emotions (Demoulin et al., 2004).

Ekman's research led him to propose that at least six basic human emotions exist—happiness, surprise, fear, sadness, anger, and disgust combined with contempt.

The quest for universals in emotion has also yielded findings of diversity across cultures (Eid & Diener, 2009; Elfenbein & Ambady, 2002). In exploring cultural differences, many researchers have considered the dimension of collectivist versus individualist cultures. Collectivist cultures emphasize group values, the family, and group harmony, which require subordinating the self to the group. Individualist cultures value individual achievement, personal goals, and development of the self. Countries such as the United States, Canada, the countries in Northern Europe, and Australia are individualist cultures, and those such as China, Japan, Korea, countries in Latin America, and many countries in Africa are collectivist. One study that explored differences in collectivist and individualist countries confirmed that people in individualist countries (U.S. and Australia) experienced more pride, whereas those in collectivist cultures (China and Taiwan) felt more guilt (Eid & Deiner, 2001). An extension of this research to collectivist cultures in Africa (Kim-Prieto & Eid, 2004) revealed that guilt was valued in the more collectivist cultures, but pride and contentment were more highly valued in collectivist cultures in Africa than in Asia. Thus, cultural variations appear, even within the classification of collectivist and individualist cultures.

Some cross-cultural research (Scherer, Wallbott, & Summerfield, 1986) included gender comparisons and revealed the expected stereotypical gender differences—women reported more expressions of emotion than men—but the differences were small. This survey also revealed some evidence against the emotional stereotypes associated with various countries: The English were very talkative rather than reticent; the Italians were very concerned with achievement rather than personal relationships; and the Swiss were very emotional rather than very reserved.

Some surprising differences appear in studies of anger, which is one of the "basic" emotions. The acceptability of anger differs substantially across cultures, and the association of anger with masculinity is not universal. For the Utku Eskimos, anger brings shame; it is considered dangerous, and its display is completely unacceptable for adults; children learn to avoid this emotion. The Vanatinai also believe that anger and aggression are unacceptable (Lepowsky, 1994). The inhabitants of this small island society in the South Pacific near New Guinea value independence and assertiveness but find physical aggression shameful; adults who commit such acts are thought to be out of control and embarrassing to their families. Fighting is rare, but women are somewhat more likely than men to be physically aggressive. This culture is not passive: The men are fierce warriors. However, women are not allowed to participate in warfare or use spears. This society holds different display rules from Western societies, placing women rather than men in the role of displaying aggression.

The cross-cultural search for emotional universals has yielded findings about similarities across cultures—the types, the antecedent situations, the labels used, and the physical reactions and facial responses people exhibit (Elfenbein & Ambady, 2002). However, when considering which emotions are valued and acceptable, large cultural differences exist. For example, emotions associated with power, such as anger and contempt, were less acceptable to Japanese participants than to participants in Canada or the United States (Safdar et al., 2009). In addition, the situations that prompt emotion and the contexts in which displays of emotion are appropriate show very large cultural differences. Cultures vary both in restricting and in prescribing the display of emotion—who should express what emotion under what circumstances: "Although there are universal patterns of expressive behavior, there also are culture-specific behavior modes, deriving from culture-specific models and from culturally based expectations regarding behavior that is appropriate under particular circumstances" (Mesquita & Frijda, 1992, p. 199). People may all feel the same emotions, but they do not express them in the same ways or under the same circumstances.

■ Summary

The stereotype of gender and emotion presents women as emotional and men as rational, but research on the different components of emotion has revealed that there may be few gender differences in the inner experience of emotion. Gender differences appear in how and when emotion is displayed.

The notion that some emotions are the result of instincts can be traced to Charles Darwin's theory of evolution. In psychology, the explanation that emotion is instinctive has faded, with the exception of beliefs about a maternal instinct and an instinct toward aggression. Belief in a maternal instinct has continued, although research by Harlow and his colleagues demonstrated that experience was critical in developing adequate maternal behaviors—monkeys deprived of contact with other monkeys during the first 6 months of their lives failed to show adequate nurturing and caregiving. Attachment is a concept related to maternal instinct but does not necessarily rely on instinct as its basis and allows for attachments between infants and others (rather than only mothers).

Research on gender differences in responsiveness to babies has shown differences in self-reports and in public displays, which are consistent with gender stereotypes. Boys are free to express their nurturance to pets, and they do. Women still have a great deal more involvement in child care than men. Self-reports indicate that the greater pleasure for women in caring for children is coupled with greater irritation in caring for them; however, men who are very involved in child care tend to report similar feelings. Although fathering has not included the type of intimate caregiving that mothering has, research indicates that fathers have increased their involvement with their children, demonstrating their interest and ability in nurturing. Therefore, the concept of maternal instinct has no support as a biologically based explanation for caregiving. Both men and women share similar emotions related to nurturing.

Aggression has also been nominated as an instinct, with the belief that men have more innate tendencies toward aggressive behavior than women. When considering the link between anger and aggression—that is, between emotion and behavior—few gender differences appear. Women and men experience anger similarly but express it differently. Boys and men tend to be more likely to use physical confrontation when they are angry, whereas girls and women are more likely not to express anger. When they do, they tend to use more indirect and relational aggression. Girls and women are more likely to cry when angry, an expression that men often misunderstand and find inappropriate.

Developmental gender differences in aggression exist, with boys more likely than girls to use physical aggression at all ages. Longitudinal studies have revealed that aggression is moderately stable over time and even over generations; aggressive children are more likely than less aggressive children to become violent adults and to have children who are more aggressive. However, both boys and girls tend to become less aggressive as they develop, and by adulthood, the gender difference in aggression has diminished.

Despite small gender differences in aggression in laboratory studies, very large gender differences exist in crime rates: Men are about 3.5 times more likely than women to be arrested for committing violent crimes. The victims of these violent crimes are likely to be other men, but women fear crime victimization more than men, especially sexual violence. Their fear has some basis. Official reports underestimate the incidence of rape, and more representative surveys show that at least 20% of women are the targets or rape or attempted rape. Attitudes of hostility toward women, an acceptance of violence, and a sense of entitlement to sex make men more likely to be sexually violent.

Although men have more experience with violence and less experience with nurturance than women, these differences relate more strongly to how emotion is expressed than to women's or men's subjective experiences of emotion. The cultural display rules that govern the behaviors associated with emotion differ for men and women, and these allow women more expression and restrain men from expressing emotions except anger, which men are more free to show than are women.

The search for universals in emotion has yielded evidence of both consistency and diversity across cultures. Research indicates that people across the world experience the same range of emotions, including the six basic emotions of happiness, surprise, fear, sadness, anger, and disgust combined with contempt. However, the situations that evoke these emotions and the rules that govern their display differ enormously across cultures. In addition, culture and gender interact in complex ways.

■ Glossary

attachment   an intimate relationship that forms between a caregiver (almost always a mother) and an infant.

bonding   an emotional attachment that develops between primary caregiver and infant within a few hours or days after birth.

display rules   learned social rules that govern who may display which emotion to whom, and in what situation each emotion may be displayed.

■ Suggested Readings

Hrdy, Sarah Blaffer. (1999). *Mother nature: A history of mothers, infants, and natural selection.* New York: Pantheon Books.
Primatologist Hrdy examines mothering from an evolutionary point of view, considering mothers, fathers, and offspring. She uses nonhuman species to provide contrasts and to draw similarities to the complexities of bearing and raising children.

Larson, Reed; & Pleck, Joseph. (1999). Hidden feelings: Emotionality in boys and men. In Dan Bernstein (Ed.), *Nebraska Symposium on Motivation, 1999: Gender and Motivation* (pp. 25–74). Lincoln: University of Nebraska Press.
Larson and Pleck review theories of emotion and present results from several studies that compare emotional responses of girls, boys, women, and men in a variety of situations. Their gender-as-process approach and innovative methodology provide an interesting presentation of gender and emotionality.

Shields, Stephanie A. (2002). *Speaking from the heart: Gender and the social meaning of emotion.* Cambridge, UK: Cambridge University Press.
Shields reviews research related to how emotion fits into social conceptualizations of gender and how emotional meaning is often sharply gendered.

Weiss, Karen G. (2009). "Boys will be boys" and other gendered accounts. *Violence Against Women, 15* (7), 810–834.
This study explores how male aggression is accepted as natural, normal, and even the victims' fault through an examination of the narratives of victims drawn from the U.S. National Crime Victimization Survey.

chapter
9 Relationships

Romantic love has been the topic of scientific research, and Jeffrey Kluger and his colleagues (2008) explored the results, including both physiological and psychological components. Their review summarized what researchers have discovered and presented a bit about why we love (and why love seems to be uniquely capable of eliciting emotions such as tenderness as well as passion). The physiological components include evidence that the senses of smell, taste, sight, and sound all play a role in finding someone attractive. Hormones also contribute; brain-imaging technology reveals a reliable pattern of responses to the feelings of exhilaration associated with passionate, romantic love.

HEADLINE
Why We Love
Time, January 28, 2008

Robert Sternberg (1986) proposed a model of love that captures many of the elements of the story by Kluger and his colleagues. Sternberg called his model the *triangular model of relationships* because he conceptualized all relationships as consisting of varying amounts of three components. Passion is one of the three components of Sternberg's triangular model. Intimacy is the second, which involves feelings of closeness. This component is also evident in romantic love. But romantic love is not the entire story of why we love. For love to last, passionate and intimacy are not enough. Commitment is essential for a continuing relationship and furnishes the third point of Sternberg's triangle.

Sternberg's triangular model is a good place to start in conceptualizing all types of relationships. His conception of intimacy encompasses feelings of closeness, passion includes romantic and sexual attraction, and commitment involves the decision that love exists and the relationship should continue. Figure 9.1 shows Sternberg's model and the different types of relationships that result from the combinations of these elements. Sternberg argued that if none of these components exists, there is no relationship.

In Sternberg's model, liking occurs when people share intimacy, but not passion or commitment. When individuals share intimacy and commitment without passion, **companionate love** results. This type of love forms the basis for love relationships that endure and may be more conducive to lasting love relationships than the type of passion that often begins intimate love relationships. However, companionate love also describes what most people regard as close friendship.

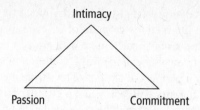

$$\text{Intimacy}$$

Passion   Commitment

Liking = Intimacy without Passion or Commitment
Companionate love = Intimacy + Commitment without Passion
Romantic love = Intimacy + Passion without Commitment
Empty love = Commitment without Passion or Intimacy
Fatuous love = Passion + Commitment without Intimacy
Infatuated love = Passion without Commitment or Intimacy
Consummate love = Passion + Commitment + Intimacy

FIGURE 9.1 *Sternberg's Triangular Theory of Love*

Source: Adapted from "A triangular theory of love," by R. J. Sternberg, 1986, *Psychological Review, 93,* pp. 123, 128. Adapted by permission of Robert Sternberg and the American Psychological Association.

Friendships

Although Sternberg's triangular theory of love makes no distinction between intimacy developed through sharing feelings or through sharing activities, these two styles tend to be associated with women and men, respectively. These gender differences have been the source of friction and contention, with men being accused of deficiencies in intimacy because their friendships are not the same style as women's friendships. That accusation has not always existed, nor do all cultures discourage intimate, emotional friendships between men (Nardi, 2007; O'Donnell & O'Rouke, 2003). The Greeks believed that true friendships could exist only between free and equal individuals, which restricted true friendship to a limited number and omitted all women, slaves, and men of lesser social standing. That view differs sharply from modern, Western society, where the type of intimacy typical of women's friendships has become the model.

Development of Styles

The basis for gender differences in friendship begins early in development, with a tendency for children to segregate themselves according to gender (Maccoby, 2002). Starting at preschool age and becoming more pronounced throughout elementary and middle school, children group themselves according to gender, even if parents or teachers do not. When girls and boys are put into situations in which they must interact, they do, but the tendency to group into same-gender associations is a persistent pattern for children and occurs in many cultures (Munroe & Romney, 2006).

The interaction patterns of boys and girls differ, beginning very early in development. A study that focused on the interactions of pairs of 33-month-old children (Jacklin & Maccoby, 1978) found that children interacted more with those of the same rather than with the other gender, in both positive and negative ways. Children in same-gender pairs were more likely to offer toys to their partners or try to take toys from their partners than the children in mixed-gender pairs. In pairs with a boy and a girl, the girls tended to be passive, standing by and watching the boys play, and the boys tended to be unresponsive, ignoring what the girls said to them. In same-gender pairs, the girls were active in their exchanges, and the boys were responsive to their partners' messages. If these reactions are typical, no wonder gender segregation occurs; playing would not be that much fun if your partner failed to react and did not listen.

Before age 3, children may show preferences for playmates, but between ages 3 and 6 years, children begin to show signs of developing friendships, such as being able to name a person as a friend and even saying who is a "best" friend (Berndt, 2004; Lindsey, 2002). Children's notion of friendship progresses, and personal characteristics become important in choosing friends. During elementary and middle school, children become more involved in friendships, relying on friends rather than siblings and parents for companionship and intimacy (Cleary, Ray, LoBello, & Zachar, 2002). The research on elementary school children has demonstrated that friends were important sources of companionship for these 2nd, 3rd, 5th, and 6th graders. Friendship is an important part of the lives of preadolescents; it can promote healthy adjustment (Waldrip, Malcolm, & Jensen-Campbell, 2008). Friends can also be a negative influence during this developmental period, providing encouragement for destructive behaviors (Berndt, 2004; Wissink, Dekovic, & Meijer, 2009).

Gender differences in the development of intimate friendship appear during elementary school. One possible basis for the gender differences in friendships during middle childhood comes from the different activities that girls and boys enjoy during these years. For example, boys are more fond of rough-and-tumble play than girls are. Such play involves play-fighting and chasing and is slightly more common among boys than girls (Scott & Panksepp, 2003). Boys also tend to play in somewhat larger groups, to spend more time outside, and to engage in activities that involve **gross motor skills**, such as running, jumping, and throwing a ball. Observing children on playgrounds demonstrates gender segregation but not overall differences in levels of activity—girls are as physically active as boys (Mota et al., 2005). However, girls both seek and value intimacy more than boys (Cleary et al., 2002; Rose, 2007). This desire may also make girls' friendships more fragile than boys' friendships; girls' friendship networks change more rapidly than boys' circles of friends (Benenson & Christakos, 2003; Chan & Poulin, 2007).

Gender is not the only basis for self-segregation during the early school years. Ethnic and racial background are also characteristics that children notice and use as a basis for forming groups. Ethnic background showed less of an effect than gender as a basis for groupings in one study (DuBois & Hirsch, 1990). When put into a position to choose, children crossed ethnic lines before gender lines. Interracial friendships form at school, but tend to be less common as children get older (Aboud, Mendelson, & Purdy, 2003). However, the patterns of crossing ethnic lines to form friends may persist into adulthood (Joyner & Kao, 2000), and cross-ethnic friendships are similar to other friendships in terms of loyalty and intimacy. Attending an integrated school increases the chances of making friends with someone from another ethnic group, but ethnicity remains a basis for grouping.

Boys tend to form friendships based on activities.

Gender segregation is a strong force during the elementary school years, and some researchers have contended that two words exist for children during this developmental period—a girls' and a boys' culture (McDougall & Hymel, 2007). Children are certainly reluctant to cross gender lines (Thorne, 1993), imposing this segregation on themselves, even when adults do not. When children cross the gender boundaries, some of the interactions are hostile, taking the form of name-calling, invading another's space, pollution games and rituals ("cooties"), and occasional fights. Situations of comfortable interaction may not represent common observations, but a study of children and adolescents (McDougall & Hymel, 2007) found that almost all the participants reported that cross-gender friendships were possible, and 93% said they had experienced such a friendship.

Preadolescents must avoid members of the other gender except under certain sanctioned circumstances, yet each gender must have sufficient contact to learn about the other. Research has suggested that friendships are important in the development of romantic relationships. One study (Furman, Simon, Shaffer, & Bouchey, 2002) analyzed friendship and parental relationships to understand formation of romantic relationships and found that characteristics of friendship were a better predictor than parental relationships. Considering that both friendships and romantic relationships are peer relationships of relative equality, this similarity makes sense. Thus, same-gender friendships during childhood may serve the function of allowing individuals to learn how to form relationships without the pressure of sexual contact. Referring back to Sternberg's model of relationships, these relationships allow the development of intimacy and commitment without passion. Childhood friendships, then, might be regarded as a type of practice for adolescent and adult romantic

Girls tend to form friendships that include emotional intimacy.

relationships. The active avoidance that children practice for the other sex changes to active interest during adolescence; contact between girls and boys becomes more common, but friendships between girls and boys remain much less common than same-sex friendships.

Friendships over the Life Span

Friendships during adolescence are similar to those of preadolescence, but adolescents intensify the intimacy in their relationships with a greater degree of personal sharing and self-disclosure than those of younger children (McDougall & Hymel, 2007). The gender differences in the value and attainment of intimacy persist, with girls more likely to be interested in forming emotionally intimate friendships with a smaller set of girls, and boys more likely to form activity-based friendships with a more extensive set of boys. The type of friendship may relate to the gender difference in competition among friends. Boys are more competitive with their friends than girls are, but competition decreases relationship satisfaction (Singleton & Vacca, 2007).

Adolescent girls use talk as a way to develop intimacy, to reveal and learn intimate knowledge about each other, which includes a greater involvement with problems and life transitions than boys' friendships do (Roy, Benenson, & Lilly, 2000). Although this type of exchange tends to make girls' friendships closer, it may serve as a way to magnify problems and increase personal distress (Calmes & Roberts, 2008). Not all relationships involve the same degree of talk-based intimacy. African American women also rated emotional communication as less important to friendship than European American and Asian American women (Samter & Burleson, 2005). African American men placed the lowest value on emotional communication.

This attitude of aloofness and withdrawal from intimacy is a set of behaviors that Richard Majors and his colleagues (Hall, 2009; Majors & Billson, 1992; Majors, Tyler, Peden, & Hall, 1994) labeled *cool pose*. Cool pose is a way that African American men present themselves, used as a compensation and coping strategy. The poses, postures, humor, readiness to use violence, and suppression of emotional displays are intended to create visibility for those who have been made invisible by a society that fails to grant African American men the status of European American men. The violence and suppression of emotion are elements of the masculine gender role, and cool pose uses an exaggeration of this role. This exaggeration allows African American men to feel a sense of masculinity. Cool pose magnifies some of the destructive elements of the masculine gender role, creating problems for those who take this pose. In addition to the violence associated with interpersonal conflicts, the emotional remoteness that is essential to the cool pose also inhibits the development of intimacy, both with women and with other men. A study of young African American men confirmed both the feelings of vulnerability and the hypermasculinity that are characteristic of cool pose (Cassidy & Stevenson, 2005).

Adherence to a traditional model of masculinity affects men of all ethnic groups because emotional closeness is a feminine behavior, and traditional men must avoid feminine behavior. Indeed, one study (Oransky & Marecek, 2009) of White adolescent boys examined how these boys concentrated on deriding and mocking displays of concern and caring in their peer groups, labeling them as "girly" and "gay." This attitude discourages men from having close friends but allows comrades or "buddies." The distinction is important: A comrade is important for the function he serves, such as playing cards, fixing cars, or being a team member, but another person can fill that position. Friends are valued as individuals in personal relationships. A study of middle-aged White men (Levy, 2005) showed that acceptance of traditional masculinity predicted having buddies but not friends.

Studies of friendship among college students (Caldwell & Peplau, 1982; Radmacher & Azmitia, 2006; Roy et al., 2000) confirmed some gender differences and similarities in friendship. These studies failed to find differences in the number or importance of friendships or in the time spent with friends. Men were more likely than women to choose an activity to do with a friend rather than "just talk" and to choose their friends on the basis of shared activities rather than shared attitudes. Some research indicates that both men and women acknowledge the importance of emotional sharing as a component of intimacy in friendship (Fehr, 2004), but women were more likely to talk about personal problems and celebrate personal accomplishments with female friends. Women in Russia reported similar patterns of friendship (Sheets & Lugar, 2005).

With the formation of committed love relationships, birth of children, and transition to the workforce, changes occur in existing friendships and the opportunities to form new friendships. Workplace settings become important in friendship formation, presenting people with similar interests with whom colleagues spend time. Research on young professionals' work-based friendships (Gibbons & Olk, 2003) indicated that young professionals readily crossed gender but not ethnic boundaries in making friends at work.

During the early years of marriage or committed relationships, both partners may relinquish other relationships to develop their relationship, seeking emotional intimacy and support from each other rather than from friends. In addition, when couples have children, the children take up time that might have been devoted to friends (or even to spouses). Young couples, especially those with children, tend to devote less time to other friendships than people who are single or childless. Thus, several circumstances can alter friendships (Fehr, 2000). If people lose proximity and fail to put effort into maintaining friendships, they tend to dissolve. Women are more likely than men to work at maintaining a network of social relationships, and the social support derived from these networks is important for happiness and even for health.

Aging produces changes in friendships, with the elderly needing more practical support while their number of friends decreases due to death. Children often become the source of this caregiving and practical support, but older people attempt to maintain social networks (Pahl & Pevalin, 2005). Older people receive different types of support from family and friends, and both are important to healthy aging (Blieszner, 2000). Women become more numerous in the social networks of the elderly because men die at younger ages, leaving more women. Thus, men's same-gender friendships tend to be replaced with relationships with women. Therefore, friendship becomes more female-based among older people.

Flexibility of Styles

Men may find emotional intimacy easier with women than with other men. As Francesca Cancian (1987) proposed, love has come to be "feminized," that is, defined in feminine terms, as the expression of feelings and as self-disclosure. These characteristics are commonly associated with women and are actually more common in women's than men's friendships. But men can also use this style of relationship and tend to do so when they relate to women, either as friends or as romantic partners.

When people think of friends, they imagine people of the same gender, so cross-gender friendships break this "rule." The model for cross-gender relationships is romance, so cross-gender friendships also break this rule. These friendships are a social development that did not exist 100 years ago when Western societies were strongly gender segregated, and women governed the home and men occupied the world of work, politics, and business. Although gender segregation still exists in some situations, school and work offer opportunities for cross-gender relationships (Sias, Smith, & Avdeyeva, 2003).

Because these friendships deviate from people's stereotypes of what friendship should be, cross-gender friendships face challenges and constraints. The friends frequently must explain "we're just good friends" to others, especially romantic partners, who may be jealous (Bevan & Samter, 2004). Some research has found that cross-gender friendships face barriers (Werking, 1997), but other research (Monsour, 2002) presented a more optimistic picture. Indeed, a survey of people in the United States indicated that cross-gender friendships have become more common and more well accepted, among both children (McDougall & Hymel, 2007) and young adults who grew up with less gender segregation than older individuals (Paul, 2003).

Individuals involved in cross-gender friendships agree that these relationships differ from same-gender friendships (McDougall & Hymel, 2007), but both men and women are usually able to use different styles of relating in different relationships (DeLucia-Waack, Gerrity, Taub, & Baldo, 2001). The ability to adapt to the situation by using a more "feminine" or "masculine" style of interaction indicates that styles of friendship are indeed roles that men and women learn. Although not all men may learn the intimate sharing and self-disclosure that are typical of women's friendships, most do; these men use this style when they form friendships with women (Werking, 1997). Men who scored higher in femininity and women whose masculinity scores were high on the Bem Sex Role Inventory were more likely than individuals with more traditional gender role beliefs to form cross-gender friendships (Reeder, 2003).

Men may feel uncomfortable in enacting this friendship style for several reasons. As several researchers have pointed out, **homophobia**—the unreasonable fear and hatred of homosexuality—restrains men from seeking emotional intimacy with other men. Even when men know the style, they may be reluctant to use it. When they use it, they may feel more comfortable in this type of relationship with women rather than with other men.

The constraints on women's behavior are not as strong; their typical style of emotional intimacy with other women carries no homosexual connotations. However, emotional intimacy between women and men often has an element of a sexual relationship, so women who seek friendships with men also often feel that they must be vigilant in maintaining these as nonsexual friendships. Women who adopt an activity-based style of relationship with men, being "one of the boys," can participate in the same activities that men enjoy with each other—playing baseball, poker, or other recreational activities. This choice creates a style of relationship typical of men and not necessarily one infused with emotional intimacy. Some men and women have chosen to break the boundaries established during preschool and form friendships with members of the other sex. The research indicates that men and women know about both friendship styles, suggesting that any limitations in creating cross-gender friendships come from reluctance to apply these styles.

Love Relationships

As the headline story on romantic love (Kluger et al., 2008) described, love relationships are an experience that occurs in all cultures. Kluger and his colleagues contacted one of the experts on love relationships, Elaine Hatfield, who has examined the history of romantic, passionate love. Hatfield and Richard Rapson (1996) contended that this type of love has not been the basis for permanent relationships until recently in industrialized Western countries. Historically, passionate, romantic love has posed a threat to the existing social structure and has rarely formed the basis for permanent relationships (Hatfield & Rapson, 1996). Many cultures have literature or legends about lovers who have died tragically as the result of their passion and the unsuitability of any permanent relationship. The story of Romeo and Juliet is an example familiar to English-speaking cultures, but Hatfield and Rapson described similar stories from ancient and modern societies around the world. Passionate love has been seen as madness rather than a good basis for marriage. The more common pattern for forming permanent relationships has been (and in many cultures remains) arranged marriages in which families choose mates for children. In such arranged marriages, financial considerations rather than love or passion have been the motivations for the match.

Several different patterns of love relationships have existed over the past several centuries in Western cultures (Cancian, 1987). Before the 1800s, agriculture was the basis for most people's livelihood, and both men and women worked together on family farms, making the family the center of both men's and women's lives. Although men were the heads of households, both men and women believed that marriage gave them the duty to love and help one another. In Sternberg's (1986) triangular model of love, this Family Duty blueprint ensured an equal relationship between the partners. Such marriages were formed around commitment, and the sharing of home life made intimacy very likely, but the component of passion might have been missing from such duty-bound relationships. In arranged marriages, this component might never be part of the relationship of a married couple.

By the 1800s, the Industrial Revolution had changed the pattern of many people's lives that affected marriage and family. Work and family became separate spheres. Men worked in jobs in factories and offices rather than around the home. Women, too, might work in factories, but the ideal pattern was for men to fulfill the Good Provider role (Bernard, 1981) and for women to be mothers and wives. This division led to the Doctrine of the Two Spheres (Welter, 1978), the view that women's place was home and family life and men's role was to go into the outside world and earn a living.

Women's role as caregivers led to the widespread perception that women were the experts in love: They were the ones who had the tender feelings and experienced the emotions; they were the ones who needed love and depended on men and children for it; they were the ones most capable of providing love to others. This type of marriage made women dependent on men for financial security, so maintaining the love of a husband became essential to women's financial security.

During the 1920s, women started to move into the male world of work, taking paid jobs outside the home. With increasing economic power, women were less dependent on men for financial security, which changed the blueprint for marriage to the Companionship model (Cancian, 1987). Cancian credited the Companionship blueprint with the feminization of love. This model focused on affection and support for each other, but women were still the experts on love and held the responsibility for the relationship: "Marriage was to be all of a woman's life but only part of a man's" (Cancian, 1987, p. 34).

The Companionship model for marriage became the standard. Spouses were supposed to love each other before they married and to choose their partners rather than relying on partners chosen by family. Using Sternberg's model to analyze these relationships, consummate love was the ideal, with an equal mixture of intimacy, passion, and commitment. However, romantic love was also a possibility, with its combination of passion and intimacy but lack of commitment. The divorce rate increased during this time, which provided evidence for the rising lack of commitment under the Companionship blueprint (Cancian, 1987).

The emphasis on personal compatibility and romance in marriage prompted a different method of selecting marriage partners. Rather than rely on the family to choose their partners or making decisions on an economic basis, individuals started to choose their own mates. Dating arose as a way of finding suitable marriage partners for Companionship-style marriages.

Dating

Dating began during the 1920s as a form of courtship but has expanded to fulfill a variety of other functions, including recreation, status, companionship, sexual exploration, and the skills to form intimate relationships (Quatman, Sampson, Robinson, & Watson, 2001).

Along with this form of courtship came a format for dating, which can be analyzed in terms of a script that guides young men's and women's behavior on dates (Morr Serewicz & Gale, 2008; Rose & Frieze, 1993). College students adhered to this script in describing first heterosexual dates. Descriptions of an actual and hypothetical first date showed a great deal of agreement between the two scripts (Rose & Frieze, 1993). However, the scripted roles for women and men differed substantially, with men leading and acting and women following and reacting. The woman's reactive role includes being concerned about her appearance, participating in the activities her partner planned, and reacting to his sexual advances, all of which matches traditional gender stereotypes. Although they do not have traditional gender stereotypes to follow on first dates, gay men's and lesbians' first dates also follow a script that is very similar to that of heterosexual couples (Klinkenberg & Rose, 1994; Rose & Zand, 2002).

Greater variety in dating began to appear after the 1940s, with girls initiating, planning, and paying for dates. Dating has evolved into a variety of activities, including mixed-gender group dating, which is popular among young adolescents (Connolly, Craig, Goldberg, & Pepler, 2004). Despite the existence of variations on the pattern of male-initiated dates, the traditional script for heterosexual dating has changed little, and most dates adhere to this scripted pattern (Laner & Ventrone, 2000; Morr Serewicz & Gale, 2008).

Dating has become an important part of adolescent life, and 57% of young people in the United States between 12 and 17 years old go out on dates regularly; about a third have a steady boyfriend or girlfriend (Fetto, 2003). Older adolescents are more likely to be involved in a romantic relationship than younger adolescents (Meier & Allen, 2009).

▢ GENDERED VOICES

I Was Terrible at Being a Girl

"I was fairly bad at being a girl when I was a child," a middle-aged woman told me. "I did tomboy-type things. But I was really terrible at it when I was a teenager and trying to date and attract boys. Dating seemed like a game, and the rules were so silly. And I was bad at the game. Flirting was a disaster—I felt so silly and incompetent.

"My mother practically despaired of my ever behaving in ways that would lead to dates. She would give me advice, such as 'Hide how smart you are, because boys don't like to date girls who are smarter than they are,' and 'Wait for him to open the door for you.' I thought both those things were pretty pointless. Why should I hide how smart I was? I had gone to school with most of the guys in my high school since we were all in elementary school, so they knew how smart I was. Besides, if I could have fooled one, I didn't think that I could have kept up the

charade. I wasn't smart enough to play dumb for all that long. Also, why would I want to date a guy who wanted a dumb girl? Sounded like a poor prospect to me.

"I know that opening doors became an issue in the 1970s feminist movement, but my objections were about 10 years earlier. It just seemed silly to me that a perfectly capable person, me, should inconvenience a guy to open a door. I was more than capable of doing so, and I never saw why I shouldn't—still don't for that matter. I now see having doors opened as a courtesy, which is O.K. I open doors for both men and women. There's probably too much made of that particular issue, but when I was a teenager, it was something my mother warned me about on numerous occasions. I just had a hard time getting the rules of the game—I was terrible at the girl stuff. I am much better at being a woman than I was at being a girl."

◼ GENDERED VOICES

Dating Strategies

Two women in their 30s were talking about their lives, and one told the other that she had gone on a date with a man but didn't see the point of continuing to do so because it didn't show much promise of turning into a serious relationship. The other woman tried to convince her friend that all dates were not prospective mates, so dating does not necessarily lead to a serious relationship.

These two attitudes reflect the research about dating, with some adults concentrating on finding lifelong partners and others dating as part of an active social life. The reluctant woman remained difficult to convince, but her friend told her, "Just think of it as your own catch-and-release program."

Younger adolescents reported that excitement was more important to their dating choices than did older adolescents, but companionship and emotional involvement were important for all ages of adolescents involved in dating.

Although dating is a highly desired activity for most adolescents, dating presents disadvantages as well as advantages (Furman, Ho, & Low, 2007). Disadvantages include stress, an increased chance of depression, and a decrease in academic motivation and achievement, and advantages include an increase in prestige and self-esteem (Quatman et al., 2001). Both the advantages and disadvantages intensified with more frequent dating. Girls who begin dating at younger ages tend to experience increased risks for problem behaviors such as smoking, alcohol use, and other sensation-seeking behaviors (Martin et al., 2007). Both boys and girls feel similar anxiety and pressures involved in dating and experience similar emotional involvement with their dating partners (Giordano, Longmore, & Manning, 2006). Having a boyfriend/girlfriend adds to prestige but does not compensate for being unpopular among same-sex peers. Early adolescents who were unpopular with peers and had a boyfriend or girlfriend were more poorly adjusted and showed more behavioral problems than unpopular adolescents who did not (Brendgen, Vitaro, Doyle, Markiewicz, & Bukowski, 2002). Therefore, for adolescents, dating and romantic relationships are important and desirable but not entirely positive experiences.

A poll of single adults (Reuters, 2008) indicated that about one-fourth had not been on a date during the past year. Adults are interested in dating to find a long-term relationship; 68% of respondents named love and marriage as a goal. Younger singles were more interested in marriage than older ones, but both older and younger adults have begun to use online dating services as a way to form a relationship. A decade ago, only about 8% of singles had used an online dating service, but that number has risen to 48% of men and 52% of women ("Survey says," 2004). Even older adults have used online dating services to seek romantic partners (Malt, 2007). However, most singles continue to rely on friends, family, and coworkers to introduce them to potential partners (Reuters, 2008).

The advent of the ability to meet people online has affected relationships for both adolescents and adults. A nationwide survey of adolescents (Wolak, Mitchell, & Finkelhor, 2002) revealed that 14% had formed a close relationship with someone online within the year. Only 2% described their online relationship as a romance, but 71% were cross-gender relationships. Despite widespread publicity about teenagers victimized by adult predators online, most teenagers are more cautious than publicity suggests (Wolak, Finkelhor, & Mitchell, 2008). A small minority (17%) qualified as unrestricted Internet users who participated in behaviors that put them at risk of receiving unwanted sexual solicitations, but the majority (51%) were cautious Internet users who interacted online only with individuals they knew personally. Nevertheless, a small percentage of young adolescents use the Internet frequently to interact with people they do not know, and forming romantic relationships is more common among this group, which places them at risk for exploitation (Peter, Valkenburg, & Schouten, 2005).

What people want in casual dating partners may differ from what they seek for long-term relationships (Sprecher & Regan, 2002). The qualities of warmth and kindness, expressivity and openness, and a good sense of humor were common across all types of relationships, but an emphasis on physical attractiveness and social status was high for dating relationships, especially long-term ones. In the study of speed dating (Luo & Zhang, 2009), physical attractiveness appeared as the strongest predictor of attraction. This result stands in contrast to stereotypes about men's emphasis on physical attractiveness, which is a prominent feature of evolutionary psychology's conceptualization of mate selection.

Evolutionary psychology is an area of psychology that examines how adaptation pressures have shaped contemporary behavior. "Evolutionary psychologists believe that females and males faced different pressures in primeval environments and that the sexes' differing reproductive status was the key feature of ancestral life that framed sex-typed adaptive problems" (Eagly & Wood, 1999, p. 408). According to this concept, remote prehuman history left gender-related differences that appear today in people's selection of mates. This view hypothesizes that men's best strategy was to reproduce as often as possible, whereas women are limited in their reproductive abilities because they can bear a limited number of children. Thus they must select mates that will help them raise their children (Buss, 1994). Preference for physical attractiveness is one of the factors that evolutionary psychology sees as a gender difference, with men valuing attractive partners because attractiveness is a sign of health and reproductive fitness. According to this view, women are less concerned with looks; women value mates who can provide resources to support them and their children.

Men tend to emphasize the attractiveness of their partner more than women do (Buss, 1994; Shackelford, Schmitt, & Buss, 2005) but perhaps not under all circumstances. When women's access to economic resources are similar to men's, the gender differences in characteristics important to mate selection decrease (Moore, Cassidy, Smith, & Perrett, 2006). In a study spanning almost 60 years (Buss, Shackelford, Kirkpatrick, & Larsen, 2001), results indicated that men are not alone—attractiveness has become more valued by both women and men. Thus, the value of attractiveness is more similar now than in the past. In addition, the adaptive advantage of attractiveness is questionable; beauty is not closely related to health and reproductive ability (Weeden & Sabini, 2005). Many women considered beautiful have fertility problems. A more reliable sign of reproductive capability is having borne children; however, the evolutionary psychologists do not hypothesize that women with young children are the most attractive potential mates, despite their demonstrated reproductive success.

Evolutionary psychology also predicts that attractiveness should be more important in heterosexual attraction than for gay or lesbian couples. A test of this hypothesis failed; few differences in partner preference appeared in the descriptions of desirable partner characteristics in male–male, female–female, as well as male–female couples (Howard,

Blumstein, & Schwartz, 1987). All said they wanted romantic partners who were kind, considerate, and physically attractive. In addition, gay men and lesbians reported preferences for characteristics of dating partners and long-term mates that were similar to preferences of heterosexuals (Regan, Medina, & Joshi, 2001). Regardless of sexual orientation, people seek similar qualities in romantic partners (Peplau & Fingerhut, 2007; Peplau & Spalding, 2000). Thus, key points in evolutionary psychology's conceptualization of mate selection have failed to gain research support.

Other characteristics that attract people to romantic partners include similarities of personal values. That is, people are romantically attracted to others who are more like than different from them. Mate selection is more a matter of "birds of a feather flock together" than "opposites attract" (Antill, 1983). These similarities include not only personal values but also ethnicity, social class, and religion (Martin, Bradford, Drzewiecka, & Chitgopekar, 2003), and the more important such characteristics are to individuals, the more satisfied they are with their relationship when they and their partners are similar (Lutz-Zois, Bradley, Mihalik, & Moorman-Eavers, 2006). Love and mutual attraction rank as the most important reason for mate selection, but intelligence, education, and a pleasing personality also receive high ratings (Buss et al., 2001).

Despite the opinion of adolescents that their dating is not oriented toward mate selection, dating is the process through which most men and women find partners. The patterns of relating to each other established during dating carry over into marriage, but marriage is a major life transition. When people marry, they assume the new roles of husband and wife.

Marriage and Committed Relationships

Marriage is not the only form of committed romantic relationship. Gay and lesbian couples cannot legally marry in most places, and heterosexual couples sometimes choose to live together without marrying. The number of cohabiting heterosexual couples has dramatically increased since the 1960s. In the United States in 1960, less than half a million heterosexual couples were cohabiting, but in 2008, almost 7 million were, representing an increase of more than 1,300% (U.S. Census Bureau, 2009b). As shown in Figure 9.2, this change is dramatic and represents the biggest change in committed relationships. For some couples, cohabitation has replaced marriage—members of these couples see more costs than benefits to marrying (McGinnis, 2003). For many cohabiting couples, cohabitation precedes marriage, and its increased social acceptance has made cohabitation a variation in intimate relationships.

Marriage and divorce have also changed over the past 50 years. The rate of marriages declined between 1980 and 2006. Divorce rates doubled between 1960 and the 1980s but began to decline in the 1990s. Both trends continue, as shown in Figure 9.3 (page 218).

Despite the increased prevalence of cohabitation, the majority of research on gender and committed relationships has focused on marriage. Several styles of marriage now exist, following the patterns Cancian (1987) called the Companionship, Independence, and Interdependence blueprints. The Companionship blueprint discussed earlier was the model for most marriages in the United States from the 1920s until the 1960s. Partners who follow this pattern tend to have well-defined and separate gender roles, with women responsible for maintaining the love relationship. This type of marriage is now considered traditional, because its adherents oppose self-development for women, a major tenet of the Independence blueprint.

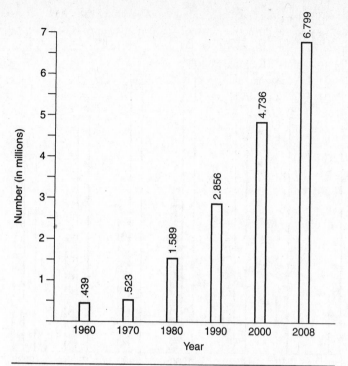

FIGURE 9.2   *Increases in Number of Unmarried Couple Households, 1960–2008*

Sources: U.S. Census Bureau, *Unmarried partners of the opposite sex, by presence of children: 1960 to present.* Retrieved September 5, 2009, from http://www.census.gov/population/www/socdemo/hh-fam.html#cps.

The Independence blueprint arose during the 1960s, a period that emphasized personal freedom and change. Increases in paid employment for women and the women's movement led to an examination of the ground rules for relationships, and both men and women started to believe that marriage should be a partnership of equals. This model emphasizes self-development over commitment and obligations, holding that a relationship is the meeting of two independent individuals. The emphasis on self-development resulted in less well-defined gender roles, and the concept of androgynous marriage arose. Cancian criticized this blueprint for encouraging empty relationships without sufficient commitment.

The Interdependence blueprint is an alternative to the Independence model. Interdependence also includes flexible gender roles, but calls for commitment based on acknowledging mutual dependence. Cancian argued that partners are always dependent on each other in marriage and that both the Companionship and Independence blueprints ignore this inevitable interdependence. Table 9.1 (page 218) shows the three blueprints and the important characteristics of each.

Sternberg's (1986) triangular model of love explains these different blueprints for marriage with differences in the three components of intimacy, passion, and commitment. Companionship-style marriages would have all three components but not in equal proportion for men and women. Under this blueprint, women seek more intimacy than men,

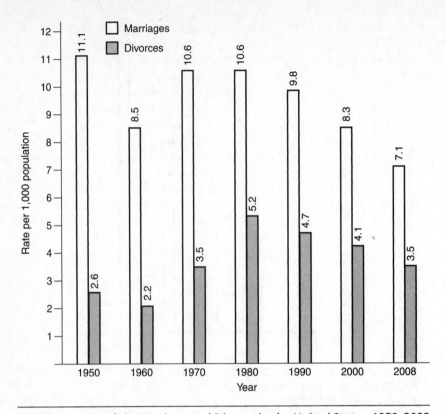

FIGURE 9.3   *Trends in Marriage and Divorce in the United States, 1950–2008*

Source: Data from *Statistical Abstract of the United States, 2006* (125th ed.), Table 72,
U.S. Census Bureau, 2006, Washington, DC: U.S. Government Printing Office, and "Births,
marriages, divorces, and deaths: Provisional data for 2008," *National Vital Statistics Reports,*
2009, vol. 57, no. 19, Table A.

TABLE 9.1   *Cancian's Blueprints for Love Relationships*

	Companionship (devotion to each other)	Independence (self-development)	Interdependence (mutual dependence)
Are traditional gender roles maintained?	Yes	No	No
Is the relationship stable?	Yes	No	Yes
Who is responsible for maintaining the relationship?	Women	Neither partner	Both partners
Who develops personal interests?	Men	Both partners	Both partners

producing an unequal balance between such partners. The Independence blueprint is short on the component of commitment, but Interdependent marriages should fit what Sternberg called consummate love, the equal balance of all three components.

Marriages and other committed relationships may follow any of the blueprints, and contemporary couples may build any of these various types of relationships. However, a longitudinal study of expectations for marriage (Botkin, Weeks, & Morris, 2000) revealed that changes have occurred in women's conceptualizations of marriage. Between the 1960s and the 1970s, a large shift occurred toward beliefs in egalitarian marriages. After the 1970s, those beliefs have persisted, and the percentage of college women who believe in egalitarian marriage relationships is over 90%. This percentage has implications for several facets of committed relationships, including men's and women's concepts of romantic love and marriage, communication between partners, division of labor in households, power and conflict in marriage, and the stability of love relationships.

Concepts of Love and Marriage.

Contrary to popular expectation (see According to the Media and According to the Research), men have more traditional concepts of love and marriage and are more romantic than women. Although men and women tend to choose partners who have similarly traditional or nontraditional beliefs about gender roles, the man of any given couple is likely to be more traditional than the woman and more likely than women to endorse statements such as "Women's activities should be confined to the home" (Glick & Fiske, 2001). This tendency for men to be more traditional concerning gender roles appears in many cultures (Hatfield & Rapson, 1996), but some research (Kalmijn, 2005; Pnina, 2009) has indicated that these discrepancies become smaller through the years of marriage by men becoming more egalitarian. The continued association of marriage partners does not produce identical beliefs, however, and the majority of the differences remain. Thus, even after years of marriage, husbands are more likely than wives to hold traditional, conservative beliefs about gender roles.

Men's idealized romantic beliefs extend across ethnic groups in the United States and exist in China (Sprecher & Toro-Mourn, 2002) and Taiwan (Lin & Raghubir, 2003). For example, men are more likely to have romantic beliefs such as "Love lasts forever" and "There is one perfect love in the world for everyone." Women, however, are more likely to report physical symptoms of being in love, such as feeling like they are "floating on a cloud." Men choose Valentine messages of praise and commitment to their beloved, whereas women's Valentines convey love and fidelity (Quintero-Gonzalez & Koestner, 2006). In other ways, men and women are similar in idealizing love; both tend to believe that their partners are better looking than they are (Swami, Steiger, Haubner, Voracek, & Furnham, 2009) and that love and mutual attraction are the most important factors for marriage (Falconi & Mullet, 2003).

Romanticism does not necessarily make men feel more favorable toward marriage (Whitehead & Popenoe, 2002). Indeed, young, single women expressed a greater desire to get married than comparable men (Blakemore, Lawton, & Vartanian, 2005). Despite men's lack of enthusiasm for marriage, married men are physically and mentally healthier than single men (de Vaus, 2002). Married women may experience more satisfaction from marriage than men do (Kiecolt-Glaser & Newton, 2001), but they also find more stresses in their marriages (Sachs-Ericsson & Ciarlo, 2000).

ACCORDING TO THE MEDIA . . .

Bad Men Can Be Transformed by Women's Love

The notion that love can be transformational reaches far beyond films, but movies are filled with images of selfish, roguish scoundrels transformed into heroes by women's love. This plot is a movie staple (Aronson & Kimmel, 1997) and an enduring myth (Galician & Merskin, 2007). Probably the ultimate transformation by love was the Beast of *Beauty and the Beast,* who was transformed—literally—from a monster into a prince by Beauty's love ("Dr. FUN," 2004).

These portrayals affect women, who come to believe that their love has the power to transform a bad man into a good one. *New York Times* columnist Anna Quindlen (reported in Aronson & Kimmel, 1997) asked female readers to choose a mate—either a kind, faithful, careful man or a roguish, self-interested scoundrel, and the vote was overwhelmingly for the nice guy. When she identified one as Ashley Wilkes and the other as Rhett Butler, however, some women felt different. One woman said, "Well, that's different . . . . Rhett Butler's never been loved by me. When I love him, he'll change" (Aronson & Kimmel, 1997, p. 32), demonstrating the belief in the media-based romantic fantasy of the transformational power of their love. One advice columnist proposed this strategy to "nice guys," suggesting that they act like "bad boys" and make "her believe that she is the one to tame you" (Marder, 2005, p. 40).

Most of the studies of marital satisfaction have questioned only European American participants, however, and this choice has limited the conclusions about attitudes toward marriage (Ball & Robbins, 1986). Investigating marital satisfaction among African Americans showed that married African American women were more satisfied with their lives than single women were, but this difference disappeared when these researchers controlled for demographic factors such as age and health. Indeed, African Americans tend to be less satisfied with their marriages than their White counterparts, with women less satisfied than men (Corra, Carter, Knox, & Houvouras, 2006).

Communication between Partners.   The issue of couples' communication in marriage has received an enormous amount of publicity. Indeed, it has become an industry; John Gray's (1992) *Men Are from Mars, Women Are from Venus* topped the best-seller list for years, prompting sequels, and allowing Gray to hold seminars, train other counselors, and present a Broadway show based on the concept. His proposal that men and women are from different planets originated from his advice to women to communicate with their husbands as if they were beings from another planet. Gray's characterization is an overstatement of gender differences in communication (Cameron, 2007), but some differences do exist.

The same gender differences that researchers have found in friendship styles also influence communication in marriage. Women create emotional intimacy through talk and self-disclosure, whereas men tend to do so through activity. In marriage, sex is often the activity that men use to create intimacy. Cancian (1987) argued that in most contemporary couples, wives do not count sex as communication or as a method for establishing intimacy. Research (Heyman, Hunt-Martorano, Malik, & Slep, 2009) has confirmed this difference: Women would like for their male partners to be more emotionally communicative, and men would like more sex. This difference can produce a discrepancy in what each thinks is the level of communication in their relationship. Her survey of couples revealed that wives

■ ACCORDING TO THE RESEARCH . . .

Bad Men Are Dangerous to the Women Who Love Them

When women hope to change bad men through love, they may put themselves in danger. Some scoundrels may be changed through love, but many remain dangerous and harm the women who love them. Women are often reluctant to leave their abusive partners, partly for the reasons that attracted them—the risk-taking associated with scoundrels may be seen as evidence of bravery, a characteristic that women find attractive (Rebellon & Manasse, 2004). Women also tell themselves that "he will change" and "this time will be the last time he will hit/be unfaithful to/humiliate me," which allows women to believe that their abusive partners will change (as they often promise) to become the men these women fantasized.

Women who do leave their abusive partners do not necessarily escape the danger they have experienced. Indeed, leaving an abusive partner puts women at increased risk for harm (Tjaden & Thoennes, 2000a). Angry, resentful, or jealous former partners may stalk and do violence to the women who have left them. Indeed, women are more likely to be killed by an intimate partner during a separation than when they lived with these violent men. Staying with them is also dangerous: Women experience more than 1.3 million physical assaults from male partners each year. The romantic notion of transformative love appears in movies; in real life, abusive partners are dangerous.

value talking about feelings more than husbands do, but husbands may feel threatened when their wives want to talk. "Talking about the relationship as she wants to do will feel to him like taking a test that she has made up and he will fail" (Cancian, 1987, p. 93).

The differences between men's and women's typical styles of communication have been proposed as a major source of conflict in marriage (and other relationships). Deborah Tannen (1990) contended that men and women use different communication styles and strategies, even when the goals are similar. Tannen argued that men and women see communication as "a continual balancing act, juggling the conflicting needs for intimacy and independence" (p. 27). She contended that women's communication is oriented toward intimacy, focusing on forming communal connections with others, whereas men's communication is oriented toward hierarchy, focusing on attaining and demonstrating status, which is consistent with the styles that develop for same-sex friendships during childhood.

Tannen is correct in believing that communication is a major task for couples, but research has not substantiated her other contentions. People do *believe* that women's speech is more emotional than men's, although that stereotype has decreased over the past 25 years (Popp, Donovan, Crawford, Marsh, & Peele, 2003). People also believe that women will be more likely to show sympathy and communicate their support in problem situations (Basow & Rubenfeld, 2003). However, in a study in which men and women offered supportive communications (a "feminine" task), few differences appeared between men's and women's style of communication (MacGeorge, Graves, Feng, & Gillihan, 2004).

A more specific test of Tannen's model (Edwards & Hamilton, 2004) yielded results that failed to support her contention that men and women make different interpretations of the same messages. This study, however, found that gender role and the characteristics associated with gender role affected the interpretation of communications in complex ways rather than in the simple ways Tannen predicted.

Another way to analyze communication focuses on communication in terms of dominance and power, which encompass gender-related factors (Barnett & Rivers, 2004; Cameron, 2007). This view holds that men typically have more power, and the powerful communicate in ways that differ from the less powerful. Thus the subordinate role is more important in the communication than sex or even gender role. Indeed, unequal power and status affect many aspects of marriage and intimate relationships.

Balance of Power.   Most dating couples believe that marriages should be an equal balance of power and decision making (Sprecher, 2001; Sprecher & Felmlee, 1997), and these attitudes are shared by married couples, high school students, gay and lesbian couples (Peplau & Fingerhut, 2007), and the general population in the United States (Thornton & Young-DeMarco, 2001). Indeed, the growth of egalitarian attitudes is a striking trend that developed over the past 40 years, changing societies from a widespread acceptance of patriarchy and men as heads of households to a culture with egalitarian ideals, which has occurred in the United States and many other countries (Schwartz & Rubel-Lifschitz, 2009). The growth of egalitarian ideology paralleled the trend of employment for women, and access to economic resources is an important factor in power in intimate relationships (Tichenor, 2005a, 2005b). However, the association of men with earnings and high status give men a type of "hidden" power, which forms a cultural background for male dominance. "The marital power equation must take both money and gender into account" (Tichenor, 2005b, pp. 192–193).

The ideal of equal power often fails to be realized in couples' relationships because the background of traditional gender roles gives men more power than women. Thus it is not surprising that a little more than half of dating couples (Sprecher, 2001) reported that the man had more power. According to an extensive survey of couples in the United States performed by Philip Blumstein and Pepper Schwartz (1983), almost 64% reported an equal balance of power, but 28% of husbands and 9% of wives said they had more power. Other studies have shown a higher percentage of male dominance in heterosexual couples (Peplau & Campbell, 1989; Sprecher & Felmlee, 1997). In addition, men's decision-making power was higher than their overall power (Sprecher & Felmlee, 1997; Tichenor, 2005a), which may lead to substantial male dominance. Table 9.2 shows the power structure in couples according to three studies.

Even in couples that report an equal balance of power, both partners may not have an equal say in all decisions. Decision-making power may be divided along traditional

TABLE 9.2   *Ideal and Actual Power Structure in Couples*

	Peplau and Campbell Study (1989)		Blumstein and Schwartz (1983)	Sprecher and Felmlee Study (1997)	
	Men	**Women**	**Couples**	**Men**	**Women**
Believe in equal power	87%	95%			
Have equal power	42	49	64%	47%	48%
Husband has more power			28	35	29
Wife has more power			9	19	24

◼ GENDERED VOICES

When I Got Sober

"The balance of power in my marriage didn't change when I went to work, but when I got sober," a woman in her 40s told me. She had been a homemaker for a number of years before she started a career, and she said that earning money didn't make much of a change in her marriage. By the time she began her job, she had already started drinking heavily, and she continued to do so.

"Everybody took care of me, so I could drink and take drugs and get away with it. So I did. My daughter took care of me for most of her childhood. My husband also let me get away with being drunk most of the time. I was dependent on them, but then I got sober, and things changed.

"When I got sober, I started being able to take care of myself, and my family wasn't used to it. The balance of power changed in my marriage, and we eventually split up. I was sober and involved in AA, and my husband was still drinking, but that wasn't the main

problem. I started to become independent, and he couldn't adjust. I realize that it was quite an adjustment: I had never taken care of myself—never in my life—and then I started.

"I remember one incident in particular. I was trying to change the batteries in my small tape recorder, and my husband came over and took the recorder out of my hands and did it for me. I thought, 'I can do that for myself.' I started thinking that about a lot of things. As I started to become more independent, our marriage changed. In fact, our entire family changed, and most of those changes were good. The kids could come to me rather than go to their father for everything. I became a responsible person. With that responsibility came a growing desire to be independent, and now I am. The marriage became an emotional power struggle, with my growing self-reliance and my husband still trying to be in control."

lines, with men making financial decisions and women making household decisions. What couples report as an equal balance of power may actually be a division of decision making into husbands' and wives' domains. Results of a survey by the Pew Research Center (Jayson, 2008) confirmed this division: women made more household decisions. However, this division does not necessarily reflect wives' power; wives may be put into the position of making decisions that their husbands consider chores. For example, wives may decide what to have for dinner and what brand of cleaning products to use, and husbands may decide which house to buy and where to live.

One drawback of a majority of research is the educational and ethnic composition of the participants; couples are often college-educated, and most are White. A consideration of other ethnic groups brings other factors relating to power. The concepts of **matriarchy** and **machismo** have been associated with African American and Hispanic American families, respectively. A review of research on families, however, found that both patterns of unequal power were more myths than descriptions of the actual balance of power in these families (Peplau & Campbell, 1989). African American families are more likely to be headed by women than White families, but African American couples' power relationships show similar discrepancies to those in White couples (Cowdery et al., 2009). An equal sharing of power, the most common pattern in a large-scale study (Blumstein & Schwartz, 1983), was also the most common pattern in African American couples. For couples with an unequal balance of power, male dominance was more common than female dominance. The same patterns appeared in Mexican American families, with the most common pattern being one of shared power. Despite the prominence of the concepts of matriarchy and machismo, a fairly equal balance of power seems to be the rule for most couples in the United States, regardless of ethnic group. For couples that immigrated to the United States, a struggle occurred between the values of egalitarianism and the tradition of higher male power (Maciel, van Putten, & Knudson-Martin, 2009).

The background of gendered expectations cannot be a factor in power differences for lesbian and gay male couples, but such couples also experience power differentials (Peplau & Fingerhut, 2007; Peplau & Spalding, 2000). The differentiating factor for these couples also applies to heterosexual couples: money. For gay men and lesbians, both partners typically are employed, but incomes may be unequal (Blumstein & Schwartz, 1983; Solomon, Rothblum, & Balsam, 2005). For gay men, the relationship between money and relationship power was clear: Those with more money had more power. The relationship between money and power was less clear for lesbians, who tried to maintain an equal monetary contribution in their relationship so as to avoid unequal power, and failure to do so was a source of problems for these women.

For heterosexual couples, paid employment is an important factor in the balance of power in marriage that interacts with gendered expectations. Women who do not have paid employment tend to have less power in their marriages than women who earn money (Deutsch, Roska, & Meeske, 2003; Steil, 2000). The amount earned is also a factor; husbands who earn more money have more power. However, wives do not gain as much power from their earnings as husbands do (Bittman, England, Folbre, Sayer, & Matheson, 2003; Tichenor, 2005a, 2005b). Women accrue more power to the point that they earn about as much money as their husbands, but ironically, wives who earn more money than their husbands actually have *less* power in their marriages. This situation occurs because both wives and husbands work toward maintaining the appearance of traditional gender roles in which the wives perform the majority of the household work and child care and the husband manages the finances and makes important decisions (Tichenor, 2005a, 2005b). Wives receive appreciation for their earnings, but husbands may minimize wives' contributions and behave in ways to preserve their power. Therefore, wives who earn no income have low power; earning money brings increased power, but achieving marital power through income is difficult for women and easy for men to achieve.

Division of Household Labor.   The division of household labor has become an area of interest to gender researchers because who does the laundry may reveal information about power and equity in relationships. In addition, performance of household chores is a source of conflict for couples. As Karen Zagor commented, "Forget the glass ceiling: the new battle of the sexes is over housework" (2006, p. 34).

Traditional gender roles include a division of labor in households, with men working outside the home for wages and women working in the home providing housekeeping and child care. Throughout the 20th century, however, an increasing number of women in industrialized countries joined the paid workforce. Now, a majority of women in the United States and Australia, even those with young children, work for wages outside the home (Singleton & Maher, 2004); throughout Western Europe, the figure is about 40% (Apparala, Reifman, & Munsch, 2003).

To maintain equity, the changes in paid labor for women should have prompted a concomitant change in the division of housework, but those changes have been slow in coming. Researchers who examined division of household labor during the 1970s and 1980s found that employed women still performed the large majority of household labor (Coltrane, 2000). Sociologist Arlie Hochschild (1989) called this arrangement the Second Shift, a situation in which women work for wages outside the home plus perform the majority of housework and child-care chores at home. This arrangement can result in a situation in which women work the equivalent number of hours of two full-time jobs. According to an extensive review completed during the 1980s (Thompson & Walker, 1989), wives did about three times more housework and child care than husbands. More recent research (Coltrane, 2000; Cunningham, 2008; Sayer, 2005; Sullivan & Coltrane, 2007) has noted changes, with women doing less and men doing somewhat more household work. However, women still perform about more household work and child care than men do.

Many factors contribute to this continuing inequity. A very important factor is the belief that household work is gendered—some chores are "women's work" and others are "men's jobs" (Coltrane, 2000). The five most time-consuming chores (preparing meals, cleaning house, shopping for groceries, washing dishes, and doing laundry) are all work associated with women. Men's chores tend to be less time-consuming and less frequently required (making household repairs, taking out the trash, mowing the lawn). When husbands or wives hold traditional gender role attitudes, men do little work around the house. Even when men hold egalitarian beliefs, they may still avoid chores or leave their female partners with the primary responsibility for household care (Singleton & Maher, 2004).

An examination of gay and lesbian couples reinforces the importance of gendered expectations for household work. Gay and lesbian couples cannot use stereotypical associations to determine who does what chores (Boren, 2007; Kurdek, 1993; Peplau & Spalding, 2000). Both gay and lesbian couples tended to share household work more equitably than heterosexual married couples (Peplau & Fingerhut, 2007; Solomon et al., 2005). Gay couples were more likely to split tasks, with each partner performing a set of chores. Lesbian couples were more likely to alternate in sharing tasks, taking turns in performing the same chores. For gay and lesbian couples, communication and negotiation were important and tended to result in a more equitable division of household labor (Boren, 2007).

In addition to ideology, family and societal factors contribute to the division of house labor. Women's employment is an important factor: Employed women do less household work (Coltrane, 2000). Wives who have high-status, highly paid employment (such as professional or managerial jobs) experience increased power in their marriages, which may give these wives the freedom to do less housework (Bittman et al., 2003; Deutsch et al., 2003). High income does not always equate to high power for women (or fewer chores), but earning a high salary is an advantage for women in their marriages (Kan, 2008).

Marital status, education, and presence of children are also factors that affect household work arrangements. Being married increases the amount of household work that women do and decreases the amount men do (Coltrane, 2000), but the amount of time a man spends living on his own before marriage tends to push his attitude toward equal participation in household work (Pitt & Borland, 2008). Education also shows different patterns of influence for women and men. Women with higher levels of education tend to do less household work than women with lower levels of education, but men with higher levels of education are likely to do more household work than men with lower levels of education. This pattern occurs in Japan as well as in Western societies (Iwama, 2005). The presence of children increases women's work and decreases men's household work in the

TABLE 9.3 *Factors Related to Division of Household Work*

Men Do More Household Work When	Men Do Less Household Work When
Wives are employed outside the home	Wives are not employed outside the home
Wives' salaries are similar to their husbands' salaries	Wives earn more money than their husbands
Wives earn money that husbands consider important to the household	Husbands or wives hold traditional gender role beliefs
Both wives and husbands have high educational levels	They are married, especially in first marriage
Both husbands and wives hold egalitarian beliefs	A first child is born
Husbands believe that it is fair to share household work	Chores are "feminine"
Men have lived as bachelors on their own before marrying	
Chores are "masculine"	
Timing of task is flexible	

United States, possibly because women tend to decrease and men tend to increase their employment when children are born (Singleton & Maher, 2004) but possibly because poor parental leave policies in the United States tend to restrict men from child care. In Sweden, with its more accessible parental leave policies, parenthood affects men and women in similar ways (Dribe & Stanfors, 2009). Table 9.3 summarizes some of the factors that relate to sharing of household work.

Men's participation in household work shows a complex relationship to social class (Coltrane, 2000; Hochschild, 1997), but ethnicity is not an important factor in attitudes toward family work. In a study of couples from a variety of ethnic groups (Stohs, 2000), conflict over household work was common. The Hispanic American women worked fewer hours per week in their jobs outside the home than African American or Asian American women did, which might lead them to feel less burdened by doing more household chores. Hispanic American wives are more likely to enlist their husbands' help when their contributions to household income were higher, which may have made these contributions more essential to the family (Pinto & Coltrane, 2009). However, husbands' help is not easy to obtain for any level of social class or ethnicity, and the feeling that husbands were not doing a fair share of household work was common and a source of dissatisfaction in relationships.

Within the issue of household work, the concept of inequity is important. A large majority of women and most men believe in an equitable distribution of household work (Apparala et al., 2003; Van Willigen & Drentea, 2001). During the 1970s and 1980s, researchers found that wives perceived that their husbands were not doing a fair share of household work, but they found rationalizations to allow them to think of this inequitable contribution as "fair" (Coltrane, 2000). That situation still exists to some degree (Braun, Lewin-Epstein, Stier, & Baumgartner, 2008), but attitudes began to change during the 1990s; researchers began to find that women reported increasing dissatisfaction with an inequitable distribution of household work. Between 25 and 33% of wives believe that their husbands are not doing a fair share of housework and want them to do more. Men tend to agree that they should share the chores, but husbands are reluctant to participate in work that they tend to see as women's domain and are not eager to give up their leisure time to do chores (Sayer, 2005). Even a mutual desire to share household work may not allow husbands and wives to negotiate this problem to the satisfaction of both. Partners who feel underbenefitted are less satisfied in their relationships; conflicts between work and family obligations and an unfair division of household work present areas increasingly mentioned as sources of couples conflict (Donaghue & Fallon, 2003; Saginak & Saginak, 2005).

Conflict and Violence.   How couples resolve conflicts reflects differentials in power. Indeed, the factor of power influences partners' physiological changes during conflicts; the partner with less power exhibited a stronger stress response (Loving, Heffner, Kiecolt-Glaser, Glaser, & Malarkey, 2004). The partner who has more power also tends to behave in different ways from the partner whose power is less. Indeed, an examination of conflict resolution strategies can reveal the power dynamics in a relationship (Gottman & Notarius, 2000). In heterosexual couples, women are more likely to start a marital conflict discussion and to direct that discussion (Solomon et al., 2005), but women reported that this behavior did not reflect their feelings of power (Gottman & Notarius, 2000). To the contrary, women said that their strategies were aimed mostly at avoiding upsetting their husbands. Another study that demonstrated women's conflict avoidance (Neff & Harter, 2002) focused on which partner sacrificed his or her own need to satisfy a partner's wishes. The results indicated that men and women are equally likely to be self-sacrificing, but men who did so said they were thinking of pleasing their partners, whereas women named conflict avoidance as their motivation. This tendency to avoid conflict also appeared in a study in which power was a factor (Solomon, Knobloch, & Fitzpatrick, 2004). This study also revealed that large power differentials exert a silencing effect that deterred aggrieved partners from seeking confrontations.

Are women justified in taking steps to avoid conflict? Men tend to display more coercive styles of conflict resolution than women (Gottman & Notarius, 2000), which can constitute the first step toward couples' violence. Historically, domestic violence has been considered appropriate, with women as targets of marital (and even premarital) violence in many societies and throughout many time periods (Bonvillain, 2000; Kar & Garcia-Moreno, 2009). Even though physical abuse is not the most common method of resolving conflicts in contemporary relationships, violence is not unusual between married, cohabiting, or even dating partners; about 23% of women and 11% of men reported that they had experienced threats of such violence (Black & Breiding, 2008). Both men and women use violence toward each other, but women are at a disadvantage in physical conflicts with men (Tjaden & Thoennes, 2000a; Weston, Temple, & Marshall, 2005). The rate of violence may even be close to equal for women and men in relationships (Archer, 2000; Hamel, 2009; Straus, 2009), but the severity and rate of injury is not; women are much more likely to be injured and to sustain serious injury as a result of domestic violence.

One way to understand the types of couples' violence is to follow Michael Johnson's (1995, 2005; Johnson & Leone, 2005) distinction between common couples violence and intimate (formerly called *patriarchical*) terrorism. Johnson used the term *common couples violence* to describe the situation in which conflicts become physical fights. This type of violence is all too common, and women may be almost as likely to instigate such violence as men.

Intimate terrorism, on the other hand, is a severe form of violence used mostly by men to control their families. Such individuals consider that they should be the unquestioned head of the family and have the right to enact any measure to maintain their dominance. Substantiating evidence appeared in an analysis of men's motives in battering their partners (Winstok & Perkis, 2009), which indicated that control was an underlying factor in their behavior.

Contrary to what people may perceive, several national surveys of couples in the United States have revealed a decreasing amount of violence between partners. A survey in the 1980s (Straus & Gelles, 1986) showed 16% of homes reported some kind of violence between spouses within the previous year, which represented a 27% decrease from a similar survey in 1975. An examination of crime victimization records (Rennison, 2003) revealed that intimate partner violence decreased by more than 40% between 1993 and 2001. Even with this magnitude of decrease, over 700,000 incidents occur in the United States each year. The majority of these incidents were minor, but discounting the acts of minor violence in domestic conflict is not wise; even minor violence is predictive of more serious violence between spouses (Feld & Straus, 1989). Furthermore, women who fight back are likely to escalate rather than halt the violence directed toward them.

Unfortunately, many people find some level of violence between partners acceptable. About 25% of wives and over 30% of husbands found violence toward each other acceptable under some circumstances (Straus, Gelles, & Steinmetz, 1980). Younger couples are at higher risk for intimate partner violence than older couples (Caetano, Vaeth, & Ramisetty-Mikler, 2008), and attitudes toward violence as a way to resolve conflict was a factor in the age difference (Bookwala, Sobin, & Zdaniuk, 2005). With these attitudes, the escalation of minor violence to abuse is not surprising, nor is it likely to change.

Marriages in which the partners have an equal balance of power are less likely to involve physical violence than marriages in which one partner is dominant (Jewkes, 2002). This is true in other countries as well (Kar & Garcia-Moreno, 2009), such as Taiwan (Xu & Lai, 2004). The tendency toward equal power in lesbians' and gay men's relationships does not exempt them from intimate partner violence. Gay men are the perpetrators and targets for intimate violence at rates somewhat higher than heterosexual couples (Greenwood et al., 2002), but lesbians experience this type of violence at rates similar to heterosexual women (Owen & Burke, 2004). Regardless of which partner has more power, nationality, or sexual orientation, both partners are more likely to be the targets of violence in couples with a dominant and a subordinate partner. Inequalities of power promote violent conflict in couples, putting both partners at increased risk.

Therefore, a connection exists among the issues of power, conflict, and violence in committed relationships. Power affects conflict and conflict management. When conflict leads to violence, women are about as likely as men to behave violently. However, women are more likely than men to be injured in a violent confrontation. As long women and men continue to find physical violence acceptable as a conflict resolution strategy, intimate partner violence will continue.

Stability of Relationships.   Relationships that involve physical violence are less stable than those with no violence, but some of these violent relationships endure with partners relatively satisfied (Williams & Frieze, 2005). Many people find it difficult to imagine why a woman would stay with a man who repeatedly abuses her, but some women do (Eisikovits, Winstok, & Gelles, 2002). Abusive men often work to isolate their partners from family and friends, depriving them of social support and alternative residences (Heise, Ellsberg, & Gottemoeller, 1999; Jewkes, 2002). Abused women who are unemployed, with few marketable skills and young children in need of financial support, may feel as though they have no options except to stay in the relationship, no matter how abusive. With the rise of shelters for women to escape abusive homes, abused women have an option, and thousands take this option each year.

Abusive relationships are an extreme case of conflict in love relationships, but all couples experience some level of conflict. Experiencing conflicts is related to decreased satisfaction in relationships (Cramer, 2002). The number of conflicts mattered but the magnitude did not; either minor or major conflicts contributed to lower ratings of satisfaction with the relationship, but the strategies for resolving conflicts are more strongly related to satisfaction and stability. John Gottman (1991, 1998) and his colleagues (Gottman & Notarius, 2000; Levenson, Carstensen, & Gottman, 1994) have investigated the elements and styles of conflicts that strengthen relationships as well as those that signal problems. They have even managed to reduce these factors to a predictive equation that has over 90% accuracy in predicting divorce (Gottman, Swanson, & Swanson, 2002).

Surprisingly, Gottman's results have indicated that marital satisfaction is not a strong predictor of separation but that the level of physical arousal during conflict is. That is, couples whose heart rates, blood pressure, sweating, and physical movement during an argument were elevated were more likely to separate within the next 3 years than couples with lower levels of arousal. Couples whose physiological reactions were calmer tended to have marriages that improved over a 3-year span.

All couples experience conflict, but how they resolve the conflict is a key to the stability of their relationship.

Behavioral factors also predicted divorce, including patterns of interaction between partners. Husbands' tendency to be unresponsive ("stonewall") by withdrawing emotionally and avoiding eye contact with their wives during an argument predicted dissolution of the marriage (Gottman 1991; Gottman & Driver, 2005; Gottman & Silver, 2000). Wives' tendency to complain, criticize, and behave defensively also constituted a danger signal. The couples headed toward separation also showed different facial expressions during their conversations, including the wives' expressions of disgust and the husbands' "miserable smile," a smile that affects only the mouth, as when people try to "put on a happy face." Gottman concluded that these patterns of interaction worked toward driving couples apart rather than allowing them to resolve conflicts. Indeed, many of the couples that exhibited these interaction patterns were in the process of dissolving their relationship emotionally, and their physiological reactions, conflict tactics, and facial expressions signaled their impending separation. These findings apply to gay and lesbian couples as well as to heterosexual ones (Gottman et al., 2003). Table 9.4 summarizes these factors.

The institution of marriage often holds couples together when they might otherwise dissolve their relationships, which means that cohabiting heterosexual, gay, and lesbian couples are more likely to end their relationships than married people are (Kurdek, 2004, 2008). However, these couples tend to exhibit similar levels of satisfaction and adjustment as well as better conflict resolution skills than married couples. Gay men and lesbians can also have stable, long-term relationships; 76% of lesbian couples and 81% of gay male couples were together during 12 years of assessments (Kurdek, 2004). In a study of heterosexual and same-sex couples who had stayed together for an average of 30 years (Mackey, Diemer, & O'Brien, 2000), several factors were related to psychological intimacy and continuation of the relationship, including lack of conflict, method of handling conflict, quality of communication, equity, and expression of affection. Lesbians reported their relationships as closer than did gay men or heterosexuals.

According to Sternberg's (1986, 1987) triangular theory of love, relationships that have only one of the components should lack stability, and the commitment component is

TABLE 9.4   *Factors Related to Marital Separation*

Factor	Prediction
Marital satisfaction	No strong relationship to separation
Physical arousal during conflict—heart rate, blood pressure, sweating, moving	Higher levels predict increased likelihood of separation; calmer reactions predict strengthening of relationship
Wives being overly agreeable	Increased likelihood of separation
Husbands participate in housework	Increased satisfaction for husbands and wives; increased health in husbands
Husbands stonewall	Increased likelihood of separation
Wives criticize and complain	Increased likelihood of separation
Husbands disagree with wives	Increased likelihood of separation
Couples are defensive	Increased likelihood of separation
Facial expressions during conflict—"miserable smile," wives' disgust, husbands' fear	Increased likelihood of separation

clearly the most strongly related to relationship stability. Commitment "can be essential for getting through hard times and for returning to better ones. In ignoring it or separating it from love, one may be missing exactly that component of loving relationships that enables one to get through the hard times as well as the easy ones" (Sternberg, 1986, p. 123). In a study of reasons that people stayed married, loving one's partner was the most common reason that participants gave (Previti & Amato, 2003).

Dissolving Relationships

Relationships go through phases of attraction, development, and sometimes dissolution. All relationships are subject to these stages, but people expect the dissolution of casual relationships and believe that such breakups pose no problems for the people involved. Unfortunately, even relationships with commitment sometimes fail to endure. When close friendships or love relationships dissolve, the two individuals are not the only ones affected. As Susan Sprecher and her colleagues (Sprecher, Felmlee, Schmeeckle, & Shu, 2006, p. 457) noted, "No breakup occurs on an island." The end of such relationships poses problems for both people involved as well as for their social network of friends and family.

Love relationships without institutional support, such as cohabitation, are more likely to break up than are marriages. Only about 10% of heterosexual cohabiting couples live together long-term without marrying (Brown & Booth, 1996). In two studies of couples (Blumstein & Schwartz, 1983; Kurdek, 2004), married couples were more likely to remain together than gay or lesbian couples. Figure 9.4 (page 232) shows the separation rates for different types of couples over time.

The institutional support for marriage is no guarantee of stability for such relationships. Although marriages have never been permanent, divorce increased dramatically over the past 50 years (U.S. Census Bureau, 2009a), hit a high level in the 1980s, decreased slightly, and remains at a high level today (see Figure 9.3). The high divorce rate is not necessarily a condemnation of marriage as much as the failure of women and men to fulfill their vision of what they believe marriage should be. Compared to dating and married couples, engaged couples expressed an idealized vision of marriage (Bonds-Raacke, Bearden, Carriere, Anderson, & Nicks, 2001), which may lead couples to unrealistic expectations that build a foundation for conflict. As research on relationship stability has indicated (Gottman, 1991; Gottman & Driver, 2005; Gottman & Notarius, 2000), how partners handle conflicts in the early years of marriage is a predictor of divorce.

Two intensive studies tell similar stories about the effects of divorce. One study, by Catherine Riessman (1990), was an interview study of divorced men and women. The other study, by Mavis Hetherington and John Kelly (2002), was a quantitative study, the Virginia Longitudinal Study of Divorce and Remarriage, which has lasted over 30 years and followed almost 1,400 families. The studies have revealed similarities in the factors that underlie divorces and the processes of adaptation and recovery. Both studies show that men and women experience similar feelings, but they also show substantial gender differences in the process of divorce.

Most people who divorce keep their ideas of marriage and what it should be (Riessman, 1990; Sandfield, 2006). That idea often matches what Cancian called the Companionship blueprint for marriage. When they separated and divorced, women and men usually failed to

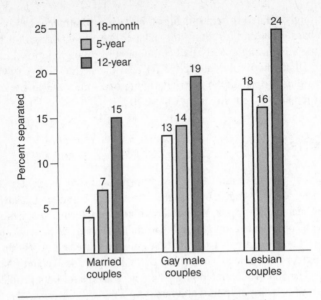

FIGURE 9.4 *Separation Rates for Couples over 18-Month, 5-Year, and 12-Year Periods*

Source: The data for 18-month period are from *American Couples,* by Philip Blumstein and Pepper Schwartz, 1983, New York: Pocket Books. The data for 5-year period are from "Relationship Outcomes and Their Predictors: Longitudinal Evidence from Heterosexual Married, Gay Cohabiting, and Lesbian Cohabiting Couples," by Lawrence Kurdek, 1998, *Journal of Marriage and Family, 60,* pp. 553–568. The data from 12-year period are from "Are Gay and Lesbian Cohabitating Couples Really Different from Heterosexual Married Couples?" by Lawrence Kurdek, 2005, *Journal of Marriage and Family, 66,* pp. 880–900.

▣ GENDERED VOICES

I Wasn't Any of His Business Anymore

A woman, talking with her friend about her ex-husband, said, "I saw Ed at a country western club last Friday night. He was there with some of his friends, drinking. I went there because I wanted to get out and have some fun. He didn't see me at first, and then he kept looking in my direction, trying to make sure he was seeing right.

"Finally, he came over to me and said, 'What are you doing in a place like this? You shouldn't be here.'

I told him that what I did wasn't any of his business anymore. We were divorced, and I could do what I wanted. I didn't need his permission to go to a bar, and he didn't have any right to say anything to me. He said some pretty ugly things, calling me a bitch and a whore, and I just walked away from him. I had enough of his ordering me around when we were married."

GENDERED VOICES

My Ex-wife Acts Like We're Still Married

"Although we were divorced three years ago, my ex-wife acts like we're still married," a man in his mid-30s said. "I understand why she calls me when something involves the kids, but she calls me when she needs things done to the house." He considered these requests inappropriate because he and his ex-wife had both remarried. "I can't help it if she married a wuss who can't fix the toilet. I don't think she should be calling me to do the chores. We're not married anymore, and taking care of her house is not part of my job now."

question the blueprint. Rather, they found fault in their own marriages, blaming either their former spouses or themselves for failing to fulfill some component of their marital ideal.

Although divorced men and women both described failures to live up to their ideals, their descriptions showed some variation (Riessman, 1990). Both women and men saw failures in achieving emotional intimacy, but they attributed the failures to different reasons. Women tended to say that their husbands had not talked and shared feelings with them as they had expected. They claimed that their husbands just didn't communicate with them.

Divorced men largely agreed with this assessment, blaming themselves for not communicating with their former wives and maintaining that they had difficulties in talking about their feelings. Divorced men also believed that their wives had failed to give them emotional support, which they tended to define as physical affection. The working-class men repeatedly said that their wives were not waiting "with their arms open and a kiss" when the men came home from work (Riessman, 1990). Such physical manifestations of intimacy were lacking, resulting in their feelings that their marriages lacked emotional intimacy. These gender-related differences reflect the talk-based versus action-based styles that are typical of women and men and highlight the importance of these differences in the dissolution of relationships.

The motives that lead to divorce have shown some changes (de Graaf & Kalmijn, 2006). Partners still believe that extramarital affairs, alcoholism, and physical abuse are reasons to divorce, but these are not the most common reasons that push people toward divorce. Instead, failures to meet partners' relationship expectations, lack of shared interests, and problems in balancing work and family demands have become more common motives for divorce. With the growing acceptability of divorce, even relatively small problems combined with a failure to receive rewards from a partner make divorce a consideration (Hetherington & Kelly, 2002).

The divorced people in both longitudinal studies mentioned problems with sex in connection with their divorce. The men mentioned dissatisfaction with the frequency of sex and resentment over their wives' refusal to have sex as often as husbands wanted. Sexual affairs were a factor in 34% of the divorced people in Riessman's study, and both women and men believed that affairs had been the impetus for the dissolution of their marriage. The women took their own as well as their husbands' affairs as a sign of emotional betrayal, signaling that their marriage was over. The men did not necessarily share that attitude, but they also acknowledged that affairs had been a factor in their divorces. Wives found it difficult to forgive husbands' affairs, and wives who had had affairs tended to leave their husbands for their lovers.

These feelings suggest that women might be the ones to initiate breakups, and findings from the Virginia Longitudinal Study and a study in Australia (Hewitt, 2009) confirmed this finding. Women initiate about two-thirds of the breakups of heterosexual couples but are less likely to do so if they have very young children. The likelihood of women initiating breakups may be due to women's tendency to be more vigilant about monitoring their relationships; they know when something is going wrong more quickly than men do. Alternatively, women's willingness to divorce may reflect their increased incomes, which allow them to leave unhappy marriages. This situation highlights a substantial asymmetry in love relationships. Women fall out of love more quickly and fall in love more slowly than men do.

Women and men both experience different lives after the dissolution of a love relationship. For partners who have been married or have cohabited, the dissolution of the relationship is usually financially as well as emotionally difficult (Avellar & Smock, 2005; Gadalla, 2009; Zagorsky, 2005). Women's lower earning power coupled with their custody of children tends to create financial hardship, whereas men's financial position may improve after divorce. Women's increasing earning power has moderated the financial impact of divorce (McKeever & Wolfinger, 2001), but women continue to experience financial disadvantage up to 3 years after divorce (Gadalla, 2009).

Many men and women search for and find positive as well as negative consequences as a result of the divorce experience (Bevvino & Sharkin, 2003; Riessman, 1990). Both said they enjoyed the freedom that came with divorce, but their feelings had different sources: Women liked being free from their husbands' dominance, whereas the men liked being free of their wives' expectations. Women were more likely than men to find something positive about the experience, but many women experienced grief and depression related to their divorce (Sakraida, 2005). Despite the depression, they also discovered heightened self-esteem and feelings of competence through performing activities their husbands had done when they were married (Riessman, 1990).

Men are more likely to "lose" in the divorce (Baum, 2004). Dissolution of marriage often deprives men not only of companionship and emotional support from their wives but also of their children and feeling of being a family (Bailey, 2007) and of their network of friends and family (a network typically maintained by women). Women tend to use these support networks after divorce, but men do not. The men in Riessman's (1990) study were surprised at the difficulties of being alone, but they also described feelings of satisfaction from developing competencies in domestic chores.

Divorced men and women are likely to feel displeased with their ex-spouses rather than with marriage itself, and most showed their endorsement of marriage by remarrying (Hetherington & Kelly, 2002). Cohabiting presents an alternative to marriage that has become increasingly common among divorced people (Wu & Schimmele, 2005). Second marriages (and cohabitations) may differ from first marriages. People in second marriages endorsed an equal sharing of power, and women tend to negotiate relationships with more equal power, greater access to resources, and more equitable sharing of household labor than their first marriages (Clarke, 2005). These marriages, however, show many more similarities than differences (Allen, Baucom, Burnett, Epstein, & Rankin-Esquer, 2001). Second marriages are even more likely to end in divorce than first marriages, which Riessman (1990) interpreted as an increased unwillingness to endure an unhappy relationship combined with the knowledge that divorce offered positive as well as negative experiences.

Considering Diversity

The blueprints for marriage have changed over time in the United States (Cancian, 1987). In the 1800s, the Family Duty blueprint was the rule; couples often entered arranged marriages for economic reasons, and their feelings revolved around a sense of duty to each other and their children. Looking further back into history and to other cultures, Nancy Bonvillain (2000) analyzed gender and marriage in a variety of settings, contrasting male-dominated and egalitarian societies. Her analysis pointed to economics as an important factor in the power that women have in their marriages and in society in general.

In societies in which women contribute significantly to household subsistence, the women have power in their personal relationships. For example, the Ju/'hoansi are a society of foraging people who live in Botswana and Namibia. Ju/'hoansi society has differences in gender roles and behaviors, but women's foraging is essential to band survival, and this contribution is reflected in Ju/'hoansi women's full participation in social decisions. The Inuit of Arctic North America are also a foraging band society, but they have a male-dominated culture. An economic analysis also applies, revealing that the scarcity of foods results in men's hunting as the main source of food. In Inuit society, women are forbidden to hunt. Consequently, women's contributions are perceived as less important, and their status is lower.

In tribal societies, both egalitarian and male-dominated societies have existed, and the economic analysis continues to maintain validity (Bonvillain, 2000). When Europeans arrived in North America, the Iroquois allowed women access to economic resources, whereas the Yanomamo of Brazil and Venezuela were a tribal society that did not allow such access. These two societies showed the predicted patterns of egalitarianism and male dominance, respectively. In even larger and more complex groups such as state and industrialized societies, the restriction of economic production to men gives them power and puts women in the position of subordinates in many ways, including in marriages. A comparative study of 27 countries (Cha & Thébaud, 2009) supported this analysis, showing a relationship between economic support for men as breadwinners and men's gender ideology—greater structural support for men as breadwinners was related to men's lower endorsement of egalitarian beliefs.

Bonvillain contended that when women's contributions are seen as minor, their status is lower, and they have little power in their relationships. Lack of power manifests itself in the inability to leave unhappy marriages or to avoid physical abuse. Consistent with the economic viewpoint, participation in the labor force is a significant predictor of divorce in nations around the world. An analysis of 71 countries on six continents (Greenstein & Davis, 2006) revealed that paid employment was a predictor of countries' divorce rate; countries with high divorce rates tend to be industrialized countries in which women comprise a high percentage of the paid labor force. Table 9.5 (page 236) presents some examples of the varying divorce rate around the world.

A cross-cultural analysis of violence against women (Heise et al., 1999; Shahidulla & Nana Derby, 2009) also related domestic violence to societies with strong male dominance. Consistent with Bonvillain's view, these analyses cited financial dependence and restriction of access to resources as contributors to domestic violence and changes in these situations to laws against such abuse. Examining domestic violence against women across cultures

TABLE 9.5 *Divorce Rate in Selected Nations*

Nation	Rate per 1,000 Population
Russia	4.5
United States	3.6
Belarus	3.3
Cuba	3.2
United Kingdom	2.8
Belgium	2.8
Switzerland	2.8
Australia	2.6
Denmark	2.6
South Korea	2.6
France	2.3
Germany	2.3
Costa Rica	2.3
Canada	2.2
Sweden	2.2
Jordan	2.1
Japan	2.0
Netherlands	1.9
Poland	1.9
Kuwait	1.8
Israel	1.6
China	1.4
Iran	1.3
Greece	1.2
Italy	0.8
Mexico	0.7
Chile	0.2

Source: Data from *Demographic Yearbook, 2006,* by United Nations, 2008, Table 25. Retrieved March 20, 2010 from http://unstats.un.org/unsd/demographic/products/dyb/dyb2006.htm. Reprinted with the permission of the United Nations.

revealed a great deal of variation in the percentage of women who reported abuse (Heise et al., 1999). In cultures that endorse men's right to control women and to "discipline" wives, the rates of abuse were high—over 40%. In such societies, men (and sometimes women, too) find a variety of justifications for abuse, including failure to obey husbands' orders, asking for money, failure to take care of children, suspicion of adultery, or refusing sex. Other societies set stricter limits on domestic violence, and these societies have a lower rate of reported partner violence. Indeed, domestic abuse does not occur in all societies.

A growing worldwide campaign against this type of abuse has arisen. Since 1993, when the United Nations General Assembly passed the Declaration on the Elimination of Violence Against Women, many countries have developed initiatives to curb domestic violence. The modernization that has occurred in many parts of the world has prompted changes in attitudes and in laws related to partner violence (Shahidulla & Nana Derby, 2009). Not only have such laws appeared in North America and Western Europe but Brazil, India, Japan, Bangladesh, and Ghana have formulated similar laws, and freedom from violence at home is coming to be seen as a human right.

■ Summary

Sternberg's triangular model of relationships provides a framework for understanding all relationships, including friendships and love relationships. Gender differences in friendship styles appear early in development; children voluntarily segregate themselves according to gender before age 5 years. Girls tend to associate in small groups, whereas boys play in larger groups with more of a hierarchical organization.

Adolescents are more concerned with developing emotional intimacy in their relationships, but girls emphasize this aspect of relationships more than boys. Men find it difficult to develop such relationships, especially with other men. Instead, they have buddies with whom they form activity-based relationships. Some men develop emotionally intimate love relationships with women, and such relationships often decrease the amount of time and emotional energy men have to devote to male friends. Some research has indicated that both men and women have a flexibility of friendship styles and that they use different styles to relate to male and female friends. Cross-gender nonsexual friendships are a recent phenomenon. Both men and women acknowledge that such relationships are possible (and even desirable) but require special rules.

Love relationships currently form through dating, an activity that first arose during the 1920s as a response to changing patterns of mate selection. Dating has now become not only a method of courting, but also a forum for recreation, socialization, and sexual exploration. Adolescents tend to choose dates similar to future mates, and men and women prefer partners who are warm and kind, expressive, intelligent, and physically attractive. People with either heterosexual or homosexual sexual orientation describe their preferred partners in similar ways.

Currently, marriage and other committed relationships can follow several different blueprints: Companionship, Independence, and Interdependence. The Companionship blueprint involves separate gender roles and emphasizes the woman's role in maintaining a love relationship. Both the Independence and Interdependence blueprints emphasize self-development for both men and women, but they differ in the importance of commitment.

Gender researchers have explored several issues in love relationships, including beliefs about love, communication, division of household labor, power and conflict, and relationship stability. Men are more romantic in their conceptualization of love than women are, and marriage tends to benefit them more, but they are not necessarily happier with their marriages. Communication is a major factor for relationships, and a great deal of publicity has focused on differences in men's and women's communication. However, research indicates that differences are more likely due to power differentials than to gender. The balance of power in marriage generally favors men, both because they have greater economic resources and because society accords men more power. Even when women make as much or more money than their husbands, they do not have equal power.

The division of household labor reflects the power difference; women perform far more of this work than men, even when women have paid employment outside the home. Women have become increasingly dissatisfied with this inequitable division, and men have begun to do more household work, but some inequity continues and produces conflict. Couples experience conflict from many sources, but some marital conflict results in violence. Men and women both behave violently toward each, but women are more likely than men to be injured as a result of relationship violence.

Violence decreases the stability of relationships, but does not necessarily end them. Stable love relationships tend to occur in couples with similar attitudes and values, and the commitment factor in marriage produces greater stability than in other love relationships. But marriages dissolve. Divorce increased dramatically during the 1980s and then decreased during the 1990s. People who have divorced tend to see the fault in their ex-spouses rather than in the institution of marriage. Although divorce brings financial and emotional problems, most women and men also find positive factors in divorce. Most remarry or cohabit, and some evidence suggests that both women and men form more equitable second marriages.

Across time and cultures, many patterns of marriage have existed. Analyzing the economic contributions of women in a variety of societies leads to the conclusion that women experience more egalitarian relationships and roles in societies in which they make significant economic contributions. Male-dominated cultures restrict women's access to resources, tend to establish restrictive marriages, allow fewer options for women to leave marriage, and condone greater intimate-partner violence. Growing labor force participation and a worldwide campaign against domestic violence is in the process of changing male–female relationships around the world.

■ Glossary

companionate love   a combination of commitment and intimacy without passion.
gross motor skills   skills involving use of large muscles of the body, producing large movements, such as throwing, kicking, running, and jumping.
homophobia   the unreasonable fear and hatred of homosexuality.

machismo   a Spanish word meaning strong and assertive masculinity and implying complete male authority.
matriarchy   a family pattern in which women are dominant or a pattern in which women are the head of the household due to the father's absence.

■ Suggested Readings

Berndt, Thomas J. (2004). Children's friendships: Shifts over a half-century in perspectives on their development and their effects. *Merrill-Palmer Quarterly, 50,* 206–222.
One of the leading researchers in the area of children's friendships provides a thorough review of this research area over the past 50 years.

Gottman, John; & Silver, Nan. (2000). *Seven Principles for Making Marriages Work.* New York: Crown.
Gottman is one of the world's leading researchers on couples' relationships. His popular book draws from his research on factors related to success and failure in marriage and formulates ways to make marriages work.

Hatfield, Elaine; & Rapson, Richard L. (1996). *Love and sex: Cross-cultural perspectives.* Boston: Allyn & Bacon.
Hatfield and Rapson's book examines love and sex across contemporary cultures as well as delves into history for additional examples. They consider attraction, the difficulties of forming relationships, and the problems involved in ending romantic relationships. Their cross-cultural and historical review adds a valuable (and fascinating) point of view to the understanding of passionate love.

Hetherington, E. Mavis; & Kelly, John. (2002). *For better or for worse: Divorce reconsidered.* New York: Norton.
Respected researcher Mavis Hetherington teams with writer John Kelly to present the findings from the Virginia Longitudinal Study on Divorce and Remarriage in a format that everyone can understand. This book offers research-based findings and advice about the impact of divorce on women, men, and children.

10 Sexuality

When Jewels Morris-Davis turned 16 years old, she was proud of being "the first person in my family to reach 16 without getting pregnant—or getting somebody pregnant" (Sullivan, 2009, p. 38). Jewels lives in a rural area in South Carolina that had a very high rate of teen pregnancy until her school instituted a sexuality education program that changed that county's teen pregnancy rate and may provide a guide for how to end the U.S. "war" over sexuality education.

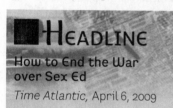

HEADLINE
How to End the War over Sex Ed
Time Atlantic, April 6, 2009

There is no argument over the problem of teen pregnancy: The United States has the highest rate in the industrialized world (Sullivan, 2009). The conflict has revolved around what type of programs can lower that statistic. In the 1996 Welfare Reform Act, the U.S. Congress provided funding for abstinence-oriented sex education, which emphasized sexual activity as an exclusive part of marriage. Proponents of this view argue that providing information on sexuality encourages questions and fantasies that push children toward sexual activity; the only acceptable message is "Don't have sex." Others believe that the abstinence approach leaves young people vulnerable and unprepared in a world filled with sex, but the federal funding limitation to abstinence-only programs has limited sexuality education in U.S. public schools.

Anderson County, South Carolina, found community funding to institute a comprehensive sexuality and relationship program (Sullivan, 2009). The county hired a professional sexuality educator (rather than follow the typical pattern of putting a coach or biology teacher in charge of sexuality education) and encouraged development of a curriculum that included not only information about pregnancy and sexually transmitted diseases (STDs) but also decision-making skills. During the first 3 years of the program, the teen birth rate stayed high, but after that, it declined sharply. Surprisingly little controversy occurred in Anderson County, but other parts of the country have been plagued by protests, and many school systems offer little or no sexuality education beyond messages to abstain (Fields & Tolman, 2006).

The controversy over sexuality education is but one of many within the area of sexuality. Other controversies include sexual orientation, childhood sexuality and abuse, and gender differences in sexuality. It seems that no area of sexuality escapes controversy, and that general principle applies even to the research on sexuality, which is the first topic for this chapter. Later sections explore the research and controversies in the development of sexuality during childhood and the development of the sexual orientations of heterosexuality, homosexuality, and bisexuality.

The Study of Sexuality

Researchers who want to know about sexual behaviors and attitudes have several options in choosing a method of investigation. They may question people about their sexual behavior, or they may directly observe people's sexual behavior. Both of these approaches present scientific, practical, and ethical problems.

Those researchers who choose to question people about their sexual behaviors or attitudes are using the survey method, which has been the most common approach to studying sexuality. People's truthfulness is a limitation to this method, which is especially problematic and may be lacking when they respond to questions about a private, personal issue such as sex. In addition, some people refuse to participate in sex surveys; these people are likely to differ from those who are willing to answer questions about their sexual attitudes and behavior. This situation describes **self-selection of participants**, which poses a problem because participants rather than researchers choose who completes the survey. This situation does not yield a **representative sample**—a group of people that reflects the characteristics of the population from which the sample was drawn. The results can still reveal interesting and important information, but self-selected participants prohibit researchers from generalizing the results to the general population. A goal of sex survey researchers is to obtain a representative of participants who report truthfully.

Another possibility for investigating sexual behavior is through direct observation of sexual activity. People are even less willing to participate in this type of research than in a survey, but nonhuman animals have (or at least have voiced) no such objections. The problems of generalizing results from these studies to humans are more serious, but a prominent example of this type of research appears in *Patterns of Sexual Behavior* (1951) by anthropologist Clellan Ford and psychologist Frank Beach. These two researchers presented not only a cross-cultural study of human sexual behavior, but cross-species comparisons as well. Only a small percentage of people have been willing to have sex in a research laboratory. Such participants allowed William Masters and Virginia Johnson (1966) to study human sexual behavior in ways that no other researchers had managed.

Despite the challenges of both approaches, researchers have attempted to understand sexual behavior by using both surveys and direct observations of sexual behavior.

Sex Surveys

Before Alfred Kinsey's groundbreaking survey of men's and women's sexual behavior in the 1930s and 1940s, several other investigators completed reports on sexuality (Brecher, 1969). For example, Henry Havelock Ellis worked in England between 1896 and 1928, and Clelia Duel Mosher began studying sexual behavior among college women in the United States in 1892 (Degler, 1974). Each conducted research that led them to question the prevailing Victorian social norms of repression and denial of sexuality that he saw around him were not reflected in people's sexual behavior. For example, Mosher found that most of the women she questions experienced both sexual desire and orgasm. Several other researchers completed small-scale sex surveys during the early 1900s, but the most famous of the surveys on sexual behavior were those completed by Alfred Kinsey and his colleagues.

The Kinsey Surveys.   In 1937, Alfred Kinsey was a professor of biology at the University of Indiana, where he began to teach a newly created course in sex education, a controversial topic at that time. Kinsey found that little systematic research existed on sexuality, and this gap prompted him to begin such a research. He started collecting data in 1938 with a preliminary interview that he later expanded to include extensive information about nine areas: social and economic background, marital history, sex education, physical characteristics and physiology, nocturnal sex dreams, masturbation, heterosexual history, history of same-sex sexual activity, and sexual contact with animals. Each of these areas included subdivisions, making the interview extensive and time consuming. Kinsey and his associates, Wardell Pomeroy, Clyde Martin, and Paul Gebhard, conducted a total of 17,500 interviews (Brecher, 1969).

Although the interviews were extensive and many people participated, Kinsey's sample was not representative. His final groups of 5,300 men and 5,940 women were White, well educated, mostly from Indiana, and largely Protestant. His failure to obtain a representative sample means that his results cannot be generalized to the U.S. population.

Kinsey's surveys managed to overcome the problem of lack of truthfulness associated with survey research. Kinsey was skilled at getting a wide variety of people to talk with him candidly about their sexual histories (Bancroft, 2004; Brecher, 1969). His technique included asking questions that required participants to admit rather than deny a practice, such as, "At what age did you first experience full intercourse?" This approach assumed that everyone had done everything. Perhaps this strategy helped to make people more comfortable and encouraged them to tell the truth. Reinterviewing some participants 18 months after their first interview revealed mostly minor inconsistencies that came from memory lapses rather than intentional deception, indicating to Kinsey that people were telling the truth.

The results from Kinsey's surveys appeared in two parts, *Sexual Behavior in the Human Male* (Kinsey, Pomeroy, & Martin, 1948) and *Sexual Behavior in the Human Female* (Kinsey, Pomeroy, Martin, & Gebhard, 1953). Kinsey's reports appeared during a time when sex was not a topic of polite conversation, when women were supposed to be reluctant to have sex, and when same-sex, premarital, and extramarital sexual activities were illegal in many areas. The results of the surveys surprised (and even shocked) many people, because the participants reported such a wide variety of sexual behaviors, including some that were socially unacceptable and even illegal.

Kinsey's results indicated that women enjoyed sex; that a substantial percentage of men had participated in male–male sexual behavior; that children experienced sexual excitement and activity; and that masturbation, premarital sex, and extramarital sex were common for both women and men. Around 90% of the women in the study had experienced orgasm by age 35 years. Of the 10% who had not, another 8% reported experiencing sexual arousal, leaving only 2% of women who had failed to enjoy sexual activity, a figure much lower than most people had imagined.

Some of Kinsey's most controversial findings concerned same-sex sexual behavior, which Kinsey referred to as *homosexual*. The term has become stigmatized because it highlights the sexual aspect of these individuals' lives and nothing else. The term **gay** is an alternative that many find preferable and that may apply to both men and women, but it is more often used to describe men who have sexual relationships with men. The term **lesbian** refers to women who have sexual relationships with women.

A total of 37% of the men in Kinsey's survey reported at least one sexual experience with another man that led to orgasm. This figure included men who had had sexual experiences with other men only as young adolescents and men who had had only one such experience. Some of these men reported that they no longer felt sexual attraction toward other men or had no subsequent sexual experiences with other men. Both the percentage of men who had some type of sexual experience with other men (37%) and the percentage of men who primarily or exclusively had sex with other men (13%) were higher than previous estimates (Brecher, 1969). Kinsey's figures on female sexual activity with other women were similar to the figures for men, but the percentages were smaller: 28% of women had at least some sexual experience with other women, but only 7% reported primarily or exclusively lesbian sexuality. Table 10.1 shows these figures. These figures for the frequency of same-sex sexual attraction and activity are part of a continuing controversy. Kinsey's figures for the number of men who primarily or exclusively have sex with other men are not only higher than previous estimates, but they are also higher than later estimates (Hunt, 1974; Laumann, Gagnon, Michael, & Michaels, 1994) and likely not representative (Bancroft, 2004).

Another controversial finding related to childhood sexuality (Bancroft, 2004). Many participants in the Kinsey survey reported that as children they had sexual feelings and sometimes acted on those feelings. The most common type of childhood sexuality was **masturbation**, manipulation of the genitals to produce sexual pleasure. Infants and young children masturbate, some to orgasm. A total of 14% of the women and 45% of the men in Kinsey's survey said that they had masturbated before age 13 years. They also remembered other-gender and same-sex exploratory play with peers as well as sexual contact with adults. Men recalled preadolescent intercourse more frequently than women did. Almost one-fourth of the women recalled incidents during which adult men had shown their genitals, touched

TABLE 10.1 *Percentage of Participants Reporting Sexual Activities in Three Sex Surveys*

Sexual Activity	Kinsey Surveys (1948, 1953)		Playboy Foundation Survey (Hunt, 1974)		National Health and Social Life Survey (Laumann et al., 1994)	
	Percentage Reporting Each Behavior					
	Men	Women	Men	Women	Men	Women
Masturbation to orgasm	92.0%	58.0%	94.0%	63.0%	—	—
Masturbation before age 13	45.0	14.0	63.0	33.0	—	—
Masturbation during marriage	40.0	30.0	72.0	68.0	57.0%	37.0%
At least one homosexual experience	37.0	28.0	—	—	7.1	3.8
Primarily homosexual orientation	13.0	7.0	2.0	1.0	4.1	2.2
Premarital intercourse	71.0	33.0	97.0	67.0	93.0	79.0
Extramarital sex	50.0	26.0	41.0	18.0	<25.0	<10.0
Sexual abuse during childhood	10.0	25.0	—	—	12.0	17.0

them, or attempted intercourse. Over half of the incidents reported by women involved acquaintances or family members. Adults' recollections of their childhood sexual activities are most likely not completely accurate, but Kinsey's results suggested that children experience sexual curiosity and exploration as well as sexual abuse by adults.

Kinsey's survey revealed that masturbation was a common sexual activity that begins for a small percentage during preadolescence and increases during adolescence. Almost all of the men and about two-thirds of the women had reached orgasm by masturbating. Married people told Kinsey that they continued to masturbate, although they also had sex with their spouses. Around 30% of married women and 40% of married men reported that they masturbated. These figures contradicted the popular notion that masturbation was primarily a practice of adolescence and that people with a sexual partner no longer masturbated, but recent research confirms Kinsey's findings. In a representative sample of U.S. adults (Das, 2007), 38% of women and 61% of men reported that they masturbate. Indeed, over half of women in the United States own and use a vibrator (Herbenick et al., 2009).

Kinsey surveyed people who lived in a society that accepted different sexual standards for men and women. Although both were supposed to be sexually inexperienced before marriage and to have sex only with their spouses, men were not held to this standard but women were. This **double standard for sexual behavior** has a history that stretches back at least a century, and Kinsey found evidence for it in the different rates for both premarital and extramarital sex. By 25 years of age, 83% of unmarried men but only 33% of unmarried women said that they had participated in intercourse. A similar discrepancy occurred in the reports of extramarital affairs—about half the men but only 26% of the women admitted having extramarital affairs.

In summary, Kinsey surveyed men and women to determine their sexual behavior. Despite Kinsey's failure to obtain a representative sample, his results showed how much sexual behavior differed from the popular view. Kinsey's participants reported that they engaged in a variety of sexual activities, beginning during childhood. The experience of orgasm was common among women; both women and men said that they masturbated and engaged in premarital and extramarital sex. He found that same-sex sexual activity was more common than imagined, especially among men. After the Kinsey reports, many other sex researchers chose the survey method of investigation.

Hunt's Playboy Foundation Survey.

In the 1970s, the Playboy Foundation commissioned a survey of sexual behavior in the United States to update the Kinsey findings and to obtain a more representative sample. This effort resulted in the 1974 publication of *Sexual Behavior in the 1970s* by Morton Hunt. Although the attempt to obtain a representative sample fell short, the final sample matched characteristics of the U.S. population in terms of ethnic background, education, age, and marital status. The 2,026 participants filled out a lengthy questionnaire about their backgrounds, including sex education, attitudes toward sex, and sexual histories. A total of 200 also participated in an even lengthier interview that was similar to the Kinsey interviews.

As Table 10.1 shows, this survey confirmed the prevalence of masturbation, with an even higher rate of preadolescent masturbation than Kinsey had found and a similar rate of masturbation during adulthood. Hunt found a lower percentage and a different pattern of same-sex sexual activity than Kinsey had found. He concluded that most such activities occur as a form of adolescent experimentation; most of the women and men who had same-sex sexual experiences discontinued this form of sexuality by age 16 years. Hunt estimated that 2% of men and 1% of women were exclusively gays or lesbians in their sexual orientation.

Hunt found some evidence for a sexual revolution in the form of increases in certain sexual activities. More unmarried people had engaged in intercourse than the Kinsey surveys reported. A total of 97% of the unmarried men and 67% of the unmarried women reported having intercourse by age 25 years, representing an increase in intercourse and a decrease in the double standard. By the 1970s, extramarital sex was more common, especially among younger women.

The Playboy Foundation survey also found evidence that more people were engaging in a wider variety of sexual activities than Kinsey reported. For example, a higher percentage of respondents in the Playboy Foundation survey reported oral–genital sexuality than in Kinsey's surveys. **Fellatio** is oral stimulation of the male genitals, and **cunnilingus** is oral stimulation of the female genitals. Kinsey found a difference in popularity of oral–genital sexuality according to educational background: 60% of people with a college education, 20% of those with a high school education, and 10% of those with a grade school education had engaged in oral–genital sexual activity. Hunt reported that 90% of the young married couples in his survey said they had engaged in oral–genital stimulation, revealing a dramatic increase in prevalence and a leveling of social class differences.

In summary, Hunt's Playboy Foundation survey obtained a more representative sample of U.S. residents and interviewed them to update Kinsey's results. The findings showed that Kinsey was correct in concluding that people's sexual behaviors are more varied than the social norms suggest and confirmed the prevalence of masturbation and childhood sexuality. Hunt's estimates for same-sex sexuality were much lower than Kinsey's figures, but Hunt found evidence for an increase in premarital, extramarital, and oral–genital sexual activity.

The National Health and Social Life Survey.   Two major U.S. sex surveys appeared during the 1990s, one conducted by Samuel and Cynthia Janus (1993) and the other by a team headed by Edward Laumann, John Gagnon, Robert Michael, and Stuart Michaels (1994) for the National Opinion Research Center, called the National Health and Social Life Survey (NHSLS). Although both groups claimed that theirs was the first survey to obtain a representative sample of adults in the United States, the NHSLS survey relied on a random sampling technique rather than on volunteers. After collecting their information, Laumann and his colleagues compared their sample to information known about U.S. adults, and they concluded their group was representative.

Results from the NHSLS revealed a slightly different picture of sex in the United States than either the Kinsey or Hunt survey had shown. One difference was a continuation of the trend toward more liberal sexual standards, with sex serving either as an important factor in love relationships (regardless of marital status) or as a recreational activity (without any necessity for a committed relationship). Only around 30% of respondents expressed the traditional, conservative view that sex outside marriage is always wrong and that procreation is the main reason for having sex.

The other difference expressed in the NHSLS indicated some degree of conservatism concerning sex. For example, a low percentage of participants reported attraction to and practice of a variety of sexual behaviors. Indeed, the NHSLS results showed that vaginal intercourse was not only the most frequent form of sexual activity with a partner but also the most appealing to both men and women. Giving and receiving oral sex and watching a partner undress were at least somewhat appealing to a majority of participants, but group sex, anal intercourse, sex with strangers, and forcing or being forced to do something sexual were not appealing to the majority of participants.

This survey also found gender differences in sexuality, just as the other surveys had done. One large gender difference related to the experience of first intercourse: 28% of women but only 8% of men said that they did not want to have intercourse at the time but either did so out of affection for their partners or were forced to do so. Men also reported more varied sexual interests and behavior, including more lifetime sex partners and a slightly higher interest in group sex, anal intercourse, watching others do sexual things, visiting sex clubs, viewing sexually explicit books or videos, and giving and receiving oral sex. Men were more likely to masturbate, but women were more likely to report feeling guilty about masturbating. Table 10.1 summarizes information from this survey.

Contrary to media depictions, "The general picture of sex with a partner in America shows that Americans do not have a secret life of abundant sex" (Michael, Gagnon, Laumann, & Kolata, 1994, p. 122). The most common category for frequency of intercourse was *a few times a month,* and only about 7% reported having sex four or more times a week. In addition, about two-thirds of both men and women said that they had only one sex partner within the past year, with reports showing only small variations across different ethnic groups, religious affiliations, or educational levels. The NHSLS results reflected a less sexually varied United States than the media or people's imaginations often present, but it also showed an acceptance of sex for pleasure and outside the boundaries of marriage.

Gender Differences (and Similarities) in Sexual Attitudes and Behavior.

The three major (and many smaller) sex surveys have shown gender differences in several sexual behaviors and in some attitudes toward sexuality. Although the more recent surveys have indicated a smaller variation in sexuality of men and women, even recent studies have indicated gender differences. A meta-analysis (Oliver & Hyde, 1993) and later summaries (Christopher & Sprecher, 2000; Fischtein, Herold, & Desmarais, 2007; Peplau, 2003) have indicated that gender differences exist in some aspects of sexuality but not in others.

Two large gender-related differences emerged from the meta-analysis (Oliver & Hyde, 1993) that were confirmed by later reviews: incidence of masturbation and attitudes toward casual premarital sex. Higher rates of masturbation and a greater acceptance of casual premarital sex occur in male than in female adolescents and adults. These researchers pointed out that the magnitude of the contrasts for these comparisons surpasses other gender-related differences, such as those in mathematics or verbal performance. (See Chapter 7 for a discussion of these cognitive differences.) The greater acceptance of casual premarital sex applies to men in a variety of cultures, including Canada, Africa, Hong Kong, Sweden, and all ethnic groups in the United States (Hatfield & Rapson, 1996). The term *casual* also seems to apply to online sex, and about 84% of those who engage in this type of sexual activity are men (Cooper, Morahan-Martin, Mathy, & Maheu, 2002). (See According to the Media/According to the Research for more about cybersex.)

According to the Media...

Sex Is Just a Mouse Click Away

Tim Fountain (2003) described the joys of Internet sex: "The World Wide Web offers us an opportunity to go to our graves having fulfilled most of our sexual fantasies" (p. 21). According to Fountain, the Web offers a sexual banquet regardless of one's tastes. For gay men such as Fountain, chat rooms offer sexually oriented "chat" as well as arrangements for people to meet online and plan for sex in the real world, including websites specializing in casual sex.

Sex on the Internet offers a number of possibilities for online sexual activity, which people of all sexual orientation use (Lever, Grov, Royce, & Gillespie, 2008). The possibilities include using the Internet to find sexual information, dating services, and sexual entertainment (Cooper, 2004). The entertainment activities consist of a variety of fantasies and interactions such as *cybersex*—using the Internet to exchange photos or sexual messages that lead to sexual gratification.

The Internet offers what Al Cooper and his colleagues (Cooper, Delmonico, Griffin-Shelley, & Mathy, 2004) called the *Triple-A Engine*—accessibility, anonymity, and affordability. The Internet has over 600 million users worldwide, and sex is the most researched topic; about a third of those online use the Internet to obtain some form of sexual information or entertainment. As Cooper suggested, the Internet may be the new sexual revolution.

As Fountain had discovered, gay, lesbian, and bisexual individuals have been enthusiastic about online sexual activities (Lever et al., 2008), along with others whose sexuality has been subject to restriction, such as individuals with disabilities or those with fetishes (Cooper, 2004). Online sexual activity opens the world to these individuals, so they are no longer restricted to their geographic location.

Other gender-related differences in sexuality were smaller, and some of the meta-analysis comparisons (Oliver & Hyde, 1993) failed to show gender variations. Table 10.2 (page 248) shows some of the behaviors and attitudes from this meta-analysis, along with the magnitude of gender-related differences. However, the gender differences in attitudes toward sex may be larger than this meta-analysis revealed. All of the studies in this analysis were based on self-reports, which draw on explicit attitudes—attitudes that people are conscious of holding. Implicit attitudes are those that are automatically activated yet not in conscious awareness, and people may hold implicit attitudes that differ from their explicit attitudes (Greenwald & Banaji, 1995). A study of implicit attitudes toward sexual words (Geer & Robertson, 2005) revealed that women held more negative implicit attitudes than men did.

Examining changes over time, gender differences have decreased in both attitudes and behaviors related to sexuality. Table 10.1 shows a decrease in variations between men's and women's sexual attitudes and behavior, along with a few continuing differences.

Gender differences in sexuality may not be as large as the research suggests. Self-reports of attitudes rely on explicit attitudes that participants reveal to researchers, and self-reports of behavior are subject to distortion and misrepresentation. For example, young men lie about the number of sex partners they have had as a way to increase their prestige (Jonason & Fisher, 2009). A procedure called the *bogus pipeline* helps researchers obtain more truthful responses by leading participants to believe that their responses are monitored by a polygraph ("lie detector"). A bogus pipeline study of sexual behavior and responses (Alexander & Fisher, 2003) showed very small differences in women's and men's responses to questions about sexual behavior; the male and female participants in

ACCORDING TO THE RESEARCH . . .

The Internet Offers New Possibilities for Sexual Addiction

The possibilities for sexual activity on the Internet are numerous, some of which are positive and others of which present problems (Whitty & Fisher, 2008). The positive possibilities include ready access to sexual information. However, most of the millions of people who use the Internet for online sex choose one of the entertainment options, viewing sexual images, participating in sexually oriented chat, or engaging in sexual fantasy activities.

For the large majority of users, online sexual activities serve as a type of recreational activity used for distraction and stress relief (Cooper et al., 2004). These users may consider their online sexual activity as entertainment, but their partners may feel that online sex is "cheating" (Zitzman & Butler, 2009), which indicates that even noncompulsive online sexual activity may present problems.

Some individuals develop compulsive involvement with online sex, which is similar to other types of compulsions. Problems arise when a person's involvement begins to create difficulties with personal relationships or work (Cooper et al., 2004). Individuals who use the Internet for sexual activities are less likely to be involved in a satisfying personal relationship.

Large gender differences exist in online sexual activity (Cooper et al., 2004). Women are not as likely as men to be involved in online sexual activities—only about 15% of those who use the Internet for sexual activities are women. Those women participate in the same range of activities that men do—viewing sexually explicit photos, sexual chat, and fantasy sexual experiences. Contrary to stereotype, a larger proportion of female than male Net users develop problems (Ferree, 2003). Therefore, online sexual activity may create problems in men's and women's lives and relationships.

this study gave similar estimates of the number of lifetime sexual partners, the age at first intercourse, voluntary exposure to sexually explicit material, and frequency of masturbation. These results suggest that men's and women's sexual behavior may be more similar than much of the research has indicated, but each tends to report behavior according to gendered expectations and social norms.

Masters and Johnson's Approach

As noted earlier, researchers who want to observe sexual behavior directly can conduct their studies on nonhuman animals, or they can enlist the cooperation of people who are willing to engage in sex in a research laboratory. Although such participants are far from average, they might furnish important information about sex, which are more objective than self-reports. The most famous researchers to take this approach were William Masters and Virginia Johnson.

Masters and Johnson recruited volunteers consisting of married couples as well as single men and women who participated in sexual activity in a research laboratory while their physiological reactions were monitored. Those who volunteered were, undoubtedly, not representative of the U.S. population, and participants were also required to regularly achieve orgasm, which further restricted the characteristics of the sample. These biases were not of great concern to Masters and Johnson; they believed that the physiological sexual responses varied little from person to person. Others (Kaschak & Tiefer, 2001; Tiefer, 1995) argued that Masters and Johnson's selection of participants biased the interpretation

TABLE 10.2 *Sexual Attitudes and Behaviors Showing and Failing to Show Gender-Related Differences*

Sexual Behaviors/Attitudes	Direction of Difference
Large Differences	
Incidence of masturbation	Higher for men
Acceptability of casual sex	Higher for men
Moderate to Small Differences	
Acceptability of sexual permissiveness	Higher for men
Incidence of sex in committed relationship	Higher for men
Incidence of intercourse by engaged couples	Higher for men
Acceptability of premarital sex	Higher for men
Age at first intercourse	Lower for men
Frequency of intercourse	Higher for men
Incidence of same-gender sexual experiences	Higher for men
Anxiety, fear, and guilt associated with sex	Higher for women
Acceptability of double standard of sexual behavior	Higher for women
Acceptability of extramarital sex	Higher for men
Number of sexual partners	Higher for men
No Differences	
Incidence of oral sex	
Incidence of kissing	
Incidence of petting	
Acceptability of masturbation	
Acceptability of same-gender sexuality	
Belief that gays and lesbians should be given civil rights	
Sexual satisfaction	

of their results. In addition, these critics have claimed that Masters and Johnson's interpretation was biased by their preconceived notions, forcing the sexual experience into stages that are not necessarily appropriate for everyone.

In these laboratory studies, the married couples had intercourse, masturbated each other, or engaged in oral–genital stimulation. The unmarried participants did not have sex with a partner; the men masturbated and the women either masturbated or were stimulated by an artificial penis designed to measure vaginal responses during sexual arousal and orgasm. In addition to collecting information by measuring genital activity during sex, Masters and Johnson gathered physiological measurements such as heart rate, muscle contraction, and dilation of the blood vessels from both men and women. They analyzed their findings (Masters & Johnson, 1966) into four phases of sexual activity—excitement, plateau, orgasm, and resolution. The two researchers contended that these four phases describe the sequence and experience of sexual arousal and orgasm for both women and men. Figures 10.1 and 10.2 show the four phases, the organs that are affected, and the responses

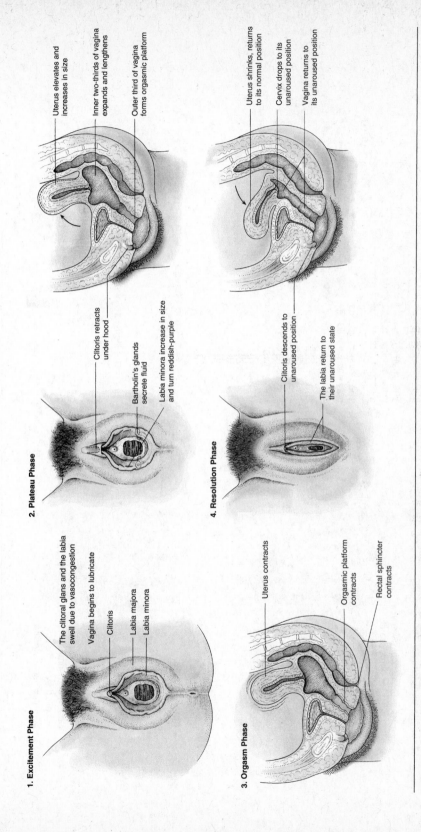

1. Excitement Phase

The clitoral glans and the labia swell due to vasocongestion

Vagina begins to lubricate

Clitoris

Labia majora

Labia minora

2. Plateau Phase

Uterus elevates and increases in size

Inner two-thirds of vagina expands and lengthens

Outer third of vagina forms orgasmic platform

Clitoris retracts under hood

Bartholin's glands secrete fluid

Labia minora increase in size and turn reddish-purple

3. Orgasm Phase

Uterus contracts

Orgasmic platform contracts

Rectal sphincter contracts

4. Resolution Phase

Uterus shrinks, returns to its normal position

Cervix drops to its unaroused position

Vagina returns to its unaroused position

Clitoris descends to unaroused position

The labia return to their unaroused state

FIGURE 10.1 *Female Genitals during the Phases of the Sexual Response Cycle*

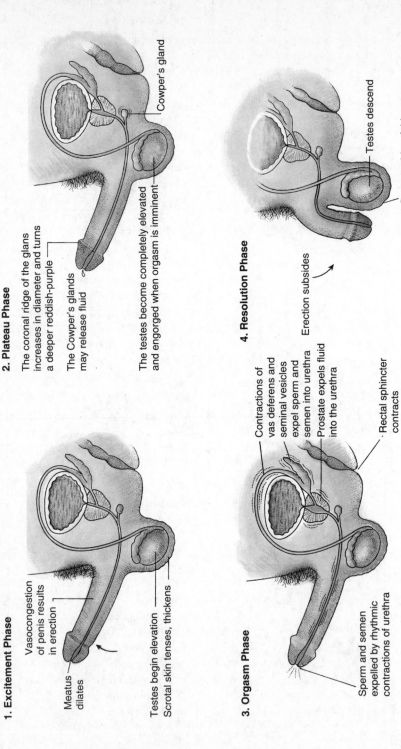

1. Excitement Phase

Vasocongestion
of penis results
in erection

Meatus
dilates

Testes begin elevation
Scrotal skin tenses, thickens

2. Plateau Phase

The coronal ridge of the glans
increases in diameter and turns
a deeper reddish-purple

The Cowper's glands
may release fluid

The testes become completely elevated
and engorged when orgasm is imminent

Cowper's gland

3. Orgasm Phase

Contractions of
vas deferens and
seminal vesicles
expel sperm and
semen into urethra

Prostate expels fluid
into the urethra

Rectal sphincter
contracts

Sperm and semen
expelled by rhythmic
contractions of urethra

4. Resolution Phase

Erection subsides

Testes descend

Scrotum thins, folds return

FIGURE 10.2 *Male Genitals during the Phases of the Sexual Response Cycle*

for both women and men. An examination of these figures reveals similarities as well as differences throughout these stages.

Not only did Masters and Johnson's research suggest that both women and men are similar in experiencing four stages of sexual response, but it also failed to support Freud's contention that women experience two types of orgasm—clitoral and vaginal orgasm. He believed that girls experience clitoral orgasm during masturbation, beginning during early childhood, but women are immature if they continue to require clitoral stimulation for orgasm. Freudian theory described women who experience orgasm through intercourse as psychologically healthier than women who have only clitoral orgasms. Masters and Johnson's results disconfirmed Freud's hypothesis, showing that women experience only one type of orgasm—a clitoral orgasm. Some women have clitoral orgasms during intercourse and some do not; intercourse may not provide sufficient clitoral stimulation to produce orgasm in some women. This important finding has not had the impact it should have had. A study on research, teaching, and popular usage of sexual terms (Ogletree & Ginsburg, 2000) revealed that the word *clitoris* is not used as the female counterpart to *penis*. Indeed, the word clitoris is not often used, and this omission may have important implications for sexuality.

Masters and Johnson's research has been influential but also controversial. As with other physiological processes, individual variations exist in the experience of these stages of sexual response, and Masters and Johnson ignored these variations (Tiefer, 1995). Their conceptualization became so well accepted that people who do not conform to these stages are open to being diagnosed with sexual dysfunctions. The Masters and Johnson research has been valuable in measuring sexual physiology, but their research findings may not be as universal as they have contended.

Childhood Sexuality: Exploration and Abuse

As the Kinsey, Playboy Foundation, and NHSLS surveys have shown, sexuality begins before puberty. Even as infants, children take part in sexual exploration, and they are sometimes the victims of sexual abuse. Infant boys have erections, and infant girls experience erections of the clitorises as well as vaginal lubrication (DeLamater & Friedrich, 2002). Infants touch their genitals as they explore their bodies, and this exploration teaches children that their bodies can produce pleasurable sensations. Preschool-aged children manipulate their genitals, sometimes several times a day.

Children's sexuality is not equivalent to adult sexual behavior; their underlying motivations and cognitions differ (Kilmer & Shshinfar, 2006). However, parents who notice their children's genital self-explorations may accept them, or they may be surprised or shocked. Their attitude and their method of dealing with their children's masturbation can convey positive or negative messages about sexuality, and these messages can have a lasting impact (DeLamater & Friedrich, 2002). Parents and other adults who say, "That's not nice," or "Nice boys and girls don't do that," or who move their children's hands away from their genitals send negative messages about sexuality (Surtees, 2005).

Another aspect of childhood sexuality that may make parents uncomfortable revolves around their children's questions about sexuality, pregnancy, and birth as well as their children's sexual exploration with other children. By age 4, most children have a concept of gender and women's and men's roles. They know that women have babies and men do not, and pregnancy and birth are topics that stimulate curiosity and questions. Parents may feel embarrassed about giving straightforward descriptions, but substitute terms may confuse children. Even with correct information, children have difficulties understanding sex and pregnancy, as the responses in Table 10.3 illustrate. Thus, formulating appropriate answers to young children's questions about sex and birth requires a delicate balance of providing the correct amount of information without excessive details. Parents' discomfort with the topic of sex complicates these discussions.

TABLE 10.3   *Examples of Children's Beliefs about Sex and Birth*

How Do People Get Babies?

According to 3- to 5-year-olds:

"You go to the baby store and buy one."

"They grow inside. I don't know how it starts. It just grows."

"The babies are in the stomach. I already have a baby in my stomach. . . . It won't grow cause I'm little. When I'm big, then it can grow . . . You have to be very careful because the baby may get loose in your stomach."

According to 4- to 6-year-olds:

"To get a baby to grow in your tummy, you just make it first. You put some eyes on it. Put the head on, and hair, some hair all curls. You make it with head stuff you find in the store that makes it for you."

"From marrying people. They put seeds in their vaginas. The mommies open up their tummy, but sometimes they open up their vaginas. So the daddies, so they can put their eggs in them, and they can put the seeds in them."

According to 7- to 10-year-olds:

"Well, I first thought, when I was seven that all you have to do is get married. And then all you would have to do is read a book, and then you would have a baby."

"The sperm is like a baby frog. It swims into the penis and makes a little hole. It bites a hole in its little mouth and swims into the vagina."

"From the daddy. He has something that helps the mommy get the baby. Some sort of medicine. I don't know what it's called, but it's here. [She pointed to her crotch.] Well, it goes in to some sort of part, I think it's the vagina, and just fixes up and helps around there, and makes it have a baby."

"I don't know much about it. Well, I know one thing. The man and the woman get together. And then they put a speck, then the man has his seed and the woman has an egg. They have to come together or else the baby, the egg won't really get hatched very well. The seed makes the egg grow. It's like plants. If you plant a seed, a flower will grow."

According to 11- and 12-year-olds:

"When the egg is fertilized it sort of comes to life. If you want to . . . the chemicals make it come to life. The sperm are injected to where the eggs are, and they just, I guess, coat them. There's some chemical in the sperms that activates another chemical in the egg, which starts the development of the baby."

"Sexual intercourse? Well, it should only be brought on by love, and it helps if you're married. And it's when the man and the woman come together, and the man sticks his penis into the lady's, near the womb, and then the egg that comes down through a little tube, down into the womb, is fertilized, and becomes a child."

From The Flight of the Stork by Anne C. Bernstein, copyright ©1978 by Anne C. Bernstein. Used by permission of Dell Publishing, a division of Random House, Inc.

"I would love for him to grow up to be a doctor, but I sure wish he'd wait another twenty years to specialize in gynecology," the mother of a 5-year-old said (Segal & Segal, 1993, p. 131). This mother humorously expressed her concern over her son and the neighbor's daughter, who were exploring each other's genitals. Such behavior is normal and more of an expression of curiosity than sexuality (Thanasiu, 2004).

Parents may be unaware that sexual explorations during childhood include same-sex as well as other-sex sexual play, but both are common. In studies with high school students (Larsson & Svedin, 2002) and college students (Whealin, Zinzow, Salstrom, & Jackson, 2007), students recalled their childhood sexual experiences, and about 80% remembered some sexual activity, most often with an age-mate. Sexual contact also occurs between siblings, and parents are not aware of most such contacts. The majority of such contact consists of examining the genitals and touching, and a low percentage of sibling sexual activity includes attempted or successful intercourse. Nonetheless, sexual activity between siblings qualifies as **incest**—sexual activity between family members. An early study (Finkelhor, 1980) reported that 15% of college women and 10% of college men recalled sexual experiences with their siblings. A later study (Whealin et al., 2007) found higher percentages— 28% of men and 26% of women. Some of these college students did not believe that the experience had harmed them, but many others evaluated this sexual contact as unwanted. A large age difference between the siblings was associated with a greater perception of harm.

Age is a critical factor in defining sexual exploitation of children (Finkelhor, 1984). When sexual contact occurs between children who are close to the same age, this activity falls into the category of *exploration*. When a child has sexual contact with an adult or an adolescent at least 5 years older than the child, that activity falls into the category of *exploitation* or *sexual abuse*. Also included as abusive are sexual relationships between adolescents and adults whose age exceeds the adolescents' age by at least 10 years.

Incest is one form of sexually abusive relationships, but children can also be sexually abused by nonrelatives, including strangers and adults in positions of authority. The Kinsey et al. (1948, 1953) surveys included questions about childhood sexual experiences with adults, and his results revealed that 25% of girls and 10% of boys reported such contact. More than half the cases involved adults whom the children did not know, but later research has indicated that most abusers are known to the children whom they target.

Beginning in the 1970s, several groups of researchers attempted to determine the rate of sexual abuse of children, but obtaining accurate numbers is difficult. Children do not participate in sex surveys (Tjaden & Thoennes, 2000b), adults who perpetrate abuse do not report their behavior (London, Bruck, Ceci, & Shuman, 2005), and adults who participate in surveys may experience memory or even honesty problems in recalling their experiences. Assessment of childhood sexual abuse has been conducted with a wide variety of people in different geographic locations using varying definitions of sexual abuse and several different research methods (Tjaden & Thoennes, 2000b). These variations have resulted in differing rates for sexual abuse, ranging from 11 to 40% for women and from 3 to 16% for men (Bagley & King, 1990; Dube et al., 2005).

Several reviews (Bagley & King, 1990; Greenfield, 1996; Tjaden & Thoennes, 2000b; Whealin et al., 2007) have shown some commonalities. Girls are sexually abused more often than boys, and men are the instigators of abuse far more frequently than women. Both girls and boys are at risk during their entire childhoods and adolescence from family members,

TABLE 10.4   *Summary of Offender and Victim Characteristics for Childhood Sexual Abuse*

Characteristic	Range of Estimated Occurrence	
	Lowest	Highest
Girls abused while under age 16 (average age 10.2–10.7 years)	11.0%	40.0%
Girls who rated the experience negatively	66.0	
Girls whose abuser was male	94.0	100
Boys abused while under age 16 (average age 11.2–12 years)	3.0	8.6
Boys who rated the experience negatively	38.0	
Boys whose abuser was male	83.0	84.0
Children whose offender was a stranger	11.0	51.0
Children whose offender was a friend or an acquaintance	33.0	49.0
Children whose offender was a relative	14.0	50.0
Girls whose offender was a sibling	15.0	
Boys whose offender was a sibling	10.0	
Children whose offender was a biological parent	1.0	6.8
Girls whose offender was a stepfather	7.6	17.0
Children who had force or threats used against them	55.0	
Children whose abuse consisted of exhibition	26.0	28.0
Children whose abuse consisted of being fondled	26.0	40.0
Children whose abuse consisted of forced fondling of offender	10.0	14.0
Children whose abuse consisted of intercourse	15.0	18.0

Source: Based on *Child Sexual Abuse: The Search for Healing,* by C. Bagley and K. King, 1990, London: Tavistock.

family friends, adult authority figures, and strangers, but the risk is not equal for all ages or from all adults. Table 10.4 shows the range of estimates and the characteristics of sexual abusers and victims.

Girls are not only more likely to be sexually abused; they are also more likely to be abused at younger ages than boys. The preadolescent years are the riskiest age period for both, with girls between ages 10 and 11 years and boys between ages 11 and 12 years at the highest risk. These ages represent the time during which the first victimization is most likely to occur. For many children, sexual abuse continues for years, often for as long as they remain in contact with their abusers.

Men are more likely to be abusers than women are. Men represented between 94 and 100% of those who abused girls and between 60 and 84% of those who abused boys. Abusers may be strangers, but more often these men are family members, family acquaintances, or adult authority figures such as neighbors, day-care workers, teachers, scout leaders, or religious leaders. Ethnicity is a factor in sexual abuse of children; Whites are more likely to be imprisoned for these offenses than African Americans or Hispanic

Americans are (Greenfield, 1996). Compared with perpetrators of other types of sexual abuse, those who abuse children are, on the average, about 5 years older.

The emphasis in research and therapy has been on boys and men as perpetrators and girls and women as victims, and this image is so prominent that people have trouble thinking of women as sexual abusers (Denov, 2003). Some women victimize boys in the guise of initiating them into sexuality, and boys may have difficulty identifying this activity as abuse (Larsson & Svedin, 2002). Women sometimes act as partners to men who sexually abuse children (Seto, 2004). However, some female sex abusers act alone and share characteristics with men who perpetrate sexual abuse. For example, a majority are family members, and most abuses are heterosexual (Seto, 2004). Female abusers tend to choose younger victims (Peter, 2009). Children have more difficulty reporting a female than a male perpetrator, and authorities have trouble recognizing such behavior in women (Denov, 2003).

Probably the most famous type of sexual abuse involves biological fathers and their daughters, but this type of sexual abuse is not the most common. Stepfathers or mothers' boyfriends are much more likely to force this type of relationship. One estimate (Russell, 1986) was that 17% of stepdaughters were molested by their stepfathers, whereas only 2% of daughters were victims of sexual abuse by their biological fathers. Cases of incest involving a father or father figure are the most damaging and may have both short-term and long-term consequences (Noll, Trickett, & Putnam, 2003; Paolucci, Genuis, & Violato, 2001). The short-term effects include fear, anxiety, depression, anger, sexually inappropriate behavior, and academic problems (Dube et al., 2005; Heise, Ellsberg, & Gottemoeller, 1999). The long-term effects include post-traumatic stress disorder, depression, suicide and suicide attempts, sexual adjustment problems, substance abuse disorders, and problems in their marriages. Few gender differences exist between boys and girls who have been the victims of sexual abuse; both suffer similar negative effects from their victimization (Dube et al., 2005; Paolucci et al., 2001).

Despite the impression that news reports have created about pedophiles, the sexual abuse of children may be declining (Jones, Finkelhor, & Halter, 2006). In the United

GENDERED VOICES

My Parents Never Said Anything Until . . .

"My parents never said anything to us about sexual abuse until my brother was molested," a teenager said. "Then our whole family talked sexual abuse. My brother had to tell us what happened, tell us what the person had done very explicitly. Maybe that wasn't a good thing for him to have to do, because he had to talk about it a lot, but we learned about what to be careful about. And they never said anything before he was molested.

"It was tough on the family, because the person who molested him was a cousin. He was about 4 or 5 years older than my brother, and our families don't speak to each other anymore. It was hard to know what to do, because the cousin had been molested when he was younger, so he was just repeating what happened to him. Should he be punished for doing what he had learned? My brother was still hurt, but it was difficult not to feel sorry for my teenage cousin.

"We went for counseling as a family, and I think it helped. I hear that it can be much worse to ignore it, because it won't go away if you don't talk about it. We talked about it afterward, but not before something happened."

States, the statistics for both reported and confirmed cases of child abuse of all types rose during the 1970s and 1980s, but during the 1990s, those rates began to decline. The decrease in number of cases for sexual abuse has been larger than for other types of violence against children; the decline represents a 36% decrease. Experts are cautious about accepting these figures as real decreases rather than problems in reporting procedures, but at least part of this decline appears to be real. Thus, these lower numbers represent some success in the efforts to stop the sexual abuse of children.

In summary, childhood sexuality is more active than most parents imagine; it begins during infancy when children explore and manipulate their own genitals and then progresses to curiosity about and exploration of others' genitals. Although parents may find these signals of sexuality distressing, such behavior is normal. Sexual exploitation also occurs when older adolescents or adults initiate sexual activity with children. Obtaining accurate estimates is difficult, but the results of various surveys indicate that at least 15% of women and 5% of men have been sexually abused as children. Girls are much more likely to be abused than boys, and men are much more likely than women to be abusers. There are few gender differences in short-term and long-term effects of childhood sexual abuse, which include post-traumatic stress disorder, depression, and suicide, as well as adult sexual and substance abuse problems. However, the rate of sexual abuse may be declining.

Heterosexuality

Most people develop erotic or sexual interests that result in attraction to people of the other sex rather than people of the same sex. That is, most people develop a heterosexual, rather than a same-sex **sexual orientation**. Signs of heterosexual erotic interest may begin during childhood, but sexual activity during childhood mainly takes the form of masturbation and exploratory play, which can be directed toward same- or other-sex children (Larsson & Svedin, 2002). Thus, children's sexuality often is not clearly heterosexual.

During late childhood and preadolescence, children seek the company of same-gender peers and avoid associating with other-gender peers (see Chapters 6 and 9). This gender segregation restricts the opportunities for heterosexual activity, but does not signal children's lack of heterosexual interest. Indeed, children often tease each other by announcing who "likes" whom and by threatening to kiss others who are unwilling (Thorne, 1993). Such games demonstrate an awareness of heterosexuality and an early knowledge of gender roles in heterosexual interactions.

During Adolescence

Although a distressing number of children are introduced to sexuality through force or coercion, adolescence is the typical period of sexual initiation. These activities consist of formal and a great deal more informal education. As the headline story for this chapter pointed out, contemporary American culture discourages adolescent sexuality, but these cultures also send many messages about sex and its pleasures. These messages pose problems for adolescents who see and hear about the promised joys of sex, but who are urged not to participate.

These messages are not equal for girls and boys. Girls receive many more messages to beware of sex than boys do (Baldwin & Baldwin, 1997), but abstinence-oriented sex education conveys information about the dangers of sexually transmitted diseases and pregnancy; some programs focus on building guilt in participants to frighten them about premarital sex (Schalet, 2009). Few question the dangers of sex for early adolescents. Teen pregnancy, sexually transmitted diseases, date rape, and sexual exploitation are possibilities for teenagers who engage in sex. But most sexuality education authorities contend that teaching children to fear sex is a bad strategy, and abstinence-only programs are much too limited to be adequate (Sullivan, 2009).

Sexuality education is more successful when the program includes information about sexual health, birth control, relationships, and decision making such as the one implemented in Anderson County, South Carolina, and described in the headline story for this chapter (Sullivan, 2009). Including an abstinence component may be desirable but not adequate (Santelli et al., 2006). Messages about the dangers of sex do not help adolescents develop knowledge or attitudes for healthy sexual relationships at some future point in their lives.

Deborah Tolman (2002) found confirmation for young women's sense of vulnerability in extensive interviews with adolescent girls about their sexuality. In these interviews,

Sexuality is an important part of people's lives, beginning during adolescence.

Tolman heard "dilemmas of desire," problems in reconciling sexual desire with being the "nice" girls that parents, peers, and schools urged them to become. The girls repeatedly mentioned the reluctance of their families to acknowledge their sexuality and the frequent reminders of the dangers that sex could bring, especially in the form of pregnancy. The image of self-centered sexuality was acceptable—even expected—for boys but not for girls. These girls felt that they had to choose either sexual desire or safety.

Despite the emphasis on marriage as the appropriate context for sexual activity, most people do not wait until marriage to have sex; premarital sex has become more common over the past decades in the United States. During the 1930s and 1940s, a majority of young men had intercourse before marriage (Kinsey et al., 1948), but a substantially smaller percentage of young women did (Kinsey et al., 1953). This discrepancy reflected the double standard, which has decreased over the past 60 years. In the 1950s, approximately 13% of girls and young women were sexually active, but by the late 1990s, the percentage had risen to 47% (Wells & Twenge, 2005). Age of first intercourse for young women also declined between the 1950s and 1990s, going from 19 years to about 15 years of age.

The changes for boys and young men have been smaller than for women. In the 1950s, over 50% of boys and men reported being sexually active, and that percentage has fallen slightly, to around 50%. The age of first intercourse decreased from 18 in the 1950s to 15 in the 1990s. Considering only intercourse biases the picture of adolescent sexuality; a larger percentage of teens engage in oral sex than vaginal intercourse (Halpern-Felsher, Cornell, Kropp, & Tschann, 2005).

Some studies have shown ethnic differences for age of first intercourse (Cavazos-Rehg et al., 2009; Upchurch, Levy-Storms, Sucoff, & Aneshensel, 1998; Wells & Twenge, 2005), but an analysis of inconsistencies in reporting (Upchurch, Lillard, Aneshensel, & Li, 2002) suggests

GENDERED VOICES

Sex De-Education

"A shiver goes up my spine remembering my "'sex education"' experience in the 6th grade. Now, I don't know if the teacher had some problems with sexuality in general, or if perhaps it was part of her job, but I'll never forget the fear of sex and sexual contact she put into about 95%, if not all, of the young girls in that class."

"The majority of the information was in reference to reproduction and sexually transmitted diseases. My teacher brought in this old, old medical book and proceeded to show these pictures of people with severe stage STDs. These pictures showed people with ulcerated sores all over their bodies; parts of their flesh were falling off, and she said, 'This is what happens to people who have sex when they're not married.' It was disgusting, not to mention terrifying."

"As if that wasn't bad enough, when she taught the section on the male genitalia, she brought another visual aid. She brought in a rubber replica of a male penis and testicles, and the thing was HUGE and she represented it as actual size. I've never heard so many young girls gasp in terror at the same time in my life. She was very quick to relay how painful sex with a man was. I never understood her motivation. She was married with three kids. Maybe her husband was that big, but it seems unlikely."

"To this day, I still wonder how many of these young girls were traumatized by their "'sex education"' and how that affected their first sexual encounter with a man. I've also wondered what techniques were used to teach the boys in our school."

that African Americans, Asian Americans, and European Americans may be more similar than some studies have indicated. Adolescents tend to misremember and misrepresent their sexual experiences to conform to gender stereotypes, just as adults do (Alexander & Fisher, 2003). Acculturation may be a significant factor in early intercourse; for example, Mexican American teens whose families were less acculturated to U.S. culture reported later ages of first intercourse than White teens (Adams, McGuire, Walsh, Basta, & LaCroy, 2005).

The decision to have intercourse may represent an attempt to make the transition to adulthood (Ott & Pfeiffer, 2009), but about two-thirds of teens who have had intercourse report regret that they did not wait longer (Martino, Collins, Elliott, Kanouse, & Berry, 2009). The reasons for girls' and boys' decisions to have sex often differ. For boys, having sex is a means not only to pleasure but also to social prestige (Baldwin & Baldwin, 1997; Jonason & Peter, 2009). "For teenage boys, their first sexual experience may be the primary symbol of manhood—a rite of passage" (Stark, 1989, p. 12). Boys feel pressure from their peers to "score," and their sharing the stories is a way to gain admiration from their peers. The pressure boys experience may be conveyed to the girls they date by demands for sex. Boys may have sex to prove a point. Girls may refuse sex to prove a point, or they may give in to this pressure and have sex. Women who readily consent to sex are at risk for being considered promiscuous, and that potential consequence may influence the decision to say "no" more than a lack of desire (Tolman, 2002). Openly acknowledging desire may lead to many unkind labels (Kreager & Staff, 2009), because the double standard for sexual behavior tends to be stronger among adolescents than adults.

Messages about the dangers of sex have some basis—forced sex, pregnancy, and sexually transmitted diseases are all too common in the lives of adolescents. **Date rape**, or **acquaintance rape**, is forced sexual activity between people who are dating or otherwise acquainted. Chapter 8 discussed rape as an aggressive crime disproportionately committed by men. Adolescents' sexual scripts conceptualize rape as an attack by a stranger (Krahé, Bieneck, & Schienberger-Olwig, 2007), but the majority of rapes and other acts involving forced or coerced sex occurs between acquaintances. Mary Koss and her colleagues (1987) surveyed college students about sexual activities and found that 54% of the young women in the survey claimed to have been the victims of some type of coerced or forced sexual activity at some time during their lives, and over 15% had been raped. A more recent survey (Gross, Winslett, Roberts, & Gohm, 2006) determined that 27% of the college women in this survey had experienced some form of unwanted sexual activity during the time they had been on campus. Over 10% of high school girls reported some forced sexual experience (Howard, Wang, & Yan, 2007). Questioning a wider age range of women, the NHSLS survey (Laumann et al., 1994) found that 22% of the women said that they had been forced to do something sexually by a man. Of these women, 46% said that they were in love with the man and another 22% said that the man who forced them was someone they knew well. Women are less likely to report sexual assaults if they know (and especially if they are dating or in love with) the perpetrator (Rickert, Wiemann, & Vaughan, 2005), leading to an underrepresentation in crime statistics of the incidence of rape by acquaintances.

Some gender differences in attitudes increase the risk for coercive sexual behavior. For example, flirting does not carry the same meaning for boys as for girls; men see flirting as more sexual than women do (La France, Henningsen, Oates, & Shaw, 2009), which may lead to different expectancies for sexual activity. Other research (Willan & Pollard, 2003) indicated that men's expectancies for sex were set early in an encounter, and those expectancies were resistant to change, regardless of protests from the women involved. Research with high school students in Israel (Geiger, Fischer, & Eshet, 2004) revealed widespread attitudes that support sexual coercion, such as blaming the situation rather than the perpetrator for rape, minimizing the seriousness of rape, and justifying rape by believing that the victim had intended to have sex. Both female and male students held these attitudes, but young men were much more likely than young women to believe in these rape myths. Thus, adolescents may hold attitudes that allow for coercive and violent sex.

Concerns over pregnancy are another issue for adolescents who have sex. This anxiety affects girls more than boys. Although some sexuality education includes the full range of birth control options, the abstinence view is more common and emphasizes the danger of sex to both girls and boys. The concern is not without reason. The United States has a higher rate of pregnancies among teens than any other industrialized country: 72.2 of every 1,000 teenaged girls between 15 and 19 years old living in the United States get pregnant each year (Ventura, Abma, & Mosher, 2008). This rate was higher 20 years ago, declined 38% between 1990 and 2001, but has begun to increase again.

Sexually transmitted diseases (STDs) represent even more of a danger for adolescents than others. One of the objections to abstinence-only sexuality education has been its failure to provide information about STDs and prevention (Santelli et al., 2006). Indeed, adolescents who made a pledge to remain sexually abstinent until marriage experience a similar rate of STDs as other adolescents (Christopher Trenholm, Devaney, Fortson, Quay, & Wheeler, 2008).

In summary, as adolescent sexuality becomes increasingly oriented toward heterosexual encounters, young people receive messages of the dangers of sex. Girls have always received messages of danger and vulnerability rather than pleasure, but all students in abstinence-only sexuality education may receive similar messages. Such programs do not best serve adolescents in preventing sexually transmitted diseases or preparing for future sexuality. First intercourse typically occurs during adolescence, and gender differences in the age of first intercourse and rates of sexual activity have diminished over the past 60 years. Nonetheless, adolescent sexuality poses risks such as pregnancy and sexually transmitted diseases.

During Adulthood

Traditionally, marriage has not only been a major transition, but also the primary context for adult sexuality, often in the form of vaginal intercourse. The more recent studies of college students and surveys with more representative samples have indicated that the standards for sexual behavior have changed. Lower ages of first intercourse, increases in sexual activity among female adolescents, and increases in the acceptability of a variety of sexual activities suggest that more frequent and more varied sexual behaviors are now accepted for both young women and men. Sexuality has become an important part of life for young adults, regardless of their marital status (Christopher & Sprecher, 2000).

Despite the importance of sexual satisfaction for adults, some are celibate. **Celibacy**, refraining from sexual activity, is sometimes a voluntary choice. For example, some religions require celibacy for clergy and for those who are not married. Inspired by religion or other codes of personal morality, some people choose celibacy, but the number of young adults who have sex before they are married is high—around 88% of men and 81% of women (Christopher & Sprecher, 2000). Research on those who are celibate (Donnelly, Burgess, Anderson, Davis, & Dillard, 2001; Netting, 1992; Netting & Burnett, 2004) revealed that reasons for refraining from intercourse include moral or religious values, fear of STDs, and lack of opportunity. Among college students (Netting & Burnett, 2004), 36% of young women chose celibacy, about one-third of whom were waiting for love, and 25% of young men, about one-third of whom were waiting for a willing partner. However, 30% of the college students who were not engaging in intercourse were having oral sex.

Between 10 and 12% of men and 14 and 16% of women reported no sex partner within the past year (Butler, 2005; Laumann et al., 1994). Lifelong celibacy is, however, unusual: Only 2.9% said they had never had a sex partner. Those who are ill or whose partners have died are especially likely to be celibate, and both circumstances are associated with increasing age. Thus, celibacy increases sharply after age 60. Older women's longer life expectancy makes them far more likely to be celibate than men of the same age.

Monogamy means having only one sexual partner in a committed love relationship. This choice represents the ideal for many people within many cultures (Christopher & Sprecher, 2001; Hatfield & Rapson, 1996), but lifelong monogamy represents the actual lifestyle for a smaller number. Some people advocate monogamy but practice **serial monogamy** in which a person has relationships with a series of partners, one at a time (Donnelly et al., 2001; Netting & Burnett, 2004). Series of exclusive dating partners and divorce and remarriage are examples of this pattern. Others believe in monogamy but have no current sexual partner, and still others say that they believe in monogamy but "cheat" by having sex with other partners. Thus, several departures from monogamy allow people to subscribe to the ideal without adhering to the practice of having one sexual partner for life.

Women tend to endorse monogamy more strongly than men. For example, a study of college students (Pedersen, Miller, Putcha-Bhagavantula, & Yang, 2002) found that 98.9% of men and 99.2% of women said that they wanted to settle down with one exclusive sexual partner at some point in their lives (but not necessarily now). Among another group of college students (Netting & Burnett, 2004), 57% of the women and 54% of the men were classified as monogamous. For married couples, monogamy is the most common style of sexuality. Indeed, 93.7% of married couples reporting in the NHSLS were monogamous in the year prior to the study (Laumann et al., 1994). Unmarried cohabiting heterosexual partners (76.7%), those who had never been married and were not cohabiting (38%), and those who were divorced or separated (40.5%) were less likely to be monogamous.

For all types of couples, failure to maintain the ideal of monogamy can cause major relationship problems. People become upset when their partners have sex with someone else (Christopher & Sprecher, 2001). One of the hypotheses of evolutionary psychology and its view of mate selection is that men and women experience jealousy, but over different behaviors. In this view, men's jealousy is prompted by sexual infidelities because such behavior would create uncertainty concerning parentage of offspring, whereas women's jealousy is sparked by emotional infidelities because such behavior would threaten continued partner support (Buss, 1994). However, several studies that tested reactions to different types of infidelities (Nannini & Meyers, 2000; Russell & Harton, 2005) failed to confirm these predictions. Women were more upset than men by both types of infidelities, and both men and women were more upset by infidelities that involved a sexual component than an emotional one.

Some people choose sexual freedom over monogamy, opting for a sexual style of free experimentation. This choice is most common among young, unmarried people (Laumann et al., 1994; Netting, 1992; Netting & Burnett, 2004). People who choose this style tend to value sexual freedom and want to participate in a variety of sexual relationships. Indeed, "hooking up" has become widespread among college students and other young adults. This term may apply to sexual activity without a personal relationship or "friends with benefits," who are nonromantic friends who have a sexual relationship (Paul, Wenzel, & Harvey, 2008). Studies of teens (Manning, Giordano, & Longmore, 2006) and college students (McGinty, Knox, & Zusman, 2007) showed that having sex with someone outside a dating relationship was common: More than 50% of sexually active participants had done so. However, many harbored hopes that these sexual relationships would develop into romantic ones. Among adults (Laumann et al., 1994), a small percentage of both men and women reported having five or more sex partners in the year prior to the survey. Table 10.5 summarizes the styles of sexuality among the college students and adults.

The sexual attitudes and behaviors of women and men show few differences, but those few differences may have larger implications for heterosexuality, especially the choices of monogamy or free experimentation. One of the large gender differences in sexuality is in the acceptability of casual sex, with men being more acceptant than women (Oliver & Hyde, 1993). Women are encouraged to associate sex with love, and they come to believe that sex should occur in the context of a committed relationship, whereas men may not be so relationship centered (McCormick, 1994). The meaning of sex for women and men may differ, but more recent research (Krahé et al., 2007) suggests that women and men are becoming more similar.

Even small gender differences may have large implications, forming areas of conflict for couples. For women, the association between commitment and sex leads them to believe that commitment should exist before having sex, but men may not share these requirements or expectations. Differing expectations about the timing of intercourse in a relationship led men to expect sex after significantly fewer dates (9 to 11) than women (15 to 18) (Cohen & Shotland, 1996). A study of dating scripts for college students (Morr Serewicz & Gale, 2008) revealed that men included expectations of more sexual activity in their first date scripts than women did. These differing expectations could be a source of conflict if men begin to pressure women to have sex and the women do not feel ready, or if women refuse sex when men believe that their relationship warrants it.

The difference in acceptability of casual sex can also have an impact on sex outside the primary relationship. Women are more likely to be monogamous than men, and they are more likely to consider sex outside the relationship as betrayals by their partners. Women tend to value monogamy, whereas men tend to consider it a sacrifice (Schmookler & Bursik, 2007). The perception of what constitutes "cheating" also follows stereotypical patterns (Sprecher, Regan, & McKinney, 1998). When the man has sex outside marriage, people predict that he will not necessarily leave his wife for his lover, but people see women's extramarital sex as more indicative of the end of the relationship. Thus, the gender difference in the acceptability of casual sex affects dating and extramarital sex and people's beliefs about what sexual affairs imply for relationships.

The other large gender difference in sexuality is the frequency of masturbation (Oliver & Hyde, 1993); men report that they masturbate more often than women say they do. At first, any relationship between masturbation and partnered sex may not seem

TABLE 10.5 *Styles of Sexuality among College Students and Adults*

Style Chosen	Percentage		Comments on Choices
	Women	Men	
College Students*			
Celibacy	36%	25%	Accepted abstinence before marriage; waiting for the right partner; waiting for an opportunity for sex (especially men)
Monogamy	25	23	Were currently monogamous
	18	15	Had had only one partner during their lives
Serially Monogamous	14	16	Currently had one sex partner but had another partner(s) during past year
Free Experimenter	7	20	Valued freedom of expression, including expression of sexuality
Never Married Adults**			
Celibacy (no sex partners)	24.5%	17.4%	Waiting for partner; believed in sex only within marriage
Monogamy (one sex partner)	50	38.3	Believed in monogamy but not in waiting for marriage to have sex
Sexually Active but Not Monogamous (2–4 sex partners)	20.9	32.1	May represent a series of partners
Free Experimenter (5 or more partners)	4.6	12.0	Young adults were much more likely than older adults to be in this group
Married Adults**			
Celibacy (no sex partners)	2.7%	1.7%	Partner absent; illness; bad relationship
Monogamy (one sex partner)	94.8	92.2	Commitment to sexual exclusivity
Sexually Active but Not Monogamous (2–4 sex partners)	2.1	4.9	Represents affairs or casual sex
Free Experimenter (5 or more partners)	0.01	1.1	Represents affairs, casual sex, and paid sex

Sources: *Data based on Netting and Burnett, 2004.
**Data based on Laumann et al., 1994, and the number of reported sex partners within the past 12 months.

apparent, but Janet Hyde (1996) explained a connection through women's guilt concerning masturbation, which results in less familiarity with their bodies and less certain knowledge of how to reach orgasm. Women's lower likelihood of experiencing orgasm during intercourse causes distress for many couples. Hyde pointed out that many sex therapists direct women who are having orgasmic difficulties to masturbate and hypothesized that women's lower frequency of masturbation may lay the foundation for women to have difficulties in reaching orgasm.

Other gender differences may also have some relationship to the problems that heterosexual couples face. One issue is desire for and frequency of intercourse. The double standard proposes that women will be less interested in sex because they are less sexual creatures than men, and evolutionary psychology (Buss, 1994, 1996) holds that women must be more sexually selective than men in order to choose mates who will be able to provide for offspring. These two views agree that women are less sexual but disagree over the reason. Determining a social or biological explanation is very difficult because society influences everyone, including sexuality, making any interpretation of "natural" sexuality is impossible.

Sarah Blaffer Hrdy (1981, 1986, 1999) criticized the view that women are less sexual than men, which she called the Myth of the Coy Female, by reporting on females unaffected by cultural expectations and the double standard—nonhuman primates. She argued that male scientists who have seen female reluctance to engage in sex have been influenced by the double standard and have projected these human differences onto nonhuman primates, revealing more about the human observer than about the observed species. Hrdy argued that the sexual behavior of nonhuman animals varies from species to species. The females of some species, such as baboons and chimpanzees, initiate multiple, brief sexual relationships and show no coy reluctance to engage in sex, whereas the females of other species, such as blue monkeys and redtail monkeys, are very selective about their mating partners. Their selectivity might appear coy, but these animals reflect only one version of primate sexuality, not a comprehensive pattern.

The double standard for sexual behavior—and women's application of it to themselves—may relate to their lower interest in sex. A meta-analysis of attitudes toward sexuality (Oliver & Hyde, 1993) showed that women accepted the double standard more strongly and felt more guilt over sex than men did, but more recent studies have shown small or inconsistent differences between women and men (Fugère, Escoto, Cousins, Riggs, & Haerich, 2008; Marks & Fraley, 2005). One study (Jonason & Marks, 2009) suggested that the double standard may have diminished for common sexual behavior but not for less common forms. If women believe that they are or should be less sexual, they may behave accordingly and become less sexual. Masters and Johnson (1966) argued that women could be just as sexual as or even more sexual than men if women were free to express their sexuality and to participate in the activities that gave them sexual pleasure.

Is sexuality really very different for women and men? Gender differences in sexual behavior have decreased, suggesting that both female and male sexuality are subject to change and are influenced by social standards. During the Victorian era, women were presumed to be less sexual than men, and so they became. In our sexualized modern culture, women are portrayed as being more sexual than in the past but still less so than men, and so they have become. Sexuality is created by each culture and shows enormous differences across cultures. Thus, women and men exhibit a wide variety of sexual behaviors depending on their physiologies, cultures, personal backgrounds, and personal expectations. Carol Tavris (1992, p. 245) summarized heterosexuality by saying, "The question is not whether women are more or less sexual than men. (The answer to that is yes, no, both, and sometimes.) The questions are: What are the conditions that allow women and men to enjoy sex in safety, with self-confidence, and in a spirit of delight? And how do we get there?"

Homosexuality

Some people develop erotic attraction toward people of the same sex and engage in same-sex sexual activities. The number of people with same-sex sexual interests, behavior patterns, and identities constitutes a minority, but estimates vary on how small a minority. Most of the variation in estimates can be explained according to the variation in definitions. Is sexual attraction to those of the same sex sufficient? Are persons lesbian or gay if they have engaged in sexual activity with persons of the same sex at any time during their lives? Does having sex primarily or exclusively with members of one's own sex define homosexuality? Or must people identify themselves as gay or lesbian? These varying criteria produce different estimates.

Kinsey and his colleagues (1948) found that 37% of the men said that they had engaged in male–male sexual activity at some time during their lives, and 28% of women reported at least one female–female sexual experience (Kinsey et al., 1953). Therefore, a substantial number of participants in the Kinsey surveys reported sexual experiences with members of their own sex, but most did not engage in such relationships as the primary form of sexuality throughout their lives. About 13% of the men and about 7% of the women in Kinsey's surveys identified themselves as primarily gay or lesbian. This estimate has been controversial (Bancroft, 2004), and other surveys have asked different questions and obtained lower estimates. Table 10.6 (page 266) presents a comparison of the various measures of homosexuality for several studies, one of which questioned people in three countries. As this table reveals, the different measures (and cultures) show variations in the percentage of people who might be classified as gay or lesbian.

Understanding homosexual sexual orientation has been a challenge for theorists and researchers. For years, psychologists failed to make a distinction between *gender role,* the social behaviors associated with one or the other gender, and *sexual orientation,* the erotic attraction to members of one or the other sex (or to both). Psychologists confused gender role and sexual orientation, incorrectly imagining that same-sex sexual orientation included an inversion of gender role (Constantinople, 1973; Lewin, 1984a, 1984b). The separation of gender role and sexual orientation clarified the process of measuring masculinity and femininity and demonstrated that same-sex sexual orientation has a far from perfect relationship to these traits. That is, men who are erotically attracted to other men are not necessarily feminine in appearance or behavior, nor are women who find other women sexually attractive necessarily more masculine than other women.

The issue of sexual orientation is socially controversial and poorly understood scientifically, possibly because of the focus on homosexuality rather than the broader concept of sexual orientation. Lisa Diamond (2003b) questioned the meaning of sexual orientation and proposed that erotic attraction and romantic attraction were separable components that usually—but not always—go together. Her questions about the underlying meaning of sexual orientation have been exceptions; most researchers have accepted the assumption that heterosexuality is the standard and thus needs no explanation, whereas homosexuality requires theory and research. This attitude of compulsory heterosexuality (Hyde & Jaffee, 2000) reflects the lack of acceptance for homosexuality in many societies. This lack of acceptance is a prominent feature of the social controversy, which also questions the underlying basis for sexual attraction to those of the same sex. Is sexual attraction biologically determined

TABLE 10.6 *Differing Estimates of Same-Sex Attraction and Behavior*

Study	Percent	
	Men	Women
Kinsey et al. (1948, 1953)		
At least one same-sex sexual experience	37%	28%
Primarily or exclusively same-sex sexual contacts	13	7
Janus and Janus (1993)		
At least one same-sex sexual experience	22	17
Primarily same-sex sex	4	2
Laumann et al. (1994, NHSLS)		
Same-sex desires or experiences	10.1	8.6
Done anything sexual with same-sex partner	9.1	4.3
Same-sex partner since puberty	7.1	3.8
Same-sex partner in past year	2.7	1.3
Attracted to same-sex individuals	7.7	7.5
Self-identified as gay or lesbian	2.8	1.4
Sell, Wells, and Wypij (1995)		
United States		
Same-sex attraction but no activity	8.7	11.1
Same-sex sexual activity since age 15	6.2	3.6
United Kingdom		
Same-sex attraction but no activity	7.9	8.6
Same-sex sexual activity since age 15	4.5	2.1
France		
Same-sex attraction but no activity	8.5	11.7
Same-sex sexual activity since age 15	10.7	3.3
Butler (2005)		
Same-sex sexual activity in past year	2.9	3.5
Turner et al. (2005)		
Same-sex sexual activity since age 18	5.7	5.4
Same-sex sexual activity in past 5 years	3.6	3.8
Same-sex sexual activity in past year	3.2	2.5

(and if so, how)? Or is sexual attraction the result of experiences (and if so, which ones)? The social controversy continues because research has not yielded clear answers concerning the basis for sexual orientation. However, theory and research are plentiful, centering around biologically based versus socially based theories.

Early biological theories of sexual orientation focused on genetics and hormones. No simple relationship exists between sexual orientation and either genetic background or hormonal levels, but both may exert influences in complex ways (Hyde, 2005b). The evidence is strong that sexual orientation has a genetic component. One large, representative study of twins (Bailey, Dunne, & Martin, 2000) found a lower rate of genetic influence for sexual orientation than in prior studies. When one of a pair of identical twins was gay, lesbian, or bisexual, about 20% of the other twins also were not heterosexual. This study also showed a higher degree of heritability for male than for female homosexual twins, suggesting the possibility than the genetic mechanisms for sexual orientation differ in men and women. How that genetic component operates remains unclear (Hyde, 2005b).

Another biologically based hypothesis centers around prenatal exposure to testosterone and how such exposure might influence the developing brain and thus affect sexual orientation (Bogaert, 2003, 2006; Cohen, 2002; Lalumiere, Blanchard, & Zucker, 2000; Rahman, 2005a, 2005b). The reasoning is that too much or too little exposure to androgens produces brain variations that underlie the development of nonheterosexual sexual orientation. Thus, studies have examined physical correlates of atypical prenatal androgen exposure and related these physical differences to sexual orientation, focusing on the ratio of the length of the second (index) and fourth (ring) fingers. Prenatal testosterone exposure affects this ratio, so finger ratio may differ for gays and lesbians compared to heterosexuals. Several studies (Hall & Love, 2003; Rahman, 2005a) have found that the finger ratios of lesbians were more like those of men than women; other studies (Rahman, 2005a; Robinson & Manning, 2000) have found that gay men's finger ratios did not match the pattern typical for men. Another approach has focused on the number of male siblings, and results have indicated that older brothers increase the likelihood of being gay (Bogaert, 2003, 2006), but only for right-handed men (Blanchard, Cantor, Bogaert, Breedlove, & Ellis, 2006). These results are consistent with the hypothesis that prenatal exposure to androgens plays a role in the development of sexual orientation.

Other theories put more emphasis on experience, such as Daryl Bem's (1996, 2000) theory, the Exotic-Becomes-Erotic. According to this view, individuals become erotically attracted to the class of people from whom they felt different during childhood. For most people, gender segregation makes the other gender that class of people; through separation from the other gender, those in that class seem different and exotic. When adolescents begin to experience sexual feelings, the objects of those feelings are those who were exotic. Thus, Bem contended that the perception of differences leads to the development of sexual interest and orientation.

For individuals who develop a same-sex sexual orientation, the Exotic-Becomes-Erotic view hypothesizes that these individuals had childhood activity preferences that were more typical of the other gender. Thus, boys who preferred playing with dolls and kitchen sets tend to associate with girls, making girls more familiar and less exotic. For girls who preferred boys' toys and games, girls would be more exotic. Therefore, this theory predicts that gay men and lesbians will have childhoods in which gender-atypical activities predominated. Many studies confirm this prediction for boys (Bailey et al., 2000; Bem, 2000), but the evidence for girls is much weaker (Peplau & Huppin, 2008). Both Bem (2000) and Phillip Hammack (2005) have argued for an interactional view that includes biological, social, and experiential components in a theory of sexual orientation. Integrated theories will remain difficult to formulate, partly because researchers remain polarized and cannot agree on what constitutes homosexuality (Savin-Williams, 2006).

During Adolescence

Adolescence is a time of sexual exploration, and adolescent sexual activity has become more common and more accepted over the past 40 years—for heterosexual individuals. Same-sex sexual activity is discouraged but still occurs. Indeed, most of the people who have same-sex sexual experiences do so as part of adolescent experimentation and not as the beginning of a gay or lesbian sexual identity. Some adolescents who are attracted to persons of the same sex do not act on these desires during adolescence (Savin-Williams & Diamond, 2000). Therefore, sexual orientation and sexual activity during adolescence do not correspond completely to sexual identity or to sexual activity during adulthood.

The process of developing a sexual identity must include the recognition of sexual attraction: labeling self as gay, lesbian, bisexual, or heterosexual; engaging in sex; and acknowledging sexual orientation (Savin-Williams & Diamond, 2000). These milestones do not necessarily occur in that order, and women and men show gender-related as well as individual variations in their trajectories of developing sexual identity. However, the recognition of sexual attraction tends to be the first milestone, which often occurs between ages 8 and 10 years.

Some gays and lesbians say they questioned if they were heterosexual or knew about their same-sex sexual attraction even before adolescence, but many of them have tried to develop heterosexual interests and fit into this accepted pattern of sexuality (Carver, Egan, & Perry, 2004). Some may succeed; as many as 90% of lesbians have entered sexual relationships with men (Rust, 2000). Also, sexual orientation in women appears to be less fixed than in men (Diamond, 2006); over 25% of young women who had identified themselves as lesbian changed that identity within a 5-year period (Diamond, 2003a). Furthermore, the milestone of identifying oneself as gay or lesbian varied for gay men and for lesbians (Savin-Williams & Diamond, 2000). Women tended to self-identify before they engaged in same-sex sexual behavior, but most gay men had a sexual experience with another man before they identified themselves as gay. The percentage of women who report sexual activity with other women has increased over the past 20 years, and this change is most obvious for younger women (Butler, 2005). These changes in women's sexual behavior are compatible with the view that women's sexuality is flexible for a longer period in their lives than men's sexual orientation, which seems to be fixed earlier in development (Baumeister, 2000).

The acceptance of same-sex attraction is a milestone that presents a major challenge for gay adolescents. They often struggle with feelings that something is wrong with them, and self-esteem may be a problem. Self-acceptance is different (and often comes more easily) than revealing one's same-sex sexual orientation or behavior to family and friends. **Coming out** is the process of personally recognizing and publicly acknowledging one's gay or lesbian orientation to others (Bohan, 1996). The term originated with the phrase "coming out of the closet," referring to the hidden (closeted) nature of sexuality for many gays and lesbians. Thus, coming out is a positive affirmation of sexuality but may nevertheless presents problems at school and within families (Rasmussen, 2004). This process may be part of adolescent development, or it may occur at any time during adulthood. One study (Savin-Williams & Diamond, 2000) indicated that the time between experiencing same-sex attraction and acknowledging gay or lesbian sexual orientation was about 10 years.

◼ GENDERED VOICES

In My School

In schools, boys and girls are the targets of name-calling and gender harassment based on sexual orientation. The basis of the name-calling is rarely related to sexual behavior.

> "If you use good grammar and good English, the kids in my school call you a faggot. It's crazy." 15-year-old African American boy attending a suburban school

> "If you belong to the drama club in my school, everybody thinks you are gay." 15-year-old White boy (in the drama club)

> "If you belong to the science fiction club, everybody thinks you are gay because those kids dress all in black and hug each other before they go to class." 14-year-old White girl attending a suburban school in a large city

> "You don't have to do anything to be called a faggot in my school. The athletes call everybody faggot, just because they are jerks who are trying to intimidate other kids." 14-year-old White boy attending a private school

Coming out includes developing a sexual self-concept, and many adolescents consult the Internet for information during this phase (Bond, Hefner, & Drogos, 2009). A public acknowledgment of sexual orientation may occur, or the revelation may be limited to friends and family. Parents may be acceptant and supportive, or they may be angry and have trouble accommodating the sexual orientation of this child; they may feel that they are being asked to accept the unacceptable (Freedman, 2008). In addition, friends may react negatively to coming out, and peer verbal or physical attacks are not unusual, especially in school (Goodenow, Szalacha, & Westheimer, 2006). Thus, gay and lesbian adolescents may be estranged from family and peers, and they are at increased risk for home- and school-related problems.

For adults, coming out often includes acceptance into the gay community. For adolescents, such acceptance is not as easy, because activities in the gay community are oriented toward adults. Charges of seducing adolescents or of promoting same-sex sexual activities present situations that make gay adults sensitive about including adolescents in the gay community.

Coming out can be a positive statement of sexuality for adolescents as well as for adults, but adolescents face many challenges in establishing a gay or lesbian identity. A longitudinal study of gay and lesbian gender identity (Rosario, Schrimshaw, Hunter, & Braun, 2006) indicated adolescents who form such an identity tend to be more comfortable and accepting of their sexual identity than those who have not yet taken that step.

During Adulthood

Women and men who engage in same-sex sexual activities face disapproval and censure. Sexual activities between people of the same sex have been illegal in many states of the United States, and the controversy over same-sex marriages reflects the lack of acceptance for these relationships (Turner, Villarroel, Chromy, Eggleston, & Rogers, 2005). Men in the United States hold more negative attitudes than women do toward homosexuality, especially regarding

GENDERED VOICES

Treated Like a Gender Traitor

"When I came out as gay, I got a lot of homophobia reactions," a college student in his 20s said. "Men were especially bad. Their reactions weren't exactly fear, although they were nervous. And it wasn't hatred. It was more like resentment. I wasn't a real man anymore and like I was some kind of traitor to the male gender."

Coming out and becoming part of the gay and lesbian community are events that are important to many lesbians and gay men.

gay men, and students in Germany (Steffens & Wagner, 2004) and Italy (Lingiardi, Falanga, & D'Augelli, 2005) showed similar gender differences in their attitudes. Both men and women with strong gender role identities tend to be more prejudiced against gays and lesbians than other people are (Whitley, 2001). Although attitudes toward gays and lesbians have become less negative over the past several years (Turner et al., 2005), implicit attitudes remain more negative than explicit attitudes (Steffens, 2005).

This lack of acceptance means that gays and lesbians face disapproval and discrimination (Sandfort, de Graaf, & Bijl, 2003), which has led to the formation of self-contained gay communities. In many large cities, such communities form the context for the lives of many gay people, who may rarely interact with the outside world of heterosexuals. Friendships and social networks become an essential part of gays' and lesbians' social lives. As they age, friendships can provide a support network that acts as a buffer between them and an outside world that stigmatizes their sexual orientation (de Vries & Megathlin, 2009).

Lesbians and gay men form love relationships that have the elements of intimacy, passion, and commitment in them, just as in heterosexual couples' relationships. Surveys

■ GENDERED VOICES

I Never Imagined the Pain

"Lesbians have been telling me about their problems in coming out," a female graduate student in counseling said. "For some reason, two women have confided in me about the problems with staying in the closet and coming out. They are women I knew and they came to trust me, but I'm not their counselor. I never imagined the pain and the problems. I guess I have led a sheltered life. I have known gays and lesbians, but I had never known or imagined the difficulties in essentially leading two lives—one for the public and the real, private one."

"One woman has been in a relationship for 17 years. During those years she and her lover have had to pretend to be 'just roommates' who share a house. She felt that she could never let the people at work know she was lesbian; she thought she would lose her job."

"She said that she felt pressured and tried to be heterosexual. She was even engaged to be married when she was in her early 20s, but her mother sensed something was wrong and told her that she didn't have to get married if she didn't want to. She broke the engagement and stopped trying to be something she wasn't, but she kept her sexual orientation secret for another 20 years."

"This woman has started to come out selectively to people she trusts. Her family still doesn't know—or at least she hasn't told them. She has found coming out a great relief and would like to be able to be completely out but does not feel comfortable enough to do so."

"The other woman has not yet come out. I guess you would say she is bisexual rather than lesbian; I'm not sure about these classifications. She is married and has a child, but she is attracted to women and has had a number of lesbian affairs, but they upset her. She says that she was 'good' when she went on a shopping trip to a large city and did not pursue a lesbian relationship, but 'bad' when she did. She is very unhappy and troubled over whether she should leave her husband and come out as a lesbian. I am really very concerned for her, because she is suicidal, and I am afraid that she might harm herself. This conflict is really a problem for her."

"In listening to these women, I was struck by their pain in essentially living a charade, pretending to be something they know they are not. That must be so difficult and so stressful. Coming out has been like removing a huge burden for the woman who has, but I see the problems in that choice, too. Talking to these two women has really been an education for me."

of gay male and lesbian couples contrasting them with heterosexual couples revealed similarities as well as differences among the various configurations of couples (Blumstein & Schwartz, 1983; Holmberg & Blair, 2009; Solomon, Rothblum, & Balsam, 2005). The surveys included questions about sexual activities and satisfaction with these activities.

Lesbian couples reported a lower level of sexual activity than any other type of couple and had some reluctance to perform cunnilingus. Lesbians' socialization as women may have influenced their sexuality, making both partners hesitant about initiating sex (Blumstein & Schwartz, 1983; Solomon et al., 2005). The result was a lower frequency of sexual activity than in couples that included a man, who would be socialized to initiate sex. Lesbians who had frequent oral sex were happier with their sex lives and with their relationships than those who had less oral sex (Blumstein & Schwartz, 1983). Nevertheless, only 39% of the lesbian couples reported having oral sex very frequently, and mutual masturbation was the most common sexual activity among these couples. Lesbians also valued nongenital physical contact, such as hugging and cuddling, activities that promoted intimacy but not orgasm. However, surveys do not count such activities as "having sex," which may reflect a heterosexual bias (Frye, 1997).

Sex is a very important part of life for gay men, and their relationships typically include a lot of sexual activity, especially early in the relationship (Blumstein & Schwartz, 1983). Fellatio is an important activity for gay men, but their sex lives are varied, and mutual masturbation is also a common activity. Anal intercourse was never as common an activity as either oral sex or manual stimulation, and its dangers for spreading HIV infection have made it less common than before the appearance of HIV. Gay men engage in a variety of sexual activities, and their frequency of sexual contact is higher than for any other configuration of couples during the early years of their relationships. The frequency of activity with their partners falls sharply after approximately the first 2 years of the relationship, but this decrease in frequency may only be a decrease in sex with their long-time partners and not in total sexual activity.

Gay men are more acceptant of casual sex than lesbians are, and even gay men who are involved in long-term relationships are more likely to have sex with men other than their partners than men in heterosexual relationships (Solomon et al., 2005). Indeed, gay men often negotiate permission to have sex with men other than their partners (Shernoff, 2006). Although all types of couples are subject to sexual jealousy (Sheets & Wolfe, 2001) and affairs can present a problem for any couple, sex outside the relationship is not as likely to be a factor in the dissolution of gay men's relationships as it is for other couples.

Many similarities appeared among all configurations of couples. For example, heterosexual, lesbian, and gay couples all reported sex as important (Blumstein & Schwartz, 1983), and couples who had sex less than once a week were not as happy as couples who had sex more often. Sex formed a physical bond for all the types of couples and helped them maintain their relationships, but it was also a common source of problems (Solomon et al., 2005). Those couples who fought about sex were less stable than those who were happy with their sexual relationships (Blumstein & Schwartz, 1983). For all of the couples, their sexual relationships reflected the problems that happened in other aspects of their relationships. Sex went well when the relationships went well, and unhappiness with the sexual activity in the relationships tended to be associated with unhappiness in the quality of affection in the relationships.

Bisexuality

In Kinsey's survey of sexual behavior (Kinsey et al., 1948), a relatively high percentage of men and women reported some same-sex experiences but did not have an exclusive same-sex sexual orientation. This situation suggested to Kinsey that sexuality should not be considered in terms of independent categories. He created a continuum for classifying people's sexual experience and attraction to members of their own and the other gender. This seven-point scale ranged from strongly heterosexual to strongly homosexual, with gradations in between representing people who have both types of sexual relationships in varying proportions. These gradations reflected people who are attracted to individuals of both genders, referred to as **bisexual**.

The status and even the existence of bisexuality remain controversial (Rieger, Chivers, & Bailey, 2005; Rust, 2000). It carries a stigma: Those who find homosexuality unacceptable will object to the same-sex element of bisexuality. For gays and lesbians, bisexuality is seen as an unwillingness to acknowledge a gay or lesbian identity by clinging to heterosexuality (McLean, 2008). Bisexuality has thus been condemned by several discrepant groups. Research has also led to questions about bisexuality. A study that measured sexual arousal (Rieger et al., 2005) found that men who identified themselves as bisexual were not equally aroused by men and women; some were more aroused by men and others by women. This finding is, however, consistent with Kinsey's concept of sexuality as a continuum rather than a category (Germon, 2008).

Although one view of bisexuality proposes that this sexual orientation represents conflict, another view focuses on its flexibility (Diamond, 2008; Zinik, 1985). Both views may be correct. For some individuals, bisexuality represents a developmental step on the way to forming a gay or lesbian sexual orientation. In a longitudinal study of nonheterosexual adolescents (Rosario et al., 2006), 18% changed their sexual orientation from bisexual to gay or lesbian, and only 15% retained a stable bisexual sexual orientation. These statistics are consistent with the view that some gay and lesbian individuals experience conflict over their sexuality, and bisexuality is a way to postpone accepting a gay or lesbian sexual identity. For others, bisexuality is a successful integration of same- and other-gender sexuality and represents flexibility. However, these individuals may not be equally attracted to both sexes (Diamond, 2008; Rieger et al., 2005).

The frequency of bisexuality is difficult to assess. Most gay men and lesbians have had heterosexual experiences at some time during their lives, which would technically place them in the category of bisexual. The prejudice in favor of heterosexuality pushes many adolescents toward heterosexual experiences, regardless of their sexual attraction. Thus, heterosexual activity may represent a type of adolescent sexual exploration among gay and lesbian adolescents rather than a sexual identity (Herdt & Boxer, 1995). Some individuals whose primary sexual orientation is heterosexual have had same-sex sexual experiences, and a behavioral criterion would count this group of individuals as bisexual. However, this criterion does not really capture the definition of attraction to both sexes.

Those who identify themselves as bisexual and who accept the possibility of romantic and sexual relationships with both women and men are much less common than those who identify themselves as gay or lesbian. According to the NHSLS results (Laumann et al., 1994), 0.8% of men and 0.5% of women identified themselves as bisexual. Studies of attitudes toward bisexuals (Herek, 2002; Steffens & Wagner, 2004) indicated that this sexual orientation was less well accepted than any other.

This number of bisexuals is so small that no community exists to offer support, and most bisexuals are not integrated into the existing gay and lesbian communities, leaving many isolated (Balsam & Mohr, 2007). This situation is beginning to change, and many gay and lesbian community centers and agencies include services oriented to bisexuals. Despite this increased acceptance, bisexuality remains the least researched, least understood, and least accepted sexual orientation.

Considering Diversity

Cultures around the world have chosen a variety of sexual activities for acceptance as "normal" and have designated other choices as abnormal, sinful, or repulsive. Cultures shape sexuality by "choosing some sexual acts (by praise, encouragement, or reward) and rejecting others (by scorn, ridicule, or condemnation), as if selecting from a sexual buffet" (Vance, 1984, p. 8). This selection from the array of available choices has resulted in virtually no universally accepted and no universally rejected set of sexual behaviors. What some cultures have found disgusting, others have found essential.

The behaviors that some cultures have considered essential include forced fellatio performed on adult men by adolescent boys, which would be the basis for criminal prosecution in many cultures. However, the Sambia in New Guinea find this practice not only acceptable but also required (Herdt, 1981). According to their beliefs, femininity is natural to girls but masculinity is not natural to boys. Thus, a preadolescent boy attains masculinity by leaving his mother and living with men. Part of the process involves swallowing semen, and the Sambia encourage boys to engage in fellatio with unmarried adolescent and adult men. The men must restrict their same-sex sexual activities to these boys, and fellatio with men their own age is strictly forbidden. When these adolescents and young men marry, they are supposed to make the transition to heterosexuality and to end all same-sex sexual activities.

A related practice occurs among the Keraki, another society in New Guinea, and for similar reasons (Kimmel, 2006). The Keraki believe that boys must receive semen to mature into men, and mature men have anal sex with boys to achieve this goal. This activity stops when the boys begin to develop secondary sexual characteristics such as facial hair and deepening voices; the process has been successful and need continue no longer.

The acceptance of these practices is difficult for people in North America and Europe to accept (Kimmel, 2006). People in Western cultures object to both same-sex behavior and sexual activity of adults with children. Students, when told of such behaviors, tend to say that they would not participate in such ritualized "homosexual" behavior, which reveals a lack of understanding of the power of culture and a tendency to interpret sexual behaviors in one's own cultural frame of reference. Searching the world and history more broadly, both behaviors have been choices for various cultures from the sexual buffet.

Another disputed choice is same-sex sexuality, but anthropologists have identified dozens of cultures that have included some sanctioned forms of same-sex sexuality (Kirkpatrick, 2000). Non-Western societies accept such behavior more than in Europe and North America, but many examples may be found among these cultures. Indeed, behaviors that accompany hazing in many fraternity initiations may be interpreted as rituals that include homosexual behaviors (Kimmel, 2006). The participants, however, deny that these hazings indicate that they are homosexual, similar to the denials of the Sambia and Keraki.

Same-sex behaviors are not limited to humans. Many species of nonhuman primates and other animals engage in some same-sex sexual behaviors (Kirkpatrick, 2000; Zuk, 2002). For example, both female and male bonobo chimpanzees engage in same-sex stimulation to orgasm. Olive baboons engage in male–male sexual stimulation. These behaviors seem to act as ways to form alliances or to soothe disagreements. However, these nonhuman primates also engage in other-sex sexual behaviors, which makes their behavior similar to most of the humans who have participated in same-sex behaviors.

Children in some societies are allowed and even expected to experiment with sex, whereas other societies restrict sexuality during childhood (Blackwood, 2000; Ford & Beach, 1951). For the societies that allow children to express their sexuality, genital touching and simulated intercourse are more likely to be allowed between peers than between a child and someone older. The Sambia and the Keraki, with their institutionalized adult–preadolescent sexuality, are exceptions, and so are the Lepcha of India, who believe that girls will not mature unless they engage in early intercourse. However, millions of children are subjected to unwanted sexual activity each year in countries throughout the world, including as many as 10 million who are forced into prostitution (Willis & Levy, 2002). In some cultures, this behavior is acceptable, but in many more it is not. However, attitudes and behavior are not the same thing, and people may condemn and yet practice a sexual behavior. Therefore, disapproval and even social sanction of any specific sexual behavior do not mean that people do not engage in that behavior.

■ Summary

Gender differences in sexual attitudes and behavior have been the object of speculation and research. Most sex research has used the survey technique—questioning people about their sexual attitudes or behavior. Problems with this method include the possibility of inaccuracy with self-reports and the problem of obtaining a representative sample that allows generalization to the population. Kinsey and his colleagues conducted the most famous sex surveys, which showed the prevalence of many sexual activities that differed from social norms. The results shocked many people. Although some of Kinsey's results are controversial, the importance of his work is not. He made the study of sexuality a legitimate part of scientific research.

The Playboy Foundation survey (Hunt, 1974) and the National Health and Social Life Survey (Laumann et al., 1994) attempted to obtain a representative sample of U.S. residents and extended Kinsey's findings. These surveys indicated some changes—especially a decrease in the double standard of sexual behavior for men and women. All of the surveys have shown that people engage in a wide variety of sexual behavior.

Masters and Johnson took another approach, measuring sexual responses directly during masturbation and intercourse in an attempt to understand the physiology of sexual response. Their 1966 book detailed four stages of the sexual response—excitation, plateau, orgasm, and resolution.

Childhood sexuality includes both exploration and the potential for abuse. Exploration begins very early in childhood, and parents may find these explorations distressing. Condemning these behaviors may convey the impression that sexual feelings and activities are unacceptable. Exploitation may also begin early in childhood. Sex surveys have revealed that at least 15% of women and 5% of men were sexually abused as children. The large majority of the perpetrators of sexual abuse of children are men, often family members or those in positions of authority, but girls and women are also perpetrators of abuse. Abuse has both short-term and long-term negative effects for male and female victims.

Adolescence is a time of increasing sexual interest and exploration. Sex education tends to emphasize the dangers rather than the pleasures of sexuality, leaving boys with information about the damage that their male sexuality can do and leaving girls with a sense of vulnerability. The average age of first intercourse had previously been higher for girls, but now that difference has disappeared. Gender differences in premarital sexual activity have decreased over the past 50 years.

Marriage is no longer the only acceptable context for sexual activity; a majority of both young men and young women now have intercourse before age 25. Celibacy may be a choice or a lack of opportunity, but monogamy is the ideal sexual relationship for many people but the reality for fewer. Choosing sexual free expression with many partners is not a common choice, but more men than women have multiple sexual partners at the same time. This difference may relate to men's greater acceptance of casual sex, which is one of the largest gender differences in sexuality. Another large difference is frequency of masturbation, which may lead to women being less likely to experience orgasm during partnered sex.

Another difference that influences sexuality is the existence of a double standard for sexual behavior, which holds that girls and women are less sexual than boys and men. Acceptance of the double standard has declined, but its continuation is a factor influencing the sexuality of women and men and contributes to conflicts in couples.

Same-sex sexual activity is not uncommon among children and adolescents, but a minority of people experience erotic attraction to only members of the same sex. Estimates vary according to the definition, but a small percentage of men and an even smaller percentage of women have primarily or exclusively gay or lesbian sexual orientation. The underlying reasons for this sexual orientation are not understood, but recent research has concentrated on biological factors such as genetics or prenatal exposure to testosterone. These biological factors may interact with personality traits and preferences to produce heterosexuality, homosexuality, or bisexuality.

Lesbian and gay sexuality is not well accepted, and adolescents who are attracted to members of their own sex may have trouble accepting themselves and their sexual orientation as well as struggling with coming out—revealing gay or lesbian interests and behavior to friends and family. The sexuality of gay men and lesbian women shows both similarities with and differences from heterosexual couples and from each other. For all types of heterosexual, gay, and lesbian couples, sex provides both a bond of pleasure and a potential for conflict in their relationships.

When individuals form romantic and sexual relationships with both men and women, they are bisexual. This sexual orientation is controversial and difficult to define because many individuals experiment with sexuality by having both male and female partners. Few, however, have a true bisexual sexual orientation, so this sexual orientation remains the least researched and most poorly understood of the sexual orientations.

Around the world, some cultures condemn the sexual behaviors that other cultures require, producing a wide variety of sexuality throughout the world. For example, behaviors such as adults having sex with children and same-sex sexuality are condemned in many societies, yet others sanction these behaviors.

■ Glossary

bisexual   a person who is sexually attracted to individuals of the same as well as the other gender.

celibacy   refraining from sexual activity.

coming out   the process of recognizing and publicly acknowledging one's gay or lesbian sexual orientation.

cunnilingus   oral stimulation of the female genitals.

date rape, or **acquaintance rape**   forced sexual activity occurring between people who are acquainted with each other.

double standard for sexual behavior   the social standard that allows men greater freedom of sexual expression than women.

fellatio   oral stimulation of the male genitals.

gay   an alternative for the term *homosexual,* emphasizing the entire lifestyle instead of only the sexual aspects of it; sometimes used to refer to both men and women, but more often to men, who feel sexual attraction for and choose sexual activity with people of the same gender.

incest   sexual activity between family members.

lesbian   a woman who feels sexual attraction for and chooses sexual activity with other women.

masturbation   manipulation of the genitals to produce sexual pleasure.

monogamy   having only one sexual partner.

representative sample   a sample (subset) of the population that reflects the characteristics of the population from which the sample was drawn.

self-selection of participants   when participants rather than researchers choose who will take part in the research. This problem biases the results and prevents generalization to a wider population.

serial monogamy   the practice of having a series of monogamous sexual relationships.

sexual orientation   the erotic attraction to members of the same or the other gender (or to both).

■ Suggested Readings

Blumstein, Philip; & Schwartz, Pepper. (1983). *American couples.* New York: Pocket Books.

Although this book is not new, its interviews with married, cohabiting, gay, and lesbian couples remain fascinating and revealing. The chapter about sex examines what couples do and enjoy as well as what role sex plays in conflict and maintenance of these relationships.

Diamond, Lisa M. (2003). What does sexual orientation orient? A biobehavioral model distinguishing romantic love and sexual desire. *Psychological Review, 110,* 173–192.

Diamond asks a provocative question concerning the meaning of sexual orientation and offers an answer that shakes the underlying assumptions of love and sex.

Hyde, Janet Shibley. (2005). The genetics of sexual orientation. In J. S. Hyde (Ed.), *Biological substrates of human sexuality* (pp. 9–20). Washington, DC: American Psychological Association.

Hyde's article provides a clear summary of the evidence concerning a genetic basis for sexual orientation, including the interesting possibility that the genetics may differ for gay men and lesbians.

Tolman, Deborah L. (2002). *Dilemmas of desire: Teenage girls talk about sexuality.* Cambridge, MA: Harvard University Press.

Tolman's extensive interviews with adolescent girls present the difficulties of developing a healthy sexuality within the current cultural context. Although the book focuses on girls, boys receive some attention.

11 School

Boy problems have always been common in school, revolving around disciplinary problems created by boys' behavior. However, the "boy problems" discussed in Ann Hulbert's headline article revolve around boys' lagging academic achievement: "boys perform consistently below girls on most tests of reading and verbal skills and lag in college enrollment and degree attainment" (Hulbert, 2005, ¶2).

HEADLINE

Boy Problems
New York Times Magazine,
April 3, 2005

These boy problems are new. Once boys dominated in school; they were the sports stars, student council presidents, valedictorians, and majority of recipients of all types of degrees. During the 1980s, many stories detailed how schools were inhospitable places for girls, and attention focused on boosting girls' school achievement, especially in math and science. Initiatives such as the "Girls Go Tech" campaign target girls, attempting to orient girls' interest to technology (Hulbert, 2005). Other efforts have been aimed at encouraging girls to take more math and science classes, and those efforts have been successful; high school girls and boys now complete about the same number of math and science courses. Now, boys are lagging behind, especially in reading and writing, which puts them at a disadvantage for most educational endeavors.

School is a setting that brings out boys' vulnerability. Sitting still, paying attention, and being quiet for extended periods of time may be difficult for boys, and when they experience problems, they receive negative attention and possibly even labels of behavior disorder or attention deficit/hyperactive disorder (ADHD). Boys may excel in sports, but they are lagging in academic achievement and obtaining degrees—everywhere from high school diplomas to master's degrees.

Some argue that, in an attempt to better serve girls, school now shortchange boys. Is it possible for schools to educate both boys and girls? What are the problems and inequities of the current system? When do they start? And what are the consequences of the school experience for women's and men's lives?

The School Experience

Even before children begin school, their parents and the society in which they live treat boys and girls differently. Chapter 3 included examples of the process of gender stereotyping: dolls for girls but trucks for boys, quiet games for girls but noisy games for boys, frilly dresses for girls but grubby jeans for boys, staying close to home for girls but venturing out for boys.

Not all girls or all boys conform to these stereotypes, but by age 4 or 5, children know what behaviors are expected and approved for each. (See Chapter 6 for a more complete discussion of the development of gender identity.) Thus, when children start preschool, they already hold beliefs about what clothes, games, and behaviors are appropriate for boys and girls, and they bring these beliefs to the school experience. Schools often reinforce these stereotypical beliefs, producing differences in attitudes and expectations about careers that result in differences in preparation to pursue careers.

Title IX of the Education Amendments of 1972 prohibits gender discrimination in school programs that receive federal funds. Although laws now prohibit sex discrimination in schools, a number of problem areas remain, especially in athletics (Acosta & Carpenter, 2009). During the 1980s and 1990s, attention to gender equity in education focused on girls and how schools may fail to meet their needs (AAUW, 1992). This attention prompted a backlash such as the one discussed in the headline story for this chapter (Hulbert, 2005), which details the problems that boys encounter in school. The publicity about gender equity has gotten the attention of many teachers (Arnot, 2000), who strive to be fair in their interactions with children in the classroom. Even so, they may fail, both in terms of student achievement (Klein, 2004) and in the eyes of their students, who see differences in how teachers treat boys and girls (Myhill & Jones, 2006; Spencer, Porche, & Tolman, 2003). Indeed, teachers tend to see their students through the lens of gender stereotypes, with girls who are good students and boys who are bad students conforming and boys who are good students failing to conform to their expectations (Jones & Myhill, 2004).

The reasons for gender inequity in schools have many roots. Gender equity is not a large part of the curriculum for prospective teachers, nor is it a frequent topic of in-service training for teachers (AAUW, 1992; Sanders, 2003). Diversity in education has been a major topic in curriculum reform, but gender equity has not (Sanders, 2003). Without specifically

◼ GENDERED VOICES

Treated Like a King

"I'm not sure why I wanted to work with kids," a young male elementary schoolteacher told me. "I started as a camp counselor, and that job was attractive because of the other counselors—lots of girls. They thought it was cool that I was a counselor and was good with kids. They seemed to think that getting along with children meant I was sensitive. I can get a line of my ex-girlfriends who will testify that I am not any more sensitive than most guys, but I do like working with kids, so I became a teacher.

"The principal and coach are both men, but there is only one other male teacher in my school, so I get a lot of attention from the students and from the female teachers. The kids love me; I'm treated like a king. When I walk down the hall, they want to be near me, and my attention is something special. Some of them live in single-parent families with their mothers, but even the ones who live with fathers seem starved for male attention. I believe that their fathers may not be too emotionally accessible, and I am, so they are drawn to me. I try to have good relationships with them, and it is work that I enjoy, but the administration keeps hinting that I should get a degree so that I can become an administrator. I don't want to; I'm satisfied doing what I'm doing."

addressing gender equity issues during teacher training, teachers bring their gender stereo-types to teaching, perpetuating unequal treatment (Brown & Evans, 2004). Such training can be effective in changing teachers' attitudes (Erden, 2009), but the tendency to view students through a lens of gender continues without specific training to minimize these issues.

Early Schooling

The problem of teachers promoting stereotypical gender roles can begin very early in the school experience and may occur even in teachers who do not realize that they are treating girls and boys differently (Garrahy, 2001). Children tend to practice gender segregation, and teachers usually allow and sometimes even encourage this separation (Thorne, 1993). In addition, children have the experience of being taught by an overwhelming majority of female kindergarten and elementary school teachers. The only man in elementary schools may be the custodian. Indeed, only about 2% of early childhood educators in the United States are men (Sargent, 2005), and this situation extends to Canada and the United Kingdom (Gosse, Parr, & Allison, 2008). These men are very aware of the female dominance in their profession and their position of providing a male role model and at the same time, behaving as nurturant "mothers," as most of the female teachers do. Male elementary teachers are thus faced with the challenge of presenting both stereotypical and counter-stereotypical behaviors.

The preponderance of female elementary school teachers has led to the "myth that early-education environments meet the needs of girls better than boys" (AAUW, 1992, p. 18).

Boys receive more teacher attention than girls, but much of that attention is oriented toward boys' misbehavior and academic problems.

A report from the American Association of University Women argued that the opposite is true: Early schooling consists of activities in which girls have more proficiency than boys, giving boys more training in the skills they lack, such as reading, while ignoring skills that girls lack, such as science investigation. Girls need practice with gross motor activities, investigatory activities, and experimental activities, but these activities tend to be considered part of "play" rather than part of their education, and thus girls have been excluded from the curriculum and tend not to develop through girls' play activities. Thus, the activities of the early elementary classroom may be difficult for boys because these activities concentrate on the skills boys lack. Girls do not have the same problems, but they also do not receive the same benefits.

To benefit from the lessons that school presents, boys must be quiet, pay attention, and concentrate. For some boys, this behavior is out of line with the gender role they are developing; that is, school requires that they act like "sissies." Either rebellion or difficulties in meeting the school requirements may contribute to the situation of boys being much more likely than girls to present behavior problems. Indeed, a great deal of the extra attention that boys receive revolves around controlling boys' misbehavior.

Few gender differences exist in school achievement during the early years of school, but the differences favor girls (Bae, Choy, Geddes, Sable, & Snyder, 2000). Tests have shown that girls outscore boys on reading and writing, and this difference persists throughout schooling (Klecker, 2006). In addition, girls make better grades. During elementary school, socioeconomic status is a more important predictor of school achievement than gender; children from lower socioeconomic levels produce consistently poorer school records than children from wealthier families. The intersection of poverty and gender may produce a particular handicap for boys during early schooling (Entwisle, Alexander, & Olson, 2007). But even controlling for socioeconomic status, girls tend to make better grades in school.

Several factors combine to predict academic success and to explain gender differences during elementary school (and beyond). Girls are more responsive to social cues and to adults' requests (Ready, LoGerfo, Burkam, & Lee, 2005), more self-disciplined (Duckworth & Seligman, 2006), and better able to delay gratification (Silverman, 2003). All of these factors contribute to being a good student. Girls' greater responsiveness to adults helps them comply with teachers' requests. The opposite also occurs; failing to comply with adults' rules and requests creates problems, and boys are more likely to behave in these ways. Indeed, conformity to gender-typical behaviors relates to both girls' success and boys' problems. However, girls tend to come to preschool with cognitive skills that better prepare them to learn to read (Ready et al., 2005).

Self-discipline is the ability to choose between conflicting impulses, and girls show higher self-discipline than boys (Duckworth & Seligman, 2006), an ability that is related to making better grades. Likewise girls' higher ability to delay gratification allows them to make choices to attend to classroom instruction and to study rather than engage in other activities (Silverman, 2003). Thus, girls have several abilities that allow them to be better students than boys, and these differences appear in elementary school and persist throughout schooling.

Boys are more likely than girls to receive referrals for special education services, and this gender difference has led to the suspicion that gender discrimination may be operating. In a study of such referrals (Wehmeyer, 2001), results indicated that gender bias was a factor. However, the bias prevented girls from receiving special education services from which they might benefit rather than producing inappropriate referrals for boys.

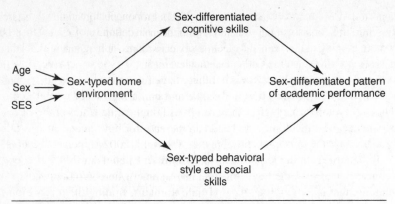

FIGURE 11.1   *Model of Social and Cognitive Abilities Predicting Academic Performance*

Source: "The Socialization of Sex-Differentiated Skills and Academic Performance: A Mediational Model," by L. A. Serbin, P. Zelkowitz, A. Doyle, D. Gold, and B. Wheaton, 1990, *Sex Roles, 23,* p. 616. Reprinted by permission of Plenum Publishing and Lisa Serbin.

Academic success is complex; both intellectual and social factors relate to success in school. Figure 11.1 shows a model of factors that one study (Serbin, Zelkowitz, Doyle, Gold, & Wheaton, 1990) related to academic success. As previous research had indicated, socioeconomic status (SES) variables predicted academic success, including mothers' occupational and fathers' educational levels. These variables also indirectly influenced the single cognitive factor most strongly related to academic success: visual–spatial ability. This study suggested that children's conformity to gender-typical behaviors plays a role in girls' academic success and in boys' poor performance. Thus, a complex picture emerges to describe academic success during elementary school, with socioeconomic factors, gender role socialization, and cognitive abilities all contributing.

Changes during Middle School

The gender differences that begin to appear during middle and junior high school relate more strongly to attitudes than to achievement and more to interests and preferences than to abilities. Girls show interest in participating in science activities, but boys are more likely to participate in and perform science, such as using microscopes, computers, and electricity meters (Kahle & Lakes, 2003). These different experiences with science activities both in and outside of the classroom relate to girls' lower achievement and decreasing interest in physical science.

These inequalities are the focus of equity education efforts, which have taken two forms: efforts aimed at equitable treatment for girls and boys in the classroom and single-sex classrooms to allow girls access to science and technology and to encourage boys to develop reading and writing skills. Attaining gender equity in the classroom has not been easy. Gender equity is not a major focus of teacher training or for most school systems, but some schools have made gender equity a focus. Unfortunately, even when administrators and teachers believe that they are offering girls and boys equal treatment, observations of classrooms and interviews with students tell a different story (Spencer et al., 2003). Proponents for single-sex classes argue that this approach is the answer, but research has not been so definitive. A review of studies (Billger, 2009) indicates only small benefits of same-sex classrooms, at best, and no advantages for most students in most areas of current and later achievement.

A great deal of attention and publicity have focused on the decline in academic confidence that girls experience during middle and junior high school. Despite this focus, the evidence for such a decline is not strong. Although some research (Bush & Simmons, 1987) indicated a decrease for girls and an increase for boys in confidence, a longitudinal study (Jacobs, Lanza, Osgood, Eccles, & Wigfield, 2002) failed to support such a decrease. This longitudinal study examined children's beliefs in their competence for language arts (a stereotypically female domain), sports (a stereotypically male domain), and mathematics (another stereotypically male domain), finding that children's confidence

Are single-sex classrooms the answer to equal access to education or a continuation of gender discrimination?

was higher when they entered school than at any other point in their education. That is, beliefs about self-competence decreased over the 12 years of schooling. Boys' self-ratings were initially higher than girls' ratings, but boys' beliefs fell faster than girls', especially in the academic domains of language, arts, and mathematics.

By junior high school, however, girls show less interest in mathematics than boys. This interest does not have a large impact on their grades or their math performance. Girls continue to make comparable or better grades in math class, and their performance is comparable (Hargreaves, Homer, & Swinnerton, 2008), but their confidence is not as great as boys', and girls come to find mathematics less interesting as a field of study (Davis-Kean, Eccles, & Linver, 2002; Jacobs, Davis-Kean, Bleeker, Eccles, & Malanchuk, 2005). One factor in their declining interest may be the perception that math is a male domain. That perception is widely shared by boys, girls, parents, and teachers (Nosek, Banaji, & Greenwald, 2002; Tiedemann, 2000). Some research (Nosek et al., 2002) has shown that this association is stronger for people who more intensely associate themselves with stereotypes of men or women. In addition, the association of men with math is not a completely conscious process, resulting in a pervasive but subtle version of stereotyping.

Athletic performance is another gendered behavior, and it becomes more gender segregated during late childhood and early adolescence. "That's a game for girls" is an insult to boys, and few girls are competent at boys' sports. The intensification of gender roles during junior high school pushes girls away from, and boys toward, athletics. In a longitudinal study (Jacobs et al., 2002), boys' beliefs in their athletic competence remained higher than beliefs about their academic abilities between 1st and 12th grade, and their beliefs about athletic abilities were higher than girls' opinions of their abilities.

Therefore, the middle school years show a continuation of better grades and academic accomplishment for girls but a decline in girls' interest in mathematics, technology, and physical sciences. Their decreased participation may be one reason for their decreased interest in science, but the continued lack of encouragement by their teachers and parents may also contribute to girls' declining interest in science and math during middle school. Both boys and girls experience a decline in confidence in their academic abilities during this time, which may affect boys more strongly than girls.

High School

High school represents a significant transition for adolescents, both in educational and social terms. Students become more focused on careers, and high school students may make choices about coursework that younger students are not allowed. The social environment revolves around school activities and heterosexuality, which may also influence the academic choices that students make. Adolescent girls believe that they will combine a family with paid employment, reflecting the current reality of contemporary family life, but they also understand that having children when they are young will affect their educational attainment (Mahaffy & Ward, 2002). Boys do not see how children might affect their educational plans.

Physical appearance and athletic ability are important to students in both public and private schools because both are ways to gain prestige in the high school social structure (Suitor & Carter, 1999; Suitor, Powers, & Brown, 2004; Suitor & Reavis, 1995). Both are avenues to status, but appearance is more important for girls and athletic ability more of an asset for boys (Weinberg, 2000). Between the 1970s and 1990s, sports became more and cheerleading less important for girls, and having a fast car became less prestigious for boys (Suitor & Reavis, 1995). Appearance remained important, especially for girls. Sociability and popularity with the other sex seem to be better ways to gain status than having sex, especially for students at private, religious high schools (Suitor et al., 2004). For both girls and boys in private and public schools, being considered intelligent and getting good grades, participating in sports, and being good looking conferred prestige.

The increased emphasis on sports for young women has resulted in the current acceptance and increased participation in sports. In 1971, girls constituted only 7.5% of athletic participants in high schools, but in 2001, the percentage had grown to 41.5% (AAUW, 2005). Not only has the number of female athletes grown, but the variety of sports in which they participate has also increased. High schools have added women's teams in cross country, gymnastics, soccer, field hockey, softball, swimming, track, volleyball, and other sports. The success of U.S. women's teams in Olympic and world competitions for soccer, basketball, and softball has provided exciting role models. Expanded opportunities for high school girls have allowed them to develop their physical abilities and talents in ways that previously were reserved for boys.

From middle to high school, girls experience more of a decrease than boys in interest and confidence concerning math, science, and computer skills. Stereotypical attitudes of parents (Bleeker & Jacobs, 2004) and teachers (Klein, 2004) push boys toward and girls away from these fields. A meta-analysis (Weinburgh, 1995) indicated that boys had more positive attitudes toward science than girls did, and the relationship between attitudes and achievement was positive. A similar relationship appeared in an analysis of Australian girls' attitudes toward advanced computing courses—girls tended to see these courses as uninteresting and not valuable to their future (Anderson, Lankshear, Timms, & Courtney, 2008). With the greater choice that high school students have about their coursework, these differences have the potential for great impact. For example, students who choose not to take advanced math and science courses will limit their access to certain college majors and careers; the choice to play sports, date, or get a job can detract from study time and affect grades, which can limit career options.

Despite their lack of enthusiasm for math during high school, overall gender differences in mathematics course enrollment have disappeared. Now, girls and boys are equally likely to take high school advanced math classes (Bae et al., 2000). Unfortunately, girls may be subject to bias and even harassment from their teachers and male students who believe that girls are not really capable of succeeding at advanced math (Abu El-Haj, 2003). Such treatment may discourage girls, leading to the situation that mathematically talented girls are less likely than comparably talented boys to pursue math or science careers (Ayalon, 2003).

The only gender difference that remains for high school course enrollment appears in science courses. Female students are more likely to enroll in advanced biology and social sciences classes, whereas boys are more likely to take physics, physical sciences, and computer courses (Bae et al., 2000). Even when enrolled in the same courses, students may have different views of how the course fits into their career plans. For example, young men who enroll in calculus and advanced science in high school are very likely to take these courses in preparation for careers in science or engineering, whereas fewer young women enrolled in the same courses pursue those careers.

◼ Gendered Voices

He Said/She Said: AP Calculus Class

The male and female students in a high school advanced placement calculus class were experiencing conflict, and part of that conflict revolved around differing preferences for classroom atmosphere (Abu El-Haj, 2003, pp. 411, 417).

He said:

> There's a guy's group that has an edge because of whatever—whether it's because they're trained to be that way or because they're really good in math, they spend more time studying it or because they're such a tight knit group that they have an edge. They really, I think, enjoy the edge. Nobody's trying to sabotage anyone. We're not ripping off people's homework or destroying people's calculators. I don't think it's competitive in that anyone's trying to defeat

anyone else. It's just that they like being one up. They like that energy. I like being better than people at something. (p. 411)

She said:

> I remember one class we had a test that I think people answered one out of four problems. That was sort of the average . . . no one got any of it. We decided to just do it in class. . . . And I remember coming away from that thinking, "God, why can't I take every test as a collaborative effort because it just—when I came away I just really understood the problems because I had contributed what I knew and this person next to me contributed what they knew and we had our combined learning." (p. 417)

A study completed in Israel explored this puzzling situation (Ayalon, 2003). Israeli students receive bonuses from universities for taking advanced courses in high school, which boosts the enrollment. Thus, many women complete advanced math and science courses and have the background to pursue science, mathematics, and engineering in college. However, they tend not to do so; women were more likely to choose psychology or humanities as majors or to pursue a career in medicine rather than mathematics or engineering. A similar pattern appeared among groups of mathematically talented youth in the United States (Benbow, Lubinski, Shea, & Eftekhari-Sanjani, 2000). Among these math-talented students, men were more likely to go on to earn doctorates in math, engineering, or physical sciences, whereas women were more likely to earn doctorates in biology, medicine, or law. Part of the reason for the difference in choices comes from different interests, but part of the difference may also be attributed to a different pattern of abilities in women and men with high math ability (Ceci, Williams, & Barnett, 2009). Women with high math ability tend to be high in verbal abilities as well, which may give them wider choices of career options.

These different choices have been considered a problem for women because these careers are high in prestige and income. When education experts judge the enrollment of women as low, they are using men and their enrollment statistics as the standard. The implication is that women's enrollment is deficient and something to be remedied. Nel Noddings (1991/1992) suggested that educators have given too little consideration both to what women are doing and to the reasons behind their choices. She pointed out that stereotypical thinking has imposed limitations on both young women and young men, restricting both from a full range of choices in coursework and careers. Most of the criticisms and research have centered on girls and how they are diverted from math and science. Fewer considerations have been directed toward boys and how they might be steered toward math and science when those subjects and careers might not be the ones for which they have the highest interest or aptitude. That is, the current situation may reflect both an underrepresentation of women and an overrepresentation of men in math and science.

Both girls and boys require information, support, and encouragement to consider nontraditional careers, including those students who do not plan to attend college. The area of career and technical education (CTE) was formerly called vocational education, which developed as a way to give boys work skills (AAUW, 1992). These careers remain more strongly gender stereotyped than others, with girls constituting over 85% of those pursuing cosmetology, health care, and child-care training and boys populating the construction, technology, and auto repair classes (Programs and Practices That Work, 2005). The salaries differ significantly for the two groups, with an hourly wage of $17.35 per hour for the male-dominated occupations and $13.85 per hour for the female-dominated jobs. Again, encouraging students to break out of these traditional jobs requires specific effort, and a number of programs have taken innovative approaches to doing so (Lufkin et al., 2007).

One factor that affects women who choose to pursue nontraditional career and technical education is sexual harassment. **Sexual harassment**, unwanted sexual attention from students and teachers, happens to both girls and boys at school. Although young men experience sexual harassment, fewer mention being troubled by unwanted sexual attention by their female peers or teachers (AAUW, 1993, 2001, 2006). Harassment involving gender may be sexually oriented or not; it consists of unwanted sexual remarks, statements about the unsuitability of women for various types of jobs, or derogatory remarks about women or men and their abilities. Same-gender sexual harassment by peers is a common experience, especially for boys. Indeed, bullying of both boys and girls tends to be sexualized (Shute, Owens, & Slee, 2008). As the AAUW reports (1993, 2001, 2006) pointed out, harassment is about power and authority, and the vast majority of incidents involve boys harassing girls.

Although sexual and other harassment that affect the educational process are prohibited by Title IX of the Education Amendments of 1972, those who harass have been allowed to continue. The attitude was often "boys will be boys," with harassment not considered a serious offense. When legal changes allowed school systems to be sued for monetary damages, school systems began to take sexual harassment more seriously (Fineran, 2002). Teachers now report negative attitudes toward harassment (Stone & Couch, 2004) but also felt reluctant to intervene in peer harassment when instructors perceived a lack of support for intervention from administrators, colleagues, and the community (Meyer, 2008). Fear of harassment may exert negative effects on girls, making them reluctant to enroll in courses with a majority of boys or to enroll in nontraditional vocational courses.

Surveys of junior high and high school students (AAUW, 1993, 2001; Asbaugh & Cornell, 2008; Timmerman, 2003) have revealed that three-fourths or more of students said they had been the target of unwelcome sexual behavior while at school or a school function. Adult school employees were the perpetrators in about one-fourth of cases, but the majority of harassment incidents are perpetrated by other students. Girls were more common targets than boys, but both girls and boys admitted perpetrating as well as being targets of sexual harassment. Student perpetrators tended to consider harassment part of school life and "no big deal" (Bryant, 1995, p. 41). The targets may feel differently. Especially when targets interpreted the harassment as intentional, they were upset (Lacasse & Mendelson, 2006). Those who are victimized may experience more than distress; the consequences may be serious (see According to the Media and According to the Research).

ACCORDING TO THE *MEDIA* ...

High School Is Near the Mouth of Hell

During its seven years of broadcasting (1997–2003), *Buffy the Vampire Slayer* sent unorthodox messages about high school and college life, family relationships, friends, and gender. The series featured Buffy Summers, who moved to a small town in southern California and enrolled in Sunnydale High School. Buffy was not part of the "in crowd" and felt like an outcast, which is not an unusual experience for the new girl in school. In *Buffy the Vampire Slayer,* Sunnydale High was located on top of one of the mouths of hell, and Buffy had superhuman powers. She was the Chosen One, a once-in-a-generation slayer who had the power to save humanity and kill the monsters that escaped from the Hellmouth. She befriended other outcast students, forming a "family" who helped in her mission to protect humanity (Burr & Jarvis, 2007).

The series used monsters as metaphors for the high school world of cliques, coolness, anti-intellectualism, and unreasoning adult authority (Early, 2001). In Buffy's high school, the bullies were literally demons. The vampires and demons were both male and female, but as the Slayer, Buffy occupied a role that is unusual for a woman: She was not only a hero but also a warrior. Female characters have occupied this role in comic books more often than on television or in movies; action heroes are usually men. Through her strength as the Chosen One and her martial arts training, this small, thin, pretty blonde was able to "kick some serious demon ass" (in Early, 2001). Buffy struggled with her mission, as heroes do, trying to do what was right. She and her "family" of outcasts patrolled Sunnydale, attempting to keep the demons from destroying humanity.

In summary, both overt and subtle forces affect adolescents during high school, with both girls and boys tending toward more traditional, stereotypical choices. Enrollment in math and science classes is now comparable for boys and girls, but attitudes about those subjects differ. Those girls who complete advanced math and science courses tend not to view these courses as part of their career preparation as boys do. Gender stereotypes exert such a powerful force that by high school, overt bias is not required to push girls and boys toward traditional courses and careers. Parents, teachers, and counselors can counteract this stereotyping by active efforts to encourage students to explore nontraditional choices. This effort is important for academic and career and technical education, which tends to guide boys toward higher-paying skilled craft jobs and girls into lower-paying business and service jobs. Girls who enroll in nontraditional courses face the possibility of bullying or sexual harassment, and, although illegal, this behavior is a common experience. Peers are more common harassers than teachers or other school personnel.

College and Professional Schools

The effects of stereotyping and gender bias influence young women and men before they enter college, creating differences in expectations and choices. Young men receive messages from society, the media, and specific people in their lives urging them to prepare for careers that will support a family. Young women get a different message: They need to be able to support themselves until they marry (and possibly after they divorce), but their careers will be less important than their husbands' employment.

ACCORDING TO THE RESEARCH...

High School May Be Close to Hell for Some Adolescents

Some adolescents may think of other students at their high schools as demons; high school is a difficult experience for many adolescents who are outcast, marginalized, bullied, and harassed. However, the difficulties experienced by those harassed about their sexual orientation are especially severe and even dangerous. Harassment and accusations of homosexuality are frequent occurrences for students who fail to conform to gender-stereotypical behaviors, even though the targets may not be gay, lesbian, or bisexual and the perpetrators know that these accusations are untrue (AAUW, 1993). The harassment sometimes goes beyond name-calling and into physical attacks, with young gay men in particular peril:

"Faggot" is the ultimate insult used by kids and teenagers all over the country to designate those who are different or simply disliked, whether they are gay or not. It was the epithet of choice the students at

Columbine High School hurled at the Trench Coat Mafia, helping to drive two of its nail-painting, Hitler-worshipping techies into their murderous rage. It was the word young gay bashers carved into the flesh of the 17-year-old Marin County lad whom they beat senseless after he founded a Gay–Straight Alliance at the high school in his supposedly liberal and tolerant community. (Ireland, 1999, p. 8)*

These incidents of harassment and violence take their toll, making school unpleasant and dangerous. Gay and lesbian students are more likely to experience depression, think about, and attempt suicide than other students (Almeida, Johnson, Corliss, Molnar, & Azrael, 2009). Some schools approach the problem by beginning counseling programs and by appointing personnel to coordinate services for gay, lesbian, and bisexual students. Some schools do not restrain the homophobia, making high school close to hell for gay and lesbian adolescents.

*Reprinted with permission from the June 14, 1999 issue of *The Nation*. For subscription information, call 1-800-333-8536. Portions of each week's Nation magazine can be accessed at http://www.thenation.com.

Before the 20th century, women rarely obtained a college education (Owens, Smothers, & Love, 2003), and if they prepared for careers, they almost always saw their careers as subordinate to their husbands' occupations. Throughout most of the 20th century, men attended college in greater numbers than women, but the number of female college students in the United States and Canada has grown to the point that women now receive more undergraduate degrees than men do (U.S. Census Bureau, 2009a). This pattern applies to a number of other industrialized countries where the percent of male and female college students is close to equal. In some developing countries, especially those in sub-Saharan Africa and in Asia, women attend college (and other schools) much less often than men. Table 11.1 (page 290) presents the percentage of college and university students who are women in various countries, but it does not reveal the number of students who are eligible to attend college yet do not. In the United States, a higher percentage of high school graduates enroll in college than in most other countries, even compared to other industrialized countries. That high percentage combined with the proportion of female U.S. college students results in U.S. women being better educated than their counterparts in many other countries (U.S. Census Bureau, 2009a).

Men have historically received the overwhelming majority of advanced degrees (master's and doctoral) and professional degrees (such as medical, dental, law, veterinary), but that pattern also has changed. In the 1960s, women earned only about 3% of professional

TABLE 11.1   *Percentage of All College and University Students Who Are Female in Various Countries*

Country	Percentage Who Are Women
Argentina	59%
Australia	54
Brazil	56
Canada	56
Denmark	57
Ethiopia	26
France	55
Germany	48
India	39
Iran	49
Israel	56
Japan	45
Kenya	34
Mexico	49
Morocco	44
Peru	49
Russia	57
Saudi Arabia	58
South Africa	53
Turkey	41
United States	55
United Kingdom	56
Vietnam	42

Source: Education for All Global Monitoring Report 2005 (2005, Table 9). United Nations Educational, Scientific and Cultural Organization, retrieved July 9, 2006, from http://portal.unesco.org/education/en/ev.php-URL_ID=35939&URL_DO=DO_TOPIC&URL_SECTION=201.html.

degrees, but by the 1980s, the percentage had grown to 33%, and in 2006, women received 60% of all master's and 48% of all doctoral degrees granted in the United States (U.S. Census Bureau, 2009a). Women have made comparable gains in earning professional degrees, such as medicine and law degrees, as Figure 11.2 shows. This growing number of women in professional fields has changed the composition of most professions, but past differences will take many years to equalize. Like undergraduate and professional degrees, doctoral degrees also show patterns of gender segregation. A greater proportion of doctoral degrees in physical sciences and engineering still go to men, whereas a greater proportion of doctoral degrees in education, humanities, and psychology go to women.

Table 11.2 (page 292) shows the percentage of degrees awarded to women in 1971 compared to 2007 for different majors. Most professions now have a larger proportion of women as a result of the changes in degrees awarded during the past 35 years. Some areas have experienced less change, some areas remain dominated by women, and some areas have become dominated by women. Whites are overrepresented and other ethnic groups

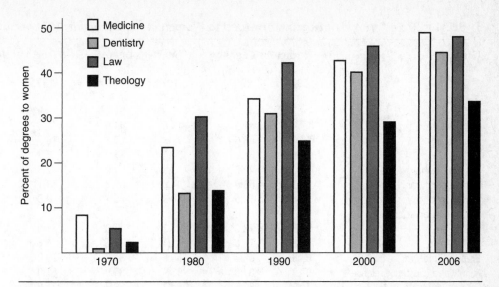

FIGURE 11.2 *Percentage of Women Earning Professional Degrees, 1970–2006*
Source: *Statistical Abstract of the United States, 2009* (128th ed., p. 183), by U.S. Census Bureau, 2009, Washington, DC: U.S. Government Printing Office.

underrepresented among those who receive master's and doctoral degrees. For example, in the year 2007 about 5.6% of doctoral degrees went to African Americans, another 5.8% to Asian Americans, 3.4% to Hispanic Americans, and 0.4% to Native Americans. In addition, African American and Hispanic American women are more likely to receive degrees than men in these ethnic groups (U.S. Census Bureau, 2009a).

Gender disparities continue to exist on college athletic fields, and the attempts to remedy these inequities have become the center of continuing, heated controversy. Title IX of the Educational Amendments of 1972 prohibited discrimination in educational programs that receive federal funding, including college athletic programs. Funding has been far from equal in athletics; men's sports receive far more scholarships, equipment, facilities, staff, and publicity than women's sports do. Colleges have struggled (and sometimes mounted legal challenges) against increased funding for women's athletics (Hall, 2008). Despite legal challenges to Title IX (Hogshead-Makar, 2003), the law has remained intact, and athletic departments have struggled to provide funding for women's athletics in times of dwindling budgets. Indeed, much of the controversy over women's athletics concerns money rather than a desire to prohibit women from participating in sport.

Increased opportunities for women to participate in competitive athletics have increased the number of women who compete. In the 1970s, only 7% of college women participated in organized athletics, but that percentage has grown to about 35%, producing more than a 400% increase (Hall, 2008). The increase has not resulted in equal participation, equal funding, or equal acceptance for women in athletics. Enforcement of Title IX has not yet resulted in equal opportunities for training, use of locker rooms, medical services, or scholarships, or even athletics funding that is proportional to the number of women who attend the school (Anderson, Cheslock, & Ehrenberg, 2006).

TABLE 11.2   *Percentage of Degrees Awarded to Women in Various Fields, 1971 versus 2007*

Field	Bachelor's Degree		Master's Degree		Doctoral Degree	
	1971	2007	1971	2007	1971	2007
Agriculture	4.2%	47.0%	5.9%	52.9%	2.9%	39.6%
Architecture	11.9	41.5	13.8	44.5	8.3	41.5
Ethnic studies	52.4	68.6	38.3	59.5	16.7	59.2
Biology	29.1	61.6	33.6	57.3	16.3	48.9
Business & management	9.1	49.2	3.9	44.0	2.8	41.4
Communications	35.3	63.0	34.6	65.8	13.1	60.8
Computer and information science	13.6	18.5	10.3	26.1	2.3	20.5
Education	74.5	78.6	56.2	77.3	21.0	67.5
Engineering	0.8	16.8	1.1	22.6	0.6	20.9
English/literature	65.6	68.3	60.6	67.2	28.8	59.4
Family and consumer science	97.3	87.8	93.9	85.9	61.0	78.3
Foreign language	74.0	69.5	64.2	69.3	34.6	58.7
Health science	77.1	85.9	55.3	80.5	16.5	73.1
Legal profession	5.0	71.9	4.8	47.9	—	45.4
Liberal studies	33.6	68.1	44.6	62.8	31.3	50.6
Library science	92.0	87.8	81.3	80.6	28.2	65.4
Math	37.9	44.1	27.1	41.5	7.6	29.7
Philosophy/religion	25.5	37.9	27.1	36.6	5.8	28.8
Physical science	13.8	40.8	13.3	39.0	5.6	31.5
Protective services	9.2	50.2	10.3	52.8	—	49.4
Psychology	44.4	77.4	40.6	79.7	24.0	73.1
Public administration	68.4	81.1	50.0	75.0	24.1	65.0
Social sciences	36.8	49.8	28.5	51.4	13.9	45.1
Visual/performing arts	59.7	61.8	47.4	57.1	22.2	54.1

Source: U.S. Department of Education, National Center for Education Statistics, 2007, Integrated Postsecondary Education Data System (IPEDS), Table 275. Retrieved October 9, 2009 from http://nces.ed.gov/programs/digest/d08/tables/dt08_275.asp.

The growing numbers of women who compete in college athletics receive support in the form of scholarships from their colleges and universities, but they have also received encouragement to develop their athletic abilities before they reach college. Mothers, older siblings, friends, and coaches in high school and junior high were all forms of social support to women who were college athletes (Hall, 2008; Weiss & Barber, 1995). Furthermore, these sources of support have improved over the past 20 years. Therefore, today's female athletes have benefited not only from the laws that mandate access to sports but also from the changes in attitudes that have made athletic competition more acceptable and admired for women.

In many ways, college amplifies the gender issues that exist in high school, making the college experience different for women and men in the classroom as well as in the locker room. Women experience more feelings of gender bias than men, and these feelings relate to the number of male instructors and classmates (Fischer & Good, 1994). Men also reported some negative feelings, including indifference and lack of recognition from their instructors. Faculty members tend to interact in different ways with male and female students (Sax, Bryant, & Harper, 2005). In addition, male students expressed a higher degree of entitlement than female students; they felt entitled to good grades, even without working for them (Ciani, Summers, & Easter, 2008). These gender differences may create a different college experience for men and women but do not keep women from doing well in college; women continue to be better students than men, for many of the same reasons that appeared during earlier schooling (Gibb, Fergusson, & Horwood, 2008).

Although men are in the minority in many college classrooms, they may still dominate. College instructors are more likely to be men, and this factor influences classroom interaction styles. Women and men tend to have different preferences for classroom interactions with teachers and peers (Abu El-Haj, 2003). Women feel more comfortable in discussions in which teachers and students collaborate than in situations in which teachers try to impose their views on students. Men feel more comfortable in classrooms with a clear hierarchy and an emphasis on specified goals. That is, women and men carry their preferences for personal interaction styles (see Chapter 9) into the classroom, and the preferences of each gender may make the other uncomfortable.

Women's uneasiness with the campus climate extends to professional and doctoral training, at which point women feel less encouraged and supported than their male colleagues (Bickel, 2001; Herzig, 2004). The majority of professors are men, and the lower percentage of female faculty presents fewer role models for female students and possibly less encouragement (Park, Minor, Taylor, Vikis, & Poenaru, 2005). Women in male-dominated doctoral programs reported lower career commitment and feeling less supported than male students in the same programs and also less supported than female students in more gender-balanced programs (Ülkü-Steiner, Kurtz-Costes, & Kinlaw, 2000).

Role models and mentoring relationships can be very important to career advancement, because young professionals benefit from the guidance and aid of older, more experienced professionals. Mentors tend to choose protégés who reflect themselves, so there is a tendency for men to choose men and women to choose women. With fewer women in high positions in academia, young women are at a disadvantage in finding mentors; male professors tend to be more helpful in supporting and encouraging their male students than their female students (Schroeder & Mynatt, 1999). Women have more female than male

⬛ GENDERED VOICES

My Professor Said . . . .

One of my students reported to me: "My engineering professor announced to the class that women should not be engineers. Women just didn't have what it takes; they weren't tough enough."

I told her that such remarks were unacceptable and probably illegal. I urged her to report this incident, but she refused even to name the professor. I reported the incident to the Dean of Engineering, who also agreed that this faculty member's behavior was unacceptable. Our concern did not solve this student's problem. By the end of the semester, she had changed her major to math education.

mentors, but male mentors may still be very influential and important, especially for women in science (Downing, Crosby, & Blake-Beard, 2005).

The close working relationships of mentoring also provide situations that can lead to sexual attraction and action. With the imbalance of power between students and faculty, sexual relationships are almost inevitably exploitative and often meet the definition of sexual harassment. A wide-scale study of sexual harassment in college (AAUW, 2006) reported that 62% of college students reported that they had experienced some type of sexual harassment while in college. Although sexual comments and jokes were the most common type of harassment, about one-third of students reported some type of physical harassment. Faculty and staff commit harassment, but the most common source was other students. The most common comment from harassers was that they thought it was funny. Targets don't think it's so funny. Female students are more distressed by the experience than male students; some female students felt embarrassed, others were angry, but a third were frightened by the harassment. These reactions make education more difficult and may lead to dropping classes, changing majors, or even leaving school.

Students are reluctant to report harassment; only 7% of students said that they had reported the harassment. About half told a friend rather than someone in authority, and about a third of harassed students told no one at all. Sexual harassment is not limited to students; both female and male faculty members are subject to harassment from students (DeSouza & Fansler, 2003). Female professors are more likely to be the target of sexual harassment by their male students than other gender combinations.

Therefore, like high school, college is another school situation in which women and men have different experiences, which relate to choices of majors and careers. The range of majors and careers is similar, but the proportion of men and women in the range of majors is not. Women more often choose majors in education and social science; men choose engineering and physical science majors more often than women do. Women now receive more undergraduate degrees than men, and their numbers of professional and doctoral degrees are approaching (and sometimes exceeding) the numbers earned by men. Women in doctoral and professional programs receive less academic attention and support (but more sexual attention) than their male peers receive. Despite legal prohibition, sexual harassment is common on campus, and women are more likely than men to be distressed by harassment from those in positions of authority, their male peers, and even their students.

Achievement

Achievement can have many meanings, including success in school. As the previous section showed, girls and women are successful in school, as measured by grades, but men are more successful when the criteria include prominence in prestigious careers and high salaries. How achievement is defined determines the extent to which women and men are high or low achievers.

Achievement Motivation

Traditionally, researchers have defined job success and recognition as achievement and have not considered personal or family relationships as comparable achievements. Therefore, neither women's nor men's roles in homemaking and family care have gained the

⬛ GENDERED VOICES

Their Children Were Their Accomplishments

I was a member of a board of directors for a civic organization with many other women (and few men). During one early meeting, we were asked to introduce ourselves and say a few words. As the introductions proceeded, one woman after another stood up and said her name and then told about her children. Most of these women were employed, and some had professional careers, but almost no one described her job. I finally realized that for these women, their jobs were not that important—their children were their accomplishments.

same type of recognition as business, scientific, and political accomplishments. Indeed, women did not play a prominent part in psychology's early studies on achievement.

David McClelland and his colleagues (McClelland, Atkinson, Clark, & Lowell, 1953) studied the motivation to achieve, formulating the concept of *need for achievement*. Results of their studies confirmed that the need for achievement not only varied among people but also was stronger in people who had chosen achievement-oriented careers and in college students who had chosen careers with high risk and high responsibility. This definition of achievement ignores forms of achievement other than business careers, which is clearly too restrictive (Hyde & Kling, 2001). In addition, the need-for-achievement construct was formulated by examining only men, even though McClelland et al. (1953) found some overlap in the achievement needs of some men and women. In researching women's achievement motivation, another concept appeared—fear of success.

Fear of Success

When Martina Horner (1969) presented women and men with a description of a successful medical student, the women sometimes imagined negative consequences for the successful female medical student, but the men usually described the successful male medical student in positive terms.

Horner interpreted the women's descriptions of negative consequences accompanying success as a **fear of success**, or a motive to avoid success. She reasoned that women equate success with loss of femininity and feel anxious about success, especially when it involves competing with men. Her investigations showed that women often do better when working alone or when in competition with other women than when they must compete against men. On the other hand, men often perform better when they are in competition than when they work alone. Horner concluded that competition is a negative factor in women's achievement and that women see achievement situations differently than men do.

Horner's terms—*fear of success* and *motive to avoid success*—are somewhat misleading because they imply that women do not wish to succeed. Women engage in self-handicapping behaviors that block their achievement, but such behaviors are more common among men (McCrea, Hirt, Hendrix, Milner, & Steele, 2008). What Horner called fear of success may have been women's acknowledgment that success in male-dominated professions is not socially well accepted for women, that success will have negative as well as positive consequences for women, and that competition may pose problems for women.

Rather than finding that women fear success, Horner may have demonstrated that women understand the social consequences of competing with men in school and careers.

The social consequences of success in nontraditional careers may be negative for both men and women. An early study (Cherry & Deaux, 1978) found that men showed fear of success when describing a man in nursing school compared to a man in medical school, and women indicated awareness of negative consequences of success for a woman in medical school but not for a woman in nursing school. A review during the 1980s (Paludi, 1984) showed that both men and women recognized the negative aspects of success at similar rates. In 64 studies on the topic, a median of 49% of women and 45% of men exhibited the "fear of success."

More recent studies have indicated that negative consequences are attached to success in nontraditional careers for both men and women. One study (Tomkiewicz & Bass, 1999) found that men showed as much fear of success as women did. Another study (Heilman, Wallen, Fuchs, & Tamkins, 2004) showed that women do not receive the same approval for being successful that men do. In particular, women who succeed in male-dominated fields are derogated rather than praised. What Horner labeled fear of success seems to be a realistic appraisal of the consequences of success for women in some occupations.

However, this situation may be changing. Women no longer receive negative evaluations when they are described as being at the top of their medical school class, and no difference exists between women's and men's fear of success imagery and achievement motivation (Krishnan & Sweeney, 1998). As Carol Tavris (2005) explained, "In the 1970s psychologists worried that women suffered from an internal 'fear of success' that was keeping them out of law and medical schools and other traditionally male careers. When discrimination was made illegal, 'fear of success' was trampled under the crush of women entering professional schools and occupations formerly closed to them, including bartending and boxing" (p. 11).

Self-Esteem and Self-Confidence

Self-esteem is conceptualized as a global evaluation of self (Kling, Hyde, Showers, & Buswell, 1999) or as an evaluation of a specific domain (Gentile et al., 2009) that can range from positive to negative. Although men and women have comparable concerns about success in nontraditional fields, their self-esteem and confidence in their own abilities show some differences and similarities.

The AAUW (1992) contended that girls experience a sharp drop in self-esteem during junior high school, which negatively influences their education and careers. Two meta-analyses (Kling et al., 1999; O'Brien et al., 1996) failed to find evidence of a dramatic decrease in self-esteem for girls during adolescence. Instead, a meta-analysis of self-esteem throughout the lifespan (Trzesniewsk, Donnellan, & Robins, 2003) and a longitudinal study (Jacobs et al., 2002) revealed a similar pattern of self-esteem development for women and men. One meta-analysis (Kling et al., 1999) specifically addressed the changes during adolescence and found that the gender difference was greatest during late, not early, adolescence. A study of adolescents from several ethnic groups (Greene & Way, 2005) found a sharp decrease in self-esteem only for boys during early adolescence.

Ethnicity is also a factor in self-esteem. Within the United States, Asian American adolescents reported lower self-esteem than Hispanic or African American students (Greene & Way, 2005). European Americans showed a small advantage for men, but for

TABLE 11.3   *Differences in Self-Esteem for Males and Females*

Age Group	Sample Population	Size of Effect	Higher In
Children	U.S. residents	Small	Males
Young adolescents	Norwegian	Small	Males
Adolescents	Chinese	Small	Females
Adolescents	Finnish	None	—
Young adults	Japanese	Small	Males
Young adults	Canadian	Small	Males
Adolescents to adults	U.S. European Americans	Small	Males
Adolescents to adults	U.S. African Americans	None	—
Adolescents and adults	Australian	Moderate	Males
Adults	U.S. residents	Small to moderate	Males
Elderly	U.S. residents	Moderate	Males

African Americans, no gender differences appeared in self-esteem for adults (Kling et al., 1999). Table 11.3 summarizes findings from several countries, showing that not all have the pattern that appears in the United States.

Applied to specific domains, self-esteem shows some gender differences (Gentile et al., 2009). Men's self-esteem is higher in the areas of physical appearance, athletics, and self-satisfaction, but women expressed higher behavioral and moral–ethical self-esteem. Furthermore, self-esteem may not be as important for school success as people have believed. Asian American children scored lowest on self-esteem of any ethnic group in the United States but had the highest grade point averages (Bankston & Zhou, 2002). African Americans scored the highest in self-esteem yet had the lowest grades. In addition, children who immigrated showed more self-esteem problems than those born in the United States, but they also made better grades than children of the same ethnicity born in the United States. Therefore, overall feelings of self-esteem may be important for self-concept but a more specific concept be more important.

Confidence in one's ability to succeed varies with the task, and the gender typing of the activity is important in this evaluation. Men express more confidence in their abilities than women do when they perceive a task as "masculine," but this advantage disappears when the task is perceived as "feminine." That is, gender stereotyping affects confidence. Women showed lower expectancy of success on a masculine task than on a feminine or neutral task (Beyer, 1998, 2002), but this bias did not apply to men. For example, men overestimated their driving ability, even when they acknowledged their risky behaviors; women's estimates were more realistic (Bergdahl, 2005).

In addition, ability for specific tasks is an individual factor differentiating the self-confidence of men and women. When such information is available, the ability estimates of men and women are similar, but when this information is absent, men estimate their ability more highly than women estimate theirs (Pallier, 2003). In a number of situations, women's low predictions represent underestimates of their performance, whereas men tend to be unrealistically confident in their abilities (Stankov & Lee, 2008).

Girls and women are also more likely to believe other people's evaluations of their performance and abilities than boys and men are (Roberts, 1991). This responsiveness might be due to women's greater social responsiveness or to lower confidence, but it may also be due to women's tendency to accept feedback from others as more informative than men do. This tendency for women to accept and men to reject others' evaluations occurs in a number of contexts (Roberts & Nolen-Hoeksema, 1994). For example, this gender difference appeared in a study of bank employees' reactions to performance evaluations (Johnson & Helgeson, 2002).

Either ignoring or accepting evaluative feedback has advantages and disadvantages. Women's typical strategy of accepting feedback may make them responsive to evaluations and eager to change, but it may also make them overly sensitive to others' opinions and allow them to rely too little on their own evaluations. Men's typical strategy of ignoring feedback may allow them to feel higher self-esteem but also makes them overly resistant to advice from others and reluctant to change their behavior when changes would improve their performance.

The tendency to be very responsive to criticism may also relate to the higher levels of distress that girls experience during school (Lloyd, Walsh, & Yailagh, 2005; Pomerantz, Altermatt, & Saxon, 2002). Despite receiving better grades and having fewer disciplinary problems, girls reported a higher degree of distress than boys during elementary and middle school. Girls evaluated their abilities as lower than boys (including the subjects in which they were making higher grades), rated their overall self-worth as lower, and showed a higher degree of anxiety related to school performance. This responsiveness may persist throughout women's lives and present a source of stress and anxiety.

Confidence and ability are not the same; one may be inappropriately confident or inappropriately unsure of one's abilities. Unduly low expectancies are more characteristic of girls and women than of boys and men. For example, women predict lower college grade point averages than men do (Beyer, 1999), women estimate their IQs as lower than men judge their own IQs, and men feel that they are more capable of learning (Furnham & Chamorro-Premuzic, 2007). In some cases, the lower estimates may be underestimates, but these judgments are more accurate in some cases (Furnham, 1999). However, men's predictions are overestimates that represent a tendency toward positive self-presentation (Brown, Uebelacker, & Heatherington, 1998). Therefore, men have a tendency to see themselves as more intelligent and academically capable than women see themselves. This tendency may lead men to be more confident in academic (and perhaps many other) situations, but it may also make them believe that they are more capable than they are.

Attributions for Success and Failure

Research has also indicated that gender differences exist in explanations for success and failure. People can attribute success or failure to either internal factors, such as ability and effort, or external factors, such as luck and the difficulty of the task. Although both ability and effort are factors that come from within each person, ability is a stable factor, whereas effort can vary from situation to situation. Persons who believe that they succeeded because they worked hard have no assurance that they will succeed again without additional, similar effort. On the other hand, those who attribute their successes to intelligence or to a "gift" for the skill should believe that similar success will continue—that is, they will still be intelligent or still have the gift next week and next year. Likewise, the external reasons for success and failure also differ in their stability. People who believe they failed because of bad luck would believe that their luck could change, leading to success on another attempt at the same task. People who attribute their failure to the difficulty of the task should believe that this

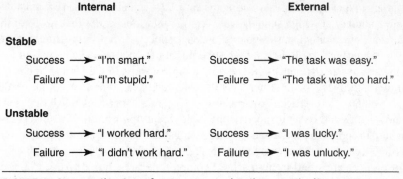

	Internal	External
Stable		
	Success ⟶ "I'm smart."	Success ⟶ "The task was easy."
	Failure ⟶ "I'm stupid."	Failure ⟶ "The task was too hard."
Unstable		
	Success ⟶ "I worked hard."	Success ⟶ "I was lucky."
	Failure ⟶ "I didn't work hard."	Failure ⟶ "I was unlucky."

FIGURE 11.3 *Attributions for Success and Failure According to Two Dimensions*

task will always be difficult and that they will fail on each attempt. Therefore, people can explain their success or failure in terms of internal or external factors, and they can see each as either stable or unstable. Figure 11.3 shows the possibilities in combining these two dimensions. These explanations, or attributions, for success and failure can affect the amount of effort and time a person is willing to expend in order to succeed.

These attributions apply to grades in college classes. When asked to explain their grades in college classes, female college students were less likely to attribute their success to ability than were male college students (Campbell & Henry, 1999). Although effort was the most common explanation for both women and men, women chose this explanation significantly more often than men did. Effort can change, and this study suggests that women tend to believe that they need to continually put forth effort to succeed, but men feel more confident in their abilities. These gender differences echo differences expressed by parents, who tend to see their sons' math performance as an expression of talent and their daughters' math achievement as the result of effort (Räty, Vänskä, Kasanen, & Kärkkäinen, 2002).

In summary, achievement has been defined as career success, which made women less achievement oriented. The concept of fear of success arose as a popular explanation for women's lower levels of achievement, but further studies have failed to confirm the validity of this concept. Instead, findings indicate that men as well as women exhibit misgivings about achievements in gender-inappropriate occupations. Research has also failed to confirm the widely publicized drop in self-esteem for adolescent girls, but women show lower levels of self-esteem in some areas than men. The gender typing of the activity is an important factor in women's and men's confidence. The gender typing of the task also influences the attributions that women and men use to explain their performance, with women tending to attribute success to effort rather than to ability, which may indicate significant gender differences in explanations for achievement.

Considering Diversity

Gender equity is a major diversity issue in education, but other diversity concerns are also important. The ethnic diversity and social class composition of the United States present problems to the educational system, and these two factors often combine to produce serious barriers to quality education. During the early 21st century, between 35 and 40% of students in elementary and high schools were ethnic minorities, and around 20% of them lived in homes in which English was not the language spoken (U.S. Census Bureau, 2009a).

Over the past 40 years, high school graduation rates have increased for all groups, but substantial differences exist among ethnic groups in the United States (U.S. Census Bureau, 2009a). Asian Americans and Whites have comparable high graduation rates (above 85%), but African Americans and Hispanic Americans finish high school at lower rates—82% and 60%, respectively. Employment opportunities have decreased for high school dropouts but increased for those who attend college, and their salaries reflect these differences; thus, those who fail to finish high school have decreasing job options. Gender differences are small in high school completion rates, but Hispanic American men are somewhat less likely than Hispanic American women and Asian American men somewhat more likely than Asian American women to graduate (U.S. Census Bureau, 2009a).

The percentage of ethnic minority students entering college increased between the 1970s and the late 1990s. By 2006, 68% of White, 56% of African American, and 58% of Hispanic American high school graduates attended college (U.S. Census Bureau, 2009a). The graduation rate showed greater discrepancies; about 13% of Hispanic Americans and 19% of African Americans earn college degrees, but 29% of Whites and 52% of Asian Americans do. Despite their growing numbers, fewer ethnic minority than White students finish high school well prepared to enter college (McCombs, 2000). Hispanic American, African American, and Native American students are not often among the highest achieving high school students, and they lack the academic records to be competitive at selective colleges. Individuals from these ethnic groups are more likely to enter 2-year colleges than White or Asian American students (U.S. Census Bureau, 2009a). The percentage of African American and Hispanic students decreases as the number of years required for college degrees increases, resulting in a very low percentage of doctoral and professional degrees granted to people from these ethnic minorities.

Ethnic minorities are underrepresented in college for all types of higher and professional education. The exception is Asian Americans, who are more numerous in college than in the population, especially in prestigious research universities. Indeed, Asian American parents not only expect their children to attend college but also to receive graduate degrees (Kuhn, 2006). Other ethnic minority students are more likely to attend public than private schools, and financing is one reason for their low college attendance and their disproportionate choice of 2-year rather than 4-year programs. The cost of college has increased rapidly (U.S. Census Bureau, 2009a), and minorities disproportionately live in poverty. Thus, even academically capable minority students may not be able to afford higher education. Ethnic minority students may be restricted to less expensive college options, even when their academic abilities and preparation are adequate to make them competitive at elite universities.

The gender differences in high school graduation rates are small, but over the past 40 years, women have become more numerous on college campuses (and at graduation ceremonies) than men (U.S. Census Bureau, 2009a). These differences are even more dramatic for ethnic minority women. For Asian Americans, the percentage of women and men who attend college is the same, but more Hispanic and Native American women than men enroll, and the gender difference for African Americans is even larger (American Council on Education, 2003).

The ethnic difference in advanced degrees affects the composition of university faculties, in which ethnic minorities are also underrepresented (Cole & Barber, 2003). Despite years of pressure to include diversity not only in curricula but also among faculty, African Americans, Hispanic Americans, and Native Americans are underrepresented among the faculty in U.S. colleges and universities (Jayakumar, Howard, Allen, & Han, 2009). Furthermore, faculty members from these ethnic groups advance more slowly and leave higher education positions at a more rapid rate than other faculty members.

The overall picture of education is one of increasing diversity but not always increased educational opportunities for diverse groups in the United States. Ethnic minority students have not enjoyed the rapid progress that women have made in gaining access to college and professional training. Asian Americans are an exception, but Hispanic American, African American, and Native American students have to face many barriers to obtaining an education. Those barriers block the academic achievement of many, as reflected in the higher dropout rates and lower college attendance and graduation rates for these students.

Around the world, girls and women experience an educational disadvantage. Indeed, many girls never make it to school at all in some countries (United Nations Children's Fund [UNICEF], 2009). The gender gap in school enrollment is largest in sub-Saharan Africa, South Asia, East Asia, and the Pacific (UNICEF, 2009). During the 1990s, that gap decreased in many countries (such as Nepal, China, and Mauritania) but remained and even widened in others (such as Pakistan, Afghanistan, and Nigeria).

Of the 101 million children who are not attending elementary school worldwide, girls account for 56% (UNICEF, 2009). They may be kidnapped and sold as wives, household workers, or sex workers while they are young enough to be in elementary school. Alternatively, they may be the victims of the tradition of educating boys but not girls. Most countries have official policies that include educating girls, but many of those countries are facing heavy debts and the burden of HIV infection, which drains money from educational efforts. However, societal attitudes that diminish the importance of education for girls are a significant underlying problem in many of these developing countries. Their education is one route to a solution.

The practice of educating boys but not girls is reflected in the lower rates of literacy for women and their lower rates of attendance in secondary schools in many countries (UNICEF, 2009). Industrialized countries tend to show patterns of women's education that are similar to the United States, in which women have overtaken men in many aspects of education (see Table 11.1). Developing countries, on the other hand, do not; girls' and women's educational levels are lower at all levels of education. The United Nations has made gender equity in education a worldwide priority, emphasizing the economic importance of access to quality education for all (UNESCO, 2005).

■ Summary

Men and women have different experiences in education. Although Title IX of the Education Amendments of 1972 prohibits discrimination based on gender in schools, girls and boys do not receive the same treatment. Beginning during the earliest school years and continuing throughout college and professional training, boys receive more attention and feedback about their performance in classroom work than girls do. Although some of this attention is negative, directed at boys' misbehavior, teachers tend to believe that boys have more ability in certain subjects, and their attention reinforces this attitude. However, beginning in elementary school, girls make better grades than boys. During junior high school, both boys and girls become less confident of their abilities.

Until recently, girls pursued advanced courses in math and science less often than boys in high school, but that gender difference has disappeared. However, girls are still less likely to take advanced physical science and computer courses. Teachers, parents, and counselors may convey higher career expectations to boys and fail to present the full range of career options to girls. Gender stereotyping tends to steer boys who enter career and technical education programs toward lucrative skilled trades, whereas women in these programs learn low-paying clerical and child-care skills. Athletics continues to be a way for boys to gain prestige, but the increase in sports participation among girls has led to greater acceptance of female athletes. Sexual harassment, especially from peers, becomes a problem for both girls and boys during high school. Gay and lesbian adolescents become targets of sexual harassment especially often, making school an unpleasant and even dangerous place for them.

Although women did not historically attend college in numbers comparable to men, that pattern has changed. Women now receive more undergraduate degrees than men, but gender differences in choices of major persist, with a small percentage of science and engineering degrees and a large percentage of education and liberal arts degrees going to women. An increasing number of women are receiving advanced and professional degrees, however, and many majors are becoming less dominated by one gender.

The campus climate is less supportive of women's than men's achievement, both in the classroom and on the athletic field. Title IX of the Educational Amendments of 1972 applies to athletics, which has provoked controversy and legal challenges. The law remains in force, mandating equitable funding for women's athletics. This situation has resulted in a large increase in the number of women involved in sports, but funding is not yet equitable.

Although achievement consists of a variety of attainments, studies of achievement have focused on career success rather than success in relationships or families. This emphasis has led to the portrayal of men as having a higher motivation for achievement than women. In considering women and achievement, the fear of success or the motivation to avoid success was once popular as a way to explain women's lower levels of achievement. Women do acknowledge that competition with men and success in nontraditional fields has negative as well as positive consequences. Men as well as women exhibit misgivings about achievements in nontraditional occupations.

Contrary to widely publicized reports, girls do not experience a sharp decrease in confidence during adolescence, but self-esteem varies by domain, with men showing greater self-esteem in some areas and women in others. Women exhibit less confidence in their ability to achieve than do men, but these gender differences in confidence depend more on the situation than on confidence as a general trait. Again, the gender typing of the situation plays a role in the confidence of both men and women, with each having more confidence in gender-typical compared to gender-atypical situations. Both men and women tend to attribute academic success to effort, but a tendency exists among teachers, parents, and others of both sexes to attribute men's success to ability and women's success to effort. This explanatory strategy places women at a disadvantage, which may relate to their lower confidence in their ability. Thus, gender role stereotypes are an important factor in achievement, with both men and women being influenced by their perceptions of the characteristics of the achievement situation.

Ethnic minorities in the United States face barriers to education. Over the past 40 years, high school graduation rates have increased for all groups, but African Americans, Hispanic Americans, and Native Americans graduate at lower rates than Asian Americans and Whites. This same disparity carries over into college, graduate, and professional training. Women from all ethnic groups attend college at higher rates than men from the same groups. Thus, at all levels, ethnic minorities—especially men—experience educational disadvantages. Around the world, girls and women experience an educational disadvantage, especially in low-income countries. A disproportionate number of girls do not go to school at all, but gender equity in access to education is becoming a worldwide priority.

■ Glossary

fear of success   negative consequences associated with success.
sexual harassment   unwanted sexual attention.

Title IX of the Education Amendments of 1972   the federal act that prohibited educational institutions that receive federal funds from discriminating on the basis of gender.

■ Suggested Readings

American Association of University Women. (2006). *Drawing the line: Sexual harassment on campus.* New York: AAUW Educational Foundation.
This new analysis of sexual harassment focuses on college and details how widespread harassment is and the harm it can do.

Connell, R. W. (1996). Teaching the boys: New research on masculinity, the gender strategies for schools. *Teachers College Record, 98,* 206–235.
The research and publicity on girls' treatment in schools has overlooked how schools can shortchange boys, too. Connell describes the problems that boys experience in school and how school can be an unfriendly place for them.

Eccles, Jacquelynne S. (2007). Gender differences in participation in physical science and engineering. In S. J. Ceci & W. M. Williams (Eds.), *Why aren't more women in science: Top researchers debate the evidence* (pp. 131–145). Washington, DC: American Psychological Association.
Eccles has worked toward understanding academic achievement and motivation for over 30 years, and this article summarizes her research and model for achievement, with an emphasis on what might produce the gender disparity in some academic areas.

chapter
12 Careers and Work

In early January 2009, the number of female CEOs in the top 500 companies in the United States (the Fortune 500) reached an all-time high—13 (Jones, 2009). Those women account for 2.6% of the CEOs in Fortune 500 companies. "It's not just that the number of female CEOs is barely inching up. Women now receive about six in 10 college degrees, yet near the top there remains slow progress in the number of female directors, officers, highest paid—and women in the pipeline" (Jones, 2009, p. 6B). The shortage of women in the pipeline means that women's progress will continue to be slow.

HEADLINE

Women Slowly Gain on Corporate America

USA Today, January 2, 2009

Not only do few women occupy the CEO offices, but women are in short supply in corporate offices and on boards of directors (Catalyst, 2008). In 2008, only about 15% of corporate officers and members of boards of directors were women. Again, little growth occurred over the prior 5 years. For women of color, the picture is bleaker: About 3% of boards of directors were Latina, African American, or Asian American women.

These dismal statistics illustrate the **glass ceiling**, the invisible barrier that prevents women and ethnic minorities from advancing in organizations, and the Fortune 500 companies represent some of the worst situations for women and ethnic minorities. To study the situation of the glass ceiling and its effect on women's advancement in business, the U.S. government established the Glass Ceiling Commission in 1991. As this headline reported, the results of studies of women and ethnic minorities in the corporate and business world paint a discouraging picture; women tend to be hired into positions traditionally associated with women, such as human relations or communications, rather than positions that put them into situations to make critical decisions and develop their management expertise (Dingell & Maloney, 2002; Petersen & Saporta, 2004). This situation puts fewer women "in the pipeline" to advance to the CEO level. Furthermore, female managers receive lower salaries than men, even when they do the same job.

Women's failure to advance to the highest levels of corporate success remains puzzling but not unique; women and ethnic minorities also advance more slowly in academic and scientific careers (Graham & Smith, 2005; Valian, 2007). At one time, few women were qualified and experienced, and holding on to stereotypes, many male executives believe that situation still exists (Catalyst, 2005). The evidence indicates otherwise; throughout the 1990s and into the 21st century, the job performance of Fortune 500 female CEOs was comparable to male CEOs (Jones, 2009). Companies with a mixture of female and

When women join the workforce, they may feel that they are forced to juggle the demands of their jobs and their families.

male executives, however, performed better than companies with few women. The mixture of women and men may be the best choice, but that balance is not on the horizon for business in the United States.

Women's careers in the Fortune 500 seem to have stalled, but is that situation representative of other business careers and of other careers?

Careers

"Career, in its broadest sense, means 'life path' and thus includes all the roles a person plays throughout life" (Farmer & Sidney, 1985, p. 338). This definition places careers in a developmental framework and emphasizes the lifelong nature of career development and the many choices and roles that contribute to this path. Ideally, all people should choose a career on the basis of their interests, abilities, and potential contributions to society, but obstacles prevent the full development of both men's and women's potentials. Gender stereotyping is one of the obstacles.

Despite the encompassing social definition of *career* as the role people play throughout their lives, the study of career development has focused on the choices and patterns that men have taken, and only recently has women's career development received attention. The framework that developed to explain men's careers does not fit women's careers, and those differences are likely to continue in the near future (Williams, 2000). One reason for this difference relates to the expectations about the types of careers each women and men will occupy.

Career choices are less sharply gendered than in the past, but most women and men continue to choose gender-traditional occupations. Another expectation is that wives' careers will be secondary to those of their husbands. If someone must stay home with a sick child or if one person must relocate due to job demands, the husband's career nearly always takes precedence, and the wife must accommodate her schedule and employment. These expectations tend to result in interruptions in the careers of women, who may take years away from employment to care for children or to support a husband's career before rejoining the workforce.

Women are more likely to hold part-time employment than men are—65% of part-time workers are women (U.S. Census Bureau, 2009a). Part-time employment means not only lower salaries for women but also puts them at a disadvantage in career advancement. Men's careers are more likely to follow a smooth line of career choices during schooling, uninterrupted employment, and continuing career advancement throughout adulthood.

Homemaking is considered a legitimate career for women, but one that excludes them from the paid workforce. However, homemaking does not compare to paid work in a number of ways—no training requirements, no wages, no retirement benefits, no job security, and no opportunity for advancement (Betz, 1993). Many mothers who choose to stay at home rather than pursuing careers have agonized over this decision and are fanatically devoted to their choice; those mothers who choose to pursue full-time employment have also found their decision difficult and are also dedicated to their choice (Blair-Loy, 2003). These two groups of women tend not to be understanding about the other's choice, and their arguments and accusations are part of what have been termed the "mommy wars" (Pollitt, 2006).

The traditional assumptions underlying careers included choices based on individual preferences and values and an orderly progression throughout careers to higher levels of responsibility and prestige. These assumptions may not apply to women's careers. Women may make career choices based on family as well as individual preferences and needs, and they may leave their careers to fulfill family obligations and not maintain a linear progression of career development. Ellen Cook, Mary Heppner, and Karen O'Brien (2002, 2005) proposed a model of career development that they called the *ecological model,* which situates a person within an environment and acknowledges the influence of environmental as well as individual factors in career development.

Exploration of children's and adolescents' career beliefs has revealed gender similarities and differences. Children between the ages of 6 and 12 perceive status differences in feminine and masculine careers (Tieg & Susskind, 2008). A study of high-achieving adolescent girls (Watson, Quatman, & Edler, 2002) found that girls' career aspirations were as high as those of boys, but a study of gifted adolescents in Germany and the United States (Fiebig, 2008) showed that career aspirations decreased as girls adopted more traditional gender roles. Indeed, the gender stereotyping of careers presents an important factor for career expectations.

Career Expectations and Gender Stereotyping

Career aspirations may be similar for girls and boys, but beliefs and expectations are not so equal; even preschool children have beliefs about the career differences of women and men (Levy, Sadovsky, & Troseth, 2000). They expressed a concept of female-dominated versus male-dominated occupations, believed that men were more competent at male-dominated and women more competent at female-dominated occupations, and said that women earn less money than men. During early adolescence, beliefs concerning competence and self-efficacy showed traditional gender differences that shaped these children's career choices over the next few years (Bandura, Barbaranelli, Caprara, & Pastorelli, 2001).

Young women's career expectations include both career and family, which represents a change over the past 60 years (Komarovsky, 1982; Konrad, 2003; Phillips & Imhoff, 1997). In the 1940s, few college women planned to continue their careers after they married, but currently, most women, regardless of their career plans, also anticipate marriage and children as part of their life goals. The requirements of combining family duties and paid work play an important role in the process of declining career aspirations and priorities for women and for more flexible careers (Ferriman, Lubinski, & Benbow, 2009; Frome, Alfeld, Eccles, & Barber, 2008).

These expectations about marriage and motherhood demonstrate what Joan Williams (2000) described as force fields that pull women toward domesticity and away from careers. Similar forces affect men, drawing them toward careers and away from family. Despite college students' beliefs that few difficulties will arise in combining career and family, research presents a different picture. Arlie Hochschild (1997) found the situation of families squeezed by a "time blind" as employed parents devoted hours to work and resented spouses and children for the time they demanded. The movement of women into nontraditional careers magnifies this problem. Women who work as managers and engineers are as devoted to their careers as the men who hold these jobs and almost as reluctant to go home to household work and child care as men are. That is, these high-prestige careers demand time and commitment from either men or women.

Women with more traditional gender role beliefs are more strongly influenced by presentation of feminine gender stereotypes (Oswald, 2008) and are more likely to choose occupations more traditional for women (Duncan, Peterson, & Ax, 2003). For example, women who value personal interaction with coworkers and providing care to others expressed less interest in science and technology careers because they perceived these fields as offering less of these valued experiences (Morgan, Isaac, & Sansone, 2001). The identification of women with caring may present a major barrier to women's success in nontraditional careers (Catalyst, 2005).

Ethnicity also plays a role in career development, but it is not a factor in career aspirations among high school students. In a meta-analysis of studies on career beliefs among high school and college students from several ethnic groups (Fouad & Byars-Winston, 2005), aspirations did not vary significantly. Students from ethnic minorities, however, perceived more limitations on their opportunities and saw more barriers to their career progress than students from the majority ethnic group. Their perceptions are most likely realistic; African American, Hispanic American, and Native American students face barriers in pursuing careers. These findings are consistent with the ecological model of career development (Cook et al., 2002) and its emphasis on the environmental circumstances that constrain career development.

The percentage of women in the U.S. workforce has risen to 48% of the total labor force (U.S. Department of Labor Statistics, 2008; see According to the Media and According to the Research), yet employed women remain concentrated in occupations that are female-dominated. Table 12.1 shows the percentage of women in various occupations in 1983 and 2007. Women occupy a range of careers but remain concentrated in a narrow range of clerical, service, or professional positions, such as clerical workers, secretaries,

TABLE 12.1   *Percentage of Women in Various Occupations, 1983 versus 2007*

Occupation	1983	2007
Managerial	41%	51%
Accountants and auditors	38	62
Advertising and promotions managers	22	56
Professional	48	56
Architects	13	28
Engineers	6	14
Lawyers	16	33
Mathematicians and computer scientists	29	27
Chemists and material scientists	21	41
Nurses	96	92
Physicians	16	30
Teachers, college	36	46
Teachers, noncollege	71	73
Social workers	64	82
Health technicians	84	76
Administrative support	80	75
Secretaries	99	97
File clerks	84	82
Sales	48	50
Mechanics	3	9
Production and skilled crafts	21	30
Construction	2	9
Labor	19	19
Service occupations	60	79
Household service	96	89
Firefighters	1	5
Police and detectives	9	23
Food preparation	63	56
Hairdressers	89	93
Machine operation	42	22
Farming, fishing, and forestry	25	25

Source: Women in the labor force: A databook, by U.S. Bureau of Labor Statistics, 2005, Table 11. Retrieved July 11, 2006, from www.bls.gov/cps/wlf-databook2005. htm; and *Women in the labor force: A databook* by U.S. Bureau of Labor Statistics, 2008, Table 11. Retrieved October 18, 2009, from www.bls.gov/cps/wlf-databook-2008.pdf.

child-care workers, teachers, nurses, and social workers. An examination of that table reveals that women are moving into male-dominated occupations at a higher rate than men
are moving into female-dominated jobs. These changes allow a gender-segregated workforce to persist, with the majority of employed women and men working in jobs occupied
by others of the same gender. This gender segregation promotes gender stereotyping and
hinders the career development of both women and men.

Career Opportunities

Women and men do not have equal career opportunities on several counts. Different encouragement, education, and training create unequal preparation for careers, which is the
beginning point for gender inequity at work (see Chapter 11 for a review of these issues).
The gender stereotyping that affects decisions related to education and training also influences hiring decisions. Discrimination in hiring represents a second point at which women
and men may be disadvantaged in careers. Again, gender stereotypes appear as a factor in
this unequal treatment.

Discrimination in Hiring.   Discrimination in hiring may be the primary factor in the
gender gap in wages, but the problems with research on the hiring process make it the
most difficult to document (Petersen, Saporta, & Seidel, 2000). Table 12.2 shows the gender gap in wages, and the differences are dramatic. For *every* occupational category,
women earned less than men.

TABLE 12.2 . *Weekly Earnings of Men and Women in Various Occupations, 2007*

Occupation	Women's Earnings	Men's Earnings
Managers	$858	$1,187
Lawyers and judges	1,381	1,783
Mathematics and computer science	1,047	1,294
Registered nurses	976	1,098
Architecture and engineering	981	1,258
Physician	1,062	1,796
Teacher, secondary school	900	1,001
Office and administrative support	570	619
Secretary	597	694
Sales	493	791
Production occupations	443	641
Construction occupations	573	648
Installation, maintenance, and repair occupations	726	750
Food service	363	403
Protective service (firefighters, police, guards)	560	754
Personal care and service	402	578
Bus drivers	476	540
Farming, forestry, and fishing	384	382

Source: Women in the labor force: A databook by U.S. Bureau of Labor Statistics, 2008, Table 18. Retrieved October
18, 2009, from www.bls.gov/cps/wlf-databook-2008.pdf.

ACCORDING TO THE MEDIA...

It's Difficult to Determine Where Women Work

Television programs frequently include characters' occupations as part of the plot, thus presenting a picture of occupations and the people who pursue those occupations. It's easier to know men's than women's occupations. For television in the 1990s (Elasmar, Hasegawa, & Brain, 1999; Signorielli & Kahlenberg, 2001) and more recently (Dozier, Lauzen, & Reyes, 2005; Shanahan, Signorielli, & Morgan, 2008; Signorielli, 2004), female major characters were less likely to be employed than male major characters; for those who were employed, their occupations were less likely to be specified. Between 30 and 40% of female characters were not employed, and the occupation of about 20% was unclear.

Women on TV with clear occupations tend to have prestigious and glamorous jobs. Although these characters are often minor characters, about 15% held jobs in the entertainment industry such as model, musician, or actress (Signorielli & Kahlenberg, 2001); less than 8% were portrayed as homemakers (Shanahan et al., 2008). However, women's jobs on television are not the ones traditionally associated with women. Female characters were more likely to have a gender-neutral job (such as artist) or a traditionally male job (such as physician, attorney, or law enforcement officer) rather than a traditionally female job (such as nurse or teacher).

This picture of high-prestige, powerful careers is more typical of White characters than of other ethnic groups. African American and Hispanic characters are less likely to be cast as holding prestigious jobs but more likely to be portrayed in law enforcement (or as criminals) (Signorielli, 2004, 2009). Overall, White men were portrayed as having jobs with the most prestige and the highest leadership.

As women have moved into the workforce in large numbers, the picture of their occupations has become less gender-stereotypical and more prestigious compared to the television portrayals of the 1970s and 1980s (Shanahan et al., 2008). However, women's work is more often absent from television. Indeed, women appear less frequently as characters on television than their numbers in the real world. Although the percentage of women on television increased between the 1970s and the early 21st century, the percentage of employed women on television did not match those gains (Shanahan et al., 2008). Television characters and TV employment remain largely a man's world.

Studies of the wage differential between men and women who worked in large companies (Gerhart, 1990; Petersen & Saporta, 2004) showed that the women's salaries were lower than men's salaries, and hiring was the point at which the difference arose and was the most prominent. The salary advancements were comparable, and women received promotions at least as rapidly as men. However, hiring allows the possibility of discrimination (1) through recruitment, (2) through who receives offers, and (3) through assignment of women and men to different jobs or with different salaries. Investigating the first two possibilities is more difficult, but several studies have explored these possibilities. One study (van Ommeren, de Vries, Russo, & van Ommeren, 2005) found that the gender composition of the applicant pool made it more difficult for a person to be hired when most of the possible hires were of the other gender. Another study (Uhlmann & Cohen, 2005) explored the processes that people use to formulate criteria for hiring and found that people adjust their criteria for merit in a biased way that gives advantages to the group they favor. Employment equity directives can increase women's chance of being hired, but only if their qualifications are higher than other applicants; when qualifications are similar, underqualified men's chances increase (Ng & Wiesner, 2007). Thus gender stereotypes work against women (and possibly additionally in favor of men) in being hired into nontraditional jobs.

ACCORDING TO THE RESEARCH . . .

Most Women Are Employed

The demographic picture of women and employment varies substantially from the television portrayal. On television, many women are not employed, whereas in the United States, employment rates for women are about 60% (U.S. Census Bureau, 2009a). In reality, women work more than they do on TV.

In some respects, women's jobs are better in real life than on television. About 30% of female characters on television hold professional or managerial jobs; employment statistics reveal that women hold about 56% of such jobs (U.S. Bureau of Labor Statistics, 2008). In other respects, the television versions of professional women's working lives are better than reality; television portrays the professional woman as a high-level executive with a prestigious jobs. In reality, only 4% of high-level corporate executives and about 5% of managing partners in law firms are women (Carli & Eagly, 2001).

For both women and men, television overrepresents some occupations and underrepresents others. The jobs of lawyers, physicians, and law enforcement officers have good potential for interesting plots, so television overrepresents these occupations. On television, 13% of characters are law enforcement officers, but only about 2% of working people actually pursue this occupation. In addition, female law enforcement officers are six times more common on television than in real life.

On television, women appear as often as men in white-collar jobs and blue-collar jobs (Signorielli & Kahlenberg, 2001). Both the proportions and the gender distribution are inaccurate. About 11% of employed characters appeared in white-collar jobs such as managers, clerks, and salespeople. In reality, over 40% of employed people have these types of jobs. About 6% of male and female characters on TV had blue-collar jobs, but the figure is really about 36%, and men are more than twice as likely as women to have these jobs.

The portrayals of women's jobs on television are all too accurate when it comes to salary disadvantages. Female characters are less likely than male characters to hold prestigious jobs with high salaries (Signorielli, 2004), which is also true for employed women (U.S. Bureau of Labor Statistics, 2008). However, women's jobs and work settings differ from the television version. Their income disadvantage is more likely to result from holding a job with a "sticky floor" than from being a desperate housewife.

Research on initial salary offers and initial job positions has indicated bias against women. Several studies (Penner, 2008b) found that women were sorted into lower-level jobs and received lower salaries than men hired by the same large companies (Petersen & Saporta, 2004). An examination of hiring in a technology organization over a 10-year period (Petersen et al., 2000) revealed no gender discrimination in hiring decisions but an 11% difference in initial salary offers. The initial salary deficit makes it difficult for women's salaries to ever catch up.

Research on the gender difference in initial salaries has revealed that women expected lower initial salaries than men did (Heckert et al., 2002). This expectation held for college students in a variety of majors. In addition, women also expected to earn less at the peak of their earnings. Other research (Solnick, 2001) concentrated on negotiation skill and found that men were more effective than women in negotiating for money. Indeed, the gender of the negotiators made a substantial difference. Women fared more poorly when they negotiated with men; men had better outcomes when they negotiated with women than with other men. However, men got more money in all pairings. These findings suggest that women may be at a disadvantage in negotiations for initial salaries and may expect to earn less than men, which constitute two situations that may contribute to women's lower salaries.

Gender stereotypes are an important source of discrimination in hiring, with both men and women subject to positive and negative discrimination on the basis of gender stereotypes (Catalyst, 2005; Pratto & Espinoza, 2001). The gender role of the job position is a major factor in discrimination; men have the advantage in applying for "masculine" jobs, and women have a disadvantage. The situation can be reversed for "feminine" jobs—a disadvantage for men and an advantage for women. Male business executives tend to perceive women as less competent (but more caring), a perception that leads them to have difficulties in seeing women as qualified for "masculine" high-level management positions (Catalyst, 2005). Gender is an ever-present factor in evaluating women's performance (Lyons & McArthur, 2007).

Stereotyping also occurs on the basis of ethnicity and sexual orientation, which may affect hiring decisions and salary offers. One study (Pratto & Espinoza, 2001) found complex effects for gender and ethnicity in ratings of job applicants. In most cases, White applicants received higher ratings than African American or Hispanic American candidates with the same qualifications. Studies of hiring discrimination (Horvath & Ryan, 2003) and wage discrepancies (Schmitt, 2008) for gay men and lesbians showed that heterosexual men received the highest and heterosexual women the lowest ratings and salaries. The gay men and lesbians received ratings between the heterosexuals. Thus men continue to have advantages in judgments about their suitability for jobs, even when their qualifications are no better than women's, and both ethnicity and sexual orientation are factors that form complex patterns of preference and bias.

Therefore, discrimination based on gender occurs in hiring decisions, especially in terms of lower status jobs and lower salaries for women. This situation puts women at a disadvantage that is difficult to overcome as their careers progress. In addition, gender stereotyping persists and makes fair hiring decisions difficult. Such discrimination is an important factor in the wage gap between men and women, but other factors also present barriers to career advancement.

Barriers to Career Advancement.   The barriers to career advancement can come from situational and organizational as well as individual sources. Alice Eagly and Linda Carli (2007) characterized women's challenge in advancing in business as negotiating a labyrinth with towering sides that obscure the route to success as well as many turns that lead to dead ends.

Ironically, women have no advantages in attaining higher positions in traditionally female-dominated fields—men have advantages for those jobs too. The advantages that men have in female-dominated fields have been referred to as the *glass escalator* (Williams, 1992). This term conveys the image that some invisible force produces an easy ascent to higher positions, in contrast with the glass ceiling, which blocks progress toward the highest levels of career achievement. Men who choose careers traditionally dominated by women face some discrimination from society in general, but these men's careers reflect a history of rapid promotion. These advantages may come as a result of the perception that men should not be in jobs that women usually perform, and thus men receive promotions to administrative or supervisory positions within that occupation.

For example, a male librarian described how happy and confident he had felt in his abilities as a children's librarian (Williams, 1992). Reading stories to children and helping them find books were part of his job, but many people mentioned to him that this was inappropriate work for a man, and he was transferred to another library and given the position

◼ GENDERED VOICES

I Never Felt Discriminated Against

A man who had gone to nursing school almost 40 years ago told me, "I decided to be a nurse when I was in the 10th grade, after I'd had surgery. The woman who lived across the street told me about the salaries of nurse-anesthetists, and the work interested me and the money sounded good. I don't remember my parents saying anything, my school counselor got information about nursing, and I didn't discuss it with my friends, so I don't recall any negative comments. There were only two men in our nursing class. Now many men go into nursing, but then it was uncommon. There had been another guy about 10 years earlier and the two of us. That's it."

"I never felt discriminated against by either the teachers or the female students. Everybody was supportive and more than fair. My fraternity brothers were another story—they gave me a lot of static about majoring in nursing. The jokes were pretty good-natured, but there were a lot of jokes. It was something that came up a lot."

"The women I have worked with were great. If anything, I think that being a man has been an advantage to me in my career. Rather than being discriminated against, I think that I was at some advantage. Maybe I got promotions and advancement faster than women, but those who chose me and recommended me were almost always women. I think I was competent and deserved the promotions, so I would have a hard time saying that I advanced in my career because I was a man, but I certainly never felt that it held me back."

I told him about the frequency of sexual harassment in jobs in which the gender ratio is far from equal and asked him if his female-dominated work situation had led to harassment. He replied, "Did I ever feel sexually harassed? That's hard to say. I never was put in the position of 'You do this or it's your job.' Never. But I've had my butt grabbed, and I've gotten a lot of offers. If that's harassment, then I guess I've been harassed, but I can't say that it really bothered me."

of research librarian. When asked why he did not consider a discrimination lawsuit, the man reported that his new job was really a promotion to a more prestigious position, so he felt benefited rather than harmed by these clearly discriminatory actions. His experience is typical of men in female-dominated careers (Budig, 2002), including men in Sweden (Hultin, 2003), where gender equity has also been actively pursued.

Gender role discrimination and occupational stereotypes provide the basis for both the glass ceiling and the glass escalator. In addition, the *sticky floor* is also a factor in women's lower wages and problems in career advancement. The concept of a sticky floor contrasts with the glass ceiling as a means to describe low-status occupations with little opportunity for advancement—that is, occupations in which employees get stuck at the lowest levels. Many of the occupations dominated by women fit this description, including clerks, secretaries, beauticians, garment workers, and household service workers. This concept also applies to women with professional careers; women are much more likely than men to get stuck at the associate level in legal firms (Reichman & Sterling, 2004).

Greater numbers of ethnic minority women tend to be concentrated in low-level jobs with a sticky floor, and both African American and Hispanic American women are more likely to occupy blue-collar jobs than White women (U.S. Census Bureau, 2009a). Ethnic differences exist within blue-collar occupations; African American women are more likely to work in health service jobs, and Hispanic American women are more likely to be employed in manufacturing. All of these jobs have lower wages than jobs typically occupied by White women or by men.

Factors other than gender stereotyping and discrimination contribute to the gender gap in wages—different educational credentials, career choices, career schedules, and workplace climate. Women occupy jobs and pursue careers that are less prestigious and not as well paid as those that men occupy. For example, only 33% of attorneys are women compared to 88% of nursing aides; only 39% of managers in marketing and advertising are women compared with 97% of secretaries and administrative assistants (U.S. Bureau of Labor Statistics, 2008). In addition, women in science, engineering, and management tend to choose public institutions rather than private industry. These situations tend to have more egalitarian attitudes and better working climates for women, but they also pay lower salaries.

The differences in women's and men's career development schedules also differ in promotions and wages. Women are more likely than men to take time off from their careers to attend to family needs, such as staying home with young children or caring for elderly parents. These employment gaps take women out of the workforce, pull them off the track to advancement, and slow their career progress (Barnett, 2004a; Fuegen, Biernat, Haines, & Deaux, 2004). Indeed, the concept of the "mommy track" assumes that women who have children will be less committed to their careers and will not achieve as much as men with comparable credentials. Little discussion has arisen over a "daddy track" because it is women and not men who are responsible for child care. The image of "working mothers" operates as a bias against women in the workplace (Güngör & Biernat, 2009; Heilman & Okimoto, 2008; King, 2008), but the same standards do not apply to fathers, who are not penalized for having children unless they interrupt their careers to care for them. If men take family leave to devote time to their families, they are penalized more severely than women (Smith, Tabak, Showail, Parks, & Kleist, 2005).

What about those women who place a high priority on their careers? Does equal emphasis on work create equal rewards for women? Answers to those questions can come from women's satisfaction with their careers or from an assessment of their career progress. A group of successful male and female MBAs (people who have earned master's degrees in business administration) showed similar motivation, involvement, and enjoyment for work as well as similar tendencies to be "workaholics" (Burke, 1999). The reality of women's commitment to their careers does not overcome the perception that they will be less committed (Catalyst, 2005), and even women without children experience discrimination because they *might* have children. Indeed, the employment advantage that lesbians experience seems to be attributable to their low likelihood of having children (Baumle, 2009). If deviating from the standard pattern does not work and following the pattern does not work, then women have no way to succeed to the extent that men do.

Another situation that affects career advancement is the work climate and the informal social structure at work, which can help or hinder the advancement of employees. Women perceive their work environments as more hostile in terms of the informal social structure, standards they must meet for advancement, sexist attitudes, and the possibility for solving problems that arise at work (Levine, 2009; Murrell & James, 2001). For example, people working in business settings demonstrated their tendency to discriminate against women by choosing a man rather than a woman as the company representative for an important assignment and a woman for a less important assignment (Catalyst, 2005; Reichman & Sterling, 2004). This behavior may be beyond the level of conscious decision; people draw on gender stereotypes without thinking about discrimination and may even voice egalitarian beliefs yet continue to behave in biased ways.

Achievement-oriented women who pursue careers in male-dominated fields are in the minority, which can put them into the category of a **token** (Kanter, 1977). The token stands out, becoming more visible than other employees, and feels pressure to succeed and to reflect well on the ability of everyone in his or her minority group. Female engineers and female CEOs of Fortune 500 companies meet the definition of tokens. As tokens try to fit into the existing corporate and social structure, the dominant group may work toward keeping them on the periphery in subtle rather than overt ways, such as excluding the token from social interactions. Tokens do not become one of the "good ol' boys" or part of the network that offers support and allows connections that may be important to career advancement. Women from ethnic minorities are at a special disadvantage because they are tokens in two ways (Murrell & James, 2001).

Tokens are also handicapped in forming mentoring relationships, the relationships between (usually) younger and less experienced and more experienced workers that offer valuable support in the form of friendship, advice, or even direct intervention in the organization. Mentor–protégé relationships tend to form within gender and ethnic lines. Neither women nor ethnic minorities are common in the upper echelons of organizations, handicapping these individual in finding mentors (Murrell & James, 2001). For example, women and ethnic minority graduates from one MBA program were less likely to have mentors than were White men who had completed the same program (Dreher & Cox, 1996). Establishing a mentor relationship with a White man was advantageous. Those

▣ GENDERED VOICES

I Was Good at Math and Science

A female chemical engineer said, "I was good at math and science, so my high school counselor suggested engineering. I looked into the various kinds of engineering. I didn't really like physics all that much, so I decided that electrical engineering would not be a good choice. I didn't consider myself very mechanical, so I ruled out mechanical engineering. I liked chemistry, so I thought chemical engineering would be a good choice, but I didn't really know what chemical engineers did. My high school had a cooperative arrangement so I could work for an engineer, but that experience didn't really let me know what the work of a chemical engineer was like. In fact, I didn't really understand the work of chemical engineers until I was a junior in college, and I learned that I didn't find the work all that interesting."

"I went to a technical college that specialized in engineering, and it was definitely male dominated; only about 25% of the students were women. But I never felt any favoritism either for or against the women.

Everybody was treated fairly. The courses during the first two years were designed to weed out students, so everybody felt that the curriculum was difficult, but the women did as well as the men, and I never felt that the professors or students showed any bias."

"What was missing on campus were ethnic minorities. The campus was very White. There just weren't any Black students, and there was one Hispanic girl. The geographic area had lots of minorities, but they didn't go into engineering at this school. I noticed the absence of minority students more than the small number of women."

"I didn't feel that being a woman was a factor in school, but it sure was on the job. I didn't necessarily feel discriminated against, but the women were very visible. There were few women, and whatever a woman did stood out. If I did a great job, I got noticed more than a man who did a great job. If I screwed up, I got noticed more than a man who made a mistake. Whatever a woman did—good or bad—came to the attention of everyone."

MBAs who did form such relationships earned over $16,000 more per year than those without mentors and those whose mentors were women or ethnic minorities. Therefore, women and minority employees are at a disadvantage and White men at an advantage in finding mentors who can further their careers.

Despite a growing number of women entering management, the perception continues that management is a position associated with the stereotypical view that "men take charge" whereas "women take care," making men more suited to be managers (Catalyst, 2005). Studies ranging from the 1980s (Heilman, Black, Martell, & Simon, 1989) to the 21st century (Catalyst, 2005) have indicated an association between men and management and negative stereotypes of women as managers.

The gender wage gap decreased from the 1970s to the present, with rapid decreases during the 1980s that slowed during the 1990s (Kongar, 2008). For young, educated women and men, the gender gap in wages is not large (Joshi, Makepeace, & Dolton, 2007), mostly due to increases in women's education plus women entering occupations traditionally held by men. However, for the workforce in general, the wage gap begins with teenaged workers (Besen-Cassino, 2008) and persists. The discrepancies in the earnings of women and men are not disappearing rapidly (Kongar, 2008). Indeed, an experimental study (Alksnis, Desmarais, & Curtis, 2008) determined that people evaluated work done by women as being worth less than work done by men—even when the work was exactly the same.

Therefore, women and ethnic minorities encounter several barriers to their career advancement. Many of those barriers relate to negative stereotypes of women and minorities, involving questions of their abilities, competence, and dedication to work. Even with similar qualifications and performance, few women and ethnic minorities attain the highest levels of career advancement, which suggests that discrimination is a continuing factor in the difference.

Balancing Career and Family.   Family demands influence career paths for both men and women. The historic association of women with household work and child care has made family concerns more of an issue for women's than men's careers. This association has created a "force field" that pulls women toward household work and child care, often decreasing the amount of time they spend on their careers (Williams, 2000; Williams & Cooper, 2004). This pull toward domesticity prevents women from fulfilling the "ideal worker" role, a worker able and willing to devote full time and overtime to work. Men who want to be involved with their families also fail as ideal workers and also may suffer penalties in their career advancement.

The large majority of people who marry and have children are faced with the task of balancing work and family demands. Figure 12.1 shows the increase in employment for married women, including women with young children. Society, employers, and many husbands assume that women will be the ones who perform most household chores and become the primary caregivers for children. Even when "family friendly" policies were in place, both corporate (Hochschild, 1997) and academic (Minerick, Wasburn, & Young, 2009) employment failed to support women's careers. Instead, the workplace climate tends to push women toward domesticity and men toward career advancement. Thus, women who chose to concentrate on their careers were perceived as neglecting their families, yet such women still do not meet the criteria for being a good employee (Ridgeway & Correll, 2004). Mothers cannot "win" as workers; they are devalued for devoting time to work and for devoting time to family.

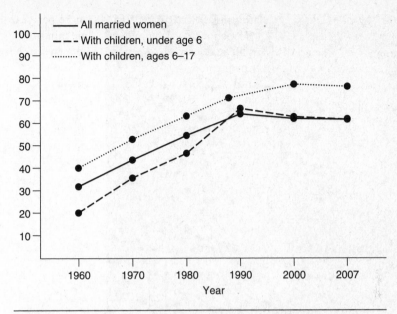

FIGURE 12.1 *Employment Trends of Married Women, Including Women with Children, 1960–2007*

Sources: *Statistical Abstract of the United States, 1999* (119th ed., p. 417), by U.S. Bureau of the Census, 1999, Washington, DC: U.S. Government Printing Office; and *Statistical Abstract of the United States, 2009* (128th ed., p. 376), by U.S. Census Bureau, 2009, Washington, DC: U.S. Government Printing Office.

On the other hand, assumptions about men place them under suspicion when they do *not* concentrate on their careers (Heyn, 2003). Men's traditional role in families is breadwinner, which puts men into careers as a way of showing devotion to their families. Ironically, family demands take men away from their families while they devote time to careers. Thus, the choice to spend time away from family has been (and remains) more socially approved for men than for women. Changes have occurred and continue to occur as men want to participate more fully in their children's lives, but even companies that have "family friendly" policies typically expect women and not men to take advantage of these provisions. As R. W. Connell (2005c) noted, the issue of work–family balance and family friendly policies are really ways of allowing women to keep their family commitments rather than ways to allow fathers time with their families.

An increasing number of people fulfill the multiple roles of partner, parent, and worker. Some theories predict problems for the individuals who do, but research has not confirmed the harmful effects (Barnett & Hyde, 2001). To the contrary, people who have both employment and family tend to be psychologically and physically healthier and happier than people who do not occupy multiple roles, but "having it all" carries a price. Career, marriage, and children are a balancing act, and overload and distress may occur; this distress affects both work and family (van Steenbergen & Ellemers, 2009). However, when people are employed, they have the opportunity to experience success, social support from others at work,

Employed women continue to perform the majority of household work and child-care chores, which may create conflict and stress.

and income. "Adding the worker role is beneficial to women, and adding or participating in family roles is beneficial for men" (Barnett & Hyde, 2001, p. 784).

What does it take to achieve a healthy balance? Flexible work schedules can help, but workers must not only know that flexible scheduling is available but also that they are free to use this option (Hayman, 2009). This situation may be difficult to achieve, especially in prestigious, high-commitment careers; either a man or a woman must be an ideal worker to succeed in such corporate, scientific, or academic careers. Indeed, these careers require someone at home serving as support for the ideal worker. The force fields that draw women away from careers may lead women growing pressure and stress, to "opting out" of such careers to pursue domesticity (Halrynjo & Lyng, 2009), or to a decision by couples to form an equal partnership without either one pursuing a high-power career

(Schwartz, 1994). Thus, most of the workplaces in the United States and many other countries make the achievement of work and family balance very difficult.

Gender Issues at Work

The gender gap in wages reflects the barriers that women face when entering and advancing in careers, but the types of jobs occupied by women and men also contribute to the wage gap. Although women have entered male-dominated professions in greater numbers in the past decades than at any previous time, women remain underrepresented in the highest levels of their professions, and women's employment remains concentrated in a narrow range of jobs. Both the unbalanced representation of women in jobs and the concentration of women in a limited number of jobs can be described as gender segregation. This situation is an important gender issue at work, but communication, power, and sexual harassment are additional factors that affect women's careers.

Gender Segregation on the Job

Gender segregation describes most job situations—the large majority of jobs are held by either men or women but not by an equal (or nearly equal) mix of both. These associations have created the perception that jobs are gendered. Regardless of the job demands, some jobs have become so associated with either men or women as to be considered male occupations or female occupations. This process contributes to the differential value of occupations because both women and men value the type of work that men do more highly than the type work that women do (Alksnis et al., 2008; Cohen & Huffman, 2003).

Women also occupy a less diversified range of occupations than men. Consequently, most employed women are concentrated in a few occupations, whereas men occupy a wider variety of jobs. Over two-thirds of women have jobs in clerical or professional fields, but the professional fields are those traditionally dominated by women—nursing and teaching (U.S. Bureau of Labor Statistics, 2008). Women are most underrepresented in skilled blue-collar jobs, such as electricians, mechanics, and plumbers. (Refer to Table 12.1 for the percentages in the "construction," "mechanics," and "production and skilled crafts" categories.)

Changes over the past 20 years have not made as large an impact on gender segregation on the job as most people imagine. The reasons for women moving into traditionally male-dominated jobs are largely economic: Male-dominated occupations pay better than female-dominated ones (Cohen & Huffman, 2003), giving women an incentive to pursue such occupations. Men have not moved into female-dominated work at a similar rate, perpetuating the unequal gender ratio in most occupations. Even when the educational and skills levels are controlled, jobs in female-dominated fields pay less than the equivalent jobs in male-dominated areas. Thus, women have an incentive to move into male-dominated jobs, and men have less incentive to seek jobs in female-dominated occupations.

The process of integrating either women or men into a gender-dominated workplace poses problems, especially during the early stages of the process. When women enter a predominantly male workplace, the organizational culture is masculine (Jandeska & Kraimer, 2005), and women may feel (and actually be) unwelcome. Women's perception of the male organizational culture and men's perception of women intruding into the workplace both contribute to a difficult transition.

The experience of integrating the military of the United States (Snyder, 2003; Yoder & Naidoo, 2006) and South Africa (van Wijk & Finchilescu, 2008) illustrates the problems of integrating a workforce. A study of changing sex ratios of symphony orchestras produced similar findings (Allmendinger & Hackman, 1995). During the early years, when women were tokens, that process was plagued by difficulties. When women held between 10 and 40% of positions within an organization, both genders were dissatisfied, and the organization did not function as effectively as it had previously. As the proportion of women increased toward 50%, many of the problems and conflicts diminished. When the workplace was integrated, no gender differences appeared in the perception of work-related demands (Hochwarter, Perrewe, & Dawkins, 1995). Although the integration process may create problems, those problems tend to diminish when gender integration progresses.

Many workplaces are not headed toward gender integration but instead remain segregated (Gatta & Roos, 2005), a situation that exists not only in the United States but also in many countries throughout Europe (Valentová, Smídová, & Katrnák, 2007). Gender segregation is especially prevalent in jobs that are traditionally female-dominated and may exist even in jobs that appear to be integrated. For example, men who pursue nursing—a female dominated field—tend to gravitate toward the specialties within nursing that they perceive as more "masculine," creating gender segregation within the field of nursing (Snyder & Green, 2008). Even people who choose occupations that are not dominated by one gender may work in companies or offices in which that occupation is. Between 1970 and 1980 gender segregation declined (Fields & Wolff, 1991), but the pattern of decrease was not consistent during the 1990s (Dolado, Felgueroso, & Jimeno, 2001). For younger, well-educated women, gender segregation diminished substantially. For others, especially for those with less education, gender segregation remains.

Jobs may be gender-segregated, but the workplace is likely to include both men and women, who, though they hold different jobs, must work together in the same setting. For example, most secretaries are women, most managers are men, and most managers have secretaries. Thus, men and women often work together but not at the same job. Indeed, the work situations often involve a power differential, with men having the more powerful positions and women the more subordinate.

Gender, Communication, and Power in the Workplace

Communication is a very important aspect of the workplace, and the notion that women's style of communication places them at a disadvantage originated in the 1970s. Robin Lakoff (1975) contended that "women's language" was more tentative and deferential, whereas men's style of communication conveys the assertive, commanding qualities necessary for leadership. The notion of gendered styles of communication received popular attention from the publications of Deborah Tannen, whose *Talking from 9 to 5* (1994) contended that men's workplace communications are oriented toward negotiations and power, whereas women's communications emphasize connection and finding commonality. Both Lakoff and Tannen argued that women's communication style may be a disadvantage in the workplace.

Would women be more successful at work if they talked like men? Although some researchers have agreed that women's communication style presents disadvantages (Basow,

2008), Elizabeth Aries's (1996, 2006) reviews on gender and communication concluded that no distinctive patterns of communication are uniquely associated with success or even with women or men. That is, the hesitant speech style that Lakoff characterized as "women's language" and the assertive style characterized as "men's language" are not specific to either but are influenced by power and situational factors. Although women and men may have different goals in speaking, the notion of a male versus a female way of talking is not supported by research. Even the tendency for men to interrupt more than women may occur more often in recently formed groups and not in more permanent groups, such as workplace groups (Mast, 2002). Furthermore, the emphasis on group differences obscures more important individual differences. Gender-related differences in communication are complex, and both the setting and situation in which communication takes place are critical factors in men's and women's speech patterns.

Conversational style also reflects power, and power is one of the situational differences that affects speech. Speakers with more power speak differently from those with less power by using more assertive language (Aries, 1996, 2006). Work roles mirror social roles, giving women less power. Thus, aspects of the female role carry over into the workplace to produce **sex role spillover** (Nieva & Gutek, 1981), gender role characteristics that spill over into the workplace, creating stereotyping and a sexualized atmosphere. Barbara Gutek (1985) expanded the concept, emphasizing that sex role spillover focuses on gender role behavior that is irrelevant (or even an impediment) to the work role. Sex role spillover can take several different forms, including the expectation that women will be more nurturant or loyal than men, that women will occupy less powerful and subordinate positions, and that women will be sexual at work.

Power in the workplace is typically associated with leadership, and leaders simultaneously occupy both the leadership role and a gender role (Eagly & Johannesen-Schmidt, 2001). For men, the leadership role is consistent with the male gender role, but the dissimilarity between these two roles for women may create conflicts, both in female leaders and in their subordinates. For example, men's experiences with women are more likely to have been women as mothers, girlfriends, wives, daughters, and secretaries, rather than as professional colleagues or as supervisors. Thus, men may rely on their prior interactions and stereotypes in their workplace interactions with women, which creates problems for female managers. Some evidence exists that women who occupy jobs most commonly filled by men adopt a male style of work-related behavior; this behavioral adaptation demonstrates how powerful situational demands can be. Meta-analytic reviews of the research on gender and leadership roles (Eagly, Johannesen-Schmidt, & van Engen, 2003; Eagly & Johnson, 1990) showed that both women and men who have attained managerial status in organizations tend to share similarities in leadership styles, but some differences also exist (van Engen & Willemsen, 2004). Especially in male-dominated workplaces, male and female leaders exhibit similar, typically masculine leadership styles, but women may be better at some behaviors related to success, such as rewarding, team building, and consulting (Catalyst, 2005). In a comparison of leadership styles, women were more likely than men to adopt leadership behaviors that included motivating subordinates by example, showing optimism and excitement, attending to individual needs, and using rewards to change behavior (Eagly & Johannesen-Schmidt, 2001). The gender differences were small, but women's leadership behaviors were associated with positive outcomes, whereas some of the behaviors associated with male leadership were associated with less effective leadership, such as concentrating on negative behaviors and problems and waiting until problems were serious before taking action.

Despite their potential as good leaders, women do not receive the opportunity to develop this potential as often as men do, and when they do, they are subject to more careful scrutiny and criticism than men in comparable positions (Eagly & Carli, 2007). Indeed, a type of double standard seems to operate in the workplace in which women are held to different standards of competence and success than men are (Catalyst, 2005).

The story of Ann Hopkins provides a dramatic example of the application of a double standard (Fiske, Bersoff, Borgida, Deaux, & Heilman, 1991). Ann Hopkins was an employee of Price Waterhouse, and she was so successful that she was nominated for partner in that company, the only woman nominated that year. She was not chosen as a partner, and she became the object of criticism for being too aggressive and "macho" as well as for not being sufficiently feminine in her behavior and appearance. Hopkins sued the company for applying different criteria to its male and female employees, contending that gender stereotyping was a factor in their decision. Eventually, the U.S. Supreme Court agreed with these arguments and condemned the double bind that women face—they are penalized for using an aggressive, powerful style when only this style can lead to success. "The official position suggests a level playing field; the personal conversation reveals that gender-based assessment of leadership creates a tilt that works against women" (Lyons & McArthur, 2007, p. 24).

If women are penalized for using the same methods to gain power that men use, how do women succeed at work? When people have the opportunity to interact and know each other on a personal basis, this information can override the stereotypes that influence judgments in the workplace (Eagly & Johannesen-Schmidt, 2001). People in organizations are often mutually dependent on each other for positive outcomes related to work, and this interdependence can build respect and recognition of competence (Goodwin & Fiske, 2001). In addition, when workers are accountable to some third party, such as an organizational hierarchy that supports female leaders, and when the organization has a good representation of female managers (Cohen, 2007), bias decreases—and so does the wage gap. Thus, women can become and function as effective leaders, but many barriers exist to block their progress.

In summary, although research has failed to support the notion of different communication styles that are unique to women or men; rather, communication styles relate to the power of the speaker and the communication situation. The issues of gender, communication, and power also relate to adherence to stereotypical gender roles in the workplace, which gives power to men and places obstacles in the way of women's career advancement. Using habitual patterns of interaction between men and women in the workplace produces a power differential, with men having the advantage. When women use the same behaviors as men to exert power, they are often perceived as behaving inappropriately and are penalized. Women have the potential to be excellent leaders, but they face many barriers in achieving their potential.

The power difference between men's and women's positions offers not only the opportunity for men to be more successful at work but also the opportunity for men to sexually exploit the women who work for them. Although sexuality at work can also be interpreted as a power issue, the term **sexual harassment** is now used as the label for sexual exploitation in the workplace.

Sexual Harassment at Work

According to Barbara Gutek (1985, p. 18), "sex role spillover facilitates the expression of sexuality at work to the extent that the sex object aspect of the female sex role and the sexual aggressor aspect of the male sex role carry over into the work setting." Thus, sexual harassment can be seen as a function of sex role spillover. Men and women also choose to enter sexual relationships in the workplace, making it difficult to distinguish between this type of sexuality and sexual harassment.

Sexual harassment became illegal as a form of gender discrimination in the United States through a court interpretation of Title VII of the 1964 Civil Rights Acts (Fitzgerald, Swan, & Magley, 1997). In 1980, the U.S. Equal Employment Opportunity Commission established guidelines on sexual harassment. The first form of sexual harassment to be recognized was **quid pro quo sexual harassment**, in which employers or supervisors demand sexual favors as a condition of employment or as a condition for promotion. This form of harassment involves a supervisor using threats or pressure toward a subordinate, making it a clear abuse of power.

In 1986, another form of sexual harassment was legally recognized in the United States—**hostile environment sexual harassment**. This concept of harassment is based on the notion that psychological harm or reduced effectiveness at work can result from unwanted sexual attention as well as from offensive or hostile behavior (Fitzgerald et al., 1997). A third classification of sexual harassment is **gender harassment**, which occurs when people are subjected to offensive or hostile behavior because of their gender. This type of harassment is distinctive because it does not necessarily involve sexuality; rather, it involves hostile or disparaging remarks directed toward a person because of that person's gender. Table 12.3 (page 324) gives examples of each type of sexual harassment.

The U.S. Supreme Court made a series of decisions that strengthened sexual harassment law, making lawsuits easier to win (Gould, 2000). During the 1990s, the number of cases filed with the Equal Employment Opportunity Commission (EEOC) more than doubled, and the monetary awards increased by more than fourfold (EEOC, 2006). Since the mid-1990s, the number of complaints filed with the Equal Employment Opportunity Commission and awards has remained fairly stable. The court decisions extended protection against sexual harassment to men as well as women, and the percentage of complaints filed by men increased to about 15%. Sexual harassment often receives comic treatment on television (Montemurro, 2003); such behavior is either portrayed as the subject of jokes or completely ignored. Increases in monetary awards and settlements have prompted real businesses to adopt attitudes different from those of TV sitcoms, and most companies in the United States have policies and training to prevent harassment.

Many countries also have laws and regulations that have been used to prohibit sexual harassment, and some countries have laws that specifically apply to sexual harassment (Barak, 1997; Sigal, 2006). The United Kingdom, Canada, Australia, Israel, Austria, Ireland, and New Zealand have laws that prohibit sex discrimination or sexual harassment, and the establishment of the European Community led to additional laws. In 2002, the European Union enacted a directive that expanded and clarified protections for employed women in the countries of the EU, which includes most of Europe (Masselot, 2004). Protections against sexual harassment were among the issues addressed by this directive. Throughout the world, some countries have passed and enforce laws against sexual harassment, such as

TABLE 12.3   *Examples of the Three Types of Sexual Harassment*

Quid Pro Quo Type

Demands for sex in exchange for hiring
Demands for sex in exchange for promotion or favorable job evaluation
Demands for sex to keep a job
Demands for sex to avoid being placed in an undesirable job

Hostile Environment Type

Sexual touching
Sexual comments and jokes
Displays of sexual material, such as drawings or photographs
Nonverbal sexual posturing, including sexual gestures
Personal remarks about sexuality
Sexually oriented comments about appearance
Discussions about a person in sexual terms in the person's presence, including comments phrased as
    though the person were not present

Gender Harassment Type

Degrading comments about the ability of women (or men)
Hostile comments about women's (or men's) behavior as a group; not confined to sexual comments
Insults directed toward women or men because of their gender, rather than because of any action or
    characteristic of the individual

Israel (Kamir, 2005) and South Africa (Govender, 2005). For other countries, sexual harassment has been controversial or not a priority, but even these countries passed laws that cover sexual harassment, including Japan, China, and countries in Latin America (Sigal, 2006). In Japan, sexual harassment is much more unacceptable among younger than older workers (Uggen & Shinohara, 2009). The world-wide trend is to enact or strengthen laws against discrimination in the workplace, including sexual harassment, yet sexual harassment remains a common experience throughout the world. For countries in which surveys have been done, the prevalence falls between 30 and 50% (Barak, 1997).

The forms of sexual harassment are not equal in frequency or in perceived severity; the hostile environment form is more common, but the quid pro quo form is perceived as more serious (Rotundo, Nguyen, & Sackett, 2001). Over time, workers have begun to identify both types of behaviors as sexual harassment (Pickerill, Jackson, & Newman, 2006). However, the two types are not independent; workplaces that spawn the hostile environment type of harassment tend to also have the quid pro quo type (Fitzgerald, 1994). As Figure 12.2 shows, all types of sexual harassment are related. Environments that allow insulting remarks and unwanted sexual attention also tend to be permissive of sexual coercion. Despite separate legal definitions for the types of sexual harassment and the differences in frequency and perceived severity, they often coexist.

Women are more frequently the targets of all sexual harassment, when defined in terms of *unwanted* sexual attention. However, both men and women are targets for sexual

▣ GENDERED VOICES

Hardly a Day Went By

In two stories I heard about sexual harassment, the behaviors of the two harassers were amazingly similar. Both harassers, a woman and a man, harassed a coworker. The behaviors of the targets were also very similar to each other.

A man told me, "I worked in a car dealership selling cars after I graduated, and one of the other salespeople was a woman—the only woman who was in sales. She sexually harassed the finance manager. It was blatant. She propositioned him in front of everybody, saying things like 'Let's go in the back room now,' and things much more vulgar."

"He seemed embarrassed and usually didn't reply; he tried to ignore her. He was married, and he never gave her any encouragement at all. She would go over and stand very close to him, never touching him, but standing close and making him uncomfortable. And she would proposition him; rarely a day went by when she didn't. The guy was clearly uncomfortable, but nobody ever did anything."

A young woman said, "I worked as a cashier in a discount store, and one of the department managers sexually harassed me. He would come over to the cash register where I was working, and he would proposition me. He made reasons to be close to me, and he kept saying what a good idea it would be for us to have sex. I didn't think it was such a good idea. I always said no, and I asked him to stop asking. His offers embarrassed me. Hardly a day went by without some sexual offer from him or some remark with sexual connotations. He never touched me or fondled me, but he made my job harder, and he embarrassed me."

"I complained to my supervisor, but she told me to just ignore him. He wasn't my boss, and he never made any threats or attacked me or anything. But I think that he shouldn't have been allowed to harass me the way he did. Nobody did one thing to stop him. I don't think that the store manager ever said a word."

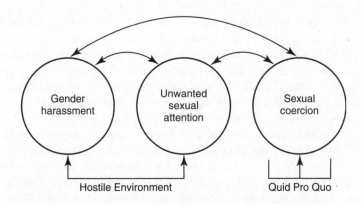

FIGURE 12.2   *A Model of Sexually Harassing Behaviors*

Source: From "But Was It Really Sexual Harassment? Legal, Behavioral, and Psychological Definitions of the Workplace Victimization of Women," by Louise F. Fitzgerald, Suzanne Swan, and Vicki J. Magley, 1997, in William O'Donohue (Ed.), *Sexual Harassment: Theory, Research, and Treatment* (p. 11). Copyright © 1997 by Allyn & Bacon. Reprinted by permission.

attention in the workplace (Gutek, 1985, 2001). Men and women receive a comparable number of sexual overtures, but women are more likely than men to judge this behavior as sexual harassment (Rotundo et al., 2001). These different standards are a factor in sexual harassment. For example, men and women disagree over whether repeated offers for dates constitute sexual harassment; men find this behavior less harassing than women do. Gutek (1985) found that the biggest gender difference concerning sexuality at work had to do with attitudes about sexual propositions. She found that two-thirds of the men in her study said that they felt flattered by such propositions, but only 17% of women felt the same way. Indeed, over 60% of the women said that they would feel insulted by a sexual proposition at work. The main problem, however, comes from the lack of understanding of each other's perceptions; neither the men nor the women in Gutek's study were aware of the perceptions of the other gender. The men believed that the women felt flattered by sexual attention when in actuality a majority of the women felt insulted or angered. During the years since Gutek's study, publicity, personal experience, and sexual harassment training have brought attitudes of women and men closer, and both have become more likely to identify unwanted sexual attention of all types as sexual harassment (Weiner, Voss, Winter, & Arnot, 2005).

Although men are the most frequent perpetrators of sexual harassment, they can also be the targets. The legal definition did not specify the gender of the target, but a 1998 U.S. Supreme Court decision (*Oncale v Sundowner Offshore Services, Inc.*) declared that men could be victims of sexual harassment. Reports of complaints to the EEOC (2006), surveys of employed men and women (Rospenda, Richman, & Shannon, 2009), and research with military personnel (Gradus, Street, Kelly, & Stafford, 2008) revealed that sexual harassment with male targets was much less common than with female targets. About 15% of the complaints filed with the EEOC (2006) come from men.

Although women often feel insulted and angered by sexual comments and propositions from supervisors and coworkers, they may have problems in labeling these behaviors as harassment (Gutek & Done, 2001; Tinkler, 2008). In addition, feeling harassed is not the same as experiencing a situation that meets the legal definition of sexual harassment. Therefore, the estimates about rates for harassment may be low if the figures are based on personal reports with a question about experiencing a specific type of sexual harassment or high if the figures are based on personal judgments of feeling harassed. When using a personal definition (Gutek & Done, 2001), between 35 and 50% of women have experienced sexual harassment at work. For men, at least 9% and up to 37% have experienced sexual harassment. However, most fail to report the harassment; some do not tell anyone, and only a small minority make use of their companies' policies to file a complaint.

Men who sexually harass women do not differ from employed men in general (Gutek, 1985, 2001), but an analysis of the situational as well as personal factors has been more useful in understanding those who harass. Men who are likely to sexually harass tend to view sex and power as linked, making them more likely to use their power at work to sexually exploit women who are their subordinates (Gutek & Done, 2001). Both men and women who were more tolerant of sexual harassment tended to hold hostile attitudes toward women (Russell & Trigg, 2004). In addition, some evidence (Done, 2000, in Gutek & Done, 2001) suggests that harassers of both genders have impulse control problems: They tend to act on rather than control their impulses to make sexual comments or overtures.

Women who are targets of harassment differ in some ways from typical women in the workforce; they are more likely to be unmarried, younger than the average employed woman, and attractive. Women who initiate sexual relationships at work are much less likely to be perceived as harassing men than vice versa, and, like the women who are the targets of harassment, they are younger and more likely to be unmarried than the average employed woman. In cases of men who reported that they were sexually harassed, their harassers were similar both to the women who initiated sex at work and to the women who were targets of harassment—young, unmarried, and attractive. These cases are consistent with Gutek's (1985) analysis of sex role spillover, when sexuality becomes part of the workplace.

Sexual harassment has both personal and professional effects. A meta-analysis of effects of workplace sexual harassment (Willness, Steel, & Lee, 2007) found that this experience has negative career and mental health consequences. The experience of sexual harassment is associated with decreased job satisfaction, increased intentions to quit, and higher job turnover; the health effects include physical health problems and mental health effects such as depression and symptoms of posttraumatic stress disorder. Even a few inappropriate questions of a sexual nature during a job interview negatively affected women's interview behavior, which demonstrates how easily sexual harassment can affect careers (Woodzicka & LaFrance, 2005). The effects on men's careers are not clear because so little research has concentrated on men's reactions to sexual harassment. However, men's experience of sexuality at work meets their definition of harassment less often than women's definition (Rotundo et al., 2001).

Perhaps the differences in consequences of sexuality at work explain the differences in perceptions of harassment; why should men feel harassed by sex at work when they are very unlikely to experience negative consequences? Why should women welcome sexual attention at work when their esteem and careers are so much more likely to be harmed? Given an equal interest in sexual relationships with people at work, the unequal consequences of sexual behavior on careers suggests that men and women should have different views of sexuality at work—and they do.

Considering Diversity

Diversity issues—more specifically, a lack of diversity—are evident in most workplaces. That lack of diversity may be traced to the concept of the "ideal worker" (Williams, 2000). The model for the ideal worker is male, which presents problems for women who pursue careers. The ideal is also White, so workers who are not White have disadvantages in hiring and career advancement. The image of the ideal worker is also able-bodied, which creates barriers for people with disabilities. Thus, many people in the workforce fail to meet this ideal in various ways. Despite the enormous changes that have made the current U.S. workforce more diverse than it has ever been, the assumption of White, male, able-bodied breadwinners continues to influence the cultural perception of workers, to the disadvantage of all the groups that fail to meet this description.

As a result, not only women but also people from various ethnic groups are less common among the upper ranks of corporate management, science, law, and technology. Figure 12.3 (page 328) shows the underrepresentation and overrepresentation in various occupations held by women, African Americans, and Hispanic Americans. (The categories of African American and Hispanic American represent both men and women from these ethnic groups, not just women, so the percentages in the *women* category overlap with the other two categories.) The under- and overrepresentations appear in terms of deviations from the center line, which ties representation to the percentage of employed people in these

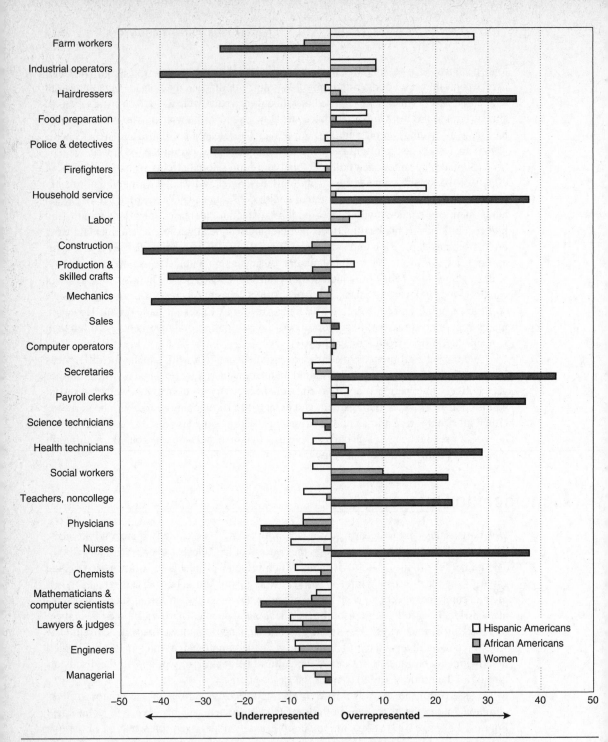

FIGURE 12.3 *Representation of Women, African Americans, and Hispanic Americans in Various Occupations*

Source: Statistical Abstract of the United States, 2002 (122nd ed., pp. 381–383), by U.S. Bureau of the Census, 2002, Washington, DC: U.S. Government Printing Office.

groups: 46.4% women, 12.8% African American, and 13.0% Hispanic American. Thus, categories for which the bars deviate little from the centerline indicate that individuals hold such jobs in about the same proportion as they participate in the workforce. Deviations indicate disproportionate numbers of women, African Americans, or Hispanic Americans in that occupation. For example, all three groups are underrepresented for most of the managerial and professional categories, meaning that women, African Americans, and Hispanic Americans do not occupy these prestigious, lucrative jobs as often as White men do. In contrast, women are overrepresented in the category of secretaries, and both African Americans and Hispanic Americans are overrepresented in the category of laborers. All three categories are overrepresented in household service. These jobs are premier examples of the "sticky floor," positions in which people get stuck at the bottom of the job hierarchy.

Some African Americans succeed in attaining the highest levels of career success (Cobbs & Turnock, 2003). But Stephen Carter (1991) contended that African Americans have to work harder than Whites to achieve, and they receive less credit when they do. The stereotyping for African Americans (just as stereotyping for women) casts African Americans as less capable and less motivated than Whites. Additional suspicion of successful African Americans comes from affirmative action, which gives ethnic minorities and women advantages in education and hiring to compensate for past (and, in many cases, continuing) discrimination. Many people believe that the only reason ethnic minorities are able to attend prestigious schools or get lucrative jobs is because of affirmative action. This policy has allowed African Americans to enter elite schools and prestigious jobs by making the entrance criteria lower than for Whites. The chances for advancement, however, have been slimmer: "Once hired, people who are not white face difficulties in finding mentors, powerful institutional figures to smooth their paths; then they will naturally advance more slowly" (Carter, 1991, p. 64).

Later research (Gilbert, Carr-Ruffino, Ivancevich, & Lownes-Jackson, 2003) confirmed Carter's beliefs: Stereotypes influence judgments and evaluations of ability and performance in much the same way that Carter himself had experienced. African American men were judged as less competent, less polite, and less committed to work than Asian Americans or African American women. Thus, this type of bias may put African American men in the position that Carter described—having to work twice as hard to be considered half as good.

Asian Americans are also subject to stereotyping, but this process can help them in certain careers. The stereotype holds that Asian Americans are hardworking, intelligent, and oriented toward science and technology, which pushes them toward careers in these areas, but hinders choices for other careers. For example, one study (King, Madera, Hebl, Knight, & Mendoza, 2006) showed that Asian Americans did not even have to submit a good resume to be considered for a high-status position, whereas even with a good resume, African Americans did not receive high evaluations. Their success has ruled Asian Americans out of the category of "real" minorities (Sakamoto, Goyette, & Kim, 2009), and workplace initiatives to diversify may thus exclude Asian Americans (Ragaza, 1999).

Women and ethnic minorities are not the only groups at a disadvantage in the world of work. People with disabilities face prejudice and discrimination, and disabled women in the workforce encounter barriers on the basis of both their gender and their handicapping condition (McLain & Perkins, 1990; Olkin, 2008; Randolph & Andresen, 2004). These biases result in unemployment and underemployment for these women. The unemployment rate among women with disabilities is about 55% for those who reported some limitation due to their disability; about 45% of men in this category were unemployed (Randolph & Andresen, 2004). When their conditions pose no limitations on employment, 25% of women were unemployed, but only 11% of men. In addition, disabled women who are employed earn less money than nondisabled women (who earned less than nondisabled men) (Olkin, 2008). Women with disabilities have disadvantages compared not only to able-bodied women but also to men who have disabilities. Such women are "at the bottom of the work heap" (McLain & Perkins, 1990, p. 54).

■ Summary

Career development has been associated with men, but women in industrialized countries now expect to pursue careers as well as have a family. Although career motivation is similar for men and women, social forces still pull women toward domesticity rather than toward careers. The limitations on women's careers come from their career choices and training, interruptions in their employment, and discrimination in hiring and promotion.

Career choices and preparation lead men into more prestigious and lucrative occupations. Women with high ability in math and science tend not to pursue engineering, science, and technology careers at the same rate as talented men do. Different pay for female-dominated occupations is a big factor in the gender wage gap, but discrimination in hiring is a major factor in the wage gap between men and women, even when they choose the same careers. Stereotyping biases perceptions of women's commitment and qualifications, and women receive lower salary offers than comparably qualified men. In addition, interruptions in employment affect careers negatively. This experience is more common to women, who more often interrupt their careers to devote time to families.

Women occupy a very small percentage of executive positions, often being blocked in their career progress by an invisible barrier called the glass ceiling, which limits women's careers throughout the world. Many factors have contributed to the formation of barriers to the advancement of women and people from ethnic minorities, but a male-dominated corporate culture is an important factor. Thus, tokens such as women or people form minority groups are excluded and have difficulty forming important mentoring relationships. Gender stereotypes influence perceptions of female managers' performance by making their gender so prominent that their competence becomes difficult to acknowledge. Gender stereotypes of competence can boost men in gender-typical careers, giving them a ride on the glass escalator that takes them to the top. Even women who have comparable training, personal backgrounds, and performance do not advance in their careers as rapidly as men do, which shows evidence of discrimination in career advancement.

Gender-based interactions at work obstruct women from gaining power and from demonstrating their competence, as these characteristics are not part of the feminine stereotype. Women who fail to adhere to traditional standards of femininity can be penalized, but by following these "feminine" standards, women cannot succeed in the corporate world. Women can gain power at work, but they have to overcome many barriers to do so.

Balancing work and family is a task for both men and women, but the gender role for women holds that they, rather than men, should devote themselves to family concerns. These social expectations lead men toward and women away from career success by placing the burdens of household chores and child care on women. Ironically, taking care of their families by being the primary breadwinner takes men away from their families. Work and family both require time and effort, but research indicates that both employment and family are positive factors in health and well-being.

The workforce is gender segregated, and few occupations have an equal proportion of men and women. Even in occupations that are not gender segregated, job situations may be. However, women have moved into traditionally male-dominated fields more rapidly than men have moved into female-dominated fields. Gender segregation on the job has resulted in certain jobs being associated with one gender, and this situation has resulted in spillover of male and female characteristics into the work environment. This gender role spillover tends to produce stereotypical patterns of interaction between men and women, rather than interaction between equal coworkers, bringing gender role stereotyping into the workplace.

Another consequence of gender stereotyping at work is sexuality and sexual harassment. Although illegal, both women and men are pressured for sexual favors from employees and supervisors and are subjected to unwanted sexual attention or hostile comments concerning characteristics and behaviors of their gender. Women are more likely than men to find sexual attention unwanted, possibly because they are more likely to be harmed by sexual relationships with coworkers. Women are more likely to label their experiences as sexual harassment than are men, especially for behaviors that fall into the hostile environment form of sexual harassment. Both men and women tend to agree that sexual coercion constitutes harassment.

Individuals from ethnic minorities also experience barriers to career success, and African Americans and Hispanic Americans are harmed by stereotyping, discrimination in hiring and promotions, and gender segregation. Asian Americans tend to be advantaged by their stereotypes. All ethnic minorities and women suffer from their discrepancy from the ideal worker model, which also poses a disadvantage for people with disabilities.

■ Glossary

gender harassment   a type of sexual harassment that occurs when people are subjected to offensive or hostile behavior because of their gender.

glass ceiling   the invisible barrier that seems to prevent women and ethnic minorities from reaching the highest levels of their professions.

hostile environment sexual harassment   the type of sexual harassment that occurs when employers allow offensive elements to exist in the work environment.

quid pro quo sexual harassment   sexual harassment in the form of demands for sexual favors in exchange for employment or promotion.

sex role spillover   the hypothesis that gender role characteristics spill over into the workplace, creating stereotyping and a sexualized atmosphere.

sexual harassment   unwanted sexual attention.

token   a symbol or an example, in this case of a minority group.

■ Suggested Readings

Catalyst. (2005). *Women "take care," men "take charge": Stereotyping of U.S. business leaders exposed.* Retrieved July 13, 2006, from www.catalyst.org/ knowledge/ alpha.shtml.
This report is based on research with U.S. businessmen and details how stereotyping continues to handicap women's career progress.

Eagly, Alice H. & Carli, Linda L. (2007). *Through the labyrinth: The truth about how women become leaders.* Boston: Harvard Business School Press.
Eagly and Carli compare the progress of women's careers to negotiating a labyrinth rather than breaking through a glass ceiling. In this readable book, these prominent researchers review the theories and research on women's careers.

Gutek, Barbara. (2001). Women and paid work. *Psychology of Women Quarterly, 25,* 379–393.
Gutek compares the field of working women in 1981 with that in 2001, noting the changes that have occurred not only for women but also for research into careers, stereotyping, leadership, and sexual harassment.

Williams, Joan C. & Cooper, Holly Cohen. (2004). The public policy of motherhood. *Journal of Social Issues, 60,* 849–865.
Williams is an attorney who has explored the complexities of gender and work. She and Cohen discuss how women vary from the ideal worker and how motherhood is an additional complication. They make some radical suggestions about how to manage this situation.

13 Health and Fitness

"The biggest fiction behind James Bond is that the fantasy master spy and world-class heartbreaker lived past 40-something. It's not just the death traps and the vodka martinis, or even the three packs of cigarettes a day, that would have shortened his life. His naked ring finger would have too" (Sheehy, 2006, p. 4). Gail Sheehy used James Bond to illustrate an interesting finding related to health: As an unmarried man, James Bond would be vulnerable both to poorer health and a shorter life.

HEADLINE

Why Marriage Is Good Medicine for Men

Parade, June 18, 2006

Marriage acts to enhance health and extend life, and men benefit more than women (Felder & Zhang, 2006). However, men do not necessarily perceive their advantages as clearly as women see them (Dempsey, 2002). Marriage benefits (and their unequal distribution) have led to an examination of how marriage might affect health and life expectancy and what occurs in marriage that benefits men more than women. As Sheehy pointed out, women provide emotional support and monitor their husbands' health-related behaviors, both of which are important to health. For husbands, wives provide the most important source of social support, urging husbands to seek medical care and maintain healthy habits such as eating a healthy diet, exercising, and not smoking. This urging, sometimes described as nagging, is the subject of many jokes but actually benefits men's health (Markey, Markey, Schneider, & Brownlee, 2005). Men do not do as well at providing emotional support for their wives, nor do husbands urge wives to seek health care. This difference in behavior is one reason that marriage improves men's health more than women's.

Not all marriages are equally beneficial. As Sheehy's article pointed out, the quality of marriage is related to health: Good marriages benefit the health of both partners. Bad marriages may be detrimental to health, especially for women (Williams, Sassier, & Nicholson, 2008), but a cumulative disadvantage appeared for both men and women in unhappy marriages (Umberson, Williams, Powers, Hui, & Needham, 2006). That is, unhappy partners really may make each other sick.

Therefore, marriage may be good medicine for men and provide benefits for women as well, but marriage itself is not the benefit. Instead, caring relationships provide a framework for healthy living, including benefits for physical health and longer life. However, men have shorter life expectancies (Simon, 2004), which indicates a complex role for gender in health and longevity.

Mortality: No Equal Opportunity

One of the puzzles in the area of health research can be summarized by the phrase "Women are sicker; men die quicker" (in Altman, 1997, p. 18). That is, women have higher **morbidity**—higher rates of illness—but they also have a lower death rate—lower **mortality**. Longer life expectancy for women is not a recent development, nor is it restricted to any ethnic group. Figure 13.1 (page 334) highlights the longer life expectancy for women in the United States over the past 100 years and projected into the near future. Notice the difference between life expectancy for Whites and nonwhites, including the small discrepancies between men and women in the early 1900s, the advantage for Whites, and the increasing discrepancy in life expectancies for nonwhite women and men after 1910.

The combination of women's longer life and poorer health is puzzling. The female gender role permits sickness to be acknowledged more readily than does men's gender role, thus providing one possibility for women's higher morbidity rates. As Sheehy's (2006) headline article described, women also tend to monitor their own health more vigilantly than men do and to seek health care when they perceive a problem. Thus, women seek and receive more health care than men, which may relate to their lower mortality rates—women are better at prevention. Also, women practice better health behaviors, which lower the risks for the leading causes of death in the United States and other industrialized countries. Three causes of death account for about 62% of all deaths in the United States, and all three show gender differences. For cardiovascular disease, cancer, and accidents, men tend to die at younger ages than women, resulting in higher overall death rates and death at younger ages for men.

Cardiovascular Disease

Cardiovascular disease (CVD) includes a group of diseases involving the heart and circulatory system, some—but not all—of which are life threatening. For example, angina pectoris is a cardiovascular disease that causes shortness of breath, difficulty in performing physical activities, and chest pain, but it poses no immediate threat to life. On the other hand, myocardial infarction (heart attack) and stroke can be immediately fatal. Cardiovascular disease is the leading cause of death, accounting for 34% of deaths in the United States in 2006 (Heron et al., 2009). Deaths from cardiovascular disease have decreased over the past 30 years, with deaths from stroke decreasing more rapidly than from heart disease.

As Table 13.1 (page 335) shows, heart disease mortality for women and men does not differ greatly over the life span—women have more fatal strokes than men do, but men die from CVD at younger ages than women do. The discrepancy in heart disease deaths for men and women between ages 35 and 74 is especially dramatic, showing how much men are affected by premature death from CVD.

The causes of cardiovascular disease are not well understood, but several physical conditions and behaviors are risk factors in the development of CVD. A **risk factor** refers to a condition associated with an increased probability that a disorder will develop. Sex is a risk factor for developing CVD before age 65, with men at elevated risk. The source of this difference is unclear, but research has focused on sex steroid hormones. Despite the

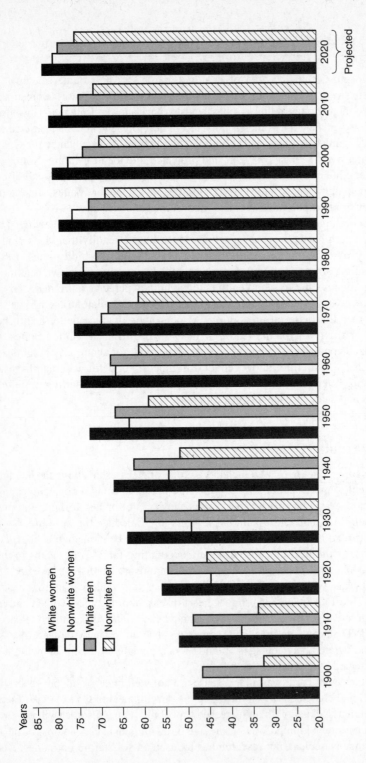

FIGURE 13.1 *Life Expectancy Increases for U.S. Women and Men from 1900 to 2020*

Sources: From Historical Statistics of the United States, Colonial Times to 1970 (p. 55), by U.S. Bureau of the Census, 1975, Washington, DC: U.S. Government Printing Office; and Statistical Abstract of the United States, 2009 (128th ed., Table 100), by U.S. Bureau of the Census, 2009, Washington, DC: U.S. Government Printing Office.

TABLE 13.1 *U.S. Death Rates for Cardiovascular Disease in Men and Women, 2005 (rates per 100,000 population)*

Age Range	Women		Men	
	Stroke	Heart Disease	Stroke	Heart Disease
15–24	0.5	1.7	0.4	3.6
25–34	1.2	5.3	1.5	10.8
35–44	5.1	17.1	5.2	40.7
45–54	13.6	49.2	16.5	131.5
55–64	27.9	129.1	38.5	306.9
65–74	90.5	372.7	113.6	692.3
75–84	349.5	1,210.5	372.9	1,829.4
85 +	1,196.1	4,610.8	1,023.3	5,143.4
All ages	57.8	218.9	38.8	221.1

Source: From *Health, United States, 2008* by National Center for Health Statistics, Tables 35 and 36. Hyattsville, MD: U.S. Government Printing Office.

belief that estrogen is protective, hormone replacement therapy carries more risks than benefits for older women (Writing Group for the Women's Health Initiative Investigators, 2002); hormone replacement is not a recommended treatment to lower the risk of CVD (Vitale, Mendolsohn, & Rosano, 2009). If hormones were the main source of heart disease, then the gender differences in CVD would apply to all times and all societies, which they do not. Indeed, the gender gap was much smaller during the 1800s, began to widen during the 1920s, and has now begun to decrease. These changes suggest that social and behavioral factors are involved in this gender difference (Weidner & Cain, 2003).

Some authorities have suggested that behaviors associated with the male gender role may be dangerous (Courtenay, 2000; Nicholas, 2000). Lifestyle factors such as smoking and eating a high-fat diet are risk factors for cardiovascular disease, and more men than women smoke and eat diets high in fat. However, lifestyle factors alone do not account for gender differences in CVD. In a study that statistically adjusted for lifestyle factors (Fried et al., 1998), men were still about twice as likely to experience CVD as women. Therefore, gender differences in CVD risk remain poorly understood.

Women who develop CVD have several disadvantages, some of which relate to the disease itself, and some of which relate to women's treatment in the medical system. Since 1984, women have died of cardiovascular disease at overall higher rates than men, but the stereotype that connects men and heart disease prevents physicians from diagnosing women (Chiaramonte & Friend, 2006; Travis, 2005). Women and men with the same symptoms of heart disease do not receive the same diagnosis or recommendations for care (Bönte et al., 2008). Physicians refer men who have symptoms of CVD for further testing, preventive interventions, and treatment more often than they refer women with similar symptoms (Vaccarino et al., 2005). Ethnicity is also a factor in diagnosis; African Americans' symptoms are undertreated compared to symptoms of Whites, and African American women's symptoms are overlooked more than those of any other group. Thus, the bias against women intersects with biases of ethnicity.

In summary, cardiovascular disease, including heart disease and stroke, is the leading cause of death in the United States and other industrialized nations, accounting for about 34% of all deaths. Men die of heart disease at younger ages than women do, but overall, more women than men die of CVD. These gender differences in risk are not clearly understood, but both physiological and lifestyle differences between the two genders contribute to differences in risk.

Cancer

Cancer is the term applied to a variety of malignant neoplasms—tissues that undergo uncontrolled growth that may form a tumor, as well as spread to other areas of the body. Such uncontrolled tissue growth can become life-threatening; cancer is the second leading cause of death in the United States, accounting for about 23% of all deaths (Heron et al., 2009).

Men have higher overall death rates from cancer than women do for most types of cancer and at most ages. Table 13.2 presents the incidence and mortality rates for women and men for various types of cancers among several ethnic groups in the United States. Incidence represents how often people develop these cancers, whereas the mortality rate reflects how deadly each type of cancer is. For example, the incidence for lung cancer is not as high as some other cancers, but its mortality rate is the highest for any cancer for both women and men. As Table 13.2 shows, differences exist for both gender and ethnicity.

Cigarette smoking is a major factor in cancer death rates, especially lung cancer. Until recently, men smoked at a much higher rate than women, but women's increased use of tobacco is a factor in the narrowing of the gender gap in longevity (Simon, 2004). Women have begun to develop lung cancer at increased rates, whereas men's rates have leveled off. In 1986, lung cancer surpassed breast cancer as the leading cause of cancer deaths among women.

Use of tobacco products accounts for about 30% of cancers, and the combination of diet, physical inactivity, and obesity for another 35% (American Cancer Society, 2008). In addition to foods that contain known or suspected carcinogens, dietary components have been implicated in the development of cancer, especially a high-fat diet. A substantial amount of evidence indicates that people who eat a high-fat diet are at increased risk for cancers of the digestive tract, plus an elevated risk for breast cancer (Brannon & Feist, 2010). On the average, women eat lower-fat diets and more fruits and vegetables than men, so this behavioral difference in diet may explain part of the discrepancy in cancer death rates.

Occupational exposure accounts for about 4% of cancer deaths. Men are at increased risk for cancer due to their exposure to workplace hazards (American Cancer Society, 2008; Courtenay, 2000). Men are more likely than women to hold jobs that bring them into contact with carcinogens such as asbestos, benzene, and various petroleum products. Exposure to such substances may also be a factor in the difference in cancer deaths between women and men.

Sexual behavior and reproduction also contribute to the development of cancer. Women who have sexual intercourse at an early age and have many sexual partners are at elevated risk for infection with the human papillomavirus, which causes cervical cancer (American Cancer Society, 2008). However, women who complete pregnancies before age 20

TABLE 13.2   *U.S. Incidence and Death Rates for Cancers in Women and Men by Ethnicity (rates per 100,00 population, 2005)*

	Women							
	Lung		Breast		Colon and Rectum		Cervix	
Ethnic Group	Incidence	Death Rate	Incidence	Death Rate	Incidence	Death Rate	Incidence	Death Rate
White	54.8	44.3	133.6	25.0	40.6	15.6	24.3	2.4
African American	56.4	39.9	113.9	33.5	51.4	22.4	19.5	7.4
Asian American	29.3	18.5	91.2	12.6	35.2	10.2	15.8	2.4
American Indian	36.7	33.8	97.2	17.1	41.9	14.2	7.2	2.8
Hispanic American	20.7	14.6	89.7	15.8	31.3	10.8	14.2	3.4

	Men							
	Lung		Prostate		Colon and Rectum		Bladder	
Ethnic Group	Incidence	Death Rate	Incidence	Death Rate	Incidence	Death Rate	Incidence	Death Rate
White	72.2	74.2	145.3	24.6	53.7	22.5	40.2	7.8
African American	93.6	93.1	220.3	59.4	62.7	31.8	19.8	5.4
Asian American	55.4	37.5	89.7	11.0	45.5	14.4	16.4	2.9
American Indian	55.5	50.2	69.5	21.1	49.7	20.5	12.5	2.6
Hispanic American	39.7	35.1	142.3	20.6	43.3	16.5	19.9	4.1

Sources: *Health, United States, 2008* by National Center for Health Statistics by National Center for Health Statistics, 2009, Hyattsville, MD, Tables 37, 38, NS 39 for incidence rates; and *U.S. and SEER Death Rates by Primary Cancer Site and Race/Ethnicity, 2001-2005* for death rates. Retrieved November 5, 2009, from http://seer.cancer.gov/csr/1975_2005/results_single/sect_01_table.11_2pgs.pdf

are at decreased risk for breast cancer compared to women with later pregnancies and women who do not bear children (Adami & Trichopoulos, 2002). Thus, early intercourse presents a risk for cancer, whereas early pregnancy is a protection against cancer.

Men's sexual behavior can place them at risk for cancer; twice as many men as women engage in risky sexual behaviors. Their behavior can also be a risk for their female sex partners (Courtenay, 2000). Men who are the receptive partner in unprotected anal intercourse are at increased risk for anal cancer as well as for infection with the human immunodeficiency virus (HIV). One of the diseases associated with HIV/AIDS is a form of cancer called Kaposi's sarcoma. Men who have many sexual partners, especially

◼ GENDERED VOICES

I Have Breast Cancer

An announcement of breast cancer is shocking but not unusual—unless the person is a man. That unusual situation happened to Robert Riter (1997), who noticed a lump in his breast. Like many other people, Riter thought it was a cyst and that it would go away. When he started bleeding from his nipple, he sought medical advice and treatment. His treatment included a biopsy, which revealed a malignancy. Although breast cancer is rare among men, the disease affects more than 1,000 men per year in the United States.

Riter's experience was both similar to and different from women's experience of breast cancer. Like many women, he had a mastectomy and chemotherapy. Unlike many women, losing the breast was not as traumatic an event for him. His greatest distress came from examining the survival statistics, which are virtually identical for men and women. Riter learned that his chances of surviving for 5 years were about 80%, but his likelihood of living 10 years was only about 60%.

Riter was the first man to join his area's support group for breast cancer survivors. "I'm probably not the only male in this area with the disease, but . . . men find it hard to discuss their prostate cancer, let alone a 'female' disease," he said (Riter, 1997, p. 14). He also encountered some surprised reactions, like the lab technician who questioned the referral slip with the diagnosis of breast cancer. He felt odd going to a "women's imaging center" to get a mammogram and he said, "My follow-up letter from the center was addressed to Ms. Robert Riter. The radiology tech did note that I had the hairiest chest she's ever seen in a mammogram room" (p. 14).

Riter noted that his experience with breast cancer had taught him more about women's health issues than he would otherwise have known, but having a life-threatening "female disease" was a difficult way for him to gain knowledge and empathy.

---

men who purchase sex, endanger their female partners by elevating the women's risk for cervical cancer by infecting them with the human papillomavirus. In addition, poor genital hygiene in men is associated with increased risk of cervical cancer in their female sexual partners.

Cancer of the genitals and reproductive tract plus breast cancer deaths account for a large proportion of women's cancer deaths during their early and middle-adult years. Indeed, before age 65, cancer is responsible for a greater proportion of women's deaths than is cardiovascular disease. The opposite pattern occurs for men, who are more vulnerable to premature death from CVD than from cancer.

Violent Deaths

Unintentional injuries (accidents) are the 5th, suicide the 11th, and homicide the 15th leading cause of death in the United States (Heron et al., 2009). Added together, these acts of violence account for about 6% of deaths in the United States. This number reflects a relatively high rate of violence compared to other industrialized, economically developed countries. Violent death rates are lower in Australia, Canada, Japan, most of the countries in Western Europe, Scandinavia, and other countries scattered throughout the world (*Britannica Book of the Year*, 2002). Moreover, violent death is the leading cause of death

TABLE 13.3 *U.S. Death Rates from Accidents and Violence, 2005 (rates per 100,000 population)*

Cause	European American		African American		Hispanic American	
	Women	Men	Women	Men	Women	Men
Motor vehicle accidents	9.4	22.0	7.6	22.5	7.8	21.3
Firearms-related injuries	2.7	15.3	3.6	36.4	1.6	13.3
Suicide	5.3	21.2	1.9	9.2	1.7	9.4
Homicide	1.8	3.5	6.1	37.3	1.8	12.1

Source: Health, United States, 2008, by National Center for Health Statistics, 2009, Hyattsville, MD: U.S. Government Printing Office.

for adolescents and young adults in the United States. Men are about three times more likely than women to die from violent deaths. This discrepancy holds for all ages, from birth until old age, but the differences are most pronounced early in life.

Ethnicity plays a major role in risk of violence. As Table 13.3 shows, African Americans in the United States are much more likely than European Americans or Hispanic Americans to die from accidents and homicides, but European Americans are more likely to die from motor vehicle crashes and suicide. African American men are disproportionately vulnerable to deaths from homicide, but gender differences are more prominent than ethnic differences.

The gender differences in risky behaviors account for the differences in violent deaths. Men tend to behave in ways that increase their risks, such as heavy alcohol use, low seat belt use, occupational risks, and illegal activities. Alcohol use increases the chances of accidents, suicide, and homicide (Rehm et al., 2003). By slowing responses and altering judgment, alcohol contributes to traffic crashes. People who have been drinking (even those who are not legally intoxicated) are more likely to be involved in fatal traffic accidents; about half of all traffic fatalities are related to alcohol. Seat belt use is an important factor in reducing traffic fatalities, and women are more likely than men to use seat belts (Eaton et al., 2008). For the same reasons that alcohol use increases the chances of traffic accidents, alcohol use is also related to deaths from falls, fires, and drownings as well as from boating, airplane, and industrial accidents. Intoxication also increases the chances of becoming a pedestrian victim of an auto accident (Courtenay, 2000).

The gender differences in percentage of drinkers has decreased, but men are more often drinkers and are more than twice as likely to binge drink than women (National Center for Health Statistics [NCHS], 2009). Younger adults tend to be heavier drinkers. These gender and age differences in drinking patterns correspond to the differential risks of violent death. With increases in women's drinking have come increases in problem drinking among women. These changes have the potential to decrease the current female advantage in avoiding violent death in alcohol-related accidents.

Men are also more likely to hold dangerous jobs than women are (Saulcy, 2005). In addition to exposure to hazardous materials, which increases the chances of cancer, men are more likely than women to have jobs that involve working around or operating dangerous machinery. More than 90% of workplace fatalities involve men. Therefore, occupational hazards and violence are substantial factors contributing to the gender difference in accidental deaths.

Women are more likely to attempt suicide, but men are more likely to actually commit suicide (NCHS, 2005). This difference in suicide rates for men and women began to appear during the 1950s, increased during the 1960s, and began to decrease during the 1970s. The ratio of attempted to completed suicides is about 10 to 1. The main reason for men's higher rates of completed suicides is the tendency to choose more lethal methods, such as guns and jumping from high places, whereas women more often attempt suicide by taking drugs. (No method is certain to be nonlethal, so any suicide attempt is serious.) The lethality of the methods chosen produces higher suicide rates among men, despite women's more frequent attempts.

Chapter 8 described gender differences in the crime rate, explaining that men are more likely than women to commit crimes. This discrepancy is even greater for crimes involving violence, in which men are more likely to both perpetrate crimes and be victims (U.S. Census Bureau, 2009a). The increase in lawbreaking among women in the past decades has not changed these figures; women's increase reflects primarily nonviolent crimes. Thus, homicide affects men to a larger degree than women and has an especially disproportionate impact on young African American men.

In summary, men are more often the victims of unintentional and intentional violence than are women. Men's increased risk comes from several sources, including their heavier use of alcohol, heightened risk of workplace accidents, greater frequency of completed suicides, and greater involvement in illegal activities. In addition, men are less likely to take protective measures, such as using seat belts. All of these causes of violent deaths put men at a survival disadvantage and account for some of women's survival advantage. Women, however, do not experience the same advantage when seeking health care; women experience greater morbidity than men and have more difficulty receiving treatment for serious conditions than men do.

The Health Care System

Women may live longer than men, but they are sick more often. Defining what constitutes being sick is not simple, but doctor visits, hospital admissions, restriction of activities, or reports of distress are some of the indicators; women meet any of these definitions of illness more often than men do (Chrisler, 2001). The combination of greater morbidity with lower mortality seems a contradiction, but sex and gender roles as well as physiology contribute to the situation. Women's reproduction and its medicalized treatment account for increased use of medical services among women: Pregnancy and childbirth are functions that now receive medical attention, require medical appointments, and prompt hospitalization. Another possibility is that women are not as healthy as men, but that their health problems are less often life threatening, producing the combination of poorer health but longer lives. A third explanation involves the difference in gender roles related to seeking and receiving health care.

Gender Roles and Health Care

People seek and receive health care from a variety of formal and informal sources, and gender roles affect receiving help from each source. Traditional male and female gender roles differ in the amounts of vulnerability each is allowed and the permissibility of seeking help. One facet of the masculine role, the Sturdy Oak, holds that men are strong and invulnerable; this aspect of the role causes men to refrain from showing signs of physical illness or seeking medical care (Brannon, 1976). The traditional female role, on the other hand, allows and even encourages weakness and vulnerability for emotional and physical problems (Lorber, 1975). Adherence to traditional gender roles may, therefore, hinder men from seeking help for their symptoms, but elements of the traditional feminine gender role relate to greater distress for women as well as to their increased readiness to seek medical care. After women and men enter the health care system, gender is also a factor in the care they receive.

Gender and Seeking Health Care. The decision to seek medical care is influenced by many factors, including the perception of symptoms and beliefs about the consequences of seeking or failing to seek treatment. People who feel healthy may enter the medical care system to receive routine exams—or not. They may find it easy to ignore checkups and screenings as long as they feel well. Men are more likely to avoid regular health care; men are less likely than women to have regular physicians (Galdas, Cheater, & Marshall, 2005). When men avoid having checkups for years, they explain these omissions in terms consistent with the masculine gender role, saying that they feel fine and thus do not need to consult physicians. This belief can be fatal; the first sign of heart disease can be a fatal heart attack; many cancers do not produce symptoms in the early stages. Nonetheless, the belief that a lack of symptoms equals good health can lead men to avoid regular contacts with the health care system.

Women, on the other hand, find it more difficult to avoid the health care system, regardless of how well they may feel. Young women must seek medical advice to obtain many forms of contraception, especially birth control pills (Chrisler, 2001). These young women count in the statistics as having consulted physicians, although their medical visits involve no illness. Such medical consultations often include physical examinations that may reveal health problems that require additional treatment. For example, blood tests may reveal anemia, and blood pressure readings may show hypertension. Each of these conditions merits further treatment, which leads these women into additional physician visits and medication. Young men receive no comparable medical attention during young adulthood that might reveal physical problems; these differences in treatment for healthy young men and women contribute to the statistics concerning gender differences in receiving health care.

The personal perception of symptoms is an important factor in seeking medical care. People who sense that their bodies are not working correctly are more likely to seek medical advice than those who sense no problems, and women are more likely than men report symptoms and physical distress (Koopmans & Lamers, 2007). Perceiving symptoms, however, is not sufficient to prompt a health care visit—most people experience some reluctance to become part of the health care system (Brannon & Feist, 2010). This reluctance may spring from costs or accessibility of medical care and anxiety over a threatening diagnosis. Scheduling of appointments and changing daily routines to keep these medical appointments are additional barriers.

The factors that influence reluctance to seek medical care may not affect men and women equally. Women are more likely than men to be outside the paid workforce and to be employed on a part-time basis, whereas men are more likely to have the types of jobs that offer health insurance benefits (Zoller, 2005). Women who are not employed can receive these benefits if they are married to men who have good insurance plans. For both men and women in these situations, continued health insurance depends on the continued employment of the spouse and the continuation of the marriage. Not only can women lose their health insurance through divorce, but children can also lose insurance coverage due to their parents' divorce. Mothers are most often granted custody, and the children may lose their coverage unless their mothers have employment that includes these benefits. Thus, women and children are less likely to have health insurance than men are, limiting their access to health care.

Men and women also seek health care from different types of providers (Kane, 1991). Both women and men are more likely to consult pharmacists than any other category of health care professional, and women make more inquiries than men, but those women may be fulfilling their role as family care giver and making inquiries for others. Men experience more injuries due to accidents and sports participation, so they are more likely to seek the services of physiotherapists than are women. On the other hand, women are more likely to seek the services of chiropractors or nutritionists (Barnes, Powell-Griner, McFann, & Nahin, 2004). Women are also more likely to use alternative health care services, such as herbal medicine and acupuncture. None of these differences is large; thus, the types of health care professionals that men and women seek vary only to a small extent.

The different preferences in seeking medical care may be partly attributable to access to medical care, with women at a disadvantage due to their more limited financial resources and poorer insurance coverage. Another difference may lie in women's greater sensitivity to symptoms, but a difference also exists in the willingness to report symptoms. These differences are consistent with gender roles, with men denying and women accepting help.

Gender and Receiving Health Care.

After a person has contacted a health care professional and becomes part of the health care system, gender becomes a factor in treatment. Gender stereotypes influence the behavior of both patient and practitioner. Although some patients and practitioners are coming to view their relationship as a collaboration, the traditional conceptualization of the patient–practitioner relationship has included the subordinate patient and the controlling practitioner. The patient role is thus more compatible with the female than the male gender role, whereas the practitioner role is more consistent with stereotypical masculinity. The combination of gender roles and patient–provider roles puts women at a disadvantage in both giving and receiving medical care; as patients, women's descriptions of symptoms are ignored, and as physicians, patients have trouble recognizing their expertise (Chrisler, 2001; Shrier et al., 2007).

Men seem to have more trouble adopting the patient role than women do (Galdas et al., 2005). Being a patient requires a person to relinquish control and follow the advice or orders of the practitioner. Gender is not a reliable predictor of patient compliance (Brannon & Feist, 2010), but the combination of the demographic factors of gender, age, ethnic background, cultural norms, religion, and educational level relates to patients' compliance with physicians' treatment advice. Therefore, gender is only one factor from a configuration of variables that relates to compliance with medical advice. Indeed, the interaction between patient and practitioner is more important to the patient's willingness to follow health advice than a patient's personal characteristics, and gender often plays a role in that interaction.

The medical profession has been criticized for its treatment of female patients, and this criticism has taken several forms. The most radical form of criticism holds that women were healers throughout history but have been replaced by technological, male-dominated forms of healing, with dominant male physicians but subordinate female nurses (Ehrenreich & English, 1973). Other criticisms (Chrisler, 2001) have claimed that negative stereotypes of female patients have led to poorer levels of medical care for women than for men. Yet other criticisms (Dijkstra, Verdonk, & Lagro-Janssen, 2008; Zoller, 2005) have cited failures to include the most current research on gender differences in disease and responses to treatment, an overemphasis on individual responsibility, and an underemphasis on social circumstances that influence health-related behaviors and treatment seeking.

Physicians often have stereotypical views of women, and these views have an impact on their treatment of female patients (Chrisler, 2001). Medical school educational standards have promoted the view that women are emotional and incapable of providing accurate information about their bodies. Indeed, gender stereotypes provide a backdrop against which physicians communicate with, diagnose, and treat patients (Andersson, Salander, Brandstetter-Hiltunen, Knutsson, & Hamberg, 2008; Flanagan & Blashfield, 2005). An increasing percentage of physicians are women, and research with female physicians (Bertakis, 2009) revealed that female physicians spent more time with their patients, recommended more preventive services, and paid more attention to emotional issues, leading to higher patient satisfaction.

The view of "emotional females" may lead physicians to discount the information provided by female patients and to believe that women cannot participate in decisions concerning their own health and treatment (Munch, 2004). One study (Benrud & Reddy, 1998) demonstrated this situation by manipulating the information supplied; problems were the same for both male and female patients. Thus any differences that appeared in the resulting attributions by physicians would be due to the use of stereotypes of women and men in making judgments. People saw women's health problems as the result of relatively uncontrollable biological and emotional factors but judged men's problems as the result of controllable behavioral and situational factors. These attributions have the potential to make big differences in health care. Women's health problems may be viewed as "emotional problems," but men may receive blame for causing their own poor health through misbehavior.

Another criticism is aimed at a more subtle type of discrimination in medicine: the view that medical training presents men as the standard by which to measure all health concerns (Munch, 2004; Tavris, 1992). Physicians receive training in how to dissect and prescribe drugs for the standard patient—a 154-pound man. Directives for medical training in the United States addressed this deficit, but a survey of directors of medical training (Spencer & Kern, 2008) indicated that students who train in internal medicine may not receive adequate training to treat women.

In addition to holding men as the standard in medicine, medical research once routinely omitted women entirely as research participants. The rationale for omitting women was that women bias the research because of their low rates of certain diseases, and their hormonal variations affect the action of drugs. For example, middle-aged women develop CVD at a rate lower than middle-aged men, so longitudinal studies that follow healthy people until they show signs of CVD would have to include many more women than men to obtain a group with this disorder. Using only male participants results in studies that are easier to complete, but these studies reveal nothing about CVD in women. Assuming that women are similar to men in their development of CVD is unwarranted, because women are excluded from these studies precisely because of their physical differences. A similar rationale applied to developing and testing new drugs, and a similar problem arose as a result; omitting women from drug trials fails to establish the safety and effectiveness of drugs for women.

During the 1980s, the practice of excluding women from medical research received increasing criticism, and pressure mounted to give women's health additional emphasis. That pressure resulted in the creation of the Office of Research on Women's Health, a part of the National Institutes of Health (Kirschstein, 1991). This office's mission is to improve the prevention and treatment of diseases in women, and one of its first steps was to attempt to end the exclusion of women from medical research studies with the help of U.S. government sponsorship.

The Office of Research on Women's Health continues to focus on women's health issues, including monitoring research to ensure that women and minorities are included in health research in the United States (Office of Research on Women's Health, 2009). One of the research projects on women's health sponsored by this organization was the Women's Health Initiative, which made headlines in July, 2002, when researchers announced that the effects of hormone replacement therapy for menopausal symptoms produced higher risks than benefits, and the trial was halted (Writing Group for the Women's Health Initiative Investigators, 2002). This finding came as a surprise because of the widespread assumption that hormone replacement therapy not only relieved the symptoms of menopause but also lowered the risk of heart disease. The results of this study indicated the opposite; women taking the combination of estrogen and progestin experienced higher rates of breast cancer, heart disease, blood clots, and stroke than did women taking the placebo. Another surprising result from the Women's Health Initiative study on hormone replacement (Shumaker et al., 2003) showed that older women who take hormones increased their risk of developing Alzheimer's disease or other types of cognitive dementia. Again, the assumptions were that hormones protected against cognitive deficits in aging people, but the results showed otherwise. The risks from hormone replacement therapy may be substantially higher for postmenopausal than premenopausal women, but most physicians recommend caution in prescribing this course of treatment (Roberts, 2009). Therefore, the creation of a special branch of the National Institutes of Health specializing in women's health has provided valuable findings and continues to advocate for women's health.

Although medicine remains male-dominated, men are not the focus of health initiatives comparable to the Women's Health Initiative (Meryn, 2009). Indeed, men may not receive optimum or even adequate care. During childhood, parents are somewhat more likely to take their sons to the doctor than their daughters, but once men are responsible for seeking their own medical care, they tend to avoid regular medical care. Men seek care for their injuries, but not for regular exams and screening tests. Men were 70% of those in a survey who had not been to a physician in 5 years (Courtenay, 2000). Men were less likely to have regular physicians than women, so getting an appointment to see a physician is a greater inconvenience for a man because he must first find a physician.

Prostate cancer kills almost as many men as breast cancer kills women, yet funding for breast cancer research is many times greater than for prostate cancer (McBride, 2007). Men have not mobilized to exert the type of political pressure that spurs funding in the same way that women have, leaving men's health issues with fewer vocal advocates.

Men's advocacy influenced the development of gender-specific medicine (Legato, 2006), but women's health researchers are also enthusiastic about this approach (Hobson, 2006). Gender-specific medicine investigates gender differences in the development and progression of disease and in responses to treatment. This specialty does not center on reproductive issues but rather focuses on research that will address leading causes of death such as heart disease and cancer, hoping to tailor more effective treatments to men's and women's specific biology.

In summary, the Sturdy Oak component of the male gender role may be a factor in men's avoiding health care; feelings of invulnerability and the belief that illness represents weakness lead men to ignore their health. Such avoidance can result in serious health problems that might be prevented or detected through routine physical exams. Men can avoid regular physical exams more easily than women can; men typically do not seek the reproductive or contraceptive medical care that women do. Thus, men seldom use the health care system until they become ill, perhaps to the detriment of their health. Not only do reproduction and contraception concerns prompt women (but not men) to seek medical care during the reproductive years, but the differences in their reproductive systems also account for a large proportion of the gender difference in seeking and receiving health care.

Reproductive Health

Many encounters with the health care system for women do not involve illness but occur as a result of contraception, pregnancy, childbirth, and menopause. In addition, sex and reproductive issues have an impact that extends to other aspects of functioning, affecting emotion, beliefs, and identity throughout the life span (Murphy, 2003). Although these functions were completed throughout history with little medical assistance, they became increasingly "medicalized" during the 19th and 20th centuries (Ehrenreich & English, 1973; Ratcliff, 2002). During this time, college education was largely restricted to men, who came to dominate the growing profession of medicine.

This expansion of medicine included attending women during childbirth, a role previously performed by midwives. Childbirth was not the only function to gain medical attention; pregnancy came to be considered an appropriate area for regular medical care. The increasing number of contraceptive technologies during the 20th century depended almost exclusively on controlling women's (rather than men's) fertility, and physicians assumed control over access to contraception techniques such as birth control pills. During the middle of the 20th century, even menopause became a "disease" that could be "cured" by hormone replacement (Wilson, 1966). Thus, medical technologies came to be involved in all facets of women's reproductive health, from contraception during adolescence to hormone replacement during and after menopause.

Some critics have argued that women are burdened by giving birth in sterile, impersonal surroundings and being subjected to increasingly large hospital bills for these services. According to this argument, birth is a natural process requiring no medical intervention. However, comparing statistics from undeveloped countries and from the United States in the years before routine medical care during pregnancy and delivery, death could also be seen as a natural process. There is no question that technological medicine has dramatically cut both maternal and infant mortality (Kane, 1991). Nonetheless, women may receive too much treatment in some areas (as in too many hysterectomies or cesarean section deliveries) and too little in other respects (as in too little testing for heart disease).

Women's more numerous consultations with health care professionals are due largely to their complex reproductive systems (Chrisler, 2001). Not only do women get pregnant and bear children, but also their reproductive organs are subject to a greater variety of problems than are male organs. Figures 13.2 and 13.3 show the female and male reproductive systems. Except for children under age 15 years, girls and women receive more treatment for problems related to their reproductive systems than boys and men do.

Both systems can develop problems during prenatal development, producing congenital conditions that are more common in boys than in girls. During infancy and early

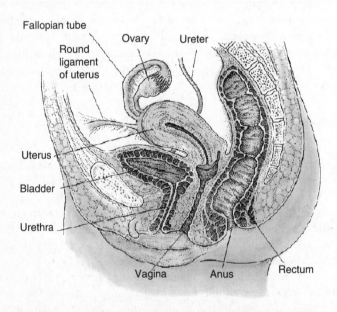

FIGURE 13.2   *Female Reproductive System*

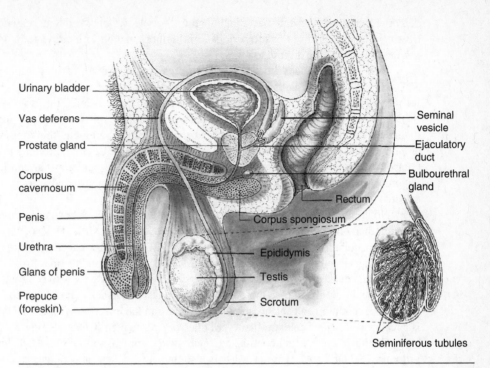

Urinary bladder

Vas deferens

Prostate gland

Corpus cavernosum

Penis

Urethra

Glans of penis

Prepuce (foreskin)

Seminal vesicle

Ejaculatory duct

Bulbourethral gland

Rectum

Corpus spongiosum

Epididymis

Testis

Scrotum

Seminiferous tubules

FIGURE 13.3 *Male Reproductive System*

childhood, boys have more problems with their genitourinary system than girls do, requiring more hospital stays and physician consultations for these problems (Kane, 1991). Beginning at age 15 years, girls make more visits to health care professionals, and require more hospitalizations regarding their reproductive systems. The majority of physician visits and hospitalizations for women during their reproductive years involve contraception, pregnancy, and childbirth; most of these contacts with the health care system are not due to illness or health problems but because women's reproductive functions have come under medical supervision (Ratcliff, 2002).

Many of the methods of contraception for women—birth control pills, implants, intrauterine devices (IUDs), diaphragms, sterilization, abortion—not only require medical supervision but also increase health risks. For example, birth control pills provide very effective contraception, but women over age 35 years who take contraceptive pills have significantly increased risks of stroke, and smoking multiplies this risk. Therefore, contraception is not only more often a woman's responsibility, but also more of a health threat to women.

Both men and women are subject to **sexually transmitted diseases (STDs)**, infectious diseases that are spread through sexual contact. The infectious agents can be bacterial, viral, fungal, or parasitic, and many can be transmitted by vaginal, oral, or anal sexual activity. These bacterial infections include gonorrhea, syphilis, and chlamydia, and they do not always produce symptoms that physicians find easy to diagnose in women (Zoller, 2005).

Although antibiotics can cure bacterial infections, people without symptoms may not receive treatment until their diseases are serious. Furthermore, delays in treatment allow infected persons to transmit the disease to others.

Delays in treatment are also likely to escalate the growth of fungal and parasitic STDs. *Candidiasis albicans,* a yeast-like fungus, produces itching and swelling of the genitals. It can be transmitted through sexual intercourse, but this infection is not always an STD; it is more common in women who take contraceptive pills or who are pregnant or diabetic. These conditions alter the chemistry of the vagina, allowing this fungus to grow at a rapid rate, producing annoying and painful symptoms. Chemical treatments exist to control this type of infection. Trichomonia is a one-celled parasite that can infect the vagina in women and the urethra in men. It is almost always sexually transmitted; an effective drug treatment exists.

No drugs exist to cure viral diseases. Thus, the viral STDs pose an even more serious problem than other types of STDs. Human immunodeficiency virus (HIV) is the virus that produces acquired immune deficiency syndrome (AIDS), a virus that can be sexually transmitted. The virus damages the immune system, leaving the body open to a variety of opportunistic diseases that eventually lead to death. Years may pass between time of infection and the development of symptoms, allowing infected persons to be unaware of the presence of the condition and able to unknowingly transmit the infection to others. HIV infection is a major worldwide health problem for both women and men (UNAIDS/WHO, 2008).

Genital herpes, viral hepatitis, and genital warts are also viral STDs. The human papillomavirus that causes genital warts is also the cause of cervical cancer, and a vaccine has been developed to prevent the transmission of this virus to those who are not infected (Pichichero, 2006). Recommendations include vaccinating girls who have not yet become sexually active to prevent infection with this virus, decreasing the incidence of cervical cancer. For those who are infected and who develop genital warts, treatments include surgical removal. Several medications exist to manage the symptoms of herpes infections. Like other viral infections, these STDs are difficult to manage and are presently without a cure. In addition, infection with any STD makes a person more vulnerable to HIV infection because genital lesions allow HIV an easy route for infection.

Not all medical problems of the reproductive organs are related to reproduction; that is, these organs can be the site of disease and cancer. Women are more likely than men to seek health care concerning problems with their reproductive organs. Although women are at greater risk for cancer of organs in the reproductive system than men are throughout young and middle adulthood, men are most likely to develop testicular cancer between ages 15 and 34 years (Brown, 2004). This form of cancer is quite rare, but rates are increasing; men are most likely to develop this form of cancer during the years when they tend to avoid regular physical checkups. A man may have no regular physician to tell about the lump he has detected on a testicle, and the tendency to hope that the problem will go away (Galdas et al., 2005) often results in a tumor that goes untreated for a dangerously long period. This form of cancer is rarely fatal if treated early, but fatality rates rise sharply with delays in treatment, going from a 90% survival rate to only a 25% survival rate. Thus, this rare form of cancer that affects men in their 20s and 30s may be fatal more often than it would be if men gave more attention to their health.

Prostate cancer is much more common than testicular cancer, and it tends to develop in older men. This form of cancer is not common until after age 75 years, when it increases sharply. Even without malignancy, prostate enlargement, which begins during puberty, can cause problems such as difficulty during urination that can require surgery. Malignant tumors of the prostate may be small and grow slowly, and many elderly men die *with* rather than *from* prostate cancer (Lowry, 2006). Other prostate tumors grow more rapidly, and early detection and treatment can extend life. The development and use of a diagnostic test, the prostate specific antigen test, has allowed earlier diagnosis, and men are beginning to mobilize as advocates for improved treatment.

Endometrial cancer affects the uterine lining, but women can also develop cancer of the cervix, ovaries, vulva, vagina, and Fallopian tubes. None of these sites is the most common site for cancer—the breast is. About 26% of the cancer diagnoses in women are breast cancer (American Cancer Society, 2008). (Even so, lung cancer is the leading cause of cancer death for both men and women due to its high fatality rate.) From ages 15 to 45, cancers of the reproductive system are a major cause of mortality for women but not for men.

During menopause, women lose their fertility; they cease ovulation and menstruation, and their production of estrogen and progesterone declines. Some women experience uncomfortable symptoms associated with menopause; the most common of these is the "hot flash," a sudden feeling of heat and skin flushing. These feelings may be uncomfortable and embarrassing but are not health threatening. Only 10% of menopausal women experience serious symptoms associated with menopause (Livingston, 1999). Hormone replacement therapy can alleviate the symptoms, but findings from the Women's Health Initiative (Shumaker et al., 2003; Writing Group for the Women's Health Initiative Investigators, 2002) have indicated that hormone replacement raises the risk for breast cancer, blood clots, cardiovascular disease, and memory deficits. These findings led many women to reconsider this therapy and to ask more critical questions and make more informed choices. However, these findings confirm the criticisms that women have been overtreated for menopause.

Men's hormone production also drops with aging, but they undergo no symptoms as visible as those of women during menopause. The decrease in hormone production in men results in the decline, but not the end, of their fertility. Men who lose the ability to get erections may receive hormone replacements or take drugs for erectile problems, but many fewer men than women receive hormone replacement therapy.

Thus, treatment for malignancies of the reproductive system accounts for only a small portion of the reproductive health care received by women, but a larger portion of that received by men. Women not only get pregnant and bear children, but they also have most of the responsibility for contraception. In addition, menstruation is often painful, and some women experience pain sufficiently serious to prompt them to consult health care professionals. The decline in hormone production associated with menopause also causes some women to seek medical treatment. Therefore, a great deal of the added health care received by women is due to their reproductive system needs; however, this is only part of the reason for women's greater number of contacts with the health care system.

Gender, Lifestyle, and Health

Men have shorter average life spans than women in all developed and most undeveloped countries. The gender gap in mortality is not static but has varied over time and place. Coexisting with this advantage, women are more likely to use health care and to report symptoms of illness. Both men's shorter lives and women's poorer health may be related to their lifestyles. That is, men may lose years from their life span by behaviors associated with the male gender role.

The female gender role may likewise endanger health. Women's role as nurturer presents both benefits and drawbacks (Barnett & Hyde, 2001). Offering and receiving social support is an important factor in health, but when people take care of others better than themselves, the role of nurturer becomes a health deficit. The demands of providing social support and nurturant care can be emotionally and physically draining, and there is no guarantee of receiving the same quality of care as that given. Women are more likely than men to be in such a situation, providing benefits to men but not as many to women, as the headline story for this chapter discussed.

Therefore, both traditional gender roles carry health risks. Women's morbidity is a factor that significantly decreases the quality of their lives (Kaplan, Anderson, & Wingard, 1991), but their more frequent illnesses are usually not ones that threaten their lives. Men, on the other hand, tend to experience health problems that are more likely to be life threatening. In other words, "One sex is 'sicker' in the short run, and the other in the long run" (Verbrugge, 1985, p. 163). The causes of death, however, are similar. Two behaviors that relate to health and longevity are eating and exercising, and these behaviors show gender-related differences.

Eating

Everyone eats, but people vary in their eating patterns and in the meanings they attach to eating (Rozin, 2007; Rozin, Bauer, & Catanese, 2003). Women's relationship with food is especially complex; women use food as comfort, but they also show more concern with eating to control weight and are more likely to diet than men. This concern with weight and their attempts to restrict food intake lead women to hold different attitudes toward eating than men do. Indeed, men's and women's brains do not respond to hunger and satiation in exactly the same ways (Del Parigi et al., 2002). Although the brain activation in response to hunger and eating were far more similar than different, some areas of brain activity differed for women and men.

Gender differences in eating patterns start during early adolescence (Caine-Bish & Scheule, 2009) and become greater during the teen years. Adolescent boys, on the average, eat enough food to obtain the required calories, but adolescent girls restrict their caloric intake to the point of risk for nutritional inadequacies. Adult women also eat less than adult men, but the discrepancy is not as great as during adolescence. Nonetheless, women may eat too little to receive adequate nutrition.

Not only do men eat more than women, but also the eating patterns of each conform to the expectations of their respective gender roles. Eating less and taking smaller bites may relate to efforts to appear feminine. Eating style can affect social perception, including impressions of femininity and personal concern about appearance (Chaiken & Pliner, 1987). In studies that paired female and male participants with same- and other-gender partners to snack and talk, women showed a tendency to eat less when paired with an attractive male partner but not with an unattractive male or with a female partner (Mori, Chaiken, & Pliner, 1987). Women's eating is thus motivated by the desire to appear feminine as well as the desire to give a good social impression. Masculinity also has an impact on men's eating, pushing men toward unhealthy food choices (Gough & Conner, 2006; Levi, Chan, & Pence, 2006). Therefore, women and men eat somewhat differently, partly due to men's greater caloric intake and partly due to the impression that women may wish to convey through their eating style.

Difference in eating styles is more than a way to make an impression; concerns with food and eating are a pervasive concern among young women (Rozin et al., 2003), whereas men are reluctant to see the risks of being overweight (Gregory, Blanck, Gillespie, Maynard, & Serdula, 2008). Women have more body fat than men, but the ideal body image for women demands thinness. Thus, women often believe that they must diet to achieve the desired body. Extreme concerns with weight and dieting can produce abnormal eating habits and serious eating disorders. A growing consensus holds that body image and eating disorders are linked; an unattainably thin body image can prompt these unhealthy eating patterns (Markey & Markey, 2005). American culture socializes women to look at their bodies as objects, with an emphasis on appearance, and an important part of that appearance is thinness (Fredrickson & Roberts, 1997). Thus women are more likely than men to be concerned, even obsessed, with body shape.

Body Image. The image of what constitutes an attractive female or male body currently emphasizes thinness for women and muscularity for men (see According to the Media and According to the Research). The contemporary ideal body image for women has developed over the past 100 years (Chernin, 1978; Wooley, 1994). Plumpness was once the ideal for women, signifying their health and wealth, but that standard has faded; overweight people are the targets of teasing and discrimination (Carr, Jaffe, & Friedman, 2008). The thin ideal arose during the early part of the 20th century with the upper classes but has spread (with varying severity) to all socioeconomic classes (Snapp, 2009) and diverse ethnic groups, including African Americans and Hispanic Americans (Bay-Cheng, Zucker, Stewart, & Pomerleau, 2002; Miller et al., 2000), Asian Americans (Barnett, Keel, & Conoscenti, 2001), and Native Americans (Neumark-Sztainer et al., 2002). A concern with thinness also exists among women in many countries (McArthur, Holbert, & Pena, 2005). Thus, the thin ideal has become widespread.

Overweight is a stigma for men as well as for women, and evidence indicates that men are also becoming body conscious. Body image discontentment appears even in preadolescent children (Lowes & Tiggemann, 2003). As young as age 6 or 7, both girls and boys chose an ideal body thinner than their own, but girls made more extreme choices. Men and boys who see themselves as overweight want to lose weight (Grogan & Richards, 2002), but even overweight men are not as dissatisfied with their bodies as women are (Markey & Markey, 2005).

A different ideal body image exists for men—muscularity. This ideal has become more influential, affecting body satisfaction for adolescent boys (Ricciardelli & McCabe, 2007), college men (Morrison, Morrison, & Hopkins, 2003), and adults (Olivardia, Pope, Borowiecki, & Cohane, 2004). Boys and college men are more likely than girls and women to enact their attitudes about muscularity by working out with weights and eating to increase bulk, but they too strive to avoid being what they consider fat. The desire to increase muscularity may also be expressed by taking anabolic steroids, drugs that can help increase muscle mass (Goldberg & Elliot, 2007). Unfortunately, these drugs have many negative side effects that can present physical and psychological risks.

▓ ACCORDING TO THE *M*EDIA . . .

Overweight People Are Repulsive

Media portrayals of beauty influence the images of how women and men want to look, and appearance is very important in all media. Examinations of magazine images reflect the thin ideal for women and the muscular ideal for men. In addition, the examples of attractive women have gotten thinner over the past years. One example of this trend appeared in analyses of the weight of *Playboy* centerfolds. Between 1959 and 1978, centerfolds became thinner (Garner, Garfinkel, Schwartz, & Thompson, 1980) but after 1979, the weight decline did not continue (Spitzer, Henderson, & Zivian, 1999). However, 99% of the centerfolds fell into the category indicating underweight close to the clinical standard for anorexia.

On television, appearance is the basis for comments from both male and female characters, and female characters are the recipients of twice as many comments about their appearance as male characters (Lauzen & Dozier, 2002). Men are also the targets of comments about appearance, which tend to be negative if they are overweight (Fouts & Vaughan, 2002). Indeed, remarks to overweight male characters are the source of laughter from the audience. However, being overweight is not common on television; only 10% of

female characters in entertainment programming are overweight, but 31% are underweight; for male characters, 17% are overweight, but only 12% are underweight (Fitzgerald, 2002).

The messages about thinness and overweight in television entertainment programming are subtle compared to the reality TV show *The Biggest Loser,* which premiered in 2004 (Bernstein & St. John, 2006). Similar to other "reality" shows, the format of *The Biggest Loser* includes a competition between teams. The competitors are all obese people; the goal is to lose the most weight, and team members vote each week to eliminate a team member who has not furthered the team's goals. Thus, this program draws from overweight individuals who not only have unhealthy weight but who also have unhealthy attitudes about weight, including the view that all their personal problems are the result of their weight and that losing weight will improve all facets of their lives. Other reality TV shows, such as *The Swan* and *Extreme Makeover,* also cultivate unhealthy body image, but *The Biggest Loser* built an audience by humiliating overweight people and sending blatant messages about the horrors of being fat.

Early research (Fallon & Rozin, 1985) indicated that women perceived the ideal female body as thinner than their own, and they believed that men found thinner female bodies attractive. However, men's preference was not as thin as the women believed. Depictions of thinness as attractive appear in the media and influence the development of unrealistic body images. This perception of thinness as attractive may be dangerous. This influence occurs early, beginning during childhood (Jung & Peterson, 2007) and intensifies during adolescence (Ata, Ludden, & Lally, 2007). Watching television featuring thin women influenced women's and men's ratings of the ideal body for women (Harrison, 2003). Similarly, viewing muscular male models decreased men's satisfaction with their own bodies (Lorenzen, Grieve, & Thomas, 2004). One study (Markey & Markey, 2005) suggested that individuals who use dangerous methods of dieting such as fasting and purging want to be unrealistically thin and are willing to use unhealthy strategies to achieve their goal.

Although men have experienced fewer problems with body image than women have, that situation is changing, and men have become subject to pressures to attain the ideal muscular body. Men tend to manage their bodies by working out and even by seeking surgery but tend to view dieting as feminine, so dieting is not a preferred strategy for men in

ACCORDING TO THE RESEARCH . . .

Women and Men Get the Media Messages about Weight, but They Still Don't Measure Up

Media images of thin women and muscular men influence how people want to look. This influence begins early, during early adolescence (Field et al., 2001) and even late childhood (Jung & Peterson, 2007). For college students, the media influence extends to specific body parts: College students who watched a lot of television had ideal measurements for hips, waists, and busts. Furthermore, those who were most influenced by the media were most receptive to the notion of surgical intervention with liposuction or breast implants to achieve these ideals (Harrison, 2003). A longitudinal study (Aubrey, 2006) showed that watching television that encourages perceiving the body as an object influenced women's and men's feelings about their bodies. Men who read men's magazines became more concerned with their own bodies and more concerned about thinness in their female partners (Hatoum & Belle, 2004). Therefore, men as well as women have accepted the media's view of ideal bodies, which had led to dissatisfaction with their own and their partners' bodies.

Adding to that dissatisfaction is the trend toward overweight: Women and men have become heavier (NCHS, 2009). The percentage of overweight U.S. residents increased from 47% during the 1970s to 67% in 2006; the number of overweight Canadians also increased during this time (Spitzer et al., 1999). The increasing percentage of overweight people and the increasing acceptance of the thin ideal creates an unhappy situation: "The ideal female weight, represented by actresses, models, and Miss Americas, has progressively decreased to that of the thinnest 5% to 10% of American women. Consequently, 90% to 95% of American women feel that they don't 'measure up'" (Seid, 1994, p. 8). This failure to "measure up" has resulted in a discontent with weight that is the norm among women and increasing among men.

The result of that dissatisfaction is depression, guilt, a growing number of eating disorders, and an increasing tendency to visit the plastic surgeon as a solution. The number of liposuction procedures has increased over 300% since the year 2000 (Matarasso, 2006). Unfortunately, this solution carries safety risks and may not yield the expected results. But for most people, not even drastic dieting will work to create the ideal body. As the title of one article on weight summarized: "Nobody's satisfied" (Raudenbush & Zellner, 1997), and the dissatisfaction has spread to both men and women.

shaping their bodies (De Souza & Ciclitira, 2005). Nonetheless, an increasing number of men diet to control their weight, including unhealthy techniques such as fasting and throwing up to lose weight (Markey & Markey, 2005).

Therefore, both women and men are subjected to pressures to have bodies that conform to the ideal, but the methods for achieving these results differ. If these messages are effective, men and women would be likely to take different strategies to achieve their ideal bodies. Women would be more likely to experience eating disorders, whereas men would be more likely to encounter exercise-related problems.

Eating Disorders.   Anorexia nervosa and bulimia are two eating disorders that have received a great deal of publicity, but these two disorders lie at the extreme on a continuum of eating problems that includes dieting (Polivy & Herman, 2002). Indeed, dieting is related to the development of the more serious eating disorders of anorexia and bulimia. **Anorexia nervosa** is a disorder caused by self-starvation in pursuit of thinness, and **bulimia** consists of binge eating followed by some method of purging (induced vomiting or excessive laxative use) to avoid gaining weight.

Dieting, anorexia, and bulimia are all more common among women than men. A survey of high school students (Eaton et al., 2008) and adult women and men (Kruger, Galuska, Serdula, & Jones, 2004) showed that dieting was more common among women. About 53% of the girls and 38% of the women were trying to lose weight, compared to about 28% of the boys in high school and 24% of the men. The gender distribution is even more divergent for eating disorders; around 90% of people who are treated for eating disorders are women (Menaster, 2002). However, some research (Striegel-Moore et al., 2009) suggests that this figure represents an underestimate for men, who fail to receive diagnosis and treatment but experience disordered eating nonetheless. Women, too, may avoid diagnosis and treatment, so eating disorders may be more common than the treatment figures reflect.

The development of eating disorders is influenced by personal and situational factors. As the rates of anorexia and bulimia suggest, both gender and age are factors, with women at a higher risk than men, and young women more subject to eating problems than older women. Social class was once a distinguishing factor, but pressures for thinness now occur in all social classes, among all ethnic groups (Polivy & Herman, 2002; Snapp, 2009), and in societies around the world (Keel & Klump, 2003). Occupation is also a factor, with young women who are in modeling or dance school more likely to have eating disorders than comparable young women whose careers do not demand thinness (Garner & Garfinkel, 1980). For men, pressures from occupation or athletics exert similar effects with wrestlers, runners, bodybuilders, rowers, and jockeys at specific risk (Menaster, 2002).

Sexual orientation shows some relationship to disordered eating in men. Gay men expressed higher body objectification than heterosexual men (Kozak, Frankenhauser, & Roberts, 2009); that is, they tended to see their bodies as the only representations of themselves. Sexual orientation is also a factor for disordered eating in women; adolescent girls who were not heterosexual were more likely to show symptoms of disordered eating and boys who were not heterosexual were less satisfied with their bodies (Austin et al., 2004). Men with eating disorders tend to be less obsessed with losing weight but similarly concerned with body shape and muscle tone (Ousley, Cordero, & White, 2008). The trajectories also vary, with men's symptoms decreasing throughout adulthood more than women's symptoms (Keel, Heatherton, Baxter, & Joiner, 2007).

The underlying causes of eating disorders are not understood, mainly because research capable of identifying causes is difficult to conduct on this topic (Polivy & Herman, 2002). Being dissatisfied with one's body is a necessary component but not a sufficient condition for developing an eating disorder. According to Janet Polivy and Peter Herman (2002), individuals must also come to see eating and weight control as solutions to their personal problems, and certain research (Evans, 2003) indicates that some women believe in a link between weight and happiness. The combination of body dissatisfaction and the belief that eating and weight control are keys to solving one's problems lays the foundation for eating disorders.

Both anorexia and bulimia are serious disorders, but anorexia is more likely to be life threatening. Indeed, anorexia has the highest mortality rate of any psychiatric disorder; between 5 and 15% of anorexics starve themselves to death (Brown, Mehler, & Harris, 2000). Furthermore, treatment for anorexia is difficult, and relapses are common. Bulimia is more easily treated because bulimics typically feel guilty about their binge eating and purging and thus want to change their behavior, but they too may experience relapses into disordered eating.

As girls enter adolescence, they become more concerned with appearance and body image.

Eating disorders, then, may be the result of concerns with body image and exaggerated attempts to achieve thinness. Because their ideal body images are thin, women are more likely than men to focus on eating and thus to develop eating disorders. Over the past several decades, both men and women have begun to feel increased pressure to attain and maintain attractive bodies, and women tend to try to achieve this goal through dieting and, to a lesser extent, through exercise; men on the other hand, use exercise as a primary means and dieting as a secondary means of shaping their bodies.

Exercise and Fitness

Physical activity is a factor in the weight maintenance equation. When dieters eat less, their basal metabolism slows, and their bodies require fewer calories, which protects against starvation but makes weight loss difficult (Pinel, 2009). Dieting is not only difficult, but it also is not as effective for weight control as dieting plus exercise. Weight control, however, is a minor factor in considering the benefits of exercise; physical activity is a basic part of life. However, people living in industrialized societies have become more sedentary.

GENDERED VOICES

I'm Afraid Some of Them Are Not Going to Be Around

"I'm afraid some of them are not going to be around," a 14-year-old dancer told her mother concerning other dancers who showed symptoms of anorexia. The dancers in her classes were encouraged to be thin, and the girl believed that several were in danger; they were so thin that she had considered them in danger of dying. Her mother was angry because she believed that the instructor was encouraging unhealthy eating in students by telling her normal-weight daughter that she needed to lose weight. The girl knew that she was heavier than many of the other dancers, but she believed that they had the problem, not her.

She had begun to hear criticisms about her weight when she was 12, and she started to become self-conscious about it, but she had resisted dieting, partly because she thought the other girls were too thin and partly because she didn't want to change her eating habits. She had also received conflicting messages about her weight, with her mother and others telling her that she wasn't too heavy, her dance teacher telling her that she needed to be thinner, and her classmates dieting to the point of anorexia.

Another girl's story confirmed the prevalence of weight consciousness among early adolescents. This 12-year-old came home from school one day and told her mother that when they had gone swimming for gym class, most of the girls had gone into the pool with their T-shirts over their bathing suits. She didn't understand why they had done so; a wet T-shirt made swimming more difficult. When she asked one why she had kept her shirt on, the other girl said, "Because I'm so fat. I don't want anyone to see me in a bathing suit." The 12-year-old told her mother, "But they're not fat." She considered her classmates' perceptions of their bodies very odd. Judging from the number of girls who had been reluctant to be seen in their bathing suits, her classmates' distorted perception was more common than her accurate assessment of what was normal and what constituted overweight.

Differences in job and leisure-time activities show gender differences, with women being less physically active than men. The overall difference in the United States is small, and both the difference and its size apply to many countries (Bauman et al., 2009).

Gender and age interact in relation to physical activity. During the preschool years, boys are more active than girls. Throughout childhood, boys are more likely to engage in physical activities requiring gross motor skills that use the large muscles of the body. Boys' preferences for baseball, football, soccer, and basketball put them into more active situations than many girls' games require. Girls' exclusion from boys' play groups decreases their opportunities to be involved in vigorous activity. Girls who do, however, engage in vigorous activity are more likely to become college athletes than girls who engage in more traditional play activities (Giuliano, Popp, & Knight, 2000). (See Chapter 9 for a discussion of gender segregation and friendships during childhood and Chapter 11 for a consideration of athletics in schools.)

Watching television and playing computer games have become popular recreational activities for children and adolescents. The computer game market was dominated initially by games aimed at boys, but companies later began to market games that girls liked (Gardyn, 2003). Now, 65% of both male and female college students play video or computer games regularly, and about 70% of those students have played since elementary school. Regardless of the content, computer games can take the place of more active games and decrease the physical activity of both boys and girls.

Gender differences in exercising increase during adolescence, with girls decreasing and boys increasing their participation in athletics. Athletic participation, with its emphasis on size, strength, and competition, is more compatible with the male than the female gender role. The traditional gender roles hold that women should look slender and dainty and should feel reluctant to compete. Men, on the other hand, should look muscular and strong and eager to compete. Adolescents feel the pressures to adopt these gender roles; thus, boys are urged to "try out" for sports, whereas girls may not receive similar encouragement.

Title IX of the Education Amendments of 1972 prohibited sex discrimination in education, which included support for school athletics. The subsequent development of athletic programs for high school girls and college women has changed opportunities and attitudes toward women's athletics. Many more women now participate in athletics, but the emphasis on sports may leave the majority of children—who are not athletically talented—without adequate encouragement to be active. Young people of both sexes who do not have the ability to excel may be allowed to be sedentary, resulting in poor fitness and an increased probability of obesity (Berkey, Rockett, Gillman, & Colditz, 2003).

A growing body of research evidence indicates that exercise provides physical and psychological benefits to both men and women (Blair, Cheng, & Holder, 2001; Warburton, Nicol, & Bredin, 2006). The benefits of physical activity seem particularly strong in terms of lowering the risk of cardiovascular disease (heart attack and stroke), but exercise also lowers the risk for several cancers, helps to prevent and to control diabetes, assists people in sleeping better, lowers depression, reduces anxiety, and buffers against stress. In addition, physical activity guards against **osteoporosis**, the process of bone demineralization. This disorder affects older individuals and is more common among women than men. Orthopedic problems such as fractures are common and can lead to decreased mobility, which is a major factor in decreased quality of life for the elderly (Robine & Ritchie, 1991; Skelton, 2006). Exercise slows and may reverse this process. Therefore, a regular program of physical activity offers many health benefits throughout the life span.

Patterns of physical activity are moderately stable across the lifespan (Friedman et al., 2008). Thus men's greater sports participation during adolescence makes them more likely than women to continue this athletic activity throughout their lives. This background is no guarantee of an active lifestyle. Those who participate in organized sports tend to discontinue physical activity when they leave school (Walters, Barr-Anderson, Wall, & Neumark-Sztainer, 2009). Enjoyment of physical activity is a better predictor of maintaining an active life.

Pressures on women to be thin have extended to fitness and exercise. This message has gotten through to women; a study that investigated reasons for exercising (Strelan, Mehaffey, & Tiggemann, 2003) found that young women's exercising may be so concentrated on appearance that their participation signals a problem in body image rather than a positive health habit. This finding is consistent with the messages aimed at women to exercise as part of weight control and body shaping rather than health promotion.

A relationship exists between exercise and eating disorders, but this relationship is complex and involves gender. People who are anorexic (usually women) are often overly concerned about exercising and may work out for hours per day in attempts to lose weight. Some people who exercise excessively (usually men) also have some eating disorder (Hausenblas & Symons Downs, 2002). Not all anorexics exercise obsessively, nor do all committed exercisers have eating disorders, but there is some concordance between these two extreme behaviors (Markey & Markey, 2005).

In this framework, men's exercise motivations may also be symptomatic of body image problems. The drive to develop muscularity can lead boys and men to exercise excessively (McCreary & Sasse, 2000; Olivardia et al., 2004), which can lead to injury and abuse of muscle-building drugs. Boys and men may be motivated to be muscular in a gender-stereotypical counterpart to girls and women, who are motivated to be thin. Exercise may allow both women and men to achieve fitness, but exercise may also provide a format for enacting body image dissatisfaction and unrealistic weight concerns. Therefore, despite the benefits of exercise, overcommitment to exercise is not healthy.

Considering Diversity

Health and mortality figures from around the world and within the United States reflect the influence of ethnicity and the economic conditions that are often related to ethnicity. One way to analyze world economies is the division into developed, high-income (or industrialized) countries, developing (middle-income) countries, and undeveloped, low-income countries. The economics of life in these countries also affects death in these countries (Lopez, Mathers, Ezzati, Jamison, & Murray, 2006). As Table 13.4 shows, life expectancy is longer in wealthy countries than in developing or low-income countries. In addition, the causes of death vary. In high-income countries, leading causes of death are CVD and cancer, which become more common as people age—they live long enough to develop these diseases. The death rates for CVD and cancer are lower for middle-income countries because many people do not live to the ages when these diseases become common; however, these diseases are becoming more prevalent in these countries and are striking people at younger ages than in high-income countries (Yach, Hawkes, Gould, & Hofman, 2004). In low-income countries, mortality is high from infectious and parasitic diseases, which are fatal for infants and young children more often than for other age groups. High mortality for infants and children lowers life expectancy and typically occurs in poor countries with inadequate nutrition and medical care.

As Table 13.4 illustrates, life expectancy and causes of death vary enormously throughout the world, but the gender gap favoring women's life expectancy appears everywhere. That gap is larger in high-income countries (5 to 8 years) and much smaller in low-income countries (a few months to 4 years), often because of problems related to pregnancy and childbirth. In several countries in sub-Saharan Africa, HIV infection is the leading cause of death and affects more women than men. In these countries, women are economically dependent on men and thus cannot refuse sex, even when they know that it will endanger them. Their social status is an important part of their risk for HIV infection. Countries with high HIV infection rates are among those that have experienced decreased life expectancies over the past decade (McMichael, McKee, Shkolnikov, & Valkonen, 2004).

Another practice that can decrease the survival advantage for girls and women is *son preference*—that is, the preference for sons over daughters. Son preference can lead to the murder of infant girls or the abortion of female fetuses, but more often it is expressed through preferential treatment for sons, including better feeding and medical attention, and the neglect of daughters (Gill & Mitra-Kahn, 2008; Shah, 2005). In countries where girls

TABLE 13.4   *Average Life Expectancies, Infant Mortality, and Causes of Death for High-, Middle-, and Low-Income Countries*

Country	Life Expectancy		Causes (per 100,000 population)				
	Men	Women	Infant Mortality (per 1,000)	Circulatory Diseases	Cancer	Accident/ Violence	Infectious/ Parasitic
High-Income Countries							
Australia	79	84	4.8	296.0	190.0	41.0	6.0
Canada	79	84	5.0	264.8	195.6	43.5	8.3
France	78	84	3.3	288.2	207.7	76.1	12.8
Germany	76	82	4.0	525.7	260.7	48.6	7.4
Japan	79	86	2.8	237.7	220.4	52.4	14.6
Sweden	79	83	2.8	525.5	234.6	48.9	8.6
United Kingdom	77	82	4.9	442.1	261.2	55.9	6.8
United States	76	81	6.3	354.4	201.6	55.9	19.6
Middle-Income Countries							
Brazil	68	76	22.6	159.0	65.9	75.9	33.5
Iran	70	73	35.8	304.0	61.0	108.0	34.0
Mexico	73	79	18.4	106.8	52.9	62.4	22.0
Thailand	71	76	17.7	89.8	49.0	73.8	27.6
Low-Income Countries							
Angola	37	39	180.2	diarrheal diseases, 25.8%; malaria, 19%; cholera, 7%			
Bangladesh	58	63	60.3	typhoid, 19.8%; tetanus, 10%; tuberculosis, 8.7%			
Haiti	59	62	59.7	11.9	malnutrition, 8.5		46
Laos	55	59	77.8	includes bronchitis, influenza, malaria, diarrhea			
Zimbabwe	46	45	32.3	40.9	28.4	44.4	64.7

Sources: Data on causes of death from *Britannica Book of the Year, 2002,* 2002, Chicago: Encyclopaedia Britannica; data on life expectancies from *The World Factbook* by Central Intelligence Agency. Retrieved November 5, 2009, from https://www.cia.gov/library/publications/the-world-factbook/rankorder/2102rank.html

and boys receive more equal treatment during infancy and childhood, girls have a survival advantage over boys, as women do when compared to men. Thus, the female survival advantage holds across many cultures. However, life expectancy varies more than the magnitude of the gender gap, which indicates that social factors are important in life expectancy.

Worldwide, men are more vulnerable to disease and death in patterns similar to those in the United States. Men's rate of CVD death is higher than that of women of comparable age, they use tobacco at a higher rate, they are more likely to drink alcohol, and they engage in risky behaviors that increase their vulnerability to violent death Wong et al., 2006). In countries in which the death rate for CVD is high, the gender gap is larger than in countries with fewer deaths from this cause. For example, the countries in Eastern Europe, including those that were part of the Soviet Union, experienced a sharp increase in CVD during the 1980s, which persisted throughout the 1990s and then began a slight decline (McMichael et al., 2004). This area of Eastern Europe has the highest CVD death rate in the world (Fonarow, 2007). The rise affected those people most vulnerable to CVD—middle-aged men. The increase in Russia was over 30%, the life expectancy in Russia declined, and the gender gap in life expectancy increased (Weidner & Cain, 2003). The CVD death rate in Russia is about 500 per 100,000 population for men, but only 80 per 100,000 for women; life expectancy is 59 and 72, respectively. The reasons for this dramatic increase in CVD are somewhat mysterious, but one hypothesis (Weidner & Cain, 2003) holds that psychosocial factors such as stress, economic uncertainty, inadequate social support, and depression are the basis of the problem; however, tobacco use and alcohol abuse also contribute.

The behaviors that put men at higher risk than women are likely to continue, so the gender gap in life expectancy is not likely to disappear in the near future (Murray & Lopez, 1997). However, that gap has narrowed recently in high-income countries (Glei & Horiuchi, 2007). The gender gap that opened during the 20th century has closed a bit during the early years of the 21st century.

The United States is among high-income nations, but some ethnic groups in the United States have patterns of disease and death that look more like those in low-income countries. The underlying reasons for these health disadvantages include poverty and discrimination, both of which affect living conditions and access to medical care. The provision of health insurance through employment or through private policies results in decreased access and often poor-quality medical care for poor people. Ethnic minority groups are affected by these circumstances more than White people are (Lasser, Himmelstein, & Woolhandler, 2006).

African Americans have higher infant mortality rates and shorter life expectancies than other ethnic groups in the United States. The infant mortality rate for African Americans is 13.7 deaths per 1,000 live births compared to a rate for Whites of 5.7 per 1,000 (U.S. Census Bureau, 2009a). That is, African American babies die at a rate comparable to those in Kuwait, Costa Rica, and Bulgaria, whereas infant mortality for White babies is comparable to that of high-income countries. Other health indicators for African Americans show that they have a shorter life expectancy and a higher rate of several diseases, including cardiovascular disease, diabetes, and liver disease. African Americans are five times more likely to die of violence than Whites (NCHS, 2009). Young men are especially likely to be the victims of unintentional and intentional injuries.

Hispanic Americans are disadvantaged by conditions similar to African Americans, but their mortality rates are more similar to non-Hispanic Whites than to African Americans. Young Hispanic American men are at elevated risk for injuries and death due to violence (NCHS, 2009), but deaths due to cardiovascular diseases and cancer are lower than for non-Hispanic Whites. The overall death rate for Hispanics was comparable to that of non-Hispanic European Americans, but as Hispanics become more acculturated, their health behaviors and health become more like other European Americans and their rates of CVD and cancer increase (Abraído-Lanza, Chao, & Flórez, 2005).

Native Americans experience a pattern of health problems that varies from other ethnic groups. Poverty and poor living conditions are major problems for the health of Native Americans, and their access to medical care is often through the Indian Health Service, which provides free medical care to Native Americans who live on reservations or in areas covered by the service (Keltner, Kelly, & Smith, 2004). This limitation restricts the health care of many Native Americans. Infant mortality is higher for Native Americans than for Whites, but lower than that for African Americans (NCHS, 2009). Youth violence is a bigger problem among Native Americans than any other ethnic group. Native Americans also have a genetic predisposition for developing diabetes, and their levels of alcohol abuse contribute to liver disease, violent deaths, and fetal alcohol syndrome.

As a group, Asian Americans experience health advantages rather than disadvantages when compared to all other ethnic groups in the United States. Infant mortality rates for Chinese Americans, Japanese Americans, and Filipino Americans are among the best in the world (NCHS, 2009). For Asian Americans as a group, CVD death rates and deaths from violence are about half of those for European Americans, and the rate of cancer deaths is lower.

Therefore, some ethnic groups within the United States have health disadvantages whereas others have advantages. The health of non-Hispanic Whites and Asian Americans compares favorably with the high-income nations throughout the world. For African Americans and Native Americans, health care and health indicators are comparable to those of low-income nations.

■ Summary

Women live longer than men. This gender difference has existed in most countries and during most time periods. In high-income countries such as the United States, Canada, Australia, and the countries of Scandinavia and Western Europe, deaths from cardiovascular disease, cancer, and violence account for the majority of deaths. Men die of these causes at younger ages than women, creating a gender gap in longevity.

Cardiovascular disease (CVD) refers to diseases of the heart and circulatory system. Heart attack and stroke account for about 32% of the deaths in the United States. Although the total mortality from CVD is similar for men and women, men are more likely to die of CVD than women are before the age of 65. This discrepancy has created a bias among physicians, who are slower to interpret women's symptoms as CVD and less likely to recommend treatment for women.

Cancer is the second most common cause of death, and men are more likely than women to die from this cause. Lung cancer, the deadliest form of cancer for both men and women, is strongly related to cigarette smoking. Until recently, men have smoked at a substantially higher rate than women. With the rise in women's smoking, their lung cancer rates have increased and will continue

to do so. Both women and men develop cancer of the reproductive organs, but women are more likely to die of such cancers, especially before age 65 years.

The gender difference in violent deaths is large; men die of unintentional injuries, suicides, and homicides at higher rates than women. The male gender role, which holds that men are supposed to be reckless and aggressive, plays a part in the high death rates from these causes. Men's greater prevalence of heavy alcohol use also increases their risk. Violent deaths also vary from country to country, with the United States having one of the higher rates of violent deaths. Within the United States, different ethnic groups are not equally affected by violence—African Americans are especially vulnerable to violent death.

Although women live longer than men, women also seek health care more often. The female gender role allows and even encourages vulnerability to illness, but the male gender role discourages the acceptance of any weakness, including illness. Women's sensitivity to physical symptoms tends to boost health care seeking, but their access to health care is diminished by lower rates of employment, lower salaries, and lower insurance coverage.

The interaction of gender roles of the patient and health care provider has an impact on the type of health care patients receive. Physicians have been the target of criticism concerning their treatment of female patients; these criticisms include being reluctant to believe female patients, using men as a standard against which all patients are judged, and omitting women from medical research. Concern over these problems has prompted the founding of the Office of Research on Women's Health. Gender-specific medicine is a newly developed specialty that devotes similar attention to men's health.

Reproductive health is a major reason for the gender difference in receiving health care. Women not only become involved in the health care system due to pregnancy and childbirth, but contraception and menopause are also reasons for consulting physicians. Both women and men are affected by sexually transmitted diseases and disorders of the reproductive organs. Both develop cancer of the genitals, and among women, breast cancer is the most frequent (but not the deadliest) cancer.

Lifestyle differences may account for some of the gender differences in morbidity and mortality. Eating and exercising are behaviors that relate to health. The thin body has become such a widespread ideal among women that dieting is now a way of life for millions of women. Because they cannot be as thin as the ideal, women develop body image problems and are more prone to eating disorders such as anorexia nervosa and bulimia. Men also experience body image dissatisfaction, but they tend to feel insufficiently muscular. Both men and women with body image problems are likely to attempt to alter their bodies through exercise and through dieting, including unhealthy dieting practices.

Exercise can be a positive factor for fitness and weight control, and men are more likely to participate in sports and physical activity than women are. The passage of Title IX of the Education Amendments of 1972 removed some barriers that prevented women from participating in athletics, and increasingly positive publicity for female athletes encourages girls to become athletic. In an increasingly technological and sedentary society, most men and women must use their leisure time to pursue fitness. Athletic activities can build fitness and contribute to health, but excessive exercise can also be symptomatic of body image problems.

Life expectancy and health vary around the world, and economic factors contribute heavily to this variation. High-income nations have longer life expectancies and the problems associated with long life—high rates of cardiovascular disease and cancer. Low-income countries have shorter life expectancies and the problems associated with poverty—high infant mortality and death from infectious diseases. But low-income countries have shown an increase in cardiovascular disease, presenting increased risk for those populations. Within the United States, Asian Americans and European Americans have longer life expectancies and better health than African Americans and Native Americans.

■ Glossary

anorexia nervosa   an eating disorder consisting of self-starvation in pursuit of thinness.

bulimia   an eating disorder consisting of binge eating, followed by some method of purging, either by induced vomiting or excessive laxative use.

cardiovascular disease (CVD)   a group of diseases involving the heart and circulatory system, some of which are life threatening; heart attack and stroke are the most common.

morbidity   illness.

mortality   death.

osteoporosis   the process of bone demineralization, resulting in greater likelihood of orthopedic problems and injuries.

risk factor   any condition or factor that increases the probability that an illness will develop.

sexually transmitted diseases (STDs)   infectious diseases that are spread through sexual contact, including bacterial infections, viral infections, fungal infections, and parasitic infections.

■ Suggested Readings

Chrisler, Joan C. (2001). Gendered bodies and physical health. In Rhoda K. Unger (Ed.), *Handbook of psychology of women and gender* (pp. 289–302). New York: Wiley.

Chrisler presents a relatively brief but fairly comprehensive summary of women's experience with illness and with the health care system. In addition, she discusses the health risks involved with the pursuit of beauty.

Courtenay, Will H. (2000). Behavioral factors associated with disease, injury, and death among men: Evidence and implications for prevention. *Journal of Men's Studies, 9,* 81–142.

Courtenay presents a lengthy, excellent summary of men's behaviors that contribute to the gender gap in mortality.

Simon, Harvey B. (2004). Longevity: The ultimate gender gap. *Scientific American, 14*(3), 18–23.

Simon's article draws too heavily on hormones as an explanation for the gender gap in longevity, but his article is short and readable, reviewing the physical, social, and behavioral factors that contribute to this gender discrepancy.

Travis, Cheryl Brown. (2005). 2004 Carolyn Sherif Award Address: Heart disease and gender inequity. *Psychology of Women Quarterly, 29,* 15–23.

Although Brown's article focuses on heart disease, her critical analysis of the biased treatment of women in health care applies to many disorders.

chapter

14 Stress, Coping, and Psychopathology

Massachusetts state senator Bob Antonioni experienced depression for years without knowing what was wrong (Scelfo, Springen, & Carmichael, 2007). He was irritable, temperamental, overly concerned with small things, and exhausted. He sought therapy after his younger brother, who was also moody, killed himself. But Antonioni kept his therapy secret because "I didn't want to sound like I couldn't take care of myself, that I wasn't a man" (in Scelfo et al., 2007, p. 43). Antonioni's experience is not unusual, and neither was his reaction—admitting to emotional problems is not part of the male gender role and keeps many men from identifying their problems as depression.

HEADLINE

Facing Darkness
Newsweek, February 26, 2007

Depression has been associated with women so closely that mental health care practitioners have difficulty in identifying a man as depressed. "The result is a hidden epidemic of despair that is destroying marriages, disrupting careers, filling jail cells, clogging emergency rooms and costing society billions of dollars in lost productivity and medical bills" (Scelfo et al., 2007, p. 45). In addition, the symptoms that depressed men exhibit differ from those of depressed women, which also makes depression difficult to diagnose in men. When men are depressed, they do not necessarily seem sad. Like Bob Antonioni, they may be angry and express their negative emotions through drinking or taking drugs. Alternatively, they may attempt or commit suicide. That is, men's expression of depression is consistent with the male gender role.

In attempting to expand the understanding of depression, researchers are considering many possibilities, including a possible role for stress. Although stress has become a popular explanation as the source of almost every psychological and medical problem, researchers strive to identify the specific role that stress may play and the disorders for which stress is a risk.

Stress and Coping

Stress has been defined in many ways, but when circumstances place people in situations that tax or exceed their resources and endanger their well-being, they feel stressed (Lazarus & Folkman, 1984). Stress is an inevitable part of life, so searching for the stresses that relate to the development of mental disorders becomes a complex task. Researchers cannot simply identify sources of stress but must investigate how people perceive various stressors and how they cope with the resulting stress in their lives.

Sources of Stress for Men and Women

The basic physiological reaction to stress is similar for men and women (Taylor et al., 2000), but sources of stress vary. The many combinations of marriage, parenthood, employment, and other activities provide women (and men) with complex roles. Men have traditionally occupied the breadwinner role and have not been involved with providing much in the way of housekeeping or child care; that situation has changed, and women are pressuring men to become more involved in performing household work and caring for children. That pressure may be one source of stress for men. Research has explored the ramifications of occupying the multiple roles of spouse, parent, and employee. Although fulfilling these roles may be satisfying, the experience may also be stressful and thus related to the development of problems. Experiences with violence present another source of stress that shows gender variations. Sexism, gender discrimination, and poverty are also potential sources of stress that have different impacts on women and men and show a relationship to the development of mental disorders.

Family Roles. The gender differences in family roles revolve around marriage, parenthood, and employment. Those roles were once different for men and women but have become more similar. Research from Australia (de Vaus, 2002) and from the United States (Hetherington & Kelly, 2002; Holt-Lunstad, Birmingham, & Jones, 2008; Williams, 2003) has indicated that being married was a mental health advantage to wives and husbands in both countries. Married people showed lower levels of mental disorders for almost every category of problem than people who were not married. In the United States, unmarried men were at higher risk for mental health problems than unmarried women (Hetherington & Kelly, 2002), but in Australia, the two groups showed similar rates of disorders (de Vaus, 2002). Husbands and wives were equally benefited by marriage in both countries (de Vaus, 2002; Williams, 2003).

Roles other than marriage may raise or lower the risk for mental disorders. Being employed was a positive factor for men and women in both countries. Indeed, the combination of marriage and employment was associated with low levels of mental health problems, and being both unmarried and unemployed raised the risks (de Vaus, 2002; Sachs-Ericsson & Ciarlo, 2000). The role of parent does not necessarily increase the risk of mental health problems, but unmarried women with children were at increased risk in both countries. In the United States, men who occupied all three roles—spouse, parent, and employee—showed the lowest risk for mental problems of any group.

As these studies demonstrate, these three family roles have the potential to improve mental health, but some combinations of roles pose risks. Satisfaction and feelings of support from a spouse make a difference. Being unhappily married presents a mental health risk for both women and men (Holt-Lunstad et al., 2008; Williams, 2003). Couples who believe that their partners contribute to the emotional work of the relationship as well as to child care and household work were more satisfied with their marriages than couples who believed that their partners were not as supportive in these domains (Edwards, 2006; Stevens, Kiger, & Mannon, 2005). When married mothers are employed and experience strain in each role,

Women report more experiences of stress than men.

their risk for mental health problems increases but not when they experience little strain in either role. When family demands are equal for employed men and women, they have comparable rates of depression and anxiety disorders (Grzywacz, Quandt, Arcury, & Marín, 2005). When the burdens of family care fall disproportionately on women, their risk increases for the development of depression. Husbands, however, may feel stressed by their wives' employment because of the changes that wives' employment bring to husbands' household work and child care responsibilities. Single fathers experience even greater burdens and also increased risks for mental health problems (Chandola et al., 2004).

The spillover of work into family and family into work affects both women and men to a similar extent, but possibly in somewhat different ways (Corwyn & Bradley, 2005). Employed women tend to have less satisfying jobs and more responsibility for child care and household work, which can make work less satisfying and create a family strain that spills over into work. Men find it easier to occupy the role of worker and father because they tend to have higher-status jobs and fewer child care and household responsibilities. Thus the unequal strain that women experience is likely due to the continuing inequality of their work and family situations (Barnett, 2004b). Both partners may experience role strain related to parenting and work, and lack of support is an important factor in the equation. Table 14.1 presents some of the influences of various roles on psychological health.

TABLE 14.1   *Influences of Various Roles on Psychological Health*

Role	Affects	Consequences
Caregiving	Women more than men	Stress; emotional and physical exhaustion
Marriage	Both genders	Positive
Parenthood	Both genders	Depends on other roles occupied and the support available
Child caregiving	Women more than men	At risk for mental and physical health problems
Employment	Both genders	Positive
Homemaker role	Women	At risk for depression
Breadwinner role	Men more than women	At risk for mental health problems
Employed wife	Men	At risk for mental health problems

Violence.   Violence researcher Mary Koss wrote, "Experiencing violence transforms people into victims and changes their lives forever. Once victimized one can never feel quite as invulnerable" (Koss, 1990, p. 374). Men and women may both be the victims of violence, but their experiences tend to differ. Men are more frequently the perpetrators as well as the victims of violence. When women are the targets, their victimization may be especially traumatic, because women are more likely to be the victims of violence by family and friends than by strangers (Pimlott-Kubiak & Cortina, 2003; Temple, Weston, Rodriguez, & Marshall, 2007). Furthermore, women are more likely to be injured in violent encounters by persons they know than by strangers.

The risk to physical health is apparent, but a growing body of research has implicated violence as a risk to mental health. Much of this research has concentrated on intimate violence in families—namely, childhood sexual abuse, rape, and marital violence. Although women's abuse has received more publicity, men may also be victims of intimate abuse; this similar victimization produces comparable effects. Indeed, a history of violence victimization is related to the development of a wide variety of psychological problems.

A meta-analysis of research on intimate partner violence (Golding, 1999) revealed that a history of such violence increases the risk for depression, suicide, posttraumatic stress disorder, and substance abuse for women. Almost half of the women in the studies showed some type of mental health problem, which represents a greatly elevated risk. A study that included a large representative sample of men and women in the United States (Pimlott-Kubiak & Cortina, 2003), another that concentrated on women in the United States (Zlotnick, Johnson, & Kohn, 2006), and another in New Zealand (Fergusson, Horwood, & Ridder, 2005) found that being the target of violence raised the risk for several types of psychopathology, especially depression. The studies showed that men and women were equally vulnerable to mental disorders when they had experienced violence. The U.S. study (Pimlott-Kubiak & Cortina, 2003) indicated different patterns of victimization for women and men, which appear in Table 14.2 (page 368). But all three studies demonstrated the mental health risks of intimate partner violence.

Sexual abuse is another type of violence that presents a risk for a variety of mental disorders, and this risk applies to both men and women who experience sexual abuse at any age (Dube et al., 2005; Koss, Bailey, Yuan, Herrera, & Lichter, 2003; Pimlott-Kubiak & Cortina, 2003). Being a victim of sexual abuse increases the chances of depression, posttraumatic

TABLE 14.2   *Patterns of Violence Victimization for Women and Men*

Type of Violence	Women	Men
Physical assault (during adulthood)	31%	45%
Physical assault (during childhood)	40	54
Emotional abuse (during adulthood)	51	48
Sexual violence (lifetime)	18	3
Stalking	32	26

Source: Data from "Gender, Victimization, and Outcomes: Reconceptualizing Risk," by S. Pimlott-Kubiak and L. M. Cortina, 2003, *Journal of Consulting and Clinical Psychology, 71,* pp. 528–539.

stress disorder, substance abuse or dependence, phobic disorder, panic disorder, and obsessive-compulsive disorder, with the magnitude of increase reaching between two and four times that of men or women who have not been abused. Childhood abuse may be more of a danger than abuse during adulthood, but both pose risks. These studies found no gender difference in likelihood of developing psychological problems following abuse, but men were more likely to experience drug and alcohol problems and women were more likely to experience depression. Sexual victimization clearly increased the risk for a variety of problems for both sexes, but women's more frequent victimization means they have greater risks.

Community violence and bullying also relate to the development of psychological disorders. Being a victim or a witness to community violence increases the risk of psychological disorders, especially posttraumatic stress disorder (PTSD) (Breslau, 2009; Foster, Kuperminc, & Price, 2004; Koss et al., 2003; Scarpa, Haden, & Hurley, 2006). Direct involvement with violence is not necessary for the development of problems; exposure to violence is also a risk. Being a victim of a violent crime was a larger risk than being a witness for men, but either experience increased the risk for women (Foster et al., 2004). More severe victimization tends to create greater risk, but all crime victims showed elevated risks of PTSD, demonstrating the psychological risks of criminal victimization. The victimization does not have to be the result of criminal behavior; bullying also creates risks for mental health. Children who were bullied experienced more unhappiness and school problems than those who were not victimized (Arseneault et al., 2006). Thus, exposure to violence as well as the experience of many types of violence presents risks to mental health.

The relationship between the experience of violence and PTSD is strong, but the link to depression is even stronger. Violence may be not only a significant contributor to the prevalence of depression among women but also may contribute to the greater number of women diagnosed with this disorder (Cutler & Nolen-Hoeksema, 1991; Wise, Zierler, Krieger, & Harlow, 2001). Childhood sexual abuse is more common for girls than boys, and evidence links childhood sexual abuse with anxiety, depression, and low self-esteem. Support for this relationship has come from two studies that compared women who were sexually abused as children to those with no history of sexual abuse (Wise et al., 2001; Yama, Tovey, & Fogas, 1993). The results from both studies demonstrated that this type of childhood abuse has lasting effects for the development of anxiety and depression.

The evidence for the relationship between violence and mental disorders is much more straightforward than risks from the various family roles; violence increases the risk for several mental disorders. Childhood victimization is especially harmful. Women are more likely to be the targets of childhood sexual abuse and rape, two types of violence that research has related to psychological disorders, but men who are victimized are at comparably elevated risk of such problems.

Discrimination.   People may be the targets of discrimination for a variety of reasons, but skin color, ethnicity, gender, and nonheterosexual sexual orientation are common reasons. A national survey of U.S. residents (Kessler, Mickelson, & Williams, 1999) revealed that the experience of discrimination was common—33.5% of the participants reported some incidence of major discrimination, and 60.9% said that they had experienced less serious discrimination. This survey included all types of discrimination and focused on participants' perception of the extent and severity of discrimination. This study showed a substantial relationship between perceptions of discrimination and mental health problems.

Sexist discrimination is also a source of stress. People may believe that sex discrimination is a practice of the past, but that perception is incorrect; many women have daily experiences of sexist discrimination, both large and small (Ross & Toner, 2003). The large traumas such as childhood sexual abuse and criminal victimization can produce problems; however, so can being subject to frequent discrimination and harassment, such as being denied a job or promotion or having to listen to sexist jokes. This type of experience has also been related to mental health problems. In one study (Klonoff, Landrine, & Campbell, 2000), women who experienced a high amount of sexist discrimination exhibited more depression, anxiety, and physical complaints than women who experienced lower levels of sexist treatment. Indeed, the women whose experience with sexism was low showed symptom levels comparable to the men in the study.

A sample of African Americans reported a high incidence of racist discrimination within the year before the study, and 100% reported having experienced racist discrimination during their lives (Hendryx & Ahern, 1997). Discrimination creates stigma, the negative consequences of which include stress and threat (Major & O'Brien, 2005).

The creation of stigma may be one route through which discrimination creates distress; individuals who perceive discrimination tend to ruminate over the experience—they think and rethink what happened—and that rumination works toward creating distress (Hatzenbuehler, Nolen-Hoeksema, & Dovidio, 2009). A meta-analysis on the effects of discrimination on health (Pascoe & Richman, 2009) showed that perceived discrimination produced heightened stress responses and also a tendency to avoid health-enhancing behaviors and to perform unhealthy behaviors. Thus, research has produced good evidence that the experience of discrimination may produce a variety of negative mental health effects. These findings may offer an explanation that sexist discrimination is a reason for women's greater levels of distress.

Poverty.   Poverty also presents a risk for mental disorders for women, men, and children (Albee, 2005; Belle & Doucet, 2003). Indeed, poverty may be the underlying factor for both physical and emotional disorders because poverty is related both to violence and discrimination (Albee, 2005; Mossakowski, 2008). The statistics indicate that those who live in poverty are at least two and a half times more likely to receive diagnoses of mental disorders than those who are not poor. Even for those who are no longer poor, a history of living in poverty increases the risk (Mossakowski, 2008).

The absolute level of poverty relates to living conditions that impinge on many factors in a person's life, but the discrepancy between lowest and highest income groups is another way to analyze the impact of poverty. That discrepancy is sharper in the United States than in many other industrialized countries, which may be a factor in health status and shows a stronger relationship to life expectancies and low rates of disease than does absolute income (Wilkinson, 1996). That is, among high-income nations, the most egalitarian have longer life expectancies than countries like the United States, with its extreme difference between wealthy and poor people. These health risks extend to mental health; this pattern appears even within the United States in states with more extreme income inequalities (Kahn, Wise, Kennedy, & Kawachi, 2000; Lieberman & Merrick, 2009). The elevated risk of mental health problems among the poor applies not only to high-income countries with large income discrepancies but to poor people in low-income countries as well (Patel & Kleinman, 2003). Being among the poor constitutes a risk.

Life circumstances associated with poverty are also associated with poor mental health (Albee, 2005; Belle & Doucet, 2003). Not only does low income create many stresses, but unemployment or underemployment, divorce, single parenthood, problems in access to services, and lack of power and resources are all sources of stress that are associated with poverty and contribute to poor mental health. In addition, low income can lead to a host of problems, such as poor housing in high-crime neighborhoods, which exposes poor people to greater risks of violence and other community dangers, a combination of stress and hazardous living conditions that Clare Ulrich (2002, p. 16) termed "the environment of poverty." People with little money also have barriers to seeking treatment, allowing their problems to become more serious before they receive care (Thoits, 2005). Poor women who are being abused by their domestic partners may be powerless to avoid this violence (Goodman, Smyth, Borges, & Singer, 2009). Thus poverty intersects with other risks and has an indirect as well as a direct link to risks that increase the likelihood for problems.

Poverty affects women and ethnic minority families more than other groups (Belle & Doucet, 2003). Single mothers are more likely to be poor than any other demographic group, not only affecting their mental and physical health but also placing their children at risk. Poverty has a negative impact on the ability to cope, depriving people of the ability to deal with other problems that can produce stress. Lack of money limits opportunities and choices, putting people in positions of dependency on government bureaucracy for housing, health care, food, and other essentials. Both problem situations and the lack of any control over them can magnify stress. The economically advantaged may be able to extricate themselves from problem situations and relationships that poor people cannot avoid—they have advantages in coping with stress.

Coping Resources and Strategies

The number and intensity of stressors are important factors in the experience of stress, but resources and strategies for coping are even more important. Those who have resources to cope with the stresses in their lives may not perceive the situations as stressful. One theory of stress (Lazarus & Folkman, 1984) proposed that each person's appraisal of a potentially stressful situation varies according to his or her perception of the personal importance of the situation plus personal resources to deal with the situation. Lacking (or believing that they lack) the resources to cope with events in their lives makes people vulnerable to stress, whereas similar experiences but better resources lead others to experience less stress. Thus, stress varies according to perception, which depends on the evaluation of resources for coping.

The resources for coping may differ for men and women; men often have more power and greater financial resources than women have. Power and money certainly offer advantages for avoiding many of life's problems and for dealing with others. For example, the loss of a job may be more stressful for a single mother of two with only a high school education and skills as a salesclerk than for a married male engineer with an employed wife and a sizable savings account. Neither of these jobless people will avoid stress; losing a job is stressful for almost everyone. However, the engineer has social and material resources for dealing with his situation that the salesclerk lacks.

One of the most important differences between the male engineer and the female salesclerk is the social support the engineer has in the form of his family. The salesclerk may receive support from her children, but she must also offer them care and support. Women's roles generally carry obligations for providing care for others, whereas men's roles more often provide them with emotional support (Belle & Doucet, 2003; Gove, 1984). Receiving support is a large advantage in coping with stress, but providing care for others can be stressful. As Deborah Belle and Joanne Doucet (2003, p. 103) commented, "Social networks can serve as conduits of stress, just as they can serve as sources of social support." Thus, involvement in social relationships carries both advantages and costs.

Social Support.   **Social support** is more than a matter of social relationships or social contacts; support implies providing emotional and material resources. Four different elements of social support are emotional concern, instrumental aid (such as money or other assistance), information and advice, and feedback (Finfgeld-Connett, 2005; House, 1984). Social support requires more than contact or acquaintanceship. People who have a high amount of social support have a wide network of people on whom they can count for emotional and material support. Poor quality of support and small network size both relate to the development of anxiety and depression (Vandervoort, 1999).

As discussed in the "Friendships" section of Chapter 9, women are more likely than men to form friendships that include emotional intimacy, which may give them the advantage in creating networks that provide them with social support. Men's friendships tend to be activity oriented, which may offer them the material support but lack the emotional intimacy that is an important component of social support. Men's social support often comes from their relationships with women; among married couples, women provided more (and more positive) social support than their male partners, creating a gender gap in social support (Verhofstadt, Buysse, & Ickes, 2007). Single and divorced men are at greater risk for mental health problems than married men (de Vaus, 2002; Sachs-Ericsson & Ciarlo, 2000), again suggesting the importance of social support. Those at greater risk typically have less social support, and those at lesser risk typically have more sources of social support.

The breadth and strength of social networks vary with culture as well as with gender. Individualistic cultures such as the United States and Australia tend to encourage different social support networks than more collectivist cultures such as those in Latin America, Asia, and some African countries. Results of cross-cultural research (Scott, Ciarrochi, & Deane, 2004) revealed that people with strong individualist values within an individualistic culture had smaller social networks, lower emotional competence, and poorer mental health than those with weaker individualistic beliefs. The collectivist influence may stay for generations in those who immigrate into individualist cultures, creating ethnic groups with stronger social support than the individualistic culture. In the United States, African American and Hispanic American families tend to have larger support networks than European Americans (Aranda, Castaneda, Lee, & Sobel, 2001; Taylor, Lincoln, & Chatters, 2005). The advantages of an extended family include a wider range of people who offer their emotional and material support and advice. The disadvantages include many demands for emotional and material support (Belle & Doucet, 2003). If these other family members are poor (and members of ethnic minorities are more likely to be poor than members of the dominant ethnic group), then being part of a support network can lead to many demands and obligations that can affect the social network (Lincoln, Chatters, & Taylor, 2005). Thus, being part of an extended family network can provide social support, but it can also impose social costs, and these advantages and disadvantages operate within a social context that includes income and ethnicity.

Coping Strategies.   **Coping** is the process of changing thoughts and behaviors to manage situations that involve potential stressors (Lazarus & Folkman, 1984). How people deal with the events in their lives makes a critical difference in the amount of stress they experience, so having coping strategies is an essential factor in managing stress. These management strategies vary among people and situations. Coping effectiveness distinguishes among people who feel more or less stress. Table 14.3 lists coping strategies and gives examples of each.

TABLE 14.3   *Examples of Coping Strategies*

Coping Strategy	Behaviors That Exemplify This Strategy
Seeking social support	Talk to someone who could help Talk to someone who has experienced similar problems Talk to friends or family who will sympathize
Problem-focused	Analyze the situation Plan a strategy to solve the problem Take action to get rid of the problem Concentrate on the problem
Emotion-focused	Become upset Express negative feelings
Denial	Refuse to accept the reality of the problem Try to ignore the problem
Turn to religion	Seek God's help Pray
Disengagement	Work on other activities Sleep more than usual Engage in distracting activities Consume alcohol or other drugs

Gender is a factor in coping with stress, but how important a factor is not currently clear. Several models hold that gender-related differences exist, but research has not furnished results that fully clarify these varying views. One view (Taylor, 2006; Taylor et al., 2000) holds that women react to stress in ways that differ from men's reactions. Rather than the "fight or flight" reaction typical of men, women's reactions to stressful situations can be described as "tend and befriend." This view ties together women's role as caregivers with neurohormonal reactions and evolutionary history, predicting that women's primary coping strategy will be seeking social support, which is classified as an emotion-focused strategy. Women are more inclined to seek social support than men are, but other gender theories of coping also account for this difference. In addition, men also "tend and befriend" under some stressful circumstances, such as soldiers during battle, so this coping strategy is not unique to women (Geary & Flinn, 2002). This theory rests on complex gender differences in hormonal responses to stress; confirmation of those responses does not yet exist (Taylor, 2006), but other findings are consistent with this view. One study (Kivlinghan, Granger, & Booth, 2005) found gender differences in hormonal responses to competition (although not exactly the elaborate differences the "tend and befriend" theory hypothesizes), and a study of workplace relationships (Morrison, 2009) found that women reported higher satisfaction from workplace friendships than men did, but men found such relationships as satisfying as women. Thus, this intriguing theory awaits clearer confirming evidence.

Other views of gender-related differences in coping include the socialization view, which holds that women and men are socialized to react to stress differently (women with emotional coping and men with active, problem-solving strategies) and the structural view, which holds that gender-related differences in coping come from the different stressful situations women and men encounter (Ptacek, Smith, & Zanas, 1992).

Consistent with the socialization view, girls used more maladaptive emotional coping (such as ruminating on their problems and lashing out at others) than boys until adolescence, when boys increased in their emotion-focused coping (Hampel & Petermann, 2005). Separating gender from gender role allowed an examination of these two factors, and results indicated that adolescents with feminine gender role orientation were more likely to use emotion-focused coping than adolescents with masculine gender role orientation (Washburn-Ormachea, Hillman, & Sawilowsky, 2004). Additional evidence in support of the socialization view comes from examinations of coping in different cultural groups. If coping differs with culture and gender within cultures, then socialization must be important in these differences. Research with African American, Asian American, and White college students (Sheu & Sedlacek, 2004) indicated both ethnic and gender differences in coping. Therefore, some evidence is consistent with the socialization view of gender differences in coping.

Consistent with the structural view, men and women tend to cope in similar ways when they are in similar situations. Early research that showed stereotypical gender differences in coping—men using problem-focused and women using emotion-focused strategies—may have been biased by the different situations of the participants. For example, in one study that showed such results (Folkman & Lazarus, 1980), the men were much more likely to be employed than the women. When studies have assessed coping strategies for men and women in comparable situations, the results have shown more similarities than differences. A longitudinal study of stress in medical school (Niemi & Vainiomäki, 2006) revealed similar stress for male and female students, and a study of first-year college students

(Pritchard & Wilson, 2006) found that coping strategies became more similar over the first semester of college, with male students beginning to use more emotion-focused strategies.

An exception to gender similarity is that women tend to use social support more than men. A study of college students (Lengua & Stormshak, 2000) and another of Spanish adults (González-Moreles, Peiró, Rodríguez, & Greenglass, 2006) showed no gender differences for active, problem-focused coping, but women were more likely to seek social support than men. Examining coping strategies among adolescents in Hungary (Piko, 2001) showed that girls were more likely than boys to seek social support, but boys who used this strategy showed fewer mental health problems than boys who used other coping strategies. In a study of workplace stress (Gianakos, 2002), women were more likely to use active coping strategies than men, and both sought social support, but men tended to rely on their workplace social networks whereas women relied on their family social networks for support. In a study of Canadian physicians (Lovell, Lee, & Brotheridge, 2009), female physicians were more likely than male physicians to seek social support for their stress.

Another possibility is that no gender differences exist in terms of coping. A study that used two methods to measure coping (Porter et al., 2000) pointed to this possibility. This study asked male and female participants to fill out questionnaires about their coping strategies, but these participants also carried electronic diaries that prompted them to make a report every 40 minutes concerning their stress and coping. The reports from the electronic diaries showed no gender differences, but the questionnaires did. This finding brings up the possibility that reports of gender differences in coping are biased by memories funneled through gender role stereotypes, and the few gender differences in coping may be research artifacts rather than genuine differences.

Therefore, situational factors and gender roles may be more important factors in coping than sex or personality traits. If so, gender differences in coping may be fairly large because men's and women's lives show many situational differences, and women report more situations as stressful than men do (Day & Livingstone, 2003). Also, gender roles place women in more situations that encourage seeking social support. Therefore, the stresses related to women's and men's lives continue to vary, and their coping strategies may also vary. The tendency of women to define more events as stressful, combined with stressors that occur more frequently in their lives, may account for some of the differences in behavior problems. Other possibilities for the source of these differences lie in the criteria and in the processes used to diagnose mental and behavioral disorders.

Diagnoses of Mental Disorders

Before a sick person can receive appropriate treatment, the person must receive a **diagnosis**, a statement of the classification of a physical or psychological problem. Without a diagnosis, treatment would be haphazard rather than connected to the problem. Thus, classification of both physical and mental problems is an essential step in receiving proper care. A good clinical classification system should provide information about the cause of the condition, enable clinicians to make predictions about the course of the disorder, and suggest a course of treatment as well as methods of prevention (Sarason & Sarason, 2001). In addition, a system of classification should provide a set of common terminology for professionals to communicate among themselves. No system of diagnosis meets these goals perfectly, but the goals are common to the diagnosis of physical and mental problems.

Diagnosis is a challenging task that consists of matching information about what constitutes a disorder against a person's symptoms. Because any person's symptoms will not match the textbook description of a disorder, clinicians' personal judgment is always a factor in the diagnosis, which allows for the possibility that personal bias can enter the diagnostic process.

Although diagnosis is a necessary part of treatment, it presents disadvantages as well as advantages (Sarason & Sarason, 2001). The advantages include providing an accepted standard that allows reliable diagnosis of the same problem by different clinicians. One of the problems involves labeling—the need to apply a label to the diagnosis. With mental disorders, many labels carry a stigma, and people who have been labeled with diagnoses of mental disorders may be the targets of discrimination. Furthermore, labeling also puts people into categories, and grouping people tends to magnify the similarities and obscure the individual differences of those within a category.

Currently, two systems exist for the classification of mental disorders—the International Classification of Diseases (ICD) of the World Health Organization and the *Diagnostic and Statistical Manual of Mental Disorders* (*DSM*) of the American Psychiatric Association. With the publication of the fourth edition of the *DSM,* the two systems became more compatible. Increasing compatibility with international psychiatry remains a priority for the fifth edition of the *DSM*, which is scheduled to appear in 2012 (American Psychiatric Association [APA], 2009).

The *DSM* Classification System

The *DSM* of the American Psychiatric Association has become the standard for professionals who provide mental health care, especially in North America. Both the first version of the manual (1952) and the second edition (1968) were relatively brief and strongly influenced by psychoanalytic theory (Sarason & Sarason, 2001). Diagnosis required the clinician to understand the patients' internal, unobservable psychological processes, which failed to provide reliable diagnoses.

The third edition of the *DSM* appeared in 1980 and represented a substantial revision. The goal was to create a description-based system of classification for mental disorders that would lead clinicians to make reliable judgments. The *DSM-IV,* which appeared in 1994, and the text revision (*DSM-IV-TR*) contained no major changes but allowed for greater compatibility with the ICD. These revision included diagnosis on the basis of five dimensions, or *axes,* which allow for comprehensive physical, psychological, and social diagnoses.

The first three axes provide the diagnosis, and the two other axes provide an evaluation of stressors and overall functioning. The manual contains over 240 different diagnoses along with descriptions of the symptoms that characterize the disorders. Information also appears concerning typical age of onset, course of the disorder, and gender ratio of the disorder—that is, how commonly the problem appears in men compared to women. In addition, the manual also contains information concerning a comparison of other, similar disorders so that clinicians can distinguish among disorders that have similar symptoms.

Axis I describes the major clinical disorders, such as schizophrenia, depression, and anxiety disorders, among others. Axis II includes mental retardation and personality disorders, such as antisocial personality, histrionic personality, and dependent personality disorders. Axis III contains a classification of physical disorders and is compatible with the ICD diagnosis system. Axis IV allows for reporting of psychosocial and environmental problems related to the diagnosis of psychopathology, including events such as death of a loved one, problems in school, homelessness, or loss of a job. Axis V provides an overall rating of functioning on the Global Assessment of Functioning Scale. Diagnosis includes a rating on each of the five axes.

For example, a diagnosis on Axis I might be **posttraumatic stress disorder (PTSD)**, a subclassification within the category of anxiety disorders. The *DSM-IV-TR* describes the diagnosis for this disorder as composed of several criteria. To be diagnosed with posttraumatic stress disorder, the person must meet five criteria: (1) "the person experienced, witnessed, or was confronted with an event or events that involved actual or threatened death or serious injury, or a threat to the physical integrity of self or others . . . [and] the person's response involved intense fear, helplessness, or horror" (APA, 2000, p. 467); (2) re-experience of the event in some form, (3) avoidance of stimuli associated with the traumatic event or numbing of responsiveness; (4) increased arousal, such as irritability, difficulty concentrating, or hypervigilance; and (5) duration of at least 1 month.

The combination of these criteria must be present and must produce "clinically significant distress or impairment in social, occupational, or other important areas of functioning" (APA, 2000, p. 468) for a diagnosis of PTSD. The *DSM-IV-TR* offers guidelines to the clinician for the different forms of re-experiencing the event, the types of avoidance and numbing that might occur, and the symptoms of increased arousal that accompany PTSD.

For a person with a diagnosis of PTSD on Axis I, the Axis II diagnosis might or might not indicate pathology; the axes are independent of each other. Thus, many people who receive a diagnosis of PTSD have no other conditions that predispose them to the disorder and might receive diagnoses of "no problem" on Axis II (Sarason & Sarason, 2001). Alternatively, people with PTSD might have other separate developmental or personality disorders, which may relate to the PTSD.

If the person with a diagnosis of PTSD has developed the disorder as a result of a combat experience or rape, then the person may also have physical injuries that stem from the same situation. The distinction between symptoms produced by PTSD and physical injury such as brain damage may be particularly difficult to distinguish during diagnosis (O'Donnell, Creamer, Bryant, Schnyder, & Shalev, 2003). The Axis III diagnosis would note injuries or other physical conditions that could affect the person's psychological functioning.

Axis IV gives the clinician an opportunity to note any social and environmental problems that might affect the development, recurrence, or exacerbation of mental disorders. The *DSM-IV-TR* instructs clinicians to note as many of these problems as are relevant and that have occurred within the prior year. PTSD is an exception, however; these events may have occurred more than a year before diagnosis and still be relevant to the problem.

Axis V allows the clinician to rate the person on the Global Assessment of Functioning Scale, based on overall psychological, social, and occupational functioning (excluding physical and environmental limitations). This scale ranges from 1 to 100, with low numbers indicating a low level of functioning and high numbers indicating less impairment. For example, a person with PTSD resulting from combat experiences might also show alcohol abuse, sleep problems, sensitivity to loud noises, and outbursts of violence with little provocation. These problem behavior indicate a moderate difficulty in social and occupational functioning, which would be reflected in the overall rating.

The *DSM* has sparked heated controversy. Criticisms include a lack of research support, adding and deleting diagnoses for political rather than scientific reasons, and adding diagnoses that may not be abnormal (Kutchins & Kirk, 1997; Marecek, 2001; Poland & Caplan, 2004). The lists of behaviors that serve as criteria for each diagnostic category gives the impression of objectivity, but little research supports these criteria (Lerman, 1996). Therefore, the impression of objectivity is an illusion. This issue is part of the discussion for *DSM-V* (APA, 2009) but also a continuing controversy within that process (MIWatch, 2009).

Gender Inequity in the Diagnosis of Mental Disorders

Criticisms of the multiaxial system of the *DSM* appeared immediately following its release in 1980, including accusations of gender bias. A number of critics (Cosgrove & Riddle, 2004; Lerman, 1996; Marecek, 2001) have asserted that the *DSM* system includes descriptions of disorders that make women likely to be diagnosed with problem behavior, even when the behavior is not due to any pathology. That situation stems from using a male standard for what is considered normal, making any behavior found more commonly in women outside the norm. The process of diagnosis is influenced by social values, and generally "professionals have used male-based norms to define healthy versus pathological behavior" (Cook, Warnke, & Dupuy, 1993, pp. 312–313). This bias has resulted in behaviors such as independence and assertiveness considered to be important for healthy mental functioning, whereas emotional expressiveness may be considered the sign of a problem.

In 1972, Phyllis Chesler proposed that diagnosis of mental disorders is fundamentally gender biased. Chesler contended that women who overconform or underconform to the traditional feminine gender role are subject to diagnosis; if they are either too aggressive or too submissive, they are deviant. Although Chesler's argument centered on the diagnosis of women's problems, the rationale can also extend to men. Those men who fail to conform to the male gender role may be at increased risk for diagnosis. Confirmation for Chesler's contention came from a study (Rosenfield, 1982) that demonstrated that gender role stereotypes relate to psychiatric diagnosis. Women and men who showed signs of psychopathology that were more typical of the other gender were more likely to be judged as candidates for hospitalization than were those who showed gender-typical disorders. A more recent study (Wirth & Bodenhausen, 2009) also found that stereotypes affect the evaluation of psychopathology. This study discovered that people evaluated a man with depression or a woman with alcohol abuse problems as more likely to have a disorder than when the man was alcoholic and the woman depressed. Both studies suggest that "deviant" deviance is seen as more serious than more "normal" deviance.

The *DSM* system has also received criticism for its failure to consider the life circumstances and culture of those receiving diagnoses (Ali, 2004; Marecek, 2001). The fourth edition of *DSM* made specific efforts to sensitize clinicians to the importance of cultural factors in diagnosis, but some critics (Dana, 2001) have contended that these efforts have not gone far enough. Despite the warnings about cultural factors in behavior, the conceptualization of diagnosis for behavior problems focuses on personal behavior. This focus assumes that disorders reside within the person, and that the person's circumstances, although possibly relevant, are not the source of the problem. Thus, if a battered woman experiences distress or depression, she will still be diagnosed by her symptoms as having depression or one of the anxiety disorders. The violence of her home life may be taken into account; however, even though the symptoms warrant a diagnosis of mental disorder, that diagnosis is given to her, not to her batterer or her home circumstances. Thus, people may receive diagnoses and then treatment for depression or substance abuse disorder without addressing the social context of the problem and without the clinician considering it appropriate to do so. A survey of clinical psychology interns (Middaugh, 1994) showed that 19% of male (but only 5% of female) interns believed that female clients must learn to adjust to their life circumstances. Although these percentages indicate that a minority of clinicians holds such attitudes, this minority holds women responsible for the behavior of others.

As noted in Chapter 13, some normal female functions, such as childbearing, have become "medicalized" and thus considered abnormal. This criticism applies to **premenstrual dysphoric disorder (PMDD)**, the diagnosis applied to symptoms that are very similar to premenstrual syndrome (PMS) (Cosgrove & Caplan, 2004; Marecek, 2001). A diagnostic category limited only to women is destined to provoke controversy; such controversy has continued with the publication of the *DSM-IV* and its inclusion of PMDD. Debate continues over the proper diagnostic criteria and appropriate treatment (Weisz & Knaapen, 2009) as well as the frequency of the disorder (Gehlert, Song, Chang, & Hartlage, 2009).

Criticisms of gender bias have been even more frequent for the Axis II personality disorders than for Axis I disorders. Part of the criticism has focused on the poorer research support for the personality disorders. Improving the research basis for personality disorders is one of the goals for *DSM-V* (Widiger, Simonsen, Krueger, Livesley, & Verheul, 2005).

◘ GENDERED VOICES

I Think I Have It

Male psychologist: "Have you read the new description of PMS that will appear in the fourth edition of the *DSM?* I'm really very concerned."

Female psychologist: "Yes, I have. *Premenstrual dysphoric disorder* will replace *late luteal phase dysphoric disorder.* I'm concerned, too. It's supposed to appear in the main body of the classification under mood disorders, and I understand that the treatment will be antidepressant drugs. It's been very controversial, and I think that this move will keep it that way. What bothers you?"

Male psychologist: "According to my reading of the diagnostic criteria, I think I have it."

Other criticism has targeted the gender, ethnic, and social class biases inherent in the description of these disorders. Indeed, the *DSM-IV* warned clinicians that they "must be cautious not to overdiagnose or underdiagnose certain Personality Disorders in females or in males because of social stereotypes about typical gender roles and behaviors" (APA, 2000, p. 688).

The *DSM* warning is warranted; the differential diagnosis for mental disorders can be conceptualized by viewing personality disorders as extensions of gender role stereotypes. For example, **schizotypal personality disorder** is characterized by "a pervasive pattern of social and interpersonal deficits marked by acute discomfort with, and reduced capacity for, close relationships as well as cognitive or perceptual distortions and eccentricities of behavior" (APA, 2000, p. 697). **Antisocial personality disorder** appears as a "pervasive pattern of disregard for, and violation of, the rights of others" (p. 701), including lying, fighting, stealing, and physical cruelty. Both these personality disorders include exaggerations of the traditional male gender role (Brannon, 1976). Indifference to social relationships resembles the Sturdy Oak facet of the role, with its emphasis on self-reliance and lack of emotion. Elements of antisocial personality disorder resemble the Give 'Em Hell facet, with its emphasis on dominance and aggression.

Dependent personality disorder features "a pervasive and excessive need to be taken care of that leads to submissive and clinging behavior and fears of separation" (APA, 2000, p. 721), which is an exaggeration of stereotypical feminine behavior. **Histrionic personality disorder** is also compatible with gender stereotypes for women, including "pervasive and excessive emotionality and attention-seeking behavior" (APA, 2000, p. 711). As Pamela Reed Gibson (2004, p. 201) observed, "our culture actually exerts pressure upon women to adopt and exhibit histrionic behavior but labels them mentally ill if they do so." Table 14.4 shows some of the personality disorders, along with their prevalence and the gender-related differences in their diagnoses.

Not surprisingly, studies that have investigated clinicians' diagnoses of these personality disorders have found biases in diagnosis that are consistent with gender stereotypes

TABLE 14.4 *Prevalence of and Gender-Related Differences in Personality Disorders*

Disorder	Estimated Rate in General Population	Gender Difference
Paranoid	0.5–2.5%	More common among men in clinical populations
Antisocial	3% men, 1% women	More common among men in both general and clinical populations
Avoidant	0.5–1.0%	Equally frequent in women and men
Borderline	2%	More common in women—75% of those diagnosed are women
Histrionic	2–3%	More commonly diagnosed in women
Narcissistic	<1%	More common among men—50–75% are men
Dependent	Most common of personality disorders	More commonly diagnosed in women.
Schizotypal	3%	Slightly more common in men

Source: Based on *Diagnostic and Statistical Manual of Mental Disorders* (4th ed., Text Revision), by American Psychiatric Association, 2000, Washington, DC: Author. Reprinted with permission from the *Diagnostic and Statistical Manual of Mental Disorders, Text Revision, Fourth Edition*, (Copyright 2000). American Psychiatric Association.

for antisocial personality disorder and histrionic personality disorder (Flanagan & Blashfield, 2005; Samuel & Widiger, 2009) as well as borderline personality disorder (Bjorklund, 2006). Rather than automatically connecting a personality disorder with a male or female client, clinicians appear to use gender as a background piece of information that skews the process of interpreting symptoms, resulting in a bias that is consistent with gender stereotypes (Flanagan & Blashfield, 2005). When this bias is enacted through the diagnosis process, the result is an exaggeration of gender differences that might actually exist in these categories.

A more fundamental criticism of diagnoses of mental disorders revolves around the concern that women will be considered less psychologically healthy than men because in any system, men constitute the standard for what is mentally healthy (Bem, 1993b). An early study (Broverman, Broverman, Clarkson, Rosenkrantz, & Vogel, 1970) laid the foundation for this concern by asking what constitutes a well-adjusted, healthy adult. The results showed that clinically trained psychologists, psychiatrists, and social workers described a well-adjusted, healthy person in different terms than a well-adjusted, healthy woman. For example, such stereotypically feminine traits as dependence and emotionality are not part of the concept for adult mental health. These researchers contended that the discrepancy between the ideal of mental health for a woman and that for an adult reflected a double standard. However, later studies (Phillips & Gilroy, 1985; Wood, Garb, Lilienfield, & Nezworski, 2002) have revealed no significant gender-related differences for standards of mental health.

Even without overall bias within the system, gender and ethnic biases may enter the diagnosis process through clinicians' personal biases and their influence on the decision about pathology (Wood, Garb, et al., 2002). This process may include two types of judgment errors—overdiagnosis and underdiagnosis (López, 1989). The most commonly studied form of diagnostic bias has been *overdiagnosis*, identifying people as having disorders when they do not. *Underdiagnosis* is the mistake of failing to identify problems by overlooking symptoms or considering them normal. Both present problems for patients by identifying problems in people who have no pathology and by failing to diagnose problems in others who have mental disorders.

Research on under- and overdiagnosis has confirmed their existence but has also found a pattern of gender bias (Horsfall, 2001; Redman, Webb, Hennrikus, Gordon, & Sanson-Fisher, 1991). Standardized assessments show a similar number of men and women as psychologically disturbed, but the diagnosis process may lead to different results. Overdiagnosis and underdiagnosis occur in both women and men. Physicians show a tendency to underrate the psychological disturbances of men and to overrate those of women but to consider men's symptoms as more serious than women's. Other research (Wood, Garb, et al., 2002) has confirmed the tendency to both overdiagnose and underdiagnose certain psychological problems, but cultural differences are more likely to contribute to over- and underdiagnosis than gender.

Therefore, both the *DSM* system and the process of diagnosis contain the potential for bias. The *DSM* contains descriptions of disorders that allow clinicians to decide which diagnosis is appropriate for a particular person. These diagnoses are included in the *DSM* through a committee decision that may be motivated by social or political reasons rather than accuracy or scientific research. The descriptions of several diagnoses seem like exaggerations of gender stereotypes, and the number of women and men who receive these diagnoses vary accordingly. In addition, clinicians' perceptions, including gender stereotypes, intrude into the diagnosis process, providing another route for gender and cultural bias in the diagnosis of mental disorders. Unfortunately, these criticisms are not often included in textbooks about abnormal psychology (Wiley, 2004), and students may be left with the impression that the *DSM* system is objective and accepted without controversy—which is not true.

Gender Comparisons in Psychopathology

Chapter 13 presented information about gender differences in seeking health care, showing that women are more likely than men to do so. This tendency also applies to psychological problems. Data from large-scale surveys of mental health problems (Kessler, Brown, & Broman, 1981; Substance Abuse and Mental Health Services Administration [SAMHSA], 2009) showed that women seek mental health care more often than men do. Several possibilities exist for this difference, including women's tendency to interpret problems as mental health problems (Kessler et al., 1981). Women's help-seeking is responsible for between 10 and 28% of the gender difference in treatment.

The circumstances that bring women and men to treatment vary. Women are more likely than men to consult general physicians about mental health problems, which opens the possibility for additional mental health consultations. Men do not make as many physician visits as women (see Chapter 13), so a comparable number of opportunities do not arise for them. The overall rate of hospitalization for mental disorders is similar for women and men (SAMHSA, 2009). Women are more likely to receive outpatient treatment, and men tend to be confined in and to stay in mental hospitals longer than women do.

In examining the patterns of gender similarities and differences for mental disorders, not all disorders show gender differences, but several do. Anxiety disorders, depression, and substance abuse disorders are among those problems that show marked gender differences, whereas schizophrenia and bipolar disorder are more evenly distributed between women and men.

Depression

The clinical diagnosis of *depression* varies from the popular conception of minor, temporary, low mood; depression is a severe, debilitating disorder that affects all aspects of functioning. In the *DSM* system, depression is classified as a type of mood disorder and appears as a diagnosis on Axis I. Two subclassifications of depressive disorders exist— major depression and dysthymia.

Symptoms of **major depression** include dissatisfaction and anxiety, loss of interest and loss of pleasure, feelings of helplessness and hopelessness, changes in sleep or eating habits, and difficulty in concentrating. These symptoms must persist for at least 2 weeks to warrant a diagnosis of major depression. **Dysthymia** is milder than major depression and tends to be a chronic condition that may last for years. This diagnosis applies to people who chronically experience depressed mood, loss of interest, or other symptoms of depression, much as they would a personality trait. Major depression and dysthymia can co-occur or can exist separately.

TABLE 14.5 *Prevalence of and Gender-Related Differences in Mood Disorders*

Disorder	Estimated Rate in General Population	Gender Difference
Major depression	10–25% for women, 5–9% for men	More common in women, with a ratio of 2:1
Dysthymia	3%	More common in women, with a ratio of 2–3:1
Bipolar disorder	0.4–1.6%	No difference

Source: Based on *Diagnostic and Statistical Manual of Mental Disorders* (4th ed., Text Revision), by American Psychiatric Association, 2000, Washington, DC: Author. Reprinted with permission from the *Diagnostic and Statistical Manual of Mental Disorders, Text Revision, Fourth Edition*, (Copyright 2000). American Psychiatric Association.

Table 14.5 shows the prevalence of and gender-related differences in mood disorders. The ratio of major depression in women compared with that in men is about 2 to 1 (Culbertson, 1997; Kessler, 2003; SAMHSA, 2009). Although most societies show a ratio of female to male depression similar to that of the United States, gender differences in depression do not occur during childhood (Twenge & Nolen-Hoeksema, 2002) but begin during adolescence (Wade, Cairney, & Pevalin, 2002). In addition, several rural, nonmodern cultures have similar rates of depression in women and men. Among these cultures are the old-order Amish, a rural farming society in the United States. In addition, university students, the elderly, and the bereaved show no gender differences in rates of depression. The explanations for these figures have included biological as well as social and cognitive theories.

Biological contributions to the development of depression include genes and hormones. Some research (Caspi et al., 2003) indicated that a specific genetic configuration interacted with the experience of stress to produce depression, both in adolescents (Åslund et al., 2009) and in adults (Brummett et al., 2008). Thus when genetically vulnerable individuals encounter environmental stressors, they are more likely to develop depression than individuals without this genetic vulnerability.

Those who have sought biological explanations for the gender differences in depression usually rely on the differences in reproductive hormones, but simple versions of hormonal theories have very little clear support (Nolen-Hoeksema, 2006). Jill Cyranowski and her colleagues (Cyranowski, Frank, Young, & Shear, 2000) hypothesized a more complex role for reproductive hormones in the development of depression. They speculated that hormones associated with the onset of puberty may constitute a type of vulnerability. Combined with girls' needs for affiliation and negative life events, adolescent girls and women become more vulnerable to depression.

Alan Booth and his colleagues (Booth, Johnson, & Granger, 1999) researched the connection between testosterone and depression in men and found a complex relationship that also points to a physiology–environment interaction. For men with low testosterone levels, the lower their hormone level, the higher their rate of depression. For men with high testosterone levels, the higher the hormone level, the higher the rate of depression. Booth and colleagues hypothesized that the relationship of negative life events and high testosterone is the basis of this association; men with high testosterone are more likely to exhibit antisocial behaviors that put them at risk for negative life events that are risk factors for mental health problems. In a similar study with children (Booth, Johnson, Granger, Crouter, & McHale, 2003), a similar interaction occurred. Good parent-child relationships moderated the risks associated with testosterone for both depression and low testosterone and antisocial behaviors and high testosterone. Therefore, hormones may be a factor in depression, but their role is quite complex, not clearly established, and not restricted to women.

Other vulnerabilities to depression come from differences in the use of cognitive strategies for dealing with distressing events that affect more women than men. Susan Nolen-Hoeksema and her colleagues (Nolen-Hoeksema, 2006; Nolen-Hoeksema, Larson, & Grayson, 1999) proposed that the gender differences in depression arise from a combination of differences in negative experiences, feelings of mastery, and strategies for dealing with negative feelings. Women have more negative experiences, lower feelings of mastery, and tend to ruminate on their feelings. Dwelling on problems and negative feelings tends to amplify the feelings, which can lead to depression. Rather than ruminate, men tend to take action, which may not solve problems but does provide distraction. Figure 14.1 shows the complex relationship among these factors. This pattern of interrelationships appeared in a large community study and suggested that women may become involved in a cycle of stress from negative events, low feelings of mastery, rumination, and depression. A meta-analysis of the studies on rumination showed that this cognitive style presents a risk for current and future depression among adolescents (Rood, Roelofs, Bögels, Nolen-Hoeksema, & Schouten, 2009). Other research on rumination (Watkins, Moulds, & Mackintosh, 2005) has indicated that this style of thinking may be related to anxiety disorders as well as depression.

Another cognitive explanation for women's higher rates of depression is that their genuine emotions, goals, and desires become suppressed or "silenced" (Jack, 1991, 1999).

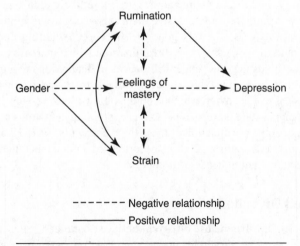

FIGURE 14.1 *Effects of Gender, Rumination, Strain, and Feelings of Mastery on Depression*

Source: Adapted from "Explaining the Gender Difference in Depressive Symptoms," by S. Nolen-Hoeksema, J. Larson, and C. Grayson, 1999, *Journal of Personality and Social Psychology, 77,* p. 1067. Copyright 1999 by the American Psychological Association. Adapted by permission of Susan Nolen-Hoeksema.

According to this view, women are more prone to depression because society devalues women and the feminine, placing women in a position in which they must deny who they really are to get along in the world and to maintain their relationships. When women conform to this standard, they lose their sense of self and become depressed. Research support for this view is less robust than for the cognitive factor of rumination, but studies have confirmed that scores on Silencing the Self Scale relate to depression (Besser, Flett, & Davis, 2003; Cramer, Gallant, & Langlois, 2005; Tan & Carfagnini, 2008). However, one important contention for the Silencing the Self concept has not been supported: the restriction of the concept to women. According to Jack (1991), this self-silencing applies to women and explains their greater depression, but in studies that included men (Cramer & Thoms, 2003; Cramer et al., 2005; Duarte & Thompson, 1999), men showed a similar relationship between self-silencing and depression as women. These findings indicate that the concept of self-silencing may be a mediating factor in the development of depression but not one unique to women.

Although gender differences exist in the diagnosis of depression, perhaps these differences represent a failure to understand men's depression, as the headline story suggested. Women and men probably experience the negative feelings that underlie depression at similar rates, but they express their feelings differently. Women tend to turn their negative feelings inward, whereas men are more likely to take action. In women, the feelings produce symptoms consistent with the female gender role and hence with the *DSM* diagnostic criteria for depression. In men, the feelings produce symptoms such as substance abuse, risk taking, and violence but may still represent depression. Thus the symptoms of depression may be seen as an expression of gender role socialization for women, but men exhibit different symptoms, which have received other diagnoses.

In summary, two types of depression appear in the *DSM* classification—major depression and dysthymia. Women from many cultures are more likely than men to report symptoms of and receive treatment for depressive disorders at a ratio of approximately 2 to 1. Several explanations exist for this gender difference, including genetic and hormonal vulnerability and the cognitive style of rumination, which increase the risk for depression. Another view holds that the gender differences in depression are a product of the ways in which women and men typically deal with distress and negative mood. Women's style includes passive behavior, which is compatible with expressing symptoms of depression, whereas men's style is to become active, expressing symptoms of risk taking, violence, drug use, or some combination of these three behaviors. Janet Hyde and her colleagues (Hyde, Mezulis, & Abramson, 2008) have proposed a model that integrates the risk factors for depression, including gender differences.

Substance-Related Disorders

Substance-related disorders involve the use of **psychoactive substances**, drugs that affect thoughts, emotions, and behavior. Examples include alcohol, amphetamines, marijuana (cannabis), cocaine, hallucinogens, opiates, and sedatives. In order to be diagnosed as having one of the types of substance-related disorders, the person not only must use the drug but also must exhibit a strong desire to use the substance and experience problems in social or occupational functioning due to drug use.

Alcohol is the most frequently used and abused substance, and men drink more than women in the categories of light, moderate, and heavy drinking (SAMHSA, 2009). Indeed, drinking and drunkenness are associated with the male, and not the female, gender role (Capraro, 2000; Monk & Ricciardelli, 2003). People expect men to drink beer and to get drunk, but the same expectation does not apply to women (Day, Gough, & McFadden, 2004). Indeed, women (and especially feminine women) are not expected to drink beer (but are expected to drink wine) and should *not* get drunk (Landrine, Bardwell, & Dean, 1988).

Alcohol is not equally intoxicating for men and women. Women tend to weigh less than men, and body weight affects intoxication, meaning that each drink has a greater effect on a smaller person. In addition, some research has indicated that women's metabolism of alcohol produces a higher alcohol concentration in their blood compared to that in men's blood, even with the body-weight factor taken into account (Ward & Coutelle, 2003). Both these factors result in greater risks to women who drink moderately or heavily than to men who do so (Mann, 2005). Because fewer women than men are heavy drinkers, however, men are more likely than women to experience the problems associated with heavy drinking, including the health risks and social problems associated with alcohol abuse.

A variety of evidence suggests that drinking is related to depression for both men and women. Alcohol and other substance abuse disorders often co-occur, but the direction of the relationship has not been clear. Several longitudinal studies have demonstrated that some people use drinking (and probably other substances) as a strategy of avoidant coping (Holahan, Moos, Holahan, Cronkite, & Randall, 2001, 2003, 2004). In a group of community adults (Holahan et al., 2001), a group of people diagnosed with depression (Holahan et al., 2003), and a contrast of the two groups (Holahan et al., 2004), drinking and depression were associated. Individuals diagnosed as depressed tended to use the strategy of drinking to cope with stress and problems, which escalated their drinking or developed alcohol-related problems over the 10 years of the study (Holahan et al., 2003, 2004). Thus, the drinking-to-cope strategy constitutes a risk of alcohol problems for depressed people. In the community sample (Holahan et al., 2001), people who reported that they used drinking as a way to cope tended to escalate their drinking and were more likely to develop problem drinking over the 10-year period of the study than people who drank for other reasons. In a study of college students (Pauley & Hesse, 2009), depression correlated with increased drinking. Therefore, the link between drinking and depression may be through the strategy of drinking to cope with stress and problems, and people who lack other coping strategies may be particularly vulnerable.

Illegal drug use is also higher among men than women, with men more likely than women to use and abuse drugs such as heroin, amphetamines, cocaine, and marijuana—a pattern that parallels their alcohol use (SAMHSA, 2009). On the other hand, women are more likely to use prescription tranquilizers and sedatives, which they receive from physicians who prescribe them for women's psychological disorders (Travis & Compton, 2001). The higher rate of prescription drug use by women and the greater use of illegal drugs by men result in similar rates but different patterns of substance use. Table 14.6 (page 386) summarizes the prevalence of and gender-related differences in substance use.

Men's drug use is more apt to be illegal, making them more likely to receive diagnoses because of their drug use. This diagnosis difference may not reflect much of a differential tendency in substance use: "The sex differences in the use of alcohol and prescription psychotropics are not inconsistent with the hypothesis that men and women are equally likely to resort to substance use for coping, and that the sex difference is merely in the choice of substances" (Biener, 1987, p. 336). Perhaps women might also resort to illegal drug use if physicians were less willing to prescribe drugs for them.

TABLE 14.6 *Prevalence of and Gender-Related Differences in Substance-Related Disorders*

Disorder	Estimated Rate in General Population	Gender Difference
Alcohol dependence	5%	More common in men, with a ratio as high as 5:1, varying with age and cultural background
Amphetamine dependence	Possibly as high as 1.5%	More common in men, with a 3:1 or 4:1 ratio
Cannabis	1.2%	More common in men
Cocaine	0.2%	More common in men, with a 1.5–2:1 ratio
Hallucinogens	0.1%	More common in men, with a 3:1 ratio
Opiates	2%	More common in men, with a ratio of 1.5–3:1
Sedatives, hypnotics, or anxiolytics	<1%	Women are at higher risk

Source: Based on *Diagnostic and Statistical Manual of Mental Disorders* (4th ed., Text Revision), by American Psychiatric Association, 2000, Washington, DC: Author. Reprinted with permission from the *Diagnostic and Statistical Manual of Mental Disorders, Text Revision, Fourth Edition*, (Copyright 2000). American Psychiatric Association.

In summary, the research indicates that a relationship exists between depression and drinking. The tendency to drink more heavily when depressed is stronger among men but not exclusive to them. Perhaps men choose this strategy for dealing with negative feelings more often than women do, so this difference in dealing with negative feelings may account for some of the gender differences in depression and substance-abuse disorders. The overall pattern of drug use for men and women probably differs little, but women tend to use legal prescription drugs, whereas men's drug use is more likely to come in the form of alcohol and illegal drugs.

Anxiety Disorders

The group of disorders labeled anxiety disorders includes panic attack, phobias, obsessive-compulsive disorder, and posttraumatic stress disorder, all involving features of anxiety and avoidance of problem situations. A survey of more than 18,000 people indicated that anxiety disorders affect more than 7% of adults in the United States (Regier, Narrow, & Rae, 1990). No gender differences exist for some types of anxiety disorders, but other types appear much more often in women than in men.

Panic attack is characterized by periods of intense fear that occur without any fear-provoking situation. These attacks are typically accompanied by physical symptoms of distress, such as sweating, dizziness, and shortness of breath. This disorder is about equally common in women and men, but panic disorder with **agoraphobia** is about twice as common in women. "The essential feature of agoraphobia is anxiety about being in places or situations from which escape might be difficult (or embarrassing) or in which help may not be available in the event of having a panic attack . . . or panic-like symptoms" (APA, 2000, p. 432). These feelings of anxiety lead people to avoid the situations that might provoke such feelings.

Agoraphobia can also occur without panic disorder, and women are also more likely to have this disorder (APA, 2000; Carlbring, Gustafsson, Ekselius, & Andersson, 2002). Other **phobias**, unreasonable fears concerning some object or situation, constitute a second category of anxiety disorder. *Social phobias* appear as persistent fears of certain social situations, such as speaking in public, in which the person is judged by others or in which the person may do something embarrassing. The gender differences are small (APA, 2000). *Specific phobias,* fears of some object or situation other than anticipating a panic attack or being in a certain social situation, are more common among women.

Obsessive-compulsive disorder is the combination of obsession, which refers to recurrent, intrusive thoughts about something the person would prefer to ignore, and compulsion, which refers to repetitive behaviors intended to ease anxiety. To receive this diagnosis, a person must be distressed by the obsessive thoughts and must spend over an hour per day on the compulsive behaviors. According to the *DSM-IV-TR* (APA, 2000), this pattern of behavior is equally common in women and men but more common among boys than girls. Other research (Fireman, Koran, Leventhal, & Jacobson, 2001) has confirmed the gender difference for children but found obsessive-compulsive disorder more common among adult women than men.

Posttraumatic stress disorder (PTSD) (defined and discussed earlier in this chapter) was originally applied to men who suffered lasting effects from their war experiences, but its applicability to a wider variety of situations became evident. Now the diagnosis is given to people experiencing the prolonged aftereffects of many different types of traumas, including natural disasters, accidents, and violent crime as well as military combat. A random sample of women revealed that over 12% met the criteria for PTSD, a much higher percentage than previous estimates (Resnick, Kilpatrick, Dansky, Saunders, & Best, 1993). Women are more likely than men to develop PTSD, possibly because of the varieties of trauma and violence by which they are victimized (Nemeroff et al., 2006).

Table 14.7 summarizes the prevalence figures presented in *DSM-IV-TR* and the differences associated with gender for anxiety disorders. Overall, more women than men receive diagnoses of some type of anxiety disorder, indicating that agoraphobia and specific phobias are sufficiently common to cause women to dominate this category.

TABLE 14.7   *Prevalence of and Gender-Related Differences in Anxiety Disorders*

Disorder	Estimated Rate in General Population	Gender Difference
Panic attack with and without agoraphobia	1–3.5%	More common in women, with a ratio of 2–3:1
Specific phobias	4–8.8%	More common in women, with a ratio of 2:1
Social phobias	2–20%	More common in women in general population; more common in men in clinical settings
Obsessive-compulsive disorder	0.5–2.1%	No difference
Posttraumatic stress disorder	8%	Not specified in *DSM-IV*

Source: Based on *Diagnostic and Statistical Manual of Mental Disorders* (4th ed., Text Revision), by American Psychiatric Association, 2000, Washington, DC: Author. Reprinted with permission from the *Diagnostic and Statistical Manual of Mental Disorders, Text Revision, Fourth Edition*, (Copyright 2000). American Psychiatric Association.

▧ ACCORDING TO THE *M*EDIA . . .

Multiple Personality Disorder Creates Violent Men

In the movies, dissociative identity disorder (DID) is a popular plot device, but DID is referred to by the older term *multiple personality disorder* and often confused with schizophrenia (Byrne, 2001). In *Me, Myself and Irene* (2000), Jim Carrey's character is called a "schizo" whose split personalities both fall for the same woman. This movie was a comedy, but DID is usually not played for laughs; instead, movies featuring characters with DID either dramatize a case study of an individual with DID or present a fictional character as part of a plot revolving around this character's disorder. The former movies usually feature female characters; the latter more often show men with DID.

The fictionalized case studies of DID include *The Three Faces of Eve* (1957), *Sybil* (1976 and 2007), and *Voices Within: The Lives of Trudi Chase* (1990). All of these movies presented stories based on women who

had experienced the symptoms typical of this disorder, including childhood trauma, memory "blackouts" during which alternate personalities dominate, and a core personality that is passive, dependent, and plagued by feelings of guilt and depression (APA, 2000). These fictionalized stories also contain a number of inaccuracies, but the movies in which DID is a plot device portray individuals with dissociative personality disorder who are typically male and murderous. In movies such as *Psycho* (1960), *Raising Cain* (1992), *Primal Fear* (1996), *Fight Club* (1999), and *Identity* (2003), men with DID commit murder (or try to get away with murder). Even in movies with fictional female characters with DID, such as *Dressed to Kill* (1980) and *Never Talk to Strangers* (1995), these female characters are killers. These movies send the message of "hidden evil in the person tainted with mental illness" (Byrne, 2001, p. 27).

Women's higher rate of anxiety disorders is not surprising, considering that anxiety and fear are more characteristic of the female than of the male gender role. Even as children and adolescents, girls show more of the sensitivity to anxiety that may underlie the development of anxiety disorders (Walsh, Stewart, McLaughlin, & Comeau, 2004). Girls learn that it is acceptable for them to express anxiety and to worry (Craske, 2003). Thus, the gender differences among the different anxiety disorders suggest varying gender-related ways of expressing anxiety, which appears in many countries around the world (Seedat et al., 2009).

Other Disorders

Several important classifications of mental disorders show few or no gender differences in prevalence, but men and women with these disorders may not exhibit identical symptoms or the same time course of the disorder. For example, **schizophrenia**—a serious and complex disorder involving thought disturbances, problems in personal relationships, and possibly hallucinations—has been diagnosed with almost equally frequency in women and men. However, male schizophrenics tend to be younger than female schizophrenics at the time of their diagnosis, less likely to be married, more likely to exhibit poor social functioning, and more likely to have been recently hospitalized (Kalisz & Cechnicki, 2002; Usall, Ochoa, Araya, & Márquez, 2003). Despite these advantages for women, they tend to have more severe symptoms than men with increasing age (Seeman, 2003). Considering these differences, male and female schizophrenics exhibited more similarities than differences. (See According to the Media and According to the Research, which present media confusion about schizophrenia.)

◼ ACCORDING TO THE RESEARCH . . .

People with Dissociative Identity Disorder Are Usually Nonviolent Women

Movie portrayals of multiple personalities as killers offer screenwriters an easy way to show bizarre, violent behavior, but these media images are inaccurate in many ways. First, the term *multiple personality disorder* is not the current diagnosis; the current term is *dissociative identity disorder* (DID). This disorder was rarely diagnosed until the 1980s (Pope, Poliakoff, Parker, Boynes, & Hudson, 2007), and its increase has made it controversial (APA, 2000). Most diagnoses of DID apply to women, who are likely to have experienced sexual abuse and trauma as children (Foote, Smolin, Kaplan, Legatt, & Lipschitz, 2006).

Second, the portrayal of individuals with DID as violent is even more inaccurate. "Confusing schizophrenia with DID is unfortunate, but the violence these films depict adds misunderstanding to misinformation. That misunderstanding equates 'split personality' with 'nice guy/murderer'" (Byrne, 2001, p. 27). Even Jim Carrey in

Me, Myself, and Irene (2000) had a violent (but comic) personality that got into a fight with himself, as did Edward Norton's character in *Fight Club* (1999). Norton's character was also a murderer.

Research on the influence of media portrayals of people with mental illness has revealed that these depictions have the power to influence people's attitudes and behaviors. The association of mental disorders and violence in the media is exaggerated; characters with mental illness are 10 to 20 times more likely to be violent than actual mental patients or former mental patients (Diefenbach, 1997). In addition, a study with college students showed a relationship between negative attitudes toward the mentally ill and watching portrayals of mental disorders on television (Granello & Pauley, 2000). Therefore, the inaccurate depictions of DID in the media serve not only to convey inaccurate information but also to perpetuate the stigma associated with mental illness.

Bipolar disorder is one of the mood disorders, along with major depression and dysthymia (see Table 14.5). Bipolar disorder is characterized by periods of mania, high activity, and elevated mood alternating with periods of depression. These drastically different mood states change in a cyclic fashion such that the affected person experiences both mania and depression over a period of weeks or months, usually interspersed with periods of normal moods. Unlike the other two mood disorders, bipolar disorder shows no gender differences in prevalence (APA, 2000). However, women may manifest symptoms somewhat differently, spending more time in both depressive and manic phases than men and cycling from manic to depressed more rapidly (Rasgon et al., 2005).

The **somatoform disorders** show some gender differences. This classification of disorders includes the experience of physical symptoms of disease, but no identifiable physical basis for those symptoms. As a group, women are more likely to receive the diagnosis of somatoform disorder, but some of the disorders within this classification show no and others show large gender differences. *Conversion disorder,* the loss of physical function without any physical basis for the disability, was originally called *hysteria* and restricted to women. In the late 1800s, this disorder was so strongly associated with women that the extension of the label to men was controversial. The *DSM-IV-TR* (APA, 2000) listed conversion disorder as substantially more common in women than in men.

Another of the somatoform disorders is *somatization disorder,* the recurrence of physical complaints and the seeking of medical attention without receiving any diagnosis of a physical problem. These complaints are often dramatic or exaggerated, and the affected person seeks care from many medical professionals. Women account for 95% of somatization disorder diagnoses in the United States (Tomasson, Kent, & Coryell, 1991), but in some other cultures, this gender discrepancy is not large. For example, the ratio of women to men in Germany is 1.6 to 1 rather than 20 to 1 (Ladwig, Marten-Mittig, Erazo, & Gündel, 2001). The *DSM-IV-TR* cautions that physical disorders that involve many variable symptoms can erroneously lead to the diagnosis of somatization disorder. Given physicians' tendency to dismiss the physical complaints of women and attribute those complaints to emotional problems (see Chapter 13), this diagnosis may be erroneously applied to women who have physical rather than mental problems (Klonoff & Landrine, 1997).

Sexual disorders consist of two groups of disorders, paraphilias and sexual dysfunctions. **Paraphilias** are characterized by intense sexual feelings in response to objects or situations, such as nonhuman objects, children, nonconsenting persons, or even the suffering of self or others. The nonhuman objects include animals or items of clothing, and the situations include exposing one's genitals to strangers, fondling strangers in public places, observing sexual activities, or dressing in gender-inappropriate clothing. Sexual masochism—experiencing pleasure from receiving pain or humiliation—and sexual sadism—experiencing pleasure from inflicting pain or humiliation on one's sexual partner—are also among the paraphilias. About 95% of sexual masochists are men (APA, 2000), and this disorder is the most common paraphilia among women, which indicates that women are rarely diagnosed with these disorders.

Sexual dysfunctions, the other subcategory of sexual disorders, consist of abnormally low (or high) levels of sexual desire, or difficulty achieving arousal or orgasm. Women are more likely to receive diagnoses indicating abnormally low levels of sexual desire or inhibited orgasm, but men also experience these sexual problems. A summary of the prevalence and gender-related differences in schizophrenia, somatoform, and sexual disorders appears in Table 14.8.

When people receive diagnoses of abnormally low (or high) sexual interest or activity, these diagnoses require a standard of comparison, which may be their previous behavior as compared with their currently decreased (or increased) interest. Some critics (Working Group on A New View of Women's Sexual Problems, 2004) have questioned the *DSM* framework of sexual problems, especially for women. The possibility exists that patients may be held to some arbitrary standard of what constitutes normal levels of sexual activity, and they may be diagnosed on the basis of behavior that is deviant merely by definition.

In summary, several mental disorders show patterns of gender differences, and some disorders that have no overall discrepancy in prevalence do show gender differences in onset or experience. The most dramatic gender differences occur for anxiety and somatoform disorders—diagnoses overwhelmingly given to women—and sexual paraphilias—diagnoses overwhelmingly given to men. Schizophrenia and bipolar disorder show no gender difference in prevalence, but men and women with schizophrenics and bipolar disorder show some behavioral differences. The gender differences in bipolar disorder relate to rapidity of cycling, with women more likely to cycle rapidly.

Although psychopathology constitutes more than exaggerated gender role behavior, all gender differences in mental disorders lend themselves to interpretations through a lens of gender. People tend to exhibit pathology related to gender stereotypes—women show

TABLE 14.8 *Prevalence of and Gender-Related Differences in Rate of Selected Axis I Disorders*

Disorder	Estimated Rate in General Population	Gender Difference
Schizophrenia	0.5–1.5%	Slightly higher rate in men
Somatoform disorders		
Conversion disorder	11–500 per 100,000	More common in women, with a ratio of 2–10:1
Somatization disorder	0.2–2% in women <0.2% in men	Rarely diagnosed in men in the United States
Body dysmorphic disorder	Unknown	Equally common in men and women
Dissociative identity disorder	Controversial	More common in women, with a ratio of 3–9:1
Sexual dysfunction		
Paraphilias	No estimate	Rarely diagnosed in women, with the ratio of men to women at 20:1

Source: Based on *Diagnostic and Statistical Manual of Mental Disorders* (4th ed., Text Revision), by American Psychiatric Association, 2000, Washington, DC: Author. Reprinted with permission from the *Diagnostic and Statistical Manual of Mental Disorders, Text Revision, Fourth Edition*, (Copyright 2000). American Psychiatric Association.

signs of weakness and physical complaints, whereas men show violence and unusual sexuality. The patterns in rates of mental disorders for men and women reflect the power of gender stereotypes. When violations of gender roles occur, clinicians are likely to perceive that these patients have more severe problems than patients who exhibit psychopathology consistent with gender stereotypes.

GENDERED VOICES

The Doctor Wouldn't Listen

The case of a young woman who was in one of my classes is a good example of a woman whose physician failed to take her complaints seriously. This young woman felt unwell, experiencing a variety of symptoms, including chest pain, abdominal pain, and lack of energy. She consulted her physician, who had been her family's doctor since she was a child. He asked her about her symptoms and about her life. She described how she felt and where it hurt, along with the stresses and problems she had recently experienced: Her parents were getting divorced, and she felt so tired that school was difficult to manage. The physician said that she was experiencing stress and told her to relax, assuring her that she would feel better.

She tried but felt no better. After several visits, the woman was convinced that she had a problem that the physician was missing, and he was equally convinced that she had a mental problem that she failed to acknowledge. She consulted another physician, who might have behaved much as the first did, but instead, the physician did a series of tests that revealed a kidney tumor, which required immediate surgery. Her many symptoms and the stresses in her life were consistent with a number of diagnoses, but her family physician failed to take her physical complaints seriously, insisting that she was experiencing psychological distress rather than organically based physical problems.

Considering Diversity

Gender stereotypes are not the only possibility for biased diagnosis with the *DSM* system; ethnic stereotypes can also influence the labeling of mental disorders. The *DSM* system represents the summary of the American Psychiatric Association's evaluation of mental disorders, and the psychiatrists who compose this organization are mostly male, mostly White, and mostly from countries in North America. The descriptions of categories within the *DSM* system have received criticisms for including not only gender but also cultural bias.

The latest edition of the *DSM* (APA, 2000) contains repeated warnings to clinicians to be sensitive to culture when making diagnoses, but such an adaptation takes knowledge and time, which may be a challenge in the current cost-conscious health care climate (Roysircar, 2005) and may not be adequate to ensure proper diagnosis (Ton & Lim, 2006). For the most part, the diagnostic categories on Axis I and II describe symptoms that people manifest in cultures around the world (U.S. Department of Health and Human Services [U.S. DHHS], 2001). However, there are errors both ways. The biggest cultural failure of the *DSM* is the omission of disorders unique to specific cultural groups from non-Western cultures. An appendix describes **culture-bound syndromes**, patterns of abnormal behavior that are unique to a specific cultural group. As Jacquelyn Flaskerud (2000, p. 5) commented, "The culture-bound syndromes represent unique illness forms with a natural history distinct from *DSM* classification."

Culture-bound syndromes include *ghost sickness,* a disorder recognized by several Native American tribes that consists of a preoccupation with death or a specific deceased person. The symptoms include nightmares, dizziness, anxiety, confusion, and even hallucinations. *Ataque de nervios* is a disorder experienced in Latin American and Mediterranean cultures and includes symptoms of uncontrollable shouting and crying, fainting episodes, a sensation of heat rising within the body, and aggressive outbursts. These behaviors are usually precipitated by some stressful event, and the affected person may have no memory afterward of the events that occurred during the attack. Women and adolescent girls are more likely than others to experience ataque de nervios, but men and even children have been identified with this disorder (Guarnaccia, Martinez, Ramirez, & Canino, 2005). The *DSM* omits these disorders from its main classification, but it includes a disorder that is culture-bound to Western cultures. Bulimia, an eating disorder described in the *DSM,* is unique to Western cultures and fails to appear in other cultures (Keel & Klump, 2003). Other disorders that seem to occur only in Western cultures include premenstrual dysphoric disorder (Chrisler, 2008) and dissociative amnesia (Pope et al., 2007). Thus, the *DSM* system consists of omissions and inclusions, both with a Western bias.

Research on clinician bias has suggested that the cultural sensitivity recommended by the *DSM* does not occur as often as it should (Jarvis, 2008; U.S. DHHS, 2001). When the ethnicity of the clinician and patient matches, clinicians reported more psychosocial events that may influence behavior and fewer Axis II diagnoses than in diagnostic situations in which White clinicians diagnosed Hispanic clients (Zayas, Cabassa, Perez, & Howard, 2005). When comparing the diagnoses for African Americans made by clinicians to diagnoses made by following a standardized assessment strictly, clinician bias became evident (Trierweiler et al., 2000). This bias is likely responsible for the findings that people of African descent receive more diagnoses of schizophrenia than White people, both in the United States (Trierweiler et al., 2000) and in the United Kingdom (Boydell et al., 2001). Even when African Americans reported symptoms consistent with depression, the tendency was to diagnose them as schizophrenic.

Other research has identified both ethnicity and social class as factors in psychiatric disorders as well as in access to treatment (U.S. DHHS, 2001). After controlling for several factors including socioeconomic level, the difference in rates of diagnosed mental illness between African Americans and White Americans disappeared. However, educational and income levels are lower for African Americans and Hispanic Americans than Whites, and thus these two factors relate to the risk of mental illness. Without statistical controls for these factors, they make a significant difference in risk for mental health problems.

Looking beyond the United States, similarities appear in psychopathology and in the factors related to its development around the world. However, different countries show different rates of problems (WHO World Mental Health Survey Consortium, 2004). For example, a much higher percentage of people in the United States (26.4%) and the Netherlands (14.9%) reported some type of psychological problem during the past year than did people in Shanghai (4.3%) or Nigeria (4.7%).

Some of the gender differences that appear in the United States also occur worldwide. For example, depression is a common mental disorder around the world and affects women more often than men (Lopez, Mathers, Ezzati, Jamison, & Murray, 2006). Some of the factors that relate to women's risk for mental disorders in the United States also operate throughout the world, including inequitable treatment in family relationships, violence, and poverty. Both women and men who live in war-torn areas are at increased risk for PTSD as a result of the violence in their countries, and women's lack of education, limited access to good jobs, and dependence on men for survival place women at risk for depression and anxiety disorders, which are more common diagnoses for women than for men throughout much of the world. Like men in the United States, men elsewhere throughout the world receive more diagnoses of drug and alcohol abuse, suggesting that the male gender role and its pressures that prompt U.S. men to cope with negative feelings by alcohol and drug use operate in many cultures. As in the United States, psychopathology tends to follow gender role patterns.

■ Summary

Women experience more stress than men, and women's roles are the most probable sources of these differences. Women's roles often obligate them to provide physical and emotional care for their families, but they may not receive as much social support as they give. An increasing body of evidence has implicated violence as a factor contributing to a variety of mental disorders. Although men are the more common targets of violent crime, women are more commonly the victims of intimate violence, including childhood sexual abuse, rape, and spouse battering. Discrimination is a pervasive experience that increases stress in the lives of both ethnic minorities and women. Poverty is related to both violence and discrimination and poses other risks that disproportionately affect women and ethnic minorities, both of whom have higher rates of mental disorders than White men.

Comparisons of women's and men's coping strategies have been complicated by the need to examine differences in stressful situations in their lives. Studies that fail to control for these factors tend to support the stereotypical view that women use emotion-focused techniques more often and men use problem-focused coping. Women use social support as a coping strategy more often than men do, but the situation is more important than gender in the selection of coping strategy.

Gender differences in patterns of psychopathology have been the source of accusations of gender bias in construction of categories and in the process of diagnosis. These criticisms have centered around the *Diagnostic and Statistical Manual of Mental Disorders* (*DSM*) of the American Psychiatric Association. This publication contains a descriptive, multiaxial system for assigning diagnoses to people's behavioral problems. Using the *DSM* system, clinicians match each patient's symptoms against a description and make diagnoses on each of five axes: (1) Axis I—major clinical disorders, (2) Axis II—mental retardation and personality disorders, (3) Axis III—a diagnosis of physical conditions, (4) Axis IV—stressors in the person's life, and (5) Axis V—an overall rating of level of functioning.

Women's higher rate of treatment and the gender differences in some categories of disorders have led some critics to argue that there is gender bias in the *DSM,* especially in the personality disorder diagnoses that appear on Axis II. The descriptions of these disorders appear to exaggerate traits of the female and male gender roles, and the expected gender differences appear.

The clinicians who apply the criteria may also be biased, holding men as the standard for both women's and men's mental health. Early research indicated that clinicians value masculine traits above feminine ones. These biases may be weakening, but physicians are more likely to overdiagnose women's and underdiagnose men's mental disorders. Although clinicians may not be personally prejudiced, gender forms a backdrop against which clinicians evaluate symptoms, creating bias in diagnoses.

Many categories of mental disorders show few gender differences, but major depression and substance-related disorders show marked gender differences, with women being more often diagnosed with depression and men more often diagnosed with substance abuse problems. Models of both disorders include biological and cognitive components—biological factors create vulnerabilities that environmental stressors and cognitive patterns precipitate into disorders. Gender differences in these two behavior problems may reflect differences in expressing similar underlying, negative feelings: Women express their negative feelings in ways that receive a diagnosis of depression, whereas men channel their negative feelings into risky behaviors such as alcohol and drug abuse.

Other mental disorders show few gender differences in prevalence, such as obsessive-compulsive disorder, schizophrenia, and bipolar disorder. Some disorders do tend to fall along gender stereotypical lines, such as phobias, which are more common among women, and paraphilias, which are far more common among men. Therefore, the patterns of abnormal behavior reflect aspects of the gender roles of women and men.

Ethnic bias may also affect diagnoses of mental disorders, and several ethnic groups in the United States receive diagnoses at higher rates than Whites do. People in these ethnic groups tend to be more burdened with risks such as poverty, violence, and discrimination. Patterns of gender difference exist throughout the world, but some mental disorders, called culture-bound syndromes, appear in one culture and not in others.

■ Glossary

agoraphobia a phobic disorder characterized by anxiety about being in places or situations in which escape might be difficult or embarrassing.

antisocial personality disorder a personality disorder that is characterized by irresponsible and antisocial behavior such as lying, fighting, stealing, and physical cruelty.

bipolar disorder one of the mood disorders, characterized by periods of mania, high activity, and elevated mood, alternating with depression.

coping the process of changing thoughts and behaviors to manage situations that involve potential stressors.

culture-bound syndromes patterns of abnormal behavior that are unique to a specific cultural group.

dependent personality disorder a type of personality disorder that features excessive desires to be cared for combined with submissive, clinging behaviors and fear of separation.

diagnosis classification of a physical or psychological problem.

dysthymia a diagnosis within the category of mood disorders that is applied to milder but chronic symptoms of depression, including depressed mood, loss of interest and pleasure, or other symptoms over an extended period, often for months or years.

histrionic personality disorder a type of personality disorder that is characterized by excessive emotionality and attention-seeking behavior, beginning in early adulthood and appearing in a variety of situations.

major depression a diagnosis within the category of mood disorders that is applied to severe symptoms of depression, such as dissatisfaction and anxiety, loss of interest and pleasure, feelings of helplessness and hopelessness, changes in eating or sleep habits, and difficulty concentrating.

obsessive-compulsive disorder the combination of obsession (recurrent, intrusive thoughts about something the person would prefer to ignore) and compulsion (repetitive behaviors intended to prevent anxiety).

panic attack one of the anxiety disorders, characterized by periods of intense fear that occur without any fear-provoking situation and accompanied by physical signals of distress.

paraphilias a type of sexual disorder characterized by intense sexual feelings in response to objects or situations that are unusual.

phobias unreasonable fears concerning some object or situation.

posttraumatic stress disorder (PTSD) one type of anxiety disorder that involves the experience of some distressing event outside the range of normal human experience, the re-experience of the event, avoidance of stimuli associated with the event, and increased sensitivity to associated experiences. These symptoms must persist for at least one month.

premenstrual dysphoric disorder (PMDD) a controversial diagnostic category that appears in an appendix of *DSM-IV*. Its symptoms are those of premenstrual syndrome, and the broad description of these symptoms presents the possibility that vast numbers of women could be diagnosed as mentally ill.

psychoactive substances drugs that affect thoughts, emotions, and behavior.

schizophrenia a serious and complex disorder involving thought disturbances, problems in personal relationships, and possibly hallucinations.

schizotypal personality disorder a personality disorder characterized by pervasive pattern of social and interpersonal deficits marked by acute discomfort with, and reduced capacity for, close relationships as well as cognitive or perceptual distortions and eccentricities of behavior.

sexual dysfunctions a subcategory of the sexual disorders that includes problems with low or high level of sexual desire, or difficulty achieving arousal or orgasm.

social support receipt of emotional and material resources from friends and family members.

somatoform disorders a classification of disorders that includes problems with physical symptoms of disease but with no physical basis for these symptoms.

stress a response that occurs when circumstances place people in situations that tax or exceed their resources and endanger their well-being.

■ Suggested Readings

Albee, George W. (2005). Call to revolution in the prevention of emotional disorders. *Ethical Human Psychology and Psychiatry, 7,* 37–44.

Albee takes a cross-cultural view of mental disorders and analyzes the underlying causes of problems in social terms, pinpointing poverty, racism, and sexism as major causes of emotional problems throughout the world.

Brooks, Gary R. (2001). Masculinity and men's mental health. *Journal of American College Health, 49,* 285–297.
Brooks discusses the "dark side of masculinity" and how fulfilling the masculine gender role may be a danger to men's mental health but also a problem for women.

Caplan, Paula J. & Cosgrove, Lisa (Eds.). (2004). *Bias in psychiatric diagnosis.* Lanham, MD: Jason Aronson.
This book is filled with articles that critique the *DSM* and the process of psychiatric diagnosis on grounds of sexism, racism, and classism.

Hyde, Janet Shibley; Mezulis, Amy H.; & Abramson, Lyn Y. (2008). The ABCs of depression: Integrating affective, biological, and cognitive models to explain the emergence of the gender difference in depression. *Psychological Review, 115* (2), 291–313.
This article works toward providing a model of depression that explains gender differences through a blending of the research from psychology and biology and a consideration of the social and environmental factors that affect women and men to different extents.

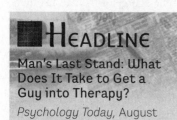

chapter
15 Treatment for
Mental Disorders

"The average man is as likely to ask for help with a psychological problem as he is to ask for directions," according to therapist Terrence Real (in Sherman, 2004, p. 71). The image of therapy is just not compatible with the male gender role. To seek therapy, a person must admit having a problem and ask for help. To participate in therapy, a person must discuss problems and feelings. These steps are difficult for most men, who are reluctant to seek help for any type of problem and who have been socialized to bury their emotions.

■ HEADLINE

Man's Last Stand: What Does It Take to Get a Guy into Therapy?

Psychology Today, August 2004

Then how do men come to therapy? Many of them are what Real described as "wife-mandated referrals" (in Sherman, 2004, p. 71). That is, many men do not exactly volunteer for therapy but make appointments because their wives, girlfriends, children, or employers have insisted. These men may experience depression, anxiety disorders, or panic attacks, but they would not seek help without some urging.

But men are seeking help for mental health problems in increasing numbers. According to a survey of U.S. residents ("Therapy in America," 2004), 22% of men sought therapy within the past 2 years. Most of the people who seek therapy are satisfied with the experience, including the reluctant men. Thus the main problem with guys and therapy is "getting in the door" (Sherman, 2004, p. 71).

Both women and men who seek therapy have a variety of options in terms of talk-based therapy, drug treatments, or a combination of these approaches. Men and women make all these choices in similar proportions ("Therapy in America," 2004), but their experiences may vary.

Approaches to Therapy

Throughout the history of therapy, the approach to treatment has been tied to the conceptualization of the source of problems. During the 19th and early 20th centuries, medicine became the model for understanding mental disorders, and the view developed that such problems were the result of problems in mental functioning. Therapies for the treatment of mental disorders arose and became part of psychiatry and psychology.

Psychoanalysis

Sigmund Freud developed a system of therapy that has influenced treatment as well as contemporary thinking about mental disorders. **Psychoanalysis** is a talk-based approach to psychotherapy that fits into Freud's comprehensive theory of personality development and functioning. (Chapter 5 presents the Freudian approach to personality development.) Freud believed that psychological problems develop when people are incapable of dealing with problems and use **repression** to push problematic material into the region of the unconscious. The unconscious does not function rationally, so repressed material has the potential to remain in the unconscious throughout childhood and adulthood and can produce problems at any time.

Psychoanalysts attempt to help patients resolve their problems by bringing unconscious material to consciousness so that patients may deal with these problems rationally. Once patients gain insight into the source of their conflicts, Freud believed that the conflict would disappear. Therefore, bringing repressed material to consciousness was a goal of psychoanalysis. Although Freud and his colleagues were physicians, psychoanalysis developed as a talk-based treatment for mental disorders; the source of mental disorders was psychological, and the treatment was accomplished through talking about the problems. Table 15.1 summarizes the elements of psychoanalytic therapy.

Dissatisfaction with some aspects of psychoanalysis prompted the development of other therapies, but they were also based on talking about problems. Karen Horney (1939), who protested the Freudian view of women, offered an alternative theory and therapeutic intervention (Westkott, 1997). (Chapter 5 also includes information about Horney's alternatives to Freudian theory.) Other talk-based therapies departed from the psychoanalytic framework, with its emphasis on early childhood and unconscious factors. Thus, these alternatives fit into other models of therapy, such as humanistic, cognitive, and behavioral therapies.

Humanistic Therapy

Humanistic theories of personality hold a more optimistic view, proposing that people are innately drawn toward fulfilling their human potential. If they fail, the reasons lie in their circumstances and in their environments, which somehow prevent the complete development of their full potentials. This context-sensitive, optimistic view of humanity is reflected in Carl Rogers's client-centered therapy.

TABLE 15.1   *Elements of Psychoanalytic Therapy*

Category	Description
Underlying source of problems	Childhood trauma plus insufficient ego to deal with trauma
Cause of problems	Repression of unconscious conflict
Immediate source of problems	Repressed material escapes from unconscious
Goal of therapy	To bring repressed material to consciousness
Techniques	Talking, free association, dream analysis
Practitioners	Psychoanalysts (who are usually psychiatrists)

Rogers (1951, 1961, 1980) proposed that human development follows a natural course toward health unless events block this development. Rogers believed that problems originate from distortions in self-concept, and these distortions arise from a lack of acceptance of true feelings. When children get messages that the feelings they experience are unacceptable, they begin to deny these feelings. Lack of acceptance of feelings leads to inaccuracies in self-concept and interferes with many facets of development.

Client-centered therapy seeks to help people develop their full potential by providing a safe therapeutic environment (Kaplan & Yasinski, 1980). To form a relationship with an empathic, acceptant, and genuine counselor is of primary importance. Thus, client-centered counselors offer three conditions to their clients—unconditional acceptance, empathy, and congruence. The most important of these is congruence, which refers to the ability to be genuine, whole, and to be what a person truly is (Feist & Feist, 2009). These three conditions are essential for clients to experience growth, and all three arise from clients' relationship with the counselor. Given these three conditions, the process of therapy occurs.

The counselor does not work directly on changing clients, who must do that for themselves. The counselor's job is to provide clients with therapeutic relationships so that clients can reclaim their abilities to move toward personal growth and development. The focus is on allowing clients to think in undistorted ways, assuming that behavior changes will follow.

Other humanistic therapies exist, and all share the view that fulfillment is a natural goal that people can reach, but barriers exist that block psychological growth. Humanistic therapists attempt to provide an atmosphere that permits clients to move in the natural direction of self-enhancement. Table 15.2 summarizes the elements of humanistic therapy.

Cognitive Therapy

Clients' thoughts are important in humanistic therapy, but these thought processes are the major focus in cognitive therapy. Cognitive therapists believe that thought processes are the basis of feelings and behavior; they create psychological problems and also provide the potential for alleviating those problems. Behavior and emotions follow from cognition, so changes in cognition provide the foundation for changes in behavior.

TABLE 15.2   *Elements of Humanistic Therapy*

Category	Description
Underlying source of problems	Discrepancy between genuine feelings and acknowledged emotions; feelings of not being whole
Cause of problems	Blockage of development toward full potential
Immediate source of problems	The problem that prompts a client to seek therapy
Goal of therapy	To provide an atmosphere that allows clients to move toward personal growth
Techniques	Empathic listening, providing unconditional positive regard, showing congruence
Practitioners	Psychologists, social workers, counselors

Ellis (1962) developed rational-emotive therapy (RET), one of the earliest cognitive therapies, in response to what he saw as the failure of psychoanalysis to solve people's problems. Ellis objected to both the length and nondirective nature of psychoanalysis, insisting instead that therapists should set goals and that therapy should be brief and problem-oriented. RET views psychological problems as a result of people's irrational beliefs and attempts to change these beliefs, assuming that changes in beliefs will produce changes in emotions and behavior.

Aaron Beck (1985) developed a cognitive therapy specifically for depression, which concentrates on the distorted, self-defeating thoughts that accompany depression. Beck contended that depressed people overgeneralize personal failures into the belief that they are worthless, and that they explain positive occurrences as exceptions to the general rule of failure. Depressed people also magnify the enormity of negative events, seeing these events as catastrophic and unchangeable. Selective perception is another cognition that adds to depression, causing depressed people to notice the negative elements of their surroundings and ignore the positive ones. These distortions of thinking magnify and maintain negative cognitions and thus perpetuate depression. Beck's cognitive therapy attempts to help clients change their negative thinking patterns by testing the beliefs to evaluate their validity and by findings ways to introduce pleasurable experience into the lives of depressed people.

Table 15.3 summarizes cognitive therapies. These therapies, such as Beck's cognitive therapy, assume that cognitions underlie psychological problems and that changing cognitions will change behavior. Rather than concentrating on behavior itself, these therapies concentrate on thoughts. Another therapeutic orientation takes an alternative approach—behavior modification emphasizes behavior rather than cognitions.

Behavior Modification

Behavior modification is a technique based on operant conditioning applied to changing undesirable behavior. Researchers who were exploring the principles of learning discovered that reinforcement and punishment are powerful forces in determining behavior. Not only do these principles apply to the nonhuman animals commonly used in laboratories, they also apply to humans and their complex behaviors. Behavior modification theory

TABLE 15.3   *Elements of Cognitive Therapy*

Category	Description
Underlying source of problems	Irrational beliefs
Cause of problems	Application of irrational beliefs to personal circumstances
Immediate source of problems	The problem that brings a person to therapy
Goal of therapy	To change irrational beliefs to more rational beliefs
Techniques	Confronting and disputing irrational beliefs; testing the validity of negative cognitions
Practitioners	Psychologists, social workers, counselors

holds that such behaviors are learned and maintained by reinforcement and punishment; application of these two principles can change unacceptable behavior. Behavior modification strives to replace inappropriate or deviant behaviors with other healthier behavior patterns through the use of reinforcement and punishment. Although both have been used in behavior modification programs, reinforcement for desirable behavior is more common than punishment for undesirable behavior.

Behavior modification is more specific and task oriented than talk-based psychotherapies are. For example, behavior modification is often the choice for various skills training, such as developing assertiveness, dealing with phobias, or changing eating patterns. In such programs, a client learns to replace maladaptive behaviors with other responses that are adaptive and acceptable in specific situations. Women are the most common clients for behavior modification because they are the ones who most often seek treatment for assertiveness problems, eating disorders, depression, and phobias.

Cognitive behavior therapy is a variation of behavior modification that accepts the importance of cognition in producing behavior and applies the principles of reinforcement to bring about behavioral changes (Fodor, 1988). As with behavior modification, this therapeutic approach assumes that problems are the result of learned patterns of maladaptive behavior, but the therapy typically differs from behavior modification by focusing on changing thought patterns and thereby change behavior. Cognitive behavior therapy tends to be more collaborative than behavior modification, with the client playing an active role by establishing goals and in developing a treatment plan. The client, rather than the therapist, may monitor and reward the desired behavior. Table 15.4 summarizes behavior modification and cognitive behavior therapy.

Medical Therapies

Talk-based psychotherapies and behavior modification are practiced by psychologists, social workers, counselors, and psychiatrists, but medical therapies are the specialty of psychiatrists and other physicians. Psychoactive drugs are the most common of the medical therapies, which take the approach of altering brain functioning in order to change thoughts and

TABLE 15.4   *Elements of Behavior Modification and Cognitive Behavior Therapy*

Category	Description
Underlying source of problems	None
Cause of problems	Behavior that is not adaptive or successful in specific situations
Immediate source of problems	The problem that brings a person to therapy
Goal of therapy	To change behavior (or cognitions that underlie behavior) to more acceptable alternative behaviors
Techniques	Reinforcement for acceptable behaviors, desensitization for phobias, assertiveness training
Practitioners	Psychologists, social workers, counselors

behavior. Psychologists are attempting to change prescribing laws so that they may gain prescription privileges for psychoactive drugs (Heiby, DeLeon, & Anderson, 2004). Practitioners may use these drugs in conjunction with psychotherapy or alone.

Since the 1950s, both the use and the number of psychoactive drugs have increased. Psychoactive drugs are prescribed to treat schizophrenia, depression, anxiety, and other disorders. Women receive more drug prescriptions than men, and this difference applies to psychoactive as well as other types of drugs (Anthony et al., 2008). A 1970 review of the patterns of prescription psychoactive drug use in Canada, the United States, and the United Kingdom showed a consistently higher rate of use for women (Cooperstock, 1970). More recent research has shown a trend toward higher rates prescription drugs for psychological problems and a continuation of gender differences in prescriptions. Over 80% of both men and women who participated in therapy received some type of medication ("Therapy in America," 2004). New drugs continue to appear for the treatment of schizophrenia, anxiety disorders, and depression; women are targeted as consumers of these drugs, both in advertising (Woodlock, 2005) and in television and magazine advertisements to consumers, urging them to ask for prescriptions (Chananie, 2005). This strategy is successful—when patients ask, physicians are much more likely to prescribe the medication (Kravitz et al., 2005). Not surprisingly, women receive more prescriptions for psychoactive drugs than men (Anthony et al., 2008).

Electroconvulsive therapy, the delivery of electrical shock to the brain, is also a medical approach to behavior problems. The resulting convulsions have a therapeutic effect, although the reasons for the beneficial effects remain unclear, and serious side effects can occur. This approach became common during the 1940s and remains in use today, mostly for major depression and bipolar depression in patients who have failed to respond to antidepressant drugs (Medda, Perugi, Zanello, Ciuffa, & Cassano, 2009). Because a majority of the cases of depression occur in women, they are the most frequent recipients of this therapy. This situation has led to the framing of electroconvulsive therapy as a form of violence against women (Burstow, 2006).

Table 15.5 summarizes medical therapies. Despite the growth of medically based treatments for behavior problems, these treatments are controversial. Drugs and electroconvulsive shock alter behavior and sometimes bring about substantial improvements, but side effects are a serious risk. In addition, these therapies decrease or diminish the severity of symptoms but do not cure mental disorders. Although the effects may be beneficial, symptoms tend to reappear when patients stop taking the drugs, and the therapeutic effects of electroconvulsive

TABLE 15.5   *Elements of Medical Therapies*

Category	Description
Underlying source of problems	Biological or biochemical abnormalities
Cause of problems	Chemical or biological malfunction in brain
Immediate source of problems	The problem that brings a person to therapy
Goal of therapy	To change biological functioning
Techniques	Psychoactive drugs, surgery, electroconvulsive therapy
Practitioners	Psychiatrists and other physicians

Men are less likely than women to receive a diagnosis of depression, but those who do may receive talk-based or drug therapy, or both.

therapy rarely last for more than a few months. In addition, medical treatments produce side effects that may produce more risks than benefits, at least for some people.

Accusations of Gender Bias in Therapy

In an early and vehement indictment of gender bias in diagnosis and therapy, Phyllis Chesler (1972) argued that diagnosis has been used to identify women who deviate from their traditional gender roles and that therapy has been used to restore women to those roles. Women may behave in many deviant ways, but when they fail to be subservient and domestic, they are sometimes labeled as needing therapy. Chesler contended that women experience problems when they either conform too little or too much to traditional gender roles and that therapy is a process used to reimpose the traditional feminine role.

According to Chesler, all therapies seek to restore women to the traditional female gender role, but therapists may exert more subtle sexist bias by imposing their own values into the therapy situation. If those values are sexist, so is the therapy. One of the respondents to a survey by the American Psychological Association (American Psychological Association [APA] Task Force on Sex Bias and Sex-Role Stereotyping in Psychotherapeutic Practice, 1978) confirmed a sexist bias by saying, "I have had women report to me that they could not continue in therapy because the objective seemed to be for them to learn to adjust better to their roles as wives, mothers, daughters (underlings of one kind or another), and they needed to become free persons" (p. 1122).

By surveying female psychologists, the APA Task Force determined that sexist bias exists in four main areas of the practice of psychotherapy (Brodsky & Holroyd, 1975). The sexist use of psychoanalytic concepts was one of the four. This gender bias comes from conceptualizing men as the standard and making female development an inferior variation of male development. These critics see psychoanalysis as inherently gender biased, but humanistic and cognitive therapies as well as behavior modification can also be conducted so as to create bias. The other areas of bias in therapy practice included fostering traditional gender roles (as Chesler claimed), including having biased expectations concerning women; devaluing women's potential; and responding to women as sex objects, including therapists' sexual exploitation of clients. Table 15.6 summarizes the potential sources of bias in various types of therapy.

Men are also subject to gender bias in therapy when practitioners urge the adoption of gender-typical behaviors. For example, when a male patient in one study described a lifestyle that included performing housework and child care, therapists tended to concentrate on these atypical behaviors, emphasizing the gender role as a potential source of problems (Robertson & Fitzgerald, 1990). A second male patient who described his role as more typical of a breadwinner received no comments on his gender role behaviors as a potential source of problems. A similar gender bias appeared in a study of marriage and family therapy (Guanipa & Woolley, 2000), and more recent research (Ro & Wampler, 2009) indicated that gender-biased attitudes still exist among therapists.

Counselors are likely to view both men and women stereotypically in terms of emotionality—women as overly emotional and men as lacking in emotion (Heesacker et al., 1999). These views influence the process of counseling when therapists blame husbands rather than wives for marital problems and when therapists set goals consistent with their own gender stereotypes. Such a bias appeared in a study in which therapists failed to encourage men to develop their expressiveness as much as they encouraged women to do so (Fowers, Applegate, Tredinnick, & Slusher, 1996).

TABLE 15.6 *Sources of Gender Bias in Therapies for Behavior Problems*

Type of Therapy	Source of Potential Gender Bias
Psychoanalysis	Psychoanalytic theory assumes that women are inferior.
Humanistic	Therapists may apply personal standards that are sexist; therapy focuses on the individual and ignores the social context of personal problems.
Cognitive	Therapists may apply personal standards that are sexist; therapy fails to address the social context of personal problems.
Behavior modification	Therapists may choose to reinforce traditional gender-related behaviors.
Medical	Women receive more prescriptions for psychoactive drugs and electroconvulsive therapy than men do.

Family therapy offers the ideal format for situating problems within a context rather than within an individual, but family systems therapists have been the target of criticism for failing to develop this opportunity (Evans, Kincade, Marbley, & Seem, 2005). For example, only 3% of the content of family practice master lectures was devoted to feminist concepts (Haddock, MacPhee, & Zimmerman, 2001). In addition, stereotypical and even overtly sexist statements occurred, such as blaming women for family problems and endorsing traditional rather than egalitarian family roles. Therefore, evidence exists that the practice of therapy is not value-free and that therapy tends to work toward preserving traditional values, for men as well as for women.

Gender Issues in Therapy

Besides therapist bias, treatment presents several other gender issues. One issue is the suitability of various types of therapy for women or men. Although women more often seek counseling and psychotherapy and tend to be better at the therapy tasks involved, their needs may not be met by the process itself. The gender bias in psychoanalytic approaches and the potential for gender bias in other therapies have presented important issues for therapy, and several alternative approaches have endeavored to correct these biases.

Recognizing the potential for bias in therapy has led to the notion that good therapy should be nonsexist (APA Task Force on Sex Bias, 1978), and professionals have worked toward the principles underlying nonsexist therapy. Feminist alternatives to therapy arose from the belief that ignoring gender issues does not make therapy gender-fair. The contention that nonsexist therapy is not an adequate answer to the gender bias in therapy prompted the development of therapies that are specifically feminist and oriented toward women's problems as well as practiced by women. "The sexism in so-called nonsexist brands of psychotherapy may be less blatant, but any approach to psychotherapy that conceptualizes women's social problems as personal pathology and promotes 'cures' for women's distress primarily through individual personal change strengthens the patriarchal status quo" (Rawlings, 1993, p. 90).

Feminist Therapy

The history of feminist therapy can be traced to the early 1970s and the women's rights movement (Enns, 2004; Truscott, 2010). Women, both inside and outside the mental health care professions, began to criticize therapy for its traditional goals and for its power in maintaining the status quo for women. Some women in professions that provide mental health care then responded by attempting to combine feminist goals with therapy; their results diverge from traditional therapy in several ways.

Principles of Feminist Therapy.   Four principles underlie the practice of feminist therapy (Worell & Remer, 2003). The first principle is that personal and social identities intersect. That is, each individual occupies several social identities (such as gender, ethnicity, sexual orientation, and physical abilities) that exist within society; all these identities influence and interact with personal identity. The second principle is borrowed from the feminist movement and states that "the personal is political." That is, personal experience is embedded within the social and political structure of the society, making the problems of

any individual woman a reflection of the wider society. The first two principles have a close relationship.

Feminist therapy strives to enact these two principles in several ways. Clients explore the influence of social roles on their individual behaviors, examining the difference between what they have been taught about appropriate behavior and what is actually appropriate. During feminist therapy, women have a forum for validating their experiences as women, including the situations and problems that are unique to women. Feminist therapists help clients reframe their problems and understand that their symptoms are a reflection of the society in which they live (Worell & Remer, 2003).

Feminist therapy is political, striving to bring about change in society. The early feminist therapists were politically active in the women's movement; indeed, such activity was a requirement for declaring oneself a feminist therapist. These therapists sought to bring about changes in the status of women and advocated political activism for their clients. Their position was that significant change was not possible in women's lives through personal changes in psychological adjustment; only change in society and in women's roles would lead to beneficial changes for women. Contemporary feminist psychotherapists may not emphasize the political as strongly as the founders did (Brown, 2006), but feminist therapists have tried to maintain the emphasis on politics by continuing to discuss power issues as part of their therapy sessions.

The third principle of feminist therapy states that therapists and clients should form an egalitarian relationship rather than the traditional therapeutic relationship in which therapists are dominant and clients are subordinate. This principle ensures that clients understand the types of therapies that they will receive and that they know about the options for other sources of assistance (Worell & Remer, 2003).

The equal relationship between client and therapist also aims to "demystify" the therapist as a person who has special knowledge and power (Gilbert, 1980). The rationale for this position lies in the attempt to counter the typical subordinate position that women occupy and to promote the belief that feminist therapy is an appropriate place for women to begin to feel a sense of personal power. Therapists who identified themselves as feminist therapists endorsed more openness and self-disclosure with their patients than did psychodynamic and other therapists (Simi & Mahalik, 1997). Clients confirmed that feminist therapists met the goal of sharing power with their clients more than therapists with other theoretical orientations (Rader & Gilbert, 2005). Feminist therapists also promote an equal relationship with clients by modeling appropriate behaviors for their female clients and by sharing personal experiences with their clients. This degree of personal openness and the advocacy of political activity on the part of the therapist differentiate the role of feminist therapists from therapists in most traditional therapies. Feminist therapists consider these differences essential to their approach.

The fourth principle states that women's perspectives are valued. Feminist therapists believe that women's viewpoint has not been valued or heard and that both value and voice can help women grow and become empowered. "Feminist therapists believe that women need to reject androcentric definitions of womanhood, to learn to value their personal characteristics, and to validate their own, woman-centered views of the world" (Worell & Remer, 2003, p. 74). Table 15.7 lists the four principles of feminist therapy.

The APA (2007) has proposed guidelines for therapy with girls and women that extend the framework of feminist therapy. These guidelines include not only rephrasings of

TABLE 15.7   *Four Principles of Feminist Therapy*

Principle 1—Personal and social identities are interdependent.
Principle 2—The personal is political.
Principle 3—Relationships between therapists and clients are egalitarian.
Principle 4—Women's perspectives are valued.

Source: Based on *Feminist Perspectives in Therapy: Empowering Diverse Women* (2nd ed., pp. 66–75), by Judith Worell and Pamela Remer, 2003. New York: Wiley. Reprinted with permission of John Wiley & Sons, Inc.

the goals of feminist therapy but also an elaboration of the importance of culture, ethnicity, and context in women's vulnerability to mental disorders, diagnosis, and treatment.

Clients of Feminist Therapy.

During the early years of feminist therapy, the majority of clients were White middle-class women—a demographic description that matches many of the clients who seek therapy (Evans et al., 2005). Questions arose over the suitability of feminist therapy for all women. After all, some women who seek therapy do not endorse feminist goals, and many are not White or middle class. Indeed, some people who seek therapy are men. Is feminist therapy appropriate for all women? And is it ever appropriate for men?

Early studies of feminist therapy evaluated the clients and problems for which this approach was suited. One study compared feminist and traditional therapy (Marecek, Kravetz, & Finn, 1979) and found that feminist therapy was more helpful to those who identified themselves as part of the women's movement, but women who did not also benefited. Other studies examined the feminist orientation of the counselor (Enns & Hackett, 1990; Hackett, Enns, & Zetzer, 1992) and found that women showed some reluctance to see radical feminist therapists but preferred more moderate feminist therapists over traditional or nonsexist therapists.

As feminist therapy developed, practitioners and researchers focused on prevention and empowerment as well as reducing specific symptoms and problems (Brown, 2008; Worell, 2001; Worell & Johnson, 2001). Research indicated some success in all these goals. Considering the goal of creating empowerment, practitioners and clients of feminist therapy were able to identify the distinct elements of feminist therapy, including empowerment for women and valuing women's point of view (Worell & Johnson, 2001). Feminist therapists have also been successful in creating egalitarian relationships with their clients (Rader & Gilbert, 2005). Feminist practitioners use a variety of specific therapy approaches and techniques, and the effectiveness of these approaches varies (Chambless & Ollendick, 2001). However, in order to be successful within the goals of feminist therapy, therapists must achieve political as well as personal goals. These criteria create an almost unattainable definition of success for feminist therapy and make the assessment of effectiveness very difficult.

Although men may seem to be unlikely clients for feminist therapy, this approach holds potential benefits for men (Brown, 2006; Walker, 2001). Traditional therapy adheres to a gendered model of mental health, but many feminist therapists adhere to a model that holds both masculine and feminine characteristics as beneficial to mental health. Research has demonstrated that people with extreme instrumental traits are at risk for mental health problems (Good, Thomson, & Brathwaite, 2005), and men who develop their expressiveness experience mental health benefits (Addis & Mahalik, 2003; Brooks, 2001). Feminist therapists have the theoretical orientation and the experience to help men make these changes. In addition, their experiences with female clients and their emotional issues have given feminist therapists valuable background that allows them to help male clients who are experiencing similar pain (Sweet, 2006; Walker, 2001).

By taking this approach with male clients, feminist therapists attempt to develop relationship skills, appropriate emotionality, empathy, and communication skills—skills that men often lack due to their masculine socialization. Feminist therapy with men also works toward altering views of gender roles and seeks to change men's attitudes concerning what is appropriate for both women and men (Szymanski, Baird, & Kornman, 2002). By examining and questioning traditional gender roles, feminist therapy with men upholds the principle that the personal is political, one of the basic principles of feminist therapy. Feminist therapists once argued that the practice of feminist therapy is restricted to women, but that position has changed (Brown, 2006). Indeed, a survey of practicing psychotherapists (Szymanski et al., 2002) revealed that 24% of male therapists identified themselves as feminist therapists. With either male or female therapists, male clients in feminist therapy can find both appropriate modeling and support through participation in group therapy.

Therefore, feminist therapy is appropriate for a wide range of people. From its beginnings as a radical therapy for women discontented with traditional therapy (both as therapists and as clients), feminist therapy has broadened its scope and clientele. Both women and men can benefit from feminist therapy by learning to develop their potential and becoming empowered in domains outside traditional gender roles.

Therapy with Men

As Terrance Real discussed in the headline story for this chapter (Sherman, 2004), therapy is not compatible with men's traditional gender role. The masculine gender role demands that men hide their vulnerabilities, whereas counseling calls for disclosing them (Brooks, 2001). Counseling urges clients to share their problems with other persons, and men have been socialized to hide their problems and approach problem solving in an intellectual rather than an emotional way. Therapy emphasizes behaviors associated with the feminine rather than the masculine role. Men who show emotion, express their vulnerability, and seek help from others fail to fit the masculine gender role, but all of these behaviors are necessary for psychotherapy.

Both clients and counselors experience difficulties in the counseling process due to male clients' stereotypically masculine behavior. Indeed, men may be in therapy because of their attitudes and unacceptable behavior associated with masculinity (Englar-Carlson, 2006; Mahalik, Good, & Englar-Carlson, 2003). These men may have followed the "Strong but Silent" or the "Tough Guy" script and become emotionally distant and uncommunicative. They may have followed the "Give 'Em Hell" script and battered their partners or children. They may have carried out parts of the "Playboy" script and experienced relationship problems or committed sexual violence. They may have enacted the "Winner" script and worked 80-hour weeks to adhere to their definition of success and developed a stress-related disorder. These men tend to be resistant to the therapy process, and therapists may

TABLE 15.8 *Barriers to Counseling Men*

Help-seeking is discouraged by elements of the masculine gender role:
- Men should not require help.
- Men should deny and suppress their emotions.
- Men should not express their vulnerability.

Therapy often takes a talk-based rather than an action-based or intellectual approach to problem solving.

Emotional sharing is difficult for many men.

Men may believe that counselors are biased against men's needs.

Psychology has responded by addressing women's needs better than it does men's needs.

Presentation of psychological services may be in a format that does not appeal to men.

have difficulties accepting such clients. Thus, men experience barriers in counseling, which Table 15.8 presents.

The goal of making psychological services more approachable for men has proven challenging. Men's attitudes about therapy are improving, but about 20% still report that they do not trust therapists ("Therapy in America," 2004). As the headline story for this chapter discussed, men are often brought to therapy by wives or girlfriends, placing them in counseling for relationships issues (Sherman, 2004), but even under threats of break-ups, men still "drag their feet" when it comes to counseling (Doss, Atkins, & Christensen, 2003).

Some strategies have succeeded in making counseling services more attractive to men. For example, avoiding the term *counseling* and substituting terms such as *classes, workshops, seminars,* and *videotapes* made these services more attractive to traditional men (Robertson & Fitzgerald, 1992; Rochlen, Blazina, & Raghunathan, 2002). Another term more compatible with the male gender role is coaching, which has developed into a way to present services to men (McKelley & Rochlen, 2007). The "Real Men. Real Depression" campaign by the National Institute of Mental Health ("NIMH launches," 2003) appealed to men by using video segments as well as radio and print publicity featuring real men instead of actors. These men told how depression affected their lives and that getting treatment was effective. A preliminary evaluation of this campaign (Rochlen, McKelley, & Pituch, 2006) indicated that men evaluated the materials favorably, especially men whose negative attitudes made them difficult to reach. Therefore, some strategies may be able to engage men with unfavorable attitudes toward counseling.

Gender-Sensitive Therapies

Good therapy must be nonsexist. The APA Task Force on Sex Bias and Sex-Role Stereotyping in Psychotherapeutic Practice (1978) recognized the need for nonsexist therapy, but therapists have disagreed over how to achieve this goal. Will vigilance against sexism be an adequate approach to making therapy gender-fair, or will it be necessary to add elements to therapies to achieve this goal? Those who follow feminist therapy believe that ignoring gender or removing objectionable elements is not sufficient to make a therapy gender-fair; a therapeutic approach must include some stated goals oriented around achieving social and personal equity.

TABLE 15.9 *Principles of Gender-Sensitive Counseling with Men: MASTERY*

*M*onitor Personal Reactions to Men and Male Behavior Styles—Therapists may have negative reactions to men's behaviors and should develop empathy with their clients to help them change.

*A*ssume That the Male Client Is Feeling Pain—Even though men may be privileged in society, their strain at maintaining the male gender role causes pain.

*S*ee the Male Client's Problems in Gender Context—Understand and help clients understand that their behavior occurs in a cultural context with gendered roles.

*T*ransmit Empathy and Understanding—Convey compassion and understanding; if possible, urge clients to become part of a men's group so that they can see they are not alone in their feelings.

*E*mpower Men to Change—Understanding is not enough; therapists must challenge men to make positive changes in their lives.

*R*espect Resistance—Accept that men in therapy are not eager to change and that change is difficult.

*Y*ield Some Control to the Larger System—Accept that many social forces push men toward traditionality, making therapeutic change slow and difficult.

Source: Based on *A New Psychotherapy for Traditional Men,* by Gary R. Brooks, 1998, San Francisco, CA: Jossey-Bass. Reprinted with permission of John Wiley & Sons, Inc.

Gender-aware therapy (GAT) was an attempt to integrate concepts of male and female gender development with the revised attitudes toward psychotherapy proposed by feminist therapists (Good, Gilbert, & Scher, 1990), but that approach has not become the dominant approach to gender-sensitive counseling. Instead, feminist therapy has continued as the major approach to dealing with gender issues in counseling for women, and new therapies for men have arisen. Gary Brooks (1998, 2001) proposed a gender-sensitive approach for counseling with traditional men that he described with the acronym MASTERY. Table 15.9 lists these principles, along with a brief description of how therapists can enact them.

More recently, Brooks (2010) has advocated for using the transtheoretical model for conducting therapy with men. This model proposes that change occurs in a sequence of stages, and Brooks argued that this type of change will engage men in the therapy process. This approach extends some elements of the MASTERY approach but shares the basic emphasis on the importance of cultural and socioeconomic context of men's problems, building empathetic relationships with clients, and empowering men.

A comparison of Tables 15.7 and 15.9 reveals many commonalities in the goals of feminist therapy and Brooks's MASTERY approach to counseling with traditional men. All of these approaches strive to be nonsexist, not by ignoring gender issues, but by finding ways to redefine gender roles, personal goals, and personal relationships. All draw attention to the social context of problem behavior, define an egalitarian relationship between client and therapist, and cultivate respect for clients' views and values. Feminist therapy and the MASTERY approach both urge political and social action to change gender roles. Therefore, sensitivity to gender-related issues is an important goal to several therapy approaches, and therapists have choices in selecting how to accomplish the goals of nonsexist therapy.

Sexual Exploitation in Therapy

The preponderance of female clients and male therapists poses a situation in which gender is nearly always either an overt or covert issue in the therapy process (see According to the Media and According to the Research). The APA Task Force on Sex Bias and Sex-Role Stereotyping in Psychotherapeutic Practice identified the treatment of clients as sex objects as a gender-related problem in therapy, which may include erotic or sexual behavior between client and therapist (Brodsky & Holroyd, 1975). Unfortunately, sex between therapist and client is not unusual. Beginning with the founding fathers of psychoanalytic therapy and continuing today, some clients are sexually exploited by the therapists to whom they come for help.

During the 1970s, a survey of licensed psychologists in clinical practice (Holroyd & Brodsky, 1977) disclosed that some therapists had engaged in erotic behavior with their clients. The percentages for this and subsequent surveys were not high—about 7% of male therapists and about 1.5% of female therapists have admitted to such behavior (Pope, 2001). The attitudes among psychologists indicated that most psychologists believed that erotic contact was *not* beneficial to clients; most professionals considered such relationships unacceptable and unprofessional. This attitude was a component in the denial of the existence of therapist–client sex. Psychologists have been reluctant to acknowledge that this problems exists (Pope, Sonne, & Greene, 2006). Initially, journals were reluctant to publish articles, and conventions were unwilling to feature presentations on the topic (Pope, 1988).

The possibility of sexual attraction on the part of clients toward therapists and for therapists toward clients is an important concept in psychoanalytical treatment, but such contact was considered unacceptable (Pope, 2001). The knowledge of this possibility did not deter several prominent early psychotherapists from forming sexual relationships with their patients. Other counseling theories do not include the likelihood of mutual attraction between therapist and client, but therapy is an intimate process, and attractions arise. Other than psychoanalytic training, the possibility of sexual attraction was not addressed, leaving therapists unprepared to deal with the possibility that they may develop sexual feelings for their clients (Pope, 1988; Pope et al., 2006).

Therapists' lack of preparation for attraction to clients contributes to entering into sexual relationships with their clients (Pope, 1988, 2000). Therapists may also rationalize such involvement, minimizing the potential harm to clients. Another factor that increases the risk of sexual exploitation is the history of sexual abuse in therapists' backgrounds; therapists who have been the victims of childhood sexual abuse are at increased risk of sexually exploiting their clients (Jackson & Nuttall, 2001).

During the 1990s, sexual relationships between therapists and clients became a widely publicized issue, and the helping professions began to address this problem. Therapists receive training concerning ethics and the unacceptability of sexual contact with their clients, but the emphasis is usually on the unacceptability of such behavior, rather than on how to deal with sexual feelings that therapists may experience (Pope et al., 2006). A survey of psychology internship programs (Samuel & Gorton, 1998) showed that 99% of programs provided some training on this topic. However, only about half of the graduates of counseling psychology programs remembered how their programs addressed this issue, and only 60% of that half thought their program's training was adequate (Blanchard & Lichtenberg, 1998).

According to the *Media* . . .

Male Therapists Are Crazy or Evil, and Female Therapists Have Sex with Their Patients

The image of psychotherapists in movies is often vague and usually not flattering (Gharaibeh, 2005). The profession of therapists is often left unclear—whether they are psychiatrists, psychologists, psychoanalysts, psychiatric social workers, or some other profession (Schultz, 2005). In addition, therapists are portrayed in unflattering ways. Therapists in the movies usually fall into one of three categories: Dr. Dippy, Dr. Evil, or Dr. Wonderful (Schneider, 1987). Dr. Dippy first appeared in a short film in 1906 as the therapist who was crazier than the patients, and about 35% of movie therapists fit into this category. Dr. Evil also appeared early in film history in a 1908 movie, *The Criminal Hypnotist*; about 15% of movie therapists fall into this category. Thus, about half the movie therapists are not good (Gharaibeh, 2005).

Dr. Wonderful is the ideal therapist—effective, caring, and available. These Dr. Wonderfuls devote large amounts of time to their on-screen patients doing talk-based therapy and rarely asking for payment. The psychiatrist in *Ordinary People* (1980) and the counselor in *Good Will Hunting* (1998) are good examples of Dr. Wonderful. Only about 22% of movie therapists fall into this category.

Female therapists are more likely to be Dr. Wonderful than Dr. Evil or Dr. Dippy, but their screen portrayals differ from male therapists. Only about 29% of therapists are female (Gharaibeh, 2005). These women are likely to be single or unhappy in their marriages, and in the movies, female therapists often "help" their male patients by becoming their lovers (Gabbard, 2000). Movies such as *Spellbound* (1945), *The Prince of Tides* (1991), *Basic Instinct* (1992), *Twelve Monkeys* (1995), and *Tin Cup* (1996) depicted such female therapists. One analysis (Gabbard & Gabbard, 1999) had trouble finding a movie female therapist who had a relationship with anyone *except* a patient or former patient.

In the movies, female therapists who have sex with their patients do not seem to violate any rules or suffer any negative consequences. The patients sustain no harm, and the therapists experience benefits by "finding their femininity" (Gabbard, 2000) and often by abandoning their professional careers. When male therapists have sex with their patients, the relationship causes more problems, but even then, the harm to the client and to the therapist's career remains off screen.

Although some therapists believe that personal and sexual relationships with clients are therapeutic for clients, research indicates otherwise. A variety of negative effects befall clients who have participated in sexual relationships with their therapists (Ben-Ari & Somer, 2004; Nachmani & Somer, 2007; Pope, 2001). Clients may not exhibit any immediate negative effects of sexual intimacy with their therapists, but evidence indicates that at least 90% will eventually experience negative effects. These effects include posttraumatic stress disorder, depression, suicide, substance abuse, disrupted personal relationships, and career problems. The effects are stronger when the relationship occurs concurrently with therapy, but clients who begin relationships with their therapists after the termination of therapy are still at risk.

The therapist–client relationship is one of trust and intimacy, but when sexual intimacy becomes part of the relationship, a betrayal of the client's trust has occurred. Thus, impaired ability to trust is a potential lifelong problem (Pope, 2001). This situation often leaves clients feeling ambivalent; they experience rage and a longing to escape combined with a fear of separation from the therapist. Sexually exploited clients may also feel guilt, isolation, emptiness, and sexual confusion. In addition, they have trouble

■ ACCORDING TO THE RESEARCH . . .

Male, Not Female, Therapists Are More Likely to Form Sexual Relationships with Patients

Movie portrayals of therapists are inaccurate in a number of ways. Therapists are not as dramatic as movie portrayals; very few therapists match the flamboyant behavior of Dr. Dippy, Dr. Evil, or even Dr. Wonderful. Effective, concerned therapists exist, but the ideal of a psychiatrist providing the amount of talk-based treatment that Dr. Wonderful's dispense is not realistic (Gabbard, 2000). Drug treatments have replaced psychotherapy for most psychiatrists, but this option appears in the movies less than 6% of the time (Gharaibeh, 2005). Of course, all types of therapists charge for their services, which makes them different from the media therapists.

Research also indicates that sexual relationships with patients are substantially different from those in the movies. A compilation of the many studies on sexual exploitation by therapists (Pope, 2001) concluded that about 7% of male and 1.5% of female therapists enter sexual relationships with their patients. This represents a substantial gender difference, which is unlike the movie version in which most of the therapists who have sex with their patients are female. In addition, one study (Holroyd & Brodsky, 1977) found that 80% of those therapists who

admitted at least one sexual relationship acknowledged more than one such relationship. This figure suggests that some therapists form a pattern of habitual sexual exploitation of their patients. In the movies, sexual relationships are usually the result of two people falling in love rather than a powerful therapist exploiting a vulnerable patient.

Another pattern of sexual relationship between client and therapist occurs as a series of steps involving boundary violations (Simon, 1999). That is, therapists begin to behave in ways that are more intimate and personal than professional, which eventually leads to sex. This process is likely to occur in gradual steps, with clients who are victims of childhood sexual abuse, and with therapists who are in a sole private practice, rather than with other configurations of clients and therapists (Somer & Saadon, 1999). This picture of sexually exploitative therapists contrasts sharply with the movie portrayal; therapists who form sexual relationships with their clients are more often male than female, tend to engage in a series of exploitative relationships, often prey on vulnerable clients, and fully understand that their behavior is a violation of their code of professional conduct.

finding help, contacting an average of 2.36 professionals before finding assistance they consider satisfactory (Luepker, 1999). Therefore, clients often experience a variety of serious problems after sexual involvement with their therapists and seek subsequent help for problems.

The growing awareness of the sexual exploitation of clients by therapists has produced changes in the codes of ethics for all of the professions that provide mental health care (Lazarus, 2003; Vasquez & Kitchener, 1988). The ethical codes that govern psychiatrists, psychologists, social workers, and marriage and family therapists all specifically prohibit sexual activity between therapists and clients.

Violations of sexual boundaries have been the most common of the ethical complaints against therapists (Gross, 2003). The typical situation involves a male therapist who forms a sexual relationship with a female client who is approximately 10 years younger than he is. This typical therapist has been the target of prior ethical complaints, but he is also at increased risk to have been involved in a sexual relationship with a teacher or supervisor. Thus, sexual exploitation during therapy may be part of a chain of sexual abuse.

The Self-Help Movement

A lack of confidence in psychotherapy, publicity of sexual exploitation of clients, increased cost, and decreased insurance coverage contribute to the reluctance to seek therapy on the part of thousands of people with personal problems ("Therapy in America," 2004). But these troubled individuals often seek the advice of others: "Across the country, in hospitals, churches, empty offices, and even shopping malls, small groups of individuals assemble to cope collectively with their unique challenges" (Davison, Pennebaker, & Dickerson, 2000, p. 205). People in self-help groups meet to share similar problems, and in the process, they receive emotional support as well as information that can assist in helping them cope.

Self-help groups began to proliferate during the 1980s. The 1987 Surgeon General's Workshop on Self-Help and Public Health brought the benefits of self-help groups to the attention of an increased number of health care providers. In 1992, the number of self-help groups was more than 500,000, and over 7 million people were involved. By the end of the 1990s, the number of people in the United States who would be involved in some type of self-help group at some time during their lives was estimated at 25 million, a number that exceeded those in other types of therapy programs (Davison et al., 2000). The United States is not unique in the popularity of self-help groups, which exist in growing numbers in all industrialized countries and in most other countries in the world (Norcross et al., 2003).

The prototype for the self-help movement is Alcoholics Anonymous (AA). Founded in 1935 by two alcoholics who had stopped drinking, AA proclaimed that people with drinking problems could stay sober through the social support of others with similar problems (Robinson, 1979). The format is a meeting in which people acknowledge their alcoholism and seek the support of others to continue in the struggle to abstain from drinking, one day at a time. This approach to dealing with problem drinking has been enormously influential, both in the treatment of problem drinking and in the formation of other self-help support groups. For example, addictions and other compulsive disorders were the concerns of early support groups such as Narcotics Anonymous, Gamblers Anonymous, and Overeaters Anonymous, but support groups now exist for a wide variety of problems, including mental disorders, physical diseases, and people living with or involved in providing care for people with mental or physical problems. "There are groups for almost every serious medical problem and almost every presenting problem that clinicians confront, plus groups for dozens of conditions virtually unserved by therapists" (Jacobs & Goodman, 1989, p. 537).

The philosophy of the self-help approach is that people with similar problems can offer each other social support and information, which can be helpful and beneficial. Rather than therapists who direct the therapy and clients who take direction, self-help and support groups may not involve professional therapists and may have no designated leaders (Gartner & Riessman, 1998). Other groups have professionals who consult or even participate in meetings (Davison et al., 2000). Groups vary in size from a few members who have formed their own group to large, nationally affiliated groups. Although the concerns of people in these groups vary, the underlying philosophies are similar.

The similarity of individuals in the group facilitates empathy and may be an important factor that draws people to support groups, especially for people with certain problems. For example, people with AIDS are 250 times more likely to join a support group than people with hypertension, and breast cancer has about 40 times as many support groups as heart

■ Gendered Voices

Of Course I've Felt Attracted to My Clients

Both a counseling intern and a counselor with 30 years of experience told me, "Of course I've felt attracted to some of my clients. I think it's almost inevitable." Both reported that the attraction made them very aware of the nature of the counseling relationship and how inappropriate these feelings were. Both also became very conscious about behaving so as to conceal signs of their attraction, because it was considered professionally unacceptable.

"Part of our training includes the ethical unacceptability of any type of personal relationship with clients, especially any sexual relationship. It's completely unacceptable," the counseling intern said. "So feeling attracted to a client raised flags and made me aware that I needed to be very careful about what I did. I didn't want to convey my feelings to my client, and I didn't want to let my feelings affect my counseling. It's a difficult situation and an inevitable conflict, I think."

The veteran counselor agreed. "It's practically inevitable, although I have been sexually attracted to very few of my clients. When I felt attracted, those feelings made counseling more difficult. I tried to conceal how I felt, which is dishonest, while remaining honest in all

other respects. And I tried very hard to do a good job in counseling the client. It made the counseling relationship more difficult."

"Nothing in our training taught me how to deal with these feelings," the intern said. "A great deal was oriented toward the ethics of counseling, but not how to handle my feelings or situations in which clients express some attraction for me. It was all 'Don't do that,' but nothing about what to do. I wouldn't feel comfortable talking to my supervisor about my feelings because of the ethical prohibition. I know it's unreasonable to imagine that counselors won't feel attracted to clients, but it's so forbidden that I feel I shouldn't have or admit to the attraction. I know that I will think about how to avoid letting any client know about my attraction, but teaching me how to deal with such feelings and what to do—no, that was lacking in my training."

The experienced counselor said that his training included how to deal with clients' attraction to him but not his toward clients. "The whole issue of sexual exploitation of clients hadn't been publicized or addressed in counselor training, so those issues were not part of my training."

disease (Davison et al., 2000). For disorders that have a social stigma or visible effects, support groups of similar others may be especially helpful, and being with others with similar experiences can be comforting (Gartner & Riessman, 1998; Humphreys, 2004).

Self-help groups may also offer economic advantages. These groups may charge participants a minimal fee or no fee at all. With the growing emphasis on cost containment, health care professionals have begun to promote cooperation between medicine and self-help groups as one way to contain treatment costs (Burti et al., 2005). Some health care providers are coming to see self-help support groups as an addition to the "toolbox" of interventions (Dadich, 2006).

Free therapy sounds cost-effective, but is it effective? A meta-analysis of bibliotherapy, providing people with reading materials, indicated that this self-help approach is effective for disorders such as anxiety and depressive disorders (den Boer, Wiersma, & Van den Bosch, 2004). However, a lack of research prevented a meta-analysis to evaluate the effectiveness of support groups. Another review (Pistrang, Barker, & Humphreys, 2008) concluded that self-help support groups can be effective in helping people with chronic mental illness, depression, and bereavement. However, another analysis (Gellatly et al., 2007) indicated that groups with some therapist guidance were more effective. Also, a 1-year follow-up assessment of people treated for substance abuse disorders found that those who participated in self-help group meetings were functioning better than those who attended no such meetings (Moos, Schaefer, Andrassy, & Moos, 2001). Thus, self-help approaches provide some benefits, boost the benefits of therapy, or both.

Self-help groups may function to alter cognitions, thus changing behavior (Dijkstra & De Vries, 2001) and boost self-efficacy and enhance coping skills (Kelly, Magill, & Stout, 2009). That is, the effectiveness of self-help groups in bringing about therapeutic change stems from the same sources that underlie therapist-assisted change (Magura et al., 2003). Specific information about changing behavior and providing ways to bring about changes are important components, regardless of the therapy format.

The cost difference between self-help and traditional therapy makes self-help attractive to a wide range of participants, but social anxiety may deter people from attending support groups meetings (Book et al., 2009). The growing accessibility of the Internet has created an even more accessible form of self-help that does not require face-to-face contact—online support groups.

Online Support Groups

Internet sites are available for a number of problems, allowing people without easy access to groups in their hometowns to meet in cyberspace. Preliminary evidence (Weinberg, Uken, Schmale, & Adamek, 1995) indicated that participants in online self-help groups receive some of the same benefits that other participants obtain. Later research has examined the participants and types of problems in online groups, the patterns of support that develop online, and the differences from and similarities to face-to-face support groups. An evaluation of the effectiveness of online groups (Rains & Young, 2009) indicated that this approach can be effective.

The formation of online groups differs from face-to-face groups. Support groups may consist of only a few people, or as many as a few dozen, but online groups may have thousands of members (Galegher, Sproull, & Kiesler, 1998). No meetings take place, but participants can enter discussions 24 hours a day, 7 days a week. Most online groups have no designated leader, but some sites have attempted to provide the "best of both worlds" by combining the online format with a mental health professional as the host (Hsuing, 2000). People can actively participate by posting comments and asking questions, or they may "lurk," reading the posted interactions but not offering comments themselves. Participants often use created names, which makes online interaction anonymous. Thus, the format for online support groups shows clear differences from other support groups.

The types of problems that prompt people to seek support on the Internet vary somewhat from those that bring people to face-to-face support groups (Davison et al., 2000). Rare and debilitating conditions are frequent topics on the Internet because sufficiently many people can meet online to form a group. Conditions such as chronic fatigue syndrome and multiple sclerosis seem well suited to online support—people with these conditions have problems that impair them from going to meetings, but online access is convenient. People who have problems with oral speech can use a computer to communicate in a medium they can master and at their own pace (Finn, 1999). For example, those with hearing impairment benefited from their involvement in an online group (Cummings, Sproull, & Kiesler, 2002).

The problems of participants in online support groups tend to center on physical health, but behavioral problems such as depression, anxiety disorders, and attention deficit disorder are also common topics. Alcohol and substance abuse treatment form a large segment of the face-to-face support groups and also appear online (Magura et al., 2003). A survey of those who participated in such services (Hall & Tidwell, 2003) indicated that people from many ethnic and age groups participated in a variety of Internet recovery services. In addition, cancer, diabetes, and AIDS bring people together online as well as in person to share information and emotional support.

The same support processes that occur in face-to-face groups also take place online (Finn, 1999). That is, online support groups also share information, work toward mutual problem solving, allow expressions of emotion, and show support and empathy. One analysis of the processes in online support groups (Finn, 1999) showed that the majority of messages (55%) could be classified as emotional or social exchanges, and 21% showed empathy. An analysis of online AA groups (VanLear, Sheehan, Withers, & Walker, 2005) indicated that emotional support was more common in AA than other online groups. Yet another analysis (Coulson, 2005) found that informational exchange was the largest part of the communications. Thus, online support groups show similarities to face-to-face groups in providing a format for the exchange of emotional support, information, and practical advice from similar others.

The gender interactions in online groups may differ from face-to-face groups. One possibility is that online anonymity might free people from gender-bound rules of interaction, but a study on this topic (Postmes & Spears, 2002) indicated that gender stereotypes affect online communication—people tended to rely on gender stereotypes to guide their interaction. A review of research on this topic (Mo, Malik, & Coulson, 2009) indicated that gender differences are more likely to appear in online groups that consist of one sex or the other; when the groups included both men and women, fewer gender differences appeared in communication.

Gender Issues in Self-Help

Just as women are more likely to seek therapy, women are also more likely than men to participate in self-help groups. More than two-thirds of those who attend support groups are women (Galegher et al., 1998). However, men are more likely than women to use the Internet, and men use online support groups more than women do. Although depression is more common among women and online support groups for depression are plentiful, only 40% of those who posted comments in such groups were women. This finding suggests that the Internet may furnish a forum in which men feel more comfortable in seeking help and participating in emotional communication than they do in formal therapy or in face-to-face support groups (Barak & Gluck-Ofri, 2007; Seale, 2006).

Gender issues are often prominent in self-help groups because many such groups are formed around women's or men's issues. Consciousness-raising groups originated as a way for women to share their unique experiences, explore the similarities of their lives, and increase interaction with other women (Morgan, 1970). These groups began to form in the mid-1960s as part of the women's movement; thus, the aims of these groups were political as well as personal. The early emphasis on political ideology shifted to personal development (Kravetz, 1978). Instead of political activism, the most important goals became a sharing of thoughts and feelings about being women, learning about other women's experiences, increasing self-awareness, receiving emotional support, and examining the traditional gender role for women. Participants rated the groups as very successful in helping them to attain these goals, and the majority of participants encouraged other women to join groups. The personal changes experienced by women during consciousness-raising groups were likely to have been therapeutic, leading to these groups' becoming substitutes for or adjuncts to therapy (Enns, 1992).

The men's movement has also devised group meetings for men to share their concerns (Andronico, 2001). In the 1970s, men's groups were similar to early women's consciousness-raising groups, with the purpose of making members more sensitive to the politics and the disadvantages of their gender role. Both concentrated on the social inequities women had experienced and how rigid gender roles had harmed men as well as women. Men sought to understand how they had participated in and had been harmed by society's mandates for their behavior.

In the 1980s, the goals of the men's movement began to diverge from those of the women's movement (Faludi, 1991). Men's oppression became the theme of many men's groups during that decade, and men sought to redefine masculinity (Andronico, 2001; Bly, 1990). The format for this discovery is often in groups in which men discuss and explore their own experiences and problems with society's definition of masculinity. Men's groups have a greater diversity than women's consciousness-raising groups, but fewer men's groups exist. Women's groups tend to be oriented toward sensitizing women to the political goals of feminism, but men's groups have a variety of possible goals. Some men's groups have political goals, such as groups organized around gay rights, divorce, or custody rights; others supplement therapy for substance abuse; still others explore social conceptions of masculinity and ways to bring about positive personal and social changes (Reddin & Sonn, 2003). Unlike traditional psychotherapy, both women's and men's groups share the goals of reexamining gender roles and seeking possible avenues of change.

Considering Diversity

The problems of mental disorders share some commonalities around the world: "Every local system of medical knowledge and healing must cope with prolonged sadness and withdrawal, with violence and irrational anger, and with seizures, emotional distress, and acute and chronic forms of madness" (Desjarlais, Eisenberg, Good, & Kleinman, 1995, p. 51). But the behaviors that lead to diagnoses of mental disorders appear in a cultural context, and the treatment that these behaviors receive are also strongly influenced by the society in which they are enacted. So the diagnosis of mental disorders varies in countries around the world, as do the frequency and type of treatment (WHO World Mental Health Survey Consortium, 2004).

Many people in Asia, Africa, and Latin America have views of treatment that are not compatible with psychiatric treatments involving drugs and psychotherapy. In some cultures, professionals using drugs and psychotherapy have little success in treating people because the individuals receiving treatment do not share the same views about their problems that the therapist holds, and they have no confidence in these therapies. In these cultures, healing processes include folk healers, ritual dramas, herbal medicine, and possession rituals (Desjarlais et al., 1995; Sorsdahl et al., 2009). For example, the Yolmo Sherpa of Nepal experience a disorder symptomized by a loss of energy; a loss of interest in eating, working, and socializing; sleep problems; and feelings of "dullness." In the United States, these symptoms would probably result in a diagnosis of depression, but the Yolmo believe that these symptoms occur because one of their spirits has left the body and wanders around the countryside. The treatment involves a lengthy and elaborate ritual performed by a shaman, who tracks the lost spirit and helps it return to the afflicted person. For the Yolmo, this course of treatment is a better choice and probably more effective than antidepressant drugs. Some international experts have considered incorporating traditional treatments into mental health treatments to make treatment more accessible.

A worldwide survey of treatment (WHO World Mental Health Survey Consortium, 2004) and an analysis of mental health services around the world (Shah & Beinecke, 2009) indicated that inadequate treatment for mental disorders is widespread. Even in high-income countries that accept Western medicine and treatment, between 40 and 50% of individuals with serious mental disorders go untreated. In middle-income countries, over 80% fail to receive treatment. These failures result in widespread disability; mental health problems such as depression and anxiety disorders disrupt people's lives (and their families' lives) and productivity. Indeed, mental disorders constitute 5 of the 10 leading causes of disability in the world (World Health Organization, 2008).

In the United States, Canada, and other high-income countries, a higher percentage of people receive treatment than in developing countries, but ethnicity plays a role in receiving treatment. A special report on mental health and care for the United States (U.S. Department of Health and Human Services [U.S. DHHS], 2001, p. 3) concluded that "Racial and ethnic minorities have less access to mental health services than do whites. They are less likely to receive needed care. When they receive care, it is more likely to be poor in quality." This discrepancy means that "*racial and ethnic minorities bear a greater burden from unmet mental health needs and suffer a great loss to their overall health and productivity*" (emphasis in original). Issues of inaccessibility of services, mistrust of health care professionals, and stigma associated with treatment create problems for ethnic minorities in the United States. However, African Americans and Native Americans are disproportionately represented in psychiatric hospitals (U.S. DHHS, 1999), which suggests that these groups are more likely to be subjected to involuntary treatment.

Therapists hold generally positive attitudes about people from ethnic minorities—at least on an overt level (Green, Hamlin, Ogden, & Walters, 2004). On a more implicit level, therapists carry the same ambivalence about women and minority ethnic groups as the majority of Whites in the United States. This situation suggests that feminist therapy may provide a model for therapy that is sensitive to the concerns of ethnic minority clients (Enns, 2004). Indeed, the desire to include diverse clients has been a goal for many feminist therapists. The sensitivity to environmental factors and the recognition of the impact of social and political factors on psychological functioning make feminist therapy better suited to ethnic minority clients than therapies that conceptualize problems as personal and internal. Feminist therapy offers African American (Greene, 1994; Hall & Greene, 2003), Native American (LaFromboise, Berman, & Sohi, 1994; Malone, 2000), Asian American (Bradshaw, 1994), Hispanic American (Vasquez, 2002), and biracial (Nishimura, 2004) women a method to help them feel empowered, to give them skills to solve their problems, and to furnish opportunities to change society.

Cultural sensitivity is also important in counseling with men from different ethnic groups. African American, Hispanic American, and Asian American men may be even more reluctant to seek therapy than White men. Their ethnic groups' conceptualizations about help-seeking and masculinity may be even stronger than for White men, exerting pressure against seeking care. For example, Hispanic men may be influenced by the concept of machismo (Casas, Turner, & Ruiz de Esparza, 2001), which calls for independence and toughness. They may struggle with ethnic stereotyping and discrimination as well a living up to the standards of their culture's concept of masculinity. Asian men (Sue, 2001) and African American men (Caldwell & White, 2001) experience similar struggles with stereotyping and discrimination. All use mental health services at lower rates than White men (U.S. DHHS, 2001), leaving men in these ethnic groups underserved.

Sexual orientation is another diversity issue, and the mental health care system has a history of failing to offer appropriate treatment to lesbians, gay men, and bisexuals. The emphasis on the social environment as a factor in psychological problems makes feminist therapy "one of few models of behavior change that intentionally perceives the variability of sexual orientations in human beings as a simple fact, rather than a matter for concern and intervention" (Brown, 1988, p. 206). Since that statement in 1988, criteria for therapies have changed to be more compatible with accepting sexual orientation as a circumstance in people's lives rather than as a problem to be treated. But, therapists in training continue to hold stereotypical view of gay men (Boysen, Vogel, Madon, & Wester, 2006), indicating some need for improvement in this area. Without sensitivity to the issues that impact gay, lesbian, bisexual, and transgendered individuals, they may otherwise receive treatment for their sexual orientation rather than for the cause of their distress. An insensitive therapist may focus on sexual orientation and miss other critical factors, rendering treatment inappropriate. Feminist therapy addresses gender stereotypes, making this approach well suited for lesbian, gay, bisexual, and transgendered individuals (Pseekos & Lyddon, 2009). Thus, sexual orientation is another diversity issue that therapy must address.

George Albee (2005) discussed the lack of access to therapy services, citing this worldwide problem as one that cannot be solved through any channel that now exists. Even in high-income countries, the number of unserved and underserved people is too great. Too few treatment facilities and too few trained personnel exist to offer appropriate treatment for mental disorders, creating a pressing need for prevention. Albee suggested that the strategies for prevention should include decreasing some of the most severe sources of stress, such as discrimination, violence victimization, and poverty. These experiences raise the risk for mental disorders such as depression, alcohol abuse, and anxiety disorders, which are leading causes of disability around the world.

■ Summary

Psychoanalysis, the treatment based on Freud's conceptualization of personality development, was an early form of treatment for mental disorders that used talk to help people bring unconscious material to consciousness. Dissatisfaction with the theory and practice of psychoanalysis prompted the development of alternative talk-based therapies, including the humanistic approach to therapy, which attempts to help people fulfill their potential by accepting their emotions and feelings. Cognitive therapy is another talk-based therapy that focuses on thoughts and holds that changing irrational and self-defeating thoughts will produce a change in behavior. Behavior modification centers on applying the principles of operant conditioning to alter undesirable behaviors. Cognitive behavior therapy is a blending of cognitive therapy and behavior modification that attempts to alter cognitions and establish more adaptive behaviors. Medical therapies are also used to treat behavior problems, including psychoactive drugs and electroconvulsive therapy. Women receive more prescriptions for psychoactive drugs and more electroconvulsive therapy than men do.

Charges of gender bias extend to all therapies; each offers a format in which therapists can enact their gender stereotypes and impose their values. In addition, all concentrate on the individual and ignore the social and political aspects of problems. Research indicates that gender stereotypes affect therapists and their delivery of therapy, tending to enforce traditional gender roles.

Nonsexist therapy was created in an attempt to remove the gender bias in therapy, but many female therapists believed that therapy should promote feminist goals. Feminist therapists hold that personal problems are reflections of wider social problems, strive to maintain equality in the relationship between client and therapist, and value the views of women as ways to empower their clients and help them bring about positive changes. From its initial position of political activism, feminist therapy has expanded to a wide variety of clients, including men.

Men are less willing to seek therapy than women are. Men's reluctance to seek therapy relates to the masculine gender role; men with more traditional values are less willing to seek help than men with less traditional values. Men find it difficult to accomplish the goals of therapy, which often include discussing emotions or acknowledging vulnerability. Therapies to help traditional men are among the gender-sensitive therapies developed in recent years.

An American Psychological Association survey of female psychologists revealed four areas of concern regarding sexism in therapy: (1) using sexist psychoanalytic concepts, (2) fostering traditional gender roles, (3) diminished expectations for female clients, and (4) treating women as sex objects, including having sex with clients.

Surveys of therapists have revealed that the sexual exploitation of clients by therapists occurs with about 7% of male therapists and about 1.5% of female therapists. The prevalence of this problem has led professional associations to include prohibitions against sexual relationships with clients, but this section nevertheless remains the most commonly violated of any of the ethical codes. A growing body of evidence indicates that intimate relationships with therapists do long-lasting harm to clients.

Rather than seeking therapy from professionals, a growing number of people join self-help groups. These groups mushroomed during the 1980s and spread worldwide. Originating with the model of Alcoholics Anonymous, self-help groups offer emotional support and access to information from others who share the same type of problem. The low cost is attractive, and increased access to the Internet has led to the proliferation of online support groups. These groups share many similarities with face-to-face groups but allow access to a wider group of participants who may not be able to attend in person. Men are more likely to participate in the online format for self-help. Gender is a factor in both online and face-to-face groups, which may be organized around gender-related issues. However, even Internet anonymity does not erase gender stereotypes in online interactions.

People in Asia, Africa, and Latin America may not have the same views of psychopathology as people in the United States and Western Europe and thus may not readily accept psychotherapy or medical treatments for behavior problems. Treatment must be compatible with a culture to be accepted and successful, and providing culturally appropriate treatment presents challenges on a worldwide basis as well as in ethnically diverse societies such as the United States. With its emphasis on social context, feminist therapy or other gender-sensitive therapies are appropriate for people from a variety of cultures as well as for gay, lesbian, bisexual, and transgendered individuals. However, the worldwide burden of mental disorders can only be solved through prevention.

■ Glossary

behavior modification the application of principles of operant conditioning to behavior, with the goal of changing undesirable behavior to more acceptable alternatives.

electroconvulsive therapy the application to the brain of electric current sufficient to induce a convulsion, which for unknown reasons produces therapeutic effects.

psychoanalysis Freud's talk-based treatment for psychological problems that consists of attempts to bring unconscious material to consciousness.

repression a defense mechanism used to push troubling material from the conscious into the unconscious.

■ Suggested Readings

American Psychological Association. (2007). Guidelines for psychological practice with girls and women. *American Psychologist, 62* (9), 949–979.

These guidelines provide a comprehensive review of issues related to girls' and women's mental health and treatment. Although focused on girls and women, these guidelines provide 11 principles for providing therapy that is culture and gender sensitive, which equals good therapy for anyone.

Brooks, Gary. (2010). *Beyond the crisis of masculinity: A transtheoretical model for male-friendly therapy.* Washington, DC: American Psychological Association. Brooks's latest book discusses the barriers that men face in therapy, men's needs for therapy, and how the transtheoretical model of behavior change can be a good model for engaging men and keeping them in therapy.

Pope, Kenneth S. (2001). Sex between therapists and clients. In Judith Worrell (Ed.), *Encyclopedia of women and gender: Sex similarities and differences and the impact of society on gender* (vol. 2; pp. 955–962). New York: Academic Press.

Pope reviews the history, harmful effects on clients, and gender differences for therapists who have sex with their clients.

Shah, Abhinav A.; & Beinecke, Richard H. (2009). Global mental health needs, services, barriers, and challenges. *International Journal of Mental Health, 38* (1), 14–29.

This review takes a worldwide view of disorders and the need for treatment in low-, middle-, and high-income countries, including factors that limit access to adequate mental health care.

16 How Different?

"The conventional wisdom is that 'men are from Mars and women are from Venus,' "said Molly Monahan Lang, a sociologist at Bloomsburg University of Pennsylvania. "On the contrary, we are from one small world that is getting smaller" (Patricia Cohen, 2007, p. A14). This statement demonstrates what participants in a conference on contemporary families described as *gender convergence*. Rather than a "war between the sexes," this notion holds that women and men are becoming more similar—and are more likely to find ways to get along with each other. Does gender convergence mean that women and men are happy with the changes to gender roles and want more? What *do* men and women want?

HEADLINE

Signs of Détente in the Battle between Venus and Mars

New York Times, May 31, 2007

What Do Women Want? What Do Men Want?

Questioning what women want became popular after Sigmund Freud asked the question of Marie Bonaparte in the 1930s (Jones, 1955). His version of the question, as many others have been, was an exasperated plea prompted by a genuine lack of understanding of women's motivations (Feist & Feist, 2009). Other men have contended that women's goals are unreasonable rather than mysterious.

Men's motives have not been subject to the same degree of scrutiny as women's, but the changes in women's roles have forced men to examine their own lives to consider what they want. Much of this examination has centered on what men want from women and the difficulties that changes in women's lives have created for men. But the concept of gender convergence suggests than women, and men are becoming more similar.

Have Women Become More Like Men?

"Why can't a woman be more like a man?" was the title of a song in the musical play *My Fair Lady* (Lerner & Loewe, 1956). Henry Higgins sang about how unreasonable women were in comparison to men. As he longed for women to be more like men, he was voicing the stereotypical belief of essential differences between women and men. Although this view was common at the time the musical appeared (and for some people, is accepted even now), that view may be incorrect. Rosalind Barnett and Caryl Rivers (2004) contended that gender differences have been exaggerated; women and men are much more similar than different. The headline article agreed with this view.

Women have begun to take the opportunity to pursue some of the goals that were once reserved for men, most notably education and paid employment. If large differences once existed between men and women, perhaps the intervening years have allowed Higgins's wish to come true. In what ways have women become more like men? And if this wish has come true, are men as comfortable with the changes as the headline article suggested?

Higgins's wishes centered around emotionality; he listed negative emotions for women and positive ones for men. Of course, Higgins himself deviated from this ideal quite a bit, and his notion of overly emotional women failed to take male violence into account. Women may report more emotional intensity than men do, but a willingness to report emotion is tied to gender stereotypes of emotionality and not necessarily to the experience of emotion (Shields, 2002). Indeed, women and men have similar experiences (but different expressions) of anger (Archer, 2004). Girls and boys spend years learning how to perform emotion in gendered ways according to the display rules of their culture. These social rules for displaying emotion shape the gender differences in emotionality.

Rather than women becoming more like men, the opposite trend has appeared in couples' relationships. As wives have joined the workforce, husbands have become more involved in household work and child care. As couples strive for intimacy, men feel the pressure to become more emotionally open. Thus, women have not become more like men in these respects, but instead, men are feeling the pressure to become more like women.

During the past 50 years, women and men have become more alike in their sexual behavior. When Alfred Kinsey and his colleagues (1948, 1953) conducted their surveys in the 1930s and 1940s, the double standard for sexual behavior constrained women from expressing their sexuality. Women were less likely to masturbate and to have intercourse outside marriage than men were. Later surveys (Hunt, 1974; Laumann, Gagnon, Michael, & Michaels, 1994) have shown a decrease in the differences, and when women and men believe that their responses are monitored by a polygraph ("lie detector"), most differences in sexual behavior disappear (Alexander & Fisher, 2003).

The sexual differences that remain may be important, with small differences creating large problems for heterosexual couples (Hyde, 1996). For example, women's lower rate of masturbation may relate to their difficulties in having orgasms during sex with their partners, a problem that prompts many couples to seek therapy and many others to experience conflict in their sexual relationships. (The advice of sex therapists often includes masturbation to learn how to have orgasms.) The difference in attitudes toward casual sex has a large influence on many relationships. When men and women bring different attitudes about commitment to sexual relationships, their varying standards can result in jealousy and conflict.

Changes in sexual attitudes have allowed women to explore their sexuality. Women made substantial changes in their sexual attitudes and behavior between the 1930s and the 1970s (Laumann et al., 1994). The conservatism of the 1980s and the growing fear of AIDS produced some decrease in the willingness for sexual exploration in both men and women, but women's exploration of their sexuality has taken them in directions that were not necessarily compatible with men's sexual preferences. Indeed, increased acceptance of sexuality other than intercourse led women to be less sexually dependent on men. This decreased dependence has become a source of men's discontent. Women have become more sexual, but not like men, and not necessarily to men's liking. Even in "hook up" relationships that are based on casual sex, women have higher expectations of emotional commitment than men do (McGinty, Knox, & Zusman, 2007).

Women have become more like men in terms of their achievements: Educational differences between men and women have reversed—women now receive more college degrees than men. Differences still persist in several areas of training and in the advanced and professional degrees awarded in some areas, but the gender gap is closing in training for prestigious careers such as law, business, and medicine. Women's gains may overcome men's current advantage, and more women than men will be qualified for high-status jobs in the future (American Council on Education, 2003). A wife's income is attractive to many men, but competing with women for good jobs is not a change that men welcome.

Employment gives women more economic advantages, but also produces greater demands. Although some women have sought employment out of a desire for personal fulfillment, economic necessity is the reason that most women join and stay in the workforce. This form of gender convergence is the most dramatic; women and men have increasingly similar ambitions and goals (Patricia Cohen, 2007). However, the degree to which women are satisfied with their employment varies according to the support they receive from their families as well as the support from their colleagues and supervisors on the job. Women whose husbands provide little assistance and emotional support for their employment are less satisfied than women with more supportive families, but gender convergence is occurring in this area, too.

In needing and providing support, women and men are now similar, but these similarities represent changes in their traditional roles. Female homemakers were the traditional caregivers, but employed women need to *receive* support from, as well as *provide* support to, their families. In the past, male breadwinners could expect the support of their wives, but they are now expected to provide their wives with emotional support and also help with household work. Through these changes, women and men have become more alike, but an increase in household chores was probably not what men like Henry Higgins had in mind. This struggle has become one of the areas of détente that the headline article described— men are becoming more involved in household work and child care. Indeed, a study of time use among women and men (Fisher, Egerton, Gershuny, & Robinson, 2007) found that each spent similar amounts of time doing at the same activities, which highlights the changes that have occurred.

The areas of gender convergence include education, employment, sexual attitudes and behavior, and achievement. Women have become more like men, but the changes have not been symmetrical—men have not adopted women's behaviors to the same extent. These asymmetric changes are not surprising when considering the situations that have produced the changes. Women have moved into the educational and employment worlds formerly occupied by men, but for the most part, men have not made corresponding moves into women's worlds. Thus, men encounter few—and women encounter many—situations that encourage the adoption of a more flexible style.

Despite superficial endorsement of the virtues of the traditional feminine role of homemaker and mother, society has accorded little value to nurturing skills or other

The large number of women entering the paid workforce has brought about changes in women's and men's relationships and family lives.

traditional feminine behaviors (Cancian & Oliker, 2000). Men's traditional masculine style of assertive, independent, agentic behavior has set the mold for behavior in a variety of situations (Barnett & Rivers, 2004). Women who enter these situations tend to adopt the style of the situation, which is usually agentic rather than communal. Society's value of masculine over feminine traits results in women receiving rewards for adopting such active, instrumental behaviors and men receiving little encouragement for becoming more expressive or communal in their behavior. Thus, women have more freedom than men to become androgynous by combining the positive aspects of masculinity with the expressive, communal behaviors of femininity.

How do women feel about these changes? A great deal of media attention has focused on the negative effects of the changes in women's lives. Stories appeared about women leaving prestigious careers to be full-time homemakers, but the publicity may not be based on valid research: "In a 24/7 media culture that doesn't always bother to wait for that next step, speculative theory can too often be fobbed off as scientific fact on the evening news or in magazine features. . . ." (Barnett & Rivers, 2004, p. 50). The stories focused on interviews with selected discontented women rather than presenting studies with more representative samples of women. Better research indicates that women would like more opportunities and options rather than a return to traditional gender roles. In a nationwide survey (CBS News Poll, 2005), women and men reported that their lives had improved because of the changes brought about by the women's movement. Neither women nor men believe that going back to the gender roles of the 1950s is desirable (Bolzendahl & Myers, 2004).

Men see more disadvantages to the changes in gender roles for men than women do for the changes for women. Men's role as breadwinner is compromised by the decreasing availability of good jobs and the increasing number of employed women who can provide for themselves (Faludi, 1999). A culture that seemed to revolve around boys and men stopped doing so, and women's concerns became preeminent. Many men expect privileges that they no longer have, leaving them feeling cheated and resentful.

Henry Higgins's wish may have come too true. Women have, indeed, become more like men, but the changes are not everything that he (and men like him) had hoped for. Most people find change difficult and anxiety provoking, and changes in expectations for men and women have come about very rapidly. Indeed, the changes have occurred faster than social institutions have been able to accommodate them. People have few models to emulate in adopting new gender roles, and they live in a society that pressures them to be more traditional. When gender roles were narrowly defined, everyone knew what to do. Although the rules were unquestionably restrictive, preventing people from performing gender-inappropriate activities, the roles were at least clear. Greater flexibility has produced uncertainty as well as options.

The power and privilege of men's traditional gender role put men in a position of having more to lose through change than women do, and men are less pleased than women with the changes that have occurred (Bolzendahl & Myers, 2004). Although some men have welcomed the opportunities to form more intimate relationships with friends and partners and to be involved in their children's lives, many others have resisted making changes or have found themselves not knowing how to enact the changes they want to make. Society offers little encouragement for men to become more feminine (R. Gross, 2003). Indeed, men continue to avoid activities associated with femininity. For example, few men want some of the new options that gender equity has offered, such as careers as elementary school teachers or secretaries. Thus, the changes in gender roles have threatened privileges that men have and given them options most do not want. However, many men want to be more involved with their children's lives, and this change has occurred to a larger extent than pursuing female-dominated careers.

Women too may not be entirely satisfied with the changes in their lives. As the many polls indicate, the majority of women favor more equal treatment in politics and jobs (Bolzendahl & Myers, 2004), but they too may resist making other changes in the roles and underlying assumptions about their relationships with men, their sexuality, and their children. Many mothers experience difficulties in becoming less involved in child care while fathers become more so. Not only does this situation violate gender-typical behavior but also women may be jealous of the bond that forms between fathers and children (Barnett & Rivers, 2004). Women do not want to lose elements of their gender role. Instead, they want to add the privileges and choices that men have enjoyed. That is, women want to "have it all" (Hoffnung, 2004).

Few women long for a return to traditionalism, but that longing is stronger in men, who believe that changes in gender roles have caused them to lose more and gain less than women have. Men tend to complain about what they have lost—services and subservience. Women tend to complain, not about what they have lost, but about what they have gained—the equivalent of two full-time jobs. As one of Lily Tomlin's characters in *The Search for Intelligent Life in the Universe* (Wagner, 1991) said, "If I had known what it was like to have it all, I might have settled for less." Table 16.1 (page 428) summarizes some of these changes.

TABLE 16.1 *Ways Men and Women Have Changed over the Past 40 Years*

Women Have Become More Like Men in	
Education	Women earn 57% of bachelor's, 60% of master's, and 48% of all doctoral degrees granted in 2006 (U.S. Census Bureau, 2009a).
Employment	48% of workforce is female (U.S. Census Bureau, 2009a).
Earnings	Women earn 80¢ for every $1 earned by men (up from 59¢ in 1970s) (U.S. Bureau of Labor Statistics, 2008).
Sexual attitudes	Age of first intercourse is similar for girls and boys across ethnic groups in the United States (Upchurch et al., 2002).
	88% of men and 81% of women engage in premarital sex (Christopher & Sprecher, 2000).
	98.9% of men and 99.2% of women want to settle down with one sexual partner at some time during their lives (Pedersen et al., 2002).
	Large majority of men and women find extramarital sex unacceptable (Laumann et al., 1994).
Physical activity	53% of women are not adequately physically active and 50% of men are not (U.S. Census Bureau, 2009a).

Men Have Become More Like Women in	
Forming intimate relationships	Women's talk-based style of intimacy has become the standard (Cancian, 1986).
Smoking rate	22.2% of men and 18.5% of women currently smoke cigarettes (U.S. Census Bureau, 2009a).
Dieting	24% of men and 38% of women are dieting (Kruger et al., 2004)

Why Can't a Man Be More Like a Woman?

Men have not embraced the changes in gender roles and behaviors that have occurred in the past 40 years to the extent that women have. Study after study has found that men hold more rigid gender stereotypes than women do (see Chapter 3). Traditional men see no advantages for themselves in women's greater freedom. Indeed, these men feel the competition for grades and jobs, and they resent the presence of women in the workplace. Traditional men have stereotypical attitudes toward their own gender role and prefer women to adhere to traditional femininity (Brooks, 2003). These men do not feel the appeal of expanding their gender role to include behaviors traditionally reserved for women, so they see nothing but disadvantages connected with changing gender roles.

These traditional men are a diminishing minority; a majority of men endorse at least some of the changes in women's roles (Bolzendahl & Myers, 2004). Age is an important factor in men's attitudes toward changing roles; traditional men are more likely to be older, whereas younger men are more acceptant of feminist goals. Many men may be considered to be in transition between traditional views of male dominance and embracing new roles for women and for men. These men tend to accept the contention that the women's movement has produced benefits for them as well as for women (CBS News Poll, 2005). They are likely to be sympathetic to individual women but unlikely to embrace women's issues.

Younger men are especially likely to endorse equality for women and greater involvement for men in family life (Galinsky, Aumann, & Bond, 2009). Young men are more likely than older ones to have grown up with a mother who was employed, giving them a model for such relationships (Bolzendahl & Myers, 2004). They are also more likely to have female partners who are less traditional than they are, pushing these young men toward egalitarian relationships. These men are unlikely to label themselves as feminists, but their values are compatible with feminist goals (CBS News Poll, 2005).

But how far do we want the convergence to go? Women have become more like men, but men have more often declined than accepted opportunities to become more like women. The asymmetry of these changes may have created a situation in which women want men to make some changes. Women are asking Henry Higgins's question from their own point of view: "Why can't a man be more like a woman?"

This question exists in two versions, one social and one personal. The first version applies to the question as a social one, challenging the wisdom of continuing to use men and masculine values as the standard and as the preferred style. For example, what makes the hierarchical, directive (sometimes autocratic) style of leadership that men typically use preferable to the cooperative, democratic style more typical of women? What is wrong with emphasizing relationships and being emotionally expressive? Why can't men accept the value of the feminine style? Why are men considered the standard and women the exception (Bem, 1993b)? The second version of the question is more personal, challenging men to include more expressiveness in personal relationships and to participate more fully in "women's work," that is, household work and child care. Women contend that both society at large, as well as their individual lives, would profit from men accepting the value of men becoming a bit more like women (Gross, 2003).

People have few problems in accepting the value of the communal qualities associated with women. Alice Eagly and her colleagues (Eagly & Johannesen-Schmidt, 2001; Eagly, Mladinic, & Otto, 1991) investigated evaluations of men and women, finding that women received more positive personal evaluations than men did. People think of women as a social category in very positive terms, but not necessarily when women exhibit these qualities in positions traditionally held by men. As Eagly et al. (1991, p. 213) put it, "Although people evidently think that these qualities are wonderful human attributes, they may value them more in close relationships than in highly paid sectors of the workforce." Thus, positive attitudes about women do not ensure the social acceptance of their style in roles other than traditional ones. This situation is unfortunate; research (Eagly & Johannesen-Schmidt, 2001) indicates that these behaviors foster positive workplace outcomes, and corporations with a mixture of male and female managers are more successful than companies with only male managers (Jones, 2009).

Although the lives of women and men are converging in a number of ways, society offers few models of couples who develop equal relationships, but many examples of traditional couples. The convergence has occurred through the effort of couples who have worked out new ways of living together and raising children, with both partners contributing in the workforce and at home. The importance of family—to both men and women—was a clear message from the results of a recent survey on work and family life in the United States (Galinsky et al., 2009).

What are the prospects for men becoming more like women? And how would women feel if they did? Currently, the rewards for men who adopt more expressive behaviors are not as great as for women who become more instrumental, which leads to the prediction that men may not change as much as women have. However, signs of convergence have emerged. Issues of gender equity have become a concern among leaders of the men's movement, with statements concerning the necessity of changes for men in order to achieve gender justice for women (Connell, 2005a, 2005b). As Rita Gross (2003) pointed out, it is not possible to free women from restrictive gender roles without changing men as well. This attitude is increasing among men, a majority of whom failed to endorse traditional views of men as breadwinners and women as homemakers (Galinsky et al., 2009).

However, women do not want men to be like women (Bloom, 2002). Women see the benefits of breaking the stereotypes, both for themselves and for men. Indeed, many examples exist of individuals who easily break these rules, such as the men who do most of the cooking and women who repair automobiles. The ideals have changed so that the ideal for women as well as men is strong, smart, and self-reliant and the ideal for men as well as women is sensitive and affectionate. But this androgyny goes only so far. Parents do not want girls to become so strong, smart, and self-reliant that they have trouble getting invited to the prom, or boys to become so sensitive that they are taunted and bullied. The gender lines may not be drawn where they were, but the lines still exist, and most men and women want some lines. Those lines can feel like a hopscotch grid when it comes to negotiating the multiple roles that have become the rule for most people's lives.

Multiple Roles Have Become the Rule

Once upon a time, women chose careers to support themselves until they married, and men devoted themselves to careers while remaining marginally involved in family life. These stereotypical patterns no longer apply to an increasing number of women and men. A growing number of women pursue careers on a full-time, uninterrupted basis. As a result, many men no longer provide the sole support for their families. With the job demands experienced by both men and women, finding the time to devote to marriage and family has become difficult. Indeed, work/life balance has become a major challenge for modern couples in most high-income countries (Galinsky et al., 2009; Zagor, 2006).

Their problems stem from social expectations and the fixed gender roles that these expectations bring (Fuwa, 2004). Despite joining the workforce of paid employment, women still are expected (and expect themselves) to occupy the role of wife and mother, including performing a majority of the household and family work. Men have experienced fewer changes in their roles, but women's employment has eroded men's role as breadwinner (Zuo, 2004). Women are pressuring men to participate more in household work and child care, with some success (Zagor, 2006). Men may struggle with these chores; they have few models for the acceptability of performing them and little practice in doing so. Instead, they have television commercials that ridicule men's efforts to do household work (Crain, 2001).

Gender stereotypes push men toward "men's work" around the house, including mowing the lawn, shoveling snow, and taking out the trash, whereas women still perform the most time-consuming chores such as grocery shopping, food preparation and cleanup, and the majority of child care (Coltrane, 2000). Even when partners plan an equitable sharing of household work, they have difficulty implementing these plans, but more couples are working toward this goal (Galinsky et al., 2009).

Some jobs are especially problematic for attaining a balance between work and family. High-level managerial and professional careers require long hours and extraordinary dedication. The corporate, male-dominated careers that women began entering in somewhat larger numbers during the 1970s have not changed to accommodate women's family duties (Connell, 2005b; Epstein, 2004). Men provided the model for these careers—men who had wives to provide a support system for their husbands' careers. These wives offered not only emotional support at home but also social support in the public functions of the organization (Williams, 2000). That is, the "corporate wife" joins auxiliaries, organizes social functions, and boosts her husband's career. Women too need "wives" to provide this support, but even husbands who are willing to be homemakers would not function as corporate "wives."

An increasing number of men have taken the role of at-home support for employed wives (Tyre et al., 2003). A few men have chosen to be "Mr. Mom" and to devote time to being with their children. However, many of these husbands have taken this role as a result of the loss of their jobs, making their wives involuntary breadwinners and creating tensions in their marriages. Even when the arrangement is voluntary, wives with corporate careers and husbands who care for children are violating gender boundaries and receive disapproval for spending too much time in tasks that are gender inappropriate (Epstein, 2004).

◼ GENDERED VOICES

I've Had This Conversation Before

Melinda was a single mother with a 2-year-old son who told me about her experiences with the woman she had hired to care for her son. She considered herself and her son extremely fortunate; the nanny was a retired pediatric nurse, ideally qualified to be a nanny, and a wonderful person. Like many other mothers with careers, Melinda felt less than enthusiastic at the thought of leaving her son in the care of someone else, and she felt fortunate not only to be able to afford a full-time, live-in nanny but also to have found a great person. Indeed, they had become like a family.

Melinda's business career was demanding but fulfilling. She had worked as a secretary during the time that she was married, but she had divorced and pursued a sales and management career and had become successful. Like other women with demanding and fulfilling careers, she worked long and sometimes irregular hours.

Her son's nanny took care of him and the house, cooking dinner for herself and the child. She said that she could easily cook for Melinda as well; she would be glad to do so, but Melinda needed to be home to eat with them.

Melinda explained that she didn't always know when she would need to work late, and she couldn't be sure about being home in time for dinner every night. "But that doesn't matter. If I'm late, just leave my dinner. It's no big deal." The nanny said that it was a big deal; she didn't want to cook dinner and have her be late and have cold food. It just wasn't right. Melinda thought, "I've had this conversation before—when I was married. Only this time I'm being the 'husband,' and last time I was the wife. My husband said all the things I'm saying and gave all the excuses I'm giving, and I said the words I'm hearing from my nanny." Melinda was now the "husband."

Pepper Schwartz (1994) studied couples who had managed to construct marriages in which each shared equitably in family life, and she contrasted these couples with more traditional marriages. One factor that distinguished these two types of couples was level of employment; few fast-track careers appeared among the marriages in which the partners shared equally. Schwartz found that these couples "maintain their relationship goals by folding work into the relationship rather than vice versa" (Pepper Schwartz, 1994, p. 181). For both men and women, the relationship was more important than career. By making their relationship and home life primary, these couples have expanded the role for men, making them into full participants in their wives' and children's lives. Younger couples are adopting this strategy more often than their parents did (Galinsky et al., 2009).

What are the consequences of this balancing act of multiple roles for men and women? Several models hypothesize different consequences of multiple roles (Barnett & Hyde, 2001). The *functionalist* view holds that families function best when men concentrate on their jobs and women specialize on caring for home and children. This view dates back to the 1950s, when this family configuration was common and deviations were considered less than ideal. In this view, multiple roles lead to role conflict because people who try to fulfill many roles experience conflict when the multiple roles produce stress in their lives. An alternative model, the *psychoanalytic* view, holds that boys develop a sense of autonomy that suits them to pursue accomplishments in the outside world, but girls do not. Thus women are unsuited for paid employment but well suited to domesticity and child care. This model also envisions a sharp division of gender roles and varying suitability for paid employment. Individuals who pursue unsuitable goals should experience problems. The view from evolutionary psychology also holds that women and men are inherently propelled toward different work and family roles by their evolutionary heritage. For example, one hypothesis drawn from this view is that women who have less contact with their families will experience more depression and mental health problems than those who stay in close contact. The *role expansion model* emphasizes the direct and indirect benefits of employment for women, proposing that the monetary benefits, the satisfaction of fulfilling several roles, and the protection of occupying several different roles will be beneficial. Table 16.2 shows these four models and the position of each on the effects of multiple roles.

TABLE 16.2   *Four Models for Multiple Role Occupancy*

Model	Result of Multiple Roles	Benefits
Functionalist	Conflict—Men should be breadwinners, and women should take care of household	None
Psychoanalytic	Conflict—Men are suited to the outside world and women to home	None
Evolutionary	Conflict and depression—"Natural" roles of breadwinning and homemaking are genetically programmed	None
Expansionist	Enhancement—Both men and women are healthier and more satisfied when they occupy roles of partner and employee	Direct and indirect

Source: Based on "Women, Men, Work, and Family: An Expansionist Theory," by Rosalind Chait Barnett and Janet Hyde, 2001, *American Psychologist, 56,* pp. 782–785.

Research supports the advantages of multiple roles, especially the benefits that come from employment. These benefits apply to women and men (Barnett & Hyde, 2001; de Vaus, 2002; Sachs-Ericsson & Ciarlo, 2000). Employment may cause stress, but its impact is similar for men and women and does not harm women more than men. Considering the economic and power benefits, women gain many advantages from occupying the role of paid employee.

Women's balance of career, household work, and child care may, indeed, produce stress, but the amount of support they receive is a mediating factor (Barnett & Hyde, 2001). For women with young children and no partner, their multiple roles of mother, head of household, and employee are often stressful, and these women tend to have more mental health problems than women with partners (Sachs-Ericsson & Ciarlo, 2000). Men are also more satisfied with their marriages and their lives when they participate in what they perceive to be a fair share of family work (Saginak & Saginak, 2005). Employed, married men with children had fewer mental health problems than any other combination of demographic characteristics for people in the United States (Sachs-Ericsson & Ciarlo, 2000).

The rule of multiple roles has resulted in women moving into careers and men becoming more involved in household work and child care. These changes have created the convergence in attitudes and behavior that the headline discussed. Then what differences remain between women and men?

Where Are the Differences?

Differences still exist between the genders in the theories used to explain psychological factors related to gender. The traditional dichotomy for theories of gender is the biological view versus the environmental view—attributing differences to either nature or nurture. Although these opposing points of view have influenced research in gender, another approach now encompasses the nature–nurture debate in gender—the maximalist versus the minimalist positions.

The maximalist view holds that men and women have large differences ("Men Are from Mars, Women Are from Venus"), whereas the minimalist view holds that the differences between men and women are small compared to their similarities ("Same Difference"). The older versions of maximalist theory are biologically based, emphasizing differences, and offering genetic, hormonal, or evolutionary explanations for behavior as well as for anatomy. Evolutionary psychology is a maximalist theory that proposes that human evolutionary history has equipped people with preprogrammed patterns of behavior that differ a great deal between women and men. These theorists tend to rationalize the disadvantaged social position of women by citing biological programming as the source of differences. Naomi Weisstein (1982, p. 41) summarized this position by saying, "Men are biologically suited to their life of power, pleasure, and privilege, and women must accept subordination, sacrifice, and submission. It's in the genes. Go fight city hall."

Not surprisingly, feminist scholars have disputed the biological basis of behavioral differences between men and women, proposing that social experiences produce differences in learning and thus in behavior. According to this view, social learning and situations, not biology, form the basis for psychological gender differences. This approach holds that behavior varies according to circumstances and surroundings, and these theorists attribute gender differences to the different situations that women and men typically encounter.

Not all maximalist theories rely on biology; social learning forms the basis for some versions of the maximalist position. Although these theorists see the differences between women's and men's behavior as learned, they believe that the differences are large and persistent. Many of these maximalist theorists are cultural feminists, advocating the superiority of women's style and characteristics. Rather than accepting the differences as deficiencies, they promote the female version as the better alternative.

Maximalist theorists such as Carol Gilligan, Nancy Chodorow, and Deborah Tannen are appealing to some women because "they offer a flattering account of traits for which they have historically been castigated" (Pollitt, 1992, p. 802). This view is a modernized version of the Doctrine of the Two Spheres, the Victorian view that women were moral, pure, spiritual, emotional, and intellectually inferior. Unfortunately, the virtues that these maximalists idealize also rationalize the continued subordination of women. What's more, the popularity of this view is ironic, given that the roles of women and men are more similar than they have been at any time during the history of the West (Barnett & Rivers, 2004; Galinsky et al., 2009).

These similarities are part of the evidence that the minimalists cite when they argue that gender differences are small. Rather than gender differences, Janet Hyde (2005a) contended that this area of research should be called *gender similarities* because meta-analyses have revealed so few differences. Rosalind Barnett and Caryl Rivers (2004) titled their analysis *Same Difference* to convey the message that gender differences have been overstated.

Both maximalists and minimalists look at the same research and find evidence to support their positions. The ability to maintain different interpretations of the same information highlights the constructed nature of theories; that is, those who support one view or the other have constructed their position in accordance with their beliefs about gender. Building and maintaining a theoretical position requires examining the research evidence, but theory goes beyond evidence. Therefore, it is possible for theorists to maintain discrepant positions with regard to gender differences, with some theorists holding maximalist and others minimalist positions.

Theories are not the only place that gender differences exist; gender-related differences also exist in behavior. The extent of gender-related differences, however, depends on the type of study considered. In considering studies on ability, few gender differences have appeared. In considering the choices that men and women have made about what to do in their lives, the gender differences are larger.

Differences in Ability

Considering the many comparisons of abilities of women and men, the gender differences are largest for physical strength. This difference relates to size and muscle mass, with men being significantly larger and stronger than women. The differences among individuals are also large; some women are stronger than other women, and some men stronger than others. However, gender differences are larger than individual differences, making gender a good predictor of strength.

In the past, physical strength made a great deal of difference for a variety of activities, especially in the world of paid employment. Currently, few positions of prestige and power require strength, but the legacy of this difference persists. In a survey and interview study of gender issues (Sigal, 1996), several men expressed the opinion that men should be paid more than women because men's jobs require more strength. Despite the high levels of skills that secretaries might need, they should receive less money, according to this view, because their jobs do not require heavy labor. The requirements for physical labor were also mentioned as a reason why men should not be expected to share household work or child care—they had already done physical labor and should not be expected to do more at home. In the years since that study, this view has diminished, especially among men (Galinsky et al., 2009).

Gender is a good predictor of physical strength but a very poor predictor of mental abilities. In both verbal abilities and mathematical abilities, only small gender differences exist. Despite the widespread belief that men have superior mathematical abilities and women have superior verbal abilities, the technique of meta-analysis has revealed that the gender differences are small (Hyde, 2005a; Hyde, Fennema, & Lamon, 1990). The largest differences in cognitive abilities are in writing and in one type of spatial task, the mental rotation task. Women have a large advantage in writing, and men have a large advantage in mental rotation, but other spatial and verbal tasks show a mixed pattern of advantages for men, women, or neither.

Research conducted in laboratory settings often shows few if any gender differences. When men and women are put into situations without gender-related cues, their behavior tends to be quite similar. For example, a literature review (Frodi, Macaulay, & Thome, 1977) and meta-analyses (Archer, 2004; Eagly & Steffen, 1986; Knight, Guthrie, Page, & Fabes, 2002) of aggression have shown that women and men are similar in their experience of anger and willingness to behave aggressively in laboratory situations, but outside the laboratory, gender differences appear. One prominent difference is the type of aggression; men tend to choose direct confrontation whereas women are more likely to use an indirect strategy of causing harm.

Thus, the evidence about gender differences in abilities indicates a few large differences and many more small differences. Table 16.3 (page 436) summarizes these few differences. When examining the behavioral choices that men and women make, gender differences are larger than when considering abilities.

Differences in Choices

Women and men make different choices about important facets of their lives, and these choices reflect the behaviors that are encouraged on the basis of gender stereotypes. Saying that women make different choices than men implies that these choices are voluntary and freely made, but such is not the case. As Joan Williams (2000) described the situation, women and men are propelled by force fields that push them toward certain options and away from others, making the traditional choices the only available options for many individuals. Many barriers that prevented women and men from attempting some activities seem to have fallen away, but constraints remain in the form of expectations and encouragement. These choices are more important than abilities in determining what happens in people's lives. The gender differences that exist in education, employment, family life, relationships, sexuality, emotionality, health-related behaviors, body image, and behavior problems reflect these different choices and the expectations that foster them.

TABLE 16.3   *Where Are the Differences?*

Differences between Men and Women Are Large in	
Size	Men are larger than women.
Strength	Men are stronger than women, especially in terms of upper body strength.
Mental rotation ability	Men are much better at mentally rotating figures in space than women are.
Writing ability	Women are better at writing than men are.
Size of sexually dimorphic nucleus	The sexually dimorphic nucleus is a brain structure that is larger in men, but its function is not currently understood.
Gender flexibility	Girls and women stereotype less and have more liberal attitudes about gender roles than boys and men do.
Crime rate	75.8% of those arrested for crimes are men; 24.2% are women (FBI, 2008).
Sexual attitudes and behavior	Men masturbate more than women do (and feel less guilty about it). Men are more acceptant of casual premarital sex than are women.
Overweight	71% of men but only 61% of women in the United States are overweight or obese (U.S. Census Bureau, 2009a).
Strategy of dealing with negative feelings	Women are diagnosed with depression twice as often as men (APA, 2000). Men are diagnosed with substance abuse disorders at ratios of 3–5:1 compared to women (APA, 2000).

Although men and women have similar mathematical ability and now have similar preparation in terms of courses completed in high school (Spelke, 2005) and an increasing number of college degrees in math (U.S. Department of Education, 2008), young men are more likely than women to pursue careers that rely on math. Even women who complete the courses required for a good math background do not choose science and engineering careers as often as men do (Ayalon, 2003; Ceci, Williams, & Barnett, 2009). These discrepancies are larger than the differences in abilities would suggest: Fewer women enter mathematics and engineering than women who have the ability to do so.

The expectation that men will pursue careers consistent with the breadwinner role and that women will seek careers compatible with family duties eliminates many options for each. Men are limited in their family involvement by careers that require dedication and long hours. Men do not receive encouragement when they make different choices, such as allotting time to family life by choosing part-time employment or by choosing to be homemakers. Indeed, this choice is considered deviant, and men who have made such decisions are encouraged to reconsider (Epstein, 2004; Robertson & Fitzgerald, 1990).

The movement of women into the paid workforce has increased their options in some ways but not in others. Women have more choices than men do concerning employment or homemaking—women may be homemakers or employed, or alternate the two, but men are still expected to be employed. However, the expectation is coming to be that women will be employed in addition to having a husband and children (Hoffnung, 2004; Konrad, 2003). Women who have chosen to have a career and family experience the strains of juggling roles as they work to develop their careers, find adequate child care, and make time for children and husbands (Paul, 2003). Women who have chosen to be homemakers feel that their choice is not as well accepted or respected as the choice of pursuing paid employment, but they feel that the job they are doing is essential for their children's well-being (Blair-Loy, 2003). Women who have paid employment but would rather be homemakers, and those who had expected to pursue careers but are instead homemakers, face conflict between their expectations and their actual lives. Thus the changes in patterns of employment for women have resulted in additional role responsibilities as well as an additional option.

Men and women tend to choose different styles of friendships, and this difference is clearly a choice. That is, most women and men are capable of adopting the style of friendship more common in the other gender. A woman can be "one of the boys," and a man can adopt the emotionally intimate friendship pattern more common among women, but each tends to choose a gender-typical style of relating to others. This choice gives women more intimate friendships with other women than with men, and it prevents men from forming intimate friendships with other men (and possibly with women). Friendships are one source of social support that brings advantages for physical and mental health. Women's style of friendship tends to provide more emotional support, whereas men's style of friendship tends to offer more material support. The advantages of social support come from both types of support and extend to both women and men.

Women's choice of achieving intimacy through emotional sharing and talk has become the accepted style for love relationships (Cancian, 1986), and men may feel deficient if they are not adept at this type of relating. Men's attempts to establish intimacy through sexual activity are not entirely compatible with women's choice to create intimacy through talk and sharing feelings. Thus, sexuality may have different meanings for women and men. Even with comparable levels of desire, men and women make different choices concerning expression of their sexuality.

Different choices also appear to be related to the varying life expectancies: Women choose healthier and safer lifestyles than men in terms of the use of health care services, diet, alcohol intake, and seat belt use. On the other hand, men tend to make better choices by exercising and avoiding unhealthy dieting. Both patterns match the interpretation that men's and women's health-related behaviors are oriented toward maintaining their gender roles. Much of women's health-related behavior is not oriented toward health but comes from their concern over body image. Likewise, men exercise to attain a muscular appearance and choose risky health-related behaviors, which match the Give 'Em Hell component of the masculine gender role.

Men's and women's strategies for handling negative feelings can lead to different outcomes. These differences appear both in statistics on violence and in rates of various types of psychopathologies. The display rules for emotion allow (and perhaps even encourage) men to openly express anger, leading to more acts of violence and crime committed by men. Women are encouraged to restrict their displays of anger, leading not to a decrease in the experience of anger, but to differences in the expression of anger. One difference is that women often cry when they are angry, whereas men typically do not.

Different choices for dealing with negative feelings may be reflected in the statistics on psychiatric diagnosis. Women are more likely to receive the diagnosis of depression than men are, but men are more likely to drink alcohol and use other illicit psychoactive substances than women are. Both types of symptoms may represent underlying depression (Scelfo, Springen, & Carmichael, 2007). For example, a pattern of avoidant coping involving alcohol use is related to developing depression (Holahan et al., 2001, 2003, 2004), which may be a more common strategy for men. Ruminating over negative events is also related to developing depression (Nolen-Hoeksema, 2006; Nolen-Hoeksema, Larson, & Grayson, 1999), but this strategy is more common among women. These different choices produce apparent differences in psychopathology, but possibly signaling similar problems with depression.

The expression of psychopathology tends to fall along gender-stereotypical lines (Chesler, 1972; Rosenfield, 1982; Wirth & Bodenhausen, 2009). The categories of psychopathology most common among women fall into the female gender role, but are exaggerated versions of the role: being dependent (dependent personality disorder), passive (major depression), self-sacrificing (self-defeating personality disorder), fearful (agoraphobia), and emotional (histrionic personality disorder). Likewise, men experience psychopathology that seems to have formed around elements of the male gender role but exaggerates these traits: being irresponsible, untruthful, and violent (antisocial personality disorder); reckless (psychoactive substance abuse disorder); and inappropriately sexual (paraphilias). Although these patterns may not represent intentional choices, they exist as reflections of gender-typical differences.

Therefore, gender stereotypes influence choices, pushing both men and women toward gender-stereotypical behaviors. Considering the similarities in abilities, the differences in choices are huge and create life courses for women that differ from those of men.

Is a Peace Plan Possible?

Carol Tavris and Carole Wade (1984) used the term (and titled their book) *The Longest War* to describe what others call the "war between the sexes." Tavris and Wade are surely correct: Of all human conflicts, this one must be the longest. Casting the relationship between men and women as a war highlights the opposition and difference that is prominent in people's thinking about sex and gender. Conflict is certainly part of male–female relationships, and some people imagine that women and men will never get along. John Gray's (1992) bestselling book tells us *Men Are from Mars, Women Are from Venus,* and Deborah Tannen's (1990) bestseller contends that *You Just Don't Understand.* These popular books influence people to believe that the longest war will continue, but research with women and men yields a more hopeful picture.

Although modern life may seem to continue to consist of two domains—male and female—with limited "visitation privileges" from one to the other, these two domains are not different planets. Rather, "the truth is, there is only one culture, and it shapes each sex in distinct but mutually dependent ways in order to reproduce itself" (Pollitt, 1992, p. 806). Cultures still shape men and women, but those forces in the United States and many other high-income countries are now "blending into equality" (Lang & Risman, 2006, p. 287).

The freedom to make cross-gender choices is still constrained by gender stereotypes. The ease of stereotype formation and the perceptions that accompany their formation produce some cognitive convenience but limit options for men and women. This limitation shares the problem posed by all stereotyping: These choices ignore the inherent complexity of individual differences and fail to allow for a wide range of individual choices. The benefit of convenience is outweighed by the cost of the limitations. The abilities of men and women demand an equally wide range of choices—wider than the choices that are available in the bipolar classification of traditional gender roles.

Although gender stereotyping remains prominent, gender convergence is also occurring. Will gender convergence lead to a peace plan for the gender wars, as the headline article suggested? Patricia Cohen's (2007) article suggested that the forays into each other's worlds has increased understanding and empathy, making men and women more similar. Unlike earlier surveys (Sigal, 1996) that had reported continued discrimination against women and little attention to gender issues by men, more recent research (Galinsky et al., 2009; Lang & Risman, 2006) has included many reports of men whose attitudes were consistent with changes in women's roles, dedicated to family involvement, discouraging sexual harassment in the workplace, respecting their female colleagues, and doing the laundry. Some men continue to complain about "the good old days" when women "knew their place," but these men are becoming less common (and less vocal). After about a generation of sharing the workplace and attempting to forge equally shared personal partnerships, changes have occurred.

The quest for gender equity is by no means finished. The gender gap remains in wages and despite men's increased family participation, in household work. A new gender gap has appeared in education, with men lagging behind women. Managing multiple roles is a current challenge for men as well as for women. Despite women's ability and education, their careers are more often interrupted than men's careers. Women are also more likely to be employed part-time, which allows them more time to devote to their families but puts them on the "mommy track" with lower expectations for career advancement. High-prestige careers have not become more flexible; these jobs are "greedy" in terms of hours and demands, and fewer women than men negotiate family arrangements that allow them to pursue such careers successfully. Increased flexibility in employment would be a giant step toward gender equity, improving the lives of women, men, and children. However, the trend in the United States is in the opposite direction—more hours at work. An increase in the number of hours worked per week makes the work/family balancing act more difficult for everyone.

Both men and women are coming to perceive the pressures of modern life as the enemy instead of each other. Many couples have worked out equitable plans for living together and have built satisfying personal relationships; others have succumbed to the pressures of trying to "have it all." Building such relationships often requires analyzing the underlying assumptions connected with gender roles and finding ways to overcome the roles that society dictates for women and men. An increasing number of couples are trying for a peace plan for themselves.

For society, peace in the gender wars is not as close. Modern society is filled with barriers to gender equality. The traditional assumptions about women's and men's roles, based on gender stereotypes, are one type of barrier. Despite many people's willingness to make individual exceptions, the rules still exist. As Williams (2000) described, these rules about gender roles exert force fields that push women and men toward traditional roles and away from equality.

■ Summary

The roles that men and women occupy have undergone changes in the past 4 decades, allowing women to move into careers that had formerly been the province of men. As women began to acquire aspirations and careers comparable with men's, some men began to imagine that women would become more like them, which would make relating to each other easier. Although some of these men have been disappointed in the ways that women have become more like men, gender convergence is occurring.

Men have long wondered what women want and have expressed the desire for women to behave in ways more similar to men. This wish has come true in several respects; women have become more like men in terms of education and occupation. Men, however, did not envision competition from women in the classroom or at work as a desirable outcome of gender similarity, but as women have moved into the worlds of higher education and paid employment, they have assumed roles and behaviors required by these situations. Gender convergence has occurred for women not only in terms of education and employment but also in sexual attitudes and behavior. Despite stereotypes, few gender differences exist in experiencing emotion, but differences remain in how emotions are displayed. Although women's style of personal relationships is the accepted one, men have experienced difficulties in becoming more like women in this way.

Women also wish for changes in men; they want men to respect the qualities women value and to feel comfortable in adopting positive behaviors traditionally associated with women. Women would like for men to be more emotionally expressive and to communicate intimate thoughts and feelings to their partners. Women would also like for men to become more active with their families, sharing household work and child care. The changes in men's lives have not been equal to the ones that women have experienced. The gender convergence for women appears in their behavior; in men, gender convergence has occurred in their attitudes. Men are coming to accept gender equality, and many are working toward becoming more involved fathers and sharing household work and child care more equally.

If women have become more like men in a number of ways, and if men have become more like women in some ways, how many gender differences remain? Differences continue in theories, with maximalist theories advocating that differences exist between the genders, and minimalist theories arguing for more similarities than differences.

Research on gender and ability has revealed relatively few differences. The largest of these differences in ability lies in men's greater physical strength, but few differences exist when measuring other abilities in laboratory situations. When examining the choices that men and women make concerning how to live their lives, larger gender differences appear. Indeed, the difference in choices may promote the idea that greater differences exist than research has confirmed.

The choices that women and men make tend to preserve well-defined gender roles rather than allow people to make freer choices and develop the most satisfying lives. Reliance on gender stereotypes may simplify thought processes, but preserving this dichotomy extracts a high price for individual women and men. On an individual level, peace between women and men is possible, and many couples have built relationships that allow them to participate fully in the workforce, household work, child care, and each other's lives. On a societal level, détente will be more difficult in the gender war because the widespread reliance on gender stereotypes exerts societal-level influence.

■ Suggested Readings

Barnett, Rosalind & Rivers, Caryl. (2004). *Same difference: How gender myths are hurting our relationships, our children, and our jobs.* New York: Basic Books.

Barnett and Rivers analyze the media outpouring of publicity about gender differences, countering the bad science with a presentation of better science. They conclude that gender similarities are more common than differences.

Connell, R. W. (2005). A really good husband: Work/life balance, gender equity and social change. *Australian Journal of Social Issues, 40,* 369–383.

Connell presents a study of work/life balance in Australia, along with his sharp analysis of this issue in the context of gender justice.

Galinsky, Ellen; Aumann, Kerstin; & Bond, James T. (2009). *Times are changing: Gender and generation at work and at home.* Families and Work Institute. Retrieved November 21, 2009, from www.familiesandwork.org/site/research/reports/Times_Are_Changing.pdf.

This report summarizes the results of a survey of men's and women's attitudes concerning how to balance the demands of work and family and provides specific confirmation for the convergence of gender-related attitudes and behavior.

References

Aboud, Frances E.; Mendelson, Morton J.; & Purdy, Kelly T. (2003). Cross-race peer relations and friendship quality. *International Journal of Behavioral Development*, 27, 165–173.

Abraído-Lanza, Ana F.; Chao, Maria T.; & Flórez, Karen R. (2005). Do healthy behaviors decline with greater acculturation?: Implications for the Latino mortality paradox. *Social Science and Medicine*, 61, 1243–1255.

Abrams, Douglas Carlton. (2002, March–April). Father nature: The making of a modern dad. *Psychology Today*, 35 (2), 38–45.

Abu El-Haj, Thea Renda. (2003). Challenging the inevitability of difference: Young women and discourses about gender equity in the classroom. *Curriculum Inquiry*, 33, 401–425.

Acosta, R. Vivian; & Carpenter, Linda Jean. (2009). Thirty-seven years later, Title IX hasn't fixed it all. *Academe*, 95 (4), 22–24.

Adami, Hans-Olov; & Trichopoulos, Dimitrios. (2002). Cervical cancer and the elusive male factor. *New England Journal of Medicine*, 346, 1160–1161.

Adams, Mary B.; McGuire, Jenifer K.; Walsh, Michele; Basta, Joanne; & LeCroy, Craig. (2005). Acculturation as a predictor of the onset of sexual intercourse among Hispanic and White teens. *Archives of Pediatrics and Adolescent Medicine*, 159, 261–265.

Addis, Michael E.; & Mahalik, James R. (2003). Men, masculinity, and the contexts of help seeking. *American Psychologist*, 58, 5–14.

Adewuya, Abiodun O.; Loto, Olabisi M.; Adewumi, Tomi A. (2009). Pattern and correlates of premenstrual symptomatology amongst Nigerian university students. *Journal of Psychosomatic Obstetrics & Gynecology*, 30 (2), 127–132.

Ahmed, Eman I.; Zehr, Julia L.; Schulz, Kalynn M.; Lorenz, Betty H.; DonCarlos, Lydia L.; & Sisk, Cheryl L. (2008). Pubertal hormones modulate the addition of new cells to sexually dimorphic brain regions. *Nature Neuroscience*, 11 (9), 995–997.

Alansari, Bader M.; Deregowski, Jan B.; & McGeorge, Peter. (2008). Sex differences in spatial visualization of Kuwaiti school children. *Social Behavior and Personality: An International Journal*, 36 (6), 811–824.

Albee, George W. (2005). Call to revolution in the prevention of emotional disorders. *Ethical Human Psychology and Psychiatry*, 7, 37–44.

Alexander, Fiona; Allen, Christine; Brooks, Jonathan; Cole, Claire; & Campbell, Anne. (2004). Reason to believe: Representations of aggression as phenomenological read-out. *Sex Roles*, 51, 647–659.

Alexander, Gerianne M. (2003). An evolutionary perspective of sex-typed toy preference: Pink, blue and the brain. *Archives of Sexual Behavior*, 32, 7–14.

Alexander, Michele G.; & Fisher, Terri D. (2003). Truth and consequences: Using the bogus pipeline to examine sex differences in self-reported sexuality. *Journal of Sex Research*, 40, 27–35.

Alfieri, Thomas; Ruble, Diane N.; & Higgins, E. Tory. (1996). Gender stereotypes during adolescence: Developmental changes and the transition to junior high school. *Developmental Psychology*, 32, 1129–1137.

Ali, Alisha. (2004). The intersection of racism and sexism in psychiatric diagnosis. In Paula J. Caplan & Lisa Cosgrove (Eds.), *Bias in psychiatric diagnosis* (pp. 71–75). Lanham, MD: Jason Aronson.

Alksnis, Christine; Desmarais, Serge; & Curtis, James. (2008). Workforce segregation and the gender wage gap: Is "women's" work values as highly as "men's"? *Journal of Applied Social Psychology*, 38 (6), 1416–1441.

Allen, Elizabeth Sandin; Baucom, Donald H.; Burnett, Charles K.; Epstein, Norman; & Rankin-Esquer, Lynn A. (2001). Decision-making power, autonomy, and communication in remarried spouses compared with first-married spouses. *Family Relations*, 50, 326–334.

Allmendinger, Jutta; & Hackman, J. Richard. (1995). The more, the better? A four-nation study of the inclusion of women in symphony orchestras. *Social Forces*, 74, 423–460.

Allport, Gordon W. (1954). *The nature of prejudice*. Reading, MA: Addison-Wesley.

Almeida, Joanna; Johnson, Renee M.; Corliss, Heather L.; Molnar, Beth E.; & Azrael, Deborah. (2009). Emotional distress among LGBT youth: The influence of perceived discrimination based on sexual orientation. *Journal of Youth and Adolescence*, 38 (7), 1001–1014.

Altman, Lawrence K. (1997, June 22). Is the longer life the healthier one? *New York Times*, Section 14 (Women's Health), p. 18.

Aluja, Anto; & Torrubia, Rafael. (2004). Hostility-aggressiveness, sensation seeking, and sex hormones in men: Re-exploring their relationship. *Neuropsychobiology, 50,* 102–107.

American Academy of Pediatrics. (2003). *Media matters: A national media education campaign.* Retrieved June 28, 2003, from http://www.aap.org/advocacy/mmcamp.htm

American Association of University Women. (1992). *The AAUW report: How schools shortchange girls.* Washington, DC: American Association of University Women Education Foundation and National Educational Association.

American Association of University Women. (1993). *Hostile hallways: The AAUW survey on sexual harassment in America's schools.* Washington, DC: American Association of University Women Educational Foundation.

American Association of University Women. (2001). *Hostile hallways: Bullying, teasing and sexual harassment in school.* Washington, DC: Author.

American Association of University Women. (2005). *Equity in school athletics.* Retrieved July 5, 2006, from http://www.aauw.org/issue_advocacy/actionpages/positionpapers/titleix_athletics.cfm

American Association of University Women. (2006). *Drawing the line: Sexual harassment on campus.* Washington, DC: Author.

American Cancer Society. (2008). *Cancer facts & figures—2008.* Atlanta: Author.

American Council on Education. (2003). *Gender equity in higher education: Are male students at a disadvantage?* Retrieved July 8, 2006, from http://www.acenet.edu/bookstore/pdf/2003_gender_equity_update.pdf

American Psychiatric Association. (2000). *Diagnostic and statistical manual of mental disorders* (4th ed., Text revision). Washington, DC: Author.

American Psychiatric Association. (2009). *DSM-V: The future manual.* Retrieved November 9, 2009, from http://www.psych.org/MainMenu/Research/DSMIV/DSMV.aspx

American Psychological Association. (2007). Guidelines for psychological practice with girls and women. *American Psychologist, 62* (9), 949–979.

American Psychological Association Task Force on Sex Bias and Sex-Role Stereotyping in Psychotherapeutic Practice. (1978). Guidelines for therapy with women. *American Psychologist, 33,* 1122–1123.

Amponsah, Benjamin. (2000). A comparison of sex differences in visual-spatial performance from preadolescence to adulthood in Ghana and Norway. *South African Journal of Psychology, 30* (4), 25–31.

Amponsah, Benjamin; & Krekling, Sturla. (1997). Sex differences in visual-spatial performance among Ghanaian and Norwegian adults. *Journal of Cross-Cultural Psychology, 28,* 81–92.

Anderson, Craig A.; & Bushman, Brad J. (2002). Human aggression. *Annual Review of Psychology, 53,* 27–52.

Anderson, Deborah J.; Cheslock, John J.; & Ehrenberg, Ronald G. (2006). Gender equity in intercollegiate athletics: Determinants of Title IX compliance. *Journal of Higher Education, 77* (2), 225–250.

Anderson, Elizabeth. (2002, Fall). Feminist epistemology and philosophy of science. In Edward N. Zalta (Ed.), *The Stanford Encyclopedia of Philosophy.* Retrieved April 28, 2003, from http://plato.stanford.edu/archives/fall2002/entries/feminism-epistemology

Anderson, G. C.; Moore, E.; Hepworth, J.; & Bergman, N. (2003). Early skin-to-skin contact for mothers and their healthy newborn infants. *Birth: Issues in Perinatal Care, 30,* 206–207.

Anderson, Kristin J.; Kanner, Melinda; & Elsayegh, Nisreen. (2009). Are feminists man haters? Feminists' and non-feminists' attitudes toward men. *Psychology of Women Quarterly, 33* (2), 216–224.

Anderson, Kristin L. (2005). Theorizing gender in intimate partner violence research. *Sex Roles, 52,* 853–865.

Anderson, Neil; Lankshear, Colin; Timms, Carolyn; & Courtney, Lyn. (2008). "Because it's boring, irrelevant and I don't like computers": Why high school girls avoid professionally-oriented ICT subjects. *Computers and Education, 50* (4), 1304–1318.

Andersson, Jenny; Salander, Pär; Brandstetter-Hiltunen, Marie; Knutsson, Emma; Hamberg, Katrina. (2008). Is it possible to identify patient's sex when reading blinded illness narratives? An experimental study about gender bias. *Journal of Equity in Health, 7* (Special Section), 1–9.

Andronico, Michael P. (2001). Mythopoetic and weekend retreats to facilitate men's growth. In Gary R. Brooks & Glenn E. Good (Eds.), *The new handbook of psychotherapy and counseling with men: A comprehensive guide to settings, problems, and treatment approaches* (pp. 664–682). San Francisco: Jossey-Bass.

Anthony, Marietta; Lee, Kwan Y.; Bertram, Carl T.; Abarca, Jacob; Rehfeld, Rick A.; Malone, Daniel C. et al. (2008). Gender and age differences in medications dispensed from a national chain drugstore. *Journal of Women's Health, 17* (5), 735–743.

Antill, John K. (1983). Sex role complementarity versus similarity in married couples. *Journal of Personality and Social Psychology, 45,* 145–155.

Antill, John K.; Goodnow, Jacqueline J.; Russell, Graeme; & Cotton, Sandra. (1996). The influence of parents and family context on children's involvement in household tasks. *Sex Roles, 34,* 215–236.

Apparala, Malathi L.; Reifman, Alan; & Munsch, Joyce. (2003). Cross-national comparison of attitudes toward fathers' and mothers' participation in household tasks and childcare. *Sex Roles, 48,* 189–203.

Aranda, Maria P.; Castaneda, Irma; Lee, Pey-Jiuan; & Sobel, Eugene. (2001). Stress, social support, and coping as predictors of depressive symptoms: Gender differences among Mexican Americans. *Social Work Research, 25,* 37–48.

Archer, John. (2000). Sex differences in aggression between heterosexual partners: A meta-analytic review. *Psychological Bulletin, 126,* 651–680.

Archer, John. (2004). Sex differences in aggression in real-world settings: A meta-analytic review. *Review of General Psychology, 8,* 291–322.

Archer, John. (2006). Testosterone and human aggression: An evaluation of the challenge hypothesis. *Neuroscience and Biobehavioral Reviews, 30,* 319–345.

Archer, John; & Coyne, Sarah M. (2005). An integrated review of indirect, relational, and social aggression. *Personality and Social Psychology Review, 9,* 212–230.

Archer, John; Graham-Kevan, Nicola; & Davies, Michelle. (2005). Testosterone and aggression: A reanalysis of Book, Starzyk, and Quinsey's (2001) study. *Aggression and Violent Behavior, 10,* 241–261.

Aries, Elizabeth. (1996). *Men and women in interaction.* New York: Oxford University Press.

Aries, Elizabeth. (2006). Sex differences in interaction: A reexamination. In Kathryn Dindia & Daniel Canary (Eds.), *Sex differences and similarities in communication* (2nd ed., pp. 21–36). Mahwah, NJ: Erlbaum.

Armesto, Jorge C. (2002). Developmental and contextual factors that influence gay fathers' parental competence: A review of the literature. *Psychology of Men & Masculinity, 3,* 67–78.

Arnot, Madeline. (2000). Gender relations and schooling in the new century: Conflicts and challenges. *Compare: A Journal of Comparative Education, 30,* 293–302.

Aronson, Amy; & Kimmel, Michael. (1997). The children's hour. *Tikkun, 12,* 32–33.

Arseneault, Louise; Walsh, Elizabeth; Trzesniewski, Kali; Newcombe, Rhiannon; Caspi, Avshalom; & Moffitt, Terrie E. (2006). Bullying victimization uniquely contributes to adjustment problems in young children: A nationally representative cohort study. *Pediatrics, 118,* 130–138.

Asbaugh, Lauren P.; & Cornell, Dewey G. (2008). Sexual harassment and bullying behaviors in sixth-graders. *Journal of School Violence, 7* (2), 21–38.

Åslund, Cecilia; Leppert, Jerzy; Comasco, Erika; Nordquist, Niklas; Oreland, Lars; & Nilsson, Kent W. (2009). Impact of the interaction between the 5HTTLPR polymorphism and maltreatment on adolescent depression, a population-based study. *Behavior Genetics, 39* (5), 524–531.

Ata, Rheanna; Ludden, Alison; & Lally, Megan. (2007). The effects of gender and family, friend, and media influences on eating behaviors and body image during adolescence. *Journal of Youth and Adolescence, 36* (8), 1024–1037.

Aubrey, Jennifer Stevens. (2006). Effects of sexually objectifying media on self-objectification and body surveillance in undergraduates: Results of a 2-year panel study. *Journal of Communication, 56,* 366–386.

Aubrey, Jennifer Stevens; & Harrison, Kristen. (2004). The gender-role content of children's favorite television programs and its links to their gender-related perceptions. *Media Psychology, 6,* 111–146.

Austin, S. Bryn; Ziyadeh, Najat; Kahn, Jessica A.; Camargo, Carlos A., Jr.; Colditz, Graham A.; & Field, Alison E. (2004). Sexual orientation, weight concerns, and eating-disordered behaviors in adolescent girls and boys. *Journal of the American Academy of Child and Adolescent Psychiatry, 43,* 1115–1123.

Auyeung, Bonnie; Baron-Cohen, Simon; Ashwin, Emma; Knickmeyer, Rebecca; Taylor, Kevin; Hackett, Gerald; et al. (2009). Fetal testosterone predicts sexually differentiated childhood behavior in girls and in boys. *Psychological Science, 20* (2), 144–148.

Avellar, Sarah; & Smock, Pamela J. (2005). The economic consequences of the dissolution of cohabiting unions. *Journal of Marriage and Family, 67,* 315–327.

Averill, James R. (1982). *Anger and aggression: An essay on emotion.* New York: Springer-Verlag.

Ayalon, Hanna. (2003). Women and men go to university: Mathematical background and gender differences in choice of field in higher education. *Sex Roles, 48,* 277–290.

Bae, Yupin; Choy, Susan; Geddes, Claire; Sable, Jennifer; & Snyder, Thomas. (2000). *Trends in educational equity for girls and women.* Washington, DC: U.S. Department of Education, National Center for Education Statistics.

Baer, John. (2008). Evidence of gender differences in creativity. *Journal of Creative Behavior, 42* (2), 78–105.

Bagley, Christopher; & King, Kathleen. (1990). *Child sexual abuse: The search for healing.* London: Tavistock/Routledge.

Bailey, J. Michael; Bechtold, Kathleen T.; & Berenbaum, Sheri A. (2002). Who are tomboys and why should we study them? *Archives of Sexual Behavior, 31,* 333–341.

Bailey, J. Michael; Dunne, Michael P.; & Martin, Nicholas G. (2000). Genetic and environmental influences on sexual orientation and its correlates in an Australian twin sample. *Journal of Personality and Social Psychology, 78,* 524–536.

Bailey, J. Michael; & Triea, Kiira. (2007). What many transgender activists don't want you to know: Any why you should know it anyway. *Perspectives in Biology and Medicine, 50* (4), 521–534.

Bailey, Sandra J. (2007). Unraveling the meaning of family: Voices of divorced nonresidential parents. *Marriage and Family Review, 42* (1), 81–102.

Baillargeon, Raymond H.; Zoccolillo, Mark; Keenan, Kate; Wu, Hong-Xing; Côté, Sylvana; Pérusse, Daniel; et al. (2007). Gender differences in physical aggression: A prospective population-based survey of children before and after 2 years of age. *Developmental Psychology, 43* (1), 13–26.

Bakan, David. (1966). *The duality of human existence.* Chicago: Rand McNally.

Baker, Kaysee; & Raney, Arthur A. (2007). Equally super?: Gender-role stereotyping of superheroes in children's animated programs. *Mass Communication & Society*, *10* (1), 25–41.

Baldwin, John D.; & Baldwin, Janice I. (1997). Gender differences in sexual interest. *Archives of Sexual Behavior*, *26*, 181–210.

Ball, Richard E.; & Robbins, Lynn. (1986). Marital status and life satisfaction among Black Americans. *Journal of Marriage and the Family*, *48*, 389–394.

Balsam, Kimberly F.; & Mohr, Jonathan, J. (2007). Adaptation to sexual orientation stigma: A comparison of bisexual and lesbian/gay adults. *Journal of Counseling Psychology*, *54* (3), 306–319.

Bancroft, John. (2002). Biological factors in human sexuality. *Journal of Sex Research*, *39*, 15–21.

Bancroft, John. (2004). Alfred C. Kinsey and the politics of sex research. *Annual Review of Sex Research*, *15*, 1–39.

Bandura, Albert. (1986). *Social foundations of thought and action: A social cognitive theory.* Englewood Cliffs, NJ: Prentice Hall.

Bandura, Albert; Barbaranelli, Claudio; Caprara, Gian Vittorio; & Pastorelli, Concetta. (2001). Self-efficacy beliefs as shapers of children's aspirations and career trajectories. *Child Development*, *72*, 187–206.

Bandura, Albert; & Bussey, Kay. (2004). Broadening the cognitive, motivational, and sociostructural scope of theorizing about gender development and functioning: Comment on Martin, Ruble, and Szkrybalo (2002). *Psychological Bulletin*, *130*, 691–701.

Banks, Terry; & Dabbs, James M., Jr. (1996). Salivary testosterone and cortisol in delinquent and violent urban subcultures. *Journal of Social Psychology*, *136*, 49–56.

Bankston, Carl L., III; & Zhou, Min. (2002). Being well vs. doing well: Self-esteem and school performance among immigrant and nonimmigrant racial and ethnic groups. *International Migration Review*, *36*, 389–415.

Barak, Azy. (1997). Cross-cultural perspectives on sexual harassment. In William O'Donohue (Ed.), *Sexual harassment: Theory, research, and treatment* (pp. 263–300), Boston: Allyn & Bacon.

Barak, Azy; & Gluck-Ofri, Orit. (2007). Degree and reciprocity of self-disclosure in online forums. *CyberPsychology and Behavior*, *10* (3), 407–417.

Barakso, Maryann; & Schaffner, Brian F. (2006). Winning coverage: News media portrayals of the women's movement, 1969–2004. *Harvard International Journal of Press/Politics*, *11* (4), 22–44.

Barnes, Patricia M.; Powell-Griner, Eve; McFann, Kim; & Nahin, Richard L. (2004). Complementary and alternative medicine use among adults: United States, 2002. *Advance Data from Vital and Health Statistics*, No. 343. Hyattsville, MD: National Center for Health Statistics.

Barnett, Heather L.; Keel, Pamela K.; & Conoscenti, Lauren M. (2001). Body type preferences in Asian and Caucasian college students. *Sex Roles*, *45*, 867–878.

Barnett, Rosalind Chait. (2004a). Preface: Women and work: Where are we, where did we come from, and where are we going? *Journal of Social Issues*, *60*, 667–674.

Barnett, Rosalind Chait. (2004b). Women and multiple roles: Myths and reality. *Harvard Review of Psychiatry*, *12*, 158–164.

Barnett, Rosalind Chait; & Hyde, Janet Shibley. (2001). Women, men, work, and family: An expansionist theory. *American Psychologist*, *56*, 781–796.

Barnett, Rosalind; & Rivers, Caryl. (2004). *Same difference: How gender myths are hurting our relationships, our children, and our jobs.* New York: Basic Books.

Barral, Jéôme; & Debû, Bettina. (2004). Aiming in adults: Sex and laterality effects. *Laterality*, *9*, 299–312.

Barres, Ben. (2006). Does gender matter? *Nature*, *442* (7099), 133–136.

Bartini, Maria. (2006). Gender role flexibility in early adolescence: Developmental change in attitudes, self-perceptions, and behaviors. *Sex Roles*, *55* (3/4), 233–245.

Bartkowski, John P. (2000). Breaking walls, raising fences: Masculinity, intimacy, and accountability among the Promise Keepers. *Sociology of Religion*, *61*, 33–54.

Bartlett, Nancy H.; Vasey, Paul L.; & Bukowski, William M. (2000). Is gender identity disorder in children a mental disorder? *Sex Roles*, *43*, 753–785.

Basow, Susan. (2008). Speaking in a 'man's world': Gender differences in communication styles. In Michele A. Paludi (Ed.), *The psychology of women at work: Challenges and solutions for our female workforce, Vol. 1: Career liberation, history, and the new millennium* (pp. 15–30). Westport, CT: Praeger.

Basow, Susan A.; & Rubenfeld, Kimberly. (2003). "Troubles talk": Effects of gender and gender-typing. *Sex Roles*, *48*, 183–187.

Bateup, Helen S.; Booth, Alan; Shirtcliff, Elizabeth A.; & Granger, Douglas A. (2002). Testosterone, cortisol, and women's competition. *Evolution and Human Behavior*, *23*, 181–192.

Baum, Nehami. (2004). On helping divorced men to mourn their losses. *American Journal of Psychotherapy*, *58*, 174–185.

Bauman, Adrian; Bull, Fiona; Chey, Tien; Craig, Cora L.; Ainsworth, Barbara E.; Sallis, James F.; et al. (2009). The International Prevalence Study on Physical Activity: Results from 20 countries. *International Journal of Behavioral Nutrition and Physical Activity*, *6*, 1–11.

Baumeister, Roy F. (2000). Gender differences in erotic plasticity: The female sex drive as socially flexible and responsive. *Psychological Bulletin*, *126*, 347–374.

Baumgardner, Jennifer; & Richards, Amelia M. (2003). The number one question about feminism. *Feminist Studies*, *29*, 448–453.

Baumle, Amanda K. (2009). The cost of parenthood: Unraveling the effects of sexual orientation and gender on income. *Social Science Quarterly*, *90* (4), 983–1002.

Baumli, Francis; & Williamson, Tom. (1997). *History of the men's movement.* National Coalition of Free Men. Retrieved November 24, 2006, from http://www.ncfm.org/hist.htm

Baxter, L. C.; Saykin, A. J.; Flashman, L. A.; Johnson, S. C.; Guerin, S. J.; Babcock, D. R.; & Wishart, H. A. (2003). Sex differences in semantic language processing: A functional MRI study. *Brain and Language, 84,* 264–272.

Bay-Cheng, Laina; Zucker, Alyssa N.; Stewart, Abigail J.; & Pomerleau, Cynthia S. (2002). Linking femininity, weight concern, and mental health among Latina, Black, and White women. *Psychology of Women Quarterly, 26,* 36–45.

Bazzini, Doris G.; McIntosh, William D.; Smith, Stephen M.; Cook, Sabrina; & Harris, Caleigh. (1997). The aging woman in popular film: Underrepresented, unattractive, unfriendly, and unintelligent. *Sex Roles, 36,* 531–543.

Beasley, Berrin; & Collins Standley, Tracy. (2002). Shirts vs. skins: Clothing as an indicator of gender role stereotyping in video games. *Mass Communications and Society, 5,* 279–293.

Beck, Aaron T. (1985). *Anxiety disorders and phobias: A cognitive perspective.* New York: Basic Books.

Bell, Emily C.; Willson, Morgan C.; Wilman, Alan H.; Dave, Sanjay; & Silverstone, Peter H. (2006). Males and females differ in brain activation during cognitive tasks. *NeuroImage, 30,* 529–538.

Bell, Leslie C. (2004). Psychoanalytic theories of gender. In Alice H. Eagly, Ann E. Beall, & Robert J. Sternberg (Eds.), *The psychology of gender* (2nd ed., pp 145–168). New York: Guilford Press.

Belle, Deborah; & Doucet, Joanne. (2003). Poverty, inequality, and discrimination as sources of depression among U.S. women. *Psychology of Women Quarterly, 27,* 101–113.

Bem, Daryl J. (1996). Exotic becomes erotic: A developmental theory of sexual orientation. *Psychological Review, 103,* 320–335.

Bem, Daryl J. (2000). Exotic becomes erotic: Interpreting the biological correlates of sexual orientation. *Archives of Sexual Behavior, 29,* 531–548.

Bem, Sandra Lipsitz. (1974). The measurement of psychological androgyny. *Journal of Consulting and Clinical Psychology, 42,* 155–162.

Bem, Sandra Lipsitz. (1981). Gender schema theory: A cognitive account of sex-typing. *Psychological Review, 88,* 354–364.

Bem, Sandra Lipsitz. (1985). Androgyny and gender schema theory: A conceptual and empirical integration. In Theo B. Sonderegger (Ed.), *Nebraska Symposium on Motivation, 1984: Psychology and Gender* (pp. 179–226). Lincoln, NE: University of Nebraska Press.

Bem, Sandra Lipsitz. (1993a). Is there a place in psychology for a feminist analysis of the social context? *Feminism & Psychology, 3,* 230–234.

Bem, Sandra Lipsitz. (1993b). *The lenses of gender.* New Haven, CT: Yale University Press.

Ben-Ari, Adital; & Somer, Eli. (2004). The aftermath of therapist-client sex: Exploited women struggle with the consequences. *Clinical Psychology and Psychotherapy, 11,* 126–136.

Benbow, Camilla Persson; Lubinski, David; Shea, Daniel L.; & Eftekhari-Sanjani, Hossain. (2000). Sex differences in mathematical reasoning ability at age 13: Their status 20 years later. *Psychological Science, 11,* 474–480.

Benbow, Camilla Persson; & Stanley, Julian C. (1980). Sex differences in mathematical ability: Fact or artifact? *Science, 210,* 1262–1264.

Benbow, Camilla Persson; & Stanley, Julian C. (1983). Sex differences in mathematical reasoning ability: More facts. *Science, 222,* 1029–1031.

Benderly, Beryl Lieff. (1987). *The myth of two minds.* New York: Doubleday.

Benderly, Beryl Lieff. (1989, November). Don't believe everything you read . . . . *Psychology Today,* 67–69.

Benenson, Joyce F.; & Christakos, Athena. (2003). The greater fragility of females' versus males' closest same-sex friendships. *Child Development, 74,* 1123–1129.

Benenson, Joyce F.; Morash, Deanna; & Petrakos, Harriet. (1998). Gender differences in emotional closeness between preschool children and their mothers. *Sex Roles, 38,* 975–986.

Benrud, Lisa M.; & Reddy, Diane M. (1998). Differential explanations of illness in women and men. *Sex Roles, 38,* 375–386.

Bentley, Jerome T.; & Wise, Donald E. (2004). *Gender differences in the careers of academic scientists and engineers.* Arlington, VA: National Science Foundation, Division of Science Resources Statistics.

Berenbaum, Sheri A. (2006). Psychological outcome in children with disorders of sex development: Implications for treatment and understanding typical development. *Annual Review of Sex Research, 17,* 1–38.

Berenbaum, Sheri A.; & Hines, Melissa. (1992). Early androgens are related to childhood sex-typed toy preferences. *Psychological Science, 3,* 203–206.

Bereska, Tami M. (2003). The changing boys' world in the 20th century: Reality and "fiction." *Journal of Men's Studies, 11,* 157–174.

Berg, Nathan; & Lien, Donald. (2002). Measuring the effect of sexual orientation on income: Evidence of discrimination? *Contemporary Economic Policy, 20,* 394–414.

Bergdahl, Jacqueline. (2005). Sex differences in attitudes toward driving: A survey. *Social Science Journal, 42,* 595–601.

Berkey, Catherine S.; Rockett, Helaine R. H.; Gillman, Matthew W.; & Colditz, Graham A. (2003). One-year changes in activity and in inactivity among 10- to 15-year-old boys and girls: Relationship to change in body mass index. *Pediatrics, 111,* 836–842.

Berman, Phyllis W. (1980). Are women more responsive than men to the young? A review of developmental and situational variables. *Psychological Bulletin, 88,* 668–695.

Bernard, Jessie. (1981). The good-provider role: Its rise and fall. *American Psychologist, 36,* 1–12.

Berndt, Thomas J. (2004). Children's friendships: Shifts over a half-century in perspectives on their development and their effects. *Merrill-Palmer Quarterly, 50,* 206–222.

Bernstein, Beth; & St. John, Matilda. (2006). HAES/The Biggest Loser. *Health at Every Size, 20* (1), 25–29.

Bernstein, Dan. (1999). Introduction. In Dan Bernstein (Ed.), *Nebraska Symposium on Motivation, 1999: Gender and motivation* (pp. vii–xxiii). Lincoln: University of Nebraska Press.

Bertakis, Klea. (2009). The influence of gender on the doctor–patient interaction. *Patient Education and Counseling, 76* (3), 356–360.

Besen-Cassino, Yasemin. (2008). The cost of being a girl: Gender earning differentials in the early labor markets. *NWSA Journal, 20* (1), 146–160.

Besser, Avi; Flett, Gordon L.; & Davis, Richard A. (2003). Self-criticism, dependency, silencing the self, and loneliness: A test of a mediational model. *Personality and Individual Differences, 35,* 1735–1752.

Bettencourt, B. Ann; & Miller, Norman. (1996). Gender differences in aggression as a function of provocation: A meta-analysis. *Psychological Bulletin, 119,* 422–447.

Betz, Nancy. (1993). Women's career development. In Florence L. Denmark & Michele A. Paludi (Eds.), *Psychology of women: A handbook of issues and theories* (pp. 627–684). Westport, CT: Greenwood Press.

Bevan, Jennifer L.; & Samter, Wendy. (2004). Toward a broader conceptualization of jealousy in close relationships: Two exploratory studies. *Communication Studies, 55,* 14–28.

Bevvino, Deborah L.; & Sharkin, Bruce S. (2003). Divorce adjustment as a function of finding meaning and gender differences. *Journal of Divorce and Remarriage, 39,* 81–97.

Beyer, Sylvia. (1998). Gender differences in self-perception and negative recall biases. *Sex Roles, 38,* 103–133.

Beyer, Sylvia. (1999). The accuracy of academic gender stereotypes. *Sex Roles, 41,* 297–306.

Beyer, Sylvia. (2002). The effects of gender, dysphoria, and performance feedback on the accuracy of self-evaluations. *Sex Roles, 47,* 453–464.

Bickel, Janet. (2001). Gender equity in undergraduate medical education: A status report. *Journal of Women's Health and Gender-Based Medicine, 10,* 261–270.

Biener, Lois. (1987). Gender differences in the use of substances for coping. In Rosalind C. Barnett, Lois Biener, & Grace K. Baruch (Eds.), *Gender and stress* (pp. 330–349). New York: Free Press.

Biernat, Monica. (1991). Gender stereotypes and the relationship between masculinity and femininity: A developmental

analysis. *Journal of Personality and Social Psychology, 61,* 351–365.

Billger, Sherrilyn M. (2009). On reconstructing school segregation: The efficacy and equity of single-sex schooling. *Economics of Educational Review, 28* (3), 393–402.

Bilodeau, Brett. (2005). Beyond the gender binary: A case study of two transgender students at a midwestern research university. *Journal of Gay & Lesbian Issues in Education, 3* (1), 29–44.

Bing, Janet. (1999). Brain sex: How the media report and distort brain research. *Women and Language, 22,* 4–12.

Bing, Stanley. (2004, October 18). There's no crying in business. *Fortune, 150* (8), 352.

Bittman, Michael; England, Paula; Folbre, Nancy; Sayer, Liana; & Matheson, George. (2003). When does gender trump money? Bargaining and time in household work. *American Journal of Sociology, 109,* 186–216.

Bjorklund, Pamela. (2006). No man's land: Gender bias and social constructivism in the diagnosis of borderline personality disorder. *Issues in Mental Health Nursing, 27,* 3–23.

Bjorkqvist, Kaj. (1994). Sex differences in physical, verbal, and indirect aggression: A review of recent research. *Sex Roles, 30,* 177–188.

Black, M. C.; & Breiding, M. J. (2008). Adverse health conditions and health risk behaviors associated with intimate partner violence—United States, 2005. *MMWR, 57* (5), 113–117.

Blackwood, Evelyn. (2000). Culture and women's sexualities. *Journal of Social Issues, 56,* 223–238.

Blair, Steven N.; Cheng, Yiling; & Holder, J. Scott. (2001). Is physical activity or physical fitness more important in defining health benefits? *Medicine and Science in Sports & Exercise, 33,* S379–S399.

Blair-Loy, Mary. (2003). *Competing devotions: Career and family among women executives.* Cambridge, MA: Harvard University Press.

Blakemore, Judith E. Owen. (1998). The influence of gender and parental attitudes on preschool children's interest in babies: Observations in natural settings. *Sex Roles, 38,* 73–94.

Blakemore, Judith E. Owen. (2003). Children's beliefs about violating gender norms: Boys shouldn't look like girls, and girls shouldn't act like boys. *Sex Roles, 48,* 411–419.

Blakemore, Judith E. Owen; Lawton, Carol A.; & Vartanian, Lesa Rae. (2005). I can't wait to get married: Gender differences in drive to marry. *Sex Roles, 53,* 327–335.

Blanchard, Christy A.; & Lichtenberg, James W. (1998). Counseling psychologists' training to deal with their sexual feelings in therapy. *Counseling Psychologist, 26,* 624–639.

Blanchard, Ray; Cantor, James M.; Bogaert, Anthony F.; Breedlove, S. Marc; & Ellis, Lee. (2006). Interaction of fraternal birth order and handedness in the development of male homosexuality. *Hormones and Behavior, 49,* 405–414.

Bleeker, Martha M.; & Jacobs, Janis E. (2004). Achievement in math and science: Do mothers' beliefs matter 12 years later? *Journal of Educational Psychology, 96*, 97–109.

Bleie, Tone. (2003). Evolution, brains, and the predicament of sex in human cognition. *Sexualities, Evolution and Gender, 5*, 149–189.

Blieszner, Rosemary. (2000). Close relationships in old age. In Clyde Hendrick & Susan S. Hendrick (Eds.), *Close relationships: A sourcebook* (pp. 85–95). Thousand Oaks, CA: Sage.

Bloom, Amy. (2002, October). Why can't a woman be more like a man? And vice versa. *O, The Oprah Magazine, 3* (10), 113+.

Blumstein, Philip; & Schwartz, Pepper. (1983). *American couples.* New York: Pocket Books.

Bly, Robert. (1990). *Iron John.* Reading, MA: Addison-Wesley.

Bobo, Lawrence D. (1999). Prejudice as group position: Microfoundations of a sociological approach to racism and race relations. *Journal of Social Issues, 55*, 445–472.

Boehnke, Klaus. (2008). Peer pressure: A cause of scholastic underachievement? A cross-cultural study of mathematical achievement among German, Canadian, and Israeli middle school students. *Social Psychology of Education, 11* (2), 149–160.

Bogaert, Anthony F. (2003). Number of older brothers and sexual orientation: New tests and the attraction/behavior distinction in two national probability samples. *Journal of Personality and Social Psychology, 84*, 644–652.

Bogaert, Anthony F. (2006). Biological versus nonbiological older brothers and men's sexual orientation. *Proceedings of the National Academy of Sciences of the United States of America, 103* (28), 10771–10774.

Bohan, Janis S. (1996). *Psychology and sexual orientation: Coming to terms.* New York: Routledge.

Bolzendahl, Catherine I.; & Myers, Daniel J. (2004). Feminist attitudes and support for gender equality: Opinion change in women and men, 1974–1998. *Social Forces, 83*, 759–789.

Bond, Bradley; Hefner, Veronica; & Drogos, Kristin. (2009). Information-seeking practices during the sexual development of lesbian, gay, and bisexual individuals: The influence and effects of coming out in a mediated environment. *Sexuality and Culture, 13* (1), 32–50.

Bonds-Raacke, Jennifer M.; Bearden, Erica S.; Carriere, Noelle J.; Anderson, Ellen M.; & Nicks, Sandra D. (2001). Engaging distortions: Are we idealizing marriage? *Journal of Psychology, 135*, 179–184.

Bönte, Markus; von dem Knesebeck, Siegrist, Johannes; Marceau, Lisa; Link, Carol; Arber, Sara; et al. (2008). Women and men with coronary heart disease in three countries: Are they treated differently? *Women's Health Issues, 18* (3), 191-198.

Bonvillain, Nancy. (2000). *Women and men: Cultural constructs of gender* (3rd ed.). Upper Saddle River, NJ: Prentice Hall.

Book, Angela S.; & Quinsey, Vernon L. (2005). Re-examining the issues: A response to Archer et al. *Aggression and Violent Behavior, 10*, 637–646.

Book, Sarah W.; Thomas, Suzanne E.; Dempsey, Jared P.; Randall, Patrick K.; & Randall, Carrier L. (2009). Social anxiety impacts willingness to participate in addiction treatment. *Addictive Behaviors, 34* (5), 474–476.

Bookwala, Jamila; Sobin, Joelle; & Zdaniuk, Bozena. (2005). Gender and aggression in marital relationships: A life-span perspective. *Sex Roles, 52*, 797–806.

Booth, Alan; Johnson, David R.; & Granger, Douglas A. (1999). Testosterone and men's depression: The role of social behavior. *Journal of Health and Social Behavior, 40*, 130–140.

Booth, Alan; Johnson, David R.; Granger, Douglas A.; Crouter, Ann C.; & McHale, Susan. (2003). Testosterone and child and adolescent adjustment: The moderating role of parent-child relationships. *Developmental Psychology, 39*, 85–98.

Booth, Alan; Shelley, Greg; Mazur, Allan; Tharp, Gerry; & Kittok, Roger. (1989). Testosterone, and winning and losing in human competition. *Hormones and Behavior, 23*, 556–571.

Boren, Justin. (2007). *Negotiating the division of household labor in same sex romantic relationships.* Paper presented at the National Communications Association.

Bosco, Andrea; Longoni, Anna M.; & Vecchi, Tomaso. (2004). Gender effects in spatial orientation: Cognitive profiles and mental strategies. *Applied Cognitive Psychology 18*, 519–532.

Botkin, Darla R.; Weeks, M. O'Neal; & Morris, Jeanette E. (2000). Changing marriage role expectations: 1961–1996. *Sex Roles, 42*, 933–942.

Bowlby, John. (1951). *Maternal care and mental health.* Geneva, Switzerland: World Health Organization.

Bowleg, Lisa. (2008). When Black + lesbian + woman Z Black lesbian woman: The methodological challenges of qualitative and quantitative intersectionality research. *Sex Roles, 59*, 312–325.

Boydell, J.; van Os, J.; McKenzie, K.; Allardyce, J.; Goel; R.; McCreadie, R. G.; & Murray, R. M. (2001). Incidence of schizophrenia in ethnic minorities in London: Ecological study into interactions with environment. *British Medical Journal, 323*, 1336–1338.

Boysen, Guy A.; Vogel, David L.; Madon, Stephanie; & Wester, Stephen R. (2006). Mental health stereotypes about gay men. *Sex Roles, 54*, 69–82.

Bradley, Susan J.; Oliver, Gillian D.; Chernick, A. B.; & Zucker, Kenneth J. (1998). Experiment of nurture: Ablatio penis at 2 months, sex reassignment at 7 months, and a psychosexual follow-up in young adulthood. *Pediatrics, 102*, 131–132.

Bradshaw, Carla K. (1994). Asian and Asian American women: Historical and political considerations in psychotherapy. In Lillian Comas-Díaz & Beverly Greene

(Eds.), *Women of color: Integrating ethnic and gender identities in psychotherapy* (pp. 72–113). New York: Guilford Press.

Brannon, Linda; & Feist, Jess. (2010). *Health psychology: An introduction to behavior and health* (7th ed.). Belmont, CA: Cengage/Wadsworth.

Brannon, Robert. (1976). The male sex role: Our culture's blueprint of manhood and what it's done for us lately. In Deborah S. David & Robert Brannon (Eds.), *The forty-nine percent majority* (pp. 1–45). Reading, MA: Addison-Wesley.

Braun, Michael; Lewin-Epstein, Noah; Stier, Haya; & Baumgartner, Miriam K. (2008). Perceived equity in the gendered division of household labor. *Journal of Marriage and Family, 70* (5), 1145–1156.

Brecher, Edward M. (1969). *The sex researchers.* Boston: Little, Brown.

Breedlove, S. Marc. (1994). Sexual differentiation of the human nervous system. *Annual Review of Psychology, 45,* 389–418.

Breedlove, S. Marc; Cooke, Bradley M.; & Jordan, Cynthia L. (1999). The orthodox view of brain sexual differentiation. *Brain, Behavior and Evolution, 54,* 8–14.

Brendgen, Mara; Vitaro, Frank; Doyle, Anna Beth; Markiewicz, Dorothy; & Bukowski, William M. (2002). Same-sex peer relations and romantic relationships during early adolescence: Interactive links to emotional, behavioral, and academic adjustment. *Merrill-Palmer Quarterly, 48,* 77–103.

Brescoll, Victoria; & LaFrance, Marianne. (2004). The correlates and consequences of newspaper reports of research on sex differences. *Psychological Science, 13* (8), 515–520.

Breslau, Naomi. (2009). The epidemiology of trauma, PTSD, and other posttrauma disorders. *Trauma, Violence, and Abuse, 10* (3), 198–210.

Bresnahan, Mary Jiang; Inoue, Yasuhiro; Liu, Wen Ying; & Nishida, Tsukasa. (2001). Changing gender roles in prime-time commercials in Malaysia, Japan, Taiwan, and the United States. *Sex Roles, 45,* 117–131.

Britannica Book of the Year, 2002. (2002). Chicago: Encyclopedia Britannica.

Brodsky, Annette; & Holroyd, Jean. (1975). Report of the Task Force on Sex Bias and Sex-Role Stereotyping in Psychotherapeutic Practice. *American Psychologist, 30,* 1169–1175.

Bronstein, Phyllis. (2006). The family environment: Where gender role socialization begins. In Judith Worell & Carol D. Goodheart (Eds.), *Handbook of girls' and women's psychological health: Gender and well-being across the lifespan* (pp. 262–271), New York: Oxford University Press.

Brooks, Gary R. (1998). *A new psychotherapy for traditional men.* San Francisco: Jossey-Bass.

Brooks, Gary R. (2001). Masculinity and men's mental health. *Journal of American College Health, 49,* 285–297.

Brooks, Gary R. (2003). Helping men embrace equality. In Louise B. Silverstein & Thelma J. Goodrich (Eds.), *Feminist family therapy: Empowerment in social context* (pp. 163–176). Washington, DC: American Psychological Association.

Brooks, Gary R. (2010). *Beyond the crisis of masculinity: A transtheoretical model for male-friendly therapy.* Washington, DC: American Psychological Association.

Broverman, Inge K.; Broverman, Donald M.; Clarkson, Frank E.; Rosenkrantz, Paul S.; & Vogel, Susan R. (1970). Sex-role stereotypes and clinical judgments of mental health. *Journal of Consulting and Clinical Psychology, 34,* 1–7.

Broverman, Inge K.; Vogel, Susan Raymond; Broverman, Donald M.; Clarkson, Frank E.; & Rosenkrantz, Paul S. (1972). Sex-role stereotypes: A current appraisal. *Journal of Social Issues, 28* (2), 59–78.

Brown, Carlton Gene. (2004). Testicular cancer: An overview. *Urologic Nursing, 24,* 83–93.

Brown, David; & Evans, John. (2004). Reproducing gender? Intergenerational links and the male PE teacher as a cultural conduit in teaching physical education. *Journal of Teaching in Physical Education, 23,* 48–70.

Brown, Jeffrey M.; Mehler, Philip S.; & Harris, R. Hill. (2000). Medical complications occurring in adolescents with anorexia nervosa. *Western Journal of Medicine, 172,* 189–193.

Brown, Laura B.; Uebelacker, Lisa; & Heatherington, Laurie. (1998). Men, women, and the self-presentation of achievement. *Sex Roles, 38,* 253–268.

Brown, Laura S. (1988). Feminist therapy with lesbians and gay men. In Mary Ann Dutton Douglas & Lenore E. A. Walker (Eds.), *Feminist psychotherapies: Integration of therapeutic and feminist systems* (pp. 206–227). Norwood, NJ: Ablex.

Brown, Laura S. (2006). Still subversive after all these years: The relevance of feminist therapy in the age of evidence-based practice. *Psychology of Women Quarterly, 30,* 15–24.

Brown, Laura S. (2008). Feminist therapy. In Jay L. Lebow (Ed.), *Twenty-first century psychotherapies: Contemporary approaches to theory and practice* (pp. 277–306). Hoboken, NJ: Wiley.

Brown, Robert D.; Clarke, Brandy; Gortmaker, Valerie; & Robinson-Keilig, Rachael. (2004). Assessing the campus climate for gay, lesbian, bisexual, and transgender (GLBT) students using a multiple perspectives approach. *Journal of College Student Development, 45,* 8–26.

Brown, Susan L.; & Booth, Alan. (1996). Cohabitation versus marriage: A comparison of relationship quality. *Journal of Marriage and the Family, 58,* 668–678.

Brown Givens, Sonja M.; & Monahan, Jennifer L. (2005). Priming mammies, Jezebels, and other controlling images: An examination of the influence of mediated stereotypes on perceptions of African American women. *Media Psychology, 7,* 87–106.

Browne, Beverly A. (1998). Gender stereotypes in advertising on children's television in the 1990s: A cross-national analysis. *Journal of Advertising*, *27*, 83–96.

Brummett, Beverly H.; Boyle, Stephen H.; Segler, Ilene C.; Kuhn, Cynthia M.; Ashley-Koch, Allison; & Jonassint, Charles R. (2008). Effects of environmental stress and gender on associations among symptoms of depression and the serotonin transporter gene linked polymorphic region (5-HTTLPR). *Behavior Genetics*, *38* (1), 34–42.

Bryant, Alyssa N. (2003). Changes in attitudes toward women's roles: Predicting gender-role traditionalism among college students. *Sex Roles*, *48*, 131–142.

Bryant, Anne. (1995, March). Sexual harassment in school takes its toll. *USA Today Magazine*, *123*, 40–41.

Budig, Michelle J. (2002). Male advantage and the gender composition of jobs: Who rides the glass escalator? *Social Problems*, *49*, 258–277.

Buntaine, Roberta L.; & Costenbader, Virginia K. (1997). Self-reported differences in the experience and expression of anger between girls and boys. *Sex Roles*, *36*, 625–637.

Burke, Ronald J. (1999). Workaholism in organizations: Gender differences. *Sex Roles*, *41*, 333–346.

Burns, Sheila L.; Peterson, Holly; Bass, Hope; & Pascoe, Neil. (2002). Gender differences on a mental rotation task: The effects of stereotype threat. *Michigan Academician*, *34*, 84–85.

Burr, Vivien; & Jarvis, Christine. (2007). Imagining the family representations of alternative lifestyles in *Buffy the Vampire Slayer*. *Qualitative Social Work*, *6* (3), 263-280.

Burstow, Bonnie. (2006). Electroshock as a form of violence against women. *Violence Against Women*, *12*, 372–392.

Burt, Keith B.; & Scott, Jacqueline. (2002). Parent and adolescent gender role attitudes in 1990s Great Britain. *Sex Roles*, *46*, 239–245.

Burti, Lorenzo; Amaddeo, Francesco; Ambrosi, Marta; Bonetto, Chiara; Cristofalo, Doriana; Ruggeri, Mirella; et al. (2005). Does additional care provided by a consumer self-help group improve psychiatric outcome? A study in an Italian community-based psychiatric service. *Community Mental Health Journal*, *41*, 705–720.

Bush, Diane M.; & Simmons, R. G. (1987). Gender and coping with the entry into early adolescence. In Rosalind C. Barnett, Lois Biener, & Grace K. Baruch (Eds.), *Gender and stress* (pp. 185–217). New York: Free Press.

Buss, David M. (1994). *The evolution of desire*. New York: Basic Books.

Buss, David M. (1996). Sexual conflict: Evolutionary insights into feminism and the "battle of the sexes." In David M. Buss & Neil M. Malamuth (Eds.), *Sex, power, conflict: Evolutionary and feminist perspectives* (pp. 296–318). New York: Oxford University Press.

Buss, David M.; Shackelford, Todd K.; Kirkpatrick, Lee A.; & Larsen, Randy J. (2001). A half century of mate preferences: The cultural evolution of values. *Journal of Marriage and Family*, *63*, 491–503.

Bussey, Kay; & Bandura, Albert. (1984). Influence of gender constancy and social power on sex-linked modeling. *Journal of Personality and Social Psychology*, *47*, 1292–1302.

Bussey, Kay; & Bandura, Albert. (1992). Self-regulatory mechanisms governing gender development. *Child Development*, *63*, 1236–1250.

Bussey, Kay; & Bandura, Albert. (1999). Social cognitive theory of gender development and differentiation. *Psychological Review*, *106*, 676–713.

Butler, Amy C. (2005). Gender differences in the prevalence of same-sex sexual partnering: 1988–2002. *Social Forces*, *84*, 421–449.

Byrne, Peter. (2001). The butler(s) DID it—Dissociative identity disorder in cinema. *Journal of Medical Ethics: Medical Humanities*, *27*, 26–29.

Caetano, Raul; Vaeth, Patrice; & Ramisetty-Mikler, Suhasini. (2008). Intimate partner violence victim and perpetrator characteristics among couples in the United States. *Journal of Family Violence*, *23* (6), 507–518.

Caine-Bish, Natalie L.; & Scheule, Barbara. (2009). Gender differences in food preferences of school-aged children and adolescents. *Journal of School Health*, *79* (11), 532–540.

Caldwell, Leon D.; & White, Joseph L. (2001). African-centered therapeutic and counseling interventions for African American males. In Gary R. Brooks & Glen E. Good (Eds.), *The new handbook of psychotherapy and counseling with men: A comprehensive guide to settings, problems, and treatment approaches* (pp. 735–753). San Francisco: Jossey-Bass.

Caldwell, Mayta A.; & Peplau, Letitia Anne. (1982). Sex differences in same-sex friendship. *Sex Roles*, *8*, 721–732.

Calmes, Christine A.; & Roberts, John E. (2008). Rumination in interpersonal relationships: Does co-rumination explain gender differences in emotional distress and relationship satisfaction among college students? *Cognitive Therapy and Research*, *32* (4), 577–590.

Camarata, Stephen; & Woodcock, Richard. (2006). Sex differences in processing speed: Developmental effects in males and females. *Intelligence*, *34* (3), 231–252.

Cameron, Deborah. (2007). *The myth of Mars and Venus*. Oxford, United Kingdom: Oxford University Press.

Campbell, Anne. (1993). *Men, women, and aggression*. New York: Basic Books.

Campbell, Anne; & Muncer, Steven. (2008). Intent to harm or injure? Gender and the expression of anger. *Aggressive Behavior*, *34* (3), 282-293.

Campbell, Anne; Shirley, Louisa; & Candy, Julia. (2004). A longitudinal study of gender-related cognition and behaviour. *Developmental Science*, *7*, 1–9.

Campbell, Anne; Shirley, Louisa; & Caygill, Lisa. (2002). Sex-typed preferences in three domains: Do two-year-olds need cognitive variables? *British Journal of Psychology*, *93*, 203–217.

Campbell, Constance R.; & Henry, John W. (1999). Gender differences in self-attributions: Relationships of gender to attributional consistency, style, and expectations for performance in a college course. *Sex Roles*, *41*, 95–104.

Campbell, Rebecca; & Wasco, Sharon M. (2000). Feminist approaches to social science: Epistemological and methodological tenets. *American Journal of Community Psychology*, *28*, 773–791.

Campenni, C. Estelle. (1999). Gender stereotyping of children's toys: A comparison of parents and nonparents. *Sex Roles*, *40*, 121–138.

Cancian, Francesca M. (1986). The feminization of love. *Signs*, *11*, 692–709.

Cancian, Francesca M. (1987). *Love in America: Gender and self-development.* Cambridge, England: Cambridge University Press.

Cancian, Francesca M.; & Oliker, Stacey J. (2000). *Caring and gender.* Thousand Oaks, CA: Pine Forge Press.

Cann, Arnie; & Vann, Elizabeth D. (1995). Implications of sex and gender differences for self: Perceived advantages and disadvantages of being the other gender. *Sex Roles*, *33*, 531–541.

Capaldi, E. J.; & Proctor, Robert W. (2005). Is the worldview of qualitative inquiry a proper guide for psychological research? *American Journal of Psychology*, *118*, 251–269.

Caplan, Paula J.; & Caplan, Jeremy B. (1994). *Thinking critically about research on sex and gender.* New York: HarperCollins.

Caplan, Paula J.; MacPherson, Gael M.; & Tobin, Patricia. (1985). Do sex-related differences in spatial abilities exist? A multilevel critique with new data. *American Psychologist*, *40*, 786–799.

Capraro, Rocco L. (2000). Why college men drink: Alcohol, adventure, and the paradox of masculinity. *Journal of American College Health*, *48*, 307–315.

Carlbring, Per; Gustafsson, Henrik; Ekselius, Lisa; & Andersson, Gerhard. (2002). 12-month prevalence of panic disorder with or without agoraphobia in the Swedish general population. *Social Psychiatry and Psychiatric Epidemiology*, *37*, 207–211.

Carli, Linda L.; & Eagly, Alice H. (2001). Gender, hierarchy, and leadership: An introduction. *Journal of Social Issues*, *57*, 629–636.

Carlo, Gustavo; Raffaelli, Marcela; Laible, Deborah J.; & Meyer, Kathryn A. (1999). Why are girls less physically aggressive than boys? Personality and parenting mediators of physical aggression. *Sex Roles*, *40*, 711–730.

Carr, C. Lynn. (2004). *Where have all the tomboys gone? Teen tales of agency and compulsory femininity.* Presented at the annual meeting of the American Sociological Association, San Francisco, CA.

Carr, C. Lynn. (2005). Tomboysim or lesbianism? Beyond sex/gender/sexual conflation. *Sex Roles*, *53*, 119–131.

Carr, C. Lynn. (2007). Where have all the tomboys gone? Women's accounts of gender in adolescence. *Sex Roles*, *56* (7/8), 439–448.

Carr, Deborah; Jaffe, Karen J.; & Friedman, Michael A. (2008). Perceived interpersonal mistreatment among obese Americans: Do race, class, and gender matter? *Obesity*, *16* (Suppl. 2), S60–S68.

Carré, Justin M.; & McCormick, Cheryl M. (2008). Aggressive behavior and change in salivary testosterone concentrations predict willingness to engage in a competitive task. *Hormones & Behavior*, *54* (3), 403–409.

Carré, Justin M.; Putnam, Susan K.; McCormick, Cheryl M. (2009). Testosterone responses to competition predict future aggressive behaviour at a cost to reward in men. *Psychoneuroendocrinology*, *34* (4), 561–570.

Carter, Jason D.; Hall, Judith A.; Carney, Dana R.; & Rospi, Janelle C. (2006). Individual differences in the acceptance of stereotyping. *Journal of Research in Personality*, *40* (6), 1103–1118.

Carter, Stephen L. (1991). *Reflections of an affirmative action baby.* New York: Basic Books.

Carver, Priscilla R.; Egan, Susan K.; & Perry, David G. (2004). Children who question their heterosexuality. *Developmental Psychology*, *40*, 43–53.

Carver, Priscilla R.; Yunger, Jennifer L.; & Perry, David G. (2003). Gender identity and adjustment in middle childhood. *Sex Roles*, *49*, 95–109.

Casas, J. Manuel; Turner, Joseph A.; & Ruiz de Esparza, Christopher A. (2001). Machismo revisited in a time of crisis: Implications for understanding and counseling Hispanic men. In Gary R. Brooks & Glen E. Good (Eds.), *The new handbook of psychotherapy and counseling with men: A comprehensive guide to settings, problems, and treatment approaches* (pp. 754–779). San Francisco, CA: Jossey-Bass.

Caspi, Avshalom; Sugden, Karen; Moffitt, Terrie E.; Taylor, Alan; Craig, Ian W.; Harrington, HonaLee; et al. (2003). Influence of life stress on depression: Moderation by a polymorphism in the 5-HTT gene. *Science*, *301*, 386–389.

Cassidy, Elaine F.; & Stevenson, Howard C., Jr. (2005). They wear the mask: Hypervulnerability and hypermasculine aggression among African American males in an urban remedial disciplinary school. *Journal of Aggression, Maltreatment and Trauma*, *11*, 53–74.

Catalyst. (2005). *Women "take care," men "take charge": Stereotyping of U.S. business leaders exposed.* Retrieved July 13, 2006, from http://www.catalyst.org/knowledge/alpha.shtml

Catalyst. (2008). *2008 Catalyst census of women board of directors of the Fortune 500.* Retrieved October 16, 2009, from http://www.catalyst.org/publication/282/2008-catalyst-census-of-women-board-directors-of-fortune-500

Cavazos-Rehg, Patricia A.; Krauss, Melissa J.; Spitznagel, Edward L.; Schootman, Mario; Bucholz, Kathleen K.; Peipert, Jeffrey F.; et al. (2009). Age of sexual debut among US adolescents. *Contraception*, *80* (2), 158–162.

CBS News Poll. (2005, October 23). *Poll: Women's movement worthwhile.* Retrieved June 24, 2010, from http://www.cbsnews.com/stories/2005/10/22/opinion/polls/main965224.shtml

Ceci, Stephen J.; & Williams, Wendy M. (Eds.). (2007). *Why aren't more women in science: Top researchers debate the evidence.* Washington, DC: American Psychological Association.

Ceci, Stephen J.; Williams, Wendy M.; & Barnett, Susan M. (2009). Women's underrepresentation in science: Sociocultural and biological considerations. *Psychological Bulletin, 135* (2), 218–261.

Cha, Youngjoo; & Thébaud, Sarah. (2009). Labor markets, breadwinning, and beliefs: How economic context shapes men's gender ideology. *Gender and Society, 23* (2), 215–243.

Chaiken, Shelly; & Pliner, Patricia. (1987). Women, but not men, are what they eat: The effect of meal size and gender on perceived femininity and masculinity. *Personality and Social Psychology Bulletin, 13,* 166–176.

Chambless, Dianne L.; & Ollendick, Thomas H. (2001). Empirically supported psychological interventions: Controversies and evidence. *Annual Review of Psychology, 52,* 685–716.

Chan, Alessandra; & Poulin, François. (2007). Monthly changes in the composition of friendship networks in early adolescence. *Merrill-Palmer Quarterly, 53* (4), 578–602.

Chananie, Ruth A. (2005). Psychopharmaceutical advertising strategies: Empowerment in a pill? *Sociological Spectrum, 25,* 487–518.

Chandola, Tarani; Martikainen, Pekka; Bartley, Mel; Lahelma, Eero; Marmot, Michael; Michikazu, Sekine; et al. (2004). Does conflict between home and work explain the effect of multiple roles on mental health? A comparative study of Finland, Japan, and the UK. *International Journal of Epidemiology, 33,* 884–893.

Chapleau, Kristine M.; Oswald, Debra L.; & Russell, Brenda L. (2008). Male rape myths. *Journal of Interpersonal Violence, 23* (5), 600–615.

Chauhan, Gargi Singh; Shastri, Jigisha; & Mohite, Prerana. (2005). Development of gender constancy in preschoolers. *Psychological Studies, 50,* 62–71.

Chavous, Tabbye M.; Harris, Angel; Rivas, Deborah; Helaire, Lumas; & Green, Laurette. (2004). Racial stereotypes and gender in context: African Americans at predominantly Black and predominantly White colleges. *Sex Roles, 51,* 1–16.

Cherland, Meredith. (2008). Harry's girls: Harry Potter and the discourse on gender. *Journal of Adolescence & Adult Literacy, 52* (4), 273–282.

Cherney, Isabelle D. (2005). Children's and adult's recall of sex-stereotyped toy pictures: Effects of presentation and memory tasks. *Infant and Child Development, 14,* 11–27.

Cherney, Isabelle D. (2008). Mom, let me play more computer games: They improve my mental rotation skills. *Sex Roles, 59* (11/12), 776–786.

Cherney, Isabelle D.; Brabec, Claire M.; & Runco, Daniel V. (2008). Mapping out spatial ability: Sex differences in way-finding navigation. *Perceptual and Motor Skills, 107* (3), 747–760.

Chernin, Kim. (1978). *The obsession: Reflections on the tyranny of slenderness.* New York: Harper & Row.

Cherry, Frances; & Deaux, Kay. (1978). Fear of success versus fear of gender-inappropriate behavior. *Sex Roles, 4,* 97–101.

Chesler, Phyllis. (1972). *Women and madness.* New York: Avon.

Chia, Rosina C.; Moore, Jamie L.; Lam, Ka Nei; Chuang, C. J.; & Cheng, B. S. (1994). Cultural differences in gender role attitudes between Chinese and American students. *Sex Roles, 31,* 23–30.

Chiaramonte, Gabrielle R.; & Friend, Ronald. (2006). Medical students' and residents' gender bias in the diagnosis, treatment, and interpretation of coronary heart disease symptoms. *Health Psychology, 25,* 255–266.

Children Now. (2006). *Children Now Publications.* Retrieved November 25, 2006, from http://publications.children-now.org/

Chodorow, Nancy. (1978). *The reproduction of mothering: Psychoanalysis and the sociology of gender.* Berkeley, CA: University of California Press.

Chodorow, Nancy. (1979). Feminism and difference: Gender, relation, and difference in psychoanalytic perspective. *Socialist Review, 46,* 42–64. Also in Mary Roth Walsh (Ed.) (1987). *The psychology of women: Ongoing debates* (pp. 249–264). New Haven, CT: Yale University Press.

Chodorow, Nancy J. (1994). *Femininities, masculinities, sexualities: Freud and beyond.* Lexington, KY: University Press of Kentucky.

Chodorow, Nancy J. (2005). Gender on the modern-postmodern and classical-relational divide: Untangling history and epistemology. *Journal of the American Psychoanalytic Association, 53* (4), 1097–1118.

Choi, Namok; & Fuqua, Dale R. (2003). The structure of the Bem Sex Role Inventory: A summary report of 23 validation studies. *Educational and Psychological Measurement, 63,* 872–887.

Choi, Namok; Fuqua, Dale R.; & Newman, Jody L. (2008). The Bem Sex-Role Inventory: Continuing theoretical problems. *Educational and Psychological Measurement, 68* (5), 881–900.

Chrisler, Joan C. (2001). Gendered bodies and physical health. In Rhoda K. Unger (Ed.), *Handbook of psychology of women and gender* (pp. 289–302). New York: Wiley.

Chrisler, Joan C. (2008). PMS as a culture-bound syndrome. In Joan C. Chrisler, Carla Golden; & Patricia D. Rozee (Eds.), *Lectures on the psychology of women* (4th ed.; pp. 155–171). New York: McGraw-Hill.

Chrisler, Joan C.; & Caplan, Paula. (2002). The strange case of Dr. Jekyll and Ms. Hyde: How PMS became a cultural phenomenon and a psychiatric disorder. *Annual Review of Sex Research, 13,* 274–306.

Chrisler, Joan C.; Rose, Jennifer Gorman; Dutch, Susan E.; Sklarsky, Katherine G.; & Grant, Marie C. (2006). The PMS illusion: Social cognition maintains social construction. *Sex Roles, 54* (5/6), 371–376.

Christakis, Dimitri A.; Zimmerman, Frederick J.; DiGiuseppe, David L.; & McCarty, Carolyn A. (2004). Early television exposure and subsequent attentional problems in children. *Pediatrics, 113,* 708–713.

Christensen, Larry B. (2004). *Experimental methodology* (9th ed.). Boston: Allyn & Bacon.

Christian, Harry. (1994). *The making of anti-sexist men.* London: Routledge.

Christopher, Andrew N.; & Mull, Melinda S. (2006). Conservative ideology and ambivalent sexism. *Psychology of Women Quarterly, 30* (2), 223–230.

Christopher, F. Scott; & Sprecher, Susan. (2000). Sexuality in marriage, dating, and other relationships: A decade review. *Journal of Marriage and Family, 62,* 999–1017.

Christopher Trenholm, Barbara; Devaney, Kenneth; Fortson, Melissa Clark; Quay, Lisa; & Wheeler, Justin. (2008). Impacts of abstinence education on teen sexual activity, risk of pregnancy, and risk of sexually transmitted diseases. *Journal of Policy Analysis and Management, 27* (2), Document No. PP08-18.

Ciani, Keith D.; Summers, Jessica J.; & Easter, Matthew A. (2008). Gender differences in academic entitlement among college students. *Journal of Genetic Psychology, 169* (4), 332–344.

Cikara, Mina; & Fiske, Susan T. (2009). Warmth, competence, and ambivalent sexism: Vertical assault and collateral damage. In Manuela Barreto; Michelle K. Ryan; & Michael T. Schmitt (Eds.), *The glass ceiling in the 21st century: Understanding barriers to gender equality* (pp. 73–96). Washington, DC: American Psychological Association.

Cisneros-Puebla, César A.; & Faux, Robert B. (2008). The deconstructive and reconstructive faces of social construction. *Forum: Qualitative Social Research, 9* (1), 1–14.

Clarke, Laura Huld. (2005). Remarriage in later life: Older women's negotiation of power, resources and domestic labor. *Journal of Women and Aging, 17,* 21–41.

Cleary, David J.; Ray, Glen E.; LoBello, Steven G.; & Zachar, Peter. (2002). Children's perceptions of close peer relationships: Quality, congruence and meta-perceptions. *Child Study Journal, 32,* 179–192.

Cobbs, Price M.; & Turnock, Judith L. (2003). *Cracking the corporate code: From survival to mastery; The revealing success stories of 32 African American executives.* New York: AMACOM.

Cochrane, Kira. (2008, June 23). Are gender stereotypes boring? *New Statesman, 137* (4902), 22–23.

Cohen, Kenneth M. (2002). Relationships among childhood sex—Atypical behavior, spatial ability, handedness, and sexual orientation in men. *Archives of Sexual Behavior, 31,* 129–143.

Cohen, Laurie L.; & Shotland, R. Lance. (1996). Timing of first sexual intercourse in a relationship: Expectations, experiences, and perceptions of others. *Journal of Sex Research, 33,* 291–299.

Cohen, Patricia. (2007, May 31). Signs of détente in the battle between Venus and Mars. *New York Times,* A14.

Cohen, Philip N. (2007). Working for the woman? Female managers and the gender wage gap. *American Sociological Review, 72* (5), 681–704.

Cohen, Philip N.; & Huffman, Matt L. (2003). Occupational segregation and the devaluation of women's work across U.S. labor markets. *Social Forces, 81,* 881–908.

Cohen-Bendahan, Celina C. C.; Buitelaar, Jan K.; van Goozen, Stephanie H. M.; Orlebeke, Jacob F.; & Cohen-Kettenis, Peggy T. (2005). Is there an effect of prenatal testosterone on aggression and other behavioral traits? A study comparing same-sex and opposite sex twin girls. *Hormones and Behavior, 47,* 230–237.

Cohen-Kettenis, Peggy T. (2005a). Gender change in 46, XY persons with 5α-reductase-2 deficiency and 17β-hydroxysteroid dehydrogenase-3 deficiency. *Archives of Sexual Behavior, 34,* 399–410.

Cohen-Kettenis, Peggy T. (2005b). Psychological long-term outcome in intersex conditions. *Hormone Research, 64* (Suppl. 2), 27–30.

Cohen-Kettenis, Peggy T.; Delemarre-van de Waal, Henriette A.; & Gooren, Louis J. G. (2008). The treatment of adolescent transsexuals: Changing insights. *Journal of Sexual Medicine, 5* (8), 1892–1897.

Colapinto, John. (2000). *As nature made him.* New York: HarperCollins.

Cole, Elizabeth R.; Jayaratne, Toby Esptein; Cecchi, Laura A.; Feldbaum, Merle; & Petty, Elizabeth M. (2007). Vive la difference? Genetic explanations for perceived gender differences in nurturance. *Sex Roles, 57* (3/4), 211–222.

Cole, Johnnetta Betsch; & Guy-Sheftall, Beverly. (2003). *Gender talk: The struggle for women's equality in African American communities.* New York: Ballantine.

Cole, Stephen; & Barber, Elinor. (2003). *Increasing faculty diversity: The occupational choices of high-achieving minority students.* Cambridge, MA: Harvard University Press.

Coley, Richard. (2001). *Differences in the gender gap: Comparisons across racial/ethnic groups in education and work.* Princeton, NJ: Educational Testing Service.

Colley, Ann; Ball, Jane; Kirby, Nicola; Harvey, Rebecca; & Vingelen, Ingrid. (2001). Gender-linked differences in everyday memory performance: Effort makes the difference. *Sex Roles, 47,* 577–582.

Coltrane, Scott. (2000). Research on household labor: Modeling and measuring the social embeddedness of routine family work. *Journal of Marriage and the Family, 62,* 1208–1233

Coltrane, Scott; & Messineo, Melinda. (2000). The perpetuation of subtle prejudice: Race and gender imagery in 1990s television advertising. *Sex Roles, 42,* 363–389.

Connell, R. W. (1987). *Gender and power: Society, the person and sexual politics.* Cambridge, England: Polity Press.

Connell, R. W. (1995). *Masculinities.* Berkeley, CA: University of California Press.

Connell, R. W. (1996). Teaching the boys: New research on masculinity, the gender strategies for schools. *Teachers College Record, 98,* 206–235.

Connell, R. W. (2001, Winter). Studying men and masculinity. *Resources for Feminist Research,* 43–56.

Connell, R. W. (2005a). Change among the gatekeepers: Men, masculinities, and gender equality in the global arena. *Signs, 30,* 1801–1825.

Connell, R. W. (2005b). Hegemonic masculinity: Rethinking the concept. *Gender and Society, 19,* 829–859.

Connell, R. W. (2005c). A really good husband: Work/life balance, gender equity and social change. *Australian Journal of Social Issues, 40,* 369–383.

Connolly, Jennifer; Craig, Wendy; Goldberg, Adele; & Pepler, Debra. (2004). Mixed-gender groups, dating, and romantic relationship in early adolescence. *Journal of Research on Adolescence, 14,* 185–207.

Constantinople, Anne. (1973). Masculinity-femininity: An exception to a famous dictum. *Psychological Bulletin, 80,* 389–407.

Cook, Ellen P.; Heppner, Mary J.; & O'Brien, Karen M. (2002). Career development of women of color and white women: Assumptions, conceptualization, and interventions from an ecological perspective. *Career Development Quarterly, 50,* 291–305.

Cook, Ellen P.; Heppner, Mary J.; & O'Brien, Karen M. (2005). Multicultural and gender influences in women's career development: An ecological perspective. *Journal of Multicultural Counseling and Development, 33,* 165–179.

Cook, Ellen Piel; Warnke, Melanie; & Dupuy, Paula. (1993). Gender bias and the DSM-III-R. *Counselor Education and Supervision, 32,* 311–322.

Cook, Jerry L.; Jones, Randall M.; Dick, Andrew J.; & Singh, Archana. (2005). Revisiting men's role in father involvement: The importance of personal expectations. *Fathering, 3,* 165–178.

Cooper, Al. (2004). Online sexual activity in the new millennium. *Contemporary Sexuality, 38,* i–vii.

Cooper, Al; Delmonico, David; Griffin-Shelley, Eric; & Mathy, Robin. (2004). Online sexual activity: An examination of potentially problematic behavior. *Sexual Addiction and Compulsivity, 11,* 129–143.

Cooper, Al; Morahan-Martin, Janet; Mathy, Robin M.; & Maheu, Marlene. (2002). Toward an increased understanding of user demographics in online sexual activities. *Journal of Sex and Marital Therapy, 28,* 105–129.

Cooperstock, Ruth. (1970). A review of women's psychotropic drug use. *Canadian Journal of Psychiatry, 24,* 29–34.

Corra, Mamadi; Carter, James; Knox, David; & Houvouras, Shannon. (2006). *Marital happiness by sex and race: A second look.* Presented at the annual meeting of the American Sociological Association, Montreal.

Corwyn, Robert Flynn; & Bradley, Robert H. (2005). The cross-gender equivalence of strains and gains from occupying multiple roles among dual-earner couples. *Parenting: Science and Practice, 5,* 1–27.

Cosgrove, Lisa. (2003). Feminism, postmodernism, and psychological research. *Hypatia, 18,* 85–113.

Cosgrove, Lisa; & Caplan, Paula J. (2004). Medicalizing menstrual distress. In Paula J. Caplan & Lisa Cosgrove (Eds.), *Bias in psychiatric diagnosis* (pp. 221–230). Lanham, MD: Jason Aronson.

Cosgrove, Lisa; & McHugh, Maureen C. (2008). A post-Newtonian, postmodern approach to science: New methods in social action research. In Sharlene Nagy Hesse-Biber & Patricia Leavy (Eds.), *Handbook of emergent methods* (pp. 73–85). New York: Guilford Press.

Cosgrove, Lisa; & Riddle, Bethany. (2004). Gender bias and sex distribution of mental disorders in the DSM-IV-TR. In Paula J. Caplan & Lisa Cosgrove (Eds.), *Bias in psychiatric diagnosis* (pp. 127–140). Lanham, MD: Jason Aronson.

Costa, Paul T., Jr.; Terracciano, Antonio; & McCrae, Robert R. (2001). Gender differences in personality traits across cultures: Robust and surprising findings. *Journal of Personality and Social Psychology, 81,* 322–331.

Côté, Sylvana M.; Vaillancourt, Tracy; Barker, Edward D.; Nagin, Daniel S.; & Tremblay, Richard E. (2007). The joint development of physical and indirect aggression: Predictors of continuity and change during childhood. *Development and Psychopathology, 19* (1), 37–55.

Côté, Sylvana M.; Vaillancourt, Tracy; LeBlanc, John C.; Nagin, Daniel S.; & Tremblay, Richard E. (2006). The development of physical aggression from toddlerhood to pre-adolescence: A nation wide longitudinal study of Canadian children. *Journal of Abnormal Child Psychology, 34,* 68–82.

Coulson, Neil S. (2005). Receiving social support online: An analysis of a computer-mediated support group for individuals living with irritable bowel syndrome. *CyberPsychology and Behavior, 8,* 580–584.

Courtenay, Will H. (2000). Behavioral factors associated with disease, injury, and death among men: Evidence and implications for prevention. *Journal of Men's Studies, 9,* 81–142.

Cowdery, Randi S.; Scarborough, Norman; Knudson-Martin, Carmen; Seshadri, Gita; Lewis, Monique E.; & Mahoney, Anne Rankin. (2009). Gendered power in cultural contexts: Part II. Middle class African American heterosexual couples with young children. *Family Process, 48* (1), 25–39.

Crain, Caleb. (2001). *American sympathy: Men, friendship, and literature in the new nation.* New Haven, CT: Yale University Press.

Cramer, Duncan. (2002). Relationship satisfaction and conflict over minor and major issues in romantic relationships. *Journal of Psychology, 136,* 75–81.

Cramer, Kenneth M; Gallant, Melanie D.; & Langlois, Michelle W. (2005). Self-silencing and depression in women and men: Comparative structural equation models. *Personality and Individual Differences, 39,* 581–592.

Cramer, Kenneth M.; & Thoms, Norm. (2003). Factor structure of the silencing the self scale in women and men. *Personality and Individual Differences, 35,* 525–535.

Craske, Michelle G. (2003). *Origins of phobias and anxiety disorders: Why more women than men?* Amsterdam: Elsevier.

Crawford, June; Kippax, Susan; Onxy, Jenny; Gault, Una; & Benton, Pam. (1992). *Emotion and gender: Constructing meaning from memory.* London: Sage.

Crawford, Mary; & Marecek, Jeanne. (1989). Psychology reconstructs the female: 1968–1988. *Psychology of Women Quarterly, 13,* 147–165.

Crouter, Ann C.; Manke, Beth A.; & McHale, Susan M. (1995). The family context of gender intensification in early adolescence. *Child Development, 66,* 317–329.

Crouter, Ann C.; Whiteman, Shawn D.; McHale, Susan M.; & Osgood, D. Wayne. (2007). Development of gender attitude traditionality across middle childhood and adolescence. *Child Development, 78* (3), 911–926.

Culbertson, Frances M. (1997). Depression and gender: An international review. *American Psychologist, 52,* 25–31.

Cummings, Jonathon N.; Sproull, Lee; & Kiesler, Sara B. (2002). Beyond hearing: Where the real-world and online support meet. *Group Dynamics, 6,* 78–88.

Cunningham, Mick. (2008). Influences of gender ideology and housework allocation on women's employment over the life course. *Social Science Research, 37* (1), 254–267.

Cutler, Susan E.; & Nolen-Hoeksema, Susan. (1991). Accounting for sex differences in depression through female victimization: Childhood sexual abuse. *Sex Roles, 24,* 425–438.

Cutter, William J.; Daly, Eileen M.; Robertson, Dene M. W.; Chitnis, Xavier A.; van Amelsvoort, Therese A. M. J.; Simmons, Andrew; et al. (2006). Influence of X chromosome and hormones on human brain development: A magnetic resonance imaging and proton magnetic resonance spectroscopy study of Turner Syndrome. *Biological Psychiatry, 59,* 273–283.

Cyranowski, Jill M.; Frank, Ellen; Young, Elizabeth; & Shear, M. Katherine. (2000). Adolescent onset of the gender difference in lifetime rates of major depression. *Archives of General Psychiatry, 57,* 21–56.

Dabbs, James M., Jr. (1992). Testosterone and occupational achievement. Social Forces, *70,* 813–824.

Dabbs, James M., Jr. (with Dabbs, Mary Godwin). (2000). *Heroes, rogues, and lovers: Testosterone and behavior.* New York: McGraw-Hill.

Dabbs, James M., Jr.; Carr, Timothy S.; Frady, Robert L.; & Riad, Jasmin K. (1995). Testosterone, crime, and misbehavior among 692 male prison inmates. *Personality and Individual Differences, 18,* 627–633.

Dabbs, James M., Jr.; Hargrove, Marian F.; & Heusel, Colleen. (1996). Testosterone differences among college fraternities: Well-behaved vs. rambunctious. *Personality and Individual Differences, 20,* 157–161.

Dabbs, James M., Jr.; Hopper, Charles H.; & Jurkovic, Gregory J. (1990). Testosterone and personality among college students and military veterans. *Personality and Individual Differences, 11,* 1263–1269.

Dabbs, James M., Jr.; & Morris, Robin. (1990). Testosterone, social class, and antisocial behavior in a sample of 4,462 men. *Psychological Science, 1,* 209–211.

Dabbs, James M., Jr.; Ruback, R. Barry; Frady, Robert L.; Hopper, Charles H.; & Sgoutas, Demetrios S. (1988). Saliva testosterone and criminal violence among women. *Personality and Individual Differences, 9,* 269–275.

Dadich, Ann. (2006). Self-help support groups: Adding to the toolbox of mental health care options for young men. *Youth Studies Australia, 25,* 33–41.

Daley, Andrea; Solomon, Steven; Newman, Peter A.; & Mishna, Faye. (2007). Traversing the margins: Intersectionalities in the bullying of lesbian, gay, bisexual and transgender youth. *Journal of Gay & Lesbian Social Services, 19* (3/4), 9–29.

Dalley, Phyllis; Campbell, Mark David. (2006). Constructing and contesting discourses of heteronormativity: An ethnographic study of youth in a Francophone high school in Canada. *Journal of Language, Identity, and Education, 5,* 11–29.

Dana, Richard H. (2001). Clinical diagnosis of multicultural populations in the United States. In Lisa A. Suzuki, Joseph G. Ponterotto, & Paul J. Meller (Eds.), *Handbook of multicultural assessment: Clinical, psychological, and educational applications* (2nd ed., pp. 101–131). San Francisco: Jossey-Bass.

Darwin, Charles. (1872). *The expression of emotions in man and animals.* New York: Philosophical Library.

Das, Aniruddha. (2007). Masturbation in the United States. *Journal of Sex and Marital Therapy, 33* (4), 301–317.

Davies, Michelle. (2004). Correlates of negative attitudes toward gay men: Sexism, male role norms, and male sexuality. *Journal of Sex Research, 41,* 259–266.

Davis-Kean, Pamela; Eccles, Jacquelynne; & Linver, Miriam. (2002, April). *Influences of gender on academic achievement.* Paper presented at the biennial meeting of the Society for Research on Adolescence, New Orleans, LA.

Davison, Kathryn P.; Pennebaker, James W.; & Dickerson, Sally S. (2000). Who talks? The social psychology of illness support groups. *American Psychologist, 55,* 205–217.

Daw, Jennifer. (2002, October). Is PMDD real? *Monitor on Psychology, 33* (9), 58–60.

Day, Arla L.; & Livingstone, Holly A. (2003). Gender differences in perceptions of stressors and utilization of social support among university students. *Canadian Journal of Behavioural Science, 35,* 73–83.

Day, Katy; Gough, Brendan; & McFadden, Majella. (2004). "Warning! Alcohol can seriously damage your feminine health." *Feminist Media Studies, 4,* 165–183.

Dean, Cornelia. (2005, February 1). For some girls, the problem with math is that they're good at it. *The New York Times,* p. F3.

Dear, Peter. (2005). What is the history of science the history of? *ISIS: Journal of the History of Science in Society, 96,* 390–406.

Deaux, Kay. (1984). From individual differences to social categories: Analysis of a decade's research on gender. *American Psychologist, 39,* 105–116.

Deaux, Kay; & Lewis, Laurie. (1984). The structure of gender stereotypes: Interrelationships among components and gender label. *Journal of Personality and Social Psychology, 46,* 991–1004.

Degler, Carl N. (1974). What ought to be and what was: Women's sexuality in the nineteenth century. *American Historical Review, 79,* 1467–1490.

de Cuypere, Griet; T'Sjoen, Guy; Beerteen, Ruth; Selvaggi, Gennaro; de Sutter, Petra; Hoebeke, Piet; et al. (2005). Sexual and physical health after sex reassignment surgery. *Archives of Sexual Behavior, 34,* 679–690.

de Graaf, Paul M.; & Kalmijn, Matthijs. (2006). Divorce motives in a period of rising divorce. *Journal of Family Issues, 27,* 483–505.

DeLamater, John; & Friedrich, William N. (2002). Human sexual development. *Journal of Sex Research, 39,* 10–14.

Del Parigi, Angelo; Chen, Kewei; Gautier, Jean-Francois; Salbe, Arline D.; Pratley, Richard E.; Ravussin, Eric; et al. (2002). Sex differences in the human brain's response to hunger and satiation. *American Journal of Clinical Nutrition, 75,* 1017–1022.

DeLucia-Waack, Janice L.; Gerrity, Deborah A.; Taub, Deborah J.; & Baldo, Tracy D. (2001). Gender, gender role identity, and type of relationship as predictors of relationship behavior and beliefs in college students. *Journal of College Counseling, 4,* 32–48.

Demoulin, Stéphanie; Leyens, Jacques-Philippe; Paladino, Maria-Paola; Dovidio, John F.; Rodriguez-Torres, Ramón; & Rodriguez-Perez, Armando. (2004). Dimensions of "uniquely" and "non-uniquely" human emotions. *Cognition and Emotion, 18,* 71–96.

Dempsey, Ken. (2002). Who gets the best deal from marriage: Women or men? *Journal of Sociology, 38,* 91–110.

den Boer, P. C. A. M.; Wiersma, D.; & Van den Bosch, R. J. (2004). Why is self-help neglected in the treatment of emotional disorders? A meta-analysis. *Psychological Medicine, 34* (6), 959–971.

Denov, Myriam S. (2003). The myth of innocence: Sexual scripts and the recognition of child sexual abuse by female perpetrators. *Journal of Sex Research, 40,* 303–314.

Désert, Michel; & Leyens, Jacques-Philippe. (2006). Social comparisons across cultures I: Gender stereotypes and high and low power distance cultures. In Serge Guimond (Ed.), *Social comparison and social psychology: Understanding cognition, intergroup relations, and culture* (pp. 303–317). New York: Cambridge University Press.

Desjarlais, Robert; Eisenberg, Leon; Good, Byron; & Kleinman, Arthur. (1995). *World mental health: Problems and priorities in low-income countries.* New York: Oxford University Press.

De Souza, Paula; & Ciclitira, Karen E. (2005). Men and dieting: A qualitative analysis. *Journal of Health Psychology, 10,* 793–804.

DeSouza, Eros; & Fansler, Gigi. (2003). Contrapower sexual harassment: A survey of students and faculty members. *Sex Roles, 48,* 529–542.

Deuster, Patricia A.; Adera, Tilahun; & South-Paul, Jeannette. (1999). Biological, social, and behavioral factors associated with premenstrual syndrome. *Archives of Family Medicine, 8,* 122–128.

Deutsch, Francine M.; Roksa, Josipa; & Meeske, Cynthia. (2003). How gender counts when couples count their money. *Sex Roles, 48,* 291–304.

de Vaus, David. (2002, Winter). Marriage and mental health: Does marriage improve the mental health of men at the expense of women? *Family Matters,* 26–32.

Devdas, Neetha R.; & Rubin, Linda J. (2007). Rape myth acceptance among first- and second-generation South Asian American women. *Sex Roles, 56* (9/10), 701–705.

Deveny, Kathleen; Kelley, Raina; Reno, Jamie; Springer, Karen; Meadows, Susannah; Underwood, Anne; & Scelfo, Julie. (2007, February 12). Girls gone bad? *Newsweek, 149* (7), 40–47.

de Vries, Brian; & Megathlin, David. (2009). The meaning of friendship for gay men and lesbians in the second half of life. *Journal of GLBT Family Studies, 5* (1/2), 82–98.

de Waal, Frans B. M. (2000). Primates—A natural heritage of conflict resolution. *Science, 289,* 586–590.

Diamond, Lisa M. (2003a). Was it a phase? Young women's relinquishment of lesbian/bisexual identities over a 5-year period. *Journal of Personality and Social Psychology, 84,* 352–364.

Diamond, Lisa M. (2003b). What does sexual orientation orient? A biobehavioral model distinguishing romantic love and sexual desire. *Psychological Review, 110,* 173–192.

Diamond, Lisa M. (2006). The evolution of plasticity in female-female desire. *Journal of Psychology and Human Sexuality, 18* (4), 245–274.

Diamond, Lisa M. (2008). Female bisexuality from adolescence to adulthood: Results from a 10-year longitudinal study. *Developmental Psychology, 44* (1), 5–15.

Dickerman, Charles; Christensen, Jeff; & Kerl-McClain, Stella Beatríz. (2008). Big breasts and bad guys: Depictions of gender and race in video games. *Journal of Creativity in Mental Health, 3* (1), 20–29.

Dickerson, Lori M.; Mazyck, Pamela J.; & Hunter, Melissa H. (2003). Premenstrual syndrome. *American Family Physician, 67*, 1743–1752.

Diefenbach, Donald L. (1997). The portrayal of mental illness on prime-time television. *Journal of Community Psychology, 25*, 289–302.

Diekman, Amanda B.; & Eagly, Alice H. (2000). Stereotypes as dynamic constructs: Women and men of the past, present, and future. *Personality and Social Psychology Bulletin, 26*, 1171–1187.

Dijkstra, Anja F.; Verdonk, Petra; & Lagro-Janssen, Antoine L. M. (2008). Gender bias in medical textbooks: Examples from coronary heart disease, depression, alcohol abuse and pharmacology. *Medical Education, 42* (10), 1021–1028.

Dijkstra, Arie; & De Vries, Hein. (2001). Do self-help interventions in health education lead to cognitive changes, and do cognitive changes lead to behavioural change? *British Journal of Health Psychology, 6*, 121–134.

Dill, Karen E.; Gentile, Douglas A.; Richter, William A.; & Dill, Jody C. (2005). Violence, sex, race, and age in popular video games: A content analysis. In Ellen Cole & Jessica Henderson Daniel (Eds.), *Featuring females: Feminist analyses of media* (pp. 115–130). Washington, DC: American Psychological Association.

Dingell, John D.; & Maloney, Carolyn B. (2002). *A new look through the glass ceiling: Where are the women?* The status of women in ten selected industries. ERIC Document Reproduction Service No. ED 468 605.

Dixon, Travis L. (2008). Who is the victim here?: The psychological effects of overrepresenting White victims and Black perpetrators on television news. *Journalism, 9* (5), 582–605.

Dixon, Travis L.; & Azocar, Cristina L. (2007). Priming crime and activating Blackness: Understanding the psychological impact of the overrerpesentation of Blacks as lawbreakers on television news. *Journal of Communication, 57* (2), 229–253.

Docter, Richard F.; & Prince, Virginia. (1997). Transvestism: A survey of 1032 cross-dressers. *Archives of Sexual Behavior, 26*, 589–605.

Doherty, Kathy; & Anderson, Irina. (2004). Making sense of male rape: Constructions of gender, sexuality and experience of rape victims. *Journal of Community and Applied Social Psychology, 14*, 85–103.

Dolado, J. J.; Felgueroso, F.; & Jimeno, J. F. (2001). Female employment and occupational changes in the 1990s: How is the EU performing relative to the US? *European Economic Review, 45*, 875–889.

Donaghue, Ngaire; & Fallon, Barry J. (2003). Gender-role self-stereotyping and the relationship between equity and satisfaction in close relationships. *Sex Roles, 48*, 217–230.

Donnelly, Denise; Burgess, Elisabeth; Anderson, Sally; Davis, Regina; & Dillard, Joy. (2001). Involuntary celibacy: A life course analysis. *Journal of Sex Research, 38*, 159–169.

Donovan, Roxanne; & Williams, Michelle. (2002). Living at the intersection: The effects of racism and sexism on Black rape survivors. *Women & Therapy, 25*, 95–105.

Doss, Brian D.; Atkins, David C.; & Christensen, Andrew. (2003). Who's dragging their feet? Husbands and wives seeking marital therapy. *Journal of Marital and Family Therapy, 29*, 165–177.

Doucet, Andrea. (2006). 'Estrogen-filled worlds': Fathers as primary caregivers and embodiment. *Sociological Review, 54* (4), 696–716.

Downing, Roberta A.; Crosby, Faye J.; & Blake-Beard, Stacy. (2005). The perceived importance of developmental relationships on women undergraduates' pursuit of science. *Psychology of Women Quarterly, 29*, 419–426.

Dozier, David; Lauzen, Martha; & Reyes, Barbara. (2005, May). *Do prime-time characters act their age? An examination of adulthood in the 2003–04 season.* Presented at the International Communication Association conference, New York.

Dreger, Alice. (2009). Gender identity disorder in childhood: Inconclusive advice to parents. *Hastings Center Report 39* (1), 26–29.

Dreher, George F.; & Cox, Taylor H., Jr. (1996). Race, gender, and opportunity: A study of compensation attainment and the establishment of mentoring relationships. *Journal of Applied Psychology, 81*, 297–308.

"Dr. FUN." (2004, February 10). *Dr. FUN's Stupid Cupid awards.* Retrieved June 25, 2006, from http://www.asu.edu/news/campus/stupidcupid_awardslist_021404.htm

Dribe, Martin; & Stanfors, Maria. (2009). Does parenthood strengthen a traditional household division of labor? Evidence from Sweden. *Journal of Marriage and Family, 71* (1), 33–45.

Drummond, Kelley D.; Peterson-Badali, Michele; Bradley, Susan J.; & Zucker, Kenneth. (2008). A follow-up study of girls with gender identity disorder. *Developmental Psychology, 44* (1), 34–45.

Duarte, Linda M.; & Thompson, Janice M. (1999). Sex differences in self-silencing. *Psychological Reports, 85*, 145–161.

Dube, Shanta R.; Anda, Robert F.; Whitfield, Charles L.; Brown, David W.; Felitti, Vincent J.; Dong, Maxia; et al. (2005). Long-term consequences of childhood sexual abuse by gender of victim. *American Journal of Preventive Medicine, 28*, 430–438.

DuBois, David L.; & Hirsch, Barton J. (1990). School and neighborhood friendship patterns of Blacks and Whites in early adolescence. *Child Development, 61*, 524–536.

Dubow, Eric F.; Huesmann, L. Rowell; & Boxer, Paul. (2003). Theoretical and methodological considerations in cross-generational research on parenting and child aggressive behavior. *Journal of Abnormal Child Psychology, 31,* 185–192.

Duckworth, Angela Lee; & Seligman, Martin E. P. (2006). Self-discipline gives girls the edge: Gender in self-discipline, grades and achievement test scores. *Journal of Educational Psychology, 98,* 19–208.

Duncan, Lauren E.; Peterson, Bill E.; & Ax, Erin E. (2003). Authoritarianism as an agent of status quo maintenance: Implications for women's careers and family lives. *Sex Roles, 49,* 619–630.

Durik, Amanda M.; Hyde, Janet Shibley; Marks, Amanda C.; Roy, Amanda L.; Anaya, Debra; & Schultz, Gretchen. (2006). Ethnicity and gender stereotypes of emotion. *Sex Roles, 54* (7/8), 429–445.

Durkin, Kevin; & Nugent, Bradley. (1998). Kindergarten children's gender-role expectations for television actors. *Sex Roles, 38,* 387–402.

Durrant, Sabine. (2008, June 11). Are men boring? *Telegraph.* Retrieved June 19, 2009, from http://www.telegraph.co.uk/news/features/3636895/Are-men-boring.html

Dweck, Carol S. (2007). Is math a gift? Beliefs that put females at risk. In Stephen J. Ceci & Wendy M. Williams (Eds.), *Why aren't more women in science: Top researchers debate the evidence* (pp. 47–55). Washington, DC: American Psychological Association.

Eagly, Alice H. & Carli, Linda L. (2007). *Through the labyrinth: The truth about how women become leaders.* Boston: Harvard Business School Press.

Eagly, Alice H.; & Johannesen-Schmidt, Mary C. (2001). The leadership styles of women and men. *Journal of Social Issues, 57,* 781–797.

Eagly, Alice H.; Johannesen-Schmidt, Mary C.; & van Engen, Marloes L. (2003). Transformational, transactional, and laissez-faire leadership styles: A meta-analysis comparing women and men. *Psychological Bulletin, 129,* 569–581.

Eagly, Alice H.; & Johnson, Blair T. (1990). Gender and leadership style: A meta-analysis. *Psychological Bulletin, 108,* 233–256.

Eagly, Alice H.; Mladinic, Antonio; & Otto, Stacey. (1991). Are women evaluated more favorably than men? An analysis of attitudes, beliefs, and emotions. *Psychology of Women Quarterly, 15,* 203–216.

Eagly, Alice H.; & Steffen, Valerie J. (1986). Gender and aggressive behavior: A meta-analytic review of the social psychological literature. *Psychological Bulletin, 100,* 309–330.

Eagly, Alice H.; & Wood, Wendy. (1999). The origins of sex differences in human behavior. *American Psychologist, 54,* 408–423.

Early, Frances H. (2001). Staking her claim: Buffy the Vampire Slayer as transgressive woman warrior. *Journal of Popular Culture, 35,* 11–27.

Easterbrook, Gregg. (1996). It's unreal: How phony realism in film and literature is corrupting and confusing the American mind. *Washington Monthly, 28* (10), 41–43.

Eaton, Danice K.; Kann, Laura; Kinchen, Steven; Shanklin, Shari; Ross, James; Hawkins, Joseph; et al. (2008). Youth risk behavior surveillance—United States, 2007. *Morbidity and Mortality Weekly Report, 57* (SS-4), 1–130.

Eccles, Jacquelynne S. (1987). Gender roles and achievement patterns: An expectancy value perspective. In June Machover Reinisch, Leonard A. Rosenblum, & Stephanie A. Sanders (Eds.), *Masculinity/femininity: Basic perspectives* (pp. 240–280). New York: Oxford University Press.

Eccles, Jacquelynne S. (2007). Gender differences in participation in physical science and engineering. In Stephen J. Ceci & Wendy M. Williams (Eds.), *Why aren't more women in science: Top researchers debate the evidence* (pp. 131–145). Washington, DC: American Psychological Association.

Eckes, Thomas. (2002). Paternalistic and envious gender stereotypes: Testing predictions from the stereotype content model. *Sex Roles, 47,* 99–114.

Edmonds, Ed M.; & Cahoon, Delwin D. (1993). The "new" sexism: Females' negativism toward males. *Journal of Social Behavior and Personality, 8,* 481–487.

Edwards, David A.; Wetzel, Karen; & Wyner, Dana R. (2006). Intercollegiate soccer: Saliva cortisol and testosterone are elevated during competition, and testosterone is related to status and social connectedness with teammates. *Physiology and Behavior, 87,* 135–143.

Edwards, Michele Rees. (2006). The role of husbands' supportive communication practices in the lives of employed mothers. *Marriage and Family Review, 40* (4), 23–46.

Edwards, Renee; & Hamilton, Mark A. (2004). You need to understand my gender role: An empirical test of Tannen's model of gender and communication. *Sex Roles, 50,* 491–504.

Egan, Susan K.; & Perry, David G. (2001). Gender identity: A multidimensional analysis with implications for psychosocial adjustment. *Developmental Psychology, 37,* 451–463.

Eggermont, Steven; Beullens, Kathleen; & van den Bulck, Jan. (2005). Television viewing and adolescent females' body dissatisfaction: The mediating role of opposite sex expectations. *Communications: The European Journal of Communication Research, 30,* 343–357.

Ehrenreich, Barbara; & English, Deirdre. (1973). *Witches, midwives, and nurses: A history of women healers.* New York: Feminist Press.

Eid, Michael; & Diener, Ed. (2001). Norms for experiencing emotions in different cultures: Inter- and intranational differences. *Journal of Personality and Social Psychology, 81,* 869–885.

Eid, Michael; & Diener, Ed. (2009). Norms for experiencing emotions in different cultures: Inter- and intranational differences. In E. Diener (Ed.), *Culture and well-being: The collected works of Ed Diener* (pp. 169–202). New York: Springer Science + Business Media.

Eisenberg, Nancy; & Lennon, Randy. (1983). Sex differences in empathy and related capacities. *Psychological Bulletin, 94,* 100–131.

Eisikovits, Zvi; Winstok, Zeev; & Gelles, Richard. (2002). Structure and dynamics of escalation from the victim's perspective. *Families in Society: The Journal of Contemporary Human Services, 83,* 142–152.

Ekman, Paul. (1984). Expression and the nature of emotion. In Klaus R. Scherer & Paul Ekman (Eds.), *Approaches to emotion* (pp. 319–343). Hillsdale, NJ: Erlbaum.

Ekman, Paul. (1992). Are there basic emotions? *Psychological Review, 99,* 550–553.

Elasmar, Michael; Hasegawa, Kazumi; & Brain, Mary. (1999). The portrayal of women in U.S. prime time television. *Journal of Broadcasting & Electronic Media, 43,* 20–42.

Elfenbein, Hillary Anger; & Ambady, Nalini. (2002). On the universality and cultural specificity of emotion recognition: A meta-analysis. *Psychological Bulletin, 128,* 203–235.

Ellis, Albert. (1962). *Reason and emotion in psychotherapy.* New York: Stuart.

Englar-Carlson, Matt. (2006). Masculine norms and the therapy process. In Matt Englar-Carlson & Mark A. Stevens (Eds.), *In the room with men: A casebook of therapeutic change* (pp. 13–47). Washington, DC: American Psychological Association.

Enns, Carolyn Zerbe. (1992). Self-esteem groups: A synthesis of consciousness-raising and assertiveness training. *Journal of Counseling and Development, 71,* 7–13.

Enns, Carolyn Zerbe. (2004). *Feminist theories and feminist psychotherapies: Origins, themes, and diversity* (2nd ed.). Binghamton, NY: Haworth.

Enns, Carolyn Z.; & Hackett, Gail. (1990). Comparison of feminist and nonfeminist women's reactions to variants of nonsexist and feminist counseling. *Journal of Counseling Psychology, 37,* 33–40.

Entwisle, Doris R.; Alexander, Karl L.; & Olson, Linda S. (2007). Early schooling: The handicap of being poor and male. *Sociology of Education, 80* (2), 114–138.

Epstein, Cynthia Fuchs. (1988). *Deceptive distinctions: Sex, gender and the social order.* New Haven, CT: Yale University Press.

Epstein, Cynthia Fuchs. (2004). Border crossings: The constraints of time norms in transgressions of gender and professional roles. In Cynthia Fuchs Epstein & Arne L. Kalleberg (Eds.), *Fighting for time: Shifting boundaries of work and social life* (pp. 317–340). New York: Russell Sage.

Equal Employment Opportunity Commission. (2006). *Sexual harassment.* Retrieved July 14, 2006, from http://www.eeoc.gov/stats/harass.html

Erden, Feyza Tantekin. (2009). A course on gender equity in education: Does it affect gender role attitudes of preservice teachers? *Teaching and Teacher Education, 25* (3), 409–414.

Eron, Leonard D. (1987). The development of aggressive behavior from the perspective of a developing behaviorism. *American Psychologist, 42,* 435–442.

Eron, Leonard D.; Huesmann, L. Rowell; Brice, Patrick; Fischer, Paulette; & Mermelstein, Rebecca. (1983). Age trends in the development of aggression, sex typing, and related television habits. *Developmental Psychology, 19,* 71–77.

Eschholz, Sarah; Bufkin, Jana; & Long, Jenny. (2002). Symbolic reality bites: Women and racial/ethnic minorities in modern film. *Sociological Spectrum, 22,* 299–334.

Esgate, Anthony; & Flynn, Maria. (2005). The brain-sex theory of occupational choice: A counterexample. *Perceptual and Motor Skills, 100,* 25–37.

Espino, Adriana Medina. (2007). New democratic exercises in Mexican feminist organizations. In Lydia Alpizar et al. (Eds.), *Building feminist movements: Global perspectives* (pp. 55–66). London, United Kingdom: Zed Books.

Eun, Ki-Soo; & Kim, Eun-Young. (2006). *The transformation of gender role within the families in Korean television commercials from 1985 to 2005.* Presented at the Annual Meeting of the American Sociological Association, Montreal, Canada. Retrieved August 4, 2009, from http://ezproxy.mcneese.edu:2139/ehost/detail?vid=6&hid=104&sid=0355f997-242b-4c1e-b09e-5d764a654ba5%40sessionmgr104&bdata=JnNpdGU9ZWhvc3QtbGl2ZQ%3d%3d#db=sih&AN=26643797

Evans, Kathy M.; Kincade, Elizabeth A.; Marbley, Aretha F.; & Seem, Susan R. (2005). Feminism and feminist therapy: Lessons from the past and hopes for the future. *Journal of Counseling and Development, 83,* 269–273.

Evans, Peggy Chin. (2003). "If only I were thin like her, maybe I could be happy like her": The self-implications of associating a thin female ideal with life success. *Psychology of Women Quarterly, 27,* 209–214.

Fagot, Beverly I.; & Hagan, Richard. (1991). Observations of parent reactions to sex-stereotyped behaviors: Age and sex effects. *Child Development, 62,* 617–628.

Fagot, Beverly I.; & Leinbach, Mary D. (1989). The young child's gender schema: Environmental input, internal organization. *Child Development, 60,* 663–672.

Fagot, Beverly I.; & Leinbach, Mary D. (1994). Gender-role development in young children. In Michael R. Stevenson (Ed.), *Gender roles through the life span: A multidisciplinary perspective* (pp. 3–24). Muncie, IN: Ball State University.

FairTest *Examiner*. (2006, October). *Test optional admissions list surges.* Retrieved November 25, 2006, from http://www.fairtest.org/examarts/2006%20October/optional.html

Falconi, Anne; & Mullet, Etienne. (2003). Cognitive algebra of love through the adult life. *International Journal of Aging and Human Development, 57,* 275–290.

Fallon, April E.; & Rozin, Paul. (1985). Sex differences in perceptions of desirable body shape. *Journal of Abnormal Psychology, 94,* 102–105.

Faludi, Susan. (1991). *Backlash: The undeclared war against American women.* New York: Crown.

Faludi, Susan. (1999). *Stiffed: The betrayal of the American man.* New York: Morrow.

Farmer, Helen S.; & Sidney, Joan Seliger. (1985). Sex equity in career and vocational education. In Susan S. Klein (Ed.), *Handbook for achieving sex equity through education* (pp. 338–359). Baltimore: Johns Hopkins University Press.

Fausto-Sterling, Anne. (2000). *Sexing the body: Gender politics and the construction of sexuality.* New York: Basic Books.

Federal Bureau of Investigation. (2008). *Crime in the United States 2007.* Retrieved August 29, 2009, from http://www.fbi.gov/ucr/cius2007/data/table_33.html

Fehr, Beverley. (2000). The life cycle of friendship. In Clyde Hendrick & Susan S. Hendrick (Eds.), *Close relationships: A sourcebook* (pp. 71–82). Thousand Oaks, CA: Sage.

Fehr, Beverley. (2004). Intimacy expectations in same-sex friendships: A prototype interaction-pattern model. *Journal of Personality and Social Psychology, 86,* 265–284.

Feingold, Alan. (1998). Gender stereotyping for sociability, dominance, character, and mental health: A meta-analysis of findings from the bogus stranger paradigm. *Genetic, Social, and General Psychology Monographs, 124,* 253–270.

Feist, Jess; & Feist, Gregory J. (2009). *Theories of personality* (7th ed.). Boston: McGraw-Hill.

Feld, Scott L.; & Straus, Murray A. (1989). Escalation and desistance of wife assault in marriage. *Criminology, 27,* 141–161.

Felder, Stefan; & Zhang, Junsen. (2006). The gender longevity gap: Explaining the difference between singles and couples. *Journal of Population Economics, 19,* 543–557.

Feng, Jing; Spence, Ian; & Pratt, Jay. (2007). Playing an action video game reduces gender differences in spatial cognition. *Psychological Science, 18* (10), 850–855.

Fennema, Elizabeth. (1980). Sex-related differences in mathematics achievement: Where and why. In Lynn H. Fox, Linda Brody, & Dianne Tobin (Eds.), *Women and the mathematical mystique* (pp. 76–93). Baltimore: Johns Hopkins University Press.

Fergusson, David M.; Horwood, L. John; & Ridder, Elizabeth M. (2005). Partner violence and mental health outcomes in a New Zealand birth cohort. *Journal of Marriage and Family, 67,* 1103–1119.

Fernández, Guillén; Weis, Susanne; Stoffel-Wagner, Birgit; Tendolkar, Indira; Reuber, Markus; Beyenburg, Stefan; et al. (2003). Menstrual cycle-dependent neural plasticity in the adult human brain is hormone, task, and region specific. *Journal of Neuroscience, 23,* 3790–3795.

Ferree, Marnie C. (2003). Women and the Web: Cybersex activity and implications. *Sexual and Relationship Therapy, 18,* 385–393.

Ferriman, Kimberley; Lubinski, David; & Benbow, Camilla P. (2009). Work preferences, life values, and personal views of top math/science graduate students and the profoundly gifted: Developmental changes and gender differences during emerging adulthood and parenthood. *Journal of Personality and Social Psychology, 97* (3), 517–532.

Fetto, John. (2003, June 1). First comes love. *American Demographics, 25* (5).

Fiebig, Jennifer Nepper. (2008). Gifted American and German adolescent women: A longitudinal examination of attachment, separation, gender roles, and career aspirations. *High Ability Studies, 19* (1), 67–81.

Field, Alison E.; Camargo, Carlos A., Jr.; Taylor, C. Barr; Berkey, Catherine S.; Roberts, Susan B.; & Colditz, Graham A. (2001). Peer, parent, and media influences on the development of weight concerns and frequent dieting among preadolescent and adolescent girls and boys. *Pediatrics, 107,* 54–60.

Fields, Jessica; & Tolman, Deborah L. (2006). Risky business: Sexuality education and research in U.S. schools. *Sexuality Research and Social Policy, 3* (4), 63–76.

Fields, Judith; & Wolff, Edward N. (1991). The decline of sex segregation and the wage gap, 1970–80. *Journal of Human Resources, 26,* 608–622.

Fiese, Barbara H.; & Skillman, Gemma. (2000). Gender differences in family stories: Moderating influence of parent gender role and child gender. *Sex Roles, 43,* 267–283.

Fineran, Susan. (2002). Sexual harassment between same-sex peers: Intersection of mental health, homophobia, and sexual violence in schools. *Social Work, 47,* 65–74.

Finfgeld-Connett, Deborah. (2005). Clarification of social support. *Journal of Nursing Scholarship, 37,* 4–9.

Finkelhor, David. (1980). Sex among siblings: A survey on prevalence, variety, and effects. *Archives of Sexual Behavior, 9,* 171–193.

Finkelhor, David. (1984). *Child sexual abuse: New theory and research.* New York: Free Press.

Finley, Gordon E.; & Schwartz, Seth J. (2008). Perceived paternal and maternal involvement: Factor structures, mean differences, and parental roles. *Fathering: A Journal of Theory, Research, and Practice about Men as Fathers, 6* (1), 62–82.

Finn, Jerry. (1999). An exploration of helping processes in an online self-help group focusing on issues of disability. *Health and Social Work, 24,* 220–227.

Fireman, Bruce; Koran, Lorrin M.; Leventhal, Jeanne L.; & Jacobson, Alice. (2001). The prevalence of clinically recognized obsessive-compulsive disorder in a large health maintenance organization. *American Journal of Psychiatry, 158*, 1904–1910.

Fischer, Agneta H. (1993). Sex differences in emotionality: Fact or stereotype? *Feminism & Psychology, 3*, 303–318.

Fischer, Agneta H.; Rodriguez Mosquera, Patricia M.; van Vianen, Annelies E. M.; & Hanstead, Antony S. R. (2004). Gender and culture differences in emotion. *Emotion, 4*, 87–94.

Fischer, Ann R.; & Good, Glenn E. (1994). Gender, self, and others: Perceptions of the campus environment. *Journal of Counseling Psychology, 41*, 343–355.

Fischtein, Dayna S.; Herold, Edward S.; & Desmarais, Serge. (2007). How much does gender explain in sexual attitudes and behavior? A survey of Canadian adults. *Archives of Sexual Behavior, 36* (3), 451–461.

Fisher, Kimberly; Egerton, Muriel; Gershuny, Jonathan I.; & Robinson, John P. (2007). Gender convergence in the American Heritage Time Use Study (AHTUS). *Social Indicators Research, 82* (1), 1–33.

Fiske, Susan T.; Bersoff, Donald N.; Borgida, Eugene; Deaux, Kay; & Heilman, Madeline E. (1991). Social science research on trial: Use of sex stereotyping research in *Price Waterhouse v. Hopkins. American Psychologist, 46*, 1049–1060.

Fiske, Susan T.; Cuddy, Amy J. C.; Glick, Peter; & Xu, Jun. (2002). A model of (often mixed) stereotype content: Competence and warmth respectively follow from perceived status and competition. *Journal of Personality and Social Psychology, 82*, 878–902.

Fitzgerald, Louise F. (1994, August). *Sexual harassment—A feminist perspective on the prevention of violence against women in the workplace.* Paper presented at the 102nd annual convention of the American Psychological Association, Los Angeles, CA.

Fitzgerald, Louise F.; Swan, Suzanne; & Magley, Vicki J. (1997). But was it really sexual harassment? Legal, behavioral, and psychological definitions of the workplace victimization of women. In William O'Donohue (Ed.), *Sexual harassment: Theory, research, and treatment* (pp. 5–28), Boston: Allyn & Bacon.

Fitzgerald, Nancy. (2002). TV's big lie: They're some of your favorite television stars, but these actresses' bodies are sending teens the wrong message about how young women are supposed to look. *Scholastic Choices, 17* (7), 6–10.

Flaherty, Mary. (2005). Gender differences in mental rotation ability in three cultures: Ireland, Ecuador, and Japan. *Psychologia: An International Journal of Psychology in the Orient, 48*, 31–38.

Flanagan, Elizabeth H.; & Blashfield, Roger K. (2005). Gender acts as a context for interpreting diagnostic criteria. *Journal of Clinical Psychology, 61*, 1485–1498.

Flaskerud, Jacquelyn H. (2000). Ethnicity, culture, and neuropsychiatry. *Issues in Mental Health Nursing, 21*, 5–29.

Flicker, Eva. (2003). Between brains and breasts? Women scientists in fiction film. *Public Understanding of Science, 12*, 307–318.

Flora, Stephen Ray; & Sellers, Melissa. (2003, May/June). "Premenstrual dysphoric disorder" and "premenstrual syndrome" myths. *Skeptical Inquirer, 27* (3), 37–42.

Flores, Lori A. (2008). A community of limits and the limits of community: MALDEF's Chicana rights project, empowering the "typical Chicana," and the question of civil rights, 1974–1983. *Journal of American Ethnic History, 27*, 81–110.

Fodor, Iris Goldstein. (1988). Cognitive behavior therapy: Evaluation of theory and practice for addressing women's issues. In Mary Ann Dutton Douglas & Lenore E. A. Walker (Eds.), *Feminist psychotherapies: Integration of therapeutic and feminist systems* (pp. 91–117). Norwood, NJ: Ablex.

Folkman, Susan; & Lazarus, Richard S. (1980). An analysis of coping in middle-aged community sample. *Journal of Health and Social Behavior, 21*, 219–239.

Fonarow, Gregg C. (2007). The global burden of atherosclerotic vascular disease. *Nature Clinical Practice Cardiovascular Medicine, 4* (10), 530–531.

Foote, Brad; Smolin, Yvette; Kaplan, Margaret; Legatt, Michael E.; & Lipschitz, Deborah. (2006). Prevalence of dissociative disorders in psychiatric outpatients. *American Journal of Psychiatry, 163*, 623–629.

Ford, Clellan S.; & Beach, Frank A. (1951). *Patterns of sexual behavior.* New York: Harper.

Ford, John, Jr. (2004). How men's movement participants view each other. *Journal of Men's Studies, 12*, 103–118.

Foster, Jennifer D.; Kuperminc, Gabriel P.; & Price, Ann W. (2004). Gender differences in posttraumatic stress and related symptoms among inner-city minority youth exposed to community violence. *Journal of Youth and Adolescence, 33*, 59–69.

Fouad, Nadya A.; & Byars-Winston, Angela M. (2005). Cultural context of career choice: Meta-analysis of race/ethnicity differences. *Career Development Quarterly, 53*, 223–233.

Fountain, Tim. (2003). Sex at the click of a mouse. *New Statesman (1996), 133* (4702), 21.

Fouts, Gregory; & Vaughan, Kimberly. (2002). Television situation comedies: Male weight, negative references, and audience reactions. *Sex Roles, 46*, 439–442.

Fowers, Blaine J.; Applegate, Brooks; Tredinnick, Michael; & Slusher, Jason. (1996). His and her individualisms? Sex bias and individualism in psychologists' responses to case vignettes. *The Journal of Psychology, 130*, 159–174.

Frawley, Timothy J. (2008). Gender schema and prejudicial recall: How children misremember, fabricate, and distort gendered picture book information. *Journal of Research in Childhood Education, 22* (3), 291–303.

Fredrickson, Barbara L.; & Roberts, Tomi-Ann. (1997). Objectification theory: Toward understanding women's lived experiences and mental health risks. *Psychology of Women Quarterly, 21,* 173–206.

Freedman, Estelle B. (2002). *No turning back: The history of feminism and the future of women.* New York: Ballantine.

Freedman, Linda. (2008). Accepting the unacceptable: Religious parents and adult gay and lesbian children. *Families in Society, 89* (2), 237–244.

Freeman, Ellen W. (2003). Premenstrual syndrome and premenstrual dysphoric disorder: Definitions and diagnosis. *Psychoneuroendocrinology, 28* (Suppl. 3), 25–37.

Freud, Sigmund. (1964). Femininity. In James Strachey (Ed. and Trans.), *New introductory lectures on psychoanalysis* (p. 112–135). New York: Norton. (Original work published 1933)

Freud, Sigmund. (1989). Some psychical consequences of the anatomical distinction between the sexes. In Peter Gay (Ed.), *The Freud reader* (pp. 670–678). New York: Norton. (Original work published in 1925)

Fried, Linda P.; Kronmal, Richard A.; Newman, Anne B.; Bild, Diane E.; Mittelmark, Maurice B.; Polak, Joseph F.; et al. (1998). Risk factors for 5-year mortality in older adults: The cardiovascular health study. *Journal of the American Medical Association, 279,* 585–592.

Friedman, Carly K. Leaper, Campbell; & Bigler, Rebecca S. (2007). Do mothers' gender-related attitudes or comments predict young children's gender beliefs? *Parenting: Science & Practice, 7* (4), 357–366.

Friedman, Howard S.; Martin, Leslie R.; Tucker, Joan S.; Criqui, Michael H.; Kern, Margaret L.; Reynolds, Chandra A. (2008). Stability of physical activity across the lifespan. *Journal of Health Psychology, 13* (8), 1092–1104.

Frieze, Irene Hanson; Ferligoj, Anuška; Kogovešek, Tina; Rener, Tanja; Horvat, Jasna; & Šarlija, Nataša. (2003). Gender-role attitudes in university students in the United States, Slovenia, and Croatia. *Psychology of Women Quarterly, 27,* 256–261.

Frodi, Ann M.; Macaulay, Jacqueline; & Thome, Pauline R. (1977). Are women always less aggressive than men? A review of the experimental literature. *Psychological Bulletin, 84,* 634–660.

Frome, Pamela M.; Alfeld, Corinne J.; Eccles, Jacquelynne S.; & Barber, Bonnie L. (2008). Is the desire for a family-flexible job keeping young women out of male-dominated occupations? In Helen M. G. Watt & Jacquelynne S. Eccles (Eds.), *Gender and occupational outcomes: Longitudinal assessments of individual, social, and cultural influences* (pp. 195–214). Washington, DC: American Psychological Association.

Frye, Marilyn. (1997). Lesbian "sex." In Maxine Baca Zinn, Pierrette Hondagneu-Sotelo, & Michael A. Messner (Eds.), *Through the prism of difference: Readings on sex and gender* (pp. 205–209). Boston: Allyn & Bacon.

Fudge, Rachel; & Tringali, Juliana. (2007). Point/counterpoint: *Veronica Mars* and its feminist stereotypes. *Bitch Magazine: Feminist Response to Pop Culture, 35* (Spring), 15.

Fuegen, Kathleen; Biernat, Monica; Haines, Elizabeth; & Deaux, Kay. (2004). Mothers and fathers in the workplace: How gender and parental status influence judgments of job-related competence. *Journal of Social Issues, 60,* 737–754.

Fugère, Madeleine A.; Escoto, Carlos; Cousins, Alita J.; Riggs, Matt L.; & Haerich, Paul. (2008). Sexual attitudes and double standards: A literature review focusing on participant gender and ethnic background. *Sexuality and Culture: An Interdisciplinary Quarterly, 12* (3), 169–182.

Furman, Wyndol; Ho, Martin J.; & Low, Sabina M. (2007). The rocky road of adolescent romantic experience: Dating and adjustment. In Rutger C. M. E. Engles, Margaret Kerr, & Håkan Stattin (Eds). *Friends, lovers and groups: Key relationships in adolescence* (pp. 61–80). New York: Wiley.

Furman, Wyndol; Simon, Valerie A.; Shaffer, Laura; & Bouchey, Heather A. (2002). Adolescents' working models and styles for relationships with parents, friends, and romantic partners. *Child Development, 73,* 241–255.

Furnham, Adrian. (1999). Sex differences in self-estimates of lay dimensions of intelligence. *Psychological Reports, 85,* 349–350.

Furnham, Adrian; Callahan, Ines; & Akande, Debo. (2004). Self-estimates of intelligence: A study in two African countries. *Journal of Psychology, 138,* 265–285.

Furnham, Adrian; & Chamorro-Premuzic, Tomas. (2007). Self-assessed intelligence and confidence for the acquisition of skills. *Zeitschrift für Personalpsychologie, 6* (1), 28–36.

Furnham, Adrian; & Mak, Twiggy. (1999). Sex-role stereotyping in television commercials: A review and comparison of fourteen studies done on five continents over 25 years. *Sex Roles, 41,* 413–438.

Furnham, Adrian; Ndlovu, Nancy P. M.; & Mkhize, Nhlanhla. (2009). South African Zulus' beliefs about heir own and their children's intelligence. *South African Journal of Psychology, 39* (2), 157–168.

Furnham, Adrian; Pallangyo, Akunda E.; & Gunter, Barrie. (2001). Gender-role stereotyping in Zimbabwean television advertisements. *South African Journal of Psychology, 31,* 21–29.

Furnham, Adrian; Reeves, Emma; & Budhani, Salima. (2002). Parents think their sons are brighter than their daughters: Sex differences in parental self-estimations and estimations of their children's multiple intelligences. *Journal of Genetic Psychology, 163,* 24–39.

Furnham, Adrian; & Saar, Alexandra. (2005). Gender-role stereotyping in adult and children's television advertisements: A two-study comparison between Great Britain and Poland. *Communications: The European Journal of Communication Research, 30,* 73–90.

Fuwa, Makiko. (2004). Macro-level gender inequality and the division of household labor in 22 countries. *American Sociological Review, 69,* 751–767.

Gabbard, Glen O.; & Gabbard, Krin. (1999). *Psychiatry and the cinema* (2nd ed.). Washington, DC: American Psychiatric Press.

Gabbard, Krin. (2000, February 11). Therapy's "talking cure" still works—in Hollywood. *Chronicle of Higher Education*, p. B9.

Gadalla, Tahany M. (2009). Impact of marital dissolution on men's and women's incomes: A longitudinal study. *Journal of Divorce and Remarriage, 50* (1), 55–65.

Galdas, Paul M.; Cheater, Francine; & Marshall, Paul. (2005). Men and health help-seeking behaviour: Literature review. *Journal of Advanced Nursing, 49,* 616–622.

Galegher, Jolene; Sproull, Lee; & Kiesler, Sara. (1998). Legitimacy, authority, and community in electronic support groups. *Written Communications, 15,* 493.

Galician, Mary-Lou; & Merskin, Debra L. (Eds.). (2007). *Critical thinking bout sex, love, and romance in the mass media.* Mahwah, NJ: Erlbaum.

Galinsky, Ellen; Aumann, Kerstin; & Bond, James T. (2009). *Times are changing: Gender and generation at work and at home.* Families and Work Institute. Retrieved November 21, 2009, from http://www.familiesandwork. org/site/research/reports/Times_Are_Changing.pdf

Gallagher, Ann; Levin, Jutta; & Cahalan, Cara. (2002). *Cognitive patterns of gender differences on mathematics admissions tests* (ETS Report No. 02–19). Princeton, NJ: Educational Testing Service.

Ganahl, Dennis J.; Prinsen, Thomas J.; & Netzley, Sara Baker. (2003). A content analysis of prime time commercials: A contextual framework of gender representation. *Sex Roles, 49,* 545–551.

Garcia-Falgueras, Alicia; & Swaab, Dick F. (2008). A sex difference in the hypothalamic uncinate nucleus: Relationship to gender identity. *Brain: A Journal of Neurology, 12* (12), 3132–3146.

Gardyn, Rebecca. (2003). Got game? *American Demographics, 25* (8), 18.

Garner, David M.; & Garfinkel, Paul E. (1980). Sociocultural factors in the development of anorexia nervosa. *Psychological Medicine, 10,* 647–656.

Garner, David M.; Garfinkel, Paul E.; Schwartz, Donald M.; & Thompson, Michael G. (1980). Cultural expectations of thinness in women. *Psychological Reports, 47,* 483–491.

Garrahy, Deborah A. (2001). Three third-grade teachers' gender-related beliefs and behavior. *Elementary School Journal, 102,* 81–94.

Gartner, Audrey; & Riessman, Frank. (1998). Self-help. *Social Policy, 28* (3), 83–86.

Gatta, Mary; & Roos, Patricia. (2005). Rethinking occupational integration. *Sociological Forum, 20,* 369–402.

Gay, Peter. (1988). *Freud: A life for our time.* New York: Norton.

Geary, David C.; & Flinn, Mark V. (2002). Sex differences in behavioral and hormonal response to social threat: Commentary on Taylor et al. (2000). *Psychological Review, 109,* 745–750.

Geer, James H.; & Robertson, Gloria G. (2005). Implicit attitudes in sexuality: Gender differences. *Archives of Sexual Behavior, 34,* 671–677.

Gehlert, S.; Song, I. H.; Chang, C.-H.; & Hartlage, S. A. (2009). The prevalence of premenstrual dysphoric disorder in a randomly selected group of urban and rural women. *Psychological Medicine, 39* (1), 129–136.

Geiger, Brenda; Fischer, Michael; & Eshet, Yovav. (2004). Date-rape-supporting and victim-blaming attitudes among high school students in a multiethnic society. *Journal of Interpersonal Violence, 19,* 406–426.

Gelfer, Joseph. (2008). Identifying the Catholic men's movement. *Journal of Men's Studies, 16* (1), 41–56.

Gellatly, Judith; Bower, Peter; Hennessy, Sue; Richards, David; Gilbody, Simon; & Lovell, Karina. (2007). What makes self-help interventions effective in the management of depressive symptoms? Meta-analysis and metaregression. *Psychological Medicine, 37* (9), 1217–1228.

Gentile, Brittany; Grabe, Shelly; Dolan-Pascoe, Brenda; Twenge, Jean M.; Wells, Brooke E.; & Maitino, Alissa. (2009). Gender differences in domain-specific self-esteem: A meta-analysis. *Review of General Psychology, 13* (1), 34–45.

Gerbner, George; Gross, Larry; Morgan, Michael; & Signorielli, Nancy. (1994). Growing up with television: The cultivation perspective. In J. Bryant & D. Zillman (Eds.), *Media effects: Advances in theory and research* (pp. 17–41). Hillsdale, NJ: Erlbaum.

Gerhart, Barry. (1990). Gender differences in current and starting salaries: The role of performance, college major, and job title. *Industrial and Labor Relations Review, 43,* 418–433.

Germon, Jennifer E. (2008). Kinsey and the politics of bisexual authenticity. *Journal of Bisexuality, 8* (3/4), 243–258.

Gharaibeh, N. M. (2005). The psychiatrist's image in commercially available American movies. *Acta Psychiatrica Scandinavica, 111,* 316–319.

Gianakos, Irene. (2002). Predictors of coping with work stress: The influences of sex, gender role, social desirability, and locus of control. *Sex Roles, 46,* 149–158.

Gibb, Sheree J.; Fergusson, David M.; & Horwood, L. John. (2008). Gender differences in educational achievement to age 25. *Australian Journal of Education, 52* (1), 63–80.

Gibbons, Deborah; & Olk, Paul. (2003). Individual and structural origins of friendship and social position among professionals. *Journal of Personality and Social Psychology, 84,* 340–351.

Gibbons, Judith L.; Hamby, Beverly A.; & Dennis, Wanda D. (1997). Researching gender-role ideologies internationally and cross-culturally. *Psychology of Women Quarterly, 21,* 151–170.

Gibson, Pamela R. (2004). Histrionic personality. In Paula J. Caplan & Lisa Cosgrove (Eds.), *Bias in psychiatric diagnosis* (pp. 201–206). Lanham, MD: Jason Aronson.

Gilbert, Jackie; Carr-Ruffino, Norma; Ivancevich, John M.; & Lownes-Jackson, Millicent. (2003). An empirical examination of inter-ethnic stereotypes: Comparing Asian American and African American employees. *Public Personnel Management, 32*, 251–266.

Gilbert, Lucia A. (1980). Feminist therapy. In Annette M. Brodsky & Rachel Hare-Mustin (Eds.), *Women and psychotherapy* (pp. 245–265). New York: Guilford Press.

Gill, Aisha; & Mitra-Kahn, Trishima. (2008). From preference to prejudice: Daughter devaluation and the missing women phenomenon in South Asia and the UK. *Pakistan Journal of Women's Studies, 15* (1), 29–46.

Gilligan, Carol. (1982). *In a different voice: Psychological theory and women's development.* Cambridge, MA: Harvard University Press.

Ginn, Sheryl R.; & Pickens, Stefanie J. (2005). Relationships between spatial activities and scores on the mental rotation test as a function of sex. *Perceptual and Motor Skills, 100*, 877–881.

Ginsburg, Herbert; & Opper, Sylvia. (1969). *Piaget's theory of intellectual development: An introduction.* Englewood Cliffs, NJ: Prentice Hall.

Giordano, Peggy C.; Longmore, Monica A.; & Manning, Wendy D. (2006). Gender and the meanings of adolescent romantic relationships: A focus on boys. *American Sociological Review, 71*, 260–287.

Giuliano, Traci A.; Popp, Kathryn E.; & Knight, Jennifer L. (2000). Footballs versus Barbies: Childhood play activities as predictors of sport participation by women. *Sex Roles, 42*, 159–182.

Glascock, Jack. (2001). Gender roles on prime-time network television: Demographics and behaviors. *Journal of Broadcasting & Electronic Media, 45*, 656–669.

Glei, Dana A.; & Horiuchi, Shiro. (2007). The narrowing sex differential in life expectancy in high-income populations: Effects of differences in the age pattern of mortality. *Population Studies, 61* (2), 141–159.

Glick, Peter; & Fiske, Susan T. (1999). The ambivalence toward men inventory: Differentiating hostile and benevolent beliefs about men. *Psychology of Women Quarterly, 23*, 519–536.

Glick, Peter; & Fiske, Susan T. (2001). An ambivalent alliance: Hostile and benevolent sexism as complementary justification for gender inequality. *American Psychologist, 56*, 109–118.

Glick, Peter; Fiske, Susan T.; Mladinic, Antonio; Saiz, José L.; Abrams, Dominic; Masser, Barbara; et al. (2000). Beyond prejudice as simple antipathy: Hostile and benevolent sexism across cultures. *Journal of Personality and Social Psychology, 79*, 763–775.

Glick, Peter; Lameiras, Maria; Fiske, Susan T.; Eckes, Thomas; Masser, Barbara; Volpato, Chiara; et al. (2004). Bad but bold: Ambivalent attitudes toward men predict gender inequality in 16 nations. *Journal of Personality and Social Psychology, 86*, 713–728.

Goldberg, Linn; & Elliot, Diane L. (2007). The prevention of anabolic steroid use among adolescents. In J. Kevin Thompson & Guy Cafri (Eds.), *The muscular idea: Psychological, social, and medical perspectives* (pp. 161–180). Washington, DC: American Psychological Association.

Golding, Jacqueline M. (1999). Intimate partner violence as a risk factor for mental disorders: A meta-analysis. *Journal of Family Violence, 14*, 99–101.

Goldsmith, Ronald E.; & Matherly, Timothy A. (1988). Creativity and self-esteem: A multiple operationalization validity study. *Journal of Psychology, 122*, 47–56.

Gonda, W.; Telek, T.; Juhász, G.; Lazary, J.; Vargha, A.; & Bagdy, G. (2008). Patterns of mood change throughout the reproductive cycle in healthy women without premenstrual dysphoric disorder. *Progress in Neuro-Psychopharmacology & Biological Psychiatry, 32* (8), 1782–1788.

Gonzales, Patricia M.; Blanton, Hart; & Williams, Kevin J. (2002). The effects of stereotype threat and double-minority status on the test performance of Latino women. *Personality and Social Psychology Bulletin, 28*, 659–670.

González-Moreles, M. Gloria; Peiró, José M.; Rodríguez, Isabel; & Greenglass, Esther R. (2006). Coping and distress in organizations: The role of gender in work stress. *International Journal of Stress Management, 13*, 228–248.

Good, Glenn E.; Gilbert, Lucia A.; & Scher, Murray. (1990). Gender aware therapy: A synthesis of feminist therapy and knowledge about gender. *Journal of Counseling & Development, 68*, 376–380.

Good, Glenn E.; & Sherrod, Nancy B. (2001). The psychology of men and masculinity: Research status and future directions. In Rhoda Unger (Ed.), *Handbook of the psychology of women and gender* (pp. 201–214). New York: Wiley.

Good, Glenn E.; Thomson, Douglas A.; & Brathwaite, Allyson D. (2005). Men and therapy: Critical concepts, theoretical frameworks, and research recommendations. *Journal of Clinical Psychology, 61*, 699–711.

Goodenow, Carol; Szalacha, Laura; & Westheimer, Kim. (2006). School support groups, other school factors, and the safety of sexual minority adolescents. *Psychology in the Schools, 43*, 573–589.

Goodkind, Sara; Wallace, John M.; Shook, Jeffrey J.; Bachman, Jerald; & O'Malley, Patrick. (2009). Are girls really becoming more delinquent? Testing the gender convergence hypothesis by race and ethnicity, 1976–2005. *Children and Youth Services Review, 31* (8), 885–895.

Goodman, Lisa A.; Smyth, Katya Fels; Borges, Angela M.; & Singer, Rachel. (2009). When crises collide: How intimate partner violence and poverty intersect to shape women's mental health and coping? *Trauma, Violence and Abuse, 10* (4), 306–329.

Goodwin, Stephanie A.; & Fiske, Susan T. (2001). Power and gender: the double-edged sword of ambivalence. In Rhoda K. Unger (Ed.), *Handbook of the psychology of women and gender* (pp. 358–366). New York: Wiley.

Gorski, Roger A. (1987). Sex differences in the rodent brain: Their nature and origin. In June M. Reinisch, Leonard A. Rosenblum, & Stephanie A. Sanders (Eds.), *Masculinity/femininity: Basic perspectives* (pp. 37–67). New York: Oxford University Press.

Gosse, Douglas; Parr, Michael; & Allison, John. (2008). Researching the halted paths of male primary school teacher candidates. *Journal of Men's Studies, 16* (1), 57–68.

Gottman, John M. (1991). Predicting the longitudinal course of marriages. *Journal of Marriage and Family Therapy, 17,* 3–7.

Gottman, John M. (1998). Psychology and the study of marital processes. *Annual Review of Psychology, 49,* 169–187.

Gottman, John M.; & Driver, Janice L. (2005). Dysfunctional marital conflict and everyday marital interaction. *Journal of Divorce and Remarriage, 43* (3/4), 63–78.

Gottman, John M.; Levenson, Robert W.; Gross, James; Frederickson, Barbara L.; McCoy, Kim; Rosenthal, Leah; et al. (2003). Correlates of gay and lesbian couples' relationship satisfaction and relationship dissolution. *Journal of Homosexuality, 45,* 23–43.

Gottman, John M.; & Notarius, Clifford I. (2000). Decade review: Observing marital interaction. *Journal of Marriage and Family, 62,* 927–947.

Gottman, John; & Silver, Nan. (2000). *Seven principles for making marriages work.* New York: Crown.

Gottman, John M.; Swanson, Catherine; & Swanson, Kristin. (2002). A general systems theory of marriage: Nonlinear difference equation modeling of marital interaction. *Personality and Social Psychology Review, 6,* 326–340.

Gough, Brendan; & Conner, Mark T. (2006). Barriers to healthy eating amongst men: A qualitative analysis. *Social Science and Medicine, 62,* 387–395.

Gould, Ketayun H. (2000). Beyond *Jones v. Clinton:* Sexual harassment law and social work. *Social Work, 45,* 237–250.

Gould, Stephen Jay. (2000). Deconstructing the "science wars" by reconstructing an old mold. *Science, 287,* 253–259.

Gove, Walter R. (1984). Gender differences in mental and physical illness: The effects of fixed roles and nurturant roles. *Social Science and Medicine, 19* (2), 77–84.

Govender, Sandra. (2005). Sexual harassment: The South African perspective. *International Journal of Discrimination and the Law, 7,* 229–251.

Grace, Diana M.; David, Barbara J.; & Ryan, Michelle K. (2008). Investigating preschoolers' categorical thinking about gender through imitation, attention, and the use of self-categories. *Child Development, 79* (6), 1928–1941.

Gradus, Jaimie L.; Street, Amy E.; Kelly, Kacie; & Stafford, Jane. (2008). Sexual harassment experiences and harmful alcohol use in a military sample: Differences in gen*der and mediating role of depression. Journal of Studies on Alcohol, 69* (3), 348–351.

Graham, John W.; & Smith, Steven A. (2005). Gender differences in employment and earnings in science and engineering in the US. *Economics of Education Review, 24,* 341–354.

Graham, Kathryn; & Wells, Samantha. (2001). The two worlds of aggression for men and women. *Sex Roles, 45,* 595–622.

Granello, Darcy Haag; & Pauley, Pamela S. (2000). Television viewing habits and their relationship to tolerance toward people with mental illness. *Journal of Mental Health Counseling, 22,* 162–175.

Gray, John. (1992). *Men are from Mars, women are from Venus.* New York: HarperCollins.

Green, Richard. (1987). *The "sissy boy syndrome" and the development of homosexuality.* New Haven, CT: Yale University Press.

Green, Robert G.; Hamlin, Hailey; Ogden, Vickie; & Walters, Kim. (2004). Some normative data on mental health professionals' attitudes about racial minorities and women. *Psychological Reports, 94,* 485–494.

Greenberg, Bradley S.; & Worrell, Tracy R. (2007). New faces on television: A 12-season replication. *Howard Journal of Communications, 18* (4), 277–290.

Greene, Beverly. (1994). African American women. In Lillian Comas-Díaz & Beverly Greene (Eds.), *Women of color: Integrating ethnic and gender identities in psychotherapy* (pp. 10–29). New York: Guilford Press.

Greene, Melissa L.; & Way, Niobe. (2005). Self-esteem trajectories among ethnic minority adolescents: A growth curve analysis of the patterns and predictors of change. *Journal of Research on Adolescence, 15,* 151–177.

Greenfield, Lawrence A. (1996). *Child victimizers: Violent offenders and their victims.* Washington, DC: U.S. Department of Justice.

Greenstein, Theodore N.; & Davis, Shannon N. (2006). Cross-national variations in divorce: Effects of women's power, prestige and dependence. *Journal of Comparative Family Studies, 37,* 253–273.

Greenwald, Anthony G. (1975). Consequences of prejudice against the null hypothesis. *Psychological Bulletin, 82,* 1–20.

Greenwald, Anthony G.; & Banaji, Mahzarin R. (1995). Implicit social cognition: Attitudes, self-esteem, and stereotypes. *Psychological Review, 102,* 4–27.

Greenwald, Anthony G.; & Farnham, Shelly D. (2000). Using the Implicit Association Test to measure self-esteem and self-concept. *Journal of Personality and Social Psychology, 79,* 1022–1038.

Greenwood, Gregory L.; Relf, Michael V.; Huang, Bu; Pollack, Lance M.; Canchola, Jesse A.; & Catania, Joseph A. (2002). Battering victimization among a probability-based sample of men who have sex with men. *American Journal of Public Health, 92,* 1964–1969.

Gregory, Cria O.; Blanck, Heidi M.; Gillespie, Cathleen; Maynard, L. Michele; & Serdula, Mary K. (2008). Perceived health risk of excess body weight among overweight and obese men and women: Differences by sex. *Preventive Medicine, 47* (1), 46–52.

Gregory, Robert J. (1987). *Adult intellectual assessment.* Boston: Allyn & Bacon.

Greven, David. (2002). Dude, where's my gender? Contemporary teen comedies and new forms of American masculinity. *Cineaste, 27* (3), 14–22.

Grogan, Sarah; & Richards, Helen. (2002). Body image: Focus groups with boys and men. *Men & Masculinities, 4,* 219–232.

Gross, Alan M.; Winslett, Andrea; Roberts, Miguel; & Gohm, Carol L. (2006). An examination of sexual violence against college women. *Violence against Women, 12,* 288–300.

Gross, Bruce. (2003). A touchy subject: Sexual intimacies between therapists and clients. *Annals of the American Psychotherapy Association, 6,* 51.

Gross, Rita M. (2003). What went wrong: Feminism and freedom from the prison of gender roles. *Cross Currents, 53,* 8–20.

Grzywacz, Joseph G.; Quandt, Sara A.; Arcury, Thomas A.; & Marín, Antonio. (2005). The work-family challenge and mental health. *Community, Work and Family, 8,* 271–279.

Guanipa, Carmen; & Woolley, Scott R. (2000). Gender biases and therapists' conceptualization of couple difficulties. *American Journal of Family Therapy, 28,* 181–192.

Guarnaccia, Peter J.; Martinez, Igda; Ramirez, Rafael; & Canino, Glorisa. (2005). Are ataques de nervios in Puerto Rican children associated with psychiatric disorder? *Journal of the American Academy of Child and Adolescent Psychiatry, 44,* 1184–1192.

Güngör, Gökce; & Biernat, Monica. (2009). Gender bias or motherhood disadvantage? Judgments of blue collar mothers and fathers in the workplace. *Sex Roles, 60* (3/4), 232–246.

Gur, Ruben C.; Alsop, David; Glahn, David; Petty, Richard; Swanson, Charlie L.; Maldjian, Joseph A.; et al. (2000). An fMRI study of sex differences in regional activation to a verbal and a spatial task. *Brain and Language, 74,* 157–170.

Gur, Ruben C.; Mozley, Lyn Harper; Mozley, P. David; Resnick, Susan M.; Kapr, Joel S.; Alavi, Abass; et al. (1995). Sex differences in regional glucose metabolism during a resting state. *Science, 267,* 528–531.

Gutek, Barbara A. (1985). *Sex and the workplace.* San Francisco: Jossey-Bass.

Gutek, Barbara A. (2001). Women and paid work. *Psychology of Women Quarterly, 25,* 379–393.

Gutek, Barbara A.; & Done, Robert S. (2001). Sexual harassment. In Rhoda K. Unger (Ed.), *Handbook of the psychology of women and gender* (pp. 367–387). New York: Wiley.

Hackett, Gail; Enns, Carolyn Z.; & Zetzer, Heidi A. (1992). Reactions of women to nonsexist and feminist counseling: Effects of counselor orientation and mode of information delivery. *Journal of Counseling Psychology, 39,* 321–330.

Haddock, Shelley A.; MacPhee, David; & Zimmerman, Toni Schindler. (2001). AAMFT master series tapes: An analysis of the inclusion of feminist principles into family therapy practice. *Journal of Marital and Family Therapy, 27,* 487–500.

Haenfler, Ross. (2004). Manhood in contradiction: The two faces of straight edge. *Men and Masculinities, 7,* 77–99.

Halari, Rozmin; Hines, Melissa; Kumari, Veena; Mehrotra, Ravi; Wheeler, Mike; Ng, Virginia; et al. (2005). Sex differences and individual differences in cognitive performance and their relationship to endogenous gonadal hormones and gonadotropins. *Behavioral Neuroscience, 119,* 104–117.

Hales, Diane. (2005, October). Big boys don't cry—and other myths about men and their emotions. *Reader's Digest, 167,* 102–107.

Hall, Gordon C. Nagayama; Teten, Andra L.; DeGarmo, David S.; Sue, Stanley; & Stephens, Kari A. (2005). Ethnicity, culture, and sexual aggression: Risk and protective factors. *Journal of Consulting and Clinical Psychology, 73,* 830–840.

Hall, Judith A.; Coats, Erik J.; & Lebeau, Lavonia Smith. (2005). Nonverbal behavior and the vertical dimension of social relations: A meta-analysis. *Psychological Bulletin, 131,* 898–924.

Hall, Lynn S.; & Love, Craig T. (2003). Finger-length ratios in female monozygotic twins discordant for sexual orientation. *Archives of Sexual Behavior, 32,* 23–28.

Hall, Margery J.; & Tidwell, Wendell C. (2003). Internet recovery for substance abuse and alcoholism: An exploratory study of service users. *Journal of Substance Abuse Treatment, 24,* 161–167.

Hall, Ronald E. (2009). Cool pose, Black manhood, and juvenile delinquency. *Journal of Human Behavior in the Social Environment, 19* (5), 531–539.

Hall, Ruth L. (2008). Sweating it out: The good news and the bad news about women in sport. In Joan C. Chrisler, Carla Golden, & Patricia D. Rozee (Eds.), *Lectures on the psychology of women* (4th ed., pp. 96–115). New York: McGraw-Hill.

Hall, Ruth L.; & Greene, Beverly. (2003). Contemporary African American families. In Louise B. Silverstein & Thelma Jean Goodrich (Eds.), *Feminist family therapy: Empowerment in social context* (pp. 107–120). Washington, DC: American Psychological Association.

Halpern, Diane F. (2000). *Sex differences in cognitive abilities* (3rd ed.). Mahwah, NJ: Erlbaum.

Halpern, Diane F. (2004). A cognitive-process taxonomy for sex differences in cognitive abilities. *Current Directions in Psychological Science, 13,* 135–139.

Halpern, Diane F.; Benbow, Camilla P.; Geary, David C.; Gur, Ruben C.; Hyde, Janet Shibley; & Gernsbacher, Morton Ann. (2007). The science of sex differences in science and mathematics. *Psychological Science in the Public Interest, 8* (1), 1–51.

Halpern-Felsher, Bonnie L.; Cornell, Joki L.; Kropp, Rhonda Y.; & Tschann, Jeanne M. (2005). Oral versus vaginal sex among adolescents: Perceptions, attitudes, and behavior. *Pediatrics*, *115*, 845–851.

Halrynjo, Sigtona; & Lyng, Selma Therese. (2009). Preferences, constraints or schemas of devotion? Exploring Norwegian mothers' withdrawals from high-commitment careers. *British Journal of Sociology*, *60* (2), 321–343.

Hamel, John. (2009). Toward a gender-inclusive conception of intimate partner violence research and theory: Part 2—New directions. *International Journal of Men's Health*, *8* (1), 41–59.

Hammack, Phillip L. (2005). The development of human sexual orientation: An integrative paradigm. *Human Development*, *48*, 267–290.

Hampel, Petra; & Petermann, Franz. (2005). Age and gender effects on coping in children and adolescents. *Journal of Youth and Adolescence*, *34*, 73–83.

Harding, Sandra. (2001). Comment on Walby's "Against epistemological chasms: The science question in feminism revisited": Can democratic values and interests ever play a rationally justifiable role in the evaluation of scientific work? *Signs*, *26*, 511–525.

Harding, Sandra. (2004). A socially relevant philosophy of science? Resources from standpoint theory's controversiality. *Hypatia*, *19*, 25–47.

Harding, Sandra. (2006). *Science and social inequality: Feminist and postcolonial issues*. Chicago: University of Illinois Press.

Harding, Sandra; & Norberg, Kathryn. (2005). New feminist approaches to social science methodologies: An introduction. *Signs*, *30* (4), 2009–2015.

Hargreaves, Melanie; Homer, Matt; & Swinnerton, Bronwen. (2008). A comparison of performance and attitudes in mathematics amongst the 'gifted'. Are boys better at mathematics or do they just think they are? *Assessment in Education: Principles, Policy and Practice*, *15* (1), 19–38,

Hare-Mustin, Rachel T.; & Marecek, Jeanne. (1988). The meaning of difference: Gender theory, postmodernism, and psychology. *American Psychologist*, *43*, 455–464.

Harlow, Harry F. (1959). Love in infant monkeys. *Scientific American*, *200* (6), 68–74.

Harlow, Harry F. (1971). *Learning to love*. San Francisco: Albion.

Harlow, Harry F.; & Harlow, Margaret Kuenne. (1962). Social deprivation in monkeys. *Scientific American*, *207*, 136–146.

Harmon, Robert J.; Bender, Bruce G.; Linden, Mary G.; & Robinson, Arthur. (1998). Transition from adolescence to early adulthood: Adaptation and psychiatric status of women with 47, XXX. *Journal of the American Academy of Child and Adolescent Psychiatry*, *37*, 286–291.

Harper, Marcel; & Schoeman, Wilhelm J. (2003). Influences of gender as a basic-level category in person perception on the gender belief system. *Sex Roles*, *49*, 517–526.

Harris, Judith Rich. (1998). *The nurture assumption: Why children turn out the way they do*. New York: Free Press.

Harrison, Kristen. (2003). Television viewers' ideal body proportions: The case of the curvaceously thin woman. *Sex Roles*, *48*, 255–264.

Harwood, Jake; & Anderson, Karen. (2002). The presence and portrayal of social groups of prime-time television. *Communication Reports*, *15*, 81–98.

Hatfield, Elaine; & Rapson, Richard L. (1996). *Love and sex: Cross-cultural perspectives*. Boston: Allyn & Bacon.

Hatoum, Jodette; & Belle, Deborah. (2004). Mags and abs: Media consumption and bodily concerns in men. *Sex Roles*, *51*, 397–407.

Hatzenbuehler, Mark L.; Nolen-Hoeksema, Susan; & Dovidio, John. (2009). How does stigma "get under the skin"? The medicating role of emotion regulation. *Psychological Science*, *20* (10), 1282–1289.

Hausenblas, Heather A.; & Symons Downs, Danielle. (2002). Exercise dependence: A systematic review. *Psychology of Sport and Exercise*, *3*, 89–123.

Hausmann, Markus. (2005). Hemispheric asymmetry in spatial attention across the menstrual cycle. *Neuropsychologia*, *43*, 1559–1567.

Hawley, Patricia H.; & Vaughn, Brian E. (2003). Aggression and adaptive functioning: The bright side to bad behavior. *Merrill-Palmer Quarterly*, *49*, 239–242.

Hayman, Jeremy R. (2009). Flexible work arrangements: Exploring the linkages between perceived usability of flexible work schedules and work/life balance. *Community, Work and Family*, *12* (3), 327–338.

Heckert, Teresa M.; Droste, Heather E.; Adams, Patrick J.; Griffin, Christopher M.; Roberts, Lisa L.; Mueller, Michael A.; et al. (2002). Gender differences in anticipated salary: Role of salary estimates for others, job characteristics, career paths, and job inputs. *Sex Roles*, *47*, 139–151.

Heesacker, Martin; Wester, Stephen R.; Vogel, David L.; Wentzel, Jeffrey T.; Mejia-Millan, Cristina M.; & Goodholm, Carl Robert, Jr. (1999). Gender-based emotional stereotyping. *Journal of Counseling Psychology*, *46*, 483–495.

Hegarty, Peter; & Pratto, Felicia. (2004). The differences that norms make: Empiricism, social constructionism, and the interpretation of group differences. *Sex Roles*, *50*, 445–453.

Heiby, Elaine M.; DeLeon, Patrick H.; & Anderson, Timothy. (2004). A debate on prescription privileges for psychologists. *Professional Psychology: Research and Practice*, *35*, 336–344.

Heilman, Madeline E.; Black, Caryn J.; Martell, Richard F.; & Simon, Michael C. (1989). Has anything changed? Current characterizations of men, women, and managers. *Journal of Applied Psychology*, *74*, 935–942.

Heilman, Madeline E.; & Okimoto, Tyler G. (2008). Motherhood: A potential source of bias in employment decisions. *Journal of Applied Psychology*, *93* (1), 189-198.

Heilman, Madeline E.; Wallen, Aaron S.; Fuchs, Daniella; & Tamkins, Melinda M. (2004). Penalties for success: Reactions to women who succeed at male gender-typed tasks. *Journal of Applied Psychology, 89*, 416–427.

Heise, Lori; Ellsberg, Mary; & Gottemoeller, Megan. (1999). Ending violence against women. *Population Reports*, Series L, No. 11. Baltimore: Johns Hopkins University, School of Public Health, Population Information Program.

Hendryx, Michael S.; & Ahern, Melissa M. (1997). Mental health functioning and community problems. *Journal of Community Psychology, 25*, 147–157.

Hentges, Beth A.; Bartsch, Robert A.; & Meier, Jo A. (2007). Gender representation in commercials as a function of target audience age. *Communication Research Reports, 24* (1), 55–62.

Herbenick, Debra; Reece, Michael; Sanders, Stephanie; Dodge, Brian; Ghassemi, Annahita; & Fortenberry, J. Dennis. (2009). Prevalence and characteristics of vibrator use by women in the United States: Results from a nationally representative study. *Journal of Sexual Medicine, 6* (7), 1857–1866.

Herdt, Gilbert H. (1981). *Guardians of the flutes: Idioms of masculinity.* New York: McGraw-Hill.

Herdt, Gilbert H. (Ed.). (1994). *Third sex, third gender: Beyond sexual dimorphism in culture and history.* New York: Zone Books.

Herdt, Gilbert H.; & Boxer, Andrew. (1995). Bisexuality: Toward a comparative theory of identities and culture. In Richard G. Parker & John H. Gagnon (Eds.), *Concerning sexuality: Approaches to sex research in a postmodern world* (pp. 69–83). New York: Routledge.

Herek, Gregory M. (2002). Heterosexuals' attitudes toward bisexual men and women in the United States. *Journal of Sex Research, 39*, 264–274.

Herlitz, Agneta; & Rehman, Jenny. (2008). Sex differences in episodic memory. *Current Directions in Psychological Science, 17* (1), 52–56.

Heron, Melonie; Hoyert, Donna L.; Murphy, Sherry L.; Xu, Jiaquan; Kochanek, Kenneth D.; & Tejada-Vera, Betzaida. (2009). Deaths: Final data for 2006. *National Vital Statistics Report, 57* (14), 1–136.

Herrmann, Douglas J.; Crawford, Mary; & Holdsworth, Michelle. (1992). Gender-linked differences in everyday memory performance. *British Journal of Psychology, 83*, 221–231.

Herzig, Abbe H. (2004). "Slaughtering this beautiful math": Graduate women choosing and leaving mathematics. *Gender and Education, 16*, 379–395.

Hetherington, E. Mavis; & Kelly, John. (2002). *For better or worse: Divorce reconsidered.* New York: Norton.

Heusel, Colleen; & Dabbs, James M., Jr. (1996, August). *Testosterone predicts engineer employment status in an oilfield service company.* Paper presented at the 104th annual convention of the American Psychological Association, Toronto, Canada.

Hewitt, Belinda. (2009). Which spouse initiates marital separation when there are children involved? *Journal of Marriage and Family, 71* (2), 362–372.

Heyman, Gail D.; & Legare, Cristine H. (2004). Children's beliefs about gender differences in the academic and social domains. *Sex Roles, 50*, 227–239.

Heyman, Richard E.; Hunt-Martorano, Ashley N.; Malik, Jill; & Slep, Amy M. Smith. (2009). Desired change in couples: Gender differences and effects on communication. *Journal of Family Psychology, 23* (4), 474–484.

Heyn, Eve. (2003, September 1). The daddy track: How more and more men are seeking a better way to balance work and family. *Parenting, 27* (7), 150.

Hill, Melanie S.; & Fischer, Ann R. (2001). Does entitlement mediate the link between masculinity and rape-related variables? *Journal of Counseling Psychology, 48*, 39–50.

Hill, Shirley A. (2002). Teaching and doing gender in African American families. *Sex Roles, 47*, 493–506.

Hines, Melissa; Ahmed, S. Faisal; & Hughes, Ieuan A. (2003). Psychological outcomes and gender-related development in complete androgen insensitivity syndrome. *Archives of Sexual Behavior, 32*, 93–101.

Hines, Melissa; Brook, Charles; & Conway, Gerard S. (2004). Androgen and psychosexual development: Core gender identity, sexual orientation, and recalled childhood gender role behavior in women and men with congenital adrenal hyperplasia (CAH). *Journal of Sex Research, 41*, 75–81.

Hines, Melissa; Golombok, Susan; Rust, John; Johnston, Katie J.; & Golding, Jean. (2002). Testosterone during pregnancy and gender role behavior of preschool children: A longitudinal, population study. *Child Development, 73*, 1678–1689.

Hiort, Olaf; Thyen, Ute; & Holterhus, Paul-Martin. (2005). The basis of gender assignment in disorders of somatosexual differentiation. *Hormone Research, 64* (Suppl. 2), 18–22.

Hobson, Katherine. (2006, March 6). Hello, his and her healthcare. *U.S. News & World Report, 140* (8), 74–76.

Hochschild, Arlie. (1997). *The time bind.* New York: Metropolitan Books.

Hochschild, Arlie (with Machung, Anne). (1989). *The second shift: Working parents and the revolution at home.* New York: Viking.

Hochwarter, Wayne A.; Perrewe, Pamela L.; & Dawkins, Mark C. (1995). Gender differences in perceptions of stress-related variables: Do the people make the place or does the place make the people? *Journal of Managerial Issues, 7*, 62–74.

Hofer, Myron A. (2006). Psychobiological roots of early attachment. *Current Directions in Psychological Science, 15*, 84–88.

Hoffman, Rose Marie. (2001). The measurement of masculinity and femininity: Historical perspective and implications for counseling. *Journal of Counseling and Development, 79*, 472–485.

Hoffnung, Michele. (2004). Wanting it all: Career, marriage, and motherhood during college-educated women's 20s. *Sex Roles, 50,* 711–723.

Hogshead-Makar, Nancy. (2003, July). The ongoing battle over Title IX. *USA Today Magazine, 132,* 64–66.

Holahan, Charles J.; Moos, Rudolf H.; Holahan, Carole K.; Cronkite, Ruth C.; & Randall, Patrick K. (2001). Drinking to cope, emotional distress and alcohol use and abuse: A ten-year model. *Journal of Studies on Alcohol, 62,* 190–198.

Holahan, Charles J.; Moos, Rudolf H.; Holahan, Carole K.; Cronkite, Ruth C.; & Randall, Patrick K. (2003). Drinking to cope and alcohol use and abuse in unipolar depression: A 10-year model. *Journal of Abnormal Psychology, 112,* 159–165.

Holahan, Charles J.; Moos, Rudolf H.; Holahan, Carole K.; Cronkite, Ruth C.; & Randall, Patrick K. (2004). Unipolar depression, life context vulnerabilities, and drinking to cope. *Journal of Consulting and Clinical Psychology, 72,* 269–275.

Holmberg, Diane; & Blair, Karen L. (2009). Sexual desire, communication, satisfaction, and preferences of men and women in same-sex versus mixed-sex relationships. *Journal of Sex Research, 46* (1), 57–66.

Holroyd, Jean Corey; & Brodsky, Annette M. (1977). Psychologists' attitudes and practices regarding erotic and nonerotic physical contact with patients. *American Psychologist, 32,* 843–849.

Holt-Lunstad, Julianne; Birmingham, Wendy; & Jones, Brandon Q. (2008). Is there something unique about marriage? The relative impact of marital status, relationship quality, and network social support on ambulatory blood pressure and mental health. *Annals of Behavioral Medicine, 35* (2), 239–244.

Honda, Akio; & Nihei, Yoshiaki. (2009). Sex differences in object location memory: The female advantage of immediate detection of changes. *Learning & Individual Differences, 19* (2), 234–237.

Hong, Zuway-R.; Veach, Patricia McCarthy; & Lawrenz, Frances. (2003). An investigation of the gender stereotyped thinking of Taiwanese secondary school boys and girls. *Sex Roles, 48,* 495–504.

Horn, Stacey S. (2007). Adolescents' acceptance of same-sex peers based on sexual orientation and gender expression. *Journal of Youth & Adolescence, 36* (3), 363–371.

Horner, Martina. (1969, November). Fail: Bright women. *Psychology Today,* pp. 36–38, 62.

Horney, Karen. (1939). *New ways in psychoanalysis.* New York: Norton.

Horror show: Scary movies are multiplying faster than ever, and getting increasingly sadistic. (2006, April 3). *Newsweek,* p. 60.

Horsfall, Jan. (2001). Gender and mental illness: An Australian overview. *Issues in Mental Health Nursing, 22,* 421–438.

Hort, Barbara E.; Fagot, Beverly, I.; & Leinbach, Mary D. (1990). Are people's notions of maleness more stereotypically framed than their notions of femaleness? *Sex Roles, 23,* 197–212.

Hort, Barbara E.; Leinbach, Mary D.; & Fagot, Beverly I. (1991). Is there coherence among the cognitive components of gender acquisition? *Sex Roles, 24,* 195–207.

Horvath, Michael; & Ryan, Ann Marie. (2003). Antecedents and potential moderators of the relationship between attitudes and hiring discrimination on the basis of sexual orientation. *Sex Roles, 48,* 115–130.

House, James S. (1984). Barriers to work stress: I. Social support. In W. Doyle Gentry, Herbert Benson, & Charles deWolff (Eds.), *Behavioral medicine: Work, stress, and health.* The Hague, Netherlands: Nijhoff.

Howard, Donna E.; Wang, Min Qi; & Yan, Fang. (2007). Prevalence and psychosocial correlates of forced sexual intercourse among U.S. high school adolescents. *Adolescence, 42* (168), 629–643.

Howard, Judith A.; Blumstein, Philip; & Schwartz, Pepper. (1987). Social or evolutionary theories? Some observations on preferences in human mate selection. *Journal of Personality and Social Psychology, 53,* 194–200.

Hrdy, Sarah Blaffer. (1981). *The woman that never evolved.* Cambridge, MA: Harvard University Press.

Hrdy, Sarah Blaffer. (1986). Empathy, polyandry, and the myth of the coy female. In Ruth Bleier (Ed.), *Feminist approaches to science* (pp. 119–146). New York: Pergamon Press.

Hrdy, Sarah Blaffer. (1999). *Mother nature: A history of mothers, infants, and natural selection.* New York: Pantheon Books.

Hsiao, Cheng-Cheng; Liu, Chia-Yih; & Hsiao, Mei-Chun. (2004). No correlation of depression and anxiety to plasma estrogen and progesterone levels in patients with premenstrual dysphoric disorder. *Psychiatry and Clinical Neurosciences, 58,* 593–599.

Hsuing, Robert C. (2000). The best of both worlds: An online self-help group hosted by a mental health professional. *CyberPsychology & Behavior, 3,* 935–950.

Hubbard, Julie A.; Smithmyer, Catherine M.; Ramsden, Sally R.; Parker, Elizabeth H.; Flanagan, Kelly D.; Dearing, Karen F.; et al. (2002). Observational, physiological, and self-report measures of children's anger: Relations to reactive versus proactive aggression. *Child Development, 73,* 1101–1118.

Hubbard, Ruth; & Wald, Elijah. (1993). *Exploding the gene myth.* Boston: Beacon Press.

Hudak, Mary A. (1993). Gender schema theory revisited: Men's stereotypes of American women. *Sex Roles, 28,* 279–293.

Huesmann, L. Rowell; Eron, Leonard D.; Lefkowitz, Monroe M.; & Walder, Leopold O. (1984). Stability of aggression over time and generations. *Developmental Psychology, 20,* 1120–1134.

Huesmann, L. Rowell; Moise-Titus, Jessica; Podolski, Cheryl-Lynn; & Eron, Leonard D. (2003). Longitudinal relations between children's exposure to TV violence and their aggressive and violent behavior in young adulthood: 1977–1992. *Developmental Psychology*, 39, 201–221.

Hulbert, Ann. (2005, April 3). Boy problems. *New York Times Magazine*, np.

Hultin, Mia. (2003). Some take the glass escalator, some hit the glass ceiling? *Work and Occupation*, 30, 30–61.

Humphreys, Keith. (2004). *Circles of recovery: Self-help organizations for addictions.* New York: Cambridge University Press.

Hunt, Morton. (1974). *Sexual behavior in the 1970s.* Chicago: Playboy Press.

Hyde, Janet Shibley. (1981). How large are cognitive gender differences? A meta-analysis using ω^2 and *d. American Psychologist*, 36, 892–901.

Hyde, Janet Shibley. (1996). Where are the gender differences? Where are the gender similarities? In David M. Buss & Neil M. Malamuth (Eds.), *Sex, power, conflict: Evolutionary and feminist perspectives* (pp. 107–118). New York: Oxford University Press.

Hyde, Janet Shibley. (2005a). The gender similarities hypothesis. *American Psychologist*, 60, 581–592.

Hyde, Janet Shibley. (2005b). The genetics of sexual orientation. In Janet Shibley Hyde (Ed.), *Biological substrates of human sexuality* (pp. 9–20). Washington, DC: American Psychological Association.

Hyde, Janet Shibley. (2007a). New directions in the study of gender similarities and differences. *Current Directions in Psychological Science*, 16 (5), 259–263.

Hyde, Janet Shibley. (2007b). Women in science: Similarities in abilities and sociocultural forces. In Stephen J. Ceci & Wendy M. Williams (Eds.), *Why aren't more women in science: Top researchers debate the evidence* (pp. 131–145). Washington, DC: American Psychological Association.

Hyde, Janet Shibley; & Durik, Amanda M. (2001). Psychology of women and gender in the 21st century. In Jane S. Halonen & Stephen F. Davis (Eds.), *The many faces of psychological research in the 21st century.* Retrieved December 12, 2001, from http://teachpsych.lemoyne.edu/teachpsych/faces/facesindex.html

Hyde, Janet Shibley; Fennema, Elizabeth; & Lamon, Susan J. (1990). Gender differences in mathematics performance: A meta-analysis. *Psychological Bulletin*, 107, 139–155.

Hyde, Janet Shibley; & Jaffee, Sara R. (2000). Becoming a heterosexual adult: The experiences of young women. *Journal of Social Issues*, 56, 283–296.

Hyde, Janet Shibley; & Kling, Kristin C. (2001). Women, motivation, and achievement. *Psychology of Women Quarterly*, 25, 364–378.

Hyde, Janet Shibley; & Linn, Marcia C. (1988). Gender differences in verbal ability: A meta-analysis. *Psychological Bulletin*, 104, 53–69.

Hyde, Janet Shibley; Mezulis, Amy H.; & Abramson, Lyn Y. (2008). The ABCs of depression: Integrating affective, biological, and cognitive models to explain the emergence of the gender difference in depression. *Psychological Review*, 115 (2), 291–313.

Iervolino, Alessandra C.; Hines, Melissa; Golombok, Susan E.; Rust, John; & Plomin, Robert. (2005). Genetic and environmental influences on sex-typed behavior during the preschool years. *Child Development*, 76, 826–840.

Imperato-McGinley, Julianne; Guerrero, Luis; Gautier, Teofilo; & Peterson, Ralph E. (1974). Steroid 5-a-reductase deficiency in man: An inherited form of male pseudohermaphroditism. *Science*, 186, 1213–1215.

Independent TeleWeb. (n.d.). *Just a question of taste.* Retrieved May 9, 2006, from http://www.users.zetnet.co.uk/itw/features/Comm3.html

Ireland, Doug. (1999, June 14). Gay ed for kids. *The Nation*, 268 (22), 8.

Ivory, James D. (2006). Still a man's game: Gender representation in online reviews of video games. *Mass Communication and Society*, 9, 103–114.

Iwama, Akiko. (2005). Social stratification and the division of household labor in Japan: The effect of wives' work on the division of labor among dual-earner families. *International Journal of Japanese Sociology*, 14, 15–31.

Jack, Dana Crowley. (1991). *Silencing the self: Women and depression.* Cambridge, MA: Harvard University Press.

Jack, Dana Crowley. (1999). Silencing the self: Inner dialogues and outer realities. In Thomas Joiner and James C. Coyne (Eds.), *The interactional nature of depression: Advances in interpersonal approaches* (pp. 221–246). Washington, DC: American Psychological Association.

Jacklin, Carol Nagy; & Maccoby, Eleanor E. (1978). Social behavior at thirty-three months in same-sex and mixed-sex dyads. *Child Development*, 49, 557–569.

Jackson, Dorothy W.; & Tein, Jenn-Yunn. (1998). Adolescents' conceptualization of adult roles: Relationships with age, gender, work goal, and maternal employment. *Sex Roles*, 38, 987–1008.

Jackson, Helene; & Nuttall, Ronald L. (2001). A relationship between childhood sexual abuse and professional sexual misconduct. *Professional Psychology: Research and Practice*, 32, 200–204.

Jackson, J. Kasi. (2008). Gender, mad scientists and nanotechnology. *Spontaneous Generations*, 2 (1), 45–55.

Jacobs, Janis E.; Davis-Kean, Pamela; Bleeker, Martha; Eccles, Jacquelynne S.; & Malanchuk, Oksana. (2005). "I can, but I don't want to": The impact of parents, interests, and activities on gender differences in math. In Ann M. Gallagher & James C. Kaufman (Eds.), *Gender differences in mathematics: An integrative psychological approach* (pp. 246–263). New York: Cambridge University Press.

Jacobs, Janis E.; & Eccles, Jacquelynne S. (1992). The impact of mothers' gender-role stereotypic beliefs on mothers' and children's ability perceptions. *Journal of Personality and Social Psychology, 63*, 932–944.

Jacobs, Janis E.; Lanza, Stephanie; Osgood, D. Wayne; Eccles, Jacquelynne S.; & Wigfield, Allan. (2002). Changes in children's self-competence and values: Gender and domain differences across grades one though twelve. *Child Development, 73*, 509–527.

Jacobs, Marion K.; & Goodman, Gerald. (1989). Psychology and self-help groups: Predictions on a partnership. *American Psychologist, 44*, 536–545.

Jacobs, Michael. (1992). *Sigmund Freud*. London: Sage.

Jakupcak, Matthew; Tull, Matthew T.; & Roemer, Lizabeth. (2005). Masculinity, shame, and fear of emotions as predictors in men's expressions of anger and hostility. *Psychology of Men and Masculinity, 6*, 275–284.

Jandeska, Kathryn E.; & Kraimer, Maria L. (2005). Women's perceptions of organizational culture, work attitudes, and role-modeling. *Journal of Managerial Issues, 17*, 461–479.

Janoff-Bulman, Ronnie; & Frieze, Irene H. (1987). The role of gender in reactions to criminal victimization. In Rosalind C. Barnett, Lois Biener, & Grace K. Baruch (Eds.), *Gender and stress* (pp. 159–184). New York: Free Press.

Jansz, Jeroen; & Martis, Raynel G. (2007). The Lara phenomenon: Powerful female characters in video games. *Sex Roles, 56* (3/4), 141–148.

Janus, Samuel S.; & Janus, Cynthia L. (1993). *The Janus report on sexual behavior*. New York: Wiley.

Jarvis, E. Eric. (2008). Changing psychiatric perception of African Americans with psychosis. *European Journal of American Culture, 27* (3), 227–252.

Jayakumar, Uma M.; Howard, Tyrone C.; Allen, Walter R.; & Han, June C. (2009). Racial privilege in the professoriate: An exploration of campus climate, retention, and satisfaction. *Journal of Higher Education, 80* (5), 538–563.

Jayson, Sharon. (2008, September 25). Women rule the roost, and that's OK with men. *USA Today*, p. 1.

Jewkes, Rachel. (2002). Intimate partner violence: Causes and prevention. *Lancet, 359*, 1423–1429.

Ji, Li-Jun; Peng, Kaiping; & Nisbett, Richard E. (2000). Culture, control, and perception of relationships in the environment. *Journal of Personality and Social Psychology, 78*, 943–955.

Johns, Michael; Schmader, Toni; & Martens, Andy. (2005). Knowing is half the battle. *Psychological Science, 16*, 175–179.

Johnson, Fern L.; & Young, Karen. (2002). Gendered voices in children's television advertising. *Critical Studies in Media Communication, 19*, 461–480.

Johnson, Maria; & Helgeson, Vicki S. (2002). Sex differences in response to evaluative feedback: A field study. *Psychology of Women Quarterly, 26*, 242–251.

Johnson, Michael P. (1995). Patriarchal terrorism and common couple violence: Two forms of violence against women. *Journal of Marriage and the Family, 57*, 283–294.

Johnson, Michael P. (2005). Domestic violence: It's not about gender—or is it? *Journal of Marriage and Family, 67* (5), 1126–1130.

Johnson, Michael P.; & Leone, J. M. (2005). The differential effects of intimate terrorism and situational couple violence: Findings from the National Violence Against Women Survey. *Journal of Family Issues, 26*, 322–349.

Jonason, Peter; & Fisher, Terri. (2009). The power of prestige: Why young men report having more sex partners than young women. *Sex Roles, 60* (3/4), 151–159.

Jonason, Peter; & Marks, Michael. (2009). Common vs. uncommon sexual acts: Evidence for the sexual double standard. *Sex Roles, 60* (5/6), 357-365.

Jones, Del. (2009, January 2). Women slowly gain on corporate America. *USA Today*, p. 6B.

Jones, Ernest. (1955). *The life and work of Sigmund Freud* (Vol. 2). New York: Basic Books.

Jones, Lisa M.; Finkelhor, David; & Halter, Stephanie. (2006). Child maltreatment trends in the 1990s: Why does neglect differ from sexual and physical abuse? *Child Maltreatment, 11*, 107–120.

Jones, Robert A. (2005). How many female scientists do you know? *Endeavour, 29* (2), 84–88.

Jones, Susan; & Myhill, Debra. (2004). "Troublesome boys" and "compliant girls": Gender identity and perceptions of achievement and underachievement. *British Journal of Sociology of Education, 25*, 547–561.

Joshi, Heather; Makepeace, Gerry; & Dolton, Peter. (2007). More or less unequal? Evidence on the pay of men and women from the British birth cohort studies. *Gender, Work and Organization, 14* (1), 37–55.

Jost, John T.; & Kay, Aaron C. (2005). Exposure to benevolent sexism and complementary gender stereotypes: Consequences for specific and diffuse forms of system justification. *Journal of Personality and Social Psychology, 88*, 498–509.

Joyner, Kara; & Kao, Grace. (2000). School racial composition and adolescent racial homophily. *Social Science Quarterly, 81*, 810–825.

Jung, Jaehee; & Peterson, Michael. (2007). Body dissatisfaction and patterns of media use among preadolescent children. *Family and Consumer Sciences Research Journal, 36* (1), 40–54.

Kahle, Jane Butler; & Lakes, Marsha K. (2003). The myth of equality in science classrooms. *Journal of Research in Science Teaching, 40* (Suppl.), S58–S67.

Kahn, Robert S.; Wise, Paul H.; Kennedy, Bruce P.; & Kawachi, Ichiro. (2000). State income inequality, household income, and maternal mental and physical health: Cross-sectional national survey. *British Medical Journal, 321*, 1311–1315.

Kalisz, Aneta; & Cechnicki, Andrzej. (2002). Gender-related prognostic factors in first admission DSM-III schizophrenic patients. *Archives of Psychiatry and Psychotherapy, 4* (3), 25–36.

Kalmijn, Matthijs. (2005). Attitude alignment in marriage and cohabitation: The case of sex-role attitudes. *Personal Relationships, 12*, 521–535.

Kamir, Orit. (2005). Sexual harassment law in Israel. *International Journal of Discrimination and the Law, 7*, 315–335.

Kan, Man Yee. (2008). Does gender trump money? Housework hours of husbands and wives in Britain. *Work, Employment and Society, 22* (1), 45–66.

Kane, Emily W. (2006). "No way my boys are going to be like that!": Parents' responses to children's gender nonconformity. *Gender and Society, 20*, 149–176.

Kane, Penny. (1991). *Women's health: From womb to tomb.* New York: St. Martin's Press.

Kanter, Rosabeth Moss. (1977). *Men and women of the corporation.* New York: Basic Books.

Kaplan, Alexandra G. (1980). Human sex-hormone abnormalities viewed from an androgynous perspective: A reconsideration of the work of John Money. In Jacquelynne E. Parsons (Ed.), *The psychobiology of sex differences and sex roles* (pp. 81–91). Washington, DC: Hemisphere.

Kaplan, Alexandra G.; & Yasinski, Lorraine. (1980). Psychodynamic perspectives. In Annette M. Brodsky & Rachel Hare-Mustin (Eds.), *Women and psychotherapy* (pp. 191–216). New York: Guilford Press.

Kaplan, Robert M.; Anderson, John P.; & Wingard, Deborah L. (1991). Gender differences in health-related quality of life. *Health Psychology, 10*, 86–93.

Kar, Heidi Lary; & Garcia-Moreno, Claudia. (2009). Partner aggression across cultures. In K. Daniel O'Leary & Erica M. Woodin (Eds.), *Psychological and physical aggression in couples: Causes and interventions* (pp. 59–75). Washington, DC: American Psychological Association.

Karniol, Rachel. (2009). Israeli kindergarten children's gender constancy for others' counter-stereotypic toy play and appearance: The role of sibling gender and relative age. *Infant & Child Development, 18* (1), 73–94.

Kaschak, Ellyn. (1992). *Engendered lives.* New York: Basic Books.

Kaschak, Ellyn; & Tiefer, Lenore. (Eds.). (2001). *A new view of women's sexual problems.* New York: Haworth Press.

Katz, Phyllis A.; & Ksansnak, Keith R. (1994). Developmental aspects of gender role flexibility and traditionality in middle childhood and adolescence. *Developmental Psychology, 30*, 272–282.

Kawahara, Debra M.; Esnil, Edna M.; & Hsu, Jeanette. (2007). Asian American women leaders: The intersection of race, gender, and leadership. In Jean Lau Chin, Bernice Lott, Joy K. Rice, & Janis Sanchez-Hulces (Eds.), *Women and leadership: Transforming visions and diverse voices* (pp. 297–313). Malden, MA: Blackwell.

Kawakami, Kerry; & Dovidio, John F. (2001). The reliability of implicit stereotyping. *Personality and Social Psychology Bulletin, 27*, 212–225.

Keel, Pamela K.; Heatherton, Todd F.; Baxter, Mark G.; & Joiner, Thomas E., Jr. (2007). A 20-year longitudinal study of body weight, dieting, and eating disorder symptoms. *Journal of Abnormal Psychology, 116* (2), 422–432.

Keel, Pamela K.; & Klump, Kelly L. (2003). Are eating disorders culture-bound syndromes? Implications for conceptualizing their etiology. *Psychological Bulletin, 129*, 747–769.

Keen, Sam. (1991). *A fire in the belly: On being a man.* New York: Bantam.

Keisner, Jody. (2008). Do you want to watch? A study of the visual rhetoric of the postmodern horror film. *Women's Studies, 37* (4), 411–427.

Keller, Evelyn Fox. (1985). *Reflections on gender and science.* New Haven, CT: Yale University Press.

Keller, Johannes. (2005). In genes we trust: The biological component of psychological essentialism and its relationship to mechanisms of motivated social cognition. *Journal of Personality and Social Psychology, 88*, 686–702.

Kelly, John Francis; Magill, Molly; & Stout, Robert Lauren. (2009). How do people recover from alcohol dependence? A systematic review of the research on mechanisms of behavior change in Alcoholics Anonymous. *Addiction Research and Theory, 17* (3), 236–259.

Keltikangas-Jarvinen, Liisa. (2002). Aggressive problem-solving strategies, aggressive behavior, and social acceptance in early and late adolescence. *Journal of Youth and Adolescence, 31*, 279–287.

Keltner, Bette; Kelley, Frances J.; & Smith, Debra. (2004). Leadership to reduce health disparities. *Nursing Administration Quarterly, 28*, 181–190.

Kennell, John; & McGrath, Susan. (2005). Starting the process of mother-infant bonding. *Acta Paediatrica, 94*, 775–777.

Kessler, Ronald C. (2003). Epidemiology of women and depression. *Journal of Affective Disorders, 74*, 5–13.

Kessler, Ronald C.; Brown, Roger L.; & Broman, Clifford L. (1981). Sex differences in psychiatric help-seeking: Evidence from four large-scale surveys. *Journal of Health and Social Behavior, 22*, 49–64.

Kessler, Ronald C.; Mickelson, Kristin D.; & Williams, David R. (1999). The prevalence, distribution, and mental health correlates of perceived discrimination in the United States. *Journal of Health and Social Behavior, 40*, 208–230.

Kidder, Louise. (1994, August). *All pores open.* Paper presented at the 102nd annual convention of the American Psychological Association, Los Angeles, CA.

Kiecolt-Glaser, Janice K.; & Newton, Tamara L. (2001). Marriage and health: His and hers. *Psychological Bulletin, 127*, 472–503.

Kiesner, Jeff. (2009). Physical characteristics of the menstrual cycle and premenstrual depressive symptoms. *Psychological Science, 20* (6), 763–770.

Kilmer, Ryan P.; & Shahinfar, Ariana. (2006). Sexuality in childhood. In M. Michele Burnette & Richard D. McAnulty (Eds.), *Sex and sexuality, Vol. 1: Sexuality today: Trends and controversies* (pp. 35–60). Westport, CT: Praeger/Greenwood.

Kim, Kwangok; & Lowry, Dennis. (2005). Television commercials as a lagging social indicator: Gender role stereotypes in Korean television advertising. *Sex Roles, 53*, 901–910.

Kimball, Meredith M. (1995). *Feminist visions of gender similarities and differences.* New York: Haworth Press.

Kimmel, Michael S. (2000). A war against boys? *Tikkun, 15* (6), 57–60.

Kimmel, Michael S. (2006). Ritualized homosexuality in a Nacirema subculture. *Sexualities, 9*, 95–105.

Kimmel, Michael S.; & Messner, Michael A. (1992). Introduction. In Michael S. Kimmel & Michael A. Messner (Eds.), *Men's lives* (2nd ed., pp. 1–11). New York: Macmillan.

Kim-Prieto, Chu; & Eid, Michael. (2004). Norms for experiencing emotions in sub-Saharan Africa. *Journal of Happiness Studies, 5*, 241–268.

Kimura, Doreen. (1989, November). How sex hormones boost—or cut—intellectual ability. *Psychology Today*, pp. 62–66.

Kimura, Doreen. (1992, September). Sex differences in the brain. *Scientific American*, pp. 119–125.

Kimura, Doreen. (2007). "Underrepresentation" or misrepresentation? In Stephen J. Ceci & Wendy M. Williams (Eds.), *Why aren't more women in science: Top researchers debate the evidence* (pp. 39–46). Washington, DC: American Psychological Association.

Kimura, Doreen; & Clarke, Paul G. (2002). Women's advantage on verbal memory is not restricted to concrete words. *Psychological Reports, 91*, 1137–1142.

King, Eden B. (2008). The effect of bias on the advancement of working mothers: Disentangling legitimate concerns from inaccurate stereotypes as predictors of advancement in academe. *Human Relations, 61* (12), 1677–1711.

King, Eden B.; Madera, Juan M.; Hebl, Mikki R.; Knight, Jennifer, L.; & Mendoza, Saaid A. (2006). What's in a name? A multiracial investigation of the role of occupational stereotypes in selection decisions. *Journal of Applied Social Psychology, 36*, 1145–1159.

King, Neal. (2005, May 26–30). *Boy jokes: Content analysis of Hollywood misogyny in mean girl and slasher movies.* Paper presented at the 55th national conference of the International Communication Association, New York.

Kinsey, Alfred C.; Pomeroy, Wardell B.; & Martin, Clyde E. (1948). *Sexual behavior in the human male.* Philadelphia: Saunders.

Kinsey, Alfred C.; Pomeroy, Wardell B.; Martin, Clyde E.; & Gebhard, Paul H. (1953). *Sexual behavior in the human female.* Philadelphia: Saunders.

Kirkpatrick, R. C. (2000). The evolution of human homosexual behavior. *Current Anthropology, 41*, 385–413.

Kirnan, Jean Powell; Alfieri, Julie Ann; Bragger, Jennifer DeNicholis; & Harris, Robert Sean. (2009). An investigation of stereotype threat in employment tests. *Journal of Applied Social Psychology, 39* (2), 359–388.

Kirschstein, Ruth L. (1991). Research on women's health. *American Journal of Public Health, 81*, 291–293.

Kissling, Elizabeth Arveda. (2002). On the rag on screen: Menarche in film and television. *Sex Roles, 46*, 5–12.

Kite, Mary E. (2001). Changing times, changing gender roles: Who do we want women and men to be? In Rhoda Unger (Ed.), *Handbook of the psychology of women and gender* (pp. 215–227). New York: Wiley.

Kivlighan, Katie T.; Granger, Douglas A.; & Booth, Alan. (2005). Gender differences in testosterone and cortisol response to competition. *Psychoneuroendocrinology, 30*, 58–71.

Klaus, Marshall H.; & Kennell, John H. (1976). *Maternal infant bonding.* St. Louis, MO: Mosby.

Klecker, Beverly M. (2006). The gender gap in NAEP fourth-, eighth-, and twelfth-grade reading scores across years. *Reading Improvement, 43*, 50–56.

Kleiber, Pamela B. (2004). Focus groups: More than a method of qualitative inquiry. In Kathleen deMarrais & Stephen D. Lapan (Eds.), *Foundations for research: Methods of inquiry in education and the social sciences* (pp. 87–102). Mahwah, NJ: Erlbaum.

Klein, Joseph. (2004). Who is most responsible for gender differences in scholastic achievements: Pupils or teachers? *Educational Research, 46*, 183–193.

Klinesmith, Jennifer; Kasser, Tim; & McAndrew, Francis T. (2006). Guns, testosterone, and aggression: An experimental test of a mediational hypothesis. *Psychological Science, 17*, 568–571.

Kling, Kristen C.; Hyde, Janet Shibley; Showers, Caroline J.; & Buswell, Brenda N. (1999). Gender differences in self-esteem: A meta-analysis. *Psychological Bulletin, 125*, 470–500.

Klinkenberg, Dean; & Rose, Suzanna. (1994). Dating scripts of gay men and lesbians. *Journal of Homosexuality, 26* (4), 23–35.

Klonoff, Elizabeth A.; & Landrine, Hope. (1997). *Preventing misdiagnosis of women.* Thousand Oaks, CA: Sage.

Klonoff, Elizabeth A.; Landrine, Hope; & Campbell, Robin. (2000). Sexist discrimination may account for well-known gender differences in psychiatric symptoms. *Psychology of Women Quarterly, 24*, 93–99.

Kluger, Jeffrey; Harrell, Eben; Kloberdanz, Kristin; & Stinchfield, Kate. (2008, January 28). Why we love. *Time, 171* (4), 54–60.

Knafo, Ariel; Iervolino, Alessandra C.; & Plomin, Robert. (2005). Masculine girls and feminine boys: Genetic and environmental contributions to atypical gender development in early childhood. *Journal of Personality and Social Psychology, 88*, 400–412.

Knafo, Ariel; & Schwartz, Shalom H. (2009). Accounting for parent-child value congruence: Theoretical considerations and empirical evidence. In U. Schönpflug (Ed.) *Cultural transmission: Psychological, developmental, social, and methodological aspects* (pp. 240-268). New York: Cambridge University Press.

Knight, George P.; Guthrie, Ivanna K.; Page, Melanie C.; & Fabes, Richard A. (2002). Emotional arousal and gender differences in aggression: A meta-analysis. *Aggressive Behavior, 28*, 366–393.

Knutson, Kristine M.; Mah, Linda; Manly, Charlotte F.; & Grafman, Jordan. (2007). Neural correlates of automatic beliefs about gender and race. *Human Brain Mapping, 28* (10), 915-930.

Koenig, Anne M.; & Eagly, Alice H. (2005). Stereotype threat in men on a test of social sensitivity. *Sex Roles, 52*, 489–496.

Koeske, Randi K.; & Koeske, Gary F. (1975). An attributional approach to moods and the menstrual cycle. *Journal of Personality and Social Psychology, 31*, 473–478.

Kohlberg, Lawrence. (1966). A cognitive-developmental analysis of children's sex-role concepts and attitudes. In Eleanor E. Maccoby (Ed.), *The development of sex differences* (pp. 52–173). Stanford, CA: Stanford University Press.

Kohlstedt, Sally Gregory. (2004). Sustaining gains: Reflections on women and science and technology in 20th-century United States. *NWSA Journal, 16* (1), 1–26.

Kokko, Katja; & Pulkkinen, Lea. (2005). Stability of aggressive behavior from childhood to middle age in men and women. *Aggressive Behavior, 31*, 485–497.

Komarovsky, Mirra. (1982). Female freshmen view their future: Career salience and its correlates. *Sex Roles, 8*, 299–313.

Komath, Sneha Sudhaa. (2008). Frames of science? *Current Science, 94* (11), 1363–1364.

Kongar, Ebru. (2008). Is deindustrialization good for women? Evidence from the United States. *Feminist Economics, 14* (1), 73–92.

Konrad, Alison M. (2003). Family demands and job attribute preferences: A 4-year longitudinal study of women and men. *Sex Roles, 49*, 35–46.

Koopmans, Gerrit T.; & Lamers, Leida M. (2007). Gender and health care utilization: The role of mental distress and help-seeking propensity. *Social Science & Medicine, 64*, 1216–1230.

Kopper, Beverly A.; & Epperson, Douglas L. (1996). The experience and expression of anger: Relationships with gender, gender role socialization, depression, and mental health functioning. *Journal of Counseling Psychology, 43*, 158–165.

Koss, Mary P. (1990). The women's mental health research agenda: Violence against women. *American Psychologist, 45*, 374–380.

Koss, Mary P.; Bailey, Jennifer A.; Yuan, Nicole P.; Herrera, Veronica M.; & Lichter, Erika L. (2003). Depression and PTSD in survivors of male violence: Research and training initiatives to facilitate recovery. *Psychology of Women Quarterly, 27*, 130–142.

Koss, Mary P.; Gidycz, Christine A.; & Wisniewski, Nadine. (1987). The scope of rape: Incidence and prevalence of sexual aggression and victimization in a national sample of higher education students. *Journal of Consulting and Clinical Psychology, 55*, 162–170.

Kozak, Megan; Frankenhauser, Heidi; & Roberts, Tomi-Ann. (2009). Objects of desire: Objectification as a function of male and sexual orientation. *Psychology of Men and Masculinity, 10* (3), 225–230.

Krahé, Barbara; Bieneck, Steffen; & Scheinberger-Olwig, Renate. (2007). Adolescents' sexual scripts: Schematic representations of consensual and nonconsensual heterosexual interactions. *Journal of Sex Research, 44* (4), 316–327.

Krahé, Barbara; Scheinberger-Olwig, Renate; & Bieneck, Steffen. (2003). Men's reports of nonconsensual sexual interactions with women: Prevalence and impact. *Archives of Sexual Behavior, 32*, 165–175.

Kravetz, Diane. (1978). Consciousness-raising groups of the 1970s. *Psychology of Women Quarterly, 3*, 168–186.

Kravitz, Richard L.; Epstein, Ronald M.; Feldman, Mitchell D.; Franz, Carol E.; Azari, Rahman; Wilkes, Michael S.; et al. (2005). Influence of patients' requests for direct-to-consumer advertised antidepressants: A randomized controlled trial. *Journal of the American Medical Association, 293*, 1995–2002.

Kreager, Derek A.; & Staff, Jeremy. (2009). The sexual double standard and adolescent peer acceptance. *Social Psychology Quarterly, 72* (2), 143–164.

Krendl, Anne C.; Richeson, Jennifer A.; Kelley, William M.; & Heatherton, Todd F. (2008). The negative consequences of threat: A functional magnetic resonance imaging investigation of the neural mechanisms underlying women's underperformance in math. *Psychological Science, 19* (2), 168–175.

Kreydatus, Beth. (2008). Confronting the "bra-burners:" Teaching radical feminism with a case study. *The History Teacher, 41* (4), 489–504.

Krieglmeyer, Regina; Wittstadt, Doris; & Strack, Fritz. (2009). How attribution influences aggression: Answers to an old question by using an implicit measure of anger. *Journal of Experimental Social Psychology, 45* (2), 379–385.

Krishnan, Ahalya; & Sweeney, Christopher J. (1998). Gender differences in fear of success imagery and other achievement-related background variables among medical students. *Sex Roles, 39*, 299–310.

Kruger, Judy; Galuska, Deborah A.; Serdula, Mary K.; & Jones, Deborah A. (2004). Attempting to lose weight: Specific practices among U.S. adults. *Journal of Preventive Medicine, 26* (5), 402–406.

Kuhn, Deanna. (2006, March 8). Does the Asian success formula have a downside? *Education Week, 25* (26), 29.

Kuhn, Deanna; Nash, Sharon C.; & Brucken, Laura. (1978). Sex role concepts of two- and three-year olds. *Child Development, 49*, 445–451.

Kühnen, Ulrich; Hannover, Bettina; Roeder, Ute; Shah, Ashiq Ali; Schubert, Benjamin; Upmeyer, Arnold; & Zakaria, Saliza. (2001). Cross-cultural variations in identifying embedded figures: Comparisons from the United States, Germany, Russia, and Malaysia. *Journal of Cross-Cultural Psychology, 32*, 365–371.

Kulik, Liat. (2002). Like-sex versus opposite-sex effects in transmission of gender role ideology from parents to adolescents in Israel. *Journal of Youth and Adolescence, 31*, 451–457.

Kurdek, Lawrence A. (1993). The allocation of household labor in gay, lesbian, and heterosexual married couples. *Journal of Social Issues, 49* (3), 127–139.

Kurdek, Lawrence A. (2004). Are gay and lesbian cohabiting couples really different from heterosexual married couples? *Journal of Marriage and Family, 66*, 880–900.

Kurdek, Lawrence A. (2008). A general model of relationship commitment: Evidence from same-sex partners. *Personal Relationships, 15* (3), 391–405.

Kurzweil, Edith. (1995). *Freudians and feminists.* Boulder, CO: Westview Press.

Kutchins, Herb; & Kirk, Stuart A. (1997). *Making us crazy. DSM: The psychiatric bible and the creation of mental disorders.* New York: Free Press.

Labre, Magdala Peixoto; & Duke, Lisa. (2004). "Nothing like a brisk walk and a spot of demon slaughter to make a girl's night": The construction of the female hero in the Buffy video game. *Journal of Communication Inquiry, 28*, 138–156.

Lacasse, Anne; & Mendelson, Morton J. (2006). The perceived intent of potentially offensive sexual behaviors among adolescents. *Journal of Research on Adolescence, 16*, 229–238.

Ladwig, Karl-Heinz; Marten-Mittag, Birgitt; Erazo, Natalia; & Gündel, Harald. (2001). Identifying somatization disorder in a population-based health examination survey: Psychosocial burden and gender differences. *Journal of Consultation Liaison Psychiatry, 42*, 511–518.

Laflamme, Darquise; Pomerleau, Andree; & Malcuit, Gerard. (2002). A comparison of fathers' and mothers' involvement in childcare and stimulation behaviors during free-play with their infants at 9 and 15 months. *Sex Roles, 47*, 507–518.

La France, Betty H.; Henningsen, David D.; Oates, Aubrey; & Shaw, Christina M. (2009). Social-sexual interactions? Meta-analyses of sex differences in perceptions of flirtatiousness, seductiveness, and promiscuousness. *Communication Monographs, 76* (3), 263–285.

LaFrance, Marianne; Hecht, Marvin A.; & Levy Paluck, Elizabeth. (2003). The contingent smile: A meta-analysis of sex differences in smiling. *Psychological Bulletin, 129*, 305–334.

LaFromboise, Teresa D.; Berman, Joan Saks; & Sohi, Balvindar K. (1994). American Indian women. In Lillian Comas-Díaz & Beverly Greene (Eds.), *Women of color: Integrating ethnic and gender identities in psychotherapy* (pp. 30–71). New York: Guilford Press.

Lahey, Benjamin B.; Goodman, Sherryl H.; Canino, Glorisa; Bird, Hector; Schwab-Stone, Mary; Waldman, Irwin D.; et al. (2000). Age and gender differences in oppositional behavior and conduct problems: Cross-sectional household study of middle childhood and adolescence. *Journal of Abnormal Psychology, 109*, 488–503.

Lakoff, Robin. (1975). *Language and woman's place.* New York: Harper & Row.

Lalumiere, Martin L.; Blanchard, Ray; & Zucker, Kenneth J. (2000). Sexual orientation and handedness in men and women: A meta-analysis. *Psychological Bulletin, 126*, 575–592.

Landrine, Hope; Bardwell, Stephen; & Dean, Tina. (1988). Gender expectations for alcohol use: A study of the significance of the masculine role. *Sex Roles, 19*, 703–712.

Lane, Jodi; Gover, Angela R.; & Dahod, Sara. (2009). Fear of violent crime among men and women on campus: The impact of perceived risk and fear of sexual assault. *Violence and Victims, 24* (2), 172–192.

Laner, Mary Riege; & Ventrone, Nicole A. (2000). Dating scripts revisited. *Journal of Family Issues, 21*, 488–500.

Lang, Molly Monahan; & Risman, Barbara J. (2006). Blending into equality: Family diversity and gender convergence. In Kathy Davis, Mary Evans, & Judith Lorber (Eds.), *Handbook of gender and women's studies* (pp. 287–303). Thousand Oaks, CA: Sage.

Langer, Susan J.; & Martin, James I. (2004). How dresses can make you mentally ill: Examining gender identity disorder in children. *Child and Adolescent Social Work Journal, 21*, 5–23.

Larson, Mary Strom. (2001). Interactions, activities and gender in children's television commercials: A content analysis. *Journal of Broadcasting & Electronic Media, 45*, 41–56.

Larson, Mary Strom. (2003). Gender, race, and aggression in television commercials that feature children. *Sex Roles, 48*, 67–75.

Larson, Reed; & Pleck, Joseph. (1999). Hidden feelings: Emotionality in boys and men. In Dan Bernstein (Ed.), *Nebraska Symposium on Motivation, 1999: Gender and motivation* (pp. 25–74). Lincoln: University of Nebraska Press.

Larsson, IngBeth; & Svedin, Carl-Goran. (2002). Sexual experiences in childhood: Young adults' recollections. *Archives of Sexual Behavior, 31*, 263–273.

Lasley Barajas, Heide; & Pierce, Jennifer L. (2001). The significance of race and genera in school success among Latinas and Latinos in college. *Gender and Society, 15*, 859–878.

Lasser, Karen E.; Himmelstein, David U.; & Woolhandler, Steffie. (2006). Access to care, health status, and health disparities in the United States and Canada: Results of a cross-national population-based survey. *American Journal of Public Health*, 96, 1300–1307.

Laumann, Edward O.; Gagnon, John H.; Michael, Robert T.; & Michaels, Stuart. (1994). *The social organization of sexuality.* Chicago: University of Chicago Press.

Lauzen, Martha; & Deiss, Douglas. (2009). Breaking the fourth wall and sex role stereotypes: An examination of the 2006–2007 prime-time season. *Sex Roles*, 60 (5/6), 379–386.

Lauzen, Martha M.; & Dozier, David M. (2002). You look mahvelous: An examination of gender and appearance comments in the 1999–2000 prime-time season. *Sex Roles*, 46, 429–437.

Lauzen, Martha M.; & Dozier, David M. (2005). Maintaining the double standard: Portrayals of age and gender in popular films. *Sex Roles*, 52, 437–446.

Lauzen, Martha M.; Dozier, David M.; & Horan, Nora. (2008). Constructing gender stereotypes through social roles in prime-time television. *Journal of Broadcasting & Electronic Media*, 52 (2), 200–214.

Lavallee, Marguerite; & Pelletier, Rene. (1992). Ecological value of Bem's gender schema theory explored through females' traditional and nontraditional occupational contexts. *Psychological Reports*, 70, 79–82.

Lazarus, Arnold A. (2003). Boundary crossings vs. boundary violations. *Annals of the American Psychotherapy Association*, 6, 24–27.

Lazarus, Richard S.; & Folkman, Susan. (1984). *Stress, appraisal, and coping.* New York: Springer.

Leahey, Erin; & Guo, Guang. (2001). Gender differences in mathematical trajectories. *Social Forces*, 80, 713–732.

Leaper, Campbell. (2002). Parenting girls and boys. In Marc H. Bornstein (Ed.), *Handbook of parenting: Vol. 1: Children and parenting* (2nd ed.; pp. 189–225). Mahwah, NJ: Erlbaum.

Leaper, Campbell; Anderson, Kristin J.; & Sanders, Paul. (1998). Moderators of gender effects on parents' talk to their children: A meta-analysis. *Developmental Psychology*, 34, 3–27.

Leaper, Campbell; & Ayres, Melanie M. (2007). A meta-analytic review of gender variations in adults' language use: Talkativeness, affiliative speech, and assertive speech. *Personality and Social Psychology Review*, 11 (4), 328–363.

Leaper, Campbell; Breed, Lisa; Hoffman, Laurie; & Perlman, Carly Ann. (2002). Variations in the gender-stereotyped content of children's television cartoons across genres. *Journal of Applied Social Psychology*, 32, 1653–1662.

Lee, Antoinette M.; So-Kum Tang, Catherine; & Chong, Catherine. (2009). A culturally sensitive study of premenstrual and menstrual symptoms among Chinese women. *Journal of Psychosomatic Obstetrics & Gynecology*, 30 (2), 105–114.

Lee, Camille. (2002). The impact of belonging to a high school gay/straight alliance. *High School Journal*, 85 (3), 13–26.

Lee, Joohee; Pomeroy, Elizabeth C.; Yoo, Seo-Koo; & Rheinboldt, Kurt T. (2005). Attitudes toward rape. *Violence Against Women*, 11, 177–196.

Leedy, M. Gail; LaLonde, Donna; & Runk, Kristen. (2003). Gender equity in mathematics: Beliefs of students, parents, and teachers. *School Science and Mathematics*, 103, 285–292.

Lefkowitz, Monroe M.; Eron, Leonard D.; Walder, Leopold O.; & Huesmann, L. Rowell. (1977). *Growing up to be violent: A longitudinal study of the development of aggression.* New York: Pergamon Press.

Legato, Marianne J. (2006, June 17). The weaker sex. *New York Times*, A13.

Lehre, Anne-Catherine; Lehre, Knut P.; Laake, Petter; & Danbolt, Niels C. (2009). Greater intrasex phenotype variability in males than in females is a fundamental aspect of the gender differences in humans. *Developmental Psychobiology*, 51 (2), 198–206.

Lengua, Liliana J.; & Stormshak, Elizabeth A. (2000). Gender, gender roles, and personality: Gender differences in the prediction of coping and psychological symptoms. *Sex Roles*, 44, 787–820.

Leonard, Christiana M.; Towler, Stephen; Welcome, Suzanne; Halderman, Laura K.; Otto, Ron; Eckert, Mark A.; et al. (2008). Size matters: Cerebral volume influences sex differences in neuroanatomy. *Cerebral Cortex*, 18 (12), 2920–2931.

Lepowsky, Maria. (1994). Women, men, and aggression in an egalitarian society. *Sex Roles*, 30, 199–211.

Lerman, Hannah. (1996). *Pigeonholing women's misery: A history and critical analysis of the psychodiagnosis of women in the twentieth century.* New York: Basic Books.

Lerner, Alan Jay; & Loewe, Frederick. (1956). *My fair lady: A musical play in two acts. Based on Pygmalion by Bernard Shaw.* New York: Coward-McCann.

Leszczynski, Jennifer Pickard; & Strough, JoNell. (2008). The contextual specificity of masculinity and femininity in early adolescence. *Social Development*, 17 (3), 719–736.

Lev, Arlene Istar. (2005). Disordering gender identity: Gender identity disorder in the DSM-IV TR. *Journal of Psychology & Human Sexuality*, 17 (3/4), 35–69.

Levant, Ronald F., Good, Glen E., Cook, Stephen W., O'Neil, James M., Smalley, K. Bryant, Owen, Karen, et al. (2006). The Normative Male Alexithymia Scale: Measurement of a gender-linked syndrome. *Psychology of Men & Masculinity*, 7 (4), 212-224.

Levant, Ronald F.; & Richmond, Katherine. (2007). A review of research on masculinity ideologies using the male role norms inventory. *Journal of Men's Studies*, 15 (2), 130–146.

Levenson, Robert W.; Carstensen, Laura L.; & Gottman, John M. (1994). The influence of age and gender on affect, physiology, and their interrelations: A study of long-term marriages. *Journal of Personality and Social Psychology, 67,* 56–68.

Lever, Janet; Grov, Christian; Royce, Tracy; Gillespie, Brian Joseph. (2008). Searching for love in all the 'write' places: Exploring internet personals use by sexual orientation, gender, and age. *International Journal of Sexual Health, 20* (4), 233–246.

Levi, Annette; Chan, Kenny K.; & Pence, Dan. (2006). Real men do not read labels: The effects of masculinity and involvement on college students' food decisions. *Journal of American College Health, 55* (2), 91–98.

Levine, Judith A. (2009). It's a man's job, or so they say: The maintenance of sex segregation in a manufacturing plant. *Sociological Quarterly, 50* (2), 257-282.

Levy, Donald P. (2005). Hegemonic complicity, friendship, and comradeship: Validation and causal processes among White, middle-class, middle-aged men. *Journal of Men's Studies, 13,* 199–224.

Levy, Gary D. (1989). Relations among aspects of children's social environments, gender schematization, gender role knowledge, and flexibility. *Sex Roles, 21,* 803–823.

Levy, Gary D. (1999). Gender-typed and non-gender-typed category awareness in toddlers. *Sex Roles, 41,* 851–874.

Levy, Gary D.; Barth, Joan M.; & Zimmerman, Barbara J. (1998). Associations among cognitive and behavioral aspects of preschoolers' gender role development. *Journal of Genetic Psychology, 159,* 121–126.

Levy, Gary D.; & Fivush, Robyn. (1993). Scripts and gender: A new approach for examining gender-role development. *Developmental Review, 13,* 126–146.

Levy, Gary D.; Sadovsky, Adrienne L.; & Troseth, Georgene L. (2000). Aspects of young children's perceptions of gender-typed occupations. *Sex Roles, 42,* 993–1006.

Levy, Lauren J.; Frick, Karyn M.; & Astur, Robert S. (2005). Men and women differ in object memory but not performance of a virtual radial maze. *Behavioral Neuroscience, 119,* 853–862.

Lewin, Catharina; Wolgers, Gerhard; & Herlitz, Agneta (2001). Sex differences favouring women in verbal but not in visuospatial episodic memory. *Neuropsychology, 15,* 165–173.

Lewin, Miriam. (1984a). "Rather worse than folly?" Psychology measures femininity and masculinity: 1. From Terman and Miles to the Guilfords. In Miriam Lewin (Ed.), *In the shadow of the past: Psychology portrays the sexes* (pp. 155–178). New York: Columbia University Press.

Lewin, Miriam. (1984b). Psychology measures femininity and masculinity: 2. From "13 gay men" to the instrumental-expressive distinction. In Miriam Lewin (Ed.), *In the shadow of the past: Psychology portrays the sexes* (pp. 179–204). New York: Columbia University Press.

Lewin, Miriam. (1984c). The Victorians, the psychologists, and psychic birth control. In Miriam Lewin (Ed.), *In the shadow of the past: Psychology portrays the sexes* (pp. 39–76). New York: Columbia University Press.

Lewin-Jones, Jenny; & Mitra, Barbara. (2009). Gender roles in television commercials and primary school children in the UK. *Journal of Children & Media, 3* (1), 35–50.

Liben, Lynn S.; & Bigler, Rebecca S. (2002). The developmental course of gender differentiation. *Monographs of the Society for Research in Child Development, 67,* vii–147.

Lieberman, Alexis; & Merrick, Joav. (2009). Comorbidity of poverty among adolescents. *International Journal of Child and Adolescent Health, 2* (1), 1–2.

Lin, Ying-Ching; & Raghubir, Priya. (2003). Gender differences in unrealistic optimism about marriage and divorce: Are men more optimistic and women more realistic? *Personality and Social Psychology Bulletin, 31,* 198–207.

Lincoln, Karen D.; Chatters, Linda M.; & Taylor, Robert Joseph. (2005). Social support, traumatic events, and depressive symptoms among African Americans. *Journal of Marriage and Family, 67,* 754–766.

Linden, Mary G.; Bender, Bruce G.; & Robinson, Arthur. (1995). Sex chromosome tetrasomy and pentasomy. *Pediatrics, 96,* 672–682.

Lindsey, Eric W. (2002). Preschool children's friendship and peer acceptance: Links to social competence. *Child Study Journal, 32,* 145–156.

Lingiardi, Vittorio; Falanga, Anthony; & D'Augelli, Anthony R. (2005). The evaluation of homophobia in an Italian sample. *Archives of Sexual Behavior, 34,* 81–93.

Linn, Marcia C.; & Petersen, Anne C. (1986). A meta-analysis of gender differences in spatial ability: Implications for mathematics and science achievement. In Janet Shibley Hyde & Marcia C. Linn (Eds.), *The psychology of gender: Advances through meta-analysis* (pp. 67–101). Baltimore: Johns Hopkins University Press.

Lippa, Richard. (2008). The relation between childhood gender nonconformity and adult masculinity-femininity and anxiety in heterosexual and homosexual men and women. *Sex Roles, 59* (9/10), 684–693.

Littlewood, Roland. (2002). Three into two: The third sex in Northern Albania. *Anthropology & Medicine, 9* (1), 37–50.

Livingston, Martha. (1999). How to think about women's health. In Carie Forden, Anne E. Hunter, & Beverly Birns (Eds.), *Readings in the psychology of women: Dimensions of the female experience* (pp. 244–253). Boston: Allyn & Bacon.

Lloyd, Jennifer E. V.; Walsh, John; & Yailagh, Manizheh Shehni. (2005). Sex differences in performance attributions, self-efficacy, and achievement in mathematics: If I'm so smart, why don't I know it? *Canadian Journal of Education, 28,* 384–408.

Lobel, Thalma E.; Bar-David, Eva; Gruber, Reut; Lau, Sing; & Bar-Tal, Yoram. (2000). Gender schema and social judgments: A developmental study of children. *Sex Roles, 43,* 19–42.

Lobel, Thalma E.; Nov-Krispin, Nohar; Schiller, Daniela; Lobel, Orly; & Feldman, Amit. (2004). Gender discriminatory behavior during adolescence and young adulthood: A developmental analysis. *Journal of Youth and Adolescence, 33,* 535–546.

Lombardo, William K.; Cretser, Gary A.; & Roesch, Scott C. (2001). For crying out loud—The differences persist into the '90s. *Sex Roles, 45,* 529–547.

London, Kamala; Bruck, Maggie; Ceci, Stephen J.; & Shuman, Daniel W. (2005). Disclosure of child sexual abuse: What does the research tell us about the ways that children tell? *Psychology, Public Policy, and Law, 11,* 194–226.

Loo, Robert; & Thorpe, Karran. (1998). Attitudes toward women's roles in society: A replication after 20 years. *Sex Roles, 39,* 903–912.

Lopez, Alan D.; Mathers, Colin D.; Ezzati, Majid; Jamison, Dean T.; & Murray, Christopher J. L. (2006). Global and regional burden of disease and risk factors, 2001: Systematic analysis of population health data. *Lancet, 367,* 1747–1757.

López, Steven Regeser. (1989). Patient variable biases in clinical judgment: Conceptual overview and methodological considerations. *Psychological Bulletin, 106,* 184–203.

Lorber, Judith. (1975). Women and medical sociology: Invisible professionals and ubiquitous patients. In Marcia Millman & Rosabeth M. Kanter (Eds.), *Another voice* (pp. 75–105). Garden City, NY: Anchor/Doubleday.

Lorber, Judith. (1997). Believing is seeing: Biology as ideology. In Maxine Baca Zinn, Pierrette Hondagneu-Sotelo, & Michael A. Messner (Eds.), *Through the prism of difference: Readings on sex and gender* (pp. 13–22). Boston: Allyn & Bacon.

Lorenzen, Lisa A.; Grieve, Frederick G.; & Thomas, Adrian. (2004). Exposure to muscular male models decreases men's body satisfaction. *Sex Roles, 51,* 743–748.

Lovas, Gretchen S. (2005). Gender and patterns of emotional availability in mother-toddler and father-toddler dyads. *Infant Mental Health Journal, 26* (4), 327–353.

Lovell, Brenda; Lee, Raymond T.; & Brotheridge, Céleste M. (2009). Gender differences in the application of communication skills, emotional labor, stress-coping and well-being among physicians. *International Journal of Medicine, 2* (3), 273–278.

Loving, Timothy J.; Heffner, Kathi L.; Kiecolt-Glaser, Janice K.; Glaser, Ronald; & Malarkey, William B. (2004). Stress hormone changes and marital conflict: Spouses' relative power makes a difference. *Journal of Marriage and Family, 66,* 595–612.

Lowes, Jacinta; & Tiggemann, Marika. (2003). Body dissatisfaction, dieting awareness and the impact of parental influence in young children. *British Journal of Health Psychology, 8,* 135–147.

Lowry, Fran. (2006). Guidelines grapple with localized prostate cancer: Review cites lack of clinical trial data. *Internal Medicine News, 39* (12), 1–2.

Lubinski, David S.; & Benbow, Camilla Persson. (2007). Sex differences in personal attributes for the development of scientific expertise. In Stephen J. Ceci & Wendy M. Williams (Eds.), *Why aren't more women in science: Top researchers debate the evidence* (pp. 79–100). Washington, DC: American Psychological Association.

Luepker, Ellen T. (1999). Effects of practitioners' sexual misconduct: A follow-up study. *Journal of the American Academy of Psychiatry and the Law, 27,* 51–63.

Lueptow, Lloyd B.; Garovich-Szabo, Lori; & Lueptow, Margaret B. (2001). Social change and the persistence of sex typing. *Social Forces, 80,* 1–36.

Lufkin, Mary E.; Wiberg, Mary M.; Jenkins, Courtney Reed; Berardi, Stefanie L. Lee; Boyer, Terri; Eardley, Ellen; et al. (2007). Gender equity in career and technical education. In Susan S. Klein et al., *Handbook for achieving gender equity through education* (2nd ed., pp. 421–443). Mahwah, NJ: Erlbaum.

Luo, Shanhong; & Zhang, Guangjian. (2009). What leads to romantic attraction: Similarity, reciprocity, security, or beauty? *Journal of Personality, 77* (4), 933–964.

Lutz-Zois, Catherine J.; Bradley, Angela C.; Mihalik, Jennifer L.; & Moorman-Eavers, Erika R. (2006). Perceived similarity and relationship success among dating couples: An idiographic approach. *Journal of Social and Personal Relationships, 23* (6), 865–880.

Lyons, Denise; & McArthur, Connie. (2007). Gender's unspoken role in leadership evaluations. *Human Resource Planning, 30* (3), 24–32.

MacCallum, Fiona; & Golombok, Susan. (2004). Children raised in fatherless families from infancy: A follow-up of children of lesbian and single heterosexual mothers at early adolescence. *Journal of Child Psychology and Psychiatry, 45,* 1407–1419.

Maccoby, Eleanor E. (1988). Gender as a social category. *Developmental Psychology, 24,* 755–765.

Maccoby, Eleanor E. (2002). Gender and group process: A developmental perspective. *Current Directions in Psychological Science, 11,* 54–58.

Maccoby, Eleanor Emmons; & Jacklin, Carol Nagy. (1974). *The psychology of sex differences.* Stanford, CA: Stanford University Press.

MacGeorge, Erina L.; Graves, Angela R.; Feng, Bo; & Gillihan, Seth J. (2004). The myth of gender cultures: Similarities outweigh differences in men's and women's provision of and responses to supportive communication. *Sex Roles, 50,* 143–175.

Maciel, Jose A.; van Putten, Zanetta; & Knudson-Martin, Carmen. (2009). Gendered power in cultural context: Part I. Immigrant couples. *Family Process, 48* (1), 9–23.

Mackey, Richard A.; Diemer, Matthew A.; & O'Brien, Bernard A. (2000). Psychological intimacy in the lasting relationships of heterosexual and same-gender couples. *Sex Roles, 43,* 201–227.

Macrae, C. Neil; & Bodenhausen, Galen V. (2000). Social cognition: Thinking categorically about others. *Annual Review of Psychology, 51,* 93–120.

Madson, Laura. (2000). Inferences regarding the personality traits and sexual orientation of physically androgynous people. *Psychology of Women Quarterly, 24,* 148–160.

Magura, Stephen; Knight, Edward L.; Vogel, Howard S.; Mahmood, Daneyal; Laudet, Alexandre B.; & Rosenblum, Andrew. (2003). Mediators of effectiveness in dual-focus self-help groups. *American Journal of Drug and Alcohol Abuse, 29,* 301–322.

Mahaffy, Kimberly A.; & Ward, Sally K. (2002). The gendering of adolescents' childbearing and educational plans: Reciprocal effects and the influence of social context. *Sex Roles, 46,* 403–417.

Mahalik, James R.; Good, Glenn E.; & Englar-Carlson, Matt. (2003). Masculinity scripts, presenting concerns, and help seeking: Implications for practice and training. *Professional Psychology: Research and Practice, 34,* 123–131.

Maher, Jill K.; & Childs, Nancy M. (2003). A longitudinal content analysis of gender roles in children's television advertisements: A 27 year review. *Journal of Current Issues and Research in Advertising, 25,* 71–81.

Mahoney, Michael J. (2003). Minding science: Constructivism and the discourse of inquiry. *Cognitive Therapy and Research, 27,* 105–123.

Major, Brenda; & O'Brien, Laurie T. (2005). The social psychology of stigma. *Annual Review of Psychology, 56,* 393–421.

Majors, Richard G.; & Billson, J. M. (1992). *Cool pose: The dilemmas of black manhood in America.* New York: Lexington.

Majors, Richard G.; Tyler, Richard; Peden, Blaine; & Hall, Ron. (1994). Cool pose: A symbolic mechanism for masculine role enactment and coping by black males. In Richard G. Majors & Jacob U. Gordon (Eds.), *The American black male: His present status and his future* (pp. 245–259). Chicago: Nelson-Hall.

Malamuth, Neil M. (1996). The confluence model of sexual aggression: Feminist and evolutionary perspectives. In David M. Buss & Neil M. Malamuth (Eds.), *Sex, power, conflict: Evolutionary and feminist perspectives* (pp. 269–295). New York: Oxford University Press.

Malinowski, Jon C. (2001). Mental rotation and real-world wayfinding. *Perceptual and Motor Skills, 92,* 19–30.

Malone, Judi L. (2000). Working with Aboriginal women: Applying feminist therapy in a multicultural counselling context. *Canadian Journal of Counselling, 34,* 33–42.

Malouf, Matthew A.; Migeon, Claude J.; Carson, Kathryn A.; Petrucci, Loredana; & Wisniewski, Amy B. (2006). Cognitive outcome in women affected by congenital adrenal hyperplasia due to 21-hydroxylase deficiency. *Hormone Research, 65,* 142–150.

Malt, Sue. (2007). Love actually! Older adults and their romantic Internet relationships. *Australian Journal of Emerging Technologies and Society, 5* (2), 84–102.

Mandara, Jelani; Murray, Carolyn B.; & Joyner, Toya N. (2005). The impact of fathers' absence on African American adolescents' gender role development. *Sex Roles, 53* (3/4), 207–220.

Manger, Terje; & Eikeland, Ole-Johan. (1998). The effects of spatial visualization and students' sex on mathematical achievement. *British Journal of Psychology, 89,* 17–25.

Mann, K. (2005). Neuroimaging of gender differences in alcohol dependence: Are women more vulnerable? *Alcoholism: Clinical and Experimental Research, 29,* 896–901.

Manning, Wendy D.; Giordano, Peggy C.; & Longmore, Monica A. (2006). Hooking up: The relationship context of "nonrelationship" sex. *Journal of Adolescent Research, 21* (5), 459–483.

Mansfield, Abigail K.; Addis, Michael E.; Cordova, James V.; & Dowd, Lynn. (2009). Emotional skillfulness as a key mediator of aggression. *Journal of Aggression, Maltreatment and Trauma, 18* (5), 221–247.

Marchel, Carol; & Owens, Stephanie. (2007). Qualitative research in psychology: Could William James get a job? *History of Psychology, 10* (40), 301–324.

Marder, Ariane. (2005). Bad boys: You may not be one, but here are seven ways to make her think you are. *Men's Fitness, 21* (10), 40.

Marecek, Jeanne. (2001). Disorderly constructs: Feminist frameworks for clinical psychology. In Rhoda K. Unger (Ed.), *Handbook of the psychology of women and gender* (pp. 303–316). New York: Wiley.

Marecek, Jeanne; Kimmel, Ellen B.; Crawford, Mary: & Hare-Mustin, Rachel T. (2003). Psychology of women and gender. In Donald K Freedheim (Ed.), *Handbook of psychology: History of psychology* (Vol. 1, pp. 249–268). New York: Wiley.

Marecek, Jeanne; Kravetz, Diane; & Finn, Stephen. (1979). Comparison of women who enter feminist therapy and women who enter traditional therapy. *Journal of Consulting and Clinical Psychology, 47,* 734–742.

Markey, Charlotte N.; & Markey, Patrick M. (2005). Relations between body image and dieting behaviors: An examination of gender differences. *Sex Roles, 53,* 519–530.

Markey, Charlotte N.; Markey, Patrick M.; Schneider, Carl; & Brownlee, Susan. (2005). Marital status and health beliefs: Different relations for men and women. *Sex Roles, 53,* 443–451.

Marks, Michael J.; & Fraley, Chris. (2005). The sexual double standard: Fact or fiction? *Sex Roles, 52,* 175–186.

Marler, Joan. (2006). The myth of universal patriarchy: A critical response to Cynthia Eller's *Myth of Matriarchal Prehistory. Feminist Theology, 14,* 163–187.

Marshall, Simon J.; Gorely, Trish; & Biddle, Stuart J. H. (2006). A descriptive epidemiology of screen-based media use in youth: A review and critique. *Journal of Adolescence, 29*, 333–349.

Martell, Richard F.; Lane, David, M.; & Emrich, Cynthia. (1996). Male-female differences: A computer simulation. *American Psychologist, 51*, 157–158.

Martin, C. A.; Lommel, K.; Cox, J.; Kelly, T.; Rayens, M. K.; Woodring, J. H.; et al. (2007). Kiss and tell: What do we know about pre- and early adolescent females who report dating? A pilot study. *Journal of Pediatric and Adolescent Gynecology, 20* (1), 45–49.

Martin, Carol Lynn. (1995). Stereotypes about children with traditional and nontraditional gender roles. *Sex Roles, 33*, 727–751.

Martin, Carol Lynn; & Fabes, Richard A. (2001). The stability and consequences of young children's same-sex peer interactions. *Developmental Psychology, 37*, 431–446.

Martin, Carol Lynn; & Halverson, Charles F., Jr. (1981). A schematic processing model of sex-typing and stereotyping in children. *Child Development, 52*, 1119–1134.

Martin, Carol Lynn; & Little, Jane K. (1990). The relation of gender understanding to children's sex-typed preferences and gender stereotypes. *Child Development, 61*, 1427–1439.

Martin, Carol Lynn; & Ruble, Diane. (2004). Children's search for gender cues: Cognitive perspectives on gender development. *Current Directions in Psychological Science, 13*, 67–70.

Martin, Carol Lynn; Ruble, Diane N.; & Szkrybalo, Joel. (2002). Cognitive theories of early gender development. *Psychological Bulletin, 128*, 903–933.

Martin, Carol Lynn; Ruble, Diane N.; & Szkrybalo, Joel. (2004). Recognizing the centrality of gender identity and stereotype knowledge in gender development and moving toward theoretical integration: Reply to Bandura and Bussey (2004). *Psychological Bulletin, 130*, 702–710.

Martin, Carol Lynn; Wood, Carolyn H.; & Little, Jane K. (1990). The development of gender stereotype components. *Child Development, 61*, 1891–1904.

Martin, Courtney E. (2007, November 26). Ugly, boring and angry? *New Statesman*. Retrieved June 23, 2009, from http://www.newstatesman.com/blogs/the-faith-column/2007/11/stereotypes-feminism-feminists

Martin, Judith N.; Bradford, Lisa J.; Drzewiecka, Jolanta A.; & Chitgopekar, Anu S. (2003). Intercultural dating patterns among young white U.S. Americans: Have they changed in the past 20 years? *Howard Journal of Communication, 14*, 53–73.

Martino, Steven C.; Collins, Rebecca L.; Elliott, Marc N.; Kanouse, David E.; & Berry, Sandra H. (2009). It's better on TV: Does television set teenagers up for regret following sexual initiation? *Perspectives on Sexual and Reproductive Health, 41* (2), 92–100.

Massa, Laura J.; Mayer, Richard E.; & Bohon, Lisa M. (2005). Individual differences in gender role beliefs

influence spatial ability test performance. *Learning and Individual Differences, 15*, 99–111.

Masselot, Annick. (2004). The new equal treatment directive: plus ça change . . . . *Feminist Legal Studies, 12*, 93–104.

Mast, Marianne Schmid. (2002). Female dominance hierarchies: Are they any different from males'? *Personality and Social Psychology Bulletin, 28*, 29–39.

Mast, Marianne Schmid; & Hall, Judith A. (2006). Women's advantage at remembering others' appearance: A systematic look at the why and when of a gender difference. *Personality and Social Psychology Bulletin, 32*, 353–364.

Masters, William H.; & Johnson, Virginia E. (1966). *Human sexual response*. Boston: Little, Brown.

Matarasso, Alan. (2006). Abdominoplasty and abdominal contour surgery: A national plastic surgery survey. *Plastic and Reconstructive Surgery, 117*, 1797–1808.

Matud, M. Pilar; Rodríguez, C.; & Grande, J. (2007). Gender differences in creative thinking. *Personality and Individual Differences, 43* (5), 1137–1147.

Maurer, Trent W.; & Pleck, Joseph H. (2006). Fathers' caregiving and breadwinning: A gender congruence analysis. *Psychology of Men and Masculinity, 7*, 101–112.

Mazur, Tom. (2005). Gender dysphoria and gender change in androgen insensitivity or micropenis. *Archives of Sexual Behavior, 34*, 411–421.

McArthur, Laura H.; Holbert, Donald; & Pena, Manuel. (2005). An exploration of the attitudinal and perceptual dimensions of body image among male and female adolescents from six Latin American cities. *Adolescence, 40*, 801–816.

McBride, Deborah. (2007). Report shows a gender gap in cancer. *ONS Connect, 22* (10), 8–9.

McClelland, David C.; Atkinson, J. W.; Clark, R. W.; & Lowell, E. L. (1953). *The achievement motive*. New York: Appleton.

McCombs, Barbara L. (2000, July). Reducing the achievement gap. *Society, 37*, 29–35.

McCormick, Naomi B. (1994). *Sexual salvation: Affirming women's sexual rights and pleasures*. Westport, CT: Praeger.

McCrea, Sean M.; Hirt, Edward R.; Hendrix, Kristin L.; Milner, Bridgett J.; & Steele, Nathan L. (2008). The worker scale: Developing a measure to explain gender differences in behavioral self-handicapping. *Journal of Research in Personality, 42* (4), 949–970.

McCreary, Donald R.; & Sasse, Doris K. (2000). An exploration of the drive for muscularity in adolescent boys and girls. *Journal of American College Health, 48*, 297–304.

McDaniel, Michael A. (2005). Big-brained people are smarter: A meta-analysis of the relationship between in vivo brain volume and intelligence. *Intelligence, 33*, 337–346.

McDougall, Patricia; & Hymel, Shelley. (2007). Same-gender versus cross-gender friendship conceptions. *Merrill-Palmer Quarterly, 53* (3), 347–380.

McFarlane, Jessica; Martin, Carol Lynn; & Williams, Tannis MacBeth. (1988). Mood fluctuations: Women versus men and menstrual versus other cycles. *Psychology of Women Quarterly, 12,* 201–223.

McFarlane, Jessica Motherwell; & Williams, Tannis MacBeth. (1994). Placing premenstrual syndrome in perspective. *Psychology of Women Quarterly, 18,* 339–373.

McGinnis, Sandra L. (2003). Cohabiting, dating, and perceived costs of marriage: A model of marriage entry. *Journal of Marriage and Family, 65,* 105–116.

McGinty, Kristen; Knox, David; & Zusman, Marty E. (2007). Friends with benefits: Women want "friends," men want "benefits." *College Student Journal, 41* (4, Part B), 1128–1131.

McGlone, Matthew S.; & Aronson, Joshua. (2006). Stereotype threat, identity, salience, and spatial reasoning. *Journal of Applied Developmental Psychology, 27* (5), 468–493.

McHale, Susan M.; Crouter, Ann C.; & Tucker, Corinna J. (1999). Family context and gender role socialization in middle childhood: Comparing girls to boys. *Child Development, 70,* 990–1004.

McHale, Susan M.; Crouter Ann C.; & Whiteman, Shawn D. (2003). The family contexts of gender development during childhood and adolescence. *Social Development, 12,* 125–148.

McHale, Susan M.; Kim, Ji-Yeon; Whiteman, Shawn; & Crouter, Ann C. (2004). Links between sex-typed time use in middle childhood and gender development in early adolescence. *Developmental Psychology, 40,* 868–881.

McHale, Susan M.; Updegraff, Kimberly A.; Helms-Erikson, Heather; & Crouter, Ann C. (2001). Sibling influences on gender development in middle childhood and early adolescence: A longitudinal study. *Developmental Psychology, 37,* 115–125.

McHale, Susan M.; Updegraff, Kimberly A.; Shanahan, Lilly; Crouter, Ann C.; & Killoren, Sarah E. (2005). Siblings' differential treatment in Mexican American families. *Journal of Marriage and Family, 67,* 1259–1274.

McHugh, Maureen C.; & Cosgrove, Lisa. (2004). Feminist research methods: Studying women and gender. In Michele A. Paludi (Ed.), *Praeger guide to the psychology of gender* (pp. 151–181). Westport, CT: Praeger/Greenwood.

McHugh, Maureen C.; Koeske, Randi D.; & Frieze, Irene H. (1986). Issues to consider in conducting nonsexist psychological research: A guide for researchers. *American Psychologist, 41,* 879–890.

McKeever, Matthew; & Wolfinger, Nicholas H. (2001). Re-examining the economic costs of marital disruption for women. *Social Science Quarterly, 82,* 202–217.

McKelley, Ryan A.; & Rochlen, Aaron B. (2007). The practice of coaching: Exploring alternatives to therapy for counseling-resistant men. *Psychology of Men and Masculinity, 8* (1), 53–65.

McKown, Clark; & Weinstein, Rhona S. (2003). The development and consequences of stereotype consciousness in middle childhood. *Child Development, 74,* 498–515.

McLain, Susan June; & Perkins, Carol O. (1990). Disabled women: At the bottom of the work heap. *Vocational Educational Journal, 65* (2), 54–63.

McLean, Kristen. (2008). Inside, outside, nowhere: Bisexual men and women in the gay and lesbian community. *Journal of Bisexuality, 8* (1/2), 63–80.

McMichael, Anthony J.; McKee, Martin; Shkolnikov, Vladimir; & Valkonen, Tapani. (2004). Mortality trends and setbacks: Global convergence or divergence? *Lancet, 363,* 1155–1159.

Medda, P.; Perugi, G.; Zanello, S.; Ciuffa, M.; & Cassano, G. B. (2009). Response to ECT in bipolar I, bipolar II and unipolar depression. *Journal of Affective Disorders, 118* (1–3), 55–59.

MediaMatters for America. (2005, June 24). Limbaugh defended his use of term "feminazi" as "right" and "accurate." Retrieved June 23, 2009, from http://mediamatters.org/research/200506240002

Meehan, Anita M.; & Janik, Leann M. (1990). Illusory correlation and the maintenance of sex role stereotypes in children. *Sex Roles, 22,* 83–95.

Mehl, Matthias R.; Vazire, Simine; Ramirez-Esparza, Nairín; Statcher, Richard B.; & Pennebaker, James W. (2007). Are women really more talkative than men? *Science, 317* (5834), 82.

Meier, Ann; & Allen, Gina. (2009). Romantic relationships from adolescence to young adulthood: Evidence from the National Longitudinal Study of Adolescent Health. *Sociological Quarterly, 50* (2), 308–335.

Melo, Angel I.; Lovic, Vedran; Gonzalez, Andrea; Madden, Melissa; Sinopoli, Katia; & Fleming, Alison S. (2006). Maternal and littermate deprivation disrupts maternal behavior and social learning of food preferences in adulthood: Tactile stimulation, nest odor, and social rearing prevent these effects. *Developmental Psychobiology, 48,* 209–219.

Melson, Gail F. (2001). *Why the wild things are: Animals in the lives of children.* Cambridge, MA: Harvard University Press.

Melson, Gail F.; & Fogel, Alan. (1988). The development of nurturance in young children. *Young Children, 43,* 57–65.

Menaster, Michael. (2002, October 1). Controversies in eating disorders among men. *Psychiatric Times,* p. 83.

Meryn, Siegfried. (2009). Global man & health. *Journal of Men's Health, 6* (1), 2–3.

Mesquita, Batja; & Frijda, Nico H. (1992). Cultural variations in emotions: A review. *Psychological Bulletin, 112,* 179–204.

Messner, Michael A. (1997). *Politics of masculinities: Men in movements.* Thousand Oaks, CA: Sage.

Meyer, Elizabeth J. (2008). Gendered harassment in secondary schools: Understanding teachers' (non) interventions. *Gender and Education, 20* (6), 555–570.

Meyer-Bahlburg, Heino F. L. (1980). Sexuality in early ado-lescence. In Benjamin B. Wolman & John Money (Eds.), *Handbook of human sexuality* (pp. 61–82). Englewood Cliffs, NJ: Prentice Hall.

Meyer-Bahlburg, Heino F. L.; Dolezal, Curtis; Baker, Susan W.; Carlson, Ann D.; Obeid, Jihad S.; & New, Maria I. (2004). Prenatal androgenization affects gender-related behavior but not gender identity in 5–12-year-old girls with congenital adrenal hyperplasia. *Archives of Sexual Behavior, 33*, 97–104.

MI Watch. (2009). *DSM-V controversy boiling.* Retrieved November 9, 2009 from http://www.miwatch.org/2009/07/dsm-v_controversy_boiling_for.html

Michael, Robert T.; Gagnon, John H.; Laumann, Edward O.; & Kolata, Gina. (1994). *Sex in America.* Boston: Little, Brown.

Middaugh, Anne. (1994, August). *Clinical psychology interns' attitudes and information about women.* Paper presented at the 102nd annual convention of the American Psychological Association, Los Angeles, CA.

Milar, Katharine S. (2000). The first generation of women psychologists and the psychology of women. *American Psychologist, 55*, 616–619.

Miletic, Michelle Price. (2002). The introduction of a feminine psychology to psychoanalysis: Karen Horney's legacy. *Contemporary Psychoanalysis, 38* (2), 287–299.

Miller, Cindy; Lurye, Leah; Zosuls, Kristina; & Ruble, Diane. (2009). Accessibility of gender stereotype domains: Developmental and gender differences in children. *Sex Roles, 60* (11/12), 870–881.

Miller, Katherine J.; Gleaves, David H.; Hirsch, Tera G.; Green, Bradley A.; Snow, Alicia C.; & Corbett, Chanda C. (2000). Comparisons of body image dimensions by race/ethnicity and gender in a university population. *International Journal of Eating Disorders, 27*, 310–316.

Miller, Laura J. (2002, June 1). Premenstrual dysphoric disorder. *Psychiatric Times, 19* (6), 54+.

Miller, Lisa; & Ramirez, Jessica. (2009, June 22). The sins of fathers. *Newsweek, 153* (25), 32.

Miller, Merry N.; & Miller, Barney E. (2001). Premenstrual exacerbations of mood disorders. *Psychopharmacology Bulletin, 35*, 135–149.

Minerick, Adrienne R.; Wasburn, Mara H.; & Young, Valerie L. (2009). Mothers on the tenure track: What engineering and technology faculty still confront. *Engineering Studies, 1* (3), 217–235.

Minton, Henry L. (2000). Psychology and gender at the turn of the century. *American Psychologist, 55*, 613–615.

Mischel, Walter. (1966). A social-learning view of sex differences in behavior. In Eleanor E. Maccoby (Ed.), *The development of sex differences* (pp. 56–81). Stanford, CA: Stanford University Press.

Mischel, Walter. (1993). *Introduction to personality* (5th ed.). Fort Worth, TX: Harcourt Brace Jovanovich.

Mitchell, Jason P.; Ames, Daniel L.; Jenkins, Adrianna C.; & Banaji, Mahzarin R. (2009). Neural correlates of stereotype application. *Journal of Cognitive Neuroscience, 21* (3), 594–604.

Mo, Phoenix K. H.; Malik, Sumaira H.; & Coulson, Neil S. (2009). Gender differences in computer-mediated communication: A systematic literature review of online health-related support groups. *Patient Education and Counseling, 75* (1), 16–24.

Moghadam, Valentine M. (2002). Islamic feminism and its discontents: Toward a resolution of the debate. *Signs, 27* (4), 1135–1171.

Molo, Mariateresa; Rizzi, Laura; Cantafio, Pietro; Cappai, Elena; Vighetti, Sergio; Castelli, Lorys; et al. (2006). Characteristics of brain activity in patients with gender identity disorder. *Journal of Sex Research, 43*, 22.

Monahan, John S.; Harke, Maureen A.; & Shelley, Jonathon R. (2008). Computerizing the mental rotations test: Are gender differences maintained? *Behavioral Research Methods, 40* (2), 422–427.

Money, John. (1986). *Venuses penuses: Sexology, sexosophy, and exigency theory.* Buffalo, NY: Prometheus Books.

Monk, Debra; & Ricciardelli, Lina A. (2003). Three dimensions of the male gender role as correlates of alcohol and cannabis involvement in young Australian men. *Psychology of Men and Masculinity, 4*, 57–69.

Monsour, Michael. (2002). *Women and men as friends: Relationships across the life span in the 21st century.* Mahwah, NJ: Erlbaum.

Montello, Daniel R.; Lovelace, Kristin L.; Golledge, Reginald G.; & Self, Carole M. (1999). Sex-related differences and similarities in geographic and environmental spatial abilities. *Annals of the Association of American Geographers, 89*, 515–534.

Montemurro, Beth. (2003). Not a laughing matter: Sexual harassment as "material" on workplace-based situation comedies. *Sex Roles, 48*, 433–445.

Moon, Michelle; & Hoffman, Charles D. (2008). Mothers' and fathers' differential expectancies and behaviors: Parent x child gender effects. *Journal of Genetic Psychology, 169* (3), 261–280.

Moore, Fhionna Rosemary; Cassidy, Clare; Smith, Miriam Jane Law; & Perrett, David Ian. (2006). The effects of female control of resources on sex-differentiated mate preferences. *Evolution and Human Behavior, 27*, 193–205.

Moos, Rudolf; Schaefer, Jeanne; Andrassy, Jill; & Moos, Bernice. (2001). Outpatient mental health care, self-help groups, and patients' one-year treatment outcomes. *Journal of Clinical Psychology, 57*, 273–287.

Morgan, Betsy Levonian. (1998). A three generational study of tomboy behavior. *Sex Roles, 39*, 787–800.

Morgan, Carolyn; Isaac, James D.; & Sansone, Carol. (2001). The role of interest in understanding the career choices of female and male college students. *Sex Roles, 44*, 295–320.

Morgan, Robin. (1970). Introduction: The women's revolution. In Robin Morgan (Ed.), *Sisterhood is powerful: An anthology of writings from the women's liberation movement* (pp. xv–xvii). New York: Vintage Books.

Mori, DeAnna; Chaiken, Shelly; & Pliner, Patricia. (1987). "Eating lightly" and the self-presentation of femininity. *Journal of Personality and Social Psychology, 53*, 693–702.

Morr Serewicz, Mary; & Gale, Elaine. (2008). First-date scripts: Gender roles, context, and relationship. *Sex Roles, 58* (3/4), 149–164.

Morrison, Rachel. (2009). Are women tending and befriending in the workplace? Gender differences in the relationship between workplace friendships and organizational outcomes. *Sex Roles, 60* (1/2), 1–13.

Morrison, Todd G.; Morrison, Melanie A.; & Hopkins, Christine. (2003). Striving for bodily perfection? An exploration of the drive for muscularity in Canadian men. *Psychology of Men & Masculinity, 4*, 111–120.

Mortimer, Ann M. (2007). The neuroscience of maternal behaviour. *Current Psychiatry Reviews, 3* (2), 129–135.

Mossakowski, Krysia N. (2008). Dissecting the influence of race, ethnicity, and socioeconomic status on mental health in young adulthood. *Research on Aging, 30* (6), 649–671.

Mota, Jorge; Silva, Pedro; Santos, Maria Paula; Ribeiro, José Carlos; Oliveira, José; & Durate, José A. (2005). Physical activity and school recess time: Differences between the sexes and the relationship between children's playground physical activity and habitual physical activity. *Journal of Sports Sciences, 23*, 269–275.

Mueller, S. C.; Temple, V.; Oh, E.; VanRyzin; C.; Williams, A.; Cornwell, B.; et al. (2008). Early androgen exposure modulates spatial cognition in congenital adrenal hyperplasia (CAH). *Psychoneuroendocrinology, 33* (7), 973–980.

Munch, Shari. (2004). Gender-biased diagnosing of women's medical complaints: Contributions of feminist thought, 1970–1995. *Women and Health, 40*, 101–121.

Munroe, Robert L.; & Romney, A. Kimbal. (2006). Gender and age differences in same-sex aggregation and social behavior: A four-culture study. *Journal of Cross-Cultural Psychology, 37*, 3–19.

Murat, Laure. (2005). The invention of the neuter. *Diogenes, 52* (4), 61–72.

Murnen, Sarah K.; Wright, Carrie; & Kaluzny, Gretchen. (2002). If "boys will be boys," then girls will be victims? A meta-analytic review of the research that relates masculine ideology to sexual aggression. *Sex Roles, 46*, 359–375.

Murphy, Elaine M. (2003). Being born female is dangerous for your health. *American Psychologist, 58*, 205–210.

Murphy, Sheila T. (1998). The impact of factual versus fictional media portrayals on cultural stereotypes. *The Annals of the American Academy of Political and Social Science, 560*, 165–178.

Murray, Christopher J. L.; & Lopez, Alan D. (1997). Alternative projections of mortality and disability by cause 1990–2020: Global Burden of Disease Study (part 4). *Lancet, 349*, 1498–1504.

Murrell, Audrey J.; & James, Erika Hayes. (2001). Gender and diversity in organizations: Past, present, and future directions. *Sex Roles, 45*, 243–257.

Myhill, Debra; & Jones, Susan. (2006). "She doesn't shout at no girls": Pupils' perceptions of gender equity in the classroom. *Cambridge Journal of Education, 36*, 99–113.

Nachescu, Voichita. (2009). Radical feminism and the nation. *Journal for the Study of Radicalism, 3* (1), 29–59.

Nachmani, Irit; & Somer, Eli. (2007). Women sexually victimized in psychotherapy speak out: The dynamics and outcome of therapist-client sex. *Women and Therapy, 30* (1/2), 1–17.

Nannini, Dawn K.; & Meyers, Lawrence S. (2000). Jealousy in sexual and emotional infidelity: An alternative to the evolutionary explanation. *Journal of Sex Research, 37*, 117–122.

Nardi, Peter M. (2007). Friendship, sex, and masculinity. In Michael Kimmel (Ed.), *The sexual self: The construction of sexual scripts* (pp. 49–57). Nashville, TN: Vanderbilt University Press.

Nassif, Atif; & Gunter, Barrie. (2008). Gender representation in television advertisements in Britain and Saudi Arabia. *Sex Roles, 58* (11/12), 752–760.

National Center for Health Statistics. (2005). *Health, United States, 2005*. Hyattsville, MD: U.S. Government Printing Office.

National Center for Health Statistics. (2009). *Health, United States, 2008*. Hyattsville, MD: U.S. Government Printing Office.

Neff, Kristin D.; & Harter, Susan. (2002). The authenticity of conflict resolutions among adult couples: Does women's other-oriented behavior reflect their true selves? *Sex Roles, 47*, 403–417.

Nemeroff, Charles B.; Bremner, J. Doublas; Foa, Edna B.; Mayberg, Helen S.; North, Carol S.; & Stein, Murray B. (2006). Posttraumatic stress disorder: A state-of-the-science review. *Journal of Psychiatric Research, 40*, 1–21.

Neto, Félix & Silva, M. Carolina. (2009). Changing patterns of gender portrayals in Portuguese television advertisements. *Journal of Applied Social Psychology, 39* (5), 1214–1228.

Netting, Nancy S. (1992). Sexuality in youth culture: Identity and change. *Adolescence, 27*, 961–976.

Netting, Nancy S.; & Burnett, Matthew L. (2004). Twenty years of student sexual behavior: Subcultural adaptations to a changing health environment. *Adolescence, 39*, 19–38.

Neumark-Sztainer, Dianne; Croll, Jillian; Story, Mary; Hannan, Peter J.; French, Simone A.; & Perry, Cheryl. (2002). Ethnic/racial differences in weight-related concerns and behaviors among adolescent girls and boys: Findings from Project EAT. *Journal of Psychosomatic Research, 53*, 963–974.

Newcombe, Nora S. (2007). Taking science seriously: Straight thinking about spatial sex differences. In Stephen J. Ceci & Wendy M. Williams (Eds.), *Why aren't more women in science: Top researchers debate the evidence* (pp. 69–77). Washington, DC: American Psychological Association.

Newman, Barry. (2008, March 17). This swimmer is in deep end of gender wars. *Wall Street Journal, 251* (63), A1, A15.

Newman, Leonard S.; Cooper, Joel; & Ruble, Diane N. (1995). The interactive effects of knowledge and constancy on gender-stereotyped attitudes. (Gender and Computers, part 2). *Sex Roles, 33,* 325–351.

Newton, Judith. (2004). *From panthers to Promise Keepers: Rethinking the men's movement.* New York: Rowman & Littlefield.

Ng, Eddy S.; & Wiesner, Willi H. (2007). Are men always picked over women? The effects of employment equity directives on selection decisions. *Journal of Business Ethics, 76* (2), 177–187.

Nguyen, Hannah-Hanh D.; & Ryan, Ann Marie. (2008). Does stereotype threat affect test performance of minorities and women? A meta-analysis of experimental evidence. *Journal of Applied Psychology, 93* (6), 1314–1334.

Nicholas, Donald R. (2000). Men, masculinity, and cancer: Risk-factor behaviors, early detection, and psychosocial adaptation. *Journal of American College Health, 49,* 27–33.

Nielsen, Laura Beth. (2002). Subtle, pervasive, harmful: Racist and sexist remarks in public as hate speech. *Journal of Social Issues, 58,* 265–280.

Niemi, P. M.; & Vainiomäki, P. T. (2006). Medical students' distress—Quality, continuity and gender differences during a six-year medical programme. *Medical Teacher, 28,* 136–141.

Nieva, Veronica F.; & Gutek, Barbara A. (1981). *Women and work: A psychological perspective.* New York: Praeger.

NIMH launches public health campaign for men with depression. (2003). Mental Health *Weekly, 13* (15), 3.

Nippold, Marilyn A.; Duthie, Jill K.; & Larsen, Jennifer. (2005). Literacy as a leisure activity: Free-time preferences of older children and young adolescents. *Language, Speech, and Hearing Services in Schools, 36,* 93–102.

Nisbett, Richard E. (2003). *The geography of thought.* New York: Free Press.

Nishimura, Nancy. (2004). Counseling biracial women: An intersection of multiculturalism and feminism. *Women and Therapy, 27* (1/2), 133–145.

Noddings, Nel. (1991/1992, December/January). The gender issue. *Educational Leadership, 49* (4), 65–70.

Nolen-Hoeksema, Susan. (2006). The etiology of gender differences in depression. In Carolyn M. Mazure & Gwendolyn Puryear Keita (Eds.), *Understanding depression in women: Applying empirical research to practice and policy* (pp. 9–43). Washington, DC: American Psychological Association.

Nolen-Hoeksema, Susan; Larson, Judith; & Grayson, Carla. (1999). Explaining the gender difference in depressive symptoms. *Journal of Personality and Social Psychology, 77,* 1061–1072.

Noll, Jennie G.; Trickett, Penelope K.; & Putnam, Frank W. (2003). A prospective investigation of the impact of childhood sexual abuse on the development of sexuality. *Journal of Consulting and Clinical Psychology, 71,* 575–586.

Norcross, John C.; Santrock, John W.; Campbell, Linda F.; Smith, Thomas P.; Sommer, Robert; & Zuckerman, Edward L. (2003). *Authoritative guide to self-help resources in mental health* (rev. ed.). New York: Guilford Press.

Nori, Raffaella; & Giusberti, Fiorella. (2006). Predicting cognitive styles from spatial abilities. *American Journal of Psychology, 119,* 67–86.

Nosek, Brian A.; Banaji, Mahzarin R.; & Greenwald, Anthony G. (2002). Math = male, me = female, therefore math Z me. *Journal of Personality and Social Psychology, 83,* 44–59.

O'Brien, Edward J.; Jeffreys, Dorothy; Leitzel, Jeff; O'Brien, Jean P.; Mensky, Larissa; & Marchese, Marc. (1996, August). *Gender differences in the self-esteem of adolescents: A meta-analysis.* Paper presented at the 104th annual convention of the American Psychological Association, Toronto, Canada.

O'Brien, Marion; Peyton, Vicki; Mistry, Rashmita; Hruda, Ludmila; Jacobs, Anne; Caldera, Yvonne; et al. (2000). Gender-role cognition in three-year-old boys and girls. *Sex Roles, 42,* 1007–1025.

O'Donnell, Katherine; & O'Rourke, Michael (Eds.). (2003). *Love, sex, intimacy and friendship between men, 1550–1800.* Basingstoke, UK: Palgrave Macmillan.

O'Donnell, Meaghan L.; Creamer, Mark; Bryant, Richard A.; Schnyder, Ulrich; & Shalev, Arik. (2003). Posttraumatic disorders following injury: An empirical and methodological review. *Clinical Psychology Review, 23,* 587–603.

Office of Research on Women's Health. (2009). *Home page.* Retrieved October 31, 2009, from http://orwh.od.nih.gov/about.html

Ogletree, Shirley Matile; & Ginsburg, Harvey J. (2000). Kept under the hood: Neglect of the clitoris in common vernacular. *Sex Roles, 43,* 917–941.

Ogletree, Shirley M.; Martinez, Cristal N.; Turner, Trent R.; & Mason, Brad. (2004). Pokémon: Exploring the role of gender. *Sex Roles, 50,* 851–859.

Olivardia, Roberto; Pope, Harrison G.; Borowiecki, John J.; & Cohane, Geoffrey H. (2004). Biceps and body image: The relationship between muscularity and self-esteem, depression, and eating disorder symptoms. *Psychology of Men & Masculinity, 5,* 112–120.

Oliver, Mary Beth; & Hyde, Janet Shibley. (1993). Gender differences in sexuality: A meta-analysis. *Psychological Bulletin, 114,* 29–51.

Olkin, Rhoda. (2008). Women with disabilities. In Joan C. Chrisler, Carla Golden, & Patricia D. Rozee (Eds.),

Lectures on the psychology of women (4th ed., pp. 190–203). New York: McGraw-Hill.

Onwuegbuzie, Anthony; & Leech, Nancy L. (2005). On becoming a pragmatic researcher: The importance of combining quantitative and qualitative research methodologies. *International Journal of Social Research Methodology, 8* (5), 375–387.

Oransky, Matthew; & Marecek, Jeanne. (2009). "I'm not going to be a girl": Masculinity and emotions in boys' friendships and peer groups. *Journal of Adolescent Research, 24* (2), 218–241.

Ortner, Tuulia; & Sieverding, Monika. (2008). Where are the gender differences? Male priming boosts spatial skills in women. *Sex Roles, 59* (3/4), 274–281.

Ostrov, Jamie M.; Crick, Nicki R.; & Keating, Caroline F. (2005). Gender-based perceptions of preschoolers' behavior: How much is aggression and prosocial behavior in the eye of the beholder? *Sex Roles, 52,* 393–398.

Oswald, Debra L. (2008). Gender stereotypes and women's reports of liking and ability in traditionally masculine and feminine occupations. *Psychology of Women Quarterly, 32* (2), 196–203.

Ott, Mary A; & Pfeiffer, Elizabeth J. (2009). "That's nasty" to curiosity: Early adolescent cognitions about sexual abstinence. *Journal of Adolescent Health, 44* (6), 575–581.

Ousley, Louise; Cordero, Elizabeth Diane; & White, Sabina. (2008). Eating disorders and body image of undergraduate men. *Journal of American College Health, 56* (6), 617–622.

Owen, Stephen S.; & Burke, Tod W. (2004). An exploration of prevalence of domestic violence in same-sex relationships. *Psychological Reports, 95,* 129–132.

Owens, Sherry Lynn; Smothers, Bobbie C.; & Love, Fannye E. (2003). Are girls victims of gender bias in our nation's schools? *Journal of Instructional Psychology, 30,* 131–136.

Paechter, Carier; & Clark, Sheryl. (2007). Who are tomboys and how do we recognise them? *Women's Studies International Forum, 30* (4), 342–354.

Pahl, Ray; & Pevalin, David J. (2005). Between family and friends: A longitudinal study of friendship choice. *British Journal of Sociology, 56,* 433–450.

Pajer, Kathleen; Tabbah, Rhonda; Gardner, William; Rubin, Robert T.; Czambel, R. Kenneth; & Wang, Yun. (2006). Adrenal androgen and gonadal hormone levels in adolescent girls with conduct disorder. *Psychoneuroendocrinology, 31* (10), 1245–1256.

Pallier, Gerry. (2003). Gender differences in the self-assessment of accuracy on cognitive tasks. *Sex Roles, 48,* 265–276.

Paludi, Michele A. (1984). Psychometric properties and underlying assumptions of four objective measures of fear of success. *Sex Roles, 10,* 765–781.

Paolucci, Elizabeth Oddone; Genuis, Mark L.; & Violato, Claudio. (2001). A meta-analysis of the published research on the effects of child sexual abuse. *Journal of Psychology, 135,* 17–36.

Park, Jason; Minor, Sam; Taylor, Rebecca Anne; Vikis, Elena; & Poenaru, Dan. (2005). Why are women deterred from general surgery training? *American Journal of Surgery, 190,* 141–146.

Parke, Ross D. (2002). Fathers and families. In Marc H. Bornstein (Ed.), *Handbook of parenting* (2nd ed., Vol. 3; pp. 27–73). Mahwah, NJ: Erlbaum.

Parlee, Mary Brown. (1973). The premenstrual syndrome. *Psychological Bulletin, 83,* 454–465.

Parmley, Maria; & Cunningham, Joseph. (2008). Children's gender-emotion stereotypes in the relationship of anger to sadness and fear. *Sex Roles, 58* (5/6), 358–370.

Parsons, Rhea. (2004). *The portrayal of PMS on television sitcoms.* Retrieved February 26, 2010 from http://www.academinist.org/mp/mp_archive/archive/december04/ampioa3.html

Parsons, Thomas D.; Larson, Peter; Kratz, Kris; Thiebaux, Marcus; Bluestein, Brendon; Buckwalter, J. Galen; et al. (2004). Sex differences in mental rotation and spatial rotation in a virtual environment. *Neuropsychologia, 42,* 555–562.

Pascoe, Elizabeth A.; & Richman, Laura Smart. (2009). Perceived discrimination and health: A meta-analytic review. *Psychological Bulletin, 135* (4), 531–554.

Patel, Vikram; & Kleinman, Arthur. (2003). Poverty and common mental disorders in developing countries. *Bulletin of the World Health Organization, 81,* 609–615.

Paul, Elizabeth L.; Wenzel, Amy; & Harvey, John. (2008). Hookups: A facilitator or a barrier to relationship initiation and intimacy development? In Susan Sprecher, Amy Wenzel, & John Harvey (Eds.), *Handbook of relationship initiation* (pp. 375–390). New York: Psychology Press.

Paul, Pamela. (2003, September 1). We're just friends. Really! *Time, 162* (9), A1.

Pauley, Perry M.; & Hesse, Colin. (2009). The effects of social support, depression, and stress on drinking behaviors in a college student sample. *Communication Studies, 60* (5), 493–508.

Pedersen, William C.; Miller, Lynn Carol; Putcha-Bhagavatula, Anila D.; & Yang, Yijing. (2002). Evolved sex differences in the number of partners desired: The long and the short of it. *Psychological Science, 13,* 157–161.

Penner, Andrew M. (2008a). Gender differences in extreme mathematical achievement: An international perspective on biological and social factors. *American Journal of Sociology, 114* (Suppl.), S138-S170.

Penner, Andrew M. (2008b). Race and gender differences in wages: The role of occupational sorting at the point of hire. *Sociological Quarterly, 49* (3), 597–614.

Peoples, Whitney A. (2008). Under construction: Identifying foundations of hip-hop feminism and exploring bridges between Black second-wave and hip-hop feminisms. *Meridians: Feminism, Race, Transnationalism, 8* (1), 19–52.

Peper, Jiska S.; Brouwer, Rachel M.; Schnack, Hugo G., van Baal, G. Caroline; van Leeuwen, Marieke; van den Berg, Stéphanie M.; et al. (2009). Sex steroids and brain structure in pubertal boys and girls. *Psychoneuroendocrinology, 34* (3), 332–342.

Peplau, Letitia Anne. (2003). Human sexuality: How do men and women differ? *Current Directions in Psychological Science, 12,* 37–40.

Peplau, Letitia Anne; & Campbell, Susan Miller. (1989). The balance of power in dating and marriage. In Jo Freeman (Ed.), *Women: A feminist perspective* (4th ed., pp. 121–137). Mountain View, CA: Mayfield.

Peplau, Letitia Anne; & Conrad, Eva. (1989). Beyond nonsexist research: The perils of feminist methods in psychology. *Psychology of Women Quarterly, 13,* 379–400.

Peplau, Letitia Anne; & Fingerhut, Adam W. (2007). The close relationships of lesbians and gay men. *Annual Review of Psychology, 58* (1), 405–424.

Peplau, Letitia Anne; & Huppin, Mark. (2008). Masculinity, femininity and the development of sexual orientation in women. *Journal of Gay and Lesbian Mental Health, 12* (1/2), 145–165.

Peplau, Letitia Anne; & Spalding, Leah R. (2000). The close relationships of lesbians, gay men, and bisexuals. In Clyde Hendrick & Susan S. Hendrick (Eds.), *Close relationships: A sourcebook* (pp. 110–123). Thousand Oaks, CA: Sage.

Perez, Beverly Encarguez. (2003). Woman warrior meets mail-order bride: Finding an Asian American voice in the women's movement. *Berkeley Women's Law Journal, 18,* 211–236.

Perrin, Paul B.; Heesacker, Martin; & Shrivastav, Rahul. (2008). Removing the tinted spectacles: Accurate client emotionality assessment despite therapists' gender stereotypes. *Journal of Social & Clinical Psychology, 27* (7), 711–733.

Perry, David G.; Perry, Louise C.; & Weiss, Robert J. (1989). Sex differences in the consequences that children anticipate for aggression. *Developmental Psychology, 25,* 312–319.

Peter, Jochen; Valkenburg, Patti M.; Schouten, Alexander P. (2005, May 26–30). *Characteristics and motives of adolescents talking with strangers on the Internet and its consequences.* Paper presented at the 55th national conference of the International Communication Association, New York.

Peter, Tracey. (2009). Exploring taboos: Comparing male- and female-perpetrated child sexual abuse. *Journal of Interpersonal Violence, 24* (7), 1111–1128.

Peters, John F. (1994). Gender socialization of adolescents in the home: Research and discussion. *Adolescence, 29,* 913–934.

Petersen, Trond; & Saporta, Ishak. (2004). The opportunity structure for discrimination. *American Journal of Sociology, 109,* 852–901.

Petersen, Trond; Saporta, Ishak; & Seidel, Marc-David L. (2000). Offering a job: Meritocracy and social networks. *American Journal of Sociology, 106,* 763–816.

Peterson, Carole; & Biggs, Marleen. (2001). "I was really, really, really mad!" Children's use of evaluative devices in narratives about emotional events. *Sex Roles, 45,* 801–825.

Petrides, K. V.; Furnham, Adrian; & Martin, G. Neil. (2004). Estimates of emotional and psychometric intelligence. *Journal of Social Psychology, 144,* 149–162.

Phillips, Roger D.; & Gilroy, Faith D. (1985). Sex-role stereotypes and clinical judgments of mental health: The Brovermans' findings reexamined. *Sex Roles, 12,* 179–193.

Phillips, Susan D.; & Imhoff, Anne R. (1997). Women and career development: A decade of research. *Annual Review of Psychology, 48,* 31–59.

Pichichero, Michael. (2006). Prevention of cervical cancer through vaccination of adolescents. *Clinical Pediatrics, 45,* 393–398.

Pickerill, J. Mitchell; Jackson, Robert A.; & Newman, Meredith A. (2006). Changing perceptions of sexual harassment in the federal workforce, 1987–94. *Law and Policy, 28,* 368–394.

Pike, Jennifer J.; & Jennings, Nancy A. (2005). The effects of commercials on children's perceptions of gender appropriate toy use. *Sex Roles, 52,* 83–91.

Piko, Bettina. (2001). Gender differences and similarities in adolescents' ways of coping. *Psychological Record, 51,* 223–235.

Pimlott-Kubiak, Sheryl; & Cortina, Lilia M. (2003). Gender, victimization, and outcomes: Reconceptualizing risk. *Journal of Consulting and Clinical Psychology, 71,* 528–539.

Pinel, John P. J. (2009). *Biopsychology* (7th ed.). Boston: Allyn & Bacon.

Pino, Nathan W.; & Meier, Robert F. (1999). Gender differences in rape reporting. *Sex Roles, 40,* 979–990.

Pinto, Katy; & Coltrane, Scott. (2009). Divisions of labor in Mexican origin and Anglo families: Structure and culture. *Sex Roles, 60* (7/8), 482–495.

Pistrang, Nancy; Barker, Chris; & Humphreys, Keith. (2008). Mutual help groups for mental health problems: A review of effectiveness studies. *American Journal of Community Psychology, 42* (1/2), 110–121.

Pitt, Richard N.; & Borland, Elizabeth. (2008). Bachelorhood and men's attitudes about gender roles. *Journal of Men's Studies, 16* (2), 140–158.

Plant, E. Ashby; Hyde, Janet Shibley; Keltner, Dacher; & Devine, Patricia G. (2000). The gender stereotyping of emotions. *Psychology of Women Quarterly, 24,* 81–92.

Pleck, Elizabeth H.; & Pleck, Joseph H. (1997). Fatherhood ideals in the United States: Historical dimensions. In Michael E. Lamb (Ed.), *The role of the father in child development* (3rd ed., pp. 33–48). New York: Wiley.

Pleck, Joseph H. (1981). *The myth of masculinity.* Cambridge, MA: MIT Press.

Pleck, Joseph H. (1984). The theory of male sex role identity: Its rise and fall, 1936 to the present. In Miriam Lewin (Ed.), *In the shadow of the past: Psychology portrays the sexes* (pp. 205–225). New York: Columbia University Press.

Pleck, Joseph H. (1995). The Gender Role Strain paradigm: An update. In Ronald F. Levant & William S. Pollack (Eds.), *A new psychology of men* (pp. 11–32). New York: Basic Books.

Pleck, Joseph H. (1997). Parental involvement: Levels, sources, and consequences. In Michael E. Lamb (Ed.), *The role of the father in child development* (3rd ed., pp. 66–103). New York: Wiley.

Pnina, Ron. (2009). The differences in role division between partners in long-term marriages and their well-being. *Journal of Family Social Work, 12* (1), 44–55.

Poland, Jeffrey; & Caplan, Paula J. (2004). The deep structure of bias in psychiatric diagnosis. In Paula J. Caplan & Lisa Cosgrove (Eds.), *Bias in psychiatric diagnosis* (pp. 9–23). Lanham, MD: Jason Aronson.

Polivy, Janet; & Herman, C. Peter. (2002). Causes of eating disorders. *Annual Review of Psychology, 53,* 187–214.

Pollack, William. (1998). *Real boys.* New York: Holt.

Pollatou, Elisana; Karadimou, Konstantina; & Gerodimos, Vasillios. (2005). Gender differences in musical aptitude, rhythmic ability and motor performance in preschool children. *Early Child Development and Care, 175,* 361–369.

Pollitt, Katha. (1992, December 28). Are women morally superior to men? *Nation,* pp. 799–807.

Pollitt, Katha. (2006, July 17/24). Mommy wars, round 587. *The Nation,* p. 10.

Pomerantz, Eva M.; Altermatt, Ellen Rydell; & Saxon, Jill L. (2002). Making the grade but feeling distressed: Gender differences in academic performance and internal distress. *Journal of Educational Psychology, 94,* 396–404.

Pontius, Anneliese A. (1997a). Lack of sex differences among east Ecuadorian school children on geometric figure rotation and face drawings. *Perceptual and Motor Skills, 85,* 72–74.

Pontius, Anneliese A. (1997b). No gender difference in spatial representation by schoolchildren in northwest Pakistan. *Journal of Cross-Cultural Psychology, 28,* 779–786.

Pope, Harrison C., Jr.; Poliakoff, Michael B.; Parker, Michael P.; Boynes, Matthew; & Hudson, James I. (2007). Is dissociative amnesia a culture-bound syndrome? Findings from a survey of historical literature. *Psychological Medicine, 37* (2), 225–233.

Pope, Kenneth S. (1988). How clients are harmed by sexual contact with mental health professionals: The syndrome and its prevalence. *Journal of Counseling and Development, 67,* 222–226.

Pope, Kenneth S. (2000). Therapists' sexual feelings and behaviors: Research, trends, and quandaries. In Lenore T. Szuchman & Frank Muscarella (Eds.), *Psychological*

perspectives on human sexuality (pp. 603–658). New York: Wiley.

Pope, Kenneth S. (2001). Sex between therapists and clients. In Judith Worrell (Ed.), *Encyclopedia of women and gender: Sex similarities and differences and the impact of society on gender* (vol. 2; pp. 955–962). New York: Academic Press.

Pope, Kenneth S.; Sonne, Janet L.; & Greene, Beverly. (2006). Therapists' sexual arousals, attractions, and fantasies: An example of a topic that isn't there. In Kenneth S. Pope, Janet L. Sonne, & Beverly Greene (Eds.), *What therapists don't talk about and why: Understanding taboos that hurt us and our clients* (pp. 27–41). Washington, DC: American Psychological Association.

Popp, Danielle; Donovan, Roxanne A.; Crawford, Mary; Marsh, Kerry L.; & Peele, Melanie. (2003). Gender, race, and speech style stereotypes. *Sex Roles, 48,* 317–325.

Porter, Laura S.; Marco, Christine A.; Schwartz, Joseph E.; Neale, John M.; Shiffman, Saul; & Stone, Arthur A. (2000). Gender differences in coping: A comparison of trait and momentary assessments. *Journal of Social and Clinical Psychology, 19,* 480–498.

Postmes, Tom; & Spears, Russell. (2002). Behavior online: Does anonymous computer communication reduce gender inequality? *Personality and Social Psychology Bulletin, 28,* 1073–1083.

Potter, Julia; Bouyer, Jean; Trussell, James; & Moreau, Caroline. (2009). Premenstrual syndrome prevalence and fluctuation over time: Results from a French population-based survey. *Journal of Women's Health, 18* (1), 31–39.

Poulin-Dubois, Diane; Serbin, Lisa A.; Eichstedt, Julie A.; Sen, Maya G.; & Beissel, Clara F. (2002). Men don't put on make-up: Toddlers' knowledge of the gender stereotyping of household activities. *Social Development, 11,* 166–181.

Powlishta, Kimberly K. (2000). The effect of target age on the activation of gender stereotypes. *Sex Roles, 42,* 271–282.

Powlishta, Kimberly K.; Serbin, Lisa A.; & Moller, Lora C. (1993). The stability of individual differences in gender typing: Implications for understanding gender segregation. *Sex Roles, 29,* 723–744.

Pratto, Felicia; & Espinoza, Penelope. (2001). Gender, ethnicity, and power. *Journal of Social Issues, 57,* 763–780.

Pratto, Felicia; Sidanius, Jim; & Levin, Shana. (2006). Social dominance theory and the dynamics of intergroup relations: Taking stock and looking forward. *European Review of Social Psychology, 17,* 271–320.

Prentice, Deborah A.; & Carranza, Erica. (2002). What women and men should be, shouldn't be, are allowed to be, and don't have to be: The contents of prescriptive gender stereotypes. *Psychology of Women Quarterly, 26,* 269–281.

Previti, Denise; & Amato, Paul R. (2003). Why stay married? Rewards, barriers, and marital stability. *Journal of Marriage and Family, 65,* 561–573.

Pritchard, Mary E.; & Wilson, Gregory S. (2006). Do coping styles change during the first semester of college? *Journal of Social Psychology 146*, 125–127.

Programs and Practices That Work. (2005). *Forging new pathways: Promising practices for recruiting and retaining students in career and technical education programs that are nontraditional for their gender.* Retrieved July 5, 2006, from http://www.nwlc.org/pdf/Report2005_PPTW_Final.pdf

Pryzgoda, Jayde; & Chrisler, Joan C. (2000). Definitions of gender and sex: The subtleties of meaning. *Sex Roles, 43*, 553–569.

Pseekos, A. Chantelle; & Lyddon, William J. (2009). The use of metaphor to address gender and sexual orientation stereotypes in counseling: A feminist perspective. *Women and Therapy, 32* (4), 393–405.

Ptacek, J. T.; Smith, Ronald E.; & Zanas, John. (1992). Gender, appraisal, and coping: A longitudinal analysis. *Journal of Personality, 60*, 747–770.

Puts, David; McDaniel, Michael; Jordan, Cynthia; & Breedlove, S. Marc. (2008). Spatial ability and prenatal androgens: Meta-analyses of congenital adrenal hyperplasia and digit ratio (2D:4D) studies. *Archives of Sexual Behavior, 37* (1), 100–111.

Quaiser-Pohl, Claudia; Geiser, Christian; & Lehmann, Wolfgang. (2006). The relationship between computer-game preference, gender, and mental-rotation ability. *Personality and Individual Differences, 40*, 609–619.

Quatman, Teri; Sampson, Kindra; Robinson, Cindi; & Watson, Cary M. (2001). Academic, motivational, and emotional correlates of adolescent dating. *Genetic, Social, and General Psychology Monographs, 127*, 211–234.

Quinn, Susan. (1987). *A mind of her own: The life of Karen Horney.* New York: Summit Books.

Quintero Gonzalez, Alexei; & Koestner, Richard. (2006). What Valentine announcement reveal about the romantic emotions of men and women. *Sex Roles, 55* (11/12), 767–773.

Raag, Tarja; & Rackliff, Christine L. (1998). Preschoolers' awareness of social expectations of gender: Relationships to toy choices. *Sex Roles, 38*, 685–700.

Rader, Jill; & Gilbert, Lucia Albino. (2005). The egalitarian relationship in feminist therapy. *Psychology of Women Quarterly, 29*, 427–435.

Radmacher, Kimberley; & Azmitia, Margarita. (2006). Are there gendered pathways to intimacy in early adolescents' and emerging adults' friendships? *Journal of Adolescent Research, 21* (4), 415–448.

Raffaelli, Marcela; & Ontai, Lenna L. (2004). Gender socialization in Latino/a families: Results from two retrospective studies. *Sex Roles, 50*, 287–299.

Ragaza, Angelo. (1999, February 8). I don't count as "diversity." *Newsweek, 133* (6), 13.

Ragland, J. Daniel; Coleman, A. Rand; Gur, Ruben C.; Glahn, David C.; & Gur, Raquel E. (2000). Sex differences in brain-behavior relationships between verbal episodic memory and resting regional cerebral blood flow. *Neuropsychologia, 38*, 451–461.

Rahman, Qazi. (2005a). Fluctuating asymmetry, second to fourth finger length ratios and human sexual orientation. *Psychoneuroendocrinology, 30*, 382–391.

Rahman, Qazi. (2005b). The neurodevelopment of human sexual orientation. *Neuroscience and Biobehavioral Review, 29*, 1057–1066.

Rains, Stephen A.; & Young, Valerie. (2009). A meta-analysis of research on formal computer-mediated support groups: Examining group characteristics and health outcomes. *Human Communication Research, 35* (3), 309–336.

Ramirez, J. Martin. (2003). Hormones and aggression in childhood and adolescence. *Aggression and Violent Behavior, 8*, 621–644.

Rammstedt, Beatrice; & Rammsayer, Thomas H. (2002). Gender differences in self-estimated intelligence and their relation to gender-role orientation. *European Journal of Personality, 16*, 369–382.

Ramsey-Rennels, Jennifer L; & Langlois, Judith H. (2006). Infants' differential processing of female and male faces. *Current Directions in Psychological Science, 15*, 59–62.

Randolph, Diane Smith; & Andresen, Elena M. (2004). Disability, gender, and unemployment relationships in the United States from the behavioral risk factor surveillance system. *Disability and Society, 19*, 403–414.

Ranke, Michael B.; & Saenger, Paul. (2001). Turner's syndrome. *Lancet, 358*, 309–314.

Rasgon, Natalie; Bauer, Michael; Groff, Paul; Gyulai, Laszlo; Elman, Shana; Glenn, Tasha; et al. (2005). Sex-specific self-reported mood changes by patients with bipolar disorder. *Journal of Psychiatric Research, 39*, 77–83.

Rasmussen, Mary Lou. (2004). The problem of coming out. *Theory Into Practice, 43*, 144–150.

Ratcliff, Kathryn Strother. (2002). *Women and health: Power, technology, inequality, and conflict in a gendered world.* Boston: Allyn & Bacon.

Räty, Hannu; Vänskä, Johanna; Kasanen, Kati; & Kärkkäinen, Riita. (2002). Parents' explanations of their child's performance in mathematics and reading: A replication and extension of Yee and Eccles. *Sex Roles, 46* (3/4), 121–128.

Raudenbush, Bryan; & Zellner, Debra A. (1997). Nobody's satisfied: Effects of abnormal eating behaviors and actual and perceived weight status on body image satisfaction in males and females. *Journal of Social and Clinical Psychology, 16*, 95–110.

Rawlings, Edna I. (1993). Reflections on "Twenty years of feminist counseling and therapy." *Counseling Psychologist, 21*, 88–91.

Read, Jen'nan Ghazal. (2003). The sources of gender role attitudes among Christian and Muslim Arab-American women. *Sociology of Religion, 64*, 207–222.

Ready, Douglas D.; LoGerfo, Laura F.; Burkam, David T.; & Lee, Valerie E. (2005). Explaining girls' advantage in kindergarten literacy learning: Do classroom behaviors make a difference? *Elementary School Journal, 106*, 21–38.

Rebellon, Cesar; & Manasse, Michelle. (2004). Do "bad boys" really get the girls? Delinquency as a cause and consequence of dating behavior among adolescents. *Justice Quarterly, 21*, 355–389.

Reddin, Julie A.; & Sonn, Christopher C. (2003). Masculinity, social support, and sense of community: The men's group experience in Western Australia. *Journal of Men's Studies, 11*, 207–223.

Reddy, Gayatri. (2005). *With respect to sex: Negotiating hijra identity in south India.* Chicago: University of Chicago Press.

Redman, Selina; Webb, Gloria R.; Hennrikus, Deborah J.; Gordon, Jill J.; & Sanson-Fisher, Robert W. (1991). The effects of gender upon diagnosis of psychological disturbance. *Journal of Behavioral Medicine, 14*, 527–540.

Reeder, Heidi M. (2003). The effect of gender role orientation on same- and cross-sex friendship formation. *Sex Roles, 49*, 143–152.

Regan, Pamela C.; Medina, Roberta; & Joshi, Anupama. (2001). Partner preferences among homosexual men and women: What is desirable in a sex partner is not necessarily desirable in a romantic partner. *Social Behavior and Personality, 29*, 625–631.

Regier, Darrel A.; Narrow, William E.; & Rae, Donald S. (1990). The epidemiology of anxiety disorders: The Epidemiologic Catchment Area (ECA) experience. *Journal of Psychiatric Research, 24* (Suppl. 2), 3–14.

Rehm, Jürgen; Room, Robin; Monteiro, Maristela; Gmel, Gerhard; Graham, Kathryn; Rehn, Nina; et al. (2003). Alcohol as a risk factor for global burden of disease. *European Addiction Research, 9* (4), 157–164.

Rehman, Jamil; Lazer, Simcha; Benet, Alexandru E.; Schaefer, Leah C.; & Melman, Arnold. (1999). The reported sex and surgery satisfactions of 28 postoperative male-to-female transsexual patients. *Archives of Sexual Behavior, 28*, 71–90.

Reichman, Nancy J.; & Sterling, Joyce S. (2004). Sticky floors, broken steps, and concrete ceilings in legal careers. *Texas Journal of Women and the Law, 14*, 27–76.

Reid, Pamela Trotman. (1993). Poor women in psychology research: Shut up and shut out. *Psychology of Women Quarterly, 17*, 133–150.

Rejskind, F. Gillian; Rapagna, Socrates O.; & Gold, Dolores. (1992). Gender differences in children's divergent thinking. *Creativity Research Journal, 5*, 165–174.

Remarks at NBER Conference on Diversifying the Science & Engineering Workforce. (2005, January 14). Retrieved March 28, 2005, from http://www.president.harvard.edu/speeches/2005/nber.html

Renk, Kimberly; Roberts, Rex; Roddenberry, Angela; Luick, Mary; Hillhouse, Sarah; Meehan, Cricket; et al. (2003). Mothers, fathers, gender role, and time parents spend with their children. *Sex Roles, 48*, 305–315.

Rennie, David L.; Watson, Kimberly D.; & Monteiro, Althea M. (2002). The rise of qualitative research in psychology. *Canadian Psychology, 43*, 179–189.

Rennison, Callie Marie. (2003). *Intimate partner violence, 1993–2001. Bureau of Justice Statistics Crime Data Briefs.* Washington, DC: Bureau of Justice Statistics.

Resnick, Heidi S.; Kilpatrick, Dean G.; Dansky, Bonnie S.; Saunders, Benjamin E.; & Best, Connie L. (1993). Prevalence of victim trauma and posttraumatic stress disorder in a representative national sample of women. *Journal of Consulting and Clinical Psychology, 61*, 984–991.

Reuters. (2008, February 12). *Engage releases first annual state of the date report.* Retrieved September 3, 2009, from http://www.reuters.com/article/pressRelease/idUS164454+12-Feb-2008+PRN20080212

Ribalow, M. Z. (1998). Script doctors. *The Sciences, 38*(6), 26–31.

Ribeiro, Michelle Lee. (2006, February). PMS makes you smarter! *CosmoGirl!, 8* (1), 67.

Ricciardelli, Lina A.; & McCabe, Marita P. (2007). Pursuit of muscularity among adolescents. In Kevin J. Thompson & Guy Cafri (Eds.), *The muscular idea: Psychological, social, and medical perspectives* (pp. 199–210). Washington, DC: American Psychological Association.

Ricciardelli, Lina A.; & Williams, Robert J. (1995). Desirable and undesirable gender traits in three behavioral domains. *Sex Roles, 33*, 637–655.

Richardson, Deborah South. (2005). The myth of female passivity: Thirty years of revelations about female aggression. *Psychology of Women Quarterly, 29* (3), 238–247.

Rickert, Vaughn I.; Vaughan, Roger D.; & Wiemann, Constance M. (2003). Violence against young women: Implications for clinicians. *Contemporary OB/GYN, 48* (2), 30–45.

Rickert, Vaughn I.; Wiemann, Constance M.; & Vaughan, Roger D. (2005). Disclosure of date/acquaintance rape: Who reports and when. *Journal of Pediatric and Adolescent Gynecology, 18*, 17–24.

Ridgeway, Cecilia L.; & Correll, Shelley J. (2004). Motherhood as a status characteristic. *Journal of Social Issues, 60*, 683–700.

Rieger, Gerulf; Chivers, Meredity L.; & Bailey, J. Michael. (2005). Sexual arousal patterns of bisexual men. *Psychological Science, 16*, 579–584.

Riessman, Catherine Kohler. (1990). *Divorce talk: Women and men make sense of personal relationships.* New Brunswick, NJ: Rutgers University Press.

Riger, Stephanie. (1992). Epistemological debates, feminist voices: Science, social values, and the study of women. *American Psychologist, 47,* 730–740.

Riggio, Heidi R.; & Desrochers, Stephan. (2005). The influence of maternal employment on the work and family expectations of offspring. In Diane F. Halpern & Susan Elaine Murphy (Eds.), *From work-family balance to work-family interaction: Changing the metaphor* (pp. 177–196). Mahwah, NJ: Erlbaum.

Risman, Barbara J. (1989). Can men "mother"? Life as a single father. In Barbara J. Risman & Pepper Schwartz (Eds.), *Gender in intimate relationships: A microstructural approach* (pp. 155–164). Belmont, CA: Wadsworth.

Riter, Robert N. (1997). I have breast cancer. *Newsweek, 130* (2), 14.

Ro, Hye-Sun; & Wampler, Richard S. (2009). What's wrong with these people? Clinicians' views of clinical couples. *Journal of Marital and Family Therapy, 35* (1), 3–17.

Roberts, Helen. (2009). Reduced use of hormones and the drop in breast cancer. *British Medical Journal, 338* (7710), 1513–1514.

Roberts, Jonathan E.; & Bell, Martha Ann. (2000). Sex differences on a computerized mental rotation task disappear with computer familiarization. *Perceptual and Motor Skills, 91,* 1027–1034.

Roberts, Tomi-Ann. (1991). Gender and the influence of evaluations on self-assessments in achievement settings. *Psychological Bulletin, 109,* 297–308.

Roberts, Tomi-Ann; & Nolen-Hoeksema, Susan. (1994). Gender comparisons in responsiveness to others' evaluations in achievement settings. *Psychology of Women Quarterly, 18,* 221–240.

Robertson, John; & Fitzgerald, Louise F. (1990). The (mis)treatment of men: Effects of client gender role and life-style on diagnosis and attribution of pathology. *Journal of Counseling Psychology, 37,* 3–9.

Robertson, John; & Fitzgerald, Louise F. (1992). Overcoming the masculine mystique: Preferences for alternative form of assistance among men who avoid counseling. *Journal of Counseling Psychology, 39,* 240–246.

Robine, Jean-Marie; & Ritchie, Karen. (1991). Healthy life expectancy: Evaluation of global indicator of change in population health. *British Medical Journal, 302,* 457–460.

Robinson, David. (1979). *Talking out of alcoholism: The self-help process of Alcoholics Anonymous.* Baltimore: University Park Press.

Robinson, S. J.; & Manning, John T. (2000). The ratio of 2nd to 4th digit length and male homosexuality. *Evolution and Human Behavior, 21,* 333–345.

Robinson, Tom; Callister, Mark; Clark, Brad; & Phillips, James. (2008). Violence, sexuality, and gender stereotyping: A content analysis of official video game web sites. *Web Journal of Mass Communication Research, 13,* 1–17.

Rochlen, Aaron B.; Blazina, Christopher; & Raghunathan, Rajagopal. (2002). Gender role conflict, attitudes toward career counseling, career decision-making, and perceptions of career counseling advertising brochures. *Psychology of Men & Masculinity, 3,* 127–137.

Rochlen, Aaron B.; McKelley, Ryan A.; & Pituch, Keenan A. (2006). A preliminary examination of the "Real Men. Real Depression" campaign. *Psychology of Men and Masculinity, 7,* 1–13.

Rodríguez, Mónica Russel Y. (2008). Accounting for MeXicana feminisms. *American Ethnologist, 35* (2) 308–320.

Rogers, Carl R. (1951). *Client-centered therapy: Its current practice, implications, and theory.* Boston: Houghton Mifflin.

Rogers, Carl R. (1961). *On becoming a person: A therapist's view of psychotherapy.* Boston: Houghton Mifflin.

Rogers, Carl R. (1980). *A way of being.* Boston: Houghton Mifflin.

Rolin, Kristina. (2004). Why gender is a relevant factor in the social epistemology of scientific inquiry. *Philosophy of Science, 71,* 880–891.

Rood, Lea; Roelofs, Jeffrey; Bögels, Susan M.; Nolen-Hoeksema, Susan; & Schouten, Erik. (2009). The influence of emotion-focused rumination and distraction on depressive symptoms in non-clinical youth: A meta-analytic review. *Clinical Psychology Review, 29* (7), 607–616.

Rosario, Margaret; Schrimshaw, Eric W.; Hunter, Joyce; & Braun, Lisa. (2006). Sexual identity development among lesbian, gay, and bisexual youths: Consistency and change over time. *Journal of Sex Research, 43,* 46–58.

Roscoe, Will. (1993). How to become a berdache: Toward a unified analysis of gender diversity. In Gilbert Herdt (Ed.), *Third sex, third gender: Beyond sexual dimorphism in culture and history* (pp. 329–372). New York: Zone Books.

Rose, Amanda J. (2007). Structure, content, and socioemotional correlates of girls' and boys' friendships. *Merrill-Palmer Quarterly, 53* (3), 489–506.

Rose, Suzanna; & Frieze, Irene Hanson. (1993). Young singles' contemporary dating scripts. *Sex Roles, 28,* 499–509.

Rose, Suzanna M.; & Zand, Debra. (2002). Lesbian dating and courtship from young adulthood to midlife. *Journal of Lesbian Studies, 6,* 85–109.

Rosenfeld, Megan. (1998, March 26). Little boys blue: Re-examining the plight of young males. *Washington Post,* p. A1.

Rosenfield, Sarah. (1982). Sex roles and societal reactions to mental illness: The labeling of "deviant deviance." *Journal of Health and Social Behavior, 23,* 18–24.

Rosenkrantz, Paul; Vogel, Susan; Bee, Helen; Broverman, Inge; & Broverman, Donald M. (1968). Sex-role stereotypes and self-concepts in college students. *Journal of Consulting and Clinical Psychology, 32,* 287–295.

Rosin, Hanna. (2008). A boy's life. *The Atlantic, 302* (4), 56–71.

Rospenda, Kathleen M.; Richman, Judith A.; & Shannon, Candice A. (2009). Prevalence and mental health correlates of harassment and discrimination in the workplace: Results from a national study. *Journal of Interpersonal Violence, 24* (5), 819–843.

Ross, Lori E.; & Toner, Brenda. (2003, Fall). Sexism & women's mental health. *Women and Environments International Magazine*, p. 34.

Rosser, Sue V. (2004). *The science glass ceiling: Academic women scientists and the struggle to succeed.* New York: Routledge.

Rotundo, Maria; Nguyen, Dung-Hanh; & Sackett, Paul R. (2001). A meta-analytic review of gender differences in perceptions of sexual harassment. *Journal of Applied Psychology, 86*, 914–922.

Rowe, Richard; Maughan, Barbara; Wortman, Carol M.; Costello, E. Jane; & Angold, Adrian. (2004). Testosterone, antisocial behavior, and social dominance in boys: Pubertal development and biosocial interaction. *Biological Psychiatry, 55*, 546–552.

Roy, Rosanne; Benenson, Joyce F.; & Lilly, Frank. (2000). Beyond intimacy: Conceptualizing sex differences in same-sex friendships. *Journal of Psychology, 134*, 93–102.

Roysircar, Gargi. (2005). Culturally sensitive assessment, diagnosis, and guidelines. In Madonna Constantine & Derald Wing Sue (Eds.), *Strategies for building multicultural competence in mental health and educational settings* (pp. 19–38). Hoboken, NJ: Wiley.

Rozin, Paul. (2007). Food and eating. In S. Kitayama & D. Cohen (Eds.), *Handbook of cultural psychology* (pp. 391–416). New York: Guilford Press.

Rozin, Paul; Bauer, Rebecca; & Catanese, Dana. (2003). Food and life, pleasure and worry, among American college students: Gender differences and regional similarities. *Journal of Personality and Social Psychology, 85*, 132–141.

Ruble, Diane N.; Lurye, Leah E.; & Zosuls, Kristina M. (2007). Pink frilly dresses (PFD) and early gender identity. *Princeton Report on Knowledge, 2* (2). Retrieved July 5, 2009, from http://www.princeton.edu/prok/issues/2-2/pink_frilly.xml

Ruble, Diane N.; & Martin, Carol Lynn. (1998). Gender development. In Nancy Eisenberg (Ed.), *Handbook of child psychology, Vol. 3: Social, emotional, and personality development* (5th ed., pp. 933–1016). New York: Wiley.

Ruble, Diane N.; Martin, Carol Lynn; & Berenbaum, Sheri A. (2006). Gender development. In Nancy Eisenberg, William Damon, & Richard M. Lerner (Eds.), *Handbook of child psychology: Vol. 3* (pp. 858–932). Hoboken, NJ: Wiley.

Ruble, Diane N.; Taylor, Lisa J.; Cyphers, Lisa; Greulich, Faith K.; Lurye, Leah; & Shrout, Patrick E. (2007). The role of gender constancy in early gender development. *Child Development, 78* (4), 1121–1136.

Rudman, Laurie A.; Greenwald, Anthony G.; & McGhee, Debbie E. (2001). Implicit self-concept and evaluative implicit gender stereotypes: Self and ingroup share desirable traits. *Personality and Social Psychology Bulletin, 27*, 1164–1178.

Russell, Brenda L.; & Trigg, Kristin Y. (2004). Tolerance of sexual harassment: An examination of gender differences, ambivalent sexism, social dominance, and gender roles. *Sex Roles, 50*, 565–573.

Russell, Diana E. H. (1986). *The secret trauma: Incest in the lives of girls and women.* New York: Basic Books.

Russell, Emily B.; & Harton, Helen C. (2005). The "other factors": Using individual relationship characteristics to predict sexual and emotional jealousy. *Current Psychology, 24*, 242–257.

Russo, Nancy Felipe. (1998). Editorial: Teaching about gender and ethnicity: Goals and challenges. *Psychology of Women Quarterly, 22*, i–vi.

Rust, Paula C. Rodriguez. (2000). Bisexuality: A contemporary paradox for women. *Journal of Social Issues, 56*, 205–222.

Ryan, Kathryn M. (2004). Further evidence for a cognitive component of rape. *Aggression and Violent Behavior, 9*, 579–604.

Sabattini, Laura; & Leaper, Campbell. (2004). The relation between mothers' and fathers' parenting styles and their division of labor in the home: Young adults' retrospective reports. *Sex Roles, 50*, 27–225.

Sable, Marjorie R.; Danis, Fran; Mauzy, Denise L.; & Gallagher, Sarah K. (2006). Barriers to report sexual assault for women and men: Perspectives of college students. *Journal of American College Health, 55* (3), 157–162.

Sachs-Ericsson, Natalie; & Ciarlo, James A. (2000). Gender, social roles, and mental health: An epidemiological perspective. *Sex Roles, 43*, 605–628.

Safdar, Saba; Friedlmeier, Wolfgang; Mutsumoto, David; Yoo, Seun Hee; Kwantes, Catherine T.; Kakai, Hisako; & Shigemasu, Eri. (2009). Variations of emotional display rules within and across cultures: A comparison between Canada, USA, and Japan. *Canadian Journal of Behavioural Science, 41* (1), 1–10.

Saginak, Kelli A.; & Saginak, M. Alan. (2005). Balancing work and family: Equity, gender, and marital satisfaction. *Family Journal, 13*, 162–166.

Sakamoto, Arthur; Goyette, Kimberly A.; & Kim, ChangHwan. (2009). Socioeconomic attainments of Asian Americans. *Annual Review of Sociology, 35* (1), 255–276.

Sakraida, Teresa J. (2005). Common themes in the divorce transition experience of midlife women. *Journal of Divorce and Remarriage, 43* (1/2), 69–88.

Salmivalli, Christina; & Kaukiainen, Ari. (2004). "Female aggression" revisited: Variable- and person-centered approaches to studying gender differences in different types of aggression. *Aggressive Behavior, 30* (2), 158–163.

Salzman, Philip C. (1999). Is inequality universal? *Current Anthropology*, *40*, 31–61.

Sampson, Helen; Bloor, Michael; & Fincham, Ben. (2008). A price worth paying? Considering the 'cost' of reflexive research methods and the influence of feminist ways of 'doing.' *Sociology*, *42* (5), 919–933.

Samter, Wendy; & Burleson, Brant. (2005). The role of communication in same-sex friendships: A comparison among African Americans, Asian Americans, and European Americans. *Communication Quarterly*, *53*, 265–283.

Samuel, Steven E.; & Gorton, Gregg E. (1998). National survey of psychology internship directors regarding education for prevention of psychologist-patient sexual exploitation. *Professional Psychology: Research and Practice*, *29*, 86–90.

Samuels, Douglas B.; & Widiger, Thomas A. (2009). Comparative gender biases in models of personality disorder. *Personality and Mental Health*, *3* (1), 12–25.

Sanchez, Kathryn; Zimmerman, Laurie; & Ye, Renmin. (2004). Secondary students' attitudes toward mathematics. *Academic Exchange Quarterly*, *8*, 56–60.

Sanders, Geoff; Sjodin, Marie; & de Chastelaine, Marianne. (2002). On the elusive nature of sex differences in cognition: Hormonal influences contributing to within-sex variation. *Archives of Sexual Behavior*, *31*, 145–152.

Sanders, Jo. (2003). Teaching gender equity in teacher education. *Education Digest*, *68* (5), 25–29.

Sanderson, Susan; & Sanders Thompson, Vetta L. (2002). Factors associated with perceived paternal involvement in childrearing. *Sex Roles*, *46*, 99–111.

Sandfield, Anna. (2006). Talking divorce: The role of divorce in women's constructions of relationship status. *Feminism & Psychology*, *16*, 155–173.

Sandfort, Theodorus G. M.; de Graaf, Ron; & Bijl, Rob V. (2003). Same-sex sexuality and quality of life: Findings from the Netherlands Mental Health Survey and Incidence study. *Archives of Sexual Behavior*, *32*, 15–22.

Sandnabba, N. Kenneth; & Ahlberg, Christian. (1999). Parents' attitudes and expectations about children's cross-gender behavior. *Sex Roles*, *40*, 249–264.

Santelli, John; Ott, Mary A.; Lyon, Maureen; Rogers, Jennifer; Summers, Daniel; & Schleifer, Rebecca. (2006). Abstinence and abstinence-only education: A review of U.S. policies and programs. *Journal of Adolescent Health*, *38*, 72–81.

Sapolsky, Barry S.; Molitor, Fred; & Luque, Sarah. (2003). Sex and violence in slasher films: Re-examining the assumptions. *Journalism and Mass Communication Quarterly*, *80*, 28–38.

Sarason, Irwin G.; & Sarason, Barbara R. (2001). *Abnormal psychology: The problem of maladaptive behavior* (10th ed.). Englewood Cliffs, NJ: Prentice Hall.

Sargent, Paul. (2005). The gendering of men in early childhood education. *Sex Roles*, *52*, 251–259.

Saucier, Deborah M.; Green, Sheryl M.; Leason, Jennifer; MacFadden, Alastair; Bell, Scott; & Elias, Lorin J. (2002). Are sex differences in navigation caused by sexually dimorphic strategies or by differences in the ability to use the strategies? *Behavioral Neuroscience*, *116*, 403–410.

Saulcy, Sara. (2005). Occupational fatalities in the U.S. *Wyoming Labor Force Trends*. Retrieved July 18, 2006, from http://wydoe.state.wy.us/LMI/0305/a1.htm

Savin-Williams, Ritch C. (2006). Who's gay? Does it matter? *Current Directions in Psychological Science*, *15*, 40–44.

Savin-Williams, Ritch C.; & Diamond, Lisa M. (2000). Sexual identity trajectories among sexual-minority youths: Gender comparisons. *Archives of Sexual Behavior*, *29*, 607–627.

Sax, Linda J.; Bryant, Alyssa N.; & Harper, Casandra E. (2005). The differential effects of student-faculty interaction on college outcomes for women and men. *Journal of College Student Development*, *46*, 642–659.

Sayer, Liana C. (2005). Gender, time and inequality: Trends in women's and men's paid work, unpaid, work and free time. *Social Forces*, *84*, 285–303.

Scali, Robyn M.; Brownlow, Sheila; & Hicks, Jennifer L. (2000). Gender differences in spatial task performance as a function of speed or accuracy orientation. *Sex Roles*, *43*, 359–376.

Scarpa, Angela; Haden, Sara Chiara; & Hurley, Jimmy. (2006). Community violence victimization and symptoms of posttraumatic stress disorder. *Journal of Interpersonal Violence*, *21*, 446–469.

Scelfo, Julie; Springen, Karen; & Carmichael, Mary. (2007). Facing darkness. *Newsweek*, *149* (9), 42–49.

Schafer, Joseph A.; Huebner, Beth M.; & Bynum, Timothy S. (2006). Fear of crime and criminal victimization: Gender-based contrasts. *Journal of Criminal Justice*, *34*, 285–301.

Schalet, Amy. (2009). Subjectivity, intimacy, and the empowerment paradigm of adolescent sexuality: The unexplored room. *Feminist Studies*, *35* (1), 133–160.

Scharrer, Erica. (2001). Tough guys: The portrayal of hypermasculinity and aggression in televised police dramas. *Journal of Broadcasting & Electronic Media*, *45*, 615–634.

Scherer, Klaus R.; Wallbott, Harald G.; & Summerfield, Angela B. (Eds.) (1986). *Experiencing emotion: A cross-cultural study*. Cambridge, England: Cambridge University Press.

Schiebinger, Londa. (1999). *Has feminism changed science*? Cambridge, MA: Harvard University Press.

Schiebinger, Londa. (2003). Introduction: Feminism inside the sciences. *Signs*, *28*, 859–867.

Schiebinger, Londa. (2007). Getting more women into science: Knowledge issues. *Harvard Journal of Law & Gender*, *30* (2), 365–378.

Schiebinger, Londa. (2008). Changing assumptions. *American Scientist, 96* (5), 428-430.

Schmader, Toni; Johns, Michael; & Barquissau, Marchelle. (2004). The costs of accepting gender differences: The role of stereotype endorsement in women's experience in the math domain. *Sex Roles, 50,* 835–850.

Schmitt, Elizabeth Dunne. (2008). Discrimination versus specialization: A survey of economic studies on sexual orientation, bender and earnings in the United States. *Journal of Lesbian Studies, 12* (1), 17–30.

Schmitz, Sigrid. (1999). Gender differences in acquisition of environmental knowledge related to wayfinding ability, spatial anxiety and self-estimated environmental competencies. *Sex Roles, 41,* 71–94.

Schmookler, Terra; & Bursik, Krisanne. (2007). The value of monogamy in emerging adulthood: A gendered perspective. *Journal of Social and Personal Relationships, 24* (6), 819-835.

Schnall, Simone; Abrahamson, Adelpha; & Laird, James D. (2002). Premenstrual syndrome and misattribution: A self-perception, individual differences perspective. *Basic and Applied Social Psychology, 24,* 215–228.

Schneider, Irving. (1987). The theory and practice of movie psychiatry. *American Journal of Psychiatry, 144,* 996–1002.

Schneider, Lawrence; Mori, Lisa; Lambert, Paul; & Wong, Anna. (2009). The role of gender and ethnicity in perception of rape and its aftereffects. *Sex Roles, 60* (5/6), 410–421.

Schroeder, Debra S.; & Mynatt, Clifford R. (1999). Graduate students' relationship with their male and female major professors. *Sex Roles, 40,* 393–420.

Schultz, Duane P.; & Schultz, Sidney Ellen. (2008). *A history of modern psychology* (9th ed.). Belmont, CA: Wadsworth/Cengage.

Schultz, Harriet T. (2005). Hollywood's portrayal of psychologists and psychiatrists: Gender and professional training differences. In Ellen Cole & Jessica Henderson Daniel (Eds.), *Featuring females: Feminist analyses of media* (pp. 101–112). Washington, DC: American Psychological Association.

Schwartz, Pepper. (1994). *Peer marriage: How love between equals really works.* New York: Free Press.

Schwartz, Shalom H.; & Rubel-Lifschitz, Tammy. (2009). Cross-national variation in the size of sex differences in values: Effects of gender equality. *Journal of Personality and Social Psychology, 97* (1), 171–185.

Scott, Eric; & Panksepp, Jaak. (2003). Rough-and-tumble play in human children. *Aggressive Behavior, 29,* 539–551.

Scott, Greg; Ciarrochi, Joseph; & Deane, Frank P. (2004). Disadvantages of being an individualist in an individualistic culture: Idiocentrism, emotional competence, stress, and mental health. *Australian Psychologist, 39,* 143–153.

Scully, Diana. (1990). *Understanding sexual violence: A study of convicted rapists.* London: HarperCollins Academic.

Seale, Clive. (2006). Gender accommodation in online cancer support groups. *Health: An Interdisciplinary Journal for the Social Study of Health, Illness and Medicine, 10,* 345–360.

Seedat, Soraya; Scott, Kate Margaret; Angemeyer, Matthias C.; Berglund, Patricia; Bromet, Evelyn J.; Brugha, Traolach S.; et al. (2009). Cross-national associations between gender and mental disorders of the World Health Organization World Mental Health Surveys. *Archives of General Psychiatry, 66* (7), 785–795.

Seeman, Mary V. (2003). Gender differences in schizophrenia across the life span. In Carl I. Cohen (Ed.), *Schizophrenia into later life: Treatment, research, and policy* (pp. 141–154). Washington, DC: American Psychiatric Publishing.

Segal, Julius; & Segal, Zelda. (1993, May). What five-year-olds think about sex: And when and how to give them the answers that they need to hear. *Parents' Magazine,* pp. 130–132.

Seid, Roberta P. (1994). Too "close to the bone": The historical context of women's obsession with slenderness. In Patricia Fallon, Melanie A. Katzman, & Susan C. Wooley (Eds.), *Feminist perspectives on eating disorders* (pp. 3–16). New York: Guilford Press.

Sell, Ingrid M. (2004). Third gender: A qualitative study of the experience of individuals who identify as being neither man nor women. *Psychotherapy Patient, 13* (1/2), 131–145.

Sell, Randall L.; Wells, James A.; & Wypij, David. (1995). The prevalence of homosexual behavior and attraction in the United States, the United Kingdom and France: Results of national population-based samples. *Archives of Sexual Behavior, 24,* 235–248.

Serbin, Lisa A.; Poulin-Dubois, Diane; Colburne, Karen A.; Sen, Maya G.; & Eichstedt, Julie A. (2001). Gender stereotyping in infancy: Visual preferences for and knowledge of gender-stereotyped toys in the second year. *International Journal of Behavioral Development, 25,* 7–15.

Serbin, Lisa A.; Poulin-Dubois, Diane; & Eichstedt, Julie A. (2002). Infants' response to gender-inconsistent events. *Infancy, 3,* 531–542.

Serbin, Lisa A.; Zelkowitz, Phyllis; Doyle, Anna-Beth; Gold, Dolores; & Wheaton, Blair. (1990). The socialization of sex-differentiated skills and academic performance: A mediational model. *Sex Roles, 23,* 613–628.

Seto, Michael C. (2004). Pedophilia and sexual offenses against children. *Annual Review of Sex Research, 15,* 329–369.

Settles, Isis H.; Cortina, Lilia M.; Malley, Janet; & Stewart Abigail J. (2006). The climate for women in academic science: The good, the bad, and the changeable. *Psychology of Women Quarterly, 30,* 47–58.

Settles, Isis H.; Pratt-Hyatt, Jennifer S.; & Buchanan, NiCole T. (2008). Through the lens of race: Black and white women's perceptions of womanhood. *Psychology of Women Quarterly*, *32* (4), 454–468.

Shackelford, Todd K.; Schmitt, David P.; & Buss, David M. (2005). Universal dimensions of human mate preferences. *Personality and Individual Differences*, *39*, 447–458.

Shah, Abhinav A.; & Beinecke, Richard H. (2009). Global mental health needs, services, barriers, and challenges. *International Journal of Mental Health*, *38* (1), 14–29.

Shah, Mussawar. (2005). Son preference and its consequences (A review). *Gender and Behaviour*, *3*, 269–280.

Shahidullah, Shahid M.; & Nana Derby, C. (2009). Criminalisation, moderinsation, and globlisation: The US and international perspectives on domestic violence. *Global Crime*, *10* (3), 196–223.

Shanahan, James; Signorielli, Nancy; & Morgan, Michael. (2008). *Television and sex roles 30 years hence: A retrospective and current look from a cultural indicators perspective*. Presented at the 2008 annual meeting of the International Communication Association.

Sheehy, Gail. (2006, June 18). Why marriage is good medicine for men. *Parade*, 4–5.

Sheets, Virgil; & Lugar, Robyn. (2005). Friendship and gender in Russia and the United States. *Sex Roles*, *52*, 131–140.

Sheets, Virgil L.; & Wolfe, Marlow D. (2001). Sexual jealousy in heterosexuals, lesbians, and gays. *Sex Roles*, *44*, 255–276.

Shellenbarger, Sue. (2006). Boys mow lawns, girls wash dishes. *Wall Street Journal Online*. Retrieved July 28, 2009, from http://208.144.115.170/columnists/workfamily/20061208-workfamily.html

Sherif, Carolyn W. (1982). Needed concepts in the study of gender identity. *Psychology of Women Quarterly*, *6*, 375–398.

Sherman, Carl. (2004). Man's last stand: What does it take to get a guy into therapy? *Psychology Today*, *37*, 71.

Sherman, Jeffrey W.; Kruschke, John K.; Sherman, Steven J.; Percy, Elise J.; Petrocelli, John V.; & Conrey, Frederica R. (2009). Attentional processes in stereotype formation: A common model for category accentuation and illusory correlation. *Journal of Personality and Social Psychology*, *96* (2), 305–323.

Shernoff, Michael. (2006). Negotiated nonmonogamy in male couples. *Family Process*, *45* (4), 407–418.

Sheu, Hung-Bin; & Sedlacek, William E. (2004). An exploratory study of help-seeking attitudes and coping strategies among college students by race and gender. *Measurement and Evaluation in Counseling and Development*, *37*, 130–143.

Shi, Jianong; Xu, Fan; Zhou, Lin; & Zha, Zixiu. (1999). Gender differences from the results of a cross-cultural study on technical creativity of children from China and Germany. *Acta Psychologica Sinica*, *31*, 428–434. (Abstract only)

Shields, Stephanie A. (1975a). Functionalism, Darwinism, and the psychology of women: A study in social myth. *American Psychologist*, *30*, 739–754.

Shields, Stephanie A. (1975b). Ms. Pilgrim's progress: The contributions of Leta Stetter Hollingworth to the psychology of women. *American Psychologist*, *30*, 852–857.

Shields, Stephanie A. (2002). *Speaking from the heart: Gender and the social meaning of emotion*. Cambridge, UK: Cambridge University Press.

Shih, Shu-Mei. (2002). Towards an ethics of transnational encounter, or "when" does a "Chinese" woman become a "feminist"? *Differences: A Journal of Feminist Cultural Studies*, *13* (2), 90-126.

Showfety, Sarah. (2008). High heels and pink? No way. *Psychology Today*, *41* (5), 43–44.

Shrier, Diane K.; Zucker, Alyssa N.; Mercurio, Andrea E.; Landry, Laura J.; Rich, Michael; & Shrier, Lydia A. (2007). Generation to generation: Discrimination and harassment experiences of physician mothers and their physician daughters. *Journal of Women's Health*, *16* (6), 532–542.

Shumaker, Sally A.; Legault, Claudine; Rapp, Stepphen R.; Thal, Leon; Wallace, Robert B.; Ockene, Judith K. et al. (2003). Estrogen plus progestin and the incidence of dementia and mild cognitive impairment in postmenopausal women: A randomized controlled trial. *Journal of the American Medical Association*, *289*, 2651–2662.

Shute, Rosalyn; Owens, Larry; & Slee, Phillip. (2008). Everyday victimization of adolescent girls by boys: Sexual harassment, bullying or aggression? *Sex Roles*, *58* (7/8), 477–489.

Sias, Patricia M.; Smith, Guy; & Avdeyeva, Tatyana. (2003). Sex and sex-composition differences and similarities in peer workplace friendship development. *Communication Studies*, *54*, 322–340.

Sibley, Chris G.; Overall, Nichola C.; & Duckitt, John. (2007). When women become more hostilely sexist toward their gender: The system-justifying effect of benevolent sexism. *Sex Roles*, *57* (9/10), 743–754.

Sibley, Chris G.; Wilson, Marc S.; & Duckitt, John. (2007). Antecedents of men's hostile and benevolent sexism: The dual roles of social dominance orientation and right-wing authoritarianism. *Personality and Social Psychology Bulletin*, *33* (2), 160–172.

Sidanius, Jim; & Pena, Yesilernis. (2003). The gendered nature of family structure and group-based anti-egalitarianism: A cross-national study. *Journal of Social Psychology*, *143*, 243–251.

Sidanius, Jim; Pratto, Felicia; & Bobo, Lawrence. (1994). Social dominance orientation and the political psychology of gender: A case of invariance? *Journal of Personality and Social Psychology*, *67*, 998–1011.

Sigal, Janet. (2006). International sexual harassment. *Annals of the New York Academy of Sciences, 1087* (1), 356–369.

Signorella, Margaret L.; Bigler, Rebecca L.; & Liben, Lynn S. (1993). Developmental differences in children's gender schemata about others: A meta-analytic review. *Developmental Review, 13,* 147–183.

Signorielli, Nancy. (1998). *A content analysis: Reflections of girls in the media: Television and the perpetuation of gender-role stereotypes.* Retrieved on June 28, 2003, from http://www.aap.org/advocacy/sign298.htm

Signorielli, Nancy. (2004). Aging on television: Messages relating to gender, race, and occupation in prime time. *Journal of Broadcasting and Electronic Media, 48,* 279–301.

Signorielli, Nancy. (2009). Race and sex in prime time: A look at occupations and occupational prestige. *Mass Communication and Society, 12* (3), 332–352.

Signorielli, Nancy; & Kahlenberg, Susan. (2001). Television's world or work in the nineties. *Journal of Broadcasting & Electronic Media, 45,* 4–22.

Silverman, Irwin W. (2003). Gender differences in delay of gratification: A meta-analysis. *Sex Roles, 49,* 451–463.

Silverman, Irwin; Choi, Jean; & Peters, Michael. (2007). The hunter-gatherer theory of sex differences in spatial abilities: Data from 40 countries. *Archives of Sexual Behavior, 36* (2), 261–268.

Silverman, Irwin; Phillips, Krista; & Silverman, Laura K. (1996). Homogeneity of effect sizes for sex across spatial tests and cultures: Implications for hormonal theories. *Brain and Cognition, 31,* 90–94.

Silverstein, Louise B. (1993). Primate research, family politics, and social policy: Transforming "cads" into "dads." *Journal of Family Psychology, 7,* 267–282.

Silverstein, Louise B.; Auerbach, Carl F.; Grieco, Loretta; & Dunk, Faith. (1999). Do Promise Keepers dream of feminist sheep? *Sex Roles, 40,* 665–688.

Silverstein, Louise B.; Auerbach, Carl F.; & Levant, Ronald F. (2002). Contemporary fathers reconstructing masculinity: Clinical implications of gender role strain. *Professional Psychology: Research and Practice, 33,* 361–369.

Simi, Nicole L.; & Mahalik, James R. (1997). Comparison of feminist versus psychoanalytic/dynamic and other therapists on self-disclosure. *Psychology of Women Quarterly, 21,* 465–483.

Simon, Harvey B. (2004). Longevity: The ultimate gender gap. *Scientific American, 14* (3), 18–23.

Simon, Robert I. (1999). Therapist–patient sex: From boundary violations to sexual misconduct. *Psychiatric Clinics of North America, 22,* 31–47.

Simon, Robin W.; & Nath, Leda E. (2004). Gender and emotion in the United States: Do men and women differ in self-reports of feelings and expressive behavior? *American Journal of Sociology, 109,* 1137–1176.

Simpson, Joe Leigh. (2001, November). Androgen insensitivity. *Contemporary OB/GYN, 46* (11), 73+.

Singleton, Andrew; & Maher, JaneMaree. (2004). The "new man" in the house: Young men, social change, and housework. *Journal of Men's Studies, 12,* 227–240.

Singleton, Royce A., Jr.; & Vacca, Jessica. (2007). Interpersonal competition in friendships. *Sex Roles, 57* (9/10), 617–627.

Skatssoon, Judy. (2005). *Do men cause PMS?* Retrieved May 9, 2006, from http://abc.net.au/health/features/pms/default.htm

Skelton, Dawn. (2006). Staying active. *Update, 72* (2), 78–81.

Slavkin, Michael; & Stright, Anne Dopkins. (2000). Gender role differences in college students from one- and two-parent families. *Sex Roles, 42,* 23–37.

Small, Kevonne. (2000). Female crime in the United States, 1963–1998. *Gender Issues, 18,* 75–90.

Smiler, Andrew P. (2004). Thirty years after the discovery of gender: Psychological concepts and measures of masculinity. *Sex Roles, 50,* 15–26.

Smiler, Andrew P.; & Gelman, Susan. (2008). Determinants of gender essentialism in college students. *Sex Roles, 58* (11/12), 864–874.

Smith, Andrea. (2005). Native American feminism, sovereignty, and social change. *Feminist Studies, 31,* 116–132.

Smith, Faye I.; Tabak, Filiz; Showail, Sammy; Parks, Judi McLean; & Kleist, Janean S. (2005). The name game: Employability evaluations of prototypical applicants with stereotypical feminine and masculine first names. *Sex Roles, 52,* 63–82.

Smith, Harriet J. (2005). *Parenting for primates.* Cambridge, MA: Harvard University Press.

Smith, Jessi L.; & White, Paul H. (2002). An examination of implicitly activated, explicitly activated, and nullified stereotypes on mathematical performance: It's not just a woman's issue. *Sex Roles, 47,* 179–191.

Smith, Tara E.; & Leaper, Campbell. (2006). Self-perceived gender typicality and the peer context during adolescence. *Journal of Research on Adolescence, 16* (1), 91–103.

Smith, Yolanda L. S.; van Goozen, Stephanie H. M; & Cohen-Kettenis, Peggy T. (2001). Adolescents with gender identity disorder who were accepted or rejected for sex reassignment surgery: A prospective follow-up study. *Journal of the American Academy of Child and Adolescent Psychiatry, 40,* 472–481.

Snapp, Shannon. (2009). Internalization of the thin ideal among low-income ethnic minority adolescent girls. *Body Image, 6* (4), 311-314.

Snodgrass, Sara E. (1985). Women's intuition: The effect of subordinate role on interpersonal sensitivity. *Journal of Personality and Social Psychology, 49,* 146–155.

Snodgrass, Sara E. (1992). Further effects of role versus gender on interpersonal sensitivity. *Journal of Personality and Social Psychology, 62,* 154–158.

Snodgrass, Sara E.; Hecht, Marvin A.; & Ploutz-Snyder, Robert. (1998). Interpersonal sensitivity: Expressivity or perceptivity? *Journal of Personality and Social Psychology, 74,* 238–249.

Snyder, Karrie Ann; & Green, Adam Isaiah. (2008). Revisiting the glass escalator: The case of gender segregation in a female dominated occupation. *Social Problems, 55* (2), 271–299.

Snyder, R. Claire. (2003). The citizen soldier tradition and gender integration of the U.S. military. *Armed Forces and Society, 29,* 185–204.

Solnick, Sara J. (2001). Gender differences in the ultimatum game. *Economic Inquiry, 39,* 189–200.

Solomon, Denise Haunani; Knobloch, Leanne K.; & Fitzpatrick, Mary Anne. (2004). Relational power, marital schema, and decisions to withhold complaints: An investigation of the chilling effect on confrontation in marriage. *Communication Studies, 55,* 146–168.

Solomon, Sondra E.; Rothblum, Esther D.; & Balsam, Kimberly F. (2005). Money, housework, sex, and conflict: Same-sex couples in civil unions, those not in civil unions, and heterosexual married siblings. *Sex Roles, 52,* 561–575.

Somer, Eli; & Saadon, Meir. (1999). Therapist-client sex: Clients' retrospective reports. *Professional Psychology: Research and Practice, 30,* 504–509.

Sommer, Iris E. C.; Aleman, André; Bouma, Anke; & Kahn, René S. (2004). Do women really have more bilateral language representation than men? A meta-analysis of functional imaging studies. *Brain: A Journal of Neurology, 127,* 1845–1852.

Sommers, Christina Hoff. (2000, May). The war against boys. *Atlantic Monthly, 285,* 59–74.

Sommers, Christina Hoff. (2008). Feminism and freedom. *American Spectator, 41* (6), 52–62.

Sorsdahl, K.; Stein, D. J.; Grimsrud, A.; Seedar, S.; Flisher, A. J.; Williams, D. R. et al. (2009). Traditional healers in the treatment of common mental disorders in South Africa. *Journal of Nervous and Mental Disease, 197* (6), 434–441.

Spelke, Elizabeth S. (2005). Sex differences in intrinsic aptitude for mathematics and science? A critical review. *American Psychologist, 60,* 950–958.

Spelke, Elizabeth S.; & Grace, Ariel D. (2007). Sex, math, and science. In Stephen J. Ceci & Wendy M. Williams (Eds.), *Why aren't more women in science: Top researchers debate the evidence* (pp. 57–67). Washington, DC: American Psychological Association.

Spence, Janet T. (1985). Gender identity and its implications for the concepts of masculinity and femininity. In Theo B. Sonderegger (Ed.), *Nebraska Symposium on Motivation, 1984: Psychology and gender* (Vol. 32; pp. 59–95). Lincoln: University of Nebraska Press.

Spence, Janet T.; & Buckner, Camille E. (2000). Instrumental and expressive traits, trait stereotypes, and sexist attitudes: What do they signify? *Psychology of Women Quarterly, 24,* 44–62.

Spence, Janet T.; & Hahn, Eugene D. (1997). The Attitudes Toward Women Scale and attitude change in college students. *Psychology of Women Quarterly, 21,* 17–34.

Spence, Janet T.; & Helmreich, Robert. (1978). *Masculinity and femininity: The psychological dimensions, correlates, and antecedents.* Austin: University of Texas Press.

Spence, Janet T.; Helmreich, Robert; & Stapp, Joy. (1974). The Personal Attributes Questionnaire: A measure of sex-role stereotypes and masculinity-femininity. *JSAS Catalog of Selected Documents in Psychology, 4,* 43 (Ms. no. 617).

Spencer, Abby L.; & Kern, Lisa M. (2008). Primary care program directors' perceptions of women's health education: A gap in graduate medical education persists. *Journal of Women's Health, 17* (4), 549–556.

Spencer, Renée; Porche, Michelle V.; & Tolman, Deborah L. (2003). We've come a long way—Maybe: New challenges for gender equity in education. *Teachers College Record, 105,* 1774–1807.

Spitzer, Brenda L.; Henderson, Katherine A.; & Zivian, Marilyn T. (1999). Gender differences in population versus media body sizes: A comparison over four decades. *Sex Roles, 40,* 545–566.

Splete, Heidi. (2005). GID patients need to be told of realities. *Clinical Psychiatry News, 33* (5), 50.

Sprecher, Susan. (2001). Equity and social exchange in dating couples: Associations with satisfaction, commitment, and stability. *Journal of Marriage and Family, 63,* 599–613.

Sprecher, Susan; & Felmlee, Diane. (1997). The balance of power in romantic heterosexual couples over time from "his" and "her" perspectives. *Sex Roles, 37,* 361–379.

Sprecher, Susan; Felmlee, Diane; Schmeeckle, Maria; & Shu, Xiaoling. (2006). No breakup occurs on an island: Social networks and relationship dissolution. In Mark A. Fine & John H. Harvey (Eds.), *Handbook of divorce and relationship dissolution* (pp. 457–478). Mahwah, NJ: Erlbaum.

Sprecher, Susan; & Regan, Pamela C. (2002). Liking some things (in some people) more than others: Partner preferences in romantic relationships and friendships. *Journal of Social and Personal Relationships, 19,* 463–481.

Sprecher, Susan; Regan, Pamela C.; & McKinney, Kathleen. (1998). Beliefs about the outcomes of extramarital sexual relationships as a function of the gender of the "cheating spouse." *Sex Roles, 38,* 301–311.

Sprecher, Susan; & Toro-Morn, Maura. (2002). A study of men and women from different sides of earth to determine if men are from Mars and women are from Venus in their beliefs about love and romantic relationships. *Sex Roles, 46,* 131–147.

Springer, Sally P.; & Deutsch, Georg. (1998). *Left brain, right brain* (5th ed.). New York: Freeman.

Stabiner, Karen. (2001, June). Lost in space. *Vogue, 191* (6), 142, 147–148.

Stangor, Charles; & Ruble, Diane N. (1987). Development of gender role knowledge and gender constancy. In Lynn S. Liben & Margaret L. Signorella (Eds.), *Children's gender schemata* (pp. 5–22). San Francisco: Jossey-Bass.

Stankov, Lazar; & Lee, Jihyun. (2008). Confidence and cognitive test performance. *Journal of Educational psychology, 100* (4), 961–976.

Stark, Ellen. (1989, May). Teen sex: Not for love. *Psychology Today*, 10–12.

Steele, Claude M. (1997). A threat in the air: How stereotypes shape intellectual identity and performance. *American Psychologist, 52*, 613–629.

Steele, Claude M.; & Aronson, Joshua. (1995). Stereotype threat and the intellectual test performance of African Americans. *Journal of Personality and Social Psychology, 69*, 797–811.

Steffens, Melanie C. (2005). Implicit and explicit attitudes towards lesbians and gay men. *Journal of Homosexuality, 49*, 39–66.

Steffens, Melanie C.; & Wagner, Christof. (2004). Attitudes toward lesbians, gay men, bisexual women, and bisexual men in Germany. *Journal of Sex Research, 41*, 137–149.

Steffensmeier, Darrel; & Allan, Emilie. (1996). Gender and crime: Toward a gendered theory of female offending. *Annual Review of Sociology, 22*, 459–477.

Steil, Janice M. (2000). Contemporary marriage: Still an unequal partnership. In Clyde Hendrick & Susan S. Hendrick (Eds.), *Close relationships: A sourcebook* (pp. 124–136). Thousand Oaks, CA: Sage.

Steinke, Jocelyn. (2005). Cultural representations of gender and science: Portrayals of female scientists and engineers in popular films. *Science Communication, 27*, 27–63.

Steinke, Jocelyn; & Long, M. (1996). A lab of her own?: Portrayals of female characters on children's educational science programs. *Science Communication, 18*, 91–115.

Stennes, Leif M.; Burch, Melissa M.; Sen, Maya G.; & Bauer, Patricia J. (2005). A longitudinal study of gendered vocabulary and communicative action in young children. *Developmental Psychology, 41*, 75–88.

Stephan, Cookie White; Stephan, Walter C.; Demitrakis, Katherine M.; Yamada, Ann Marie; & Clason, Dennis L. (2000). Women's attitudes toward men: An integrated threat theory approach. *Psychology of Women Quarterly, 24*, 63–73.

Sternberg, Robert J. (1986). A triangular theory of love. *Psychological Review, 93*, 119–135.

Sternberg, Robert J. (1987). Liking versus loving: A comparative evaluation of theories. *Psychological Bulletin, 102*, 331–345.

Stevens, Daphne Pedersen; Kiger, Gary; & Mannon, Susan E. (2005). Domestic labor and marital satisfaction: How much or how satisfied? *Marriage and Family Review, 37*, 49–67.

Stewart, Abigail J. (2003). Gender, race, and generation in a midwest high school: Using ethnographically informed methods in psychology. *Psychology of Women Quarterly, 27*, 1–11.

St. John, Warren. (2002, May 12). With games of havoc, men will be boys. *New York Times*, p. ST1.

Stohs, Joanne Hoven. (2000). Multicultural women's experience of household labor, conflicts, and equity. *Sex Roles, 42*, 339–362.

Stone, Marilyn; & Couch, Sue. (2004). Peer sexual harassment among high school students: Teachers' attitudes, perceptions, and responses. *High School Journal, 88*, 1–13.

Straus, Murray A. (2009). Gender symmetry in partner violence: Evidence and implications for prevention and treatment. In Daniel J. Whitaker & John R. Lutzker (Eds.), *Preventing partner violence: Research and evidence-based intervention* (pp. 245–271). Washington, DC: American Psychological Association.

Straus, Murray A.; & Gelles, Richard J. (1986). Societal change and change in family violence from 1975 to 1985 as revealed by two national surveys. *Journal of Marriage and the Family, 48*, 465–479.

Straus, Murray A.; Gelles, Richard J.; & Steinmetz, Suzanne K. (1980). *Behind closed doors: Violence in the American family*. Garden City, NY: Anchor.

Strelan, Pater; Mehaffey, Sarah J.; & Tiggemann, Marika. (2003). Self-objectification and esteem in young women: The mediating role of reasons for exercise. *Sex Roles, 48*, 89–95.

Stremikis, Barbara A. (2002). The personal characteristics and environmental circumstances of successful women musicians. *Creativity Research Journal, 14*, 85–92.

Striegel-Moore, Ruth H.; Rosselli, Francine; Perrin, Nancy; DeBar, Lynn; Wilson, G. Terence; May, Alexis; et al. (2009). Gender difference in the prevalence of eating disorder symptoms. *International Journal of Eating Disorders, 42* (5), 471–474.

Strine, Tara W.; Chapman, Daniel P.; & Ahluwalia, Indu B. (2005). Menstrual-related problems and psychological distress among women in the United States. *Journal of Women's Health, 14*, 316–323.

Strough, JoNell; Leszczynski, Jennifer Pickard; Neely, Tara L.; Flinn, Jennifer A.; & Margrett, Jennifer. (2007). From adolescence to later adulthood: Femininity, masculinity, and androgyny in six age groups. *Sex Roles, 57*, 385-396.

Struckman-Johnson, Cindy; & Struckman-Johnson, David. (1994). Men pressured and forced into sexual experience. *Archives of Sexual Behavior, 23*, 93–114.

Subramaniam, Mangala. (2004). A symposium: Bridging scholarship: The Indian women's movement. *Contemporary Sociology, 33* (6), 635–639.

Substance Abuse and Mental Health Services Administration (SAMHSA). (2009). *Results from the 2008 National Survey on Drug Use and Health: National Findings.* (Office of Applied Studies, NSDUH Series H-36, HHS Publication No. SMA 09-4434). Rockville, MD: U.S. Government Printing Office.

Sue, David. (2001). Asian American masculinity and therapy: The concept of masculinity in Asian American males. In Gary R. Brooks & Glen E. Good (Eds.), *The new handbook of psychotherapy and counseling with men: A comprehensive guide to settings, problems, and treatment approaches* (pp. 780–795). San Francisco, CA: Jossey-Bass.

Sugihara, Yoko; & Katsurada, Emiko. (2002). Gender role development in Japanese culture: Diminishing gender role differences in a contemporary society. *Sex Roles, 47,* 443–452.

Suitor, J. Jill; & Carter, Rebecca S. (1999). Jocks, nerds, babes and thugs: A research note on regional differences in adolescent gender norms. *Gender Issues, 17,* 88–101.

Suitor, J. Jill; Powers, Rebecca S.; & Brown, Rachel. (2004). Avenues to prestige among adolescents in public and religiously affiliated high schools. *Adolescence, 39,* 229–241.

Suitor, J. Jill; & Reavis, Rebel. (1995). Football, fast cars, and cheerleading: Adolescent gender norms. *Adolescence, 30,* 265–272.

Sullivan, Amy. (2009, April 6). How the end the war over sex ed. *Time Atlantic, 173* (14), 28–31.

Sullivan, Michele G. (2003, February 1). Revised guidelines address hypogonadism in men. *Family Practice, 33* (3), 34.

Sullivan, Oriel; & Coltrane, Scott. (2007). *Men's changing contributions to housework and child care.* Paper presented at the annual meeting of the American Sociological Association.

Surtees, Nicola. (2005). Teacher talk about and around sexuality in early childhood education: Deciphering an unwritten code. *Contemporary Issues in Early Childhood, 6,* 19–29.

Survey says: Half of today's singles have used a dating service. (2004, September 24). *PR Newswire.*

Susskind, Joshua E. (2003). Children's perception of gender-based illusory correlations: Enhancing preexisting relationships between gender and behavior. *Sex Roles, 48,* 483–494.

Sutfin, Erin; Fulcher, Megan; Bowles, Ryan; & Patterson, Charlotte. (2008). How lesbian and heterosexual parents convey attitudes about gender to their children: The role of gendered environments. *Sex Roles, 58* (7/8), 501–513.

Swaab, D. F.; & Fliers, E. (1985). A sexually dimorphic nucleus in the human brain. *Science, 228,* 1112–1115.

Swaab, D. F.; Gooren, L. J. G.; & Hofman, M. A. (1995). Brain research, gender, and sexual orientation. *Journal of Homosexuality, 28,* 283–301.

Swami, Viren; Stieger, Stefan; Haubner, Tanja; Voracek, Martin; & Furnham, Adrian. (2009). Evaluating the physical attractiveness of oneself and one's romantic partner: Individual and relationship correlates of the love-is-blind bias. *Journal of Individual Differences, 30* (1), 35–43.

Sweet, Holly. (2006). Finding the person behind the persona: Engaging men as a female therapist. In Matt Englar-Carlson & Mark A. Stevens (Eds.), *In a room with men: A casebook of therapeutic change* (pp. 69–90). Washington, DC: American Psychological Association.

Sweetland, Annalise. (2004, April 19). *Afghan diary: Afghan apartheid.* Retrieved May 9, 2006, from http://afghandiary.org.uk/?p=diary.tem&page=4

Szollos, Alex; Thyrum, Elizabeth; & Martin, Betty. (2006). College women's perceptions of anxiety and menstrual distress across the menstrual cycle. *College Student Journal, 40,* 186–194.

Szymanski, Dawn M.; Baird, M. Kathleen; & Kornman, Christopher L. (2002). The feminist male therapist: Attitudes and practices for the 21st century. *Psychology of Men & Masculinity, 3,* 22–27.

Tager, David D.; & Good, Glenn E. (2005). Italian and American masculinities: A comparison of masculine gender role norms. *Psychology of Men and Masculinity, 6,* 264–274.

Tan, Josephine; & Carfagnini, Brooke. (2008). Self-silencing, anger and depressive symptoms in women: Implications for prevention and intervention. *Journal of Prevention and Intervention in the Community, 35* (2), 5–18.

Tannen, Deborah. (1990). *You just don't understand: Women and men in conversation.* New York: William Morrow.

Tannen, Deborah. (1994). *Talking from 9 to 5: Women and men at work: Language, sex and power.* New York: Avon Books.

Tashakkori, Abbas; & Teddlie, Charles. (2003). Issues and dilemmas in teaching research methods courses in social and behavioural sciences: US perspective. *International Journal of Social Research Methodology, 6* (1), 61–77.

Tavris, Carol. (1992). *The mismeasure of woman.* New York: Simon & Schuster.

Tavris, Carol. (2005). Brains, biology, science, and skepticism: On thinking about sex differences (again). *Skeptical Inquirer, 29* (3), 11–12.

Tavris, Carol; & Wade, Carole. (1984). *The longest war: Sex differences in perspective* (2nd ed.). New York: Harcourt Brace Jovanovich.

Taylor, Robert Joseph; Lincoln, Karen D.; & Chatters, Linda M. (2005). Supportive relationships with church members among African Americans. *Family Relations, 54,* 501–511.

Taylor, Shelley E. (2006). Tend and befriend: Biobehavioral bases of affiliation under stress. *Current Directions in Psychological Science, 15* (6), 273–277.

Taylor, Shelley E.; Klein, Laura Cousino; Lewis, Brian P.; Gruenewald, Tara L.; Gurung, Regan A. R.; & Updegraff, John A. (2000). Biobehavioral responses to stress in females tend-and-befriend, not fight-or-flight. *Psychological Review, 107*, 411–429.

Taylor, Tiffany; & Risman, Barbara J. (2006). Doing deference or speaking up: Deconstructing the experience and expression of anger. *Race, Gender & Class, 13* (3/4), 60-80.

Temple, Jeff R.; Weston, Rebecca; Rodriguez, Benjamin F.; & Marshall, Linda L. (2007). Differing effects of partner and nonpartner sexual assault on women's mental health. *Violence Against Women, 13* (3), 285–297.

Tennenbaum, Harriet R.; & Leaper, Campbell. (2002). Are parents' gender schemas related to their children's gender-related cognitions? A meta-analysis. *Developmental Psychology, 38*, 615–630.

Terlecki, Melissa S.; & Newcombe, Nora S. (2005). How important is the digital divide? The relation of computer and videogame usage to gender differences in mental rotation ability. *Sex Roles, 53*, 433–441.

Terman, Lewis M.; & Merrill, Maud A. (1937). *Measuring intelligence.* Boston: Houghton Mifflin.

Thanasiu, Page L. (2004). Childhood sexuality: Discerning healthy from abnormal sexual behaviors. *Journal of Mental Health Counseling, 26*, 309–319.

Therapy in America 2004. (2004). Retrieved July 31, 2006, from http://www.psychologytoday.com/pto/press_release_050404.html

Thoits, Peggy A. (2005). Differential labeling of mental illness by social status: A new look at an old problem. *Journal of Health and Social Behavior, 46*, 102–119.

Thompson, Becky. (2002). Multiracial feminism: Recasting the chronology of second wave feminism. *Feminist Studies, 28*, 337–360.

Thompson, Linda; & Walker, Alexis J. (1989). Gender in families: Women and men in marriage, work, and parenthood. *Journal of Marriage and the Family, 51*, 845–871.

Thompson, Teresa L.; & Zerbinos, Eugenia. (1995). Gender roles in animated cartoons: Has the picture changed in 20 years? *Sex Roles, 32*, 651–674.

Thompson, Teresa. L.; & Zerbinos, Eugenia. (1997). Television cartoons: Do children notice it's a boy's world? *Sex Roles, 37*, 415–432.

Thorne, Barrie. (1993). *Gender play: Girls and boys in school.* New Brunswick, NJ: Rutgers University Press.

Thornton, Arland; & Young-DeMarco, Linda. (2001). Four decades of trends in attitudes toward family issues in the United States: The 1960s through the 1990s. *Journal of Marriage and Family, 63*, 1009–1037.

Thunberg, Monika; & Dimberg, Ulf. (2000). Gender differences in facial reactions to fear-relevant stimuli. *Journal of Nonverbal Behavior, 24*, 45–51.

Tichenor, Veronica Jaris. (2005a). *Earning more and getting less: Why successful wives can't buy equality.* New Brunswick, NJ: Rutgers University Press.

Tichenor, Veronica. (2005b). Maintaining men's dominance: Negotiating identity and power when she earns more. *Sex Roles, 53*, 191–205.

Tiedemann, Joachim. (2000). Parents' gender stereotypes and teachers' beliefs as predictors of children's concept of their mathematical ability in elementary school. *Journal of Educational Psychology, 92*, 144–151.

Tiefer, Lenore. (1995). *Sex is not a natural act and other essays.* Boulder, CO: Westview Press.

Tieg, Stacey; & Susskind, Joshua. (2008). Truck driver or nurse? The impact of gender roles and occupational status on children's occupational preferences. *Sex Roles, 58* (11/12), 848–863.

Timmerman, Greetje. (2003). Sexual harassment of adolescents perpetrated by teachers and by peers: An exploration of the dynamics of power, culture, and gender in secondary schools. *Sex Roles, 48*, 231–244.

Tinkler, Justine E. (2008). "People are too quick to take offense": The effects of legal information and beliefs on definitions of sexual harassment. *Law and Social Inquiry, 33* (2), 417–445.

Tjaden, Patricia; & Thoennes, Nancy. (2000a). *Extent, nature and consequences of intimate partner violence: Findings from the National Violence Against Women Survey.* Washington, DC: U.S. Department of Justice.

Tjaden, Patricia; & Thoennes, Nancy. (2000b). *Full report of the prevalence, incidence, and consequences of violence against women: Findings from the National Violence Against Women Survey.* Washington, DC: U.S. Department of Justice.

Tlauka, Michael; Williams, Jennifer; & Williamson, Paul. (2008). Spatial ability in secondary school students: Intro-sex differences based on self-selection for physical education. *British Journal of Psychology, 99* (3), 427–440.

Tolman, Deborah L. (2002). *Dilemmas of desire: Teenage girls talk about sexuality.* Cambridge, MA: Harvard University Press.

Tomasson, Kristinn; Kent, D.; & Coryell, W. (1991). Somatization and conversion disorders: Comorbidity and demographics at presentation. *Acta Psychiatrica Scandinavica, 84*, 288–293.

Tomkiewicz, Joe; & Bass, Kenneth. (1999). Changes in women's fear of success and fear of appearing incompetent in business. *Psychological Reports, 85*, 1003–1010.

Ton, Hendry; & Lim, Russell F. (2006). The assessment of culturally diverse individuals. In Russell F. Lim (Ed.), *Clinical manual of cultural psychiatry* (pp. 3–31). Arlington, VA: American Psychiatric Publishing.

Trautner, Hanns M.; Gervai, Judit; & Németh, Rita. (2003). Appearance-reality distinction and the development of gender constancy understanding in children. *International Journal of Behavioral Development, 27,* 275–283.

Trautner, Hanns M.; Ruble, Diane N.; Cyphers, Lisa; Kirsten, Barbara; Behrendt, Regina; & Hartmann, Petra. (2005). Rigidity and flexibility of gender stereotypes in childhood: Developmental or differential? *Infant and Child Development, 14,* 365–381.

Travis, Cheryl Brown. (2005). 2004 Carolyn Sherif Award Address: Heart disease and gender inequity. *Psychology of Women Quarterly, 29,* 15–23.

Travis, Cheryl Brown; & Compton, Jill D. (2001). Feminism and health in the decade of behavior. *Psychology of Women Quarterly, 25,* 312–323.

Trencansky, Sarah. (2001). Final girls and terrible youth: Transgression in 1980s slasher horror. *Journal of Popular Film and Television, 29,* 63–73.

Trierweiler, Steven J.; Neighbors, Harold W.; Munday, Cheryl; Thompson, Estina E.; Binion, Victoria J.; & Gomez, John P. (2000). Clinician attributions associated with the diagnosis of schizophrenia in African American and non-African American patients. *Journal of Consulting and Clinical Psychology, 68,* 171–175.

Trzesniewsk, Kali H.; Donnellan, M. Brent; & Robins, Richard W. (2003). Stability of self-esteem across the life span. *Journal of Personality and Social Psychology, 84,* 205–220.

Truscott, Derek. (2010). Feminist. In Derek Truscott, *Becoming an effective psychotherapist: Adopting a theory of psychotherapy that's right for you and your client* (pp. 127–140). Washington, DC: American Psychological Association.

Turner, Charles F.; Villarroel, Maria A.; Chromy, James R.; Eggleston, Elizabeth; & Rogers, Susan M. (2005). Same-gender sex among U.S. adults. *Public Opinion Quarterly, 69,* 439–462.

Tweedie, Neil. (2008, June 12). And you call us boring? *Telegraph.* Retrieved June 19, 2009, from http://www.telegraph.co.uk/news/features/3636899/And-you-call-us-boring.html

Twenge, Jean M. (1997). Attitudes toward women, 1970–1995. *Psychology of Women Quarterly, 21,* 35–51.

Twenge, Jean M.; & Nolen-Hoeksema, Susan. (2002). Age, gender, race, socioeconomic status, and birth cohort differences on the Children's Depression Inventory: A meta-analysis. *Journal of Abnormal Psychology, 111,* 578–588.

Tyre, Peg; McGinn, Daniel; Springen, Karen; Wingert, Pat; Pierce, Ellise; Joseph, Nadine Juarez; et al. (2003, May 12). She works, he doesn't. *Newsweek, 141* (19), 45+.

Uggen, Christopher; & Shinohara, Chika. (2009). Sexual harassment comes of age: A comparative analysis of the United States and Japan. *The Sociological Quarterly, 50* (2), 210–234.

Uhlmann, Eric Luis; & Cohen, Geoffrey L. (2005). Constructed criteria. *Psychological Science, 16,* 474–480.

Ülkü-Steiner, Beril; Kurtz-Costes, Beth; & Kinlaw, C. Ryan. (2000). Doctoral student experiences in gender-balanced and male-dominated graduate programs. *Journal of Educational Psychology, 92,* 296–307.

Ulrich, Clare. (2002). High stress and low income: The environment of poverty. *Human Ecology, 30* (4), 16–18.

Umberson, Debra; Williams, Kristi; Powers, Daniel A.; Liu, Hui; & Needham, Belinda. (2006). You make me sick: Marital quality and health over the life course. *Journal of Health and Social Behavior, 47,* 1–16.

UNAIDS/WHO. (2008). *Toward universal access: Scaling up priority HIV/AIDS interventions in the health sector: A progress report 2008.* Geneva: World Health Organization.

Unger, Rhoda K. (1979). Toward a redefinition of sex and gender. *American Psychologist, 34,* 1085–1094.

Unger, Rhoda K. (1983–1984). Sex in psychological paradigms—From behavior to cognition. *Imagination, Cognition, and Personality, 3,* 227–234.

Unger, Rhoda K. (1995). Conclusion: Cultural diversity and the future of feminist psychology. In Hope Landrine (Ed.), *Bringing cultural diversity to feminist psychology* (pp. 413–431). Washington, DC: American Psychological Association.

United Nations Children's Fund. (2009). Monitoring the situation of women and children. *Childinfo.* Retrieved October 13, 2009, from http://www.childinfo.org/education.html

United Nations Educational, Scientific and Cultural Organization. (2005). *Education for all global monitoring report 2005.* Retrieved July 9, 2006, from http://portal.unesco.org/education/en/ev.php-URL_ID=35939&URL_DO=DO_TOPIC&URL_SECTION=201.html

Upchurch, Dawn M.; Levy-Storms, Lene; Sucoff, Clea A.; & Aneshensel, Carol S. (1998). Gender and ethnic differences in the timing of first sexual intercourse. *Family Planning Perspectives, 30,* 121–127.

Upchurch, Dawn M.; Lillard, Lee A.; Aneshensel, Carol S.; & Li, Nicole Fang. (2002). Inconsistencies in reporting the occurrence and timing of first intercourse among adolescents. *Journal of Sex Research, 39,* 197–206.

Uray, Nimet; & Burnaz, Sebnem. (2003). An analysis of the portrayal of gender roles in Turkish television advertisements. *Sex Roles, 48,* 77–87.

Usall, J.; Ochoa, S.; Araya, S.; & Márquez, M. (2003). Gender differences and outcome in schizophrenia: A 2-year follow-up study in a large community sample. *European Psychiatry, 18,* 282–284.

U. S. Bureau of Justice Statistics. (2008, December). Criminal victimization, 2007. *Bureau of Justice Statistics Bulletin,* NCJ224390, 1-12. Retrieved August 28, 2009 from http://www.ojp.usdoj.gov/bjs/abstract/cv07.htm

U.S. Bureau of Labor Statistics. (2008). *Women in the labor force: A databook.* Retrieved October 18, 2009, from www.bls.gov/cps/wlf-databook-2008.pdf.

U.S. Census Bureau. (2009a). *Statistical Abstract of the United States, 2009* (128th ed.). Washington, DC: U.S.

Government Printing Office. Retrieved August 30, 2009, from hhttp://www.census.gov/compendia/statab/2009/2009edition.html

U.S. Census Bureau. (2009b). *Unmarried partners of the opposite sex, by presence of children: 1960 to present.* Retrieved September 5, 2009, from http://www.census.gov/population/www/socdemo/hh-fam.html#cps

U.S. Department of Education. (2008). *Digest of Educational Statistics*, Table 311. Retrieved June 24, 2010 from http://nces.ed.gov/programs/digest/d08/tables/dt08_311.asp

U.S. Department of Health and Human Services. (1999). *Mental health: A report of the Surgeon General.* Washington, DC: U.S. Government Printing Office.

U.S. Department of Health and Human Services. (2001). *Mental health: Culture, race, and ethnicity—A supplement to Mental health: A report of the Surgeon General.* Rockville, MD: Author.

Vaccarino, Viola; Rathore, Saif S.; Wenger, Nannette K.; Frederick, Paul D.; Abramson, Jerome L.; Barron, Hal V.; et al. (2005). Sex and racial differences in the management of acute myocardial infarction, 1994 through 2002. *New England Journal of Medicine, 353,* 671–682.

Valentová, Marie; Šmídová, Iva; Katrňák, Tomáš. (2008). Gender segregation in the labour market placed in the context of educational segregation: Cross-national comparison. *Sociologia, 39* (3), 214–244.

Valian, Virginia. (2007). Women at the top in science—and elsewhere. In Stephen J. Ceci & Wendy M. Williams (Eds.), *Why aren't more women in science: Top researchers debate the evidence* (pp. 27–37). Washington, DC: American Psychological Association.

Valles, Nizete-Ly; & Knutson, John F. (2008). Contingent responses of mothers and peers to indirect and direct aggression in preschool and school-aged children. *Aggressive Behavior, 34* (5), 497–510.

Valls-Fernández, Federico; & Martínez-Vicente, José Manuel. (2007). Gender stereotypes in Spanish television commercials. *Sex Roles, 56* (9/10), 691–699.

van Anders, Sari M. (2004). Why the academic pipeline leaks: Fewer men than women perceive barriers to becoming professors. *Sex Roles, 51,* 511–521.

Van Bokhoven, Irene; van Goozen, Stephanie H. M.; van Engeland, Herman; Schaal, Benoist; Arseneault, Louise; Séguin, Jean R.; et al. (2006). Salivary testosterone and aggression, delinquency, and social dominance in a population-based study of adolescent males. *Hormones & Behavior, 50* (1), 118–125.

Vance, Carole S. (1984). Pleasure and danger: Toward a politics of sexuality. In Carole S. Vance (Ed.), *Pleasure and danger: Exploring female sexuality* (pp. 1–27). Boston: Routledge & Kegan Paul.

Vandello, Joseph A.; Bosson, Jennifer K.; Cohen, Cov; Burnaford, Rochelle M.; & Weaver, Jonathan, R. (2008). Precarious manhood. *Journal of Personality and Social Psychology, 95* (6), 1325–1339.

Vandervoort, Debra. (1999). Quality of social support in mental and physical health. *Current Psychology, 18,* 205–222.

van Engen, Marloes L.; & Willemsen, Tineke M. (2004). Sex and leadership styles: A meta-analysis of research published in the 1990s. *Psychological Reports, 94* (1), 3–18.

VanLear, C. Arthur; Sheehan, Megan; Withers, Lesley A.; & Walker, Robert A. (2005). AA online: The enactment of supportive computer mediated communication. *Western Journal of Communication, 69,* 5–26.

Van Ommeren, Jos; de Vries, Reinout E.; Russo, Giovanni; & van Ommeren, Mark. (2005). Context in selection of men and women in hiring decisions: Gender composition of the applicant pool. *Psychological Reports, 96,* 349–360.

van Steenbergen, Elianne F.; & Ellemers, Naomi. (2009). Is managing the work–family interface worthwhile? Benefits for employee health and performance. *Journal of Organizational Behavior, 30* (5), 617–642.

van Wijk, Charles H.; & Finchilescu, Gillian. (2008). Symbols of organisational culture: Describing and prescribing gender integration of navy ships. *Journal of Gender Studies, 17* (3), 237–249.

Van Willigen, Marieke; & Drentea, Patricia. (2001). Benefits of equitable relationships: The impact of sense of fairness, household division of labor, and decision making power on perceived social support. *Sex Roles, 44,* 571–597.

Vasquez, Melba J. T. (2002). Latinas: Exercise and empowerment from a feminist psychodynamic perspective. *Women and Therapy, 25* (2), 23–38.

Vasquez, Melba J. T.; & Kitchener, Karen Strohm. (1988). Introduction to special feature: Ethics in counseling: Sexual intimacy between counselor and client. *Journal of Counseling and Development, 67,* 214–217.

Ventura, Stephanie J.; Abma, Joyce C.; & Mosher, William D. (2008). Estimated pregnancy rates by outcome for the United States, 1990–2004. *National Vital Statistics Report, 56* (15), 1–28.

Verbrugge, Lois M. (1985). Gender and health: An update on hypotheses and evidence. *Journal of Health and Social Behavior, 26,* 156–182.

Verhofstadt, Lesley L.; Buysee, Ann; & Ickes, William. (2007). Social support in couples: An examination of gender differences using self-report and observational methods. *Sex Roles, 57* (3/4), 267–282.

Vermeersch, Hans; T'Sjoen, Guy; Kaufman, Jean-Marc; & Vincke, John. (2008). The role of testosterone in aggressive and non-aggressive risk-taking in adolescent boys. *Hormones & Behavior, 53* (3), 463–471.

Viki, G. Tendayi; Abrams, Dominic; & Hutchinson, Paul. (2003). The "true" romantic: Benevolent sexism and paternalistic chivalry. *Sex Roles, 49,* 533–537.

Vitale, Cristiana; Mendelsohn, Michael E.; & Rosano, Giuseppe M. C. (2009). Gender differences in the cardiovascular effect of sex hormones. *Nature Reviews Cardiology, 6* (8), 532–542.

von Stumm, Sophie; Chamorrro-Premuzic, Tomas; & Furnham, Adrian. (2009). Decomposing self-estimates of intelligence: Structure and sex differences across 12 nations. *British Journal of Psychology, 100* (2), 429–442.

Voyer, Daniel; Voyer, Susan; & Bryden, M. Philip. (1995). Magnitude of sex differences in spatial abilities: A meta-analysis and consideration of critical variables. *Psychological Bulletin, 117,* 250–270.

Wade, M. Leslie; & Brewer, Marilynn B. (2006). The structure of female subgroups: An exploration of ambivalent stereotypes. *Sex Roles, 54* (11/12), 753–765.

Wade, Terrance J.; Cairney, John; & Pevalin, David J. (2002). Emergence of gender differences in depression during adolescence: National panel results from three countries. *Journal of the American Academy of Child and Adolescent Psychiatry, 41,* 190–198.

Wagner, Jane. (1991). *The search for intelligent life in the universe.* New York: Harper Paperbacks.

Waldrip, Amy M.; Malcolm, Kenya T.; & Jensen-Campbell, Lauri A. (2008). With a little help from your friends: The importance of high-quality friendships on early adolescent adjustment. *Social Development, 17* (4), 832–852.

Walker, Lenore E. A. (2001). A feminist perspective on men in emotional pain. In Gary R. Brooks & Glenn E. Good (Eds.), *The new handbook of psychotherapy and counseling with men: A comprehensive guide to settings, problems, and treatment approaches* (pp. 683–695). San Francisco: Jossey-Bass.

Wallentin, Mikkel. (2009). Putative sex differences in verbal abilities and language cortex: A critical review. *Brain & Language, 108* (3), 175–183.

Walsh, Mary Roth. (1985). Academic professional women organizing for change: The struggle in psychology. *Journal of Social Issues, 41* (4), 17–28.

Walsh, Trudi M.; Stewart, Sherry H.; McLaughlin, Elizabeth; & Comeau, Nancy. (2004). Gender differences in Childhood Anxiety Sensitivity Index (CASI) dimensions. *Journal of Anxiety Disorders, 18,* 695–706.

Walters, Stephanie; Barr-Anderson, Daheia J.; Wall, Melanie; Neumark-Sztainer, Dianne. (2009). Does participation in organized sports predict future physical activity for adolescents from diverse economic backgrounds? *Journal of Adolescent Health, 44* (3), 268–274.

Wang, Rong; & Bianchi, Suzanne. (2009). ATUS fathers' involvement in childcare. *Social Indicators Research, 93* (1), 141–145.

Warburton, Darren E. R.; Nichol, Crystal Whitney; & Bredin, Shannon S. D. (2006). Health benefits of physical activity: The evidence. *CMAJ: Canadian Medical Association Journal, 174,* 801–809.

Ward, L. Charles; Thorn, Beverly E.; Clements, Kristi L.; Dixon, Kim E.; & Sanford, Stacy D. (2006). Measurement of agency, communion, and emotional vulnerability with the Personal Attributes Questionnaire. *Journal of Personality Assessment, 86,* 206–216.

Ward, Roberta J.; & Coutelle, Ch. (2003). Women and alcohol susceptibility: Could differences in alcohol metabolism predispose women to alcohol-related diseases? *Archives of Women's Mental Health, 6,* 231–238.

Warin, Jo. (2000). The attainment of self-consistency through gender in young children. *Sex Roles, 42,* 209–232.

Washburn-Ormachea, Jill M.; Hillman, Stephen B.; & Sawilowsky, Shlomo S. (2004). Gender and gender-role orientation differences on adolescents' coping with peer stressors. *Journal of Youth and Adolescence, 33,* 31–40.

Watkins, Ed; Moulds, Michelle; & Mackintosh, Bundy. (2005). Comparisons between rumination and worry in a non-clinical population. *Behaviour Research and Therapy, 43,* 1577–1585.

Watson, Cary M.; Quatman, Teri; & Edler, Erik. (2002). Career aspirations of adolescent girls: Effects of achievement level, grade, and single-sex school environment. *Sex Roles, 46,* 323–335.

Watson, Neil V.; Freeman, Louise M.; & Breedlove, S. Marc. (2001). Neuronal size in the spinal nucleus of the bulbocavernosus: Direct modulation by androgen in rats with mosaic androgen insensitivity. *Journal of Neuroscience, 21* (3), 1062–1066.

Wattendorf, Daniel J.; & Muenke, Maximilian. (2005). Klinefelter syndrome. *American Family Physician, 72,* 2559–2562.

Weeden, Jason; & Sabini, John. (2005). Physical attractiveness and health in Western societies: A review. *Psychological Bulletin, 131,* 635–653.

Wehmeyer, Michael L. (2001). Disproportionate representation of males in special education services: Biology, behavior, or bias? *Education and Treatment of Children, 24,* 28–45.

Weidner, Gerdi; & Cain, Virginia S. (2003). The gender gap in heart disease: Lessons from Eastern Europe. *American Journal of Public Health, 93,* 768–770.

Weil, Shalva. (2008). Is there a "legitimation crisis" in qualitative methods? *Forum: Qualitative Social Research, 9* (2), 1–13.

Weinberg, Nancy; Uken, Janet S.; Schmale, John; & Adamek, Margaret. (1995). Therapeutic factors: Their presence in a computer-mediated support group. *Social Work with Groups, 18* (4), 57–69.

Weinberg, William T. (2000). The role of sports as a determinant of popularity among high school students. *Research Quarterly for Exercise and Sport, 71* (1), A84.

Weinburgh, Molly. (1995). Gender differences in student attitudes toward science: A meta-analysis of the literature from 1970 to 1991. *Journal of Research in Science Teaching, 32,* 387–398.

Weiner, Richard L.; Voss, Amy M.; Winter, Ryan J.; & Arnot, Lucy. (2005). The more you see it, the more you know it: Memory accessibility and sexual harassment judgments. *Sex Roles*, *53*, 807–820.

Weiss, Karen G. (2009). "Boys will be boys" and other gendered accounts. *Violence Against Women*, *15* (7), 810–834.

Weiss, Maureen R.; & Barber, Heather. (1995). Socialization influences of collegiate male athletes: A tale of two decades. *Sex Roles*, *33*, 129–140.

Weisstein, Naomi. (1970). "Kinde, küche, kirche" as scientific law: Psychology constructs the female. In Robin Morgan (Ed.), *Sisterhood is powerful: An anthology of writings from the women's liberation movement* (pp. 228–245). New York: Vintage Books.

Weisstein, Naomi. (1982, November). Tired of arguing about biological inferiority? *Ms.*, pp. 41–46, 85.

Weisz, George; & Knaapen, Loes. (2009). Diagnosing and treating premenstrual syndrome in five western nations. *Social Science & Medicine*, *68* (8), 1498–1505.

Welch-Ross, Melissa K.; & Schmidt, Constance R. (1996). Gender-schema development and children's constructive story memory: Evidence or a developmental model. *Child Development*, *67*, 820–835.

Wells, Brooke E.; & Twenge, Jean M. (2005). Changes in young people's sexual behavior and attitudes, 1943–1999: A cross-temporal meta-analysis. *Review of General Psychology*, *9*, 249–261.

Welter, Barbara. (1978). The cult of true womanhood: 1820–1860. In Michael Gordon (Ed.), *The American family in social-historical perspective* (2nd ed., pp. 313–333). New York: St. Martin's Press.

Werking, Kathy. (1997). *We're just good friends.* New York: Guilford Press.

West, Candace; & Zimmerman, Don H. (1987). Doing gender. *Gender and Society*, *1*, 125–151.

Westkott, Marcia C. (1997). On the new psychology of women: A cautionary view. In Mary Roth Walsh (Ed.), *Women, men, and gender: Ongoing debates* (pp. 362–372). New Haven, CT: Yale University Press.

Weston, Rebecca; Temple, Jeff R.; & Marshall, Linda L. (2005). Gender symmetry and asymmetry in violent relationships: Patterns of mutuality among racially diverse women. *Sex Roles*, *53*, 553–571.

Whealin, Julia M.; Zinzow, Heidi M.; Salstrom, Seoka A.; & Jackson, Joan L. (2007). Sex differences in the experience of unwanted sexual attention and behaviors during childhood. *Journal of Child Sexual Abuse*, *16* (3), 41–58.

Whelan, Emma. (2001). Politics by other means: Feminism and mainstream science studies. *Canadian Journal of Sociology*, *26*, 535–582.

Whitehead, Barbara Dafoe; & Popenoe, David. (2002). *The state of our unions: The social health of marriage in America.* Piscataway, NJ: National Marriage Project. Retrieved on July 18, 2003, from http://marriage.rutgers.edu

Whitley, Bernard E., Jr. (2001). Gender-role variables and attitudes toward homosexuality. *Sex Roles*, *45*, 691–721.

Whitty, Monica T.; & Fisher, William A. (2008). The sexy side of the Internet: An examination of sexual activities and materials in cyberspace. In Azy Barak (Ed.), *Psychological aspects of cyberspace: Theory, research, applications* (pp. 185–208). New York: Cambridge University Press.

WHO World Mental Health Survey Consortium. (2004). Prevalence, severity, and unmet need for treatment of mental disorders in the World Health Organization world mental health survey. *Journal of the American Medical Association*, *291*, 2581–2590.

Widiger, Thomas A.; Simonsen, Erik; Krueger, Robert; Livesley, W. John; & Verheul, Roel. (2005). Personality disorder research agenda for the DSM-V. *Journal of Personality Disorders*, *19*, 315–338.

Wieringa, Saskia E. (1994). The Zuni man-woman. *Archives of Sexual Behavior*, *23*, 348–351.

Wilansky-Traynor, Pamela; & Lobel, Thalma E. (2008). Differential effects of an adult observer's presence on sex-typed play behavior: A comparison between gender-schematic and gender-aschematic preschool children. *Archives of Sexual Behavior*, *37* (4), 548–557.

Wiley, Autumn. (2004). Abnormal psychology textbooks exclude feminist criticism of the DSM. In Paula J. Caplan & Lisa Cosgrove (Eds.), *Bias in psychiatric diagnosis* (pp. 41–46). Lanham, MD: Jason Aronson.

Wilkinson, Richard G. (1996). *Unhealthy societies: The afflictions of inequity.* London: Routledge.

Wilkinson, Sue. (1999). Focus groups: A feminist method. *Psychology of Women Quarterly*, *23*, 221–244.

Willan, V. J.; & Pollard, Paul. (2003). Likelihood of acquaintance rape as a function of males' sexual expectations, disappointment, and adherence to rape-conducive attitudes. *Journal of Social and Personal Relationships*, *20*, 637–661.

Williams, Christine L. (1992). The glass escalator: Hidden advantages for men in the "female" professions. *Social Problems*, *39*, 253–267.

Williams, Dmitri. (2003). The video game lightning rod: Constructions of a new media technology, 1970–2000. *Information, Communication, and Society*, *6*, 523–550.

Williams, Joan. (2000). *Unbending gender: Why family and work conflict and what to do about it.* New York: Oxford University Press.

Williams, Joan C.; & Cooper, Holly Cohen. (2004). The public policy of motherhood. *Journal of Social Issues*, *60*, 849–865.

Williams, John E.; & Best, Deborah L. (1990). *Measuring sex stereotypes: A multination study* (r. ed.). Newbury Park, CA: Sage.

Williams, John E.; Satterwhite, Robert C.; & Best, Deborah L. (1999). Pancultural gender stereotypes revisited: The Five Factor Model. *Sex Roles*, *40*, 513–526.

Williams, Kristi; Sassier, Sharon; & Nicholson, Lisa M. (2008). For better or for worse? The consequences of marriage and cohabitation for single mothers. *Social Forces*, *86* (4), 1481–1511.

Williams, Stacey L.; & Frieze, Irene. (2005). Patterns of violent relationships, psychological distress, and marital satisfaction in a national sample of men and women. *Sex Roles*, *52*, 771–784.

Willingham, Warren W.; & Cole, Nancy S. (1997). *Gender and fair assessment*. Mahwah, NJ: Erlbaum.

Willingham, Warren W.; Cole, Nancy S.; Lewis, Charles; & Leung, Susan Wilson. (1997). Test performance. In Warren W. Willingham & Nancy S. Cole, *Gender and fair assessment* (pp. 55–126). Mahwah, NJ: Erlbaum.

Willis, Brian M.; & Levy, Barry S. (2002). Child prostitution: Global health burden, research needs, and interventions. *Lancet*, *359*, 1417–1422.

Willness, Chelsea R.; Steel, Piers; & Lee, Kibeom. (2007). A meta-analysis of the antecedents and consequences of workplace sexual harassment. *Personnel Psychology*, *60* (1), 127–162.

Wilson, Robert A. (1966). *Feminine forever*. New York: M. Evans.

Winstok, Zeev; Eisikovits, Zvi; & Gelles, Richard. (2002). Structure and dynamics of escalation from the batterer's perspective. *Families in Society: The Journal of Contemporary Human Services*, *83*, 129–141.

Winstok, Zeev; & Perkis, Eila. (2009). Women's perspective on men's control and aggression in intimate relationships. *American Journal of Orthopsychiatry*, *79* (2), 169–180.

Wirth, James H.; & Bodenhausen, Galen V. (2009). The role of gender in mental-illness stigma: A national experiment. *Psychological Science*, *20* (2), 169–173.

Wise, Lauren A.; Zierler, Sally; Krieger, Nancy; & Harlow, Bernard L. (2001). Adult onset of major depressive disorder in relation to early life violent victimisation: A case-control study. *Lancet*, *358*, 881–887.

Wiseman, Rosalind. (2002). *Queen bees and wannabes: Helping your daughter survive cliques, gossip, boyfriends, and other realities of adolescence*. New York: Crown.

Wissink, Inge B.; Dekovic, Maja; & Meijer, Anne Marie. (2009). Adolescent friendship relations and developmental outcomes. *Journal of Early Adolescence*, *29* (3), 405–425.

Witelson, S. F.; Beresh, H.; & Kigar, D. L. (2006). Intelligence and brain size in 100 postmortem brains: Sex, lateralization and age factors. *Brain: A Journal of Neurology*, *129* (2), 386–398.

Witkin, Herman A.; Mednick, Sarnoff A.; Schulsinger, Fini; Bakkeström, Eskild; Christiansen, Karlo O.; Goodenough, Donald R.; et al. (1976). Criminality in XYY and XXY men. *Science*, *193*, 547–555.

Witt, Susan D. (1997). Parental influence on children's socialization to gender roles. *Adolescence*, *32*, 253–259.

Witt, Susan D. (2000). The influence of television on children's gender role socialization. *Childhood Education*, *76*, 322–324.

Wolak, Janis; Finkelhor, David; & Mitchell, Kimberly. (2008). Is talking online to unknown people always risky? Distinguishing online interaction styles in a national sample of youth Internet users. *CyberPsychology and Behavior*, *11* (3), 340–343.

Wolak, Janis; Mitchell, Kimberly J.; & Finkelhor, David. (2002). Close online relationships in a national sample of adolescents. *Adolescence*, *37*, 441–455.

Wolfson, S.; & Neave, N. (2004). Effects of venue on testosterone, territoriality and performance in soccer. *Journal of Sports Sciences*, *22*, 577–578.

Wong, Mitchell D.; Chung, Anne K.; Boscardin, W. John; Li, Ming; Hsieh, Hsin-ju; Ettner, Susan L.; et al. (2006). The contribution of specific causes of death to sex differences in mortality. *Public Health Reports*, *121* (6), 746–754.

Wong, Y. Joel; Pituch, Keenan A.; & Rochlen, Aaron B. (2006). Men's restrictive emotionality: An investigation of associations with other emotion-related constructs, anxiety, and underlying dimensions. *Psychology of Men and Masculinity*, *7*, 113–126.

Wood, Eileen; Desmarais, Serge; & Gugula, Sara. (2002). The impact of parenting experience on gender stereotyped toy play of children. *Sex Roles*, *47*, 39–49.

Wood, James M.; Garb, Howard N.; Lilienfeld, Scott O.; & Nezworski, M. Teresa. (2002). Clinical assessment. *Annual Review of Psychology*, *53*, 519–544.

Wood, Jeffrey J.; & Repetti, Rena L. (2004). What gets dad involved? A longitudinal study of change in parental child caregiving involvement. *Journal of Family Psychology*, *18*, 237–249.

Woodhill, Brenda Mae; & Samuels, Curtis A. (2003). Positive and negative androgyny and their relationship with psychological health and well-being. *Sex Roles*, *48*, 555–565.

Woodlock, Delanie. (2005). Virtual pushers: Antidepressant internet marketing and women. *Women's Studies International Forum*, *28*, 304–314.

Woodzicka, Julie; & LaFrance, Marianne. (2005). The effects of subtle sexual harassment on women's performance in a job interview. *Sex Roles*, *53*, 67–77.

Wooley, O. Wayne. (1994). . . . And man created "woman": Representations of women's bodies in Western culture. In Patricia Fallon, Melanie A. Katzman, & Susan C. Wooley (Eds.), *Feminist perspectives on eating disorders* (pp. 17–52). New York: Guilford.

Woollett, Anne; & Marshall, Harriette. (2001). Motherhood and mothering. In Rhoda K. Unger (Ed.), *Handbook of the psychology of women and gender* (pp. 170–182). New York: Wiley.

Worell, Judith. (1996). Opening doors to feminist research. *Psychology of Women Quarterly*, *20*, 469–485.

Worell, Judith. (2001). Feminist interventions: Accountability beyond symptom reduction. *Psychology of Women Quarterly, 25,* 335–343.

Worell, Judith; & Etaugh, Claire. (1994). Transforming theory and research with women: Themes and variations. *Psychology of Women Quarterly, 18,* 443–450.

Worell, Judith; & Johnson, Dawn. (2001). Therapy with women: Feminist frameworks. In Rhoda K. Unger (Ed.), *Handbook of the psychology of women and gender* (pp. 317–329). New York: Wiley.

Worell, Judith; & Remer, Pam. (2003). *Feminist perspectives in therapy: Empowering diverse women* (2nd ed). New York: Wiley.

Working Group on a New View of Women's Sexual Problems. (2004). A new view of women's sexual problems. In Paula J. Caplan & Lisa Cosgrove (Eds.), *Bias in psychiatric diagnosis* (pp. 233–239). Lanham, MD: Jason Aronson.

World Health Organization. (2008). *The global burden of disease: 2004 update.* Geneva, Switzerland: Author.

Wraga, Maryjane; Helt, Molly; Jacobs, Emily; & Sullivan, Kerry. (2007). Neural basis of stereotype-induced shifts in women's mental rotation performance. *Social Cognitive and Affective Neuroscience, 2* (1), 12–19.

Writing Group for the Women's Health Initiative Investigators. (2002). Risks and benefits of estrogen plus progestin in healthy postmenopausal women: Principal results from the Women's Health Initiative randomized controlled trial. *Journal of the American Medical Association, 288,* 321–333.

Wu, Zheng; & Schimmele, Christoph M. (2005). Repartnering after first union disruption. *Journal of Marriage and Family, 67,* 27–36.

Xu, Feng. (2009). Chinese feminisms encounter international feminisms. *International Feminist Journal of Politics, 11* (2), 196–215.

Xu, Xiaohe; & Lai, Shu-Chuan. (2004). Gender ideologies, marital roles, and marital quality in Taiwan. *Journal of Family Issues, 25,* 318–355.

Yach, Derek; Hawkes, Corinna; Gould, C. Linn; & Hofman, Karen J. (2004). The global burden of chronic diseases: Overcoming impediments to prevention and control. *Journal of the American Medical Association, 291,* 2616–2622.

Yama, Mark F.; Tovey, Stephanie L.; & Fogas, Bruce S. (1993). Childhood family environment and sexual abuse as predictors of anxiety and depression in adult women. *American Journal of Orthopsychiatry, 63,* 136–141.

Yee, Doris K.; & Eccles, Jacquelynne S. (1988). Parent perceptions and attributions for children's math achievement. *Sex Roles, 19,* 317–333.

Yoder, Janice D.; Christopher, Jessica; & Holmes, Jeffrey D. (2008). Are television commercials still achievement scripts for women? *Psychology of Women Quarterly, 32* (3), 303–311.

Yoder, Janice D.; & Kahn, Arnold S. (1993). Working toward an inclusive psychology of women. *American Psychologist, 48,* 846–850.

Yoder, Janice D.; & Naidoo, Loren. (2006). Psychological research with military women. In David A. Mangelsdorff (Ed.), *Psychology in the service of national security* (pp. 211–223). Washington, DC: American Psychological Association.

Yonkers, K. A.; Pearlstein, K.; & Rosenheck, R. A. (2003). Premenstrual disorders: Bridging research and clinical reality. *Archives of Women's Mental Health, 6,* 287–292.

Young, Robert; & Sweeting, Helen. (2004). Adolescent bullying, relationships, psychological well-being, and gender-atypical behavior: A gender diagnosticity approach. *Sex Roles, 50,* 525–537.

Zagor, Karen. (2006, May 29). I declare a chore war. *Maclean's, 119* (22), 34–36.

Zagorsky, Jay L. (2005). Marriage and divorce's impact on wealth. *Journal of Sociology, 41,* 406–424.

Zavos, Alexandra; & Biglia, Barbara. (2009). Embodying feminist research: Learning from action research, political practices, diffractions, and collective knowledge. *Qualitative Research in Psychology, 6* (1/2), 153–172.

Zayas, Luis H.; Cabassa, Leopoldo J.; Perez, M. Carmela; & Howard, Matthew O. (2005). Clinician–patient ethnicity in psychiatric diagnosis: A pilot study with Hispanics. *Journal of Ethnic and Cultural Diversity in Social Work, 14,* 93–109.

Ziegler, Albert; & Stoeger, Heidrun. (2008). Effects of role models from films on short-term ratings of intent, interest, and self-assessment of ability by high school youth: A study of gender-stereotyped academic subjects. *Psychological Reports, 102* (2), 509–531.

Zinik, Cary. (1985). Identity conflict or adaptive flexibility? Bisexuality reconsidered. *Journal of Homosexuality, 11,* 7–19.

Zitzman, Spencer T.; & Butler, Mark H. (2009). Wives' experience of husbands' pornography use and concomitant deception as an attachment threat in the adult pair-bond relationship. *Sexual Addiction and Compulsivity, 16* (3), 210–240.

Zlotnick, Caron; Johnson, Dawn M.; & Kohn, Robert. (2006). Intimate partner violence and long-term psychological functioning in a national sample of American women. *Journal of Interpersonal Violence, 21,* 262–275.

Zoller, Heather M. (2005). Women caught in the multi-causal web: A gendered analysis of *Healthy People 2010. Communication Studies, 56,* 175–192.

Zosuls, Kristina M.; Ruble, Diane N.; Tamis-LeMonda, Catherine S.; Shrout, Patrick E.; Bomstein, Marc H.; & Greulich, Faith K. (2009). The acquisition of gender labels in infancy: Implications for gender-typed play. *Developmental Psychology, 45* (3), 688–701.

Zucker, Kenneth J. (2001). Biological influences on psychosexual differentiation. In Rhoda K. Unger (Ed.), *Handbook of psychology of women and gender* (pp. 101–115). New York: Wiley.

Zucker, Kenneth J. (2002). A factual correction to Bartlett, Vasey, and Bukowski's (2000) "Is gender identity disorder in children a mental disorder?" *Sex Roles, 46,* 263–264.

Zucker, Kenneth J.; & Bradley, Susan J. (1995). *Gender identity disorder and psychosexual problems in children and adolescents.* New York: Guilford Press.

Zucker, Kenneth J.; Bradley, Susan J.; & Sanikhani, Mohammad. (1997). Sex differences in referral rates of children with gender identity disorder: Some hypotheses. *Journal of Abnormal Child Psychology, 25,* 217–227.

Zucker, Kenneth J.; & Spitzer, Robert L. (2005). Was the gender identity of childhood diagnosis introduced into DSM-III as a backdoor maneuver to replace homosexuality? A historical note. *Journal of Sex and Marital Therapy, 31,* 31–42.

Zucker, Kenneth J.; Wilson-Smith, Debra N.; Kurita, Janice A.; & Stern, Anita. (1995). Children's appraisals of sex-typed behavior in their peers. *Sex Roles, 33,* 703–725.

Zuk, Marlene. (2002). *Sexual selections: What we can and can't learn about sex from animals.* Berkeley: University of California Press.

Zuo, Jiping. (2004). Shifting the breadwinning boundary: The role of men's breadwinner status and their gender ideologies. *Journal of Family Issues, 25,* 811–832.

Name Index

A

Abma, Joyce C., 260
Aboud, Frances E., 206
Abrahamson, Adelpha, 91
Abraído-Lanza, Ana F., 360
Abrams, Dominic, 65
Abrams, Douglas Carlton, 71, 92
Abramson, Lyn Y., 384, 396
Abu El-Haj, Thea Renda, 285, 286, 293
Acosta, R. Vivian, 279
Adamek, Margaret, 416
Adami, Hans-Olov, 337
Adams, Mary B., 259
Addis, Michael E., 187, 408
Adera, Tilahun, 89
Adewumi, Tomi A., 91
Adewuya, Abiodun O., 91
Ahern, Melissa M., 369
Ahlberg, Christian, 133
Ahluwalia, Indu B., 89
Ahmed, Eman I., 76, 86
Akande, Debo, 153
Alansari, Bader M., 174
Albee, George W., 369, 370, 395, 420
Aleman, André, 78
Alexander, Fiona, 190
Alexander, Gerianne M., 138
Alexander, Karl L., 281
Alexander, Michele G., 246, 259, 424
Alfieri, Julie Ann, 64
Alfieri, Thomas, 134
Ali, Alisha, 378
Alksnis, Christine, 316, 319
Allan, Emilie, 193
Allen, Christine, 190
Allen, Elizabeth Sandin, 234
Allen, Gina, 213
Allen, Walter R., 301
Allison, John, 280
Allmendinger, Jutta, 320
Allport, Gordon W., 64
Almeida, Joanna, 289
Altmatt, Ellen Rydell, 298
Altman, Lawrence K., 333

Aluja, Anto, 96
Amato, Paul R., 231
Ambady, Nalini, 201
Ames, Daniel L., 62
Amponsah, Benjamin, 174
Anderson, Craig A., 186
Anderson, Deborah J., 291
Anderson, Elizabeth, 41
Anderson, Ellen M., 231
Anderson, G. C., 182
Anderson, Irina, 195
Anderson, John P., 350
Anderson, Karen, 57
Anderson, Kristin J., 141
Anderson, Kristin L., 189, 192, 193
Anderson, Neil, 285
Anderson, Sally, 261
Anderson, Timothy, 402
Andersson, Gerhard, 386
Andersson, Jenny, 343
Andrassy, Jill, 416
Andresen, Elena M., 329, 330
Andronico, Michael P., 418
Aneshensel, Carol S., 258
Angold, Adrian, 96
Anthony, Marietta, 402
Antill, John K., 141, 216
Antonioni, Bob, 364
Apparala, Malathi L., 224, 226
Applegate, Brooks, 404
Aranda, Maria P., 372
Araya, S., 388
Archer, John, 95, 97, 186, 187, 189,
    190, 191, 193, 197, 227, 424, 435
Arcury, Thomas A., 366
Aries, Elizabeth, 321
Armesto, Jorge C., 185
Arnot, Lucy, 326
Arnot, Madeline, 279
Aronson, Amy, 220
Aronson, Joshua, 62, 171
Arseneault, Louise, 368
Asbaugh, Lauren P., 287
Åslund, Cecilia, 382

Astur, Robert S., 163
Atkins, David C., 409
Atkinson, J. W., 295
Aubrey, Jennifer Stevens, 145, 353
Auerbach, Carl F., 13, 184
Aumann, Kerstin, 429, 441
Avdeyeva, Tatyana, 210
Avellar, Sarah, 234
Averill, James R., 178, 187
Ax, Erin E., 307
Ayalon, Hanna, 285, 286, 436
Ayres, Melanie M., 155
Azmitia, Margarita, 209
Azocar, Cristina L., 57
Azrael, Deborah, 289

B

Bachman, Jerald, 193
Bae, Yupin, 281, 285
Baer, John, 167
Bagley, Christopher, 253
Bailey, J. Michael, 133, 139, 149, 267, 273
Bailey, Jennifer A., 367
Bailey, Sandra J., 234
Baillargeon, Raymond H., 188
Baird, M. Kathleen, 408
Bakan, David, 52
Baker, Kaysee, 114
Baldwin, Janice I., 256, 259
Baldwin, John D., 256, 259
Ball, Jane, 166
Ball, Richard E., 220
Balsam, Kimberly F., 224, 272, 274
Banaji, Mahzarin R., 62, 160, 246, 284
Bancroft, John, 82, 241, 242, 265
Bandura, Albert, 113, 114, 115, 116,
    117, 120, 123, 307
Banks, Terry, 94
Bankston, Carl L., III, 297
Barak, Azy, 323, 324, 417
Barbaranelli, Claudio, 307
Barber, Elinor, 300
Barber, Heather, 292

507

Subject Index

Photo Credits